CW00369954

THE
WAITE'S CO
OF NATAL ASTROLOGY

with Ephemeris for 1880–1990
and Universal Table of Houses

by
COLIN EVANS

B.A. (first-class hons.) London
Diploma, Faculty of Astrological Studies
Chief Examiner, Federation of British Astrologers

Revised and brought up to date by
BRIAN E. F. GARDENER

SAMUEL WEISER, INC.,
York Beach, Maine

Original edition by Herbert T. Waite
first published in 1917
Reprinted 1924, 1929 and 1936
This edition rewritten 1953 by Colin Evans
and published by Routledge & Kegan Paul plc,
London, Melbourne and Henley
Revised and brought up to date 1967 and 1971
by Brian Gardener
First published in the United States of America, 1974
by Samuel Weiser, Inc.
Box 612, York Beach, Maine 03910
Reprinted 1976, 1985
Printed in Great Britain

ISBN 0 87728 125 4

THE NEW WAITE'S COMPENDIUM
OF NATAL ASTROLOGY

CONTENTS

CONTENTS

II. ASTROLOGICAL JUDGMENT OF PLANETS

III. ASPECTS

IV. CHARACTER DELINEATIONS OF THE SIGNS

V. THE TWELVE HOUSES OF THE CHART

VI. THE RIVAL SYSTEMS OF HOUSE-DIVISION

VII. CASTING THE HOROSCOPE

VIII. CASTING THE HOROSCOPE, CONTINUED: THE CUSPS

CONTENTS

INTRODUCTION

THE following is the main part of the original preface by Herbert Waite (first edition, 1917):

'As a student of astrology I always resented the fact that it was impossible to carry about with me ephemerides for sixty or seventy years, and tables of houses for most of the civilised world, with which to erect the horoscopes of the sceptics I met, and so silence them then, there, and for ever. . . . I therefore set to work to remedy the evil and make my own astrological pocket friend and companion. . . . I succeeded in compiling really useful condensed ephemeris and tables of houses sufficiently accurate for the purpose for which they were intended. Having encountered many students who envied me my possession, I decided to publish it to the astrological world; but . . . I realised that while advanced students would be concerned only with the bare ephemeris and tables of houses, there would be many who would appreciate some explanations and instructions, and others who would make their first acquaintance with the science through this little book. I have sought, therefore, in the small space at my command, to satisfy these three classes of readers. The simple rules given will enable those who have not ready access to the complete ephemeris for the year in question and tables of houses for the place, to erect a horoscope correctly to within a very small fraction of a degree. Those who know anything of astrology will appreciate the usefulness of the book while realising its limitations. . . . The complete ephemeris is a *sine qua non* for complete calculations, and the beginner will be well advised to bear this in mind if attempting the calculation of directions. . . .'

The great value of Waite's idea, explained above, and the excellence of the way he carried it out, are sufficiently attested by the success and popularity of editions constantly reprinted without change over thirty years and the clamorous demand for a new edition now; although from 1917 to 1951 the book had rapidly been losing part of its practical utility by the mere fact that the condensed ephemeris was never carried beyond 1916. The publishers' intention of adding data for the subsequent years, in order to issue a more useful edition about 1948 or 1949, was frustrated because nobody could answer the anxious questionings of admirers of his work by ascertaining whether the author was still among us in this disordered post-war world, or, if so, get into communication with him.

Meanwhile I had been planning another work on more or less similar lines, though reluctant to compete, as if in rivalry, with the deservedly well-established work of Waite. Under these circumstances, it was finally decided that my own work should take the place, and perpetuate the name, of his.

In so far as it faithfully keeps to the general purpose and plan outlined in the foregoing excerpts from Waite's preface, the present work, therefore, is in fact a new and up-to-date edition of *Waite's Compendium*. In almost every other respect, however, it is an entirely new and original work.

The ephemeris I now give covers ninety-one years: from 1870 to 1960, inclusive. The annoying need to turn from one section of the book to

another in the middle of finding the planets' positions for a given date, as was necessary when Waite's lay-out involved giving the Moon's positions on entirely different pages from those on which the longitudes of the Sun and other planets were given, has been eliminated. On each one-year page of the new condensed ephemeris, the Moon now occupies the right-hand columns, while the Sun and the 'planets proper' are given in the left-hand portion of the same page. Waite's original arrangement, superior planets at intervals of fourteen days, and inferior planets and the Sun at intervals of seven days, involved the confusing printing of each alternate week's longitude for Sun, Mercury, and Venus, half a line lower than the preceding week, and in entirely separate columns—whereas the plan I have adopted makes it possible to vary the length of interval used for each planet more suitably, in view of relative speeds and uniformities of motion, and to avoid wasting space by repetition of dates, while giving a complete section of the page to each planet. Mercury, swiftest and most irregular of all, is now given for every six days; Sun and Venus for every eight days; Mars, Jupiter, Saturn, Uranus, Neptune, for every twelve days (less at the end of each month); Pluto (not known when Waite's work was compiled) once a month; and, of course, the Moon, still, every two days. Such slips of calculation as do (one knows by sad experience) often result from too quickly estimating the number of days from (say) February 25th to March 7th, 1924 (eleven days), and February 25th to March 7th, 1925 (ten days), and March 25th to April 7th (thirteen days), and April 25th to May 7th (twelve days), are avoided by the fact that *every* planet is given on the *first* of *every* month, besides whatever later days of the same month are tabulated, so that only days of the same month have to be allowed for in calculating positions on unlisted dates. The Node (the Moon's Ascending Node, or 'Dragon's Head') omitted by Waite, has now been included. And instead of giving the stations of Mercury, Venus, and Mars, only, the stations of all planets (except Pluto) are now given; without which, longitudes at intervals of over ten days can be seriously misleading.

With regard to the tables of houses, the maddening plan, commonly adopted (following Raphael's lead) in England, of giving the cusps at irregular broken intervals of minutes and seconds of sidereal time (for the sake of making the M.C. always an exact degree), and of giving tables for latitudes of important towns, in broken degrees (odd minutes) of latitude, has been abandoned. It has always led to the student's having the alternatives of (a) calculating the correct interpolations for latitude and sidereal time between (for example) latitude 56°28' and 57°9', and between 1h.47m.49s. and 1h.51m.38s., in order to find the Ascendant for latitude 56°53' at sidereal time 1h.49m.15s., or (b) using the *nearest* latitude and time as a rough approximation. The former involves such tiresome arithmetic as finding $\frac{86}{229}$ of 0°37', and $\frac{25}{41}$ of 0°26'. The latter involves such errors, often, in the Ascendant, that it becomes worse than useless to attempt going closer than the nearest whole degree, if as close. The plan here adopted includes the selection of geographical latitudes of whole degrees only, except that an extra table is given for London (51°30'), and sidereal times at uniform regular intervals of twelve minutes (much less than the *average* interval used by Waite). This enormously simplifies the arithmetic needed for accurate interpolation: a doubly important matter in *condensed* tables.

An even more important criticism of the tables of houses as originally

given, though one in which Herbert Waite simply did what everybody else was then doing, is that they perpetuated the deplorable error of encouraging the ordinary student to look on the 'publishers' system' of house-division as if it were the one and only established, standard, universally recognised, or traditional system; or as if the house-cusps given were simply records of natural or astronomical facts, as objective and non-controversial as the long-itudes of the planets in an ephemeris. Today, no good teacher of astrology, in touch with the thought of the leading workers in this field, would dream of letting even a beginner receive or retain such a fallacious impression.

The Ascendant is, indeed, a simple fact of mathematical astronomy about which there is no dispute. It is the longitude used for the cusp of the first house in all generally and widely known systems of house-division employed from the earliest times, long before Christ, to the present day. The M.C. is similarly a simple and non-controversial fact of mathe-matical astronomy, and while the most ancient system of house-division, still advocated and used today by a few, though not most, of the leading authorities, does not employ the M.C. as cusp of the tenth house, all other house-systems in at all wide usage do, and always have. So, for houses 1 and 10 (and consequently for the opposite houses, 7 and 4) the usual published tables of houses may justifiably be looked on as 'standard'. When it comes, however, to the intermediate houses, 11, 12, 2, 3, and their 'opposite numbers' west of the meridian, there is no one system that has any right to be so regarded. At the very least, six entirely different systems, often giving quite different signs on these intermediate house-cusps, are in current daily use, for standard 'orthodox' astrology, by leading astro-logers of today in England, and on the continent of Europe, and in America. Four of these are much more ancient than, and one of them much newer than, the system of Placidus. And Placidus is the one most hotly attacked by almost all sound theoreticians on this feature of western astrology. But it is the system which happened to be in vogue when the first Raphael, by no means a specialist authority on the subject, 'took it for granted' in compiling his tables of houses for some important cities, which became the basis of the complete tables published by the firm who acquired his copyrights; and these, filling an urgent need for published tables, to save the individual calculation of all house-cusps, and making no mention that they represented one system in particular, arbitrarily selected, rather than others with better claim to be considered 'standard', led to the average student's omitting any study of the house-division question whatever, and simply accepting the 'published tables of houses' as blindly as the ephemeris. Let those who, for what they deem sound reasons, still prefer the Placidean system by all means continue to use it; they may be right; but let it be for some better reason than that they do not know at all what system it is nor what other systems there are, but simply use 'the published tables of houses'! That is the view of all the best teachers today, and in fighting for it I have the support of the Federation of British Astrologers, and of the leading and most responsible officers in the Faculty of Astrological Studies and in the Astrological Lodge of the Theosophical Society (London).

I have therefore planned and compiled the tables of houses with a view to presenting side by side, with complete impartiality, the necessary cusps for erecting a horoscope by any of the following systems (named here in chronological order of their first known use), all in current use today for

standard astrology: Equal Houses, Porphyry, Regiomontanus*, Campanus, Placidus, and Natural Graduation (my own system). I have also included a short chapter explaining, as simply as possible, the principles of these systems and their differences, without arguing for or against any one system.

The changes here outlined have meant that it has been impossible to use any of the pages compiled by Waite for either the Ephemeris or the tables of houses. In computing these afresh, full use has been made of astronomical facts and mathematical results already computed by others, and ascertainable from their publications, which it would have been stupid, as well as heroically laborious, for an individual to attempt to calculate all over again quite independently, giving, if correctly done, precisely the same figures, with no evidence that he *had* done the work afresh! (Though I have *had* to do this for Regiomontanus, Campanus, and Natural Graduation cusps.†) But no such use of other published work as would involve plagiarising the manner of presentation of any of the data, or infringing any legal or moral rights, has, it is hoped, been made. This does not prevent its seeming a becoming courtesy and an expression of real gratitude to acknowledge how invaluable have been the abundant data made available for such uses in *Planetary Co-ordinates*, 1940–1960 (H.M. Stationery Office), *American Astrology Tables of Houses* (by Hugh S. Rice), Le Riche's *L'Influence des Astres*, Reverchon's condensed ephemerides and *Ephemerides Cycliques*, the *Deutsche Ephemeride*, the *Astrologers' Ephemeris* (Chicago), *Raphael's Ephemeris*, Fagan's *Sidereal Ephemeris*, A. Muir's *Pluto Ephemeris*, Koppenstätter's *Pluto Ephemeride*, and Leo Knegt's *Astrologie: Weltenschapenluke Techniek*. As far as they cover the same ground, all of these have been compared and collated to check the accuracy of my own figures, and they have all been used where suitable for data on which to base my own calculations of details they do not actually give for the exact intervals wanted or in the geocentric form required.

For geographical and time data I used *Philips's Handy* and *The Times* Gazetteers of the World; the 1952 *Annuaire du Bureau des Longitudes*; Ed. Koppenstätter's *Zonen und Sommerzeiten*, and I. H. Taylor's 1942 *Supplement* to *World Daylight Saving Time*; fifty-odd back numbers of *Whitaker's Almanack* (by its Editor's kindness, with hospitality of his private office many long hours); and direct information from—with trouble generously taken by—the Home Office, the Colonial Office, the U.S.A. National Bureau of Standards, many foreign consulates, embassies and ministries (especially Portugal, Norway, Eire, Germany), and observatories (especially Brussels and Madrid), and, above all, the B.B.C.—unsparing in prolonged co-operation.

Greenwich refused any data or help, disapproving of astrology.

Waite's delineations of the twelve character-types represented by the twelve signs are so much loved and admired, by some colleagues whose views I value, that I have retained these. They are virtually all of his own work that I *have* retained, in what I hope that he, if, still on this plane, he comes across my new structure built on his foundation, or if, on some higher plane, he has awareness of it, will not find a too unworthy new fulfilment of his own original aims.

1952   COLIN EVANS

---

* Regiomontanus himself (Johan Müller of Königsberg) is much later than Campanus but the *system* of the former is much the older, having been used centuries earlier by Ibn Ezra.
† Involving almost 30,000 separate new computations.

Preface to the 1981 Edition

If you have read the introduction to this book written in 1952 by Colin Evans, you may understand how much regard he had for Herbert Waite's work in naming his essentially new book *The New Waite's Compendium of Natal Astrology*. For sixty-four years this book, originally conceived by Herbert Waite in his 1917 edition and re-written in its present form by Colin Evans in 1953, has constantly withstood the test of time and its increasing demand in these days of scientific advancement and computer technology by astrologers and students alike, pays tribute to the author's excellent work.

Since 1965, I have periodically been asked by the publisher to revise and up-date the book and this I have done, being careful not to offend the existing text. With this aim in mind, and in addition to revising the Ephemeris up to 1990 I have, over the years, extended Chapter 5 and added Appendix III. The amount of research and interpretation required, particularly for the more distant spheres of Neptune, Uranus and Pluto, prompted me to extend the chapter entitled 'The Twelve Houses on the Chart' to include a more detailed analysis of these three planets. The addition of Appendix III, which deals with 'Planets in Signs', is intended to act as a modifying influence on Chapter 5, for students who are already familiar with the fundamental principles of Astrology.

Apart from the above additions the form of the text is still the same as that followed by Evans, including excerpts from Waites's edition of 1917.

The problem of preparing the Ephemeris from 1961 to 1990 was more arduous than corresponding calculations for previous editions. The reason for this was the lack of a direct transposition for these years. Consequently 13,000 calculations had to be performed and I would like to offer my appreciation to Dr G. Kempson, Mrs L. Stevens and Mrs W. Smith for assisting me in some of this work. Each calculation has been checked but with so many, the possibility of errors exist. Should any be found, I apologise to readers in advance. Data for the calculations was taken from *The Complete Planetary Ephemeris,* which quoted planets' positions at midnight and these were then transposed to noon G.M.T.

The accuracy of the Ephemeris must, therefore, be as quoted by Evans in the notes preceding the Ephemeris with the exception of Mercury and the Moon which are subject to a tolerance of 0 degrees 4 minutes. Pluto is quoted in degrees and minutes, but no indication of stations is given as this appeared to be unnecessary, bearing in mind the speed of travel of this planet.

Daylight saving time tables once again presented a special problem, since sources of information are unreliable and scarce. Daylight saving time from 1970 onwards has therefore been omitted as with so many countries now making almost annual changes both in the amount of adjustment and dates, any information prepared could only lead the student into confusion. It is better nowadays for the subject to check through friends and relatives for more reliable information. Information

up to 1970 although brief is included and for this I am indebted to Miss A. W. Elliott of the B.B.C. and to those embassies who were able to help. The accuracy of this table nevertheless still remains suspect since it is inevitable that certain countries, in addition to those listed, observe time changes.

I gratefully acknowledge the use of data from *Raphael's Ephemeris 1970–1971, Raphael's Longitudes and Declinations 1900–2001* and *Complete Planetary Ephemeris*. I would finally like to acknowledge the excellent work of Herbert Waite and Colin Evans, whose contributions to Astrology contained within these pages have been an inspiration to my own humble efforts.

Brian E. F. Gardener

I

ESSENTIAL PRELIMINARIES

1. Astronomy, Pure and Applied. Pure astronomy is the science that deals with the physical natures, positions, and movements of the celestial bodies. Applied astronomy, including navigation, astrology, and chronometry (the three arts from which the study of pure astronomy later developed), makes practical use of some of the facts studied by pure astronomy.

2. Astrology is thus an art based on a science. It uses the facts revealed by astronomy as to the relative positions and apparent movements of the Sun, Moon, and planets (mainly), in the local sky, as indicators of influences affecting human consciousness and experience in life on earth. It does not depend at all on the acceptance or non-acceptance of any of the theories sometimes held about whether such influences are actually caused by the planets, etc., with which astrology associates them, or whether the skies simply furnish a 'clock' (as it were) to time the complex recurrences of cyclic developments in psychology and history, or whether the unity of the universe as a self-consistent Divine Idea is what makes symbolic analogies reliable means of prediction.

3. The Horoscope, in the sense in which the word is currently used by people with a reputable position in astrology, is a complete chart or diagram of the solar system in relation to a particular place on earth (such as the place of a person's birth) at a given moment of time (such as the birth time), along with a full and reasoned judgment of what is to be inferred from it as to the nature of, and probable developments from, an event occurring at that place and time; for example, a man's character, and the general tendencies of his life. The name horoscope may also be used for the chart or diagram itself. It is wrong to use the word horoscope for a stock reading, or generalisation, applied to everyone born with the Sun in a certain part of the zodiac, without taking account of the other factors that make all the difference to an individual case, however good a purpose such readings may serve.

4. To Cast a Horoscope, or draw up a diagram or chart of the kind referred to above, it is necessary to know the place, date, and time of birth. This includes knowing what system of time was used when that birth-time was recorded (*e.g.*, Central European Time? British Summer Time?). This is one reason the *place* matters. Also, geographical latitude determines the parts of the heavens 'rising' and 'setting' at a given moment, and, thus, which parts of the star-pattern in the skies were on the eastern horizon, which overhead, and so on. What, in the eastern sky, might denote the personality of the native, would, at another place, be in mid-sky, denoting the sort of public reputation he attains, and at another place would be in the west and indicate the kind of second person he gets paired with. All this will be briefly taught in the pages that follow.

1

5. The two Equinoxes (vernal and autumnal) are the points in the heavens where, or the moments in the year when, the Sun is exactly over the earth's own middle line, the equator, in spring and autumn. It then shines equally on the northern and southern hemispheres of the earth, and makes night the same length as day all over the world.

6. The two Solstices are the points or times at which the Sun is midway between the two equinoxes, and therefore is farthest north or south from the equator, and makes the longest night and shortest day, or the reverse, the inequality being greatest for places farthest from the equator.

7. The Ecliptic is the circle among the 'fixed' stars marked out by the Sun's successive positions during the year, as seen from the earth.

8. The Zodiac is a belt of space round the celestial sphere having the ecliptic as its middle line, and thought of as, at least, 'wide' enough to include the paths or orbits of all planets and the Moon. It *may* be thought of as covering the whole celestial sphere, considered as divided up with reference to the ecliptic as its middle line, just as the equator is the middle line of the earth itself.

9. Quarters of the Zodiac. The zodiac begins at the spring equinox (vernal equinoctial point) where the ecliptic crosses the equator from south to north. It is divided into four quarters at the equinoxes and solstices, each quarter showing one of the alternate processes of separation and convergence of the ecliptic and equator. Each quarter is divided into three parts—a cardinal sign, which begins the process of separation or convergence, a fixed sign, which persists in the same process; and a mutable sign, which completes it in readiness to commence the opposite process in the next quarter. This divides the whole zodiac into twelve parts, the twelve signs.

10. Longitude on earth (geographical longitude) is distance measured along or parallel to the equator *on earth*, starting from the longitude of Greenwich Observatory. The nearest point on the equator to Greenwich (which is a long way north from the equator) is also the nearest place on the equator to all places from the South Pole to the North Pole that have the same longitude as Greenwich, longitude 0°. Other places are so many degrees (anything up to 180°) east or west (from Greenwich) in longitude. But longitude in the heavens (celestial or zodiacal longitude) is distance similarly measured along the ecliptic, not the equator, starting at the beginning of the zodiac, and measured always in the same direction, up to 360°, the direction in which the Sun seems to move round the ecliptic, which may be called 'eastward'.

11. Right Ascension or R.A. is distance *in the heavens* measured along or parallel to the equator (like *longitude* on *earth*), but starting at the beginning of the zodiac. As the earth rolls over on itself completely (axial rotation) in one day, this point of the celestial equator (and ecliptic) is carried round the *earth's* equator from 0° geographical longitude to 180° west and then the rest of the way back to 0°.

12. Sidereal Time is measured by this apparent movement of the sky as a whole, caused by the earth's axial rotation. As 360° of R.A. pass over a particular place in twenty-four sidereal hours (a sidereal day), an hour of sidereal time corresponds to 15° of R.A.; one degree of R.A. to four minutes of time.

13. True Solar Time. As the Sun moves round the entire 360° of the ecliptic in a year, it advances in the signs by (roughly) 1° per day. Noon

is when the Sun is halfway between rising and setting. So when the ecliptic point in which the Sun was at noon yesterday is itself halfway between rising and setting today, it is not yet quite noon but will be when the *next* degree of the ecliptic gets there, which *now* contains the Sun. This makes a true solar day a little longer than a sidereal day, and a true solar hour a fraction longer than a sidereal hour. It also makes the sidereal time at noon about four minutes more every day—about two hours more each month.

14. Mean Time. The length of a true solar day or hour varies a little at different seasons of the year; a sundial shows true solar time. For practical convenience, our ordinary clocks show 'mean time', making a mean hour always the same length, the *average* length of a true solar hour. 'Mean noon' is the moment when it would be noon if the Sun really kept mean time instead of true solar time.

15. The Numbering of Hours of sidereal time starts from the moment when the beginning of the zodiac is midway between rising and setting. This is 0h.0m.0s.* (no hours, no minutes, no seconds) of S.T. (sidereal time) at the place concerned. The numbering of hours of mean time starts at mean midnight (twelve hours earlier than mean noon), when the Sun, if its speed were uniform so that it kept mean time, would be halfway from setting to rising again. This is 0h.0m.0s. of (local) mean time, for the place concerned. So S.T. at mean noon is anything from 0h. to 24h. according to the day of the year.

16. Local, Standard, and Greenwich Time; Zone Time. As the Sun, or any star, or any point on the ecliptic, rises, sets, and 'culminates' (reaches its midway point between rising and setting above the earth, or between setting and rising below the earth), owing to earth's axial rotation (rolling over on itself), it is obvious that when it is noon here, because the Sun is culminating, it will not yet be noon at a place farther west, but will be later than noon at a place farther east. This makes the difference of local mean time at different places. The same is true if we are talking about a certain point of the ecliptic as rising or culminating, making a similar difference to local sidereal time according to the geographical longitude of the place. Fifteen degrees of longitude on earth correspond to one hour of whichever kind of time (mean or sidereal) we are discussing. So when the local mean time at Philadelphia (75° W. from Greenwich) is 13h.0m., or 1 p.m., the mean time at Greenwich will be 18h.0m., or 6 p.m. And when sidereal time at Philadelphia is 13h. 0m., then sidereal time at Greenwich is 18h.0m. 'Standard time' is the mean time used all over a large area, though not the real local time except for one part of that area. Thus all over England the standard time is Greenwich mean time, though the local time at Yarmouth (east coast) is nearly seven minutes more than the time at Greenwich. The modern idea is to adopt everywhere as standard time a 'zone time' which differs from Greenwich mean time by an exact number of hours or half-hours instead of by odd minutes and seconds. **Summer Time**, or **Daylight-Saving Time**, is standard time (usually zone time) with an hour (sometimes two hours) added by law, to economise artificial lighting and heating by getting the working day started earlier.

17. The Planets, of which the earth on which we live is one, swing round the Sun at various speeds, according to distance. The earth takes a year to complete the 'orbit' along which it travels right round the Sun. It is

---

* In technical works the 'h' ,'m', and 's' are written small and high up, like the 'degrees' symbol. In this book the notation used here is preferred for small print.

this orbital movement of the earth, causing the Sun to be seen in different directions, that 'moves' the Sun from one part of the zodiac to another. The movement, of planets (other than earth) in the zodiac are the combined results of the earth's own movement and the planets' movements in their respective orbits. The Moon swings round the earth, while its own orbit is carried round the Sun by the earth, the combination of the Moon's and the earth's orbital movements causing the Moon's movement through the zodiac.

18. Direct and Retrograde Motion, Stations. The Sun's and Moon's changes of position in the zodiac are always direct, that is, forward, or eastward. But the relative positions of earth and the other planets cause the planets' movements in the zodiac to be sometimes direct (forward) and sometimes retrograde (backwards). When direct motion is just changing to retrograde, or the reverse, the planet is stationary, or in its station.

19. Latitude and Declination. Latitude *on earth* (geographical latitude) is distance northward or southward from the equator. Distance from a circle to any point on a sphere is measured from the nearest point on that circle along a line that is part of a circle perpendicular to the former one. All circles on a sphere perpendicular to one circle meet at two opposite points called the poles of that one. Thus lines perpendicular to the equator, called meridians, pass through the poles of the equator, which (on earth) are the geographical North and South Poles. If a place has latitude 45°, this means that the place is 45° (an eighth of a circle) distant from the nearest point on the equator towards one of the poles— the North Pole, if the place has latitude 45° N.—measured along *a* meridian (*the* meridian of the place). Declination is distance from the Equator in the heavens, measured the same way. Thus if the declination of a star is the same as the latitude of my home, then the star is exactly over my home when it culminates. If not, the star passes over my meridian somewhere north or south from my home. Latitude *in the heavens* (celestial latitude) means distance north or south from the ecliptic, not the equator, measured similarly. Lines perpendicular to the ecliptic are ecliptic secondaries, and meet at the poles of the ecliptic, or ecliptic poles, which are about 23°27′ (roughly a sixteenth of a circle) away from the poles of the equator (celestial poles in the heavens, or geographical poles on the earth). This 23°27′ is the obliquity of the ecliptic, and the distance apart between ecliptic and equator at the solstices, and maximum declination of the Sun. The orbits of the Moon and planets are tilted southwards and northwards through the plane (or level) of the ecliptic, so that the Moon, or a planet, is only on the ecliptic (where it has 0° latitude) twice in the time it takes to go round its orbit. The rest of the time it 'has latitude', meaning that it is some way north or south from the ecliptic.

20. Nodes are the points where a planet or the Moon crosses the ecliptic. The Moon's nodes move backwards through the zodiac at the rate of about one degree in 19 days, roughly. The Ascending Node is the one where the planet or Moon is crossing the ecliptic from south to north; the other, the Descending Node. These two nodes of the Moon are sometimes called the Dragon's Head and Tail (*Caput,* and *Cauda, Draconis,* in the traditional Latin).

21. The Fixed Stars are so called because the pattern they make, as seen from earth, does not change (noticeably) in a short enough time to be

observed by one generation of mankind. The 'wanderers' (original meaning of 'planets') are the Sun and Moon and the planets proper, which can easily be seen to be moving about in the star pattern, all on or near the ecliptic circle, owing to the orbital motions of the earth, Moon, and planets. Some astrologers use the 'fixed stars' (though only the more prominent of those which are near the ecliptic) in horoscopes. But the main practice of astrology confines itself to Sun, Moon, and planets, and to certain points in the heavens that take their significance from the orbits of these (such as the nodes). The earth's daily axial rotation causes stars, as part of the entire sky-pattern, to wheel round once a day, without altering their relative positions in that pattern. Those stars that are exactly on the equator go round the circle of the equator itself in the sidereal day; the others, round smaller circles, parallel to the equator.

22. Rising and Setting. If the star's declination, added to the geographical latitude of a place on earth, makes more than 90°, the star does not rise or set; the whole circle round which it is carried in one sidereal day is either in the sky above that place or else under the earth. Otherwise the star rises and sets once a day. The same is true of any point on the ecliptic circle, and of any other point in the heavens. If we disregard the amount by which a planet or the Sun or Moon changes its place in the zodiac and in the star-pattern during one day (a small amount, in any case), then the same is true for Sun, Moon, and planets. Their rising, passing over the sky, setting, passing under the earth, and rising again, has nothing to do with the orbital movements which carry them from one sign of the zodiac to another, but only with the passage of sidereal time, which measures the earth's axial rotation.

23. The Solar System consists mainly of the Sun, Moon, and planets (including earth)—all near enough together for light to take only a matter of minutes going from one to another. The 'fixed stars' are so unimaginably far away that the light from the nearest of them takes four years to reach us, from others many hundreds.

24. Loose Use of Words. The word 'stars' is sometimes, in popular language, loosely applied to all the celestial bodies used in astrology, including Sun, Moon, and planets, besides the 'fixed stars'. The name 'planets', now restricted by astronomers to bodies that swing round the Sun, is still, for convenience, used by astrologers in its proper original sense of 'wanderers', for the planets (other than earth), *and* the Sun, *and* the Moon.

25. The Horizon of a place is the circle round the sphere which divides it (as viewed from that place on earth) into upper and lower hemispheres, separating 'above' from 'below'. All along one half of this circle are the points where different stars 'rise' (come up into the sky from below the earth); that semi-circle is the eastern horizon. The East Point is the middle point of the eastern horizon, where the equator crosses it. Stars set on the western horizon, the other half of the same circle, whose mid-point is the West Point, where the equator crosses it again. Stars 'culminate' above the earth when they reach the upper (half of the) meridian, the midway line between east and west, and 'culminate' below when they cross the lower meridian (under the earth).

26. The Zenith and Nadir are the points exactly over and under our place on earth, the middle points of the upper and lower hemispheres of the sky. They are therefore on the meridian. They are where it crosses

the prime vertical, the line that runs east and west round the sphere exactly over and under our place on earth and that meets the equator where prime vertical and equator both cut the horizon, at the East and West Points. The North and South Points of the horizon are where the meridian cuts it. Verticals are lines perpendicular to the horizon, and meet at the Zenith and Nadir, the poles of the horizon circle. So 'the' meridian is both 'a' meridian (perpendicular to equator) and a vertical (perpendicular to the horizon).

27. Ascendant and M.C. (Midheaven), and their Opposite Points. The Ascendant and Descendant are the two opposite points where the ecliptic cuts the eastern and western horizon; the M.C. and I.C. (abbreviations of Latin phrases for 'midheaven' and 'deepest heaven') are where ecliptic cuts meridian above and below. The degree of the zodiac (as measured on the ecliptic) that is the Ascendant is different every moment for the same place, and different at the same moment for places with different geographical latitudes. M.C. and I.C. are the same for all places, at the same sidereal time, but change according to the sidereal time, all round the zodiac, in a day. The Ascendant and Descendant, on the contrary, differ according to the geographical latitude of the place, as well as according to time.

28. Houses and Cusps. 'Houses' are the twelve divisions of a chart representing different departments of life and consciousness. The 'cusp' of each house is the chief longitude (degree of the zodiac) in that house. A planet near a cusp has more effect on affairs of that house than a planet anywhere else. Traditionally, in European astrology, the cusp is also the beginning of the house, though authorities who take this view still allow a planet a few degrees (about five) before a cusp to be reckoned as belonging to the house. Another view, adopted lately by users of some systems (see below) of house-division, is that the same cusps are the 'centres' of the houses, half the house being before the cusp. Different methods of dividing the sky into houses are preferred by different authorities (see pp. 45-49).

?9. Angular Cusps, Quadrants, Kinds of Houses. 'Angular cusps' or 'angles' is the usual name for the four most important house-cusps: the first and tenth, and the opposite ones, seventh and fourth. These are the beginnings of the four quadrants of the chart. Most systems of house-division use Ascendant and Descendant as cusps of first and seventh houses, and M.C. and I.C. as cusps of tenth and fourth houses. All systems differ as to where the other (intermediate) cusps come. Some astrologers prefer one system and some another. The house after each angular house is the succedent house; that before each angular house is the cadent house. If we compare the twelve houses to the twelve signs, then angular, succedent, and cadent houses may be compared to cardinal, fixed, and mutable signs, respectively.

30. Elements and Polarities. The first four signs of the zodiac (all three signs of the first quarter and the cardinal sign of the next) represent the four traditional 'elements' of man's make-up and of the universe: Fire, Earth, Air, Water (in that order). The next four signs, the same elements in the same order. Similarly the last four signs. This causes each quarter of the zodiac to begin with a cardinal sign of a different element, in the order Fire, Water, Air, Earth (1st, 4th, 7th, 10th signs). Signs are alternately of the two opposing polarities, positive and negative, so that Fire

and Air signs are positive, Water and Earth signs negative, with a Fire sign always opposite an Air sign, and Water always opposite Earth.

31. The Names and Symbols of the Planets, in their order outward from the Sun, with the 'shorthand symbol' used by astronomers and astrologers for each planet, are: ☿ MERCURY, ♀ VENUS, (⊕ EARTH), ♂ MARS, ♃ JUPITER, ♄ SATURN (all known to the ancients); and beyond these, recently discovered: ♅ URANUS, ♆ NEPTUNE, ♇ (Pl. or other symbols) PLUTO.

31a. Other Important Symbols are: ☉ the SUN, ☽ the MOON; ☊ and ☋ the ASCENDING NODE and the DESCENDING NODE (of the Moon, unless otherwise specified).

32. The Part of Fortune. The astronomical symbol ⊕ shown above for Earth is, in astrology, used for the 'Part of Fortune'. This is the point of the sky where the Moon would be if it were the same distance in front of or behind the Ascendant, in the zodiac, as it actually is in front of or behind the Sun. In a symbolic sense, though not quite accurately, it stands for the position of the Moon at sunrise.

33. The Names and Symbols of the Signs, their qualities and elements and polarities (+ positive and − negative), and the symbols used for them in astronomy and astrology are:

First Quarter: Spring		opposite	Third Quarter: Autumn
Cardinal ARIES (Fire) +	♈	,,	♎ (Air) + LIBRA Cardinal
March–April			September–October
Fixed TAURUS (Earth) −	♉	,,	♏ (Water) − SCORPIO Fixed
April–May			October–November
Mutable GEMINI (Air) +	♊	,,	♐ (Fire) + SAGITTARIUS Mut.
May–June			November–December

Second Quarter: Summer		,,	Fourth Quarter: Winter
Cardinal CANCER (Water) − ♋		,,	♑ (Earth) − CAPRICORN Card.
June–July			December–January
Fixed LEO (Fire) +	♌	,,	♒ (Air) + AQUARIUS Fixed
July–August			January–February
Mutable VIRGO (Earth) −	♍	,,	♓ (Water) − PISCES Mutable
August–September			February–March

The seasons and months named above are those in which the Sun is in each quarter or sign. It enters each sign *about* the 20th (roughly) of each month. It is important to know which sign is opposite which.

34. The Zodiacal Constellations, Equinox Zodiac, and Stellar Zodiac. A constellation is some fixed stars grouped by the eye into a fanciful picture. The traditional constellations round the ecliptic circle, and roughly covering the width formerly attributed to the zodiac (which must now be thought of as wider, since Pluto, discovered 1931, goes farther north and south from the ecliptic than any planet known before) have the names that are given above as names of the signs. If we did not bother about the fact that the vernal equinoctial point is slowly moving backwards through the constellations, we might find it convenient to identify one sign of the zodiac with one group of stars which are seen in that sign, and to form that group of stars into a fanciful picture denoting the life-type which experience has shown to be associated with that sign of the zodiac, and

then to name both sign and constellation by an allegorical name suggesting that life-type. After some centuries, however, the same sign, as defined by distance from the vernal equinoctial point, would cover a different, or partly different, group of stars. That is what has actually happened. Thus the signs no longer correspond to the constellation of the same names. A large school of Hindu astrologers and a very few European astrologers do, however, use a 'stellar' zodiac, in which the signs are made to coincide with what they believe to have been the same fixed-star positions with which they formerly coincided. So this 'stellar' zodiac does not begin at the vernal equinox now, and its quarters and signs no longer have any special relation to the separation and convergence of ecliptic and equator.

A table (based on computations published by Cyril Fagan, chief advocate of a stellar zodiac in western astrology) is given after the ephemeris in this book ('The Stellar Zodiac') for those who wish to experiment by converting the zodiacal positions in the standard European equinox-zodiac into positions in the Hindu fixed-star zodiac.

II

ASTROLOGICAL JUDGMENT OF PLANETS

35. 'Good' and 'Bad' Planets. All forces in the created universe are in themselves good; all can be misused to make them bad. However, one may be violent, another restrictive, and these present difficulties to cope with. These, rightly coped with and used, may be fruitful in great achievement. A third may be pleasant, harmonious, easy, and seem to make any effort on our part unnecessary. This, if we are content to drift, may make us idle and self-indulgent, with fruitless lives. Superficially, the two former may be called 'bad' or 'unlucky', and the latter 'good' or 'lucky'. There is no fatalism in astrology. With the very same winds, two sailing ships can be steered from the same port to very different destinations, if the captain knows the winds and uses them with skill and with a clear idea of the course he wishes to take. It is the same with the influences shown in a horoscope. The so-called 'good' ones will only prove really good if wise use is made of the opportunities they present. The so-called 'bad' ones, disastrous if we ignore them, may be the very means of producing the greatest good if we recognise their nature and deal with them accordingly. We are not fated to good or evil; at most, 'fated' to have certain factors to deal with, from which we can either make good or evil; but we need to know what those factors are, and this, to a large extent, a horoscope can show us. Mars denotes aggressive virility and force; Neptune, the vision and imagination that are not bound to the material world; the combination may produce either a Crusader-Saint, with deeds of martial heroism and experience of mystical spiritual vision, or else a murderous gangster drug-addict, who escapes from reality in the fantasies of the opium dream and returns to shoot up bank-managers. Though, for brevity and concreteness, phrases are used in what follows that might suggest good or evil fortune or character, as if fatalistically shown by the skies, yet this paragraph must always be borne in mind.

36. Benefics and Malefics. Traditionally, Venus and Jupiter are the two benefics, the 'Lesser Fortune' and the 'Greater Fortune', fortunate or 'lucky' planets; Mars and Saturn are the two malefics, the 'Lesser' and 'Greater Infortune', 'evil' or 'unlucky'; Sun, Moon, and Mercury are 'variable', becoming 'good' or 'bad' according to their positions and the other planets that are combined in any way with them. Uranus, Neptune, Pluto, all of recent discovery, have naturally no 'traditional' character, but each when newly known tended to be regarded as 'bad'; which by no means now describes their more fully studied effects. (Comparably, electricity, before understood at all, simply connoted the deadly thunderbolt; now, it is our means of light and warmth and broadcast music.)

37. The Significance of Each Body.

THE SUN denotes the fundamental ego, the real spiritual character, according to its position in the zodiac and the houses, and its aspects.

THE MOON denotes the instincts, the subconscious, the desire-nature and the feelings and reactions.

MERCURY denotes the mentality, memory, intelligence, and brainwork.

VENUS denotes the sense of beauty and the affections, love-life, artistic taste.

MARS denotes the virile passions, aggression, impulse, maleness, daring.

JUPITER represents expansion, 'joviality', exaltation, success.

SATURN represents restriction, restraint, duration, depth, seriousness.

URANUS is individualistic, occult, inspired, unconventional, disruptive, and explosive.

NEPTUNE is mystical, visionary, spiritual or sensually 'escapist', unworldly, nebulous.

PLUTO (discovered in 1931) is by a few astrologers still considered as not yet sufficiently understood to be used at all in judging a horoscope, and they omit it. But it seems to be the planet of far-reaching change, destruction and reconstruction, death and rebirth, the grave and the womb.

38. The Moon's Ascending Node (Dragon's Head)

and the opposite point (Descending Node, Dragon's Tail) are by some authorities ignored; by others the former is considered a fortunate or helpful, and the latter an unfortunate or hindering, influence.

39. Use of the Part of Fortune.

Not used by all astrologers, but, when used, considered an indication of worldly good fortune in connection with the matters denoted by the part of the chart where it occurs.

40. The Sun as Significator

also denotes people in authority and important positions, the husband in a female horoscope, the father; and is a symbol of vitality, prosperity, when well-placed and not badly aspected. Esoterically, it is the physical symbol (for earth-dwellers) of the Creative Spirit, Centre and Source of Life, Deity.

41. The Moon as Significator

also denotes the wife in a male horoscope, the masses or 'common people', the mother.

42. Rulership, Dignities, Debilities.

Each sign of the zodiac is said to have a certain planet as its 'ruler'. This means two things: (1) the planet is 'dignified' when in that sign; that is, its influence is made stronger and more harmonious and beneficial; (2) the planet, even when in any other sign, 'represents' its own rulership sign, as it were. If a certain sign is on the cusp of the house dealing with possessions and income, and the ruling planet of that sign is in some other house and some other sign, then the matters denoted by that other house, and the characteristics indicated by that other sign, will affect the finances, just as will the characteristics denoted by the sign on the house of possessions and the influence denoted by the ruling planet of this sign. The opposite sign to a planet's rulership is the planet's 'detriment', where it is debilitated—acts undesirably, distortedly, or weakly.

43. Exaltations.

Each planet also has one sign where it is traditionally 'exalted'—where its good influence is markedly emphasised. (Traditionally, it is exalted in a *particular degree* of that sign, though the exaltation *degrees* are now usually ignored.) The opposite sign is its 'fall', where its influence is made weak or injurious.

44. 'Strong by Sign'.

Apart from and less important than the rulership,

exaltation. detriment, and fall, there are certain signs which have enough affinity with a particular planet for it to be strengthened when in them.

45. The 'New' Planets' Dignities. The three 'new' planets (♅, ♆, Pl.) have no traditional rulership, but may be considered joint rulers of certain signs without deposing the traditional rulers.

46. Two Rulership-Series. The Sun rules only one sign, Leo; the Moon only one, Cancer. Planets in order outward from the Sun (☿ ♀ ♂ ♃ ♄) rule signs in order from the next after Leo, forward in the zodiac (♍ ♎ ♏ ♐ ♑); and in order *towards* the Sun the remaining signs (so that ♄ ♃ ♂ ♀ ☿ rule ♒ ♓ ♈ ♉ ♊). Uranus and Neptune are probably joint rulers of Aquarius and Pisces respectively, and Pluto of Scorpio. Table:

47.

Sign	Ruler	Exaltation	Strong	Detriment	Fall
♈	♂	☉	♃	♀	♄
♉	♀	☽	♃ (♄)	♂ (Pl.)	(? ♅)
♊	☿	♌	♄	♃	♋
♋	☽	♃	☿ (♆)	♄	♂
♌	☉	(? Pl.)	♂	♄ (♅)	(? ♆)
♍	☿	☿	♄	♃ (♆)	♀
♎	♀	♄	♃	♂	☉
♏	♂ (Pl.)	(? ♅)	☉	♀	☽
♐	♃	♋	♀ (☉)	☿	♌
♑	♄	♂	☿	☽	♃
♒	♄ (♅)	(? ♆)	(♀)	☉	(? Pl.)
♓	♃ (♆)	♀	(☽)	☿	☿

Brackets ( ), not traditional; brackets with query (? . .), merely tentative suggestions.

48. Personal Characteristics Shown by the Planets. As every planet is in everybody's horoscope (and everybody has in his character the germs of all qualities), the following must be interpreted as meaning that the characteristics are likely to be *marked* in the case of a person in whose chart the planet mentioned is specially *prominent* by position—especially if it is rising at birth, or is the ruling planet (or joint ruler) of the sign that is on the Ascendant, or is in strong aspect to the Sun or to the ruling planet of the Ascendant, or to the Moon:

SUN: pride, generosity, egoism, honour, loyalty, ardour, vitality.

MOON: sensitiveness, sentiment, maternal instinct, femininity, changeableness.

MERCURY: quickness, sharpness, braininess, ready wit, flow of words.

VENUS: beauty, grace, charm, artistic tastes, affection, sociability.

MARS: virility, energy, courage, initiative, impulsiveness, passion, aggression.

JUPITER: optimism, cheer, generosity, joviality, sport, strength, nobility, ceremoniousness.

SATURN: caution, taciturnity, pessimism, self-restraint, profundity, steadfastness.

URANUS: originality, inspiration, eccentricity, individualism.

NEPTUNE: mysticism, vagueness, fantasy, imagination, clairvoyance.

PLUTO: transformation, regeneration, the manifesting of the subconscious by way of sudden change like 'death' and 'rebirth'. Drastic alterations to predetermined ideas and ethics.

III

ASPECTS

49. Planets in Combination. Influences denoted by different planets interact and combine, either 'harmoniously' (beneficially) or 'discordantly' (injuriously)—but compare 35—according to their distance apart in the zodiac, which is, really, the kind of angle between the two lines from two planets to us, and therefore the manner in which the two 'rays of influence' impinge on one another when reaching us. Harmonious are the aspects equal to the angle in an equilateral triangle, a zodiacal distance of 120° or four whole signs, as when two planets are in the same part of two signs of the same element (Fire, Earth, Air, Water); and half or a quarter of that angle (60°, 30°); two signs, one sign, apart.

Discordant, difficult, or 'bad' are the aspects based on halving and quartering the zodiac; 90° (three signs) apart (same 'quality', cardinal, fixed, or mutable), and opposition (six signs apart, opposite one another, 180° apart, in the same parts of opposite signs), and half of the former (45°, one and half signs apart), and one and a half times the 'square' or 90° aspect (135°, four and a half signs, apart). Traditionally regarded as 'bad' or discordant, not always so regarded by the moderns, and perhaps too difficult to interpret correctly for the beginner to be advised to notice it at all, is the aspect called 'Inconjunct', or 'Quincunx', five signs apart (150°). Of these, the aspects of two, three, four, six, whole signs are strong and important, the others relatively weak and unimportant.

The 'conjunction' is when two planets are together in the zodiac (0° apart). It is 'good' between two good planets or a neutral and a good planet; bad between two bad ones or a neutral and a bad one, and mixed in its effects between a good planet and a bad one. But note again that 'good' and 'bad' are really wrong descriptions (35).

50. Table of Aspects, with the 'short-hand' symbol used for each aspect:

Name of aspect	Symbol used	Signs apart	Degrees apart	Strength of aspect	Nature of aspect
CONJUNCTION ...	☌	0	0	Strong	Variable
SEXTILE ...	✳	2	60	Strong	Harmonious
SQUARE	□	3	90	Strong	Discordant
TRINE	△	4	120	Strong	Harmonious
OPPOSITION ...	☍	6	180	Strong	Discordant
SEMI-SEXTILE ...	⌄	1	30	Weak	Harmonious
SEMI-SQUARE ...	∠	1½	45	Weak	Discordant
SESQUI-SQUARE ...	⬚	4½	135	Weak	Discordant
INCONJUNCT ...	⌃	5	150	Weak	Discordant ?

13

'New' Aspects, introduced by Kepler:

Name of aspect	Symbol used	Signs apart	Degrees apart	Strength of aspect	Nature of aspect
QUINTILE ...	Q	$2\frac{2}{5}$	72	Weak	Harmonious
SEMI-QUINTILE ...	⊥	$1\frac{1}{5}$	36	Very Weak	Harmonious
BIQUINTILE ...	±	$4\frac{4}{5}$	144	Very Weak	Harmonious

51. Orbs of Aspects. An aspect need not be exact; if one planet is within a certain number of degrees of being in a certain aspect to another, that aspect is considered to exist between them. The margin of inexactitude allowed is called the 'orb' of the aspect. How many degrees of orb to allow is a vexed question; as a rough and ready guide for the beginner the following orbs may be used:

The Strong Aspects: about 8° (up to 10° if Sun or Moon is involved).
Weak Aspects, about 3° at most. Very weak aspects, 1° or 2°.
Less in all cases if the inexactitude puts planets in signs in which they would not be if the aspect were exact. For instance, if one planet is in Aries and the other in Gemini, the aspect would be sextile if exact: but if the first is in 3° Aries and the other in 27° Taurus, this is only 6° short of the exact aspect that would exist if the second planet were in 3° Gemini; but it is probably a much weaker aspect than if there were only 6° orb between one in 10° Aries and the other in 4° or 16° Gemini, that is, both in the signs that make sextile aspect to one another.

51a. Two planets are in 'mutual reception' (equivalent to a harmonious aspect, fairly strong) if each is in the other's rulership sign, or if each is in the other's exaltation sign; ♃ ♉, ♀ ♐ .

52. Tendencies Indicated by Harmonious Aspects (for Conjunctions see Section 54). (*a*) SUN OR MOON WITH A PLANET OR ONE ANOTHER.

☉ and ☿: strength of intellect, subject to signs they are in: literary, mathematical, good memory.

☉ and ♀: affectionate, lucky, pleasure-loving, artistic.

☉ and ♂: vitality, energy, health, gift of command, courage, initiative.

☉ and ♃: morality, honour, charity, generosity, sympathy, ceremonious, cheery.

☉ and ♄: prudence, honesty, faithfulness, patience, endurance, seriousness.

☉ and ♅: genius, originality, and individualism, independence of outlook and character, occultism.

☉ and ♆: spiritual, musical, sensuous, lucky, charming, intuitive.

☉ and Pl.: (more research needed) perhaps: mediumistic, liable to undergo some drastic and complete reorientation, becoming a 'new man'.

☉ and ☽: subconscious instincts in harmony with conscious reason; success, ambition, public recognition, good luck.

☽ and any planet: similar to ☉ and same planet, but more affecting feelings and subconscious inclinations than fundamental character and conscious or deliberate choice.

(*b*) MERCURY WITH ANOTHER PLANET:

☿ and ♀: artistic, poetical, musical, kind, happy.

☿ and ♂: witty, sarcastic, clever at technical things, engineering, etc.

☿ and ♃: just, philosophical, religious, potentiality for fame.

☿ and ♄: serious-minded, scientific, profound in study, intellectual.

☿ and ♅: inventive genius, fine original mind, aptitude for occult studies.
☿ and ♆: poetical, idealistic, gifted for imaginative literature, fiction.
☿ and Pl.: (more research needed) mediumship? drastic change of mental
activity?

(c) VENUS WITH ANOTHER PLANET:

♀ and ♂: strong animal nature, 'great lover', free with money, good
marriage.
♀ and ♃: very fortunate, fine lovable nature, happy in marriage.
♀ and ♄: virtue, steadfast affections, fidelity, serene patience.
♀ and ♅: sudden gains and journeys, peculiar but happy love-episodes,
original if eccentric artistic genius.
♀ and ♆: refined, dreamer, imaginatively artistic, idealistic love; sensuous,
fascinating.
♀ and Pl.: (more research needed) a drastic change in life through love?

(d) MARS WITH ANOTHER PLANET:

♂ and ♃: generous, just, enthusiastic, free with money, great fighters.
♂ and ♄: brave endurance, persistent energy, able to command, vigorous
old age.
♂ and ♅: great energy, often unpredictable in action, constructive genius
or invention, inspired fighter.
♂ and ♆: magnetic, pushing, confident, fascinating, changeable.
♂ and Pl.: (more research needed) fighting spirit developed by some
revolutionary spiritual 'rebirth'?

(e) JUPITER AND ANOTHER PLANET:

♃ and ♄: religious, profoundly philosophical, charitable, financially
fortunate, apt for political success.
♃ and ♅: sudden gains, originality, unconventionality, independent outlook in religion and philosophy, probably with occult leanings.
♃ and ♆: psychic, perhaps mediumistic, spiritual, sensuous, emotional,
lucky.
♃ and Pl.: (more research needed) religious conversion?

(f) SATURN WITH ANOTHER PLANET:

♄ and ♅: occult gifts and interests, magnetic, aptitude for revolutionary
politics.
♄ and ♆: psychic gifts, if utilised, mystical philosophy, self-control,
mental concentration, gift for meditation (spiritual).
♄ and Pl.: (more research needed) a revolutionary change in philosophical
outlook?

(g) URANUS, NEPTUNE, AND PLUTO:

♅ and ♆: exalted nature, psychic and occult, originality especially in
matters of spiritual vision or imaginative fantasy.
♅ and Pl.: (more research needed) 'spiritual rebirth', begetting a revolt
against established routine or conventions?
♆ and Pl.: (more research needed) mediumship? trance? revolutionary
reorientation of spiritual vision?

53. Tendencies Suggested by Discordant Aspects (for Conjunctions, see
section 54).

(a) SUN AND MOON WITH PLANETS AND ONE ANOTHER:

☽ and ☿: an uncharitable tongue, gossip. (Remark: ☉ and ☿ cannot make
a discordant aspect.)

⊙ and ♀: love difficulties, social restrictions.

⊙ and ♂: hastiness, rashness, bad-temper, accidents, operations, fevers, sensuality or lust, violence, combativeness.

⊙ and ♃: extravagance, religious differences, litigation, disappointments, exaggeration, boasting.

⊙ and ♄: selfish, despondent, taciturn, thwarted, oppressed with responsibilities, sluggish.

⊙ and ♅: sudden disasters, eccentricity, love-sorrows, estrangements, nerve troubles.

⊙ and ♆: treachery from others, disappointments, sensuality, impracticability.

⊙ and Pl.: (more research needed) loss of faith in some great crisis?

⊙ and ☽: psychological tensions and conflict, reason at variance with desire or instinct with will.

☽ and any planet: similar to ⊙ and same planet, but rather affecting subconscious inclinations and instinctive reactions, and feelings, than conscious or deliberate choice or experience.

(b) MERCURY AND ANOTHER PLANET

☿ and ♀: conceited, perhaps especially with musical interests, bad taste in art.

☿ and ♂: impulsive, harsh, turbulent, self-assertive, neurotic, too subtle, sarcastic and ironic, sharp and clever.

☿ and ♃: hypocrisy, scepticism, bad judgment, litigation, grandiose lying.

☿ and ♄: worry, enmity, over-seriousness, pessimistic philosophy, political trickery.

☿ and ♅: neurotic, erratic, eccentric if clever, a rebel in intellectual matters, abrupt speech, curt and brusque.

☿ and ♆: diffuse and scattered mind and thoughts, nebulous and confused, sensuous, especially in fantasies, dishonesty or untruthfulness or theft.

☿ and Pl.: (more research needed) bad memory? loss of memory?

(c) VENUS AND ANOTHER PLANET:

♀ and ♂: loose morals, oversexed, intemperate, separations.

♀ and ♃: extravagance, treachery from others, religious strife.

♀ and ♄: obstacles, frustration or sorrows, in love-affairs; losses, sensuality.

♀ and ♅: dangerous or unconventional and illicit love episodes, losses, estrangements in emotional relationships, or bereavements.

♀ and ♆: sensuality, drink, drugs, deceiving or being deceived in love, the 'eternal triangle'.

♀ and Pl.: (more research needed) character blighted by love affair?

(d) MARS AND ANOTHER PLANET:

♂ and ♃: extravagance, litigation, losses.

♂ and ♄: danger through recklessness, unwisely enthusiastic, unlucky accidents, losses, violent, sarcastic, churlish.

♂ and ♅: nerve troubles, love dangers, rash eccentric impulses, sudden accidents, partings, and bereavements, brusque manners.

♂ and ♆: sensuality, intemperance, drugs, immorality, unhealthy imagination.

♂ and Pl.: (more research needed) fanaticism and bigotry after a 'conversion'?

(*e*) JUPITER AND ANOTHER PLANET:

♃ and ♄: melancholy, misfortune, losses, bigotry.

♃ and ♅: sudden losses and accidents, litigation, eccentric religious views.

♃ and ♆: superstition, credulity, sensuality, pride, intemperance.

♃ and Pl.: (more research needed) vain ceremonialism after a 'conversion'?

(*f*) SATURN AND ANOTHER PLANET:

♄ and ♅: eccentricity in tastes and opinions and beliefs, unsociable individualism.

♄ and ♆: selfish, temperamentally moody, pessimistically imaginative, self-deception, cowardice.

♄ and Pl.: (more research needed) conversion to a pessimistic philosophy?

(*g*) URANUS, NEPTUNE, AND PLUTO:

♅ and ♆: sudden, unpredictable and eccentric, moods and fancies.

♅ and Pl.: (more research needed) anti-social after a tragedy?

♆ and Pl.: (more research needed) black magic?

54. How to Interpret a Conjunction.

☉ conjunct with ☽: this 'new moon' position is favourable to beginnings, new enterprises, etc.

☉ conjunct with ♀, ♃: harmonious (see 52).

☉ conjunct with ♂, ♄: discordant (see 53).

☉ conjunct with ♅, ♆: mixture of the good and bad effects of discordant and harmonious aspects (see 52–53).

☽ in conjunction with any planet: see ☉ in conjunction with same planet, above, but affecting feelings more than fundamental character.

☿ in conjunctions: see ☉ in same conjunctions; but specially affecting communications (speech, writing) and brainwork.

♀ or ♃ in conjunction with ♂ or ♄: mixture of the harmonious and discordant aspects (see 52–53).

♀ or ♃ in conjunction with ♅ or ♆: mixture of harmonious and discordant aspects, the former predominating (see 52–53).

♂ or ♄ in conjunction with ♅ or ♆: discordant (see 53).

♅ in conjunction with ♆: mixture of discordant and harmonious effects (see 52–53).

N.B. Any conjunction is made more definitely discordant or harmonious by discordant or harmonious aspects with a third planet.

Pl.: needs more research.

55. Character not Doomed. Nobody is condemned at birth by his horoscope to be immoral, dishonest, etc. Such qualities or tendencies indicated by any aspect are to be interpreted as warnings that such a fault might, with that horoscope, be too easily developed if not guarded against. The need to guard against it may result in a conspicuous freedom from it and possession or cultivation of the opposite virtue.

IV

CHARACTER DELINEATIONS OF THE SIGNS
OF THE ZODIAC

56. Waite's 'Signs'. The following descriptions (60–72) of the characters denoted by the twelve signs of the zodiac are those written by Herbert Waite for the original edition of this *Compendium*. They are so highly thought of by eminent leaders in the teaching of astrology in England that it was decided to retain them, without change, in the present work.

57. In Judging Character from the horoscope we have to consider:

(i) The sign containing the Ascendant; the sign containing the ruling planet of the sign containing the Ascendant; planets *in* the Ascendant *sign*, or within about 10° of the Ascendant itself if in an adjoining sign. All these may be taken as depicting the type of personality which the native outwardly represents—in appearance, behaviour, relations with other people. The Ascendant sign is primary, and the other factors mentioned may be regarded as modifying it to various extents, needing experience to estimate well. Aspects to the ruling planet of the Ascendant sign and to planets in the Ascendant sign or near the Ascendant must also be taken into account.

(ii) The sign in which the Sun is placed, with the aspects to the Sun, as denoting the fundamental character or ego of the person, which may or may not be like the surface personality shown by the Ascendant, but gives his real motivation, in his reason and spiritual nature.

(iii) The sign in which the Moon is placed, with aspects to the Moon, as showing the desire-nature, the subconscious psychological tendencies, or the involuntary reactions and feelings, of the person.

(iv) The sign-position and aspects of Mercury, as indicating the type of mentality and thought-processes in the earth-mind whose organ is the brain.

Each of the following sign character-readings must be, therefore, taken as denoting the basic character (if it is the Sun-sign), the emotional nature (if it is the Moon-sign), the manifested personality (if it is Ascendant-sign), or a second superimposed and fainter manifested personality modifying the predominant manifested personality, if it is the sign containing the Ascendant-ruler. Any of these receives additional modifications from any planets in the sign and from aspects to Sun, Moon or ruling planets.

58. Sign-Characters Classified by Quality:

Cardinal signs give restlessness and activity of mind and body, somewhat at the expense of thoroughness of detail as a rule. An enterprising and independent spirit is produced, inclined to constant moving about.

Fixed signs denote stubbornness, fixity of purpose, self-reliance, will-power, and great determination to overcome obstacles to the ambition.

Mutable signs give the power of dispassionate judgment, great versatility and adaptability, ability in detail work and criticism; some indecision, excess of subtlety, vacillation, and pessimism, may be shown, with the disposition to leave undertakings uncompleted. (*Waite.*)

59. Sign-Characters Classified by Element:

Fire signs tend to produce more or less headstrong natures, emotional, intuitional, exaggerative, enthusiastic, energetic, aspiring, and ambitious. Usually noble aims.

Air signs incline to intellectual work, principally, giving the ability to receive a good education. The nature is humane and refined, and there is innate wisdom.

Water signs give excess of emotion and extreme sensitiveness, and impressionability. The nature is naturally sociable and there is love of home comforts.

Earth signs give the 'earthy', practical, nature, and incline to caution, method, shrewdness, and diplomacy. (*Waite.*)

(*Note*: Water signs usually give some psychic power, clairvoyance, etc.; especially true of Pisces.—*Evans.*)

60. The Twelve Signs of the Zodiac. A brief description of the characteristics given by each of the twelve signs, and of the type of body produced by each sign when rising on the eastern horizon.

For the convenience of the reader the following is repeated:

THE ASCENDANT, or the sign rising on the eastern horizon at the moment of birth, denotes the type of body and brain, the physical temperament and mental outlook.*

THE MOON ☽, through the sign in which it was placed at birth, denotes the personal characteristics; the senses and the functioning of the body as a whole; the Soul.

THE SUN ☉, through the sign in which its rays vitalised the earth at the time of birth, denotes the real self, the Ego—that part of the Universal Spirit imprisoned, for purposes of tuition in constructive Love and Wisdom, in the body of flesh.

The physical body and brain (Asc.) act as the vehicle and limiting factor for the expression of as much of the pure or real mind (☉) as the Soul (☽) reflects and modifies through the desires.

Limitations of space preclude anything like a complete treatment of any part of the judgment of a horoscope, but the following brief descriptions may be taken as showing (1) Individual characteristics, when ☉ is in a sign. (2) Personal characteristics (in a general sense) when ☽ is in a sign. (3) Mental outlook, or 'what is bred in the bone', when Ascendant is in a sign.

ASPECTS to the Sun modify the individual characteristics; aspects to

---

* Planets rising near the Ascendant very considerably alter the type of body and general appearance. The Sun and Moon also modify the type of body. Saturn near the Ascendant gives a short stature, even when a tall sign is rising. Mars generally gives red or sandy hair. Venus gives roundness to the face.

It should be clearly understood that the descriptions of types of body given in the following pages are applicable to the *rising sign*: for instance, anyone born between March 21st and April 20th would not necessarily have the sign Aries rising.

(*Waite.*)

the Moon modify the personal characteristics; aspects to the Ascendant and ruling planet affect the physical body and brain and mental outlook.
(*Waite.*)

61. ♈ **The Sign Aries** ♈ : *the Positive House of its Ruler,* ☉ in ♈ March 21st to April 20th.

This sign belongs to the *Fiery* Element, and is of the cardinal or movable quality. Aries individuals are characterised by intellectuality, self-reliance, activity, energy, and impulsiveness. They are pioneers in the realms of thought and action, though they are more idealistic than practical. Always wilful and headstrong when young, most of them fail to achieve the necessary measure of caution even in mature life, and continue to go to extremes. Self-restraint, calmness, coolness, and consideration for the feelings of others are not virtues of these people, as a rule, though what they lack in this respect they gain in dauntless courage, enthusiasm, and zeal, either for their own work or for any cause they may take up.

Aries people love approbation, and if this is given them, they are tireless in their efforts for their employers; but they resent being driven, and if this is attempted, either throw up their posts in indignation or take revenge by means of acting and deception, for when perverting the influence of the sign they are arch-deceivers. It may be said that it takes an Arian to deceive an Arian, as they are extremely perceptive and intuitive, being able to sense others to an extraordinary degree. When acting up to the highest in them they are prophetic and clairvoyant, and should the Moon be in Libra clairvoyance is very often produced. They usually have too much self-esteem, more especially when the Moon is also in a fiery sign, though the Moon in Capricorn renders them lacking in this respect. Interference and restriction they find hard to endure, and independence, freedom of action, and constant change and novelty seem to be the breath of life to them. Usually there are many changes of occupation during their lives.

New ideas and schemes crowd on top of one another in their brains, and they are always embarking on fresh enterprises, great or small, according to their station in life. If they can visualise the end of an enterprise they are rarely swerved from the determination to carry it through; but it is this mental picture of a work completed in a short time which spurs them on to the finish. Thus they are not adapted for work requiring patient application over a long period, and unless the horoscope is strong for detail they are better fitted to create, organise, and lead, rather than to personally work out their schemes in practical detail.

They are intellectual, but, as a rule, their great activity of mind and body leads to diffusion and the inability to marshal their thoughts sufficiently to show all that is in them.

Voluble and often brilliant in conversation, they do not always adhere strictly to truth, and in this, as in all they do, exaggeration and imagination can generally be discerned.

None are more alive to their own interests than Aries people, and unless the individual character is stronger than the personal, this trait results in jealousy and covetousness, often putting them back in life. There is much danger of this with the combination of ☉ in ♈, ☽ in ♏. In this, as in all the signs, there will be found people who *use* the influence, and those who *abuse* it. The first are the pioneering and reforming leaders of men;

frank, candid, intense, intellectual, aspiring; perhaps a little too 'touchy', assertive, exaggerative, and venturesome. The second place self-interest above principle, are aggressive, presumptuous, too changeable, inconstant, and sensitive, yet inconsiderate of others; magnifying everything that engages their attention, as well as their own powers. They ape their superiors, ever seeking to place themselves on an equality with them, are unduly familiar and personal, and if one gives them the proverbial 'inch' they promptly take a 'yard'. These personal Arians are typical usurpers.

Health. Aries governs the head and brain. Though the general health is usually good and the constitution sound, Aries people are always highly strung, and their natural inclination to go to extremes often results in severe headaches, toothache, brain-fever, neuralgia, etc. Prolonged worry and the physical and mental excesses to which their nature renders them liable sometimes completely unhinge their minds.

Occupation. Actors, designers, herbalists, nature-cure doctors, guides and travellers, surveyors, architects, electricians, agents of all kinds, company promoters, free-lance journalists, novelists, etc., are found amongst the Aries people.

Type of body. Average stature; spare, lean, but with strong body and large bones; head broad at top, narrowing down somewhat noticeably at chin; visage and neck rather long, and complexion dusky or ruddy; thick shoulders; hair light to reddish in those having the nose pinched or 'button-holed', dark in those having the ram-like face with bushy eyebrows; eyes blue to grey, sometimes light brown; quick sight.

62. ♉ The Sign Taurus ♉ : *the Negative House of its Ruler,* ♀. ☉ in ♉ April 21st to May 20th.

This sign belongs to the *earthy* element, and is of the *fixed* quality. Taurean individuals are *practical,* sure, plodding, secretive, reserved, fixed in purpose, possessing as a rule more vitality of mind and body than those born under any other sign. Extremely strong-willed, they can be led but never driven. They are the manufacturers, the builders, those who make and mould things. While the Arian nature is to create the *idea,* the main scheme, and to lead and inspire others to put it into practical use, the Taurean nature is to handle the materials for the scheme, mould and erect them. The Arian is the architect, the Taurean the builder. Though the terms may be interpreted in their actual meaning, they are used in their broadest sense. For instance, let the Arian be the company promoter, then the Taurean is the mathematician and the financial expert.

Taureans are averse to change, not very adaptable, and the knowledge and skill they obtain is largely bought at the price of experience, as they stick to their own conservative methods long after a more flexible mentality would have lined up in the ranks of advancing science. They are usually slow to anger, but when once aroused lose all control, becoming furious and violent, though the combination of ☉ in ♉ and ☽ in either ♈, ♌ or ♐ renders them quick to anger and violence. The latter combinations, while stirring the Taurean into action, also incline to bring out some of the lower Venusian tendencies, such as gambling, over-eating, and drinking, sensuality, conceit, etc.

When it is remembered that this is a fixed and earthy sign and represents the negative side of Venus, some idea of the laziness, love of sensuous and worldly pleasures, fondness for the table, obstinacy (pig-headedness),

and even slovenliness, latent within the Taurean may be gleaned. If they are living principally in the personal or *Desire* part of their nature, these tendencies will obtain more or less sway over them. On the other hand, the more individualised they become the more real *Will* they show, displaying wonderful powers of concentration and indomitable persever-ance. Though rarely anything but practical and objective, they are then generous, kind, and full of feeling for others.

Fixed 'earthly' or objective *feeling* being the main feature of this sign, the Taureans are either faithful and kind friends, or somewhat relentless enemies, only appeasable, if at all, through an appeal to their feelings. In their family life it will often be noticed that they seem to provoke quarrels for the sake of the pleasure it evidently affords them to 'patch it up again'. All Taureans should be very careful in their choice of a marriage partner, for they are more liable than most to err in this direction, more especially when they marry young.

The Venus influence inclines them to a love of music, and they are generally very good vocalists. Taurus also gives a gift for mathematics and finance. The Taurean is usually somewhat of a fatalist, even when professing indifference or scepticism with regard to occult subjects. If at all religious they incline to ceremony and ritual, but the average personal Taurean evinces little interest in religious observances.

Health. Taurus governs the neck and the throat. The constitution is usually exceptionally strong and robust. The neck and throat being the weakest parts, Taureans are subject to sore throats, diphtheria, mumps, quinsy, tumours in the region of the throat. They are also liable to heart and kidney troubles, diabetes, etc. Laziness is fatal to their health, work their best medicine.

Occupation. Cashiers, financial agents, municipal accountants, and collectors, stock-brokers, etc., are found among Taureans. Their great vitality and magnetism make them good masseurs, doctors, nurses. Many have good mechanical ability and succeed well either in the actual manual work connected with mechanism or as foremen. Manufacturers of paper, sweet-stuffs, chemicals, etc., are also found amongst them as are many following agricultural pursuits. They make excellent chefs and cooks.

Type of body. Average to short stature; heavy, strong and thick-set body, inclining to stoutness; broad and full forehead, big mouth and usually thick lips with fleshy cheeks and jaw; big and prominent eyes; black or coarse sandy hair, usually wavy or curly; nose sometimes aquiline, though usually broad and full.

63. ♊ The Sign Gemini ♊: *the Positive House of its Ruler,* ☿. ☉ in ♊ May 21st to June 20th.

This sign is of the *Airy* element and mutable quality.

Gemini individuals are *dual in nature*, intellectual, clever, inspirational, nervous, and restless. Happy, elusive, brilliant, charming, with wonderful powers of imagination, they are so contradictory in nature that one might, at times, think them stolid materialistic pessimists. This is due to their airy, mutable, and mercurial disposition, which makes them reflect every phase and change in their environment. They live mostly in the mind and have a great love of intellectual pursuits, though the knowledge they gain is more often than not the result of picking the brains of others and lightly skimming over books, never sticking for long to any one study.

At times, however, they have a fit of enthusiasm and go to extremes in mental studies. They are active, positive, very adaptable and versatile, and very clever with their hands.

When acting along purely personal lines, they are cunning, acute, very clever, neither over-scrupulous, nor truthful, materialistic, yet always elusive and difficult to understand. A typical personal Gemini subject was Jay Gould, the American multi-millionaire.

The combination of ⊙ in ♊ with ☽ in ♈, ♌, or ♐ increases the positiveness and acuteness of the nature and inclines in many ways to extremes, though giving much force and ability. There is also danger with these combinations of over-assertiveness, which is harmful to the Gemini nature, as there is not the inherent fixity and stamina behind them to enable them, if put to the test, to meet much opposition without great depletion of the nervous system. ⊙ in ♊ is perhaps best combined with ☽ in either Airy or Earthy signs. With ☽ in Watery signs the sensational tendencies need combating.

It has been said of Mercurian people that they can be 'all things to all men', and this is certainly true of Gemini subjects, their versatility being remarkable; but in this lies their greatest weakness, for so volatile is their nature that they find great difficulty in remaining long enough at any one post or undertaking to extract the maximum of success from it. In this way worry through instability of finance often comes upon them. As a rule, they lack the one-pointedness which makes for success, though they are extremely capable workers in many spheres. In affairs of the heart and friendship they are often considered false, yet they are usually honest in intention, and their fickleness is due to the fact that they can love with one side of their twin nature (their symbol is The Twins), while the other side starts to reason out sensations and criticise, thus nullifying the love impulse. They have great powers of expression, and when nervousness has been overcome make eloquent public speakers, diplomats, and actors. They delight in hearing or telling a good story or pun.

Health. Gemini governs the lungs, arms, hands, and nerves. The constitution is not very strong and the health quickly breaks up when the nerves are affected by worry, overwork, shock, etc. There is often catarrhal trouble with the nose and bronchial tubes, while pneumonia and diseases of the lungs generally need to be guarded against. Stammering and very quick speech are also associated with this sign.

Occupation. Their quick, keen, and subtle mentality renders Gemini people excellent brokers, dealers, and auctioneers, while they also excel as public speakers, reporters, journalists, barristers, book-keepers, clerks; in fact, in any mental work which combines change with the necessity of keenness of brain rather than solid, patient effort.

Type of body. Tall stature; thin, upright body; long face and features; sanguine complexion as a rule, though sometimes obscure and dark; when complexion is dark the eyes are very handsome, usually hazel, big and piercing; hair light in first 10° of sign; after, dark, sometimes black; long arms and hands, very quick and active in movement and carriage.

64. ♋ The Sign Cancer ♋: *the House of its Ruler,* ☽. ⊙ in ♋ June 21st to July 21st.

This sign is of the *Watery* element, and cardinal quality. Cancer individuals are very emotional and sensitive, intensely romantic, with vivid

imagination. Like the crab, their symbol in the zodiac, they are extremely tenacious. They are nearly always political and apt to make an idol of some sensational political opportunist.

Cancer persons seem to be drawn to football or cricket matches, political meetings and similar functions where sensation is the main feature; and there they can be studied to advantage. The dignified and quiet man of business then reveals much of his nature; first, the staunch supporter of a particular *party* is seen, then one notices how his tense features and excited gestures reflect every ebb and flow of the fortunes of that party; then, completely under the sway of sensation, he shouts the names of his particular idols, admiringly, coaxingly, fiercely, according to his mood, but always in a personal way, though he has never met them in his life. All this is typical of the Cancerian's glory in movement, action and sensation, besides which it shows up his tendency to be prejudiced, to tinge with the personal element all that comes into his life, thus limiting and cramping his vision.

Where Gemini would take ideas from a novel, history, or person, and from them elaborate some mental vision, Cancer would live and *feel* the part; and thus we often find Cancerians playing a role, *imagining* themselves martyrs or heroes. Similarly they are often plagiarists and copyists, reproducing the thoughts of others, while a short time spent by them in any fresh locality often results in their unconsciously 'absorbing' the manners and vocal intonation of the people they have contacted most. This liability to absorb the nature of others should warn the Cancerian to choose carefully his environment and friends. Deep down within there is a love of all things mystical and occult, antique and curious. They appreciate home comforts, ease and luxury. Sensitiveness about their families, relations, and friends is a very marked feature with them. Retentiveness and tenacity are part of them, and even in the faculty of memory this will be noticed, for they can recall in exact detail minute incidents that have happened many years ago.

They are inventive and original, and many great organisers are found among them. In business, and matters to do with real estate, they show much aptitude. They have a good sense of value, and their economy in small things is often taken to extremes; but in the spending of big sums their sense of proportion is sometimes somewhat lacking.

Of warm affections and sociable nature, they are really shy at bottom, and their ambitions and desires are usually more idealistic than passionate, sensual and worldly; though they are apt to be impressed by ceremony and the gaudy trappings and pompous pretensions of temporal power.

Always eloquent when at their ease, they often give proof of their gifts on the public platform. The combination of ⊙ in ♋ and ☽ in ♐ and ♍ gives much ability in this respect. They take great interest in gardening of all kinds. Music especially appeals to them, and they are often very accomplished in this direction.

Health. Cancer rules the breast and stomach. Giving way to excessive emotion and sensitiveness often causes Cancerians to suffer from gastric and stomach troubles. Pleurisy, dropsy, and all watery and inflammatory diseases are associated with this sign. Vitality is not over strong.

Occupation. Cancerians love the sea and make excellent sailors and naval captains. Their strong domesticity makes women under this sign the best of housekeepers, hotel-keepers, midwives, etc., while they love

to deal in liquids, making good barmaids, laundresses, etc. Dealers in all manner of second-hand articles, curios, etc., real-estate agents, builders' merchants, are also found under Cancer.

Type of body. Average to small stature; somewhat fleshy body, upper part larger than lower; round and full face, forehead usually prominent or even bulging, wide at temples; pale complexion; small blue or grey eyes; hair brown; usually short nose, slightly upturned; somewhat ungainly carriage, especially in mature life.

65. ♌. The Sign Leo ♌: *the House of its Ruler,* ☉. ☉ in ♌ July 22nd to August 21st.

This sign is of the element *Fire,* and of fixed quality. Leo individuals are proud, passionate, ambitious, masterful, honourable, irrepressible, delighting in all that is really big in life. It has been said that they are the born commanders, rulers and kings as much in the material universe as in the realms of the heart, this being their birthright gained through loyalty and the mastery of true obedience. However this may be, Leo persons certainly rank amongst the best organisers and methodisers of the world. They are also usually capable of exercising authority.

Faith seems inherent with them, though it assumes a great variety of forms. Many are staunch upholders of ancient religious doctrines, and will tell one, with evident sincerity, 'I *know* my belief is the only one'. Others subscribing to totally different and often absurd doctrines will say the same thing. Though many people express belief, none leave one so impressed by their sincerity as do the Leo types. They are generous and warm-hearted, cheerful and sociable, and there is a sterling worth about most of them which cannot pass long unnoticed. They rarely go totally to the bad, though many have to pass through the Fire of uncontrolled desire before they realise the Divine Spark within them; for the strength, vitality, and intensity of Leo when turned into sensual and dissolute channels is a terrible force, such a torrent as only Leo himself can stem. But the fall of Leo is more often due to the influence of others than inherent vice. Leo people are particularly subject to disillusionments with regard to their friends.

They generally show pride, though this varies with the type—personal or individual. The personal type is either haughty and boastful, assuming a superiority which he is far from possessing, or accomplished yet discontented or disdainful, looking down on others and showing no desire to give proof of his accomplishments; while the pride of the individual type is neither supercilious aloofness nor empty conceit, but the outward sign of a certain good opinion of himself, quite legitimate and natural.

The combination of ☉ in ♌ and ☽ in ♈, ♌ or ♐ is very good in many respects. With ☽ in ♉ or ♏ the Leo person needs much self-control to combat the lower tendencies of two very strong signs, in order to derive the best from the combination.

Getting to the root of a matter with wonderful directness, Leo people are practical and hard-headed, yet ever ready to obey the dictates of a warm heart, for they are sensitive and emotional as well as intuitive.

Unlike the first fixed sign, Taurus, Leo, though quick to take offence, as quickly forgives; and while Leo likes luxury and pleasure, sometimes too much, it is usually of a very different kind to the sensuous variety favoured by Taurus.

These people are capable of long-sustained effort and the carrying out of great schemes. They seem to do best when having authority over others, as chiefs, managers, or foremen. Their will-power and self-control are usually very strong and they are faithful and trustworthy, sticking hard and fast to their principles and their work. Reverses to them are but the spur to victory. More often than not they appeal to the best in a man to obtain what is due to them, though there is the domineering spirit latent within them and some tendency to dramatic display.

Health. Leo governs the heart and the back. Discord, contention, and excess are enemies to the normally strong Leo constitution. Under their influence the heart suffers. Affections of the ribs, side and back, pleurisy, fevers and convulsions are other illnesses to which Leo people are subject, while they are often troubled with their eyes. Rest in solitude and peace is a wonderful curative agent with them.

Occupation. They excel as organisers, leaders, managers, or foremen. Many social welfare workers are found amongst them, especially women; organists and musicians showing preference for the really grand and inspiring in their art; artists, actors. They do not like manual labour and usually do better in a professional rather than a business career.

Type of Body. Tall to average stature; big-boned and well-knit body, usually lean in young life, inclining to fulness later; somewhat narrow hips; yellow or dark flaxen hair; sanguine or florid complexion; big round head; usually blue or grey, or grey-brown eyes; quick sight; commanding and brisk carriage.

66. ♍ **The Sign Virgo** ♍: *the Negative House of its Ruler,* ☿. ☉ in ♍ August 22nd to September 21st.

This sign is of the element *Earth*, and of mutable quality. Virgo individuals are shrewd, discriminative, diplomatic, quietly active and reserved. They are often thought harsh and taciturn, but the fact is they conceal behind a cold and matter-of-fact exterior the peculiar nervousness of their negative, mercurial temperament. At bottom they are extremely kind and sympathetic, yet so nervous and retiring that, many times, when expected to say a word in consolation, they refrain for fear the mention of the subject should revive sorrowful remembrances in their friends; in some cases their fear is that they may appear too sympathetic and not sufficiently worldly and businesslike. They, more than those born in any other sign, usually feel the need to bolster themselves up and even repress some of their finer instincts in order to keep their equilibrium. It may be said that they maintain their cool and dignified attitude and often impressive presence at the expense of an ill-deserved reputation for coldness of feeling; and thus their true nature is rarely, if ever, seen. When in authority over others they are rather too exacting, though just to a fault.

This is said to be the sign of Service, but since all life is service in some form or other, the statement that Virgo is the servant and not the master is very misleading. As a matter of fact, so industrious, scientific, and adaptable is the Virgo man that very often he rises rapidly to a position of command.

Mr Asquith [later the Earl of Oxford and Asquith] is a Virgo man—and a typical one.

They are essentially methodical and logical, and with suitable training possess the power to tabulate in clear and precise form the most involved

schemes and statistics. Their mental abilities are very good, and they have the analytical type of mind; are very clever in detail work, and their mental working capacity is often extraordinary.

They delight in quoting from famous authors, and history and statistics especially appeal to them. Drugs, patent foods and the like have a strange fascination for them.

Shrewd and subtle, when too material they are amongst the sharpest and least scrupulous of business men. With their positive Mercurian brother, Gemini, they constitute a combination that would hoodwink the world if so inclined. But the good type of Virgo is the most conscientious, methodical, reliable, and hardworking man that could be desired.

Virgo people know instinctively when a thing can be improved upon, and they generally bring about the improvement, being very inventive. They are gifted with manual dexterity and are excellent technicians, but their sphere seems to be more the office and the archive than the field of construction.

Their faults are vacillation and lack of self-confidence, often held in check by innate conscientiousness, but the best of them have, at times, to recognise a certain inclination to give way before difficulties. It is always more or less a struggle for Virgo people to make up their minds, as their nature is to discriminate; and seeing so many points which are hidden from other minds it is all the harder for them to decide on any particular line of action. It is owing to this that responsibility is sometimes a strain on them, but none could say that they are more suited to be servants than masters without a careful consideration of the horoscope as a whole. With the Moon in fixed and fiery signs they make capable and practical leaders.

Health. Virgo rules the bowels, and worry and overwork usually causes diarrhœa, flatulence, and other affections of this part of the body. Care in diet is essential to the health of Virgo people. They are much given to worry, which reacts on their nerves. Drugs and alcohol are very harmful to them.

Occupation. Virgo people do well in all business connected with food and drugs. They make splendid analytical chemists. Editors and literary critics of the solid rather than the superficial class are found amongst them. They are fitted by their tact, mental ability, and business aptitude for practically any professional or business vocation.

Type of body. Tall to average stature; well-knit and often plump body; ruddy or dark complexion; hair and eyes dark; oval face, round forehead; peculiar nose, outstanding, with pronounced curves at side of nostrils.

67. ♎ **The Sign Libra** ♎: *the Positive House of its Ruler,* ♀. ☉ in ♎ September 22nd to October 22nd.

This sign is of the element *Air*, and of cardinal quality. Libra individuals are refined, artistic, very perceptive, intuitive, lovers of pleasure, beauty and elegance, harmony and order. They seem to have the ability to mentally balance (♎ the balance), and seek to arrive at an impartial judgment on most things. They will be found to compare and criticise everything they see, and in the lower order of Libran this is carried to excess, becoming irksome to those about them. This class, though often the very best judges of style, elegance, and beauty of dress, fabrics, and most ornamental things, too often spend the greater part of their lives in prying into other people's affairs and 'picking them to pieces'. Their curiosity seems

insatiable, and they will be found in their element at every sale, bazaar, church service, wedding, or funeral of note, observing and comparing every detail of their surroundings *always seeking to draw conclusions*; fashion, ceremony, convention, family histories and social scandal seem to be the breath of life to the personal Libran. These people show much the same dislike of contention to be noted in the better type of Libran, but while they would go out of their way to avoid a brawl where the differences of others are concerned, are very bitter and go to extremes if provoked themselves. In love and marriage their critical nature soon destroys their happiness.

The combination ⊙ in ♎ and ☽ in ♋ or ♏ needs much control to combat the undesirable traits of Libra; though a very careful study of the horoscope is necessary before it can be pronounced a wholly personal one. And the innate refinement of Libra must always be borne in mind, as it gives a certâin indefinable elegance and charm to all its children, making even the moral lapses which many a Libran fails to guard against far removed from the ordinary conception of vulgarity and vice. Many 'fops', fast-livers, and gamblers are Librans, but their airy elegance, natural politeness and bonhomie, does much to disarm their critics. Their nature is flexible and sensitive, the feelings and emotions very strong, swaying them to such a degree that association and union with others to a large extent moulds their lives.

The good type of Libra shows much sweetness and harmony of nature —justice, courtesy, kindness, generosity, and charming manners being very marked.

Their mental powers are good and they are desirous of mental improvement, often becoming very accomplished. It is rarely, however, that they study anything outside their profession very deeply, being changeable and subject to many moods and fancies, unless the horoscope as a whole shows marked perseverance and will-power.

They show great interest in all occult matters.

When combined with strong influences, Libra gives some noble characters, an instance of which was the late Lord Roberts, whose individual Libran character gave him the highest form of perception, clairvoyance, enabling him to warn the country of the coming of the Great War. It has been remarked of Lord French that he could sense the temper and strength and detect the weakest points of the enemy to a remarkable degree. This is another example of Libra intuition, for he also is a typical individual Libran.

Libra gives a gift for music, poetry, and painting, and an inclination for the law and the higher professions generally.

Libra people are inclined, at times, to vacillate and delay their decisions until too late. They would do well to cultivate concentration.

Health. Libra rules the reins and kidneys. The constitution is usually strong but excess in eating and especially drinking affects the kidneys and the bladder, sometimes causing stone or gravel. Pains in the loins, weakness of the lower part of the back, and humid feet are also associated with this sign. Libra people often fret and allow themselves to get into a very melancholy state. Beautiful and peaceful surroundings are their best medicine.

Occupation. Barristers, lawyers, musical and theatrical people generally and those having the direction and management of the artistic side of

public amusements are found amongst Librans. Secretarial work is also to their liking, and they are clever as artists and decorators. In trade they are antique and art dealers, and have much to do with perfumery, fabrics, fancy stationery, etc.

Many nuns and Sisters of Mercy are Librans.

Type of body. Tall to average stature; well-formed, usually beautiful body; round face, generally lovely, with fine soft red-and-white complexion; smooth long hair, sometimes flaxen, but often dark in latter half of sign; inclining to stoutness after youth; blue eyes as a rule, though sometimes hazel or brown, and full of feeling,

68. ♏ The Sign Scorpio ♏ : *the Negative House of its Ruler, ♂. ⊙ in ♏* October 23rd to November 21st.

This sign is of the element *Water*, and of fixed quality. Scorpio individuals are determined, tenacious, very secretive, critical, cautious, keen, and shrewd. They are very magnetic and many possess a strange hypnotic power over others. It may be said that the most powerful natures, for good or for evil, belong to this sign.

There will be noticed in the higher class of Scorpions a silent watchfulness, something unfathomable, yet all-comprehensive in the eyes, a calmness and quiet intensity and determination bespeaking some wonderful force hidden within them. There is an impressive dignity about them, warning all that no liberty may be taken there. The most magnetic and emotional orators and preachers, the most capable diplomats and the greatest seers are found amongst this class; but there are all too few of them. A deep study of the sign is necessary to form any idea of the wonderful power of the regenerated Scorpion, but it will here suffice to say that Scorpio represents the Sex principle, and when it is remembered that this is a *Watery* or sensational and emotional sign of *fixed* quality, we can imagine the debauchery and degradation of which these Martians are capable when perverting that principle; moreover, we are enabled to understand something of their dramatic nature and of that extraordinary power of attraction and attachment which any observer of human nature will have noticed in Scorpions of both sexes.

The generality of Scorpions are strong-willed, bold, and self-confident, somewhat too direct in manner, showing a masterful temper on the slightest provocation, and resenting anything like a liberty from their fellows. When these people dislike anything they are very bitter and dogmatic. Endowed with all the perceptive and critical qualities of Libra, they lack the elegance and relative harmlessness of the latter sign, and are often relentless and destructive in their criticisms, being capable of biting sarcasm unequalled by any other sign. Thus they make many enemies.

There is always an element of secrecy about them, and they seem to take a delight in baulking the curiosity of others; yet they will unravel the life of another, being natural detectives. More often than not there are tragic and secret love-affairs in their lives, and few of them seem to escape having the works of the devil pushed right under their noses at some period of their careers.

For all their strength of character most of them are very sensitive, fear the opinion of the world too much, and dread the very thought of being ill; while they can generally be swayed through their deep emotions. Their innate fixity of purpose, excellent abilities, and dislike of change

nearly always result in a secure and often influential position in life; yet, although they display a desire to dominate and govern others, it is doubtful if the majority of them are ambitious, beyond the point that gives a certain ease and security of circumstances. If once ambition is awakened, however, their whole energies go to the one point and great things are accomplished, their working power then becoming enormous.

Though they are given to delay matters, when once they have made up their minds they are resistless in their determination to attain their object. They are cool, collected, and resourceful, in fact, resoucefulness in word and deed is an outstanding feature of their character and they are at their best in an emergency. They make firm friends and passionate and jealous lovers, inclining to acts of violence if crossed in love, while they will brook no interference from parents or others in such matters.

They spend money freely on themselves and cannot, as a class, be considered generous, but when they have succeeded in amassing money, often do great good without courting publicity.

The mentality is subtle and acute, capable of great persistence in the unravelling of mysteries of any kind. Thus they are excellent research workers, detectives, occultists, doctors, and being also endowed with manual dexterity, make splendid surgeons. The combination of ☉ in ♏ and ☽ in ♋ inclines much to the medical profession. Many of the cleverest chess players are Scorpions, and there seems little doubt that Napoleon's great military genius was largely due to this sign rising at his birth.

The faults of the Scorpion are many, not least amongst which are pride, harshness, and scepticism, and a tendency to be too exacting, selfish, dogmatic, violent, and unforgiving; but the power for good within him is probably greater than that possessed by any other, since he is endowed with great magnetism, invincible will, and executive ability beyond the ordinary to carry out the work of destroying evil and constructing good.

Health. Scorpio governs the secret parts. The constitution is usually strong, with great powers of resisting disease. Scorpions suffer from all diseases and infections of the generative organs, discharges from the private parts, affections of the bladder and poisoning of the blood, pains in the groin, kidney troubles, etc.

Occupation. Scorpions succeed in all martial employments, such as doctor, surgeon, butcher, mechanical engineers, ironmongers, smiths, etc. They are also hypnotists and magnetic healers, occultists, chemists, inventors of all kinds, detectives, etc. They are in their element at sea and make good naval officers and sailors.

Type of Body. Average to tall stature; corpulent and strong body, usually very hairy; hair rarely fine and generally coarse, thick, and curling; bullet-shaped top part of head, prominent over eyes; square face, aquiline or sometimes ill-shapen 'squashed-out' type of nose, the face often reminding one of an eagle. As a rule, the higher the type, the finer the hair.

69. ♐ **The Sign Sagittarius** ♐ : *the Positive House of its Ruler*, ♃. ☉ **in** ♐ November 22nd to December 20th.

This sign is of the element *Fire*, and of mutable quality. Sagittarius individuals are optimistic, cheerful, honourable, loyal, independent, enterprising, and very active. They possess a natural gift for prophecy

and wonderful intuition. The higher class of Sagittarian combines a keen sense of justice with a philosophical, innately religious, kind and merciful nature; his character is reflected in his face and his bearing, giving to the eyes a marked openness, kindness, and honesty of expression; to the bearing a lofty and noble dignity. They will be found amongst the most merciful judges, the most loved of religious and social workers, the greatest mystics, seers, and philosophers. People seem to gravitate to them for guidance in both spiritual and material matters, for they are Nature's teachers, philosophers and friends, the perfect arbitrators and lawgivers, finding their greatest pleasure in life in showing others that All is Law, and that all pain and discord are due to the fact that this great truth has yet to be internally realised by the majority of mankind. But it is by Law that the Sagittarian comes into his heritage, and he has to learn through rebelliousness, diffusiveness, and other abuses of his higher nature. Thus we find the true rebel against everything, in this sign, and even the religious hypocrite, the advertising philanthropist, and the worst of the toadies to power, especially that of the orthodox clergy and the law.

In this latter stage we see the Sagittarian at his worst, the worshipper of form, enslaved by ritual, ceremony, and convention. His impressionable nature is then working only through the senses; outer perception rules his life, inner perception is not yet his. And it is just this that makes him the hypocrite, for though he is honestly swayed through his senses, he is yet aware of the white flame of truth within him, there to light his way through the dark maze of conventionality and hollow ceremony; but material ambition and desire for preferment have a strong hold on him, and thus he becomes the plausible toady and hypocrite, chiefly in the domains of the Church, the law, and politics, since these constitute his natural bent.

In the rebel we get the awakening of the inner-self. Thomas Carlyle was typical of the class. The inherent honesty of the Sagittarian has triumphed at last, revolting against hypocrisy and the blind worship of form, power, and authority; his intuition now enables him to see through the hollow sham of most things in this material world, and he becomes a dangerous enemy to the established order of things, principally to the lower Sagittarians installed in their lucrative posts in the Church and the law. But gradually he reduces his militant and rebellious activities, for he has glimpsed the Great Law working in All, and his philosophy has made him more tolerant of the weaknesses of others. And so he comes into his heritage to *guide and uplift*, rather than destroy and cast down.

This is a contradictory sign, in many ways similar to its opposite, Gemini, though showing its changeableness in advancing and relatively permanent states of consciousness, causing the Sagittarian to modify his views and change his profession or trade, always once, and mostly many times during his life. Sagittarians are born teachers, and no sooner do they gain knowledge than they are eagerly imparting it to others. Even the lower order of them will rarely abuse a personal trust. They like one to place implicit confidence in them, and through this characteristic and their innate honesty are probably trusted more than any other class. They are far too outspoken, causing annoyance to sensitive people and often putting themselves back in life through making their ambitions too evident. Somewhat hasty and impulsive, their fiery anger is soon aroused

when their great intuition enables them to wound and cover their enemies with confusion in a very few words, for they know instinctively the weakest points of others and shoot their mental arrows straight to the vulnerable spot. Morally they know no fear, and are great lovers of liberty, freedom of speech, and justice that, either in their own defence or in the cause of another, they will fight to the end to redress an injury, though avoiding physical violence if at all possible, as they are really peaceable and humane in nature.

Their nature seems to oblige them to seek the company of others, and they are splendid companions, showing great insight into human nature and possessing a keen sense of humour.

They have strong will-power, and work feverishly to complete a task, yet they are generally better adapted to work in partnership or co-operation with others than by themselves, though they are very independent, dislike restraint, and always seek to rule and lead others. They have splendid foresight and are born organisers, combining these qualities with dash and precision. It is typical of them to say that they like to do something big, difficult and even dangerous, but soon over and done with! For they love change and novelty.

As a class they are generous, but where money is concerned are always on their guard, and through their intense dislike of being imposed upon are often thought niggardly. Music always appeals to them, and many are very accomplished musicians, while all things artistic have a marked fascination for them and they are amongst the best judges of beauty and ornamentation.

The mentality is of high order, fitting them for all the higher professions, philosophy and the most abstruse subjects. They have a gift for languages, good executive ability and manual dexterity. Amongst their faults are irritability, restlessness, and a tendency to be too assertive, intolerant, defiant, distant, and casual; while they go to extremes, often dissipate their energies on too many schemes, are a little inclined to exaggeration, and lack concentration unless fairly individualised.

Health. Sagittarius governs the thighs and hips. This sign gives a sound and wiry constitution, but Sagittarians are always highly strung; excesses, worry or overwork cause nervous breakdowns. Fistulas, tumors, and all diseases affecting the hips and thighs are associated with this sign; sciatica, rheumatism, varicose veins, too-heated blood, fevers, etc. Fresh air and exercise are absolutely essential for the well-being of Sagittarians.

Occupation. Military officers, civil engineers, politicians, clergymen, college professors, and barristers are found among Sagittarians; also commercial travellers, advertising and advance agents, inspectors, horse-dealers, book-makers, etc.

Type of Body. Above the average stature and usually tall; wiry and well-formed body; generally good looking, with very expressive and open-looking eyes; sunburnt colour of complexion; hair light brown or chestnut to dark; inclined to baldness; peculiarity about front teeth. Eyes usually blue or hazel, sometimes brown; high forehead, oval face; dignified and commanding carriage.

70. ♑ The Sign Capricorn ♑ : *the Negative House of its Ruler,* ♄. ☉ in ♑ December 21st to January 19th.

This sign is of the element *Earth,* and of cardinal quality.

Capricorn individuals are economical, practical, persevering, shrewd, diplomatic, reserved, cautious. They are essentially plodders, and a self-made man of business who has started with nothing and created a huge store is typical of the class. The higher type of Capricornians impress one by their solidity, gravity, faithfulness, impartiality, and wonderful capacity for plodding, patient, and thorough industry. They are just, but one must not look to them for allowances for failings, nor the mercy of the Sagittarian for the wrong-doer. Justice, hard and stern, they give, as judges or as men of business. They expect from an employee what he was engaged to do; they ask no more, but they will accept no less. They give the exact value for money and they expect it from others. To waste time or material is a crime to them; not even the crumbs from their tables are wasted; yet, if careful, they are certainly not mean. Neatness and tidiness are born in them. One might sum them up as the most eminently sensible, practical, and exact of the human type, possessing stability, endurance, calm, and earnest perseverance probably unequalled by any other sign. They will be found amongst the greatest financiers and bankers, real-estate brokers, government contractors and officials, judges and scientists. Though they are brisk, there is nothing dashing or assertive about them, and their bearing is more often solid and heavy than dignified, the dominant notes being gravity and reflection, with occasional lapses into sparkling but quiet wit, gaiety and even eloquence.

The lower type of Capricorn is easily recognisable, for Saturn leaves his mark on his unwilling pupils for all to see. The sallow, discontented and gloomy face; the miserly, deceitful, surly, distant and repining nature; the humility of a Uriah Heep and the avarice of a Gaspard, are the signs; and some of them are always to be seen.

The average Capricornians are self-possessed and somewhat self-centred people, very firm-willed, subtle, cautious and suspicious. Very subject to moods, they have at times to fight hard against discontent and melancholy. Ambition is very strong with them, and it is a poor specimen of their class who does not leave this world far richer than he entered it. As a rule their lives are not altogether happy, and there is generally a lot of enmity towards them from many sources, partly through their own self-centred natures and partly because they are misunderstood by others.

They have much force of character and strong temper though nothing like the irresistible nature of the fixed signs; but when they encounter a stronger will than their own they can wait a long while and attain their object by subtle and roundabout routes. They are fitted to rule and manage, and are never happy unless exercising authority and power, no matter what their sphere in life. Usually they lead more or less public lives and have much to do with the masses, often working great good amongst them, according to their peculiar and Saturnine lights.

Though they make good friends and are sociable in their own circle, they do not take easily to strangers, and are very reserved and uncommunicative with them. They always hold people at a distance until quite sure of them, and those who offend them usually rue it and do not get the chance to repeat the offence, for they make bad enemies. The mentality is clever, subtle, acute, and profound, fitting them either for entirely mental pursuits or for business organisation and management, as they also possess executive ability, great tact, diplomacy, prudence, and method. The

combination of ☉ in ♋ and ☽ in ♌ gives many successful speculators, while ☽ in ♐ inclines to legal matters and oratory, though lessening concentration.

Capricornians make subtle and often brilliant debaters, and delight in getting the best of an argument. Like Cancer people, they are nearly always political, and are not as a rule inclined to worry about the moral aspect of the power that subjugates peoples and builds empires so long as it is orthodox and has been ordained by the powers that be; for they are fatalists and compulsionists at heart, and when in power themselves often become the greatest despots, even when they have obtained their power by fighting despotism.

They always look up to intellect, but are usually too material-minded to be much affected by others, anything unconventional and unorthodox being their *bête noire*. They run in a groove mentally, and quickly bridle if anyone dares to suggest that their ideas are wrong.

They are not idealistic, and their mission seems to be to *conserve* what is conventional and orthodox in order that the more advanced and inspirational element of humanity may not revolutionise the world in too great a hurry. If all the world consisted of Capricornians it would be a hive of industry and order; but we should be offering up human sacrifices to wooden gods as of old and doing much as we did thousands of years ago; for Capricorn does not *create*, at most it improves, organises, methodises and sacrifices.

The key-notes of Capricorn seem to be ambition, duty, and sacrifice. These self-centred people, strange as it may be, though they sacrifice others, will sacrifice themselves more than most, when what they consider to be their duty calls. Kind and affectionate and yearning for sympathy, Saturn yet seems to withhold something from them, for they are usually more feared than liked, more respected than loved.

Their faults are malice and revengefulness, a tendency to go to extremes to satisfy ambition, to badger and nag at others, and to be cold and inconsiderate of the feelings and wishes of others, fanatical in regard to some religious creed, toadies to the aristocracy, even when railing at them, worshippers of power.

Health. Capricorn rules the knees. The constitution is fairly strong, but Capricornians are usually subject to much ill-health, especially women, often becoming very despondent and melancholy. All diseases of the knees, itch, cutaneous complaints, and rheumatism are associated with this sign.

Occupation. Managers and organisers of all huge enterprises requiring persistent and long-sustained effort, contractors, real-estate agents and brokers, lawyers, farmers and agricultural workers and dealers, researchers, landed-proprietors, etc., are found amongst Capricornians.

Type of body. Average to short stature, usually dry and bony body; face angular and long, with long chin and nose; long, small neck; narrow chest and weak or slightly deformed knees; some peculiarity of carriage; lank and thin hair and beard, usually dark.

71. ♒ The Sign Aquarius ♒: *the Positive House of its Ruler,* ♄. ☉ in ♒ January 20th to February 18th.

This sign is of the element *Air*, and of fixed quality. Aquarius individuals are refined, artistic, intellectual, faithful and humane. The higher type of Aquarian combines all the practical and persevering qualities of Capricorn

with much intuition, very exalted ideals of life, and the natural ability to read character.

They are quiet but very intense, strong and forceful characters, impressing one with their strange magnetism and a wonderful mentality combined with a disposition delightfully open and naïve. Typical representatives of this class were Ruskin and Charles Dickens. Each showed, in his own peculiar way, a vast understanding of humanity and the splendid literary gift of the sign. The marked magnetism of Aquarians makes them in many ways as strong and forceful as Scorpions, yet the impression they give is quite unlike Scorpio, for there is an airy-mental electrifying 'something' about them which ever eludes the understanding of even the most intuitive of character-readers. This quality of theirs, and the fact that they exhibit inventiveness, idealism, and the power to transcend the material and think far ahead of the times in which they live, seems conclusive proof that Uranus the Awakener is to a great extent the ruler of this sign.

In the lower types of Aquarius the Uranian influence is even more marked, for then we see the fiery and erratic temper, extreme independence, sudden fits of eccentricity and seething internal unrest, reminding one of a volcano which may erupt at any minute, perverse and threatening in its silence as it gives off the fumes of anger. These fits of strange and often unaccountable silence are a marked feature of the sign, and even in the more evolved types they will occasionally be noticed, making the Aquarian a very difficult person to understand and get on with when in these moods.

In the lower type we get the extreme egoist, false, scheming and selfish, using his mental gifts and inflexible will for ambition and personal aggrandisement only, entirely regardless of principle. Such a man is Wilhelm II of Germany. In his case the combination of ⊙ in ♒ and ☽ in ♏, both strong and *fixed* signs, will give the intuitive reader an idea of the tremendous power for good or evil imprisoned within him. He chose to live on the personal side of his nature (☽ in ♏), perverting instead of strengthening his individual self (⊙ in ♒).

The average Aquarians are fixed, strong-willed, and intellectual characters, generally reserved, quiet, and thoughtful in mien, though, at times, showing a naïveté and apparent frivolousness of character which deceives others as to their true worth. Nervous and highly strung, they are very quick and active, and capable of enormous temporary resistance to fatigue, often injuring their health through incessant and prolonged application to some particular work.

Some of their peculiarities are a desire to be quite alone at times; to resent the interference or even help of others in their work unless they are in command; to be very reserved and secretive if questioned on any matter, when if left to tell their tale at their own time they would be quite frank. They are also subject to many disappointments and disillusionments with regard to other people, for they read character so quickly that the outer veneer of society does not hold them long entranced, and they seem to feel, as a consequence, a kind of mental isolation and solitude. If they become attached to others they are very faithful and seem to be able to hold their friends and lovers in a very marked manner. At the same time, they do not readily give their confidence to other people, and it is practically impossible for them to 'make friends' again if once offended or

deceived, so deep is their resentment and sensitiveness. Though their friendships are usually life-long and no sacrifice is too great for those they love, they are generally undemonstrative. They are always found declaiming against snobbishness, but, to others, they often appear to ignore or be too casual or condescending to those below them in station; yet they delight to engage in humanitarian works, and freely give both their time and money.

All things intellectual and artistic appeal to them strongly, and they will be found to frequent, very much, public lectures and meetings, the opera, theatres, etc., and they make very good entertainers, impersonators, etc.

The mentality is very clear and profound, fitting them for literary and scientific pursuits. There is much originality and usually a marked gift for character impersonation, poetry, novel-writing, or music, while they are capable of controlling others as managers or inspectors, more especially in any position in which they can instruct as well as direct.

Electrical work in any of its branches seems to appeal especially to them, and in the higher types the literary gift is sure to come out.

They show a horror of cruelty in any form, and are great lovers of dumb animals.

Their faults include scepticism, a tendency to be too fixed and self-opinionated, strange and sudden fits of waywardness and silence, and concentrated and lasting dislike for those who offend them. Often they make their lives sad, gloomy, and lonely through their own strange and erratic temperaments, living in the mind far too much for their well-being, while some of the worst religious fanatics are found in this sign, generally inclining to form and ceremony, though sometimes evincing egotism and megalomania.

Health. Aquarius rules the ankles and legs. The constitution is not very strong, though wiry. Swollen legs and ankles and all diseases and weaknesses of these parts, poor circulation, cramps, pains through flatulence, spasmodic and nervous diseases, are peculiar to this sign. The Moon in Aquarius, especially when badly aspected, gives trouble with the eyes. The quiet and peaceful contemplation of nature is the best medicine for those born in this sign.

Occupations. Railway, post-office and telegraph employees, managers, engineers, and surveyors, are largely recruited from Aquarians. Reformers and revolutionists in many spheres are amongst them, and they will be found much in evidence in all public companies and associations. Musicians, poets, astronomers, astrologers, literary workers, artists, secretaries, etc., are other occupations of this sign.

Type of Body. Average to short stature, thick-set and usually plump and well-made; good complexion, from pearly pink-and-white to sanguine; hair flaxen or sandy when young, going darker as life advances; somewhat long face, often very good looking; hazel or blue and magnetic eyes.

72. ♓ The Sign Pisces ♓ : *the Negative House of its Ruler,* ♃. ☉ in ♓ February 19th to March 20th.

This sign is of the element *Water,* and of mutable quality. Pisces individuals are patient, emotional, sympathetic, honourable, generous, and hospitable. Very sensitive and impressionable, they possess subtlety and a natural power of persuasion, having a wonderful capacity for

quiet and tactful persistence when dealing with others, serving as an asset against an often painful sensitiveness which tends to keep them in the background in life. This excessive sensitiveness is usually noticed when the Moon is in a watery or Earthy sign.

The higher types of the sign impress one by their ready sympathy, broad-mindedness, patience, and quietness of mien. Marked features about them are their quickness of understanding and willingness to listen to and learn from others. They show great interest in archæology, geology, and, in fact, all nature studies, and are very psychic and mediumistic characters. Occultism especially appeals to them.

As they like to combine the practical with the theoretical, they are very useful and well-informed people on a great variety of subjects, while their literary abilities are often pronounced. Typical of this class was Dr. Richard Garnett, the Keeper of the Printed Books at the British Museum and a noted student of astrology.

In the lower types the duality of the sign is more easily seen than in the more individualised Piscurians, though in all a certain contradiction and duality of nature will be noted. The less evolved type is either a very weak and dissipated person, his own worst enemy, knocked about from pillar to post by circumstances which he seems powerless to control; or impetuous, assertive and seemingly confident, but unable to do what he professes and easily beaten in a test of strength and spirit. Deceit, hypocrisy, lying, lack of self-confidence and initiative, fretfulness, peevishness, and morbid fear of reverses; a feeling that fate is against them and everyone conspiring to do them harm; alcoholism, and all the vices of the senses will be found in these types; while they quickly absorb the magnetism from evil associates and are often led to their ruin. Yet this is a Jupiterian sign, and it will be noticed that the schemer and the thief amongst Piscurians often voluntarily returns what he has stolen and in many ways atones for any evil act. Similarly their enemies usually become their friends, so difficult is it to harbour resentment against them, for they have no inherent vice; while they themselves quickly forgive an injury. These personal Piscurians are great talkers and boasters, and of them it may truly be said that one 'cannot get a word in edge-ways', in vivid contrast to their quiet, reserved and somewhat silent individualised brethren. They are, like the lower type of their positive brothers, the Sagittarians, much swayed by form and ceremony.

The average Piscurians are good-natured, friendly, sympathetic, and benevolent people, kind and easy-going, loving beauty and refinement in everything. Somewhat timid and shy at bottom, they are nevertheless capable of taking care of themselves and show much spirit and dignity if anyone presumes to take advantage of their good nature and inoffensiveness, though they detest anything violent and vulgar. The fact that a very large number of nurses, hospital attendants, and officials of charitable institutions and organisations are found amongst Piscurians is significant of their sympathetic and humane natures. They seem to be fated to have something to do with charity and nursing at some period of their lives.

They are usually best fitted to fill some post under others, and though frequently fretting under authority, know instinctively that if having to rely entirely on their own initiative they would be liable to worry, apprehension, and failure. Through this they often make the fortunes of more self-confident men, remaining frequently but ill rewarded for their labours.

When seeking their fortunes otherwise than in the employment of others, they should join with a suitable partner.

They are mentally ambitious, being very desirous of perfection in their studies, though somewhat lacking in concentration. Their material ambition might be said to work from point to point, as they rarely set out with a fixed idea of what they want, their careers, more often than not, being moulded by circumstances. They often follow two or more occupations at the same time, travel entering largely into their lives, while the more change and novelty they get in their employment the happier they are.

The mentality is good, *method* and order being much in evidence, fitting them for organisation in many spheres. Their vivid imagination, excellent powers of expression, and understanding of the inner meaning of words, make them capable literary workers, while their considerable adaptability and versatility open up a large and varied field for their activities. Music, singing, painting, and drawing very much appeal to them, and they generally show aptitude in one or more of these accomplishments.

Their main object should be to cultivate concentration and fixity of purpose, and combat excessive sensitiveness. Their faults, like those of the Sagittarians, are usually such as can easily be forgiven, but they are too ready to vacillate and be discouraged and despondent, often feeling themselves somewhat of martyrs, incline to dissipate their energies in too many schemes, and seem to wait for approbation to spur them on, being very disappointed if it is not forthcoming.

Health. Pisces governs the feet. The constitution is rarely strong, and there is usually much trouble with the feet through lameness and pains, swellings, and rheumatism proceeding from impure blood.

Other marked features of the sign are blotches, boils, ulcers, tumours, mucous diseases and discharges of the bowels, and colds and chills caught through the feet, often leading to consumption. Fresh air and exercise, and the avoidance of low-lying and damp localities, are essential for the health of Pisces people.

Occupations. Chiefs of department, organising agents and secretaries, agents of all descriptions, literary workers, book-keepers, librarians, nurses, sailors and naval officers, caterers, hotel-keepers, etc., are found amongst Piscurians.

Type of Body. Average to short stature; fleshy and lymphatic body; short thick limbs; pale complexion; rather large face; hair ranging from light brown to dark; usually prominent and sleepy-looking eyes, often subject to styes and redness on the lids; often a peculiarity about the feet.

V

THE TWELVE HOUSES OF THE CHART

73. The Three Kinds of Houses. The horoscope chart is divided into twelve houses (sections), namely:

Four ANGULAR HOUSES: Houses I, IV, VII, X.

Four SUCCEDENT HOUSES: Houses II, V, VIII, XI.

Four CADENT HOUSES: Houses III, VI, IX, XII.

One house of each kind (angular, succedent, cadent) make up a quadrant of the horoscope, if each house be considered to begin at its cusp. (If the other view be taken, that the cusp is the centre of the house, then a quadrant begins and ends at cusps of angular houses, and contains the second half of one angular house, the whole of one succedent, and one cadent house, and the first half of another angular house.)

74. Houses and Signs. The houses are sometimes regarded as being so analogous to the twelve signs of the zodiac that the ruler (Mars) of the first sign (Aries) is called the 'natural ruler' of the first house, even though the sign Aries be nowhere near the first house; Venus (ruler of Taurus) the natural ruler of the second house; and so on. The so-called 'accidental ruler' of the first house is the ruler of whatever sign may be on the cusp of house I. Thus if the cusp of the second house is 25° Sagittarius, then Venus (ruler of Taurus, the second sign) is 'natural ruler', and Jupiter (ruling planet of Sagittarius) is 'accidental ruler', of the second house. But the planet that is actually *in* the house is probably the 'effective', or more important, 'ruler' of that house, if any planet *is* in the house. As ruling or most important planet of a house, therefore, consider:

(i) The planet contained in the house itself, if any; if more than one, the one nearest to the cusp, or, of one before and one after the cusp, the one after the cusp, if at least in the half-house that starts at the cusp.

(ii) If there be no planet in the house, the 'accidental ruler' (ruling planet of the sign on the cusp of the house).

75. Influences in Houses. The matters dealt with by a particular house, however, are subject to the combined influences inferred from the most important or ruling planet (as above), the aspects to that planet, the sign containing the accidental ruler, the aspects, house-positions, and sign-position of the 'natural ruler'; and the nature and aspects of any other planets that are actually in the house, and the signs *they* are in (because part of the house may be in a sign not on the cusp).

76. Subject-Matter of each House.

House 1. The person himself (the Native); his personal appearance, the character he *shows*, his personality as manifested in life on earth; his

behaviour and manner in general, and general tendencies as to personal relations with others.

House 2. Money and movable possessions; income and expenditure; financial fortunes.

House 3. Brainwork, communications, going about, brethren and neighbours (including studies, speech, languages, writing, publicity, agencies, retail trade, short journeys, and relationships with brothers, sisters, cousins, etc.).

House 4. Home environment, closing years of retirement from public work, dwelling place, houses and landed property, and one of the parents (probably the mother).

House 5. Creation, recreation, procreation; love affairs, courtship; childbirth and the begetting of children; children and the young in general, creative artistic work; amusements and pleasures; business or professional work connected with amusement and pleasure (the stage, screen, concert-platform, etc.); sexual compatibility in married life; gambling or speculation.

House 6. Servants and employees; or relations with employer and work, as a subordinate employee; service and healing; sickness and recovery; which parts of the body are most likely to suffer in illness or injury.

House 7. Pairing with an equal; marriage, and agreed partnerships (domestic or professional or commercial); joint undertakings, company business; war, litigation, open conflict with an opponent (as in an election or competition); one's 'opposite number', in fact.

House 8. Death (one's own or anyone else's affecting one); inheritance of goods or money or characteristics etc.; any activities or interests concerned with death or the dead (undertaker's business, position as executor of will, mediumship, for communication with the departed, etc.); 'other people's money' (position as custodian or manager of it; finances as affected by husband's or wife's or partner's affairs); bequests and legacies.

House 9. 'Remote exploration' in either a geographical or metaphysical sense: foreign travel, relations with foreigners, foreign interests or people; religious and philosophical outlook and experiences and interests; the law and lawyers; the Church and Churchmen; predictive dreams.

House 10. Fame or notoriety, reputation, public work, career, professional business and position in the world; the other parent (probably father).

House 11. Position in social organisation—friends, acquaintances, socia contacts, interests in open societies or organisations for social reform or idealistic or altruistic or philanthropic purposes.

House 12. The secret inner life; secret societies (Freemasonry, etc.); places of seclusion and restraint (hospitals, prisons, asylums, orphanages and similar 'institutions'); life of fantasy and daydream; conspiracies and intrigue, secret enemies or enmities; idle dreams.

77. Element-Affinities of Houses. Adventurous and creative houses, corresponding to the Fire signs of the zodiac, are the first, fifth, and ninth. Materialistic houses, corresponding to the Earth signs, are the second, sixth, and tenth. Mental houses corresponding to the Air signs are the third, seventh, eleventh. Psychic houses corresponding to the Water signs are the fourth, eighth, twelfth.

Planets in Houses

Subject to modifications by aspects and by the sign each planet is in, and other considerations, the following give an idea of the meaning of each planet in or ruling each house (numbers, 1–12, show the houses):

78. Sun in:

1. Health, vitality, honour, courage, success.
2. Financial prosperity.
3. Success in writing or the like, in going about, in dealings with kindred and neighbours.
4. Good auguries for matters of residence, home-life, and real estate.
5. Richness of love-life and emotional experience, speculation; good for pleasure, children, social functions.
6. Success in employment; possibly delicate health.
7. Good for marriage, partnership or company business, popularity.
8. Success in other things *through* marriage or partners, or inheritance.
9. Success in law or the Church, or abroad.
10. Success in occupation and career, positions of responsibility.
11. Social and material success through friends and superiors.
12. Retired life and occupation, much withdrawn.

79. Moon in:

1. Changeable, imaginative, acquisitive, journeys.
2. Fluctuating 'ups and downs' in finances (aspects, good or bad, make great difference).
3. Many journeys or removals; enquiring, active mind.
4. Good for real estate, inheritance, and domestic life; changes.
5. Many love-affairs, some fickleness perhaps, tends to large family.
6. Best as employee, gain in service; sometimes not very strong vitality.
7. Success in marriage and partnership (if with good aspects to Moon), popularity, and publicity.
8. Legacies; gain or loss (according to aspects) through deaths.
9. Much travel, or changeable outlook in matters of religion and philosophy; success in these things if well aspected.
10. Fluctuating variations of success (good, with good aspects) in profession and public life, with changes probable; popularity in profession.
11. Popularity socially, many associates, woman friends.
12. Good for interests associated with hospitals, prisons, etc.; some seclusion.

80. Mercury in:

1. Witty, quick-witted, good speaker, good dealer.
2. Financial gain through brainwork.
3. Good brain, excellent for brainworking professions.
4. Many changes of residence.
5. Clever children, mental pleasures.
6. Good as employee in brainwork.
7. Marriage with mental interests shared; good for businesses (companies or partnerships) in Mercurian lines (journalism, publishing transport, etc.).
8. Nerviness; gain or loss through deaths.

9. Good intellect, professional abilities (especially law or Church): much travel.

10. Professional career in Mercury lines (literary, publishing, commerce, transport).

11. Clever, not always reliable, friends.

12. Worries, mental distractions.

81. Venus in:

1. Pleasing disposition, popular, artistic, sociable, good looks.

2. Financial success, if no bad aspects.

3. Harmony with relatives of same generation; success in studies and in things involving going from place to place in own country; perhaps in literary work, especially of artistic or romantic kinds.

4. Harmonious closing years of life; good fortune in matters of real estate; peaceful home life.

5. Good for love, children, pleasure, artistic or musical work.

6. Good for health and for employment.

7. Success in marriage and partnership.

8. Money by legacies or marriage, if not badly aspected.

9. Gain through travel, or happiness in religion.

10. Gain through parents, happiness in career.

11. Pleasure and profit through friendships.

12. Charitable, or gain from charity; secret love-affairs.

82. Mars in:

1. Enterprising spirit, quick temper, quick worker, energetic, plucky.

2. Extravagance, heavy expenses or losses, wealth needs effort to gain.

3. Combative mind, quarrels with kindred, perhaps literary.

4. Troubled home-life; losses in real estate.

5. Trouble through children, love-affairs, pleasure, gambling; if with good aspects, male children.

6. Trouble through servants or with employers; illnesses, if any, feverish or inflammatory—wounds, cuts, burns.

7. Passionate or unfortunate marriage; conflict; possible loss of spouse.

8. Legacies; if with bad aspects, possibilities of disputes *re* legacies or inheritance, or of violent manner of death; bereavements.

9. Militant in religious and philosophical matters; litigation; dangers in foreign travel.

10. Masterful; warlike, or surgical, or engineering, or similar occupations; difficulties or troubles regarding career or business, or parents (or one).

11. Unpopularity, or trouble with, or death of, friends.

12. Dangers of persecution, treachery, self-undoing literal or metaphorical.

83. Jupiter in:

1. Noble nature, wise, merciful, religious.

2. Best indication of financial prosperity, if no bad aspects; some extravagance possible, especially with bad aspects.

3. Refined mind, good for going about, and relations with kinsmen.

4. Domestic happiness, prosperity from parents, or from real estate.

5. Fortunate in children and speculation, expansive in social pleasures.
6. Success as employer or employee; health good if not badly aspected.
7. Excellent for marriage and partnership.
8. Legacies, money by marriage.
9. Success in religion, law, the Church, voyages abroad.
10. Rise to affluence, fame.
11. Influential friends, social popularity.
12. Success in occultism or Freemasonry; benevolence.

84. Saturn in:

1. Cautious, worldly, acquisitive, persistent.
2. Economy, restricted means, gain difficult, and needs hard work.
3. Slow but thoughtful mind; on cold terms with relatives.
4. Unhappy or cramped home-life.
5. Sorrow through children; losses in speculation; frustration in love.
6. Trouble with servants, or in employment; ill-health if with bad aspects, especially lingering or chronic maladies, or through cold.
7. Late, not always happy, marriage, or with discrepancy in age or social rank.
8. If with bad aspects, many losses by death; slow death.
9. Troubles through, or frustration in, travel or religion; if with good aspects, very serious philosophical mind.
10. Slow rise in life; if with bad aspects, risks of ultimate downfall.
11. Friends faithful and few, or (with bad aspects) lost through death.
12. Morbid introspection or fantasies; risks through treachery.

85. Uranus in:

1. Strong will, independence, originality, although restless and highly strung.
2. Speculation, financial independence.
3. Inventiveness, exaggeration, contradiction of ideas.
4. Domestic instability, enforced changes.
5. Creative originality, sudden infatuations.
6. Unusual career; unusual health symptoms.
7. Competitive nature; sudden attachments in love, erratic romances, jealousy.
8. Unexpected financial gains through legacy, sudden accidents.
9. Unorthodox philosophical outlook; unexpected journeys.
10. Versatile; seeks freedom; powerful position through advancement.
11 Sudden friendships and attachments; high ideals.
12. Intuitive nature.

86. Neptune in:

1. Visionary, idealistic, receptive, imaginative, changeable.
2. Financial compunctions, indifferent to money.
3. Impressionable, intuitive.
4. Strong parental ties, seclusion in latter years.
5. Pleasure seeking, though easily bored.
6. Lack of effort; sensitive to environment.
7. Sacrificial demands in marriage.
8. Sensitivity, financial disappointments.
9. Mystical, idealistic, inconclusive.
10. Artistic occupation, impractical, high inspirations.
11. Demanding nature with friends.
12. Charitable, sympathetic, contemplative.

87. Pluto in:

1. Sense of adventure, good potentialities, courage, stable, learns by experience.
2. Sensationai and unusual activities.
3. Versatile, original, revolutionary.
4. Many changes in home and environment.
5. Impulsive creative urge.
6. Resourceful career in help to others.
7. Co-operative, self-sufficient, secretive.
8. Desire for truth, shrewd, philosophical.
9. Quest for knowledge, love of travel.
10. Independence, self-assertive, quest for power.
11. Prefers company of others, influential.
12. Mystical interest, suppressed emotions.

VI

THE RIVAL SYSTEMS OF HOUSE-DIVISION

N.B. You cannot fully understand this Chapter without having read pp. xi–xii (Introduction) and mastered pp. 2–6, *especially paragraphs 5, 6, 10, 11, 12, 19, 22, 25, 26, 27, 28.*

90. Placidus. The system most widely used at the present day is that of Placidus, seventeenth century, generally adopted in England in the eightteenth century, and now (quite mistakenly) supposed, by those no better informed, to be the standard traditional system, simply because tables of houses based on it, but not mentioning this fact or containing any hint that it is merely one system of many, were published a century ago, and have since been imitated and continued, and enable students to copy the houses from them without any inquiry as to what they mean. The ordinary tables of houses on sale are really tables of the 'Houses According to Placidus'.

91. Placidus System Applied to 0° Aries or Libra. Ascendant and M.C. are used as cusps of houses 1 and 10. If the Ascendant happens to be 0° of Aries, it will be the M.C. six sidereal hours later, the Descendant six hours after that, the I.C. six hours later still, and the Ascendant again after another six hours, completing the twenty-four hours. From eastern horizon (where it is Ascendant) to the meridian over the earth (where it is M.C.) and from there to western horizon (where it is Descendant) are the two 'diurnal semi-arcs' of this degree; and under the earth are its two nocturnal semi-arcs. This degree, and also 0° of Libra, takes thus an equal period of six hours to go through each semi-arc, which corresponds to one quadrant of the horoscope chart. So Placidus makes 0° of Aries or Libra each cusp in turn, in reverse numerical order, namely, cusps* I, XII, XI, X, IX, VIII, VII, VI, V, IV, III, II, and I again at equal intervals of two hours sidereal time.

92. Applied to other Degrees and Signs. But at the geographical latitude of London, for instance, 0° of Gemini, as a random example, takes nearly eight hours going through each diurnal semi-arc (or backwards through the two quadrants from I to X and from X to VII), and only about four hours going through each of the other two semi-arcs (or quadrants of the chart), under the earth. So, for London, Placidus makes 0° Gemini cusp I at S.T. 20h.0m., XII at 22h.37m., XI at 1h.14m., X at 3h.51m., taking about 2h.37m. from cusp to cusp above the earth, and then at the shorter interval of about 1h.24m. (all these times are only roughly approximate) he makes it reach in turn each of the remaining cusps below the earth. This system is therefore based on *artificially equalised* subdivisions of the

---

* It is convenient often to use Roman figures for houses (II for 'second' etc.), as will often be done in the following pages.

naturally unequal amounts of time a degree of the zodiac spends in each quadrant. Taking each degree in turn, after the time when it is Ascendant at a given place has been calculated, as well as the time when it is M.C. (the same at all places), it is easy, by this system, to make a complete table of houses for that place. But without such a complete table it would be far too difficult for most people to calculate what are the twelve cusps at a given moment. So this is a good 'publisher's system' for 'tables of houses'!

93. Notes on Placidus. This is the only system that is not geometrical: does not divide the entire celestial sphere into areas, equal or unequal, by lines meeting at any two opposite points (which would be poles of whatever primary circle might be used as basis of a system of house-division. No such primary circle is the basis of the Placidus system). All other systems are geometrical, and divide the whole sphere into areas bounded by lines perpendicular to, and meeting at the poles of, one primary circle. As some degrees of the zodiac are never Ascendant or Descendant (cusps I and VII) at geographical latitudes greater than 66°33′, those degrees, at such places, have no time-interval from cusp I to cusp X to divide (and similarly in the other three quadrants), so cannot be given any house-position, and if not exactly M.C. or I.C. (cusp X or IV), have to be left out of the horoscope, along with any planet, or even the Sun or Moon, happening to be in those degrees. A well-known New York lady, author and lecturer, has no Jupiter in her horoscope by this system, for that reason, having been born at latitude 70° N. in Greenland. But astrologers (except those now busily developing astrology in Finland and nearby places) seldom have to study horoscopes for such far-north or far-south places; in the days of Placidus, they *never* had to.

94. The Equal-House System simply uses Ascendant as cusp I and then divides the whole zodiac into twelve equal parts for the twelve houses, by putting the same degree of the next sign on the next cusp (II), the same degree of the sign after that on cusp III, and so on all round. As the M.C. is usually more or less than 90° (or three signs) from the Ascendant, the M.C., by this system, is not usually cusp X or any other cusp, but is by modern users of the system considered an important point in the sky and marked wherever it comes, which may be in *any* house above the horizon. Then perhaps the Equal-House cusp X is judged as indicating the career to which the native's personality inclines him, while the M.C. in another part of the chart may show the career into which worldly conditions force him. This system (but with no use of the M.C. at all in olden days) is the most ancient of all.

95. The Porphyry System (the second oldest of all, still in use) simply divides into three equal parts that section of the zodiac, whether less or more than 90°, that is contained in each quadrant, after allotting the M.C. to cusp X and the Ascendant to cusp I, so that if there be 54° of the zodiac between M.C. and Ascendant, and 135° between Ascendant and I.C., the degrees between cusps will be: 15° between each pair of cusps from X to I, 45° between each pair from I to IV.

96. The Natural Graduation System, discovered or invented, and introduced, by the present writer (Colin Evans) some years ago, and now adopted by some (not many, yet) of the leading authorities, aims at improving on the Porphyry system by abolishing the arbitrary method of

making artificially equal subdivisions of naturally unequal quadrants. Dividing the horoscope chart into twenty-four half-houses (because the middle point of each quadrant is halfway between a cusp and another, and it is a disputed question whether the cusp is the beginning or the centre of a house), this system assumes that these (or any smaller fractions into which we might divide houses) are *gradually* and *continuously* increasing, as measured in degrees of the zodiac, in both directions, from a minimum at the middle of a quadrant holding less than 90° of the zodiac, to a maximum at the middle of each neighbouring quadrant, which holds more than 90°. If the second half-house from the middle of a quadrant is (say) one and a half times as 'big' (in the zodiac) as the one nearest the middle of that quadrant, then the one that is third from the middle of the quadrant will be one and a half times as great as the one second from the middle. And so on till the maximum is reached at the middle of the next quadrant. Joining these half-houses two-and-two gives the houses.

97. Campanus and Regiomontanus are the names associated with the other two systems in common use. The Campanus system is now the most favoured in England by those who reject Placidus (it dates from the thirteenth century); Regiomontanus is more used on the Continent (dating from Ibn Ezra in the eleventh century, but made more widely known by Regiomontanus, fourteenth century) but was the one used by the greatest English astrologers before the general adoption of Placidus. Both these systems reflect the idea that as we look eastward for the first house, midway between east and west in the upper sky for the tenth, west for the seventh, and so on, the primary circle to which house-boundaries should be perpendicular must be the line that runs east and west from our place on earth, the prime vertical. After all (it may be argued), the Ascendant and the M.C. are on the horizon and the meridian, which are perpendicular to the prime vertical, and meet at its poles, which are the North and South Points of the horizon. So Campanus and Regiomontanus make all the other cusps also points on lines perpendicular to the prime vertical and meeting at the North and South Points of the horizon. The difference between these two systems is that Campanus sets these lines equally wide apart, thus dividing the prime vertical itself into twelve equal parts between the twelve cusps, while Regiomontanus spaces them unequally, so as to divide the *equator* equally. (Horizon and meridian are the only two lines perpendicular to the prime vertical that can divide *both* it *and* the equator equally at the same time.)

98. Other Systems. There are other systems, but none that the beginner need bother with for purely practical purposes. Full treatment of this subject can be found in *Time-Saver Tables and House-Division Made Clear*, by Colin Evans, now in preparation (Whitman Publishing Co., London). The tables of houses now given in the present book provide for the use of any or all of the systems mentioned here, leaving the choice to the student. Those who feel they do not yet know enough of the subject to make a well-guided choice are advised to start with the Equal-House system, as being the simplest of all, but to experiment soon with Natural Graduation and either Regiomontanus or Campanus (or both). If under a teacher, you should use the system that teacher advises till you outgrow tuition. For any reader who flatteringly regards the present writer as his teacher, that system will be Natural Graduation.

99. When Systems are the Same. At geographical latitude 0° (*i.e.* at places on the equator) there is no difference between the systems of Placidus, Regiomontanus, and Campanus, and relatively little difference between Equal Division, Porphyry, and Natural Graduation, or between these three and the other three. At 6h. and 18h., the Ascendant is the same at all geographical latitudes, and exactly 90° from the M.C. There is then no difference at all (whatever the geographical latitude) between the Equal Division, Porphyry, and Natural Graduation systems, and less difference than at other times between Placidus, Campanus, and Regiomontanus, or between these and the three former systems.

100. When Planets 'have Latitude'. Any planet is on the ecliptic only at two moments in the whole time taken for its orbital journey round the Sun (from about three months for Mercury to about 250 years for Pluto). At all other times the planet 'has latitude'. Boundary lines of houses or parts of houses in the Equal Division, Porphyry, and Natural Graduation systems, being perpendicular to the ecliptic, the zodiac's middle line, are also boundary lines of signs or degrees or other fractions of the zodiac. So even if a planet has much latitude, its place in the zodiac gives its real house-position (house-position of the planet's bodily location in the heavens) in these three systems. But the boundary-lines of houses or any parts of houses in the Regiomontanus, Campanus, and Placidus systems slant obliquely across the ecliptic and across lines perpendicular to it, and therefore slope away from one degree or sign of the zodiac into another as they extend northward or southward from the ecliptic. Hence when a planet has latitude (when it is not exactly on the ecliptic) the house-position of the actual body of the planet is different from the house-position of the point on the ecliptic that has the same zodiacal longitude. However, users of these systems still represent the planets in a chart by the zodiacal degrees the planets occupy, as if the planets were on the ecliptic. This is called the 'zodiacal position' of each planet. The house-position of the planet's true bodily place in the heavens is called its 'mundane' position and needs very elaborate mathematical calculation to determine, when these systems of house-division are used. It is employed only in some advanced techniques of timing predicted events. In the Equal-House, Porphyry, and Natural Graduation systems there is no distinction between 'zodiacal' and 'mundane' positions of planets.

101. Difficulty of Choice. On theoretical grounds good cases can be made out for all systems, though there are specially serious difficulties about Placidus. The test of practical use seems to give excellent results for each actually used system, in the hands of the best astrologers who use it. So there, for the moment, this controversial question must be left.

102. Cusps as Centres or as House-Boundaries. At the present day, users of the Equal-House, Placidus, and Regiomontanus systems generally regard the cusp as the beginning of the house, though allowing planets a few degrees before it (up to perhaps 5° of the zodiac so long as that is only a small fraction of a whole house) to be considered as belonging to the house. This is the traditional view in European astrology (not in Indian). Users of the Natural Graduation, Porphyry, and Campanus systems now mostly regard the half-house before a cusp as belonging to the same house as that cusp, so that the cusp becomes the 'centre' of the house. Some of the exponents of these systems take the pains to mark on the chart not only the twelve cusps (as most important points in the

twelve houses) but also the twelve 'midcusps', or points in between the cusps where half-houses beginning at cusps end, and half-houses which end at cusps begin, thus showing the actual beginning and end (as well as centre) of each house, according to the theory that the cusp is the centre of the house. Other (perhaps most) users of these systems, while regarding the cusp as centre of the house, do not think it important to mark the exact point where they consider the house begins, because house-influence any really considerable distance from the cusp seems to be rather weak, and, such as it is, to spread a good deal over both the adjoining houses. Space in this book has made it quite impossible to provide for the 'mid-cusps' or half-house boundaries in the tables of houses, but after the tables of houses will be found a page of special tables by which those willing to take a little more trouble (hardly any for Natural Graduation, rather more for Regiomontanus and Placidus, most for Campanus) can find cusps in *degrees and minutes* by *all* systems and *midcusps* for Natural Graduation and Campanus.

103. The Overlap Theory. The present writer (Colin Evans) is much inclined towards, and largely uses, the theory (his own) that the half-house before a cusp is an area of overlapping between two houses, while the half-house following the cusp belongs exclusively to that house.

VII

CASTING THE HOROSCOPE

104. Information Needed:

Item i: Date of birth. This is the year, month, and day of month.

Item ii: Moment of birth. This is the hour and minute and (for great exactitude, hardly ever obtainable) second of time; for most practical purposes, the hour and approximate minute as nearly as known.

Item iii: Place of birth. This means the geographical latitude and longitude, or longitude-equivalent, of birth-place, and the standard-time area or zone of birth-place.

105. Notes on Date and Time. Note on Item i: seldom any difficulty about this (except that a Russian birth may possibly involve a doubt whether it is an old-style or a new-style date—see p. 247).

Note on Item ii: fortunately *very great* exactitude about this item seldom makes any appreciable difference to the reading of a natal, or birth, horoscope, though in special cases it may (and it does, for some advanced methods of predicting future events or tendencies with correct dates of their likely occurrence where even a few seconds difference can matter greatly). 'Fortunately' is said because really exact birth-time is so seldom obtainable. Opinions differ as to the values of various methods of 'rectification' (theoretical calculation of birth-time, by astrological methods, more exactly than the time is recorded), but all of them are too difficult for the beginner to tackle, besides being more or less disputable as to which methods are valid. So the horoscope must be treated as more or less exact according to how closely birth-time can be found out by making inquiries of relatives, etc.

106. Note on Place. Item iii: 'standard-time area' or 'zone', means whether the birth-place is in a country that uses (or did at date of birth) Greenwich mean time, or Paris mean time, or Dublin mean time, or Indian standard time, or American 'Eastern Zone Time', or 'Mountain Time', etc. Particulars of standard zone times for different countries, and in some cases for before and after certain dates when a country changed its standard time, are given near the end of this book. When possible, and when it seems necessary, make inquiries as to the kind of time meant in the reported time of birth. Often the official standard or zone time was used on railways, etc., from the official date, but ignored by ordinary people in their private lives, who continued for some years to use the same kind of time as before the official adoption of 'railway time'. The geographical latitude is needed because it alters the Ascendant and other house-cusps, and so means using a different page of the tables of houses given in this book. The geographical longitude or longitude-equivalent is wanted because when Greenwich sidereal time at the moment of birth has been found as explained below, this has to be turned into

local sidereal time of birth by adding or subtracting the longitude-equivalent. This is one hour for every 15° of longitude, and 4 minutes for every extra 1° of longitude, one minute for every 15′ of longitude, and four seconds of time for every 1′ of longitude. Or it may be found from the table at the foot of page 92. This longitude-equivalent (with + for East, and − for West) is given, instead of actual geographical latitude, to save you trouble, in the lists of 'Places in Great Britain and Abroad' given near the end of this book. For places not named in these lists, look up latitude and longitude in the atlas or gazetteer, or inquire about nearest big cities, one of which is probably in the lists, and use latitude and longitude of that (if possible, with a correction according to miles east or west, south or north, from it, the amount of longitude or latitude for miles being tabulated for different parts of the world in a little table on p. 243).

107. Precision and Correctness are two different things. Whole degrees in a horoscope are *more correct* than degrees-and-minutes, *if* the whole degrees are *reliable* and the minutes are *not*. Roughly, a difference of four minutes of time in a moment of birth makes a difference of about one degree on house-cusps (may be double this in some cases, or even more). So Ascendant worked out in fractions of a degree, or in degrees and minutes, is absolutely *incorrect*, because it *is* so precise, if birth-time is uncertain to within about five minutes either way. Similarly a degree error in the geographical longitude, or latitude, of birth-place may in some cases make up to three degrees (most often about one degree) of difference to the Ascendant and other house-cusps. And in places like London, every mile from the official *centre* of the town, whose latitude and longitude are given in gazetteers, etc., may make about 1′ of difference to the latitude and longitude of the actual birth-place. And it is a number of miles from Hampstead to Kennington, if the birth-place is merely given as London! Slovenly lack of precision is bad in what professes to be exact and careful work, but really worse is a misleading amount of precision that ignores probable margins of error unavoidable from incomplete information. NEVER TRY TO BE MORE PRECISE THAN JUSTIFIED BY RELIABLE, ACCURATE, PRECISION OF INFORMATION AVAILABLE, or you will be *less* correct than you would be with less precision.

108. The Two 'Birth-Times'. These, of course, are really two methods of stating one birth-moment. Out of the many different ways that might be used for stating the moment of birth, two different ones must be used in casting the horoscope, and have to be arrived at from the reported time of birth, which may be given in some third way. The two ways in which birth-moment must be expressed for casting a horoscope are:

(1) GREENWICH MEAN TIME of birth (G.M.T.), for finding the planet's places from an ephemeris; and

(2) LOCAL SIDEREAL TIME OF BIRTH for finding the house-cusps from the tables of houses.

Of these, No. (1) (G.M.T.) is found from reported time of birth by steps I and II (below) in most cases (*special* cases will be easy for anyone with common sense to handle IF he can get hold of the information needed for each case, often difficult in those 'special ones').

No. (2) (local sidereal time) is found from No. (1) (G.M.T.), after that has been found, by the further steps II, III, IV.

Step I: Turning Summer Time into Standard or Zone Time (never needed for births in a year before 1916). Make sure whether the reported time is the standard or zone time of the land of birth, or whether it is the legal 'summer time', 'daylight saving time', etc., which is the standard time or zone time with one hour (occasionally, as in British Double Summer Time, two hours) added. Details of this kind of 'summer time' are given after the list of 'Standard and Zone Times' in this book, but are in some cases incomplete through confusion and lack of records due to wartime conditions in some countries. Details of *British* summer time are at top of each page of ephemeris, 1916–1951. From the reported time of birth in such cases SUBTRACT THE EXTRA HOUR, ETC., OF SUMMER TIME. Result is standard or zone time.

Step II: Turning Standard or Zone Time into G.M.T. Details of standard and zone times for different countries are given after the last page of the ephemeris in this book, as far as ascertainable. They are given in the form plus (+) or minus (–) so much (hours and minutes, and occasionally seconds, as for Paris in certain years). This means how fast (+) or slow (–) the standard or zone time is compared with Greenwich. If the amount is ' + ' (more than Greenwich) it must be SUBTRACTED, making it less, to turn it into Greenwich time: if it is less than Greenwich, marked ' – ', it must be ADDED, to increase it and make it into Greenwich time. This step is never needed in Great Britain, nor in Ireland (or Eire, or Northern Ireland), after October, 1916.

Steps I and II, or whichever, if either, is needed, give you the G.M.T. of birth. Use this for finding planets' places. And use it as starting point for the following additional steps which find the local sidereal time of birth, but note (see step III) the possibility of the Greenwich-time *date* being the day before or after the reported *day* of birth.

Step III: Finding Greenwich Sidereal Time at the Nearest '12 o'clock' (Midnight or Noon) of Greenwich Mean Time before Moment of Birth. If G.M.T. of birth found by steps I and II is a.m. (before noon) you want the Greenwich sidereal time at midnight (0h.); if the G.M.T. is p.m. (after noon) you want the Greenwich sidereal time at noon. Usually this means midnight (0h., the beginning of the day by Greenwich time) or noon, of the *day of birth*; but it may occasionally mean midnight or noon of the Greenwich-time date of birth. That would be in such a case as birth at 2.30 a.m., January 1st, 1901, at a place with zone time ' + 5h.', because taking away 5h. for step II will make it 8.30 p.m. of the previous day by G.M.T., so the Greenwich-time date will be December 31st, 1900; or a birth in New York (where the zone time used is ' – 5h') will, by step II, become the day after, changing (for example) from June 30th to July 1st, if hour of birth by New York time was later than 7 p.m., so that adding 5h. makes it some time a.m. next morning. Or an English birth at 12.30 a.m. Summer Time = 11.30 p.m. of the day before by G.M.T. So take sidereal time at midnight (0h.) for birth a.m. by G.M.T., or at noon for birth p.m. by G.M.T., of the day of birth if not changed by steps I and II, or of the Greenwich-time date if steps I and II have changed the day. The bottom right-hand corner of the page for the year required, in the ephemeris in this book, gives the sidereal time (for Greenwich) at both midnight and noon on January 1st for that year. The differences for any other month of the same year and for any other day of the month are given on page 86 before the first page of the ephemeris and apply

equally to all years, and these differences must be added to the sidereal time (midnight or noon) of January 1st to give Greenwich sidereal time for midnight or noon on day of birth (or on Greenwich-time date if different from day of birth).

Step IV: Turning Greenwich Sidereal Time at Midnight or Noon into Greenwich Sidereal Time at Moment of Birth. Add to the Greenwich sidereal time found in step III the hours and minutes of G.M.T., of birth a.m. or p.m. (as found by steps I and II) *plus* the acceleration. This 'acceleration' is the difference between a certain amount of time expressed in figures as *mean time* and the same actual length of time expressed as hours and minutes and seconds of *sidereal time*. It is:

TEN SECONDS FOR EVERY HOUR OR ONE MINUTE FOR EVERY SIX HOURS, less one second for anything from 3½ to 10½ hours, and less another second for anything over 10½ hours. But it may be found at sight from the table on same page as the additions for month and day (p. 92).

Step V: Turning Greenwich Sidereal Time into Local Sidereal Time. To or from the Greenwich sidereal time found by step IV, add or subtract the longitude-equivalent of the birth-place. Add if the place is east of Greenwich (longitude-equivalent marked ' + ' in this book's list of places, or longitude marked E. in atlas or gazetteer) and subtract if west (marked ' – ' or W.). The result of this addition or subtraction is the local sidereal time of birth.

109. Examples of Finding the 'Two Birth-Times':

Example A: Born in Cardiff, Wales (Britain), long. (from gazetteer) 3°10′ W.; long.-equivalent (calculated from this) 12m.40s. (given in List of Places in Britain as – 12m.40s.), 7.30 p.m., July 2nd, 1910.

STEP I. Not needed.

STEP II. Not needed.

G.M.T. for Planets is therefore 7.30 p.m.

	h.	m.	s.
STEP III. Birth G.M.T. is p.m., so use noon sid. time.			
From ephemeris for 1910, sid. time noon Jan. 1....	18	41	2
From p. 86 add for July (common year)........	11	53	36
And for 2nd of month.....................		3	56
	30	34	38
STEP IV. G.M.T. p.m........................	7	30	0
Acceleration for 7h.30m.....................		1	14
	38	5	52
STEP V. Longitude-equivalent (subtract because W. or –)		12	40
	37	53	12
As this is more than 24h., take away..........	24	0	0
(because time cannot be more than 24h.)			
LOCAL SIDEREAL TIME	13	57	12

The seconds are not correct, because seconds of birth-time were not given in the reported time, but we used seconds in adding the different items (six items added) because omitting 20s., for example every time

might possibly have added up to an error of 2m. Now, however, we 'round off' by calling more than 30s. a minute, or less than 30s. 'no minutes', and say:

Local sidereal time of birth (used for houses) is 13h.53m.

Example B: Born in Yarmouth, Norfolk, England, long. 1°43′ E., long.-equivalent +6m.52s., July 2nd, 1951, at 10.24 a.m.

	h.	m.	s.
STEP I. Reported time.............................	10	24	0
British Summer Time.........................	1	0	0
Standard time	9	24	0

STEP II. Not needed, so time just found is G.M.T.

	h.	m.	s.
STEP III. From ephemeris for 1917, sid. time MIDNIGHT..	6	39	21
Addition for July (as in Ex. A.)................	11	53	56
2nd day......................................		3	ʻ57
STEP IV. G.M.T. a.m..............................	9	24	0
Acceleration for 9h.24m......................		1	33
STEP V. Longitude-Equivalent (add for E. or +)......		6	52
	28	9	39
Deduct 24h. and 'round off' to whole minutes....	24	0	0
LOCAL SIDEREAL TIME AT BIRTH	4	10	

Example C: Born in New York, U.S.A., 'Eastern Standard Time' (–5h.), long. 74° W., long.-equivalent—4h.56m., 10.24 p.m., July 31st, 1951.

	h.	m.	s.
STEP I. From reported time, Summer Time...........	10	24	0
Take Summer Time.........................	1	0	0
Zone time (Eastern Standard Time, U.S.A.).....	9	24	0
STEP II. Add the zone time difference...............	5	0	0
G.M.T. of birth is therefore p.m. (after noon) July 31st...............................	14	24	0
Which is a.m. of the Greenwich-time date, Aug. 1st, 1951...............................	2	24	0
STEP III. (Remember Greenwich-time date, Aug. 1st, so use midnight S.T., ephemeris, 1951, Jan. 1)..	6	39	21
Add for August (common year)	13	57	50
STEP IV. G.M.T. of birth........................	2	24	0
Acceleration for 2h.24m......................			24
Greenwich sidereal time of birth...............	23	1	35
STEP V. Subtract for west long. (–long.-equiv.).......	4	56	0
LOCAL SIDEREAL TIME ('rounded off' to whole minutes)	18	6	

Example D: Born in Pekin (long. 116°30′E.: long.-equivalent 7h.46m.0s.; but zone time is +8h.), on Jan. 1st, 1952, at 7 a.m.

	h.	m.	s.
STEP I. Not needed.			
STEP II. Reported time........................a.m.	7	0	0
Subtract zone time (because east)..............	8	0	0
Eight hours before 7 a.m. is, previous day...p.m.	11	0	0
Which gives G.M.T. on Greenwich-time date Dec. 31st, 1951.			
STEP III. Noon (because G.M.T. is p.m.), Jan. 1st, 1951	18	41	19
Add for Dec. (common year).................	21	56	49
and for 31st...............................	1	58	17
Noon, Dec. 31st, 1951 (dropping out 24h.).......	18	40	22
STEP IV. G.M.T. of birth........................	11	0	0
Acceleration................................		1	48
STEP V. Long.-equivalent (ADDED because east or +)...	7	46	0
LOCAL SIDEREAL TIME AT BIRTH (say 14h.24m.)	14	24	3

VIII

CASTING THE HOROSCOPE, CONTINUED:
THE CUSPS

110. Finding the Cusps of the houses depends on the system of house-division chosen. Whichever system this is, the Ascendant will be cusp I. And, except in the Equal-House system, the M.C. will be cusp X. Even in the Equal-House system it is necessary to find the M.C., though it is not a cusp of any house, because it should be marked inside a house, or against the outside of the 'wheel', to show where it comes. It is customary in careful work to aim at a standard of precision giving the nearest 1′ (one-sixtieth of a degree) on the Ascendant and M.C., and for all planets, etc., but only the nearest degree on the cusps of the intermediate houses. For them, that is all that is permitted by the most-used tables of houses (Placidus) published in Britain. In quick or short work, it is usually sufficient to give whole degrees only for everything—including Ascendant, M.C., and planets. In many cases, in fact, greater precision would be definitely wrong, as not being justified by precision of available data.

111. The Condensed Tables of Houses in this book give M.C. and Ascendant in degrees and minutes, and the intermediate cusps (XI, XII, II, III) in whole degrees (to nearest degree), for every twelve minutes of sidereal time, with a separate table (occupying two pages) for each latitude. The intermediate-house cusps are given four times over, according to four different systems of house-division: Regiomontanus, Campanus, Placidus, Natural Graduation (in what is believed to be their order of age). It is usually easy to see at a glance whether the differences between cusps at two consecutive latitudes for which tables are provided is sufficient to make it advisable to correct those for the nearest latitude given by a proportionate part of the difference between the cusps given for that latitude and the cusps given for the next following or preceding latitude, or whether cusps given for the nearest latitude are good enough without correction. If birth-time is known only to within about ten minutes either way, the nearest time given in the tables is good enough; if known more accurately, take cusps at two consecutive times between which the birth-time lies, and use a proportion of the difference to get them correct for actual birth-time. The working out of Ascendant and M.C. and all cusps by each system in the Example Horoscope below will show what is meant, and will illustrate a way of arranging the work. In working these out the standard of precision used will be closer than usually worth while. In presenting final results, however, minutes, even when found, will not be given for the intermediate cusps; these will be rounded off to the nearest degree.

112. The Example Horoscope: Ascendant and M.C. (wanted whatever system of house-division be used):

Man born at Cardiff, Wales; lat. 51°28′ N.; long. 3°10′ W.; 7.26 p.m., G.M.T., July 2nd, 1910. This is not, by the way, the horoscope of any real person but an imaginary case.

Local sidereal time (found as shown in the preceding chapter): 13h.53m. As this is between 13h.48m. and 14h.0m., and the latitude is between 51° and 52°, we extract from the tables of houses the M.C. at both sidereal times given there, and the Ascendant at both times and both latitudes, to see how much difference 12m. of time makes (and thence estimate how much difference 5m. makes, to be added to 13h.48m. in order to make the required 13h.53m.), and how much difference 1° of latitude makes (to adjust the Ascendant given in tables for lat. 51° and make it correct for lat. 51°28′, by allowing for a proportionate part of the difference for 1° lat.). We find:

Sidereal time	Ascendants lat. 51°	lat. 52°	Diff. for 1°	28′	Asc. for 51°28′	M.C. long.
13h.48m.......	25 ♐ 12	24 ♐ 4	−1°8′	32′	24 ♐ 40	29♎ 3
14h.0m........	27 ♐ 51	26 ♐ 40	−1°11′	33′	27 ♐ 18	2♏11
Diff. for 12m.					2°38′	3°8′
Diff. for 5m. (half above less ⅕th of half)					1° 6′	1° 18′
Add diffs. for 5m. to Asc. and M.C. 13h.48m.					24 ♐ 40	29♎ 3
RESULTS WANTED FOR 13h.53m., lat. 51°28′......					25 ♐ 46	0♏21
					Asc.	M.C.

Remarks: Note whether Ascendant moves forward or backward in the zodiac when the geographical latitude increases: backwards always if sidereal time is between 6h. and 18h.; otherwise forwards; in the present example backwards, so the difference for 28′ has to be taken away from Ascendant at lat. 51°, not added. In the four systems of house-division for which cusps XI, XII, II, III are given in the condensed tables of houses, those cusps sometimes move forward and sometimes backwards, sometimes some cusps one way and some the other at the same sidereal time, when the latitude of a place increases. A glance at tables for two consecutive latitudes shows which. Differences that are to be subtracted are marked ‘ − ’ as done above. Difference for difference of time is always to be added, for changing any cusp at an earlier time to what is wanted for a later time.*

113. Opposite Cusps. In the following sections, where we find the other cusps (XI, XII, II, III) by various systems of house-division, we do not bother to calculate cusps from IV to IX inclusive, for the simple reason that once cusps X, XI, XII, I, II, III, have been found, all that has to be done

* As an example in 'interpolation' (finding intermediate amounts between amounts given in a table) we have dealt with 51°28′ as if the tables of houses gave nothing between 51° and 52°. As a matter of fact, because of the great number of London births, a table has been given for lat. 51°30′ (for London) which is close enough to 51°28′ to have rendered this work unnecessary.

is to put the same degrees (and minutes if any) of the opposite signs on the opposite cusps. Opposite cusps are those that differ by 6—the first and seventh, the third and ninth, the fourth and tenth, for example. Opposite signs, if not already known, should have been learned from 33.

114. Southern Latitudes. The condensed tables of houses are calculated for northern latitudes. When a horoscope has to be erected for a south latitude proceed thus: pretend the sidereal time is twelve hours earlier or later, and pretend that the latitude is the equal northern latitude. Calculate the cusps accordingly, but change every sign to the opposite sign. This gives correct cusps for the real latitude (south) and time. For example, if a horoscope is needed for 51°28′ S., at sidereal time 1h.53m., we pretend it is for 51°28′ N. at 13h.53m., and find Ascendant and M.C. as above to be 25 ♐ 46 and 0♏21, but changing these to the opposite sign we give the real Ascendant and M.C. as 25♊46 and 0♉21. If we found cusp XI was (let us suppose) 18♏39, by a certain system of house-division, we should take this to mean that cusp XI is really 18♉39, by that system.

115. 'Intercepted' Signs. These cannot occur in the Equal-House system; in other systems it may happen that the same sign is on more than one cusp, and some other sign (perhaps more than one in the same half of the horoscope) seems to be omitted altogether. For example, there may be ♒ on one cusp and ♈ on the next, with ♓ omitted. In this case, the 'omitted' sign is said to be intercepted—it begins after one cusp, and ends before the next cusp. It is usual to mark it between the cusps, roughly nearer to whatever cusp it is really near (for example, if the cusp in ♒ was near the end of ♒ and the cusp in ♈ was near the beginning of ♈, obviously ♓ begins nearer to the preceding cusp than the following one). If a sign is intercepted the opposite sign must also be intercepted between the opposite cusps. Thus in the case just mentioned, ♍ is intercepted as well as ♓.

116. For Latitude 0° (which is omitted in the tables of houses here) the following rule will prove very simple. M.C. is the same as at any other latitude—take it from a table of houses for some other latitude. Ascendant is the same as M.C. at sidereal time six hours later. The methods which will be taught for the Equal-House and Porphyry systems will then apply. For the Natural Graduation system, the difference from Porphyry houses is so slight at lat. 0° as not to matter greatly, but a condensed table of Natural Graduation cusps for houses XI, XII, II, III is given on p. 85. For all other systems: XI is M.C. two hours later; XII is M.C. four hours later; II eight hours later; and III is the M.C. ten hours later.

Special example for latitude 0°: sid. time 3h.48m.; Placidus system:

X (M.C.) is the M.C. at 3h.48m.................... .	29♉13
XI is the M.C. at 5h.48m............................	27♊15
XII is the M.C. at 7h.49m...........................	25♋3
I (Asc.) is the M.C. at 9h.48m.......................	21♌37
II is the M.C. at 11h.48m...........................	26♍44
III is the M.C. at 13h.48m..........................	29♈3

All these 'M.C.'s' used as different cusps are found in the M.C. column of the table of houses for any latitude.

117. Example Horoscope continued: Cusps by Equal-House System. The Ascendant is cusp I. The signs of the zodiac are put in their proper order on all the other cusps, starting at the sign on the Ascendant, and continuing

all round. For the sake of giving, for every system, the houses X, XI, XII, I, II, III here, we have worked backwards from Ascendant to cusp X (which in this system is not the M.C.) and forwards from Ascendant to cusp III. But in practice you can simply go forward from I to XII in consecutive order right round the 'wheel'. The same degree is put on every cusp, and the same minutes if minutes are used. Here, for the sake of giving results in a similar form (for comparison) by all systems, we are keeping degrees and minutes on houses X and I but rounding off '25°44″' on other cusps to nearest degree, 26°. Thus we get:

House:	X	XI	XII	I	II	III
Cusp:	25♍46	26♎	26♏	25♐46	26♑	26♒

M.C.   0♏21 (between cusps XI and XII in this example)

118. Example Horoscope: Houses According to the Porphyry System. For this system the distance in the zodiac from the M.C. to the Ascendant must be found, and divided by 3, and the result added to the M.C. to give the cusp of house XI, and added again to XI to give XII. Two whole signs forward from XII is II. Four whole signs forward from XI is III. Of course, X is the M.C. and I is the Ascendant.

From M.C. (0♏21) to end of sign (♏)............... 29° 39′
From beginning of Asc. sign (♐) to Asc. (25♐46).. 25   46
30° for every whole sign between (none in this case)

                                                3)55° 25′
                                                18   28
Add this to the M.C..................... 0♏21 cusp X

Result is............................... 18♏49 cusp XI
Again add the 18   28

Result is............................... 7♐17 cusp XII
The Ascendant is....................... 25♐46 cusp I
XII(7♐17) plus 2 signs is................ 7♒17 cusp II
XI(18♏49) plus 4 signs is................ 18♓49 cusp III

Notice that as cusp X is in ♏, cusp IV will be in the opposite sign, ♉, and therefore, between cusps III (in ♓) and IV (♉) there is ♈ intercepted —which you might have overlooked, though seeing at once that ♒ is intercepted between ♑ and ♓. So we have:

House:	X	XI	XII	I	II	III
Cusp:	0♏21	19♏	7♐	25♐46	7♑	19♓

Intercepted...♑ ....♈.

(In finding a third of 55°25′ we ignored a third of one minute. Strictly we should have added 1′ (for *two* thirds) to cusp XII, therefore.)

119. Example Horoscope by Regiomontanus System. Use Ascendant and M.C. as cusps I and X as in the Porphyry system, but simply copy cusps XI, XII, II, III, as given under those house-numbers* and under the name REGIOMONTANUS, in the tables of houses. A glance will usually be enough to show whether any correction is needed, for a sidereal time or a geographical latitude in between the nearest ones given in the tables, when using the nearest time and latitude in the tables; and, if it is, a mental

---

* Arabic numerals (11, 12, 2, 3) in the tables of houses.

estimate of how much the correction should be is usually quite easy, as we are only working in whole degrees. But we will, for form's sake, do the work more elaborately, with an arrangement of the work that can be used in all cases:

time	lat. 51° (in tables)				lat. 52° (in tables)				lat. 51°28' (estimated)			
	XI	XII	II	III	XI	XII	II	III	XI	XII	II	III
13h.48m.	19♏	5♐	2♒	26♓	18♏	4♐	1♒	25♓	19♏	5♐	2♒	26♓
14h.0m.	21♏	7♐	6♒	0♈	20♏	6♐	5♒	0♈	21♏	7♐	6♒	0♈

12m. time makes difference of...................... 2° 2° 4° 4°

So 5m. time (nearly half 12m.) makes diff........ 1 1 2 2
Adding these differences (to 13h.48m.)........... 19♏ 5♐ 2♒ 26♓

Gives us for cusps XI, XII, II, III.............. 20♏ 6♐ 4♒ 28♓

We found cusps for 51°28' by comparing those for 51 and 52 N. lat. at each time in turn, noting that in this example greater latitude moves cusps *backwards* in the zodiac (it may move them either backwards or forwards, or some cusps one way and the others the other), and so subtracting from cusps at 51° lat. 28/60ths of the difference made by 1° lat. (slightly less than half the difference). In this particular example, as the difference made by 1° lat. is 1° or 0°, less than half that difference is always 0° in whole degrees, we need not have bothered with the table for lat. 52° but simply used cusps for lat. 51°, for these houses, though not for the Ascendant (but see footnote to section 112).

Thus we get, for the Regiomontanus system:

House:	X	XI	XII	I	II	III
Cusp:	0♏21	20♏	6♐	25♐46	4♒	28♓

Intercepted............... ♑ .... ♈ ....

120. Example Horoscope by the Campanus System. Method is exactly the same as that explained and shown above for the Regiomontanus system (115), only copying cusps from columns under 'CAMPANUS' in the tables of houses. For the Example Horoscope this gives:

House:	X	XI	XII	I	II	III
Cusp:	0♏21	14♏	28♏	25♐46	27♒	11♈

Intercepted.................................♑ .... ♓ ....

121. Example Horoscope by the Placidus System. Exactly the same method of work as for the Regiomontanus and Campanus systems, 114 and 115, only copying the cusps from columns under the name 'PLACIDUS' in the tables of houses.
For the Example Horoscope this gives:

House:	X	XI.	XII	I	II	III
Cusp:	0♏21	21♏	9♐	25♐46	7♑	26♓

Intercepted.. ♒ ..... ♈ .

122. Example Horoscope by the Natural Graduation System. Exactly the same method as for Regiomontanus, Campanus, or Placidus. This gives:

House:	X	XI	XII	I	II	III
Cusp:	0♏21	21♏	5♐	25♐46	1♒	25♓

Intercepted............................... ♑ .... ♈

IX

CASTING THE HOROSCOPE, CONCLUDED:
PLANETS, ETC:

123. Finding the Planets' Places. In the Condensed Ephemeris the longitude (zodiacal position) of each planet, etc., is given on the first of each month, and also in most cases on other days of the month: at intervals of eight days for the Sun, six days for Mercury, eight days for Venus, twelve days for Mars, Jupiter, Saturn, Uranus, and Neptune, and two days for the Moon. At the end of a month the days are usually fewer. Pluto and the Node are given only for the first of the month. All these positions are given for noon (Greenwich mean time). Midnight would be better, as now used by astronomers, and in some Continental astrological ephemerides for years later than 1930; but errors are often caused when people already in the habit of consulting the noon ephemerides in common use in England make an occasional reference to a different ephemeris calculated for midnight. It is, however, best, when casting a horoscope, to obtain from the ephemeris positions for the '12 o'clock' before time of birth—that is, for the *midnight* before a birth at Greenwich mean time '*a.m.*', and for the *noon* before a birth that was '*p.m.*' by G.M.T. After this midnight or noon position has been found, it is converted into the position at actual time of birth by a proportional part of the planet's movement in twelve hours (a half-day). Various examples will now be worked out to show the method in different types of case, for particular planets, etc., before working out the positions of them all together for the Example Horoscope.

124. Example E: Moon's place wanted for 7.40 p.m. (G.M.T.) on Feb. 4th, 1891. As the time is p.m. we find position at noon on Feb. 4th, 1891, first:

In condensed ephemeris:	Feb. 5th	26 ♐ 56	(noon)
,,　　　,,　　　,,	Feb. 3rd ☽	29 ♏ 50	(,,)
Subtracting.....................		27° 6′	in 2 days
Dividing by 2....................		13° 33′	in 1 day
Add the above to position on Feb. 3rd			
(noon).....................		29 ♏ 50	
Position on Feb. 4th (noon) is......		13 ♐ 23	

We now have to add to this the movement in 7h.40m We could (in

this case) say, an hour is three periods of 20m., and so 7h.40m. is 3 times 7 or 21, and another 2, making 23, periods of 20m., while a day (24h.) is 72 such periods, so we want 23/72nd parts of one day's movement; but most of those readers who need any instruction at all in this part of the calculation will probably find it easier to separate 7h.40m. into 6h. + 1h. + 30m. + 10m.:

1 day (above), 13°33′; so 6h. (a quarter of 1 day)........	3° 23′
1h. (a sixth of 6h.)...................................	0 34
30m. (half of 1 h.)..................................	0 17
10m. (a third of 30m.)................................	6
Total for 7h.40m....................................	4° 20′
Add this to position at noon..........................	13 ♐ 23
POSITION REQUIRED...................................)	17 ♐ 43

(This is not *quite* correct, but in most cases near enough. It assumes that the movement of 27°6′ in 2 days was at a uniform speed, and so was exactly 13°33′ each day, and 34′ each hour. Actually, from noon on Feb. 3rd to noon on the 4th the Moon covered 13°19′ only, and from noon 4th to noon 5th covered 13°47′—moving more quickly the second day than the first. When it really matters much to be slightly more accurate, this can be done by making a correction by a method to be taught later in the present chapter. In this example the correction would make a difference of 12′.)

125. Example F: Find Mercury's place at 7 a.m. (G.M.T.) on Nov. 16th, 1884. For an a.m. G.M.T., we want a 0h. (midnight) position, namely a half-day later than the previous noon, noon of Nov. 15th:

From Ephemeris, Nov. 19th, 1884..	5 ♐ 57
„ „ Nov. 13th, 1884..............☿	26 ♏ 37 (noon)
In 6 days....................................	9° 20′
In 1 day.....................................	1° 33′
In 2 days (2 times 1 day)....................	3° 6′
In half-day (half of 1 day)..................	0 46
Total for 2½ days...........................	3° 52′
Add position on Nov. 13th (noon)........... .	26 ♏ 37
Position on Nov. 16th (midnight 0h.)...........	0 ♐ 29
Add for 6h. (half of ½ day)...................	23
Add for 1h. (6th of 6h.).....................	4
Position required (7 a.m., Nov. 16th)...........	0 ♐ 56

126. Example G: Find position of Mars at 10 p.m. (G.M.T.) on April 7th, 1888. The most important thing to notice; the moment you look for

Mars in the Ephemeris for April, 1888, is that it is retrograde: moving backwards. So movements have to be subtracted instead of added. As a constant reminder of this, mark every movement ' – ' (minus):

From Ephemeris, April 1st, 1888 (noon)...............	25≏19
„ „ April 13th, 1888 „	20 56
Subtracting: 12 days.................................	– 4 23
6 days	– 2 11
Subtract from position on April 1st....................	25≏19
Position for noon, April 7th..........................	23≏ 8
1 day (6th of 6 days)........ –22' ;	
Therefore 6h. (quarter of day).......................	– 5
4h. (two-thirds of 6h.)...............................	– 3
Total for 10h...	– 8
Take this from noon position (April 7th)...............	23≏ 8
Position required (10 p.m., April 7th).................	23≏ 0

(With even Jupiter, and certainly with slower planets (♄ ♅ ♆ Pl.), movement in two or three hours is hardly enough to matter for most work, so it would do as a rule to find position at *nearest* (earlier or later) half-day, noon or midnight. Here, midnight (0h.) of April 8th would have been nearest—6½ days movement from position at noon, April 1st.)

127. Example H: Find place of Venus at 1 p.m. G.M.T., May 20th, 1889. Here the condensed ephemeris gives for ♀ 3 ♉ 9 at noon, May 17th, and 2 ♉ 51 at noon, May 25th; you might think a movement retrograde of 18' in eight days, and so 7' in three days, making position required 3 ♉ 2. But this would be a mistake—overlooking one important fact: Venus is retrograde on May 17th but direct on May 25th, so must have been stationary some time between those dates. Looking in the lower right-hand section of the 1889 page of the condensed ephemeris, for 'Stations', we find under ♀: May 22nd, 2 ♉ 40. As the date we want (May 20th) is between 17th and 22nd, we ignore May 25th and proceed as if the ephemeris gave positions for May 17th and May 22nd:

May 17th (noon)....................................♀	3 ♉ 9
May 22nd (noon).....................................	2 40
5 days (retrograde)	– 0° 29'
1 day (a fifth).......................................	– 0° 6'
3 days	– 0° 18'
Take from (May 17th)...............................	3 ♉ 9
Position wanted is........	2 ♉ 51

(Although often good enough, this is still not quite right, for a planet near its station goes much slower the day or two before and after station than a few days earlier or later still. A method for use in such cases, with the faster planets, for getting greater accuracy, is given later in this chapter.)

128. Example I: Find position of Pluto for July 20th, 1900:

Aug. 1st...Pl. 17♊13
July 1st .... 16♊38

35 days .... 0° 35′

It is really not worth while to find 19/31sts of this by multiplying by 19 and dividing by 31; it is so obvious that treating 20 days as two-thirds of a month is quite near enough and saves trouble: ⅔ of 35′ is 23′. So (adding 23′ to 16♊38) we say at once: 17♊1, for any hour of the day.*

129. Finding the 'Part of Fortune'. Add the Moon's zodiacal longitude to the Ascendant and subtract the Sun's longitude or place in the zodiac. But how can you add (say) 13 ♉ to 29♒, and subtract 14♍? Only by remembering that 13 ♉ really means 'one sign and 13° from the beginning of the zodiac', and 29♒ means '9 signs and 29°', and 14♍ means '5 signs and 14°'. Of course, ♍ is the sixth sign, but we say '5ₐ14°' because there are only five whole signs before Virgo, and then the 14° of Virgo are added. Make sure you can say off-hand how many signs from the beginning of the zodiac any sign is:

> ♈ is 1st sign, so before it there are   0 signs;
> ♉ is 2nd „   „   „   „   „ is   1 sign;
> ♊ is 3rd „   „   „   „   „ are   2 signs;
>   and so on.

Another way is to memorise how many degrees from the beginning of the zodiac is 0° of each sign, thus:

0♈ = 0°	0♋ = 90°	0♎ = 180°	0♑ = 270°
0♉ = 30°	0♌ = 120°	0♏ = 210°	0♒ = 300°
0♊ = 60°	0♍ = 150°	0♐ = 240°	0♓ = 330°

then add the degrees and minutes in the sign to the degrees equivalent to 0° of that sign. For example, 17♐23 is 240° (for 0♐) + 17°23′—making 257°23′.

130. Example J: Find Part of Fortune when Ascendant is 17♎43, ☽ is in 11♌46, and ☉ in 14♑34:

Either this way				Or this way		
17♎43 is	6ₐ17°43′	Asc.		17♎43 is	197°43′	Asc.
11♌46 is	4ₐ11°46′	☽		11♌46 is	131°46′	☽
Add:	10ₐ29°29′				329°29′	
14♑34 is	9ₐ14°34′	☉		14♑34 is	284°34′	☉
Subtract:	1ₐ14°55′				44°55′	

Result: ⊕   14♉55

* If we *had* reckoned 19/31sts of 35′ the result would have differed by 2′. Does it matter?

131. Example K: Find the Part of Fortune for noon, January 1st, 1912, lat. 50° N. Sidereal time is found to be 18h.39m., and at this S.T. and lat. 50° N., the Ascendant is 21♈30, and so:

	Either this way		*Or this way*
Asc.	0ˢ21°30′	(21♈30)	21°30′
☽ add	1ˢ20°41′	(20♉41)	50°41′
	1ˢ42°11′		72°11′
☉ subt.	9ˢ 9°44′	(9♐11)	279°44′

We cannot subtract the Sun's longitude from LESS longitude; so we add 12ˢ or 360° (the whole zodiac) to make subtraction possible:

Asc. + ☽	1ˢ42°11′	or	72°11′
add	12ˢ	or	360°
	13ˢ42°11′		432°11′
☉	9ˢ 9°44′		279°44′
	4ˢ32°27′		152°27′
which is	5ˢ 2°27′		

Making the result 2♍27

(If Ascendant and ☽ add up to more than twelve signs or more than 360°, we take away or drop twelve signs or 360° before proceeding, unless we shall need them because the Sun is more than the remaining signs and degrees would be.)

132. Completing the Example Horoscope. It is convenient, when finding the places of all the planets for one horoscope, to put together those for which the ephemeris gives positions on the same date and at the same length of interval. Thus we shall find ☽ separately, ☿ separately, ☉ and ♀ together, and ♂ ♃ ♄ ♅ ♆ together, and then Pl. and Node together; and finally the Part of Fortune separately.

For 7.30 p.m. (G.M.T.), July 2nd, 1910:

Moon ☽			
July 1st (noon)	25♈58		
July 3rd ,, ...	24♉47		
2 days	28	49	
1 day	14	24	
6h. (quarter).......	3	36	
1h. 30m.	0	54	(quarter of 6h.)
Total	18° 54′		(1 day 7h.30m.)
Add to...................	25♈58		
	☽ 14♉52		(7.30 p.m. July 2nd, 1910)

Mercury ☿

July 1st (noon).............	20♊0	
July 7th..................	0♋42	
6 days	10° 42′	
1 day	1° 47′	
6h.	0 27	
1h. 30m.	0 7	
Total	2° 21′	(for 1 day 7h. 30m.)
Add to....................	20♊11	(position on July 1st at noon)
☿ 22♊33		(7.30 p.m., July 2nd, 1910)

	Sun ☉	Venus ♀	
July 1st (noon).............	8♋55	1♊58	
July 9th..................	16 23	11 20	
8 days	7° 28′	9° 22′	
1 day	0° 56′	1° 10′	
6h.	0 14	0 18	
1 h. 30m..................	0 4	4	
Total	1° 14′	1° 32′	(for 1 day 7h. 30m.).
Add to....................	8♋55	1♊58	(noon, July 1st)
	☉ 10♋ 9	♀ 3♊30	at 7.30 p.m., July 1st, 1910

	Mars ♂	Jupiter ♃	Saturn ♄	Uranus ♅	Neptune ♆
July 1st	7♌43	5♎54	4♉35 (ʀᴇᴛ)	23♑51	18♋40
July 13th....	15 15	7 4	5 25	23 22	19 7
12 days	7 32	1 10	0 50	−0 29	0 27
1 day	0° 38′	0° 6′	0° 4′	−0° 2′	0° 2′
6h.	0 9	0 1	0 1	−0 0	0 0
1h.30m......	0 2				
Total	0° 49′	0° 7′	0° 5′	−0° 2′	0° 2′
Add to......	7♌43	5♎54	4♉35	23♑51	18♋40
	♂ 8♌32	♃ 6♎ 1	♄ 4♉40	♅ 23♑49	♆ 18♋42

	Pluto Pl. or ♇	Node ☊	Part of Fortune ⊕	
July 1st	26♊38	(Ret.) 26♉ 9	Asc.	25♐45 = 265° 45'
Aug. 1st	27 18	24 31	☽	+ 14♉52 = 44 52
31 days	0° 40'	– 1° 38'		310° 37'
1 day	0° 1'	– 0° 3'	subtract ☉	– 99 59
Add to......	26♊38	24♉ 9		
			Part of Fortune	210° 38'
July 2nd ...Pl.	26♊39	☊ 24♉ 6	That is	⊕ 0♏38

133. Faster Planets near Stations. The table below shows what fraction of so many days' movement is made in so many days, reckoned backwards or forwards from the day of station. Look in the column headed with the number of days from the ephemeris-date before the station to the day of the station, or from the day of the station to the ephemeris-date after that; and look in the line for the number of days from the day of birth to the day of the station, or from the day of the station to the day of birth. The fraction found is what proportion of the movement that is made in the number of days named at the head of the column occurs in the number of days shown at the beginning of the line.

For days	of 12 days	of 11 days	of 10 days	of 9 days	of 8 days	of 7 days	of 6 days	of 5 days	of 4 days	of 3 days	of 2 days
1	$\frac{1}{64}$	$\frac{1}{50}$	$\frac{1}{45}$	$\frac{1}{32}$	$\frac{1}{30}$	$\frac{1}{22}$	$\frac{1}{16}$	$\frac{1}{12}$	$\frac{1}{8}$	$\frac{1}{5}$	$\frac{2}{5}$
2	$\frac{1}{25}$	$\frac{1}{20}$	$\frac{1}{16}$	$\frac{1}{12}$	$\frac{1}{11}$	$\frac{1}{8}$	$\frac{1}{6}$	$\frac{1}{5}$	$\frac{1}{3}$	$\frac{1}{2}$	...
3	$\frac{1}{12}$	$\frac{1}{10}$	$\frac{1}{8}$	$\frac{1}{7}$	$\frac{1}{6}$	$\frac{1}{5}$	$\frac{1}{3}$	$\frac{2}{5}$	$\frac{3}{5}$	...	...
4	$\frac{1}{8}$	$\frac{1}{7}$	$\frac{1}{6}$	$\frac{1}{6}$	$\frac{1}{4}$	$\frac{1}{4}$	$\frac{1}{2}$	$\frac{2}{3}$	...	...	...
5	$\frac{1}{6}$	$\frac{1}{5}$	$\frac{1}{5}$	$\frac{1}{3}$	$\frac{2}{5}$	$\frac{1}{2}$	$\frac{2}{3}$	...	...	...	...
6	$\frac{1}{4}$	$\frac{1}{4}$	$\frac{1}{3}$	$\frac{2}{5}$	$\frac{3}{5}$	$\frac{2}{3}$	...	...	...	...	...
7	$\frac{1}{3}$	$\frac{2}{5}$	$\frac{2}{5}$	$\frac{2}{3}$	$\frac{3}{4}$	...	...	...	...	...	...
8	$\frac{1}{2}$	$\frac{3}{5}$	$\frac{3}{5}$	$\frac{4}{5}$	...	...	...	...	...	...	...
9	$\frac{3}{5}$	$\frac{2}{3}$	$\frac{4}{5}$	...	...	...	...	...	...	...	...
10	$\frac{3}{4}$	$\frac{4}{5}$	...	...	...	...	....	...	...	...	...
11	$\frac{4}{5}$	...	...	...	...	...	...	...	...	...	...

Example: Wanted, Mercury's place at noon, Aug. 11th, 1912.

Ephemeris gives station Aug. 9th, 6♍33, and ephemeris-date Aug. 13th, 5♍29: a movement of 1°4' in four days. From the station-date Aug. 9th to the birth-date Aug. 11th is two days; the line for 'in 2 days' and column for 'of 4 days' in table above shows the fraction ⅓: one-third of 1°4' is 21'. This taken from longitude at station, 6♍33, gives longitude required as 6♍12. This happens to be exactly correct by the full (day-to-day) ephemeris, though the example was taken at random before working it out. The method and table do not always give quite such accurate results, but always 'near enough', except for advanced precision work,

for which a condensed ephemeris would never be used. Note that whether the birthday is BEFORE or AFTER the station-date, we always SUBTRACT the fractional part of total movement if station is where planet changes from direct to retrograde, but ADD if planet is changing from retrograde to direct.

(Apology to mathematicians and astronomers: this table professes to be nothing better than *roughly* approximate *convenient* fractions, based empirically on a few typical cases. It is a development of the method given by Waite in his original work, though much extended and re-arranged.)

134. Correction of Moon's Position for Varying Speed. If this optional method of obtaining a little closer accuracy for the Moon's place is adopted, it is necessary to copy from the ephemeris in this book FOUR days' noon positions of the Moon: the two between which the time and date of the horoscope fall, and the one before those and one after those. We thus have (usually) three intervals of two days each. Near the end or the beginning of a month it may be one interval of one day and two intervals of two days each; cases which are to be dealt with in a special way; see below. Using first the ordinary method of finding the position as if speed were uniform, taught above, we get an UNCORRECTED POSITION, based solely on the Moon's movements during the middle interval (the interval inside which is our required birth-date or birth-time). For the correction: FIND THE DIFFERENCE BETWEEN THE DISTANCE MOVED IN THE PRECEDING AND IN THE FOLLOWING PERIOD (ignoring that middle period). TAKE A FRACTION OF THIS DIFFERENCE (as shown in the brief table below) and ADD IT OR SUBTRACT IT TO OR FROM THE UNCORRECTED POSITION: *add* if Moon is moving more SLOWLY after the birth-date, *subtract* if Moon is moving more QUICKLY after the birth-date (that is ADD if movement is LESS in third period; SUBTRACT if movement is MORE in third period than in first period).

Example: Required Moon's place at noon on Aug. 4th, 1912. Ephemeris gives:

movement in 2 days:

Aug. 1st	15♓6	
Aug. 3rd	9♈21	first period 24°15′
Aug. 5th	4♉29	second period 25°8′
Aug. 7th	1♊4	third period 26°35′

For the uncorrected position, using only the movement in the second or middle period, within which noon of Aug. 4th comes, we find: 21♈55; this is the uncorrected position.

For the correction we ignore that middle period, and comparing the first period (movement is 24°15′) and third period (26°35′) we find a difference between these of 2°20′. The part of a period wanted to reach noon on Aug. 4th from noon on Aug. 3rd is 24 hours. The fraction given in table below for 24h is $\frac{1}{16}$. So we take $\frac{1}{16}$ of the difference found between movements in the first and third periods, namely, $\frac{1}{16}$ of 2°20′. This is 9′. As movement is increasing or becoming quicker (more in the third period than in the first) we SUBTRACT it from the uncorrected position (21♈55), giving us the CORRECTED POSITION: 21♈46. This is exactly correct by an ephemeris giving positions every day at noon, and thus remedies the slight inaccuracy caused by using a condensed ephemeris giving the Moon only every two days. (The fractions in the table are convenient fractions

roughly approximating the Besselian interpolation-coefficients for second differences, adapted for use with parts of two-day intervals.)

If the first or third period in the condensed ephemeris is one day (31st of a month to 1st of next month, for example), double the movement in that period, before finding difference of movements in first and third periods.

If the time of birth is in a day which happens to be a one-day period in the condensed ephemeris, the correction is not needed.

TABLE OF CORRECTION FRACTIONS FOR MOON

For or	3h. 45h.	6h. 42h.	9h. 39h.	12h. 36h.	15h. 33h.	18h. 30h.	21h. 27h.	24h. 24h.
Fraction	0	$\frac{1}{36}$	$\frac{1}{25}$	$\frac{1}{21}$	$\frac{1}{18}$	$\frac{1}{16}$	$\frac{1}{16}$	$\frac{1}{16}$

135. Day of Week. Most astrologers (and the present writer thinks wisely) ignore the day of the week in horoscope-work, except when it serves to help determine an uncertainly remembered date of birth ('I *think* it was January 3rd, 1942, but I *know* it was a Wednesday'). Some, however, attach importance to the 'ruling planet' of each day of the week: ⊙ SUNDAY, ☽ MONDAY, ♂ TUESDAY, ☿ WEDNESDAY, ♃ THURSDAY, ♀ FRIDAY, ♄ SATURDAY. For either purpose, the condensed ephemeris in this book gives (under the position of the Node) the day of the week on first of each month. From this it is very easy to find the weekday for any later day of the month: 8th, 15th, 22nd, 29th, same as first; count forwards on your fingers from the nearest one of these before the day wanted.

136. The Chart Itself is in modern practice almost always circular in shape; a 'wheel' with twelve spokes representing the cusps, usually a small circle in the middle, and the outer rim consisting of two circles between which are written the longitudes on the cusps of the houses. Inside the wheel, against the spokes, are written the planets etc., with their degrees in their signs—the sign itself seldom needs writing, being indicated by that on the cusp. Planets in intercepted signs are written parallel to the rim of the wheel, against the intercepted sign; others, parallel to the nearest cusp-line or 'spoke', on the correct side of it (before or after the cusp). On pages 76 to 81 are shown the charts for the Example Horoscope according to the six different systems of house-division catered for in this book. For the sake of clear legibility in charts reproduced on the small scale needed to print them here, only whole degrees have been given, even for Ascendant and M.C. and planets.

137. The Aspects in the Example Horoscope. These should be tabulated after filling in the chart, and before trying to 'judge' the horoscope:

SUN is in 10 ♋ (to nearest whole degree). Allowing fairly wide orbs for major aspects (conjunction, sextile, square, trine, opposition) we look for bodies in from 2° to 18° of any sign except those adjacent to the one the Sun is in, and those adjacent to the Sun's opposite sign. This allows an orb of 8° either way (8° more or less than Sun's 10°). In same sign (conjunction) is Neptune. For sextile aspects, look in next-but-one sign on either side of Cancer (in Taurus and Virgo), and we find Moon and Saturn (15 ♉ and 5 ♉). Look next for squares, in signs of the same

'qualities' (cardinal, fixed or mutable; in this case, cardinal) as Sun's sign (Cancer), other than the opposite sign. We find Jupiter in Libra. For trines we look in signs of the same element (in this case Water), or four signs away in either direction, namely in Scorpio and Pisces, but find nothing; Sun has no trine aspects. We write Sun's aspects thus:

$$\odot: \; ☌ \; ♆; \; ✶ \; ☽ \; ♄; \; □ \; ♃.$$

A similar search for aspects to the other bodies gives us:

☽: ✶ ⊙ ♆; □ ♂.

☿: ☌ Pl.

♀: (as this is *very* near the beginning of a sign, in addition to looking in the proper signs for aspects, we must also make sure whether anything is very near the end of a sign preceding the sign that would make an aspect): ✶ ♂; △ ♃.

♂: ✶ ♀ ♃; □ ☽ ♄.

♃: ✶ ♂; □ ⊙; △ ♀.

♄: ✶ ⊙; □ ♂.

♅: 0° ♆.

♆: 0° ♅.

Pl. ☌ ☿.

(Students sufficiently advanced or experienced to make *proper use* of the *minor* aspects need no instruction in *finding* them.)

To obviate oversights, a table in this form is useful:

	⊙	☽	☿	♀	♂	♃	♄	♅	♆	P
⊙		✶				□	✶		☌	
☽	✶				□				✶	
☿										☌
♀					✶	△				
♂		□		✶		✶	□			
♃	□			△	✶					
♄	✶				□					
♅									☍	
♆	☌	✶						☍		
P			☌							

Note: In the above table, each aspect has been inserted twice: once under each of the two bodies concerned. This is not usual, and not neces-

sary; it has been done here so that the beginner may not overlook any major aspect, whether looking down a column or along a row to find aspects to a single planet. The normal, and for more experienced students, the better way is to enter each aspect only in the row belonging to the planet first in order, and in the column under the other planet.

138. Summary: Example Horoscope by Six Systems.

House	X	XI	XII	I	II	III	Notes
Equal-House System	25♍46	26♎	26♏	25♐46	26♑	26♒	M.C.: 0♏21
Porphyry System	0♏21	19♏	7♐	25♐46	7♒	19♓	Intercepted: ♑♈
Regiomontanus System	0♏21	20♏	6♐	25♐46	4♒	28♓	,, ♑♈
Campanus System	0♏21	14♏	28♏	25♐46	27♒	11♈	,, ♑♓
Placidus System	0♏21	21♏	9♐	25♐46	7♑	26♓	,, ♒♈
Natural Graduation System	0♏21	21♏	5♐	25♐46	1♒	25♓	,, ♑♈

⊙ 10♋9; ☽ 14♉52; ☿ 22♊33; ♀ 3♊30; ♂ 8♌32; ♃ 6♎1; ♄ 4♉40; ♅ 23♑49; ♆ 18♋42; Pl. 26♊39; ☊ 24♉6; ☋ 24♏6; ⊕ 0♏38.

Harmonious Aspects	Doubtful Aspects	Discordant Aspects
⊙✶☽; ⊙✶ ♄;	⊙☌♆;	⊙□♃
☽✶ ♆;	. . .	☽□♂
. . .	☿☌Pl.	. . .
♀✶♂; ♀△ ♃	. . .	. . .
♂✶ ♃	. . .	♂□♄
. . .	. . .	♅☍♆

(Each aspect is here entered once only.)

X

THE JUDGMENT OF THE HOROSCOPE

139. Scheme. With experience, it will be found best not to *follow* any cut-and-dried scheme in writing out a judgment of a chart. The *having* of such a scheme, however, from which to depart as and when it seems desirable, is useful. For the beginner and for short, 'summary' readings, the following may be suggested:

I. *You as portrayed in the skies at birth:*

1. CHARACTER: the Sun sign, aspects to the Sun.
2. DISPOSITION: the Moon sign; aspects to the Moon.
3. PERSONALITY: the Ascendant sign; sign-position of the ruling planet of the Ascendant; aspects to that planet; planet(s) in the Ascendant sign or rising; aspects to it or them.
4. MENTALITY: Mercury's sign- and house-position and aspects.
5. AFFECTIONS: Venus in sign-position and with aspects.

II. *Your life-pattern potentialities:*

1. MONEY: sign on cusp of second house; planet(s) in that house, and aspects; ruling planet of that sign, its sign-position and aspects.
2. PEOPLE: parents (tenth and fourth houses), relatives (third house), friends (eleventh house), lovers and children (fifth house), husband or wife (seventh house) (also, Moon in man's horoscope, Sun in woman's).
3. CAREER: business, fame, success (tenth house); any indications in second house of kind of activity associated with income; in sixth house, of work as employee; in seventh house, of partnership business.
4. HEALTH: sixth house mostly; any physical inferences from Ascendant and aspects to Sun.
5. RELIGIO-PHILOSOPHICAL AND SPIRITUAL DEVELOPMENTS: ninth house; Neptune and Jupiter.
6. TRAVEL: third and ninth houses.

140. The Specimen 'Reading' which follows does not keep to the foregoing scheme, or any other fixed scheme, and the numbering of its paragraphs has nothing to do with the numbering of the foregoing headings. It simply illustrates the way one student might read the chart at first sight. Another might, quite as legitimately, pick out as most outstanding quite other factors, and in some details differently interpret the same factors. As this is not the horoscope of a real person, about whom it would be important to arrive at as true a conclusion as possible, but merely an imaginary horoscope dealt with for illustrative purposes, it

does not matter what system of house-division is used to obtain a chart on which to practise. The present writer's own system (Natural Graduaion) has been used, as it happens. It would, however, be instructive, and useful practice for the student, to see what differences, in his opinion, would be made in the reading if the chart according to one of the other systems had been used instead.

141. A Short Judgment of the Example Horoscope (according to the Natural Graduation System). For the chart see Appendix I, Fig. 6.

1. Ascendant in Sagittarius suggests a vigorous, energetic, rather many-sided, personality, and possibly a fairly tall man, though height may be reduced by Sun's square aspect to the Ascendant-sign ruler, Jupiter. His air and manner are likely as a rule to be 'jovial', optimistic, cheery, and sociable; he is likely to be of a hospitable type, and possibly fond of horses and outdoor sport. But the planet Uranus rising is apt to suggest that a certain brusquerie or an occasionally offensive abruptness may come as a nasty change to his normally genial manner, and he can prove extremely independent and individualistic, not always co-operative.

2. Sun in Cancer makes his real fundamental character, even though not always shown as near the surface as the Ascendant personality, one marked by great sensitiveness, with feelings more easily hurt than the Sagittarian exterior would lead casual acquaintances to suspect, and with much capacity for sympathy and perhaps intuition, and a feminine streak of sentiment in his make-up. This may include a strong sentiment for things of historical and antiquarian interest or associations. The conjunction of Neptune with the Sun adds to his intuitive gifts and, possibly, psychic faculties, especially being in Cancer (a sign congenial to mediums, for example).

3. Moon in Taurus gives an instinctive resistance against any change in his set ways or opposition to his purposes, a certain obstinacy, a taste and need for the material pleasures of the senses, including good food (and drink, probably, with Neptune conjunct Sun), and the company of the opposite sex (especially as the Moon is in his fifth house). Moon's square aspect to Mars can make the love-instinct, in its more physical manifestations, a very strong one, and a source of much temptation at times. A gift of artistic imagination, besides a further indication of possible psychic powers, is indicated by Moon's sextile aspect to Neptune.

4. The financial fortunes may be marked by considerable difficulties during his life, with Uranus in the second house, and Saturn, traditional ruler of Aquarius (sign on cusp II) square to Mars, making for losses. On the other hand, Uranus being well-placed by sign in its own joint-rulership, Aquarius, and Saturn being in good aspect (sextile) to the Sun, makes for an influence of prosperity, if real wisdom is used to cope with the Saturn-Mars risks and tribulations in money-matters.

5. With Taurus on the fifth-house cusp, and Moon and Ascending Node there, and with Venus, ruler of Taurus, in good aspect to the passionate and virile Mars and to the expansive and prospering Jupiter, creative art, the professions or businesses dealing with pleasure and amusement, and the bringing up of his children if he has any (probably daughters) and the emotional life, can be sources of rich benefit and enjoyment, provided that too much self-indulgent misuse of the capacity for a very full love-life is not allowed to bring penalties too easily risked; for he is probably very 'successful' and popular with women. And some fickleness

and changeability in matters of the affections may be likely with 'inconstant Moon' in the fifth house, and that house's accidental ruler (Venus), which is also the love-planet, in the dualistic and changeful sign of Gemini.

6. Marriage may be something which, or the opportunity for it, will be more than once a factor in this man's life, with the dualistic signs of Sagittarius and Gemini on the horizon, especially with Gemini on the seventh house, and its ruler Mercury almost on the cusp itself. Pluto conjunct Gemini on this cusp may possibly point (but our knowledge is too incomplete to speak with any positiveness) to bereavement and remarriage and a very great change in general outlook and life following this.

7. Venus in the sixth house in good aspect to Jupiter, ruler of the Ascendant, makes for the utmost beneficial influences for the best possible treatment and recuperation if illness is experienced at any time, but there is no real indication of more illness than is perhaps common to all mankind, in this particular map. Much caution, however, with Uranus rising, Gemini on the sixth cusp, and Jupiter (the expansive and exaggerating) square to the Sun, is called for, to guard against excesses, rash risks, and especially nerve-strain and nervous tension. Too foolhardy a disregard of any such caution *could* even give the Mars-in-eighth-house influence an opportunity to work out in terms of death by violence, though there could be no justification at all for predicting that such an end is more than a possibility. This position of Mars, in strong good aspects to the two most fortunate planets, Venus and Jupiter, but discordant (square) aspect to Moon and Saturn, may very probably point to much benefit from inheritance or legacies or the handling of wife's or partner's business or finances, but much grief from bereavements.

8. Pisces on the third house, with its ruler Jupiter on the overlap of the ninth and tenth houses, and its co-ruler Neptune conjunct with the Sun, and with Virgo on the ninth house, its ruler Mercury strongly placed on an angular cusp and dignified in its other rulership sign of Gemini, a sign favourable to movement and travel and to intellectual activities, all point to the likelihood of much travel, with beneficial effects both on career (tenth house) and on intellectual, and philosophic-religious, developments (ninth house).

9. In spite of the mixed influences affecting the house of money, referred to above, the potentialities for a successful career in the eyes of the world seem very good with Jupiter elevated, not far from the Midheaven, and the Part of Fortune situated there.

APPENDIX I

CHARTS OF EXAMPLE HOROSCOPE
ACCORDING TO SIX SYSTEMS

The following six illustrations give the chart, or figure of the heavens, or map, of the Example Horoscope, according to the six different systems of house-division in current use for general astrological purposes in Europe and America.

Simply because a diagram overcrowded with numerals is not very easy for the unaccustomed person to follow at a glance when reduced to very small size to fit these pages, all longitudes have been rounded off to nearest whole-degree value—even the Ascendant and M.C. (and cusp X of the Equal-House chart), and the planets,* although in Chapters VIII and IX these were found in degrees and minutes. Printed blank forms for the chart in various slightly varied designs and of various sizes can be bought at many places, including those bookshops which specialise in astrological or occult works. A very simple wheel, with no lettering or printed numbers at all, can be had from the Whitman Publishing Co., a larger one, with dotted lines (that can be used or ignored) for 'midcusps' (dividing each house into two half-houses) and with the cusps boldly numbered, but no wording, as used in the reduced-scale reproductions here, can be had from the present writer, Colin Evans, c/o the Publishers. Most of the printed forms on sale (different types can usually be seen on the literature stall at the Astrological Lodge of the Theosophical Society, London) contain spaces with printed words for calculating and recording purposes, and sometimes for a table of aspects.

To draw one's own 'wheel' with a pair of compasses and a ruler is not difficult, and it is not very expensive to get a rubber stamp made of the horoscope-wheel to one's own design or requirements and of the size one prefers (limited by size of inking-pads obtainable—they are made up to about six inches square, which is large enough for anyone). The 'wheel' is usually drawn with an extreme diameter of from 3 inches (or a little less) to 5 inches (or a little more).

'Zenith', often printed against tenth cusp is wrong; 'East Point', sometimes put as an alternative to 'Ascendant' against cusp I, is equally wrong. So are 'North Point', and 'South Point', printed sometimes against cusps X and IV. If you get horoscope-blanks so printed do not let these wordings mislead you.

---

* In the charts the long. of ☿ is given as 22 ♊. To nearest minute it is 22 ♊ 33, so to nearest degree should be 23 ♊ —a slip discovered after charts were printed.

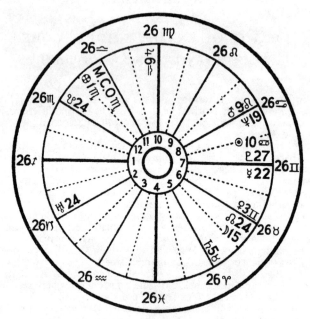

Figure 1.—The Example Horoscope by the EQUAL-HOUSE SYSTEM. Ignore dotted lines (not usually printed on horoscope-chart blanks) if cusps considered beginnings of houses.

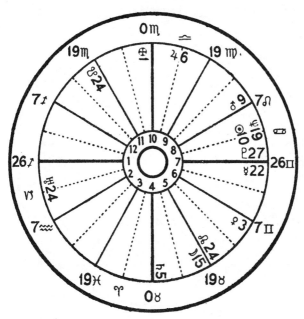

Figure 2.—The Example Horoscope by the
PORPHYRY SYSTEM. Dotted lines are boundaries
between houses when cusps considered centres
of houses.

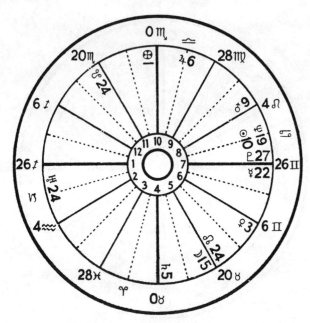

Figure 3.—The Example Horoscope by the REGIOMONTANUS SYSTEM. Ignore dotted lines, as cusps are (usually) considered beginnings of houses.

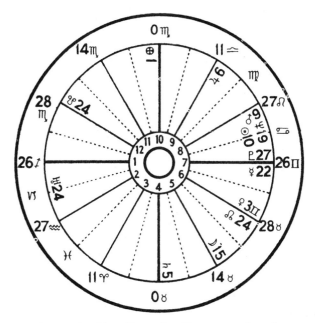

Figure 4.—The Example Horoscope by the
CAMPANUS SYSTEM. Cusps usually considered
centres of houses, so dotted lines represent
house-boundaries.

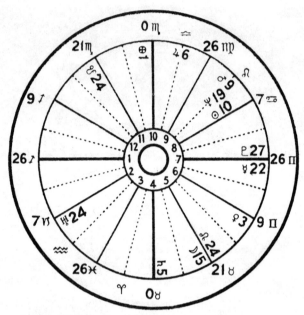

Figure 5.—The Example Horoscope by the
PLACIDUS (SEMI-ARC) SYSTEM. Cusps usually considered beginning of houses; dotted lines
ignored.

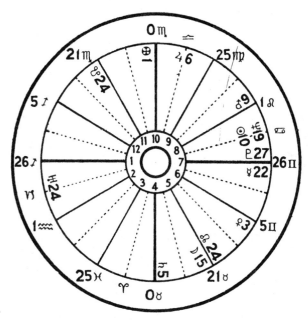

Figure 6.—The Example Horoscope by the NATURAL GRADUATION SYSTEM. Cusps usually considered centres of houses, then dotted lines are where houses begin.

APPENDIX II

LOVE, MONEY, AND HEALTH

(i) LOVE AND MARRIAGE. The good or bad aspects to planets in the fifth house and to the ruling planet of the sign on the fifth house are indications of helpful or unhelpful tendencies in regard to the opposite sex, and of ease or difficulty in establishing happy relations with that sex. The general fortunes in courtship and 'romance' are judged also from the character-istics of the sign itself that is on cusp V; and some further indication is to be found in the aspects to Venus and her house-position, and in Mars-Venus aspects, and whether Venus and/or Mars is debilitated or dignified (in rulership, exaltation, strong by sign, in detriment, or in fall). The seventh house deals more with marriage as a contract of partnership, and less specially with the love-making side. Delays, frustration, discrepancies of age or social status may be indicated by Saturn, unless it has only strong good aspects (when it may show steadfast loyalty), whether as planet in the house, planet aspecting planet in the house, or ruler of the sign on the cusp. Harmony, affection, co-operation, by Venus (or, badly aspected and debilitated, sensuality and pleasure-seeking); good and normal or bad and excessive manifestations of the more animal side of sexual impulse, either in connection with love-affairs (fifth house) or marriage (seventh house) are to be judged by Mars, its sign-position, house-position, and aspects; especially significant if either in or ruling the seventh or fifth house. If the interpretation is corroborated by other indications, Mars or Uranus not very harmoniously aspected in either house may show either quarrels or bereavement.

The Moon is said to symbolise the female marriage-partner in a male chart, and the Sun the male spouse in a woman's horoscope. The first planet making aspect to either, after birth, and the kind of aspect, denote the type of partner, and the success or otherwise of the match. In com-paring two people's horoscopes of birth, Mars in one chart with Venus in the other, making strong aspect (good or bad) to one another, is significant of likelihood of amorous attraction, desirably or the reverse; aspect between Sun in one chart and Moon in the other is very significant for marriage. Ascendant signs and/or Sun-signs in good or bad aspect are significant for general compatibility or incompatibility. But no one factor alone is at all conclusive.

(ii) MONEY in general is denoted in the second house; Taurus is a specially favourable sign here; Libra, Leo, Sagittarius, are rather fortunate. Any planets in the second house are important as indicating a tendency to be subject to good or bad fortunes in financial matters (Mars bad through losses, extravagance, rashness; Saturn, through restriction of means, losses, frustration, meanness; Uranus, through the unforeseen and sudden,

unless very well aspected—then equally unforeseen strokes of luck; Neptune, more 'luck' than judgment, some muddle; Jupiter, extremely fortunate unless ill-aspected—then extravagance or great expenditure; Moon, changeable fortunes; Venus very fortunate unless very badly aspected, then loss through self-indulgence or females; Mercury, gain through brainwork if well aspected, or through commerce, and some fluctuations of fortune). The planet ruling the sign on cusp II is equally important—and is *most* important if no planets are in the second house. Financial speculation or 'gambles' are influenced by the same factors that affect love-affairs, in the fifth house. The tenth house, especially when it is related in any way to the second (by a planet in, or ruling, one of them and aspecting a planet in, or ruling, the other, for example) shows the factors primarily connected with career or public position or profession as affecting financial fortunes. Eighth house shows legacies, inheritance, and other people's money you handle or are affected by, especially husband's or wife's.

(iii) HEALTH. It is wrong and dangerous for any but the most experienced and expert student to be at all detailed or definite on matters of health and longevity. Only very tentative suggestions of possibilities should be made by any student who still needs such instruction as this book can give. Good planets and aspects affecting sixth house point to favourable protecting and helping influences to secure good recovery and recuperation in cases of illness. Saturn's influence makes rather for chronic (that is, more or less permanent—not *necessarily* very bad) illnesses, and Mars more for acute (short and sharp) ones; Saturn, for chills and effects of cold, weakness; Mars for feverish conditions, cuts, burns; Uranus for shock, physical or mental, neuroses (bad aspects to Mercury here are an indication also), and hurts from electricity or explosions, and sudden unlooked-for accidents; Neptune, to toxins, drugs, drink, delusions; Jupiter, to protection, immunity, or, badly aspected, ill effects of excess or overdoing things. Below is a table of parts of the body ruled by each sign. The sign on the Ascendant or containing the Sun, or containing the ruler of the Ascendant, or on the sixth house, or containing its ruler, are all to be looked at in judging parts of the body most liable to be affected by illness or injury:

♈ ARIES: head and face.
♉ TAURUS: throat and neck.
♊ GEMINI: lungs, nervous system, hands, arms, shoulders.
♋ CANCER: breast and stomach.
♌ LEO: heart, sides, upper back.
♍ VIRGO: bowels, solar plexus.
♎ LIBRA: loins, kidneys, ovaries.
♏ SCORPIO: bladder, anus, genitals.
♐ SAGITTARIUS: liver, hips, thighs.
♑ CAPRICORN: knees, spleen.
♒ AQUARIUS: calves, ankles.
♓ PISCES: feet, reactions of body to fluids, medicine, drugs, alcohol, tobacco.

APPENDIX III

THE PLANETS IN THE ZODIAC SIGNS

(i) INTERPRETATION: The descriptions given in chapter V, under the heading 'Planets in Houses', should be interpreted only in general terms, as experience will justify. Only by co-ordinating the influences of the aspects with the relationships of the signs and the signs in which the planets appear can a detailed analysis be made. This will be fully appreciated from experience, but initially it is necessary to master the fundamental influences of the planets in the houses of the chart.

(ii) A GOOD ASTROLOGER will consider all influences before attempting to make an interpretation. He will consider a planet in a sign to have a comparatively weak influence in the horoscope if it is not supported by an aspect or an appropriate sign.

(iii) EXAMPLE: Mars is aggressive, combative, ardent and bold. Detriment in Libra is both pleasure and beauty-loving. The discord between the planet and the sign of its detriment emphasizes the less desirable aspect of both—the violent, pleasure-seeking 'lover' and the sensual artist or the workshy gangster, in the extreme case, but the sign of Mars, which is virile, heroic, courageous and adventuresome in the Fire sign of Sagittarius, which is cheerful, enterprising and energetic, produces a person who is very active, a traveller and one who is prepared to fight doggedly for his opinion in matters of religious or philosophical belief. In contrast to sign Venus in the sign of Sagittarius (in which this planet is 'strong') will produce a gentler, idealistic and more artistic type of person with the ability to appreciate beauty, metaphysical ideas and capable of achieving success abroad.

The following information may help to clarify the associations between planets and signs:

(iv)   THE SUN IN: (Denotes the fundamental ego of an individual).

Sign	General	Good Aspects	Bad Aspects
ARIES	Originality Independence	Leadership	Egotism Selfishness
TAURUS	Creative Practical Constructive	Enterprising	Possessiveness Laziness Complacency
GEMINI	Awareness Intellectual Duality	Inventiveness Adaptability	Lack of concentration Impatience
CANCER	Emotional Imaginative	Protective Shrewd	Possessiveness Anxiety
LEO	Creative Self-expressive	Inspiring Organizing	Egotism Vanity

Sign	General	Good Aspects	Bad Aspects
VIRGO	Dutiful Dedicated	Analytical Discriminating	Intolerant Fussy Vague
LIBRA	Harmonious Just	Helpful Diplomatic	Suspicious Disbelieving
SCORPIO	Energetic Determined	Self Control	Jealousy Ruthlessness
SAGITTARIUS	Joviality Purposeful	Wisdom Understanding	Superficial Careless
CAPRICORN	Dutiful Integrity	Cautious Dependable Practical	Suspicious Snobbish
AQUARIUS	Knowledge-seeking Intellectual	Humanitarian Co-ordinating	Remote Vacant
PISCES	Sympathetic Understanding	Placid Adaptable Imaginative	Lazy Unstable

(v)   THE MOON IN: (Controls instincts and desires)

Sign	General	Good Aspects	Bad Aspects
ARIES	Hasty Enthusiastic Impetuous	Independence	Restless Militant
TAURUS	Endurance Determined	Resourceful Intuitive	Over-Sensuous Reminiscing
GEMINI	Poetic Self-Expressive Unusual pursuits	Alert Conversationalist Controlling influence	Crafty Scheming Moody
CANCER	Imaginative Romantic Sociable	Sympathetic	Idealistic
LEO	Generous Loyal	Optimism in leadership	Fame-Seeking Conceited Outspoken
VIRGO	Industrious Fastidious	Re-assuring Comforting	Over-critical Nagging
LIBRA	Pacifist Tolerant Accommodating	Hospitable Friendly Self-reliant	Evasive Sulky
SCORPIO	Sexually Attractive Seductive	Capable Enthusiastic	Tormenting
SAGITTARIUS	Forthright Enthusiastic Impulsive	Independent Jovial	Superficial Unstable ideas Easily led
CAPRICORN	Prudent Reliable Ambitious	Austere Diligent	Habit-forming Slow to rouse Jealous Pessimistic Self-centred
AQUARIUS	Humanitarian Unconventional Unpredictable	Progressive Ingenious Friendly	Obstinate Erratic

Sign	General	Good Aspects	Bad Aspects
PISCES	Passive Sentimental Gentle	Intense Kind Cheerful	Lazy Indecisive Restless

(vi) MERCURY IN: (The mental activity)

Sign	General	Good Aspects	Bad Aspects
ARIES	Alert Forceful	Good concentration Decisive Conclusive	Argumentative
TAURUS	Practical Diplomatic	Organized Inspired Fluent	Inflexible Dogmatic
GEMINI	Active Lively	Inventive Versatile Witty	Easily misled Superficial
CANCER	Receptive Imaginative	Expressive Dedicated	Uninspired
LEO	Authoritative Comprehensive	Creative Self-sufficient	Diversified
VIRGO	Logical Observant Scientific	Accurate Attentive Decisive	Hesitating Dithering Hypercritical
LIBRA	Surmising Judicial Rational	Good Concentration Suave	Easily dis- tracted Perfectionist
SCORPIO	Thorough Shrewd Secretive	Resourceful Astute Searching	Intolerant Bitter Critical
SAGITTARIUS	Inspiring Independent	Impulsive Enthralling Encouraging Good teacher	Argumentative Reactionary Sarcastic
CAPRICORN	Cautious Profound Painstaking Careful	Methodical Precise	Suspicious Dogmatic
AQUARIUS	Warm Poetic Clever	Original Tolerant	Uncertain Vague Detached
PISCES	Humorous Illogical Prejudiced	Subtle Diplomatic	Confused Wandering

(vii) VENUS IN: (Affections and artistic taste)

Sign	General	Good Aspects	Bad Aspects
ARIES	Impetuous Impulsive	Devoted	Fickle (Changes of heart)
TAURUS	Steadfast Obedient	Generous Sociable Charming	Slow Slothful
GEMINI	Spontaneous	Humorous Sympathetic	Flirtatious

Sign	General	Good Aspects	Bad Aspects
CANCER	Devoted Materialist	Romantic Gentle Warm-hearted	Possessive
LEO	Inspiring Reliable Sincere Noble	Generous	Indecisive Self-satisfying
VIRGO	Moral Pure	Dutiful	Fear of self- indulgence
LIBRA	Refined Idealistic	Sense of Proportion Charming	Inflexible
SCORPIO	Passionate Direct	Loyal Expressive	Jealous Self-indulgent Desirous Secret
SAGITTARIUS	Adventurous High-spirited Impulsive	Freedom-loving Sincere	Evasive
CAPRICORN	Consistent Protective	Sincere	Stubborn
AQUARIUS	Impersonal Artistic	Altruistic	Insecure Unenterprising
PISCES	Devoted Changeable	Self-sacrificial	Lack of will power

(vii) MARS IN: (Dynamic activity, impulses)

ARIES	Forceful Positive Direct	Independent Spontaneous	Impatient Aggressive Quick-tempered
TAURUS	Persistent	Determined Enterprising	Inflexible Single-minded
GEMINI	Spontaneous Excitable	Observant Quick-witted	Vulnerable Fearful of criticism
CANCER	Emotional Imaginative	Conservative Sympathetic	Resentful Spiteful
LEO	Dominating Dramatic	Respected	Rebellious Self-indulgent
VIRGO	Calculating Self-disciplined Scientific	Diplomatic Consulting	Hypercritical Scheming
LIBRA	Co-ordinated	Compromising Courteous	Easily influenced Intolerant
SCORPIO	Perservering Energetic Probing	Regimented Perceptive Authoritarian	Callous Insidious
SAGITTARIUS	Frank Spontaneous Optimistic	Courteous Dedicated Just	Insatiable Unscrupulous

Sign	General	Good Aspects	Bad Aspects
CAPRICORN	Orthodox Persistent Organizing	Efficient Suave Conscientious	Slow-witted No sense of humour Unimaginative
AQUARIUS	Original Dynamic Theoretical	Understanding Humane	Disturbing Susceptible to changes of heart
PISCES	Receptive Unassuming Co-operative	Intuitive Humorous	Shy Devious Scheming

(ix) JUPITER IN: (Energy in expansion)

ARIES	Active desire for freedom, adventurous
TAURUS	Constructive, acquiring, self-helping
GEMINI	Creative, witty, scientific
CANCER	Domestic abilities, power of expression, good actor, diplomatic, fanciful
LEO	Assertion through example, vital, generous, vain, autocratic
VIRGO	Probing, researching, expansion through discovery
LIBRA	Harmonious, artistic expression, philosophical, humanitarian approach
SCORPIO	Attractive, inspiring devotion
SAGITTARIUS	Physically active, socially accepted, sporting interests
CAPRICORN	Devoted to duty, organizing, responsible, orthodox
AQUARIUS	Philosophical, original, reformer
PISCES	Receptive, sympathetic care of others

(x) SATURN IN: (Limitation, restrictions, discipline, caution)

ARIES	Overwrought, difficult in reconciliation, frustration, self-reliant
TAURUS	Determined, insecure, fear of dependence, prudent
GEMINI	Seeks unification, fear of being stereotyped, happy in situations requiring versatility and quick thought
CANCER	Emotional, opinionated, intolerant, fear of suppression
LEO	Sense of honour, jealous, hypocritical, dread of being ignored or over-looked
VIRGO	Cautious, discriminating, lack of confidence, seeking security, fear of unknown
LIBRA	Judgement, honourable, dislike of sentimentality, impartial
SCORPIO	Egotistical, exacting, self-disciplined, with bad aspects, callous, intolerant, afraid of becoming emotionally dependent
CAPRICORN	Well-controlled, organizing ability, seeks recognition, lacks originality
AQUARIUS	Detached, reserved, treasures independence, dread of over-involvement
PISCES	Intuitive, passive, pessimistic, dislikes own company, fear of being isolated

(xi) URANUS IN any sign adds a touch of inspiration, expressiveness, will-power and inventiveness. It is the spark from which the fire is kindled. As joint ruler of Aquarius it encourages originality, progressive thinking and analysis, whilst in the sign of Leo, Uranus produces over-confidence, pride and a quest for power.

(xii) NEPTUNE IN a sign produces intuitiveness, imagination, mysticism and the ability to overcome obstacles associated with the sign and the house in which it appears. This planet causes self-sacrifice, renunciation, expansion and achievement beyond normal boundaries, the breaking down of conventions, spiritualism and vagueness.

(xiii) PLUTO in a sign represents the potential for transformation, re-juvenation or rebirth within the sign, or house in which it appears. It enables one to start afresh to find new beginnings. Pluto works well in Scorpio where the regenerative process is in harmony, but in Taurus it finds conflict with the steadfast, unchanging attitudes of Taurus.

ERRATA

P. 163, SUN on Aug. 1st: *for* ♋ *read* ♌. Similar mistyped *signs* now and then on other pages—easily corrected by comparing preceding and following entries—make some attention advisable, in using ephemeris and Tables of Houses.

IN THE TABLES OF HOUSES (pages 195–235 inclusive): a discrepancy of one unit sometimes observable between an item at foot of either page and same item at top of facing page only shows inconsistent rounding-off of a critical fraction; for example, where 15 and 16 are both good approximations for a value almost exactly $15\frac{1}{2}$. But some real errors are:

P. 197, M.C.; 19h.0m., read: 13 49.

P. 199, PLACIDUS cusp 2, from sid. time 20h.12m. to end of column, read: 10 13 16 19 / 22 25 27 ♋0 3 / 6 8 11 14 16 / 19 22 25 27 ♌0 / 3 /. (*Note: the stroke, /, above, denotes the line ruled across the page.*)

P. 200, REGIOMONTA. cusp 2, 8h.12m. to end of column, read: 27 ♐0 2 5 / 8 10 13 16 18 / 21 24 26 29 ♑2 / 5 7 10 13 16 / 19 /.

P. 201, REGIOMONTA. cusp 2, 12h.0m., read: 19.

P. 201, SID. TIME, immediately under 21 12, read: 21 24.

P. 204, PLACIDUS cusp 11, 11h.48m. and 12h.0m., read: 27 / 29 /.

P. 206, CAMPANUS cusp 3, 0h.0m., read: 7 (not 17).

P. 197, NAT. GRAD. cusp 12, 23h.12m. to end of column, read: 9 12 14 17 / 19 /.

P. 213, REGIOMONTA. cusp 3, 12h.0m., read: 17.

P. 229, PLACIDUS cusp 3, 12h.0m., read: 27.

P. 231, PLACIDUS (all cusps), 23h.0m. to end of column, read:

11	12	2	3
21	14	4	21
25	16	6	23
29	19	9	26
♉3	22	11	28
7	25	13	♍1
11	28	15	3

Pp. 233–5, M.C., 19h.24m., read: 19 24.

P. 234, CAMPANUS cusp 3, 12h.0m., delete the sign before the figure 8.

P. 235, CAMPANUS cusp 2, 24h.0m., read: / ♍1 /.

Pp. 238–9 : Longitude-equivalents for Cardiff and Yarmouth respectively: read −12m.40s., +6m.52s. (as used on pp. 53–54).

THE AUTHOR will thank readers who point out any other substantial error among the more than forty-three thousand longitudes that had to be computed and copied for these tables of houses (for about three-quarters of which there existed no published tables available as a check).

CONDENSED EPHEMERIS
1 8 8 0 – 1 9 9 0 both years inclusive
CALCULATED FOR GREENWICH MEAN NOON
with
RAPID TABLES FOR FINDING SIDEREAL TIME
and
TABLE FOR CONVERTING FROM MOVING–EQUINOX ZODIAC TO FIXED–STAR ZODIAC

NOTES:

LONGITUDES of the Moon (every two days) and Sun (every eight days) and Mercury (every six days) and Venus (every eight days) and Mars Jupiter Saturn Uranus and Neptune (every twelve days) and Pluto and the North Node of the Moon (first of every month) — all in degrees and minutes and shown thus: 23♈15 means 23°15' of ♈ (Aries).

RETROGRADE is indicated by R. Direct (after being Retrograde) shown by D. The sign is not shown if it is the same as in preceding line; so the R or D is placed in space left vacant by sign. When change of sign leaves no room the R or D is given in next line if it is still applicable. If not it is omitted. As this happens fairly often in a condensed ephemeris, watch should always be kept for longitudes that decrease or for those that have just stopped decreasing. Otherwise retrograde motion or its termination may be overlooked.

STATIONS of all planets except Pluto are given below the columns for the Moon but are only approximate. They are intended merely to give better interpolation between a tabulated date in the main columns of the ephemeris and the date of a planet's change of motion.

YEARS 1954 to 1960: as the usual authoritative sources for checking — and especially any close data for Pluto — were not available when computing for these years Pluto is given only in whole degrees — and the minutes of longitude for the Moon and occasionally for Mercury — though seldom, it is thought — may be subject to a possible marginal error of about 0°3'. Other entries, of about 0°1'.

SIDEREAL TIME for the first day of January in each year is given for Greenwich Mean Midnight (0h., beginning of the calendar year) and is also given for Greenwich Mean Noon (12h.) with a note that the year is common or LEAP. See lowest right-hand corner of each page, under the STATIONS. The sidereal time at Greenwich for any time of any day of any month is found by the simple addition to one of these of the amounts for day of month and for month and the time elapsed since the preceding noon or midnight and the acceleration, all given on p.86. Adding (for east longitude) or subtracting (for west) the longitude-equivalent will then give local sidereal time (of birth etc.)

THE DAY OF THE WEEK for the first of each month is given at the foot of the column for that month which contains positions of Sun and the planets; see under the longitude of Node each month.

FOREIGN SUMMER TIME AND DAYLIGHT SAVING TIME: see special pages near end of book. Students should write in data as to British and foreign summer-time etc. as ascertained for years after 1951 and for places or years for which information could not be given accurately here.

TABLES FOR SIDEREAL TIME

The "Addition for Month" and "Addition for Day" given below, when added to Sidereal Time at Greenwich Mean Midnight or Noon for 1st of January as given on each year's page of the Ephemeris, furnish the Sidereal Time at G.M.Midnight or Noon for any other month, or day. For any time after midnight or noon add the mean time, a.m., or p.m., and also the Acceleration for that amount of Mean Time. The result is Greenwich Sidereal Time, and this becomes the Local S. T. (of birth, for example) when Longitude-Equivalent of place is added (if longitude is East) or subtracted (if West).

ADDITION FOR MONTH

Kind of Year	FEB.	MAR.	APR.	MAY	JUNE
(See Ephemeris)	h m s	h m s	h m s	h m s	h m s
Common Year	2 2 13	3 51 37	5 54 50	7 53 7	9 55 20
LEAP YEAR	2 2 13	3 56 33	5 58 46	7 57 3	9 59 16

Kind of	JUL.	AUG.	SEP.	OCT.	NOV.	DEC.
Year	h m s	h m s	h m s	h m s	h m s	h m s
Common	11 53 36	13 55 50	15 58 3	17 56 19	19 58 33	21 56 49
LEAP	11 57 33	13 59 46	16 1 59	18 0 16	20 4 29	22 0 46

ADDITION FOR DAY

day	m s	day	m s	day	m s	day	h m s	day	h m s
2nd	3 57	8th	27 36	14th	0 51 15	20th	1 14 56	26th	1 38 34
3rd	7 53	9th	31 32	15th	0 55 12	21st	1 18 51	27th	1 42 30
4th	11 50	10th	35 29	16th	0 59 8	22nd	1 22 48	28th	1 46 27
5th	15 46	11th	39 26	17th	1 3 5	23rd	1 26 44	29th	1 50 24
6th	19 43	12th	43 22	18th	1 7 1	24th	1 30 41	30th	1 54 20
7th	23 39	13th	47 19	19th	1 10 58	25th	1 34 37	31st	1 58 17

ACCELERATION

Mean Time min.	Whole hours of Mean Time											
	0h.	1h.	2h.	3h.	4h.	5h.	6h.	7h.	8h.	9h.	10h.	11h.
	m s	m s	m s	m s	m s	m s	m s	m s	m s	m s	m s	m s
0	0 0	0 10	0 20	0 30	0 39	0 49	0 59	1 9	1 19	1 29	1 39	1 48
6	0 1	0 11	0 21	0 31	0 40	0 50	1 0	1 10	1 20	1 30	1 40	1 49
12	0 2	0 12	0 22	0 32	0 41	0 51	1 1	1 11	1 21	1 31	1 41	1 50
18	0 3	0 13	0 23	0 33	0 42	0 52	1 2	1 12	1 22	1 32	1 42	1 51
24	0 4	0 14	0 24	0 34	0 43	0 53	1 3	1 13	1 23	1 33	1 43	1 52
30	0 5	0 15	0 25	0 34	0 44	0 54	1 4	1 14	1 24	1 34	1 43	1 53
36	0 6	0 16	0 26	0 35	0 45	0 55	1 5	1 15	1 25	1 35	1 44	1 54
42	0 7	0 17	0 27	0 36	0 46	0 56	1 6	1 16	1 26	1 36	1 45	1 55
48	0 8	0 18	0 28	0 37	0 47	0 57	1 7	1 17	1 27	1 37	1 46	1 56
54	0 9	0 19	0 29	0 38	0 48	0 58	1 8	1 18	1 28	1 38	1 47	1 57
60	0 10	0 20	0 30	0 39	0 49	0 59	1 9	1 19	1 29	1 39	1 48	1 58

LONGITUDE-EQUIVALENT

After each degree of long. are given h. and m. of equivalent time (for minutes of long., read ° as ', and h. m. as m. s. of time). For long. exceeding 90° use 6h. plus equivalent of excess.

°	h m	°	h m	°	h m	°	h m	°	h m	°	h m	°	h m	°	h m
1	0 4	13	0 52	25	1 40	37	2 28	49	3 16	61	4 4	73	4 52	85	5 40
2	0 8	14	0 56	26	1 44	38	2 32	50	3 20	62	4 8	74	4 56	86	5 44
3	0 12	15	1 0	27	1 48	39	2 36	51	3 24	63	4 12	75	5 0	87	5 48
4	0 16	16	1 4	28	1 52	40	2 40	52	3 28	64	4 16	76	5 4	88	5 52
5	0 20	17	1 8	29	1 56	41	2 44	53	3 32	65	4 20	77	5 8	89	5 56
6	0 24	18	1 12	30	2 0	42	2 48	54	3 36	66	4 24	78	5 12	90	6 0
7	0 28	19	1 16	31	2 4	43	2 52	55	3 40	67	4 28	79	5 16	EXAMPLE
8	0 32	20	1 20	32	2 8	44	2 56	56	3 44	68	4 32	80	5 20	106°32'
9	0 36	21	1 24	33	2 12	45	3 0	57	3 48	69	4 36	81	5 24	=6h0m0s
10	0 40	22	1 28	34	2 16	46	3 4	58	3 52	70	4 40	82	5 28	+1h4m0s
11	0 44	23	1 32	35	2 20	47	3 8	59	3 56	71	4 44	83	5 32	+0h2m8s
12	0 48	24	1 36	36	2 24	48	3 12	60	4 0	72	4 48	84	5 36	=7h6m8s

Noon		JAN	FEB	MAR	APR	MAY	JUN
☉	1	10♑31	12♒ 4	11♓20	12♈ 9	11♉27	11♊18
	9	18 40	20 10	19 20	20 1	19 12	18 58
	17	26 49	28 15	27 18	27 50	26 55	26 36
	25	4♒57	6♓19	5♈14	5♉38	4♊36	4♋14
☿	1	18♐ 9	2♒43	24♓45	5♈50	15♈15	10♊ 5
	7	25 30	12 43	4♈37	2R14	23 17	23 13
	13	3♑44	23 13	11 24	1D37	2♉38	5♋39
	19	12 27	4♓12	13 41	3 58	13 14	16 53
	25	21 34	15 29	11R24	8 41	25 4	26 43
	31	1♒ 5	...	6 38	...	7♊54	...
♀	1	25♏43	2♑10	7♒14	15♓ 4	21♈47	29♉43
	9	4♐57	11 47	16 58	24 51	1♉34	9♊31
	17	14 20	21 27	26 44	4♈39	11 21	19 19
	25	23 48	1♒ 9	6♓31	14 26	21 9	29 8
♂	1	14♉38	24♉20	7♊47	24♊21	11♋29	29♋48
	13	17 33	29 33	14 0	1♋ 7	18 31	7♌ 1
	25	21 35	5♊17	20 29	8 0	25 37	14 19
♃	1	9♓ 9	15♓26	22♓11	29♓41	6♈36	12♈50
	13	11 25	18 10	25 5	2♈31	9 10	14 50
	25	13 54	21 0	28 0	5 16	11 32	16 33
♄	1	9♈21	11♈15	14♈ 9	17♈54	21♈38	25♈ 7
	13	9 54	12 20	15 33	19 24	23 4	26 15
	25	10 41	13 35	17 1	20 54	24 24	27 13
♅	1	8♍52	7♍59	6♍46	5♍33	4♍54	5♍ 2
	13	8R36	7R31	6R15	5R12	4D51	5 19
	25	8 15	6 59	5 47	4 58	4 56	5 43
♆	1	9♉21	9♉19	9♉45	10♉39	11♉45	12♉52
	13	9R16	9 26	10 4	11 5	12 12	13 16
	25	9D16	9 39	10 25	11 31	12 38	13 36
Pl.	1	25♉37	25♉17	25♉25	25♉52	26♉26	27♉ 7
☊	1	15♑57	14♑19	12♑47	11♑ 8	9♑33	7♑55
	1st	Thu	Sun	Mon	Thu	Sat	Tue

Noon		JUL	AUG	SEP	OCT	NOV	DEC
☉	1	9♋57	9♌32	9♍23	8♎40	9♏28	9♐44
	9	17 35	17 13	17 9	16 34	17 30	17 52
	17	25 13	24 54	24 57	24 30	25 34	26 0
	25	2♌51	2♍36	2♎46	2♏28	3♐39	4♑ 9
☿	1	5♌ 8	16♌10	25♌ 7	19♎12	2♐40	24♏26
	7	12 0	11R35	6♍11	28 41	8 6	25D33
	13	17 2	8 32	17 37	7♏43	10 22	0♐56
	19	19 47	9D19	28 42	16 18	7R16	8 21
	25	19R45	14 33	9♎14	24 21	29♏36	16 40
	31	16 51	23 24	...	1♐35	...	25 27
♀	1	6♋30	14♌40	22♍58	0♏ 4	8♐19	15♑ 7
	9	16 20	24 33	2♎52	9 57	18 10	24 52
	17	26 11	4♍26	12 46	19 50	27 59	4♒34
	25	6♌ 2	14 19	22 39	29 41	7♑47	14 12
♂	1	17♌58	7♍11	26♍52	16♎28	7 22	28♏15
	13	25 21	14 45	4♎39	24 29	15 38	6♐48
	25	2♍48	22 23	12 30	2♏35	24 1	15 27
♃	1	7♈17	19♈28	18♈37	15♈18	11♈24	9♈37
	13	18 27	19R31	17R30	13R41	10R21	9R45
	25	19 14	19 5	16 5	12 10	9 44	10 22
♄	1	27♈38	28♈54	28♈32	26♈49	24♈24	22♈35
	13	28 18	28R57	27R59	25R53	23R33	22R13
	25	28 45	28 46	27 14	24 56	22 51	22D 7
♅	1	5♍57	7♍30	9♍23	11♍13	12♍47	13♍39
	13	6 29	8 13	10 8	11 53	13 13	13 46
	25	7 7	8 57	10 52	12 28	13 32	13R46
♆	1	13♉45	14♉16	14♉16	13♉48	13♉ 0	12♉11
	13	14 0	14 20	14R 8	13R31	12R40	11R56
	25	14 12	14R19	13 55	13 12	12 21	11 43
Pl.	1	27♉42	28♉ 7	28♉14	28♉ 1	27♉35	27♉ 2
☊	1	6♑19	4♑41	3♑ 2	1♑27	29♐49	28♐13
	1st	Thu	Sun	Wed	Fri	Mon	Wed

d.		JAN	FEB	MAR	APR
☽	1	24♌ 5	14♎14	8♏53	2♑15
	3	20♍10	12♏ 7	7♐15	0♒ 1
	5	17♎22	10♐29	5♑24	26 57
	7	15♏46	9♑ 7	3♒11	23♓ 7
	9	15♐ 6	7♒35	0♓27	18♈31
	11	14♑40	5♓18	26 58	13♉ 7
	13	13♒31	1♈48	22♈29	7♊ 3
	15	10♓57	26 59	17♉ 0	0♌39
	17	6♈47	21♉ 8	10♊48	24 29
	19	1♉18	14♊48	4♋28	19♌14
	21	25 6	8♋42	28 43	15♍33
	23	18♊48	3♌26	24♌13	13♎43
	25	12♋56	29 24	21♍20	13♏18
	27	7♌52	26♍37	19♎52	13♐15
	29	3♍45	24♎42	19♏ 4	12♑30
	31	0♎33	...	18♐ 2	...

d.		MAY	JUN	JUL	AUG
☽	1	10♒28	29♓51	3♉51	18♊ 8
	3	7♓ 9	24♈44	27 47	11♋47
	5	2♈48	18♉52	21♊23	5♌54
	7	27 38	12♊34	15♋ 3	0♍47
	9	21♉50	6♋ 9	9♌ 7	26 32
	11	15♊34	29 56	3♍51	23♎10
	13	9♋ 8	24♌17	29 30	20♏40
	15	2♌59	19♍42	26♎21	19♐ 1
	17	27 42	16♎36	24♏32	18♑ 0
	19	23♍53	15♏12	23♐53	17♒ 8
	21	21♎57	15♐ 8	23♑47	15♓36
	23	21♏38	15♑27	23♒12	12♈43
	25	22♐ 1	14♒57	21♓16	8♉17
	27	21♑49	12♓52	17♈36	2♊36
	29	20♒13	9♈ 3	12♉26	26 16
	31	17♓ 0	...	6♊20	20♋ 0

d.		SEP	OCT	NOV	DEC
☽	1	2♌ 6	5♍13	23♎55	1♐ 2
	3	26 59	1♎46	22♏52	1♑ 9
	5	22♍58	29 33	22♐17	0♒58
	7	19♎56	28♏ 0	21♑19	29 37
	9	17♏33	26♐32	19♒28	26♓47
	11	15♐35	24♑46	16♓36	22♈35
	13	13♑52	22♒33	12♈48	17♉22
	15	12♒13	19♓49	8♉ 8	11♊28
	17	10♓18	16♈19	2♊41	5♋11
	19	7♈36	11♉52	26 37	28 47
	21	3♉40	6♊25	20♋12	22♌36
	23	28 27	0♋14	13♌55	17♍ 4
	25	22♊20	23 50	8♍23	12♎41
	27	15♋58	17♌53	4♎12	9♏55
	29	10♌ 3	13♍ 6	1♏48	8♐54
	31	...	9♎54	...	9♑ 7

STATIONS	☿	♀	♂	♃
	20Mar 13♈36 / 12Apr 1♈30 / 23Jul 26♌ 6 / 16Aug 8♌22 / 14Nov 10♐16 / 4 Dec 24♏17	None	None	9Aug 19♈33 / 5 Dec 9♈36
		♄	♅	♆
		11Aug 28♈58 / 25Dec 22♈ 7	12May 4♍51 / 19Dec 13♍47	19Jan 9♉16 / 19Aug 14♉20
		SIDER. TIME 6h 40m 9s / 18h 42m 7s / LEAP YEAR		1 Jan Midn. / Noon / 1880

Noon		JAN	FEB	MAR	APR	MAY	JUN
☉	1	11♑17	12♒50	11♓ 5	11♈54	11♉13	11♊ 4
	9	19 26	20 56	19 5	19 46	18 58	18 44
	17	27 35	29 1	27 3	27 36	26 40	26 22
	25	5♒43	7♓ 4	4♈59	5♉24	4♊22	4♋ 0
☿	1	26♐57	17♒21	26♓26	15♓21	23♈55	27♊23
	7	6♑ 4	28. 7	24R21	20 9	5♉11	7♋42
	13	15 27	8♓48	18 55	26 43	17 29	16 23
	19	25 8	18 20	14 15	4♈38	0♊31	23 19
	25	5♒10	24 49	12D51	13 44	13 29	28 15
	31	15 35	...	14 45	...	25 31	...
♀	1	22♒34	28♓23	27♈20	19♉15	14♉17	5♉58
	9	2♓ 2	7♈ 7	4♉27	21 12	9R24	9 7
	17	11 21	15 32	10 45	20R44	5 55	13 49
	25	20 31	23 31	15 56	17 45	4D53	19 39
♂	1	20♐32	13♑30	4♒42	28♒30	21♓34	15♈ 2
	13	29 21	22 32	13 53	7♓44	0♈43	23 56
	25	8♑15	1♒39	23 6	16 58	9 48	2♉41
♃	1	10♈57	15♈ 6	20♈31	27♈32	4♉43	11♉56
	13	12 16	17 16	23 8	0♉24	7 33	14 33
	25	13 58	19 40	25 53	3 16	10 21	17 0
♄	1	22♈10	23♈29	25♈54	29♈28	3♉15	7♉ 1
	13	22 29	24 24	27 12	0♉58	4 46	8 19
	25	23 3	25 30	28 36	2 30	6 12	9 29
♅	1	13♍42	12♍55	11♍46	10♍30	9♍44	9♍44
	13	13R29	12R27	11R15	10R 7	9R38	9 58
	25	13 9	11 56	10 45	9 50	9D40	10 19
♆	1	11♉38	11♉33	11♉57	12♉49	13♉54	15♉ 2
	13	11R32	11 40	12 15	13 14	14 21	15 26
	25	11D31	11 52	12 36	13 41	14 48	15 47
Pl	1	26♉34	26♉20	26♉25	26♉47	27♉22	28♉02
☊	1	26♐35	24♐56	23♐27	21♐49	20♐13	18♐35
	1st	Sat	Tue	Tue	Fri	Sun	Wed

Noon		JUL	AUG	SEP	OCT	NOV	DEC
☉	1	9♋43	9♌19	9♍ 9	8♎26	9♏14	9♐30
	9	17 21	16 59	16 55	16 20	17 16	17 37
	17	24 58	24 40	24 42	24 16	25 19	25 45
	25	2♌37	2♍22	2♎32	2♏14	3♐25	3♑54
☿	1	0♌49	21♋33	10♍12	29♎30	23♏ 0	20♏57
	7	0R41	26 4	21 20	7♏30	16R30	29 28
	13	27♋58	4♌ 6	1♎48	14 41	9 46	8♐25
	19	24 0	14 42	11 37	20 33	8D57	17 35
	25	21 5	26 29	20 50	24 6	13 34	26 53
	31	21D10	8♍17	...	23R37	...	6♑20
♀	1	24♉36	24♊49	29♋14	4♍40	12♎36	20♏ 0
	9	1♊46	3♋25	8♌31	14 21	22 31	0♐ 2
	17	9 26	12 14	17 56	24 7	2♏29	10 4
	25	17 30	21 14	27 27	3♎57	12 29	20 7
♂	1	7♉ 0	28♉23	17♊45	3♋23	13♋53	14♋11
	13	15 28	6♊10	24 28	8 20	15 27	10R54
	25	23 42	13 36	0♋36	12 14	15R 7	6 21
♃	1	18♉10	23♉11	25♉57	25♉46	22♉44	18♉47
	13	20 19	24 34	26 14	24R53	21R 8	17R31
	25	22 13	25 34	26R 3	23 37	19 32	16 38
♄	1	10♉ 1	11♉58	12♉23	11♉13	8♉56	6♉43
	13	10 56	12 20	12R 5	10R25	7R59	6R6
	25	11 39	12R26	11 34	9 30	7 6	5 42
♅	1	10♍31	11♍59	13♍51	15♍42	17♍21	18♍20
	13	11 2	12 41	14 36	16 24	17 50	18 31
	25	11 37	13 25	15 21	17 1	18 12	18R34
♆	1	15♉57	16♉30	16♉32	16♉ 7	15♉20	14♉31
	13	16 13	16 35	16R25	15R50	14R59	14R14
	25	16 25	16R35	16 14	15 31	14 40	14 1
Pl.	1	28♉38	29♉03	29♉11	29♉0C	28♉33	27♉59
☊	1	17♐ 0	15♐21	13♐43	12♐ 7	10♐29	8♐53
	1st	Fri	Mon	Thu	Sat	Tue	Thu

d.	JAN	FEB	MAR	APR
☽ 1	24♑21	16♓54	24♓50	13♉48
3	24♒18	14♈45	22♈41	9♊ 4
5	22♓43	10♉44	18♉48	3♋13
7	19♈19	5♊14	13♊24	26 53
9	14♉23	28 57	7♋10	20♌46
11	8♊29	22♋32	0♌48	15♍29
13	2♋ 8	16♌26	24 54	11♎22
15	25 45	10♍57	19♍52	8♏24
17	19♌37	6♎11	15♎44	6♐14
19	14♍ 0	2♏10	12♏25	4♑28
21	9♎ 8	29 4	9♐44	2♒48
23	5♏21	27♐ 1	7♑39	1♓ 0
25	2♐59	26♑ 2	6♒ 6	28 49
27	2♑ 7	25♒37	4♓50	25♈56
29	2♒15	...	3♈15	22♉ 1
31	2♓18	...	0♉39	...

d.	MAY	JUN	JUL	AUG
☽ 1	16♊59	1♌ 3	3♍20	19♎ 9
3	11♋ 4	24 46	27 34	14♏56
5	4♌45	19♍ 0	22♎47	12♐15
7	28 40	14♎21	19♏30	11♑15
9	23♍27	11♏15	17♐59	11♒32
11	19♎33	9♐47	17♑56	11♓55
13	17♏ 6	9♑26	18♒20	11♈ 5
15	15♐46	9♒16	17♓56	8♉21
17	14♑51	8♓19	15♈54	3♊50
19	13♒41	6♈ 1	12♉ 7	28 6
21	11♓49	2♉22	7♊ 0	21♋48
23	9♈ 4	27 35	1♋ 4	15♌28
25	5♉22	22♊ 0	24 46	9♍24
27	0♊45	15♋55	18♌27	3♎48
29	25 17	9♌35	12♍19	28 49
31	19♋13	...	6♎41	24♏42

d.	SEP	OCT	NOV	DEC
☽ 1	8♐ 5	16♑ 9	9♓40	18♈ 9
3	5♑53	14♒49	8♈ 5	15♉ 1
5	5♒ 7	14♓ 8	5♉53	11♊ 0
7	5♓12	13♈15	2♊37	6♋ 5
9	4♈59	11♉16	28 5	0♌23
11	3♉18	7♊41	22♋29	24 11
13	29 45	2♋38	16♌18	17♍59
15	24♊36	26 37	10♍ 8	12♎22
17	18♋32	20♌20	4♎37	7♏55
19	12♌11	14♍24	0♏11	5♐ 4
21	6♍ 7	9♎14	27 3	3♑43
23	0♎37	5♏ 1	25♐ 1	3♒17
25	25 49	1♐41	23♑36	2♓44
27	21♏45	29 5	22♒14	1♈17
29	18♐28	27♑ 3	20♓31	28 35
31	...	25♒25	...	24♉44

STATIONS	☿	♀	♂	♃
	3Mar 26♓18	13Apr 21♉18	18Nov 15♋33	16Sep 26♉14
	25Mar 12♓51	25May 4♉53	...	...
	5Jul 1♌ 2	♄	♅	♆
	29Jul 20♋44	25Aug 12♉26	18May 9♍38	20Jan 11♉21
	29Oct 24♏21	...	24Dec 18♍34	22Aug 16♉35
	...	SIDER. TIME 6h 43m 8s		1 Jan Midn.
	...	18h 45m 6s		Noon
		Common Year		1881

Noon		JAN	FEB	MAR	APR	MAY	JUN
☉	1	11♑ 2	12♒35	10♓50	11♈40	10♉59	10♊50
	9	19 12	20.41	18 50	19 31	18 43	18 29
	17	27 20	28 46	26 49	27 21	26 26	26 8
	25	5♒29	6♓49	4♈45	5♉ 9	4♊ 8	3♋46
☿	1	7♑55	29♒23	26♒58	16♓23	10♉ 3	4♋17
	7	17 37	6♓51	24R59	25 13	23 1	9 1
	13	27 34	9 43	26D43	5♈ 1	5♊30	11 14
	19	7♒45	6R41	1♓ 8	15 46	16 38	10R45
	25	18 3	0. 25	7 24	27 28	25 57	8 2
	31	27 52	•••	15 0	•••	3♋16	•••
♀	1	28♐55	7♒52	12♓56	21♈30	28♉29	6♋16
	9	8♑58	17 54	22 55	1♉24	8♊17	15 56
	17	19 2	27 55	2♈53	11 17	18 3	25 34
	25	29 5	7♓56	12 50	21 7	27 47	5♌10
♂	1	3♋37	26♊58	0♋52	12♋ 3	26♋23	13♌ 6
	13	29♊40	27D39	4 35	17 29	2♌40	19 55
	25	27R24	29 51	9 7	23 20	9 12	26 54
♃	1	16♉21	17♉ 2	20♉12	25♉39	2♊ 7	9♊17
	13	16D14	18 8	22 7	28 8	4 52	12 5
	25	16 36	19 37	24 17	0♊46	7 39	14 50
♄	1	5♉35	6♉10	8♉ 5	11♉19	15♉ 3	18♉59
	13	5D36	6 50	9 13	12 46	16 35	20 25
	25	5 53	7 44	10 31	14 17	18 7	21 45
♅	1	18♍32	17♍52	16♍46	15♍28	14♍36	14♍28
	13	18R22	17R26	16R15	15R 3	14R27	14 38
	25	18 5	16 57	15 44	14 44	14D25	14 56
♆	1	13♉55	13♉48	14♉10	15♉ 0	16♉ 4	17♉12
	13	13R48	13 54	14 26	15 24	16 31	17 37
	25	13D46	14 5	14 47	15 50	16 58	17 59
Pl.	1	27♉31	27♉15	27♉20	27♉41	28♉17	28♉58
☊	1	7♐15	5♐36	4♐ 7	2♐29	0♐54	29♏15
	1st	Sun	Wed	Wed	Sat	Mon	Thu

Noon		JUL	AUG	SEP	OCT	NOV	DEC
☉	1	9♋29	9♌ 5	8♍54	8♎12	8♏59	9♐14
	9	17 7	16 44	16 40	16 5	17 1	17 22
	17	24 45	24 26	24 28	24 1	25 5	25 30
	25	2♌23	2♍ 8	2♎18	1♏59	3♐10	3♑39
☿	1	4♋33	24♋56	24♍11	3♏46	22♎47	0♐35
	7	2R20	6♌42	3♎44	7 41	26 6	9 58
	13	2D51	19 0	12 34	8R14	3♏15	19 22
	19	6 36	0♍56	20 39	4 3	11 58	28 50
	25	13 39	12 7	27.51	26♎48	21 12	8♑25
	31	23 7	22 32	•••	22 48	•••	18 9
♀	1	12♌19	18♍45	23♎42	24♏38	18♐19	17♐34
	9	21 49	27 57	2♏20	1♐56	21 19	12R50
	17	1♍15	7♎ 2	10 44	8 35	22R 8	8 47
	25	10 37	16 0	18 49	14 20	20 24	6 56
♂	1	0♍27	19♍17	9♎ 0	28♎53	20♏19	11♐54
	13	7 38	26 49	16 51	7♏ 5	28 51	20 46
	25	14 58	4♎28	24 51	15 24	7♐31	29 44
♃	1	16♊10	22♊40	27♊51	0♋53	1♋ 9	28♊34
	13	18 48	24 52	29 21	1 22	0R25	27R 0
	25	21 17	26 50	0♋28	1R22	29♊16	25 23
♄	1	22♉23	24♉58	26♉ 8	25♉41	23♉47	21♉23
	13	23 31	25 36	26R 9	25R 5	22R49	20R33
	25	24 29	26 1	25 54	24 18	21 51	19 53
♅	1	15♍ 7	16♍30	18♍19	20♍11	21♍54	23♍ 1
	13	15 35	17 10	19 4	20 54	22 25	23 15
	25	16 8	17 53	19 49	21 33	22 51	23 21
♆	1	18♉ 8	18♉43	18♉49	18♉25	17♉39	16♉50
	13	18 25	18 49	18R42	18R 9	17R19	16R32
	25	18 38	18R50	18 32	17 51	16 59	16 18
Pl.	1	29♉34	♊01	♊10	29♉58	29♉32	28♉59
☊	1	27♏40	26♏ 1	24♏23	22♏47	21♏ 9	19♏34
	1st	Sat	Tue	Fri	Sun	Wed	Fri

d.		JAN	FEB	MAR	APR
☽	1	7♊27	23♋29	2♌28	16♍48
	3	2♋21	17♌21	26 12	10♎56
	5	26 40	11♍ 6	20♍ 1	5♏25
	7	20♌34	4♎57	14♎ 4	0♐56
	9	14♍17	29 13	8♏35	27 8
	11	8♎14	24♏25	3♐53	24♑27
	13	2♏57	21♐ 7	0♑25	22♒58
	15	29 5	19♑42	28 35	22♓24
	17	27♐ 2	19♒54	28♒16	21♈54
	19	26♑41	20♓33	28♓38	20♉31
	21	27♒ 6	20♈11	28♈19	17♊36
	23	26♓55	17♉57	26♉20	13♋ 7
	25	25♈12	13♊53	22♊30	7♌29
	27	21♉46	8♋31	17♋14	1♍18
	29	17♊ 2	•••	11♌10	25 9
	31	11♋27	•••	4♍53	•••

d.		MAY	JUN	JUL	AUG
☽	1	19♎30	6♐24	12♑45	6♓ 4
	3	14♏38	3♑42	11♒50	5♈48
	5	10♐39	1♒52	11♓ 7	4♉16
	7	7♑33	0♓25	9♈49	1♊17
	9	5♒15	28 53	7♉31	27 4
	11	3♓37	26♈56	4♊14	22♋ 0
	13	2♈20	24♉20	0♋ 6	16♌21
	15	0♉55	20♊55	25 12	10♍17
	17	28 48	16♋35	19♌38	3♎58
	19	25♊32	11♌18	13♍33	27 43
	21	21♋ 0	5♍20	7♎15	22♏ 4
	23	15♌25	29 6	1♏16	17♐39
	25	9♍17	23♎12	26 15	15♑ 1
	27	3♎10	18♏15	22♐49	14♒19
	29	27 39	14♐44	21♑12	14♓47
	31	23♏11	•••	20♒59	15♈ 4

d.		SEP	OCT	NOV	DEC
☽	1	29♈44	6♊38	24♋16	26♌54
	3	27♉44	3♋10	18♌54	20♍48
	5	24♊ 4	28 14	12♍46	14♎31
	7	19♋ 7	22♌23	6♎28	8♏38
	9	13♌25	16♍ 8	0♏28	3♐38
	11	7♍17	9♎51	25 4	29 46
	13	1♎ 0	3♏49	20♐27	26♑54
	15	24 45	28 16	16♑44	24♒45
	17	18♏50	23♐28	13♒56	22♓58
	19	13♐44	19♑46	12♓ 3	21♈15
	21	10♑ 0	17♒29	10♈54	19♉24
	23	8♒ 3	16♓37	9♉59	17♊ 8
	25	7♓48	16♈33	8♊36	14♋ 5
	27	8♈20	16♉15	6♋ 6	9♌56
	29	8♉17	14♊43	2♌ 9	4♍40
	31	•••	11♋30	•••	28 35

STATIONS	☿	♀	♂	♃
	14Feb 9♓37	17Nov 22♐ 8	3Feb 26♊58	11Jan 16♉13
	8Mar 25♒ 2	27Dec 6♐23	••• •••	20Oct 1♋25
		♄	♅	♆
	16Jun 11♋19	8Jan 5♉33	23May 14♍25	24Jan 13♉46
	10Jul 2♋12	9Sep 26♉11	••• •••	23Aug 18♉50
	12Oct 8♏27	SIDER. TIME 6h 42m 10s		1 Jan Midn.
	1Nov 22♎47	18h 44m 8s		Noon
		Common Year		1882

Noon		JAN	FEB	MAR	APR	MAY	JUN
☉	1	10♑47	12♒20	10♓35	11♈25	10♉45	10♊36
	9	18 57	20 27	18 36	19 17	18 30	18 16
	17	27 6	28 32	26 34	27 7	26 12	25 54
	25	5♒14	6♓35	4♈30	4♉55	3♊54	3♋32
☿	1	19♑47	21♒30	13♒30	26♓52	26♉51	20♊17
	7	29 36	14R59	19 41	7R59	6♊38	17R22
	13	9♒ 9	9 18	27 11	19 57	14 7	14 15
	19	17 33	7D55	5♓39	2♉34	19 3	12 46
	25	22 46	10 22	14 58	15 12	21 13	13D54
	31	22R13	...	25 6	...	20R37	...
♀	1	7♐27	26♐28	24♑22	29♒ 7	4♈15	11♉13
	9	10 12	3♑52	3♒ 6	8♓24	13 45	20 50
	17	14 44	11 47	12 1	17 45	23 16	0♊28
	25	20 34	20 6	21 5	27 10	2♉50	10 7
♂	1	5♑ 1	28♑49	20♒40	14♓58	8♈14	1♉43
	13	14 10	8♒ 9	0♓ 5	24 19	17 25	10 35
	25	23 24	17 32	9 29	3♈37	26 29	19 19
♃	1	24♊28	21♊40	21♊42	24♊32	29♊20	5♋36
	13	23R 6	21R22	22 28	26 15	1♋39	8 14
	25	22 4	21D32	23 40	28 15	4 7	10 55
♄	1	19♉36	19♉24	20♉43	23♉30	27♉ 3	1♊ 2
	13	19R19	19 48	21 39	24 51	28 35	2 33
	25	19D17	20 27	22 47	26 18	0♊ 8	4 1
♅	1	23♍21	22♍49	21♍47	20♍27	19♍30	19♍13
	13	23R15	22R25	21R16	20R 1	19R18	19 21
	25	23 1	21 57	20 45	19 39	19 13	19 35
♆	1	16♉12	16♉ 2	16♉22	17♉10	18♉13	19♉22
	13	16R 4	16 8	16 38	17 34	18 41	19 47
	25	16 2	16 18	16 59	18 0	19 7	20 9
Pl.	1	28♉29	28♉14	28♉16	28 38	29♉12	29♉53
☊	1	17♏55	16♏17	14♏48	13♏ 9	11♏34	9♏55
	1st	Mon	Thu	Thu	Sun	Tue	Fri

Noon		JUL	AUG	SEP	OCT	NOV	DEC
☉	1	9♋15	8♌51	8♍41	7♎58	8♏45	9♐ 0
	9	16 53	16 31	16 26	15 51	16 46	17 7
	17	24 31	24 12	24 14	23 47	24 50	25 15
	25	2♌ 9	1♍54	2♎ 4	1♏45	2♐55	3♑24
☿	1	17♊51	11♌40	3♎39	19♎22	24♎ 4	11♐55
	7	24 28	23 33	10 55	12R54	3♏40	21 19
	13	3♋30	4♍33	16 55	7 34	13 22	0♑43
	19	14 37	14 39	21 2	8D 4	22 59	10 8
	25	27 1	23 55	22R15	13 55	2♐29	19 24
	31	9♌36	2♎20	...	22 30	...	28 1
♀	1	17♊23	25♋11	3♍25	10♎46	19♏30	27♐ 2
	9	27 6	5♌ 1	13 21	20 45	29 31	7♑ 2
	17	6♋50	14 52	23 18	0♏45	9♐31	17 1
	25	16 36	24 45	3♎16	10 45	19 31	27 0
♂	1	28♉37	15♊ 8	5♋16	23♋ 1	8♌37	19♌10
	13	2♊ 5	23 7	12 37	29 27	13 32	21 21
	25	10 23	0♋52	19 38	5♌25	17 34	21R55
♃	1	12♋16	19♋12	25♋36	0♌40	3♌55	4♌23
	13	14 59	21 47	27 48	2 12	4 27	3R45
	25	17 40	24 14	22 46	3 24	4R31	2 42
♄	1	4♊43	7♊50	9♊44	10♊ 4	8♊45	6♊27
	13	6 2	8 44	10 4	9R44	7R54	5R30
	25	7 13	9 26	10R 8	9 11	6 57	4 38
♅	1	19♍45	21♍ 1	22♍47	24♍40	26♍26	27♍40
	13	20 10	21 40	23 32	25 24	27 0	27 57
	25	20 41	22 22	24 18	26 4	27 28	28 7
♆	1	20♉20	20♉57	21♉ 5	20♉43	19♉59	19♉ 9
	13	20 37	21 4	20R59	20R28	19R38	18R51
	25	20 51	21 6	20 50	20 10	19 18	18 36
Pl.	1	♊31	♊56	1♊05	♊56	♊30	29♉58
☊	1	8♏20	6♏42	5♏ 3	3♏28	1♏49	0♏14
	1st	Sun	Wed	Sat	Mon	Thu	Sat

	d.	JAN	FEB	MAR	APR
☽	1	10♎25	24♏10	2♐22	19♑21
	3	4♏14	19♐22	27 27	16♒49
	5	28 51	16♑16	24♑14	16♓ 3
	7	24♐47	14♒54	22♒57	16♈23
	9	22♑12	14♓34	23♓ 1	16♉35
	11	20♒43	14♈ 9	23♈16	15♊32
	13	19♓35	12♉46	22♉30	12♋46
	15	18♈ 6	10♊ 9	20♊11	8♌25
	17	15♉59	6♋30	16♋24	2♍55
	19	13♊11	2♌ 0	11♌31	26 47
	21	9♋43	26 49	5♍53	20♎25
	23	5♌31	21♍ 1	29 47	14♏ 9
	25	0♍28	14♎46	23♎25	8♐16
	27	24 37	8♏22	17♏ 6	3♑ 4
	29	18♎17	...	11♐13	28 57
	31	12♏ 2	...	6♑17	...

	d.	MAY	JUN	JUL	AUG
☽	1	26♒11	19♈13	28♉ 9	19♋38
	3	24♓54	18♉32	26♊32	16♌ 5
	5	24♈43	17♊42	24♋11	11♍28
	7	24♉43	15♋53	20♌37	5♎50
	9	23♊49	12♌35	15♍44	29 33
	11	21♋19	7♍45	9♎48	23♏14
	13	17♌ 8	1♎50	3♏27	17♐35
	15	11♍39	25 29	27 23	13♑15
	17	5♎25	19♏20	22♐13	10♒30
	19	29 3	13♐53	18♑20	9♓ 5
	21	22♏58	9♑26	15♒40	8♈15
	23	17♐31	5♒59	13♓49	7♉11
	25	12♑53	3♓20	12♈14	5♊24
	27	9♒10	1♈16	10♉31	2♋47
	29	6♓27	29 36	8♊31	29 20
	31	4♈45	...	6♋ 5	25♌ 4

	d.	SEP	OCT	NOV	DEC
☽	1	7♍37	10♎44	24♏58	28♐ 0
	3	2♎ 5	4♏24	18♐49	22♑51
	5	25 54	27 58	13♑15	18♒31
	7	19♏28	21♐52	8♒40	15♓13
	9	13♐21	16♑40	5♓30	13♈10
	11	8♑14	12♒57	3♈59	12♉20
	13	4♒43	11♓ 2	3♉52	12♊13
	15	2♓59	10♈43	4♊15	11♋47
	17	2♈34	11♉ 6	3♋53	9♌58
	19	2♉28	10♊57	1♌53	6♍20
	21	1♊41	9♋23	28 2	1♎ 7
	23	29 39	6♌ 9	22♍43	24 56
	25	26♋21	1♍28	16♎32	18♏29
	27	21♌56	25 48	10♏ 5	12♐23
	29	16♍40	19♎35	3♐49	7♑ 0
	31	...	13♏10	...	2♒28

STATIONS	☿	♀	♂	♃
	29Jan 23♒ 9	None	24Dec 21♌56	16Feb 21♊21
	19Feb 7♒55		... ...	21Nov 4♌33
		♄	♅	♆
	28May 21♊15	21Jan 19♉ 1	28May 19♍13	26Jan 16♉ 2
	21Jun 12♊50	23Sep 10♊ 8	... ...	26Aug 21♉ 6
	25Sep 22♎15	SIDER. TIME		1 Jan
	16Oct 7♎ 1	6h 41m 13s		Midn.
		18h 43m 11s		Noon
		Common Year		1883

Noon		JAN	FEB	MAR	APR	MAY	JUN
☉	1	10♑32	12♒ 6	11♓21	12♈10	11♉29	11♊20
	9	18 42	20 12	19 21	20 2	19 13	18 58
	17	26 50	28 17	27 19	27 52	26 56	26 37
	25	4♒59	6♓20	5♈15	5♉39	4♊37	4♋15
☿	1	29♑19	21♑15	19♒27	14♈29	0♊19	22♉49
	7	5♒32	23 12	28 36	26 54	1R27	25 2
	13	6R57	28 3	8♓28	8♉41	29♉43	29 45
	19	1 54	4♒39	19 3	18 39	26 26	6♊42
	25	24♑40	12 22	0♈22	26 0	23 33	15 41
	31	21 18	...	12 25	...	22D42	...
♀	1	5♒43	14♓ 4	19♈11	25♉10	26♊56	22♋12
	9	15 39	23 51	28 40	4♊ 1	4♋30	26 4
	17	25 34	3♈34	8♉ 1	12 37	11 28	28 5
	25	5♓27	13 13	17 14	20 56	17 39	27R48
♂	1	21♌22	12♌ 5	3♌16	4♌41	14♌ 8	28♌18
	13	18R55	7R31	2D30	7 46	19 13	4♍32
	25	14 51	4 9	3 27	11 49	24 50	11 4
♃	1	1♌55	27♋54	25♋ 4	24♋43	27♋ 8	1♌46
	13	0R25	26R30	24R34	25 24	28 43	3 58
	25	28♋49	25 24	24D32	26 28	0♌34	6 19
♄	1	4♊12	3♊12	3♊52	6♊ 8	9♊23	13♊18
	13	3R37	3D18	4 35	7 20	10 51	14 51
	25	3 17	3 39	5 30	8 40	12 23	16 23
♅	1	28♍ 9	27♍45	26♍45	25♍25	24♍24	24♍ 0
	13	28R 6	27R23	26R14	24R57	24R 9	24 5
	25	27 55	26 57	25 43	24 33	24 1	24 17
♆	1	18♉29	18♉17	18♉35	19♉22	20♉25	21♉34
	13	18R21	18 21	18 51	19 46	20 52	21 59
	25	18 17	18 30	19 10	20 11	21 19	22 21
Pl.	1	29♉28	29♉12	29♉14	29♉35	0♊ 9	0♊49
☊	1	28♎35	26♎57	25♎25	23♎46	22♎11	20♎32
1st		Tue	Fri	Sat	Tue	Thu	Sun

Noon		JUL	AUG	SEP	OCT	NOV	DEC
☉	1	9♋59	9♌34	9♍24	8♎42	9♏30	9♐46
	9	17 36	17 14	17 10	16 36	17 32	17 53
	17	25 14	24 55	24 58	24 32	25 36	26 2
	25	2♌52	2♍38	2♎48	2♏30	3♐41	4♑11
☿	1	26♊33	28♌18	4♎34	21♍41	7♏26	24♐16
	7	8♋51	7♍48	5R40	27 1	17 8	3♑ 8
	13	21 45	16 19	3 2	5♎41	26 37	11 24
	19	4♌17	23 44	27♍11	15 38	5♐57	18 7
	25	15 57	29 49	21 56	25 48	15 10	21 14
	31	26 37	4♎ 5	...	5♏47	...	18R 5
♀	1	25♋57	11♋49	25♋ 6	22♌56	27♍24	3♏13
	9	21R41	12D37	1♌40	1♍27	6♎47	12 59
	17	16 47	15 33	8 57	10 16	16 18	22 49
	25	13 8	20 6	16 47	19 19	25 56	2♐42
♂	1	14♍27	2♎48	22♎31	12♏43	4♐43	26♐58
	13	21 23	10 17	0♏28	21 6	13 30	6♑ 5
	25	28 32	17 57	8 36	29 39	22 27	15 20
♃	1	7♌33	14♌12	20♌58	27♌ 2	2♍10	5♍14
	13	10 4	16 50	23 28	29 12	3 40	5 45
	25	12 40	19 27	25 53	1♍ 9	4 48	5R49
♄	1	17♊ 8	20♊39	23♊10	24♊13	23♊36	21♊38
	13	18 34	21 46	23 47	24R11	22R57	20R39
	25	19 55	22 43	24 8	23 54	22 6	19 41
♅	1	24♍25	25♍36	27♍19	29♍11	1♎ 1	2♎19
	13	24 48	26 13	28 4	29 56	1 36	2 39
	25	25 17	26 54	28 49	0♎38	2 7	2 52
♆	1	22♉32	23♉11	23♉20	23♉ 0	22♉16	21♉26
	13	22 50	23 18	23R15	22R45	21R56	21R 8
	25	23 4	23 21	23 6	22 28	21 36	20 53
Pl.	1	1♊26	1♊51	2♊ 1	1♊52	1♊27	0♊54
☊	1	18♎57	17♎19	15♎40	14♎ 5	12♎26	10♎51
1st		Tue	Fri	Mon	Wed	Sat	Mon

d.	JAN	FEB	MAR	APR
☽ 1	15♒30	6♈21	0♉47	24♊ 5
3	12♓ 8	4♉21	29 23	21♋57
5	9♈29	2♊33	27♊31	18♌38
7	7♉36	0♋47	25♋ 1	14♍15
9	6♊25	28 45	21♌46	9♎ 1
11	5♋29	25♌56	17♍38	3♏ 8
13	3♌59	21♍56	12♎33	26 52
15	1♍ 9	16♎43	6♏41	20♐33
17	26 44	10♏38	0♐22	14♑37
19	21♎ 1	4♐16	24 8	9♒37
21	14♏40	28 21	18♑39	6♓ 4
23	8♐24	23♑29	14♒28	4♈15
25	2♑52	20♒ 1	11♓54	3♉55
27	28 25	17♓50	10♈46	4♊10
29	25♒ 2	16♈25	10♉21	3♋48
31	22♓27	...	9♊43	...

d.	MAY	JUN	JUL	AUG
☽ 1	2♌ 0	20♍38	23♎52	7♐44
3	28 34	15♎ 9	17♏38	1♑40
5	23♍47	8♏58	11♐17	26 16
7	18♎ 6	2♐36	5♑18	21♒44
9	11♏55	26 24	29 54	18♓ 3
11	5♐35	20♑36	25♒11	15♈ 6
13	29 21	15♒25	21♓13	12♉49
15	23♑32	11♓ 4	18♈10	11♊ 8
17	18♒32	7♈56	16♉12	9♋52
19	14♓47	6♉16	15♊16	8♌28
21	12♈40	5♊56	14♋50	6♍15
23	12♉11	6♋ 8	13♌54	2♎44
25	12♊36	5♌37	11♍34	27 51
27	12♋40	3♍25	7♎31	21♏59
29	11♌14	29 21	2♏ 5	15♐43
31	7♍56	...	25 54	9♑43

d.	SEP	OCT	NOV	DEC
☽ 1	22♑ 0	25♒18	14♈ 8	21♉24
3	17♒20	22♓11	13♉29	21♊57
5	13♓51	20♈26	13♊34	22♋18
7	11♈22	19♉31	13♋15	21♌10
9	9♉31	18♊41	11♌36	18♍ 8
11	7♊56	17♋14	8♍26	13♎30
13	6♋18	14♌50	3♎59	7♏50
15	4♌19	11♍25	28 39	1♐41
17	1♍41	7♎ 4	22♏46	25 24
19	28 7	1♏55	16♐34	19♑12
21	23♎30	26 7	10♑17	13♒16
23	17♏55	19♐53	4♒11	7♓53
25	11♐45	13♑37	28 44	3♈30
27	5♑32	7♒50	24♓30	0♉38
29	29 51	3♓ 8	22♈ 2	29 34
31	...	0♈ 2	...	29♊54

STATIONS

☿	♀	♂	♃
6May 1♊29	20Jun 28♋17	12Mar 2♌29	21Mar 24♋29
30May 22♉40	3Aug 11♋48	...	23Dec 5♍50
6Sep 5♎43	**♄** 5Feb 3♊12	**♅** 3Jan 28♍ 9	**♆** 31Jan 18♉17
28Sep 21♍ 3	7Oct 24♊14	31May 24♍ 0	28Aug 23♉21
26Dec 21♐11	SIDER. TIME		1 Jan
...	6h 40m 16s		Midn.
...	18h 42m 14s		Noon.
	LEAP YEAR		1884

1885

Noon		JAN	FEB	MAR	APR	MAY	JUN
☉	1	11♑19	12♒52	11♓ 7	11♈56	11♉15	11♊ 6
	9	19 28	20 58	19 7	19 47	18 59	18 45
	17	27 37	29 3	27 5	27 37	26 42	26 23
	25	5♒45	7♓ 6	5♈ 1	5♉25	4♊23	4♋ 1
☿	1	16♑57	18♑40	0♓41	29♈10	5♉50	17♉36
	7	9R14	26 29	11 25	7♉ 3	3R 0	26 20
	13	5 9	5♒ 1	22 50	11 28	2D37	6♊41
	19	6D19	14 9	4♈46	12R 7	4 56	18 32
	25	10 56	23 52	16 42	9 41	9 38	1♋24
	31	17 28	...	27 33	...	16 19	...
♀	1	11♐21	19♑54	24♒47	3♈18	10♉23	18♊32
	9	21 17	29 52	4♓44	13 12	20 15	28 22
	17	1♑14	9♒50	14 41	23 6	0♊ 6	8♋11
	25	11 11	19 48	24 37	2♉59	9 56	17 59
♂	1	20♑45	15♒ 5	7♓12	1♈30	24♈32	17♉34
	13	0♒ 8	24 34	16 39	10 47	3♉33	26 15
	25	9 34	4♓ 3	26 3	19 59	12 26	4♊47
♃	1	5♍38	3♍ 9	29♌33	26♌29	25♌59	28♌13
	13	4R59	1R39	28R 8	25R57	26 32	29 43
	25	3 55	0 4	26 59	25D51	27 30	1♍29
♄	1	19♊ 9	17♊30	17♊26	19♊ 0	21♊49	25♊32
	13	18R21	17R18	17 51	20 0	23 11	27 5
	25	17 45	17D22	18 31	21 10	24 39	28 38
♅	1	2♎55	2♎38	1♎44	0♎25.	29♍19	28♍48
	13	2R55	2R19	1R14	29♍56	29R 2	28D49
	25	2 47	1 54	0 43	29R30	28 51	28 58
♆	1	20♉46	20♉32	20♉48	21♉33	22♉34	23♉44
	13	20R37	20 35	21 2	21 56	23 1	24 9
	25	20 32	20 44	21 20	22 21	23 28	24 32
Pl.	1	0♊24	0♊ 9	0♊10	0♊30	1♊ 4	1♊44
☊	1	9♎13	7♎34	6♎ 5	4♎26	2♎51	1♎13
1st		Thu	Sun	Sun	Wed	Fri	Mon

Noon		JUL	AUG	SEP	OCT	NOV	DEC
☉	1	9♋44	9♌20	9♍10	8♎28	9♏15	9♐31
	9	17 22	17 0	16 56	16 21	17 17	17 38
	17	25 0	24 41	24 44	24 17	25 21	25 47
	25	2♌38	2♍24	2♎34	2♏15	3♐26	3♑56
☿	1	14♋25	6♍12	11♍38	27♍ 6	19♏ 7	0♑44
	7	26 45	12 23	6R25	7♎44	28 17	4 58
	13	8♌ 2	16 44	4D57	18 14	7♐12	4R 0
	19	18 11	18 35	8 52	28 21	15 48	27♐ 4
	25	27 12	17R12	16 57	8♏ 7	23 52	20 23
	31	5♍ 1	12 36	...	17 34	...	19D19
♀	1	25♋20	3♍13	10♎50	16♏48	23♐10	26♑36
	9	5♌ 7	12 57	20 29	26 17	2♑20	4♑54
	17	14 54	22 41	0♏ 5	5♐43	11 20	12 48
	25	24 41	2♎22	9 39	15 4	20 9	20 7
♂	1	9♊ 0	0♋13	20♋24	8♌48	26♌18	10♍58
	13	17 20	8 9	27 54	15 48	2♍30	15 52
	25	25 31	15 56	5♌13	22 31	8 16	19 59
♃	1	2♍28	8♍14	14♍46	21♍13	27♍26	2♎21
	13	4 34	10 42	17 21	23 43	29 34	3 50
	25	6 51	13 15	19 56	26 6	1♎29	4 58
♄	1	29♊25	3♋13	6♋17	8♋ 4	8♋16	6♋52
	13	0♋56	4 31	7 10	8 21	7R53	5R58
	25	2 24	5 41	7 49	8R23	7 15	5 0
♅	1	29♍ 5	0♎ 9	1♎48	3♎40	5♎32	6♎56
	13	29 25	0 44	2 32	4 25	6 9	7 19
	25	29 51	1 23	3 17	5 8	6 42	7 34
♆	1	24♉43	25♉24	25♉36	25♉18	24♉35	23♉45
	13	25 2	25 32	25R32	25R 3	24R15	23R26
	25	25 17	25 36	25 26	24 46	23 55	23 11
Pl.	1	2♊21	2♊48	2♊57	2♊48	2♊24	1♊52
☊	1	29♍37	27♍59	26♍21	24♍45	23♍ 7	21♍31
1st		Wed	Sat	Tue	Thu	Sun	Tue

d.	JAN	FEB	MAR	APR
☽ 1	15♋13	7♍29	15♍27	3♏38
3	15♌15	4♎57	12♎40	28 38
5	13♍33	0♏40	8♏26	22♐48
7	9♎53	25 5	3♐ 0	16♑36
9	4♏42	18♐52	26 52	10♒36
11	28 38	12♑38	20♑41	5♓25
13	22♐19	6♒49	15♒ 0	1♈31
15	16♑ 8	1♓40	10♓14	29 1
17	10♒19	27 17	6♈31	27♉36
19	5♓ 0	23♈41	3♉46	26♊36
21	0♈21	20♉56	1♊44	25♋19
23	26 42	19♊ 4	0♋ 4	23♌17
25	24♉22	17♋56	28 29	20♍23
27	23♊26	16♌59	26♌37	16♎38
29	23♋23	...	24♍ 9	12♏ 5
31	23♌ 5	...	20♎44	...

d.	MAY	JUN	JUL	AUG
☽ 1	6♐47	21♑11	23♒49	10♈ 5
3	0♑51	14♒57	18♓ 6	6♉ 5
5	24 37	9♓10	13♈20	3♊35
7	18♒35	4♈27	10♉ 7	2♋39
9	13♓20	1♉25	8♊47	2♌45
11	9♈30	0♊16	8♋57	2♍43
13	7♉24	0♋29	9♌28	1♎27
15	6♊44	0♌47	8♍57	28 27
17	6♋35	29 56	6♎39	23♏51
19	5♌51	27♍22	2♏38	18♐ 9
21	3♍52	23♎17	27 21	11♑58
23	0♎34	18♏ 9	21♐23	5♒45
25	26 12	12♐22	15♑ 9	29 52
27	21♏ 5	6♑15	8♒57	24♓32
29	15♐24	0♒ 0	2♓59	19♈58
31	9♑19	...	27 31	16♉20

d.	SEP	OCT	NOV	DEC
☽ 1	29♉55	8♋45	2♍ 5	9♎53
3	27♊58	7♌15	29 39	6♏ 4
5	27♋ 0	5♍48	26♎34	1♐31
7	26♌27	3♎58	22♏42	26 17
9	25♍26	1♏15	17♐54	20♑24
11	23♎12	27 20	12♑13	14♒ 4
13	19♏26.	22♐13	5♒58	7♓45
15	14♐19	16♑15	29 43	2♈ 3
17	8♑21	10♒ 0	24♓10	27 44
19	2♒ 6	4♓ 5	19♈57	25♉16
21	26 9	29 5	17♉25	24♊37
23	20♓53	25♈22	16♊13	24♋51
25	16♈33	22♉53	15♋45	24♌39
27	13♉11	21♊13	14♌47	23♍ 8
29	10♊39	19♋47	12♍51	20♎ 7
31	...	18♌ 6	...	15♏53

STATIONS	☿	♀	♂	♃
	15Jan 5♑ 2	None	None	22Apr 25♌29
	18Apr 12♉16			...
				...
	21Aug 18♍31	♄	♅	♆
	12Sep 4♍47	17Feb 17♊17	8Jan 2♎56	30Jan 20♉32
	10Dec 5♑18	21Oct 8♋24	7Jun 28♍28	28Aug 25♉36
	30Dec 19♐ 8	SIDER. TIME 6h 43m 14s		1 Jan Midn.
		18h 45m 12s		Noon.
		Common Year		1885

Noon		JAN	FEB	MAR	APR	MAY	JUN
☉	1	11♑ 4	12♒37	10♓52	11♈41	11♉ 0	10♊52
	9	19 13	20 43	18 52	19 33	18 45	18 31
	17	27 22	28 48	26 50	27 23	26 28	26 9
	25	5♒30	6♓51	4♈46	5♉11	4♊ 9	3♋47
☿	1	19♐42	26♑50	15♓11	23♈39	15♈35	28♉26
	7	23 54	6♒15	26 46	20R29	20 33	10♊56
	13	0♑22	16 10	7♈51	16 3	27 20	24 5
	19	8 2	26 36	16 59	13 4	5♉39	6♋58
	25	16 24	7♓34	22 36	12D55	15 23	18 53
	31	25 18	...	23R51	...	26 28	...
♀	1	25♒52	7♓53	24♒16	29♒41	24♓53	27♈31
	9	1♓29	5R24	22R20	5♓19	2♈55	6♉25
	17	5 40	0 55	22D57	11 52	11 16	15 27
	25	7 55	26♒ 8	25 48	19 7	19 51	24 36
♂	1	21♍56	24♍57	17♍51	7♍24	7♍ 8	16♍ 7
	13	24 20	22R59	13R10	5R57	9 45	21 11
	25	25 14	19 20	9 6	6D20	13 30	26 51
♃	1	5♎27	5♎46	3♎36	29♍44	26♍46	26♍11
	13	5 56	5R 5	2R10	28R20	26R12	26 43
	25	5R58	4 1	0 37	27 12	26D 3	27 39
♄	1	4♋25	2♋15	1♋27	2♋14	4♋28	7♋51
	13	3R28	1R44	1D32	2 58	5 41	9 20
	25	2 39	1 28	1 54	3 55	7 1	10 52
♅	1	7♎40	7♎31	6♎43	5♎25	4♎16	3♎37
	13	7 43	7R14	6R14	4R55	3R56	3D35
	25	7R38	6 52	5 43	4 28	3 42	3 41
♆	1	23♉ 3	22♉47	23♉ 0	23♉43	24♉44	25♉53
	13	22R53	22 49	23 14	24 6	25 10	26 18
	25	22 48	22 57	23 31	24 31	25 37	26 42
Pl.	1	1♊22	1♊06	1♊07	1♊27	2♊00	2♊40
☊	1	19♍53	18♍14	16♍45	15♍ 7	13♍32	11♍53
	1st	Fri	Mon	Mon	Thu	Sat	Tue

Noon		JUL	AUG	SEP	OCT	NOV	DEC
☉	1	9♋31	9♌ 6	8♍56	8♎14	9♏ 1	9♐16
	9	17 8	16 46	16 42	16 7	17 3	17 24
	17	24 46	24 27	24 30	24 3	25 6	25 32
	25	2♌24	2♍10	2♎20	2♏ 1	3♐11	3♑41
☿	1	29♋34	0♍47	20♌55	10♎49	28♏47	14♐ 0
	7	8♌57	29♌42	28 4	20 58	6♐40	6R15
	13	17 0	25R46	8♍ 2	0♏40	13 33	3 17
	19	23 33	20 51	19 6	9 57	18 24	6D 1
	25	28 16	18 14	0♎10	18 52	19R12	12 2
	31	0♍39	20D 7	...	27 24	...	19 36
♀	1	1♊31	7♋59	15♌25	22♍25	1♏ 9	8♐51
	9	10 49	17 33	25 14	2♎23	11 12	18 54
	17	20 12	27 11	5♍ 5	12 22	21 15	28 59
	25	29 39	6♌53	14 58	22 22	1♐18	9♑ 3
♂	1	29♍53	17♎13	6♏40	27♏ 5	19♐30	12♑13
	13	6♎18	24 32	14 40	5♐37	28 29	21 31
	25	13 6	2♏ 7	22 54	14 20	7♑37	0♒54
♃	1	28♍15	2♎31	8♎15	14♎33	21♎14	27♎16
	13	29 41	4 37	10 43	17 9	23 44	29 25
	25	1♎24	6 52	13 16	19 45	26 8	1♏20
♄	1	11♋39	15♋37	19♋ 6	21♋31	22♋31	21♋50
	13	13 12	17 3	20 12	22 6	22R26	21R 8
	25	14 44	18 23	21 8	22 27	22 6	20 17
♅	1	3♎46	4♎43	6♎17	8♎ 7	10♎ 1	11♎31
	13	4 3	5 16	7 0	8 52	10 40	11 56
	25	4 26	5 53	7 44	9 36	11 15	12 15
♆	1	26♉53	27♉36	27♉51	27♉35	26♉54	26♉ 4
	13	27 13	27 45	27R48	27R21	26R34	25R45
	25	27 29	27 50	27 40	27 5	26 14	25 28
Pl.	1	3♊17	3♊45	3♊56	3♊50	3♊23	2♊51
☊	1	10♍18	8♍39	7♍ 1	5♍26	3♍47	2♍11
	1st	Thu	Sun	Wed	Fri	Mon	Wed

d.		JAN	FEB	MAR	APR
☽	1	28♏26	14♑ 5	22♑52	6♓45
	3	23♐ 1	7♒47	16♒29	1♈ 0
	5	17♑ 5	1♓26	10♓15	26 6
	7	10♒49	25 19	4♈29	22♉ 8
	9	4♓25	19♈46	29 24	19♊ 4
	11	28 19	15♉14	25♉13	16♋46
	13	23♈ 6	12♊13	22♊11	15♌ 6
	15	19♉25	10♋54	20♋22	13♍51
	17	17♊41	10♌55	19♌38	12♎34
	19	17♋39	11♍14	19♍19	10♏40
	21	18♌14	10♎38	18♎30	7♐33
	23	18♍ 4	8♏21	16♏21	3♑ 1
	25	16♎16	4♐21	12♐34	27 20
	27	12♏45	29 0	7♑20	21♒ 2
	29	7♐53	...	1♒13	14♓49
	31	2♑ 9	...	24 51	...

d.		MAY	JUN	JUL	AUG
☽	1	9♈18	26♉51	3♋44	27♌ 9
	3	4♉56	24♊59	3♌20	26♍57
	5	1♊45	23♋51	2♍53	25♎29
	7	29 30	22♌42	1♎35	22♏29
	9	27♋42	21♍ 0	29 7	18♐ 8
	11	25♌59	18♎36	25♏33	12♑48
	13	24♍ 9	15♏31	21♐ 4	6♒49
	15	22♎ 2	11♐39	15♑48	0♓29
	17	19♏20	6♑56	9♒53	24 6
	19	15♐43	1♒22	3♓33	18♈ 0
	21	10♑58	25 9	27 10	12♉39
	23	5♒13	18♓46	21♈16	8♊33
	25	28 54	12♈53	16♉29	6♋ 5
	27	22♓42	8♉10	13♊22	5♌16
	29	17♈19	5♊ 7	12♋ 4	5♍30
	31	13♉17	...	12♌ 2	5♎38

d.		SEP	OCT	NOV	DEC
☽	1	20♎19	26♏55	14♑16	16♒30
	3	18♏27	23♐30	8♒42	10♓13
	5	14♐50	18♑29	2♓24	3♈55
	7	9♑48	12♒27	26 4	28 17
	9	3♒51	6♓ 3	20♈20	23♉51
	11	27 29	29 49	15♉32	20♊45
	13	21♓ 7	24♈ 8	11♊45	18♋40
	15	15♈ 5	19♉13	8♋47	17♌ 2
	17	9♉37	15♊ 7	6♌22	15♍22
	19	5♊ 2	11♋53	4♍23	13♎28
	21	1♋36	9♌34	2♎44	11♏12
	23	29 33	8♍11	1♏13	8♐23
	25	28♌50	7♎28	29 18	4♑43
	27	28♍51	6♏41	26♐22	0♒ 1
	29	28♎33	4♐54	22♑ 4	24 20
	31	...	1♑33	...	18♓ 1

STATIONS	☿	♀	♂	♃
	31Mar 23♈51	30Jan 8♓ 6	27Jan 25♍13	21Jan 6♎ 0
	23Apr 12♈38	11Mar 22♒16	17Apr 5♍53	25May 26♍ 3
		♄	♅	♆
	3Aug 0♍46	5Mar 1♋26	14Jan 7♎43	1Feb 23♉47
	27Aug 18♍19	5Nov 22♋31	12Jun 3♎35	1Sep 27♉51
	24Nov 19♐27	SIDER. TIME		1 Jan
	14Dec 3♐24	6h 42m 17s		Midn.
		18h 44m 15s		Noon
		Common Year		1886

Noon		JAN	FEB	MAR	APR	MAY	JUN
☉	1	10♑49	12♒22	10♓37	11♈27	10♉46	10♊38
	9	18 58	20 28	18 37	19 19	18 31	18 17
	17	27 7	28 33	26 36	27 9	26 14	25 56
	25	5♒15	6♓36	4♈32	4♉57	3♊55	3♋34
☿	1	20♐57	8♒35	27♓55	24♓ 0	16♈47	16♊41
	7	29 23	19 1	4♈30	23D51	26 13	29 11
	13	8♑14	29 52	6R19	26 41	6♉49	10♋26
	19	17 26	10♓58	3 22	1♈46	18 35	20 14
	25	26 58	21 40	28♓12	8 35	1♊21	28 31
	31	6♒54	...	24 21	...	14 31	...
♀	1	17♑50	26♒45	1♈38	9♉43	15♊46	21♋44
	9	27 54	6♓45	11 31	19 26	25 12	0♌42
	17	7♒57	16 43	21 22	29 4	4♋32	9 29
	25	17 59	26 40	1♉11	8♊39	13 46	18 4
♂	1	6♒24	0♓52	22♓52	16♈47	9♉15	1♊39
	13	15 51	10 20	2♈12	25 51	18 1	10 6
	25	25 20	19 45	11 26	4♉49	26 40	18 25
♃	1	2♏20	5♏22	5♏44	3♏26	29♎44	26♎41
	13	3 48	5 49	5R 8	2R 1	28R20	26R 7
	25	4 54	5R50	4 10	0 29	27 11	25D59
♄	1	19♋43	17♋16	15♋49	15♋46	17♋21	20♋15
	13	18R44	16R30	15R35	16 14	18 21	21 38
	25	17 46	15 57	15D38	16 55	19 31	23 5
♅	1	12♎23	12♎23	11♎40	10♎25	9♎13	8♎27
	13	12 28	12R 9	11R13	9R54	8R50	8R22
	25	12R28	11 48	10 43	9 26	8 34	8D24
♆	1	25♉20	25♉ 2	25♉12	25♉53	26♉53	26♉ 2
	13	25R10	25D 3	25 25	26 15	27 19	28 28
	25	25 3	25 9	25 42	26 40	27 46	28 52
Pl.	1	2♊20	2♊ 2	2♊ 4	2♊ 3	2♊55	3♊36
☊	1	0♍33	28♌55	27♌25	25♌47	24♌12	22♌33
	1st	Sat	Tue	Tue	Fri	Sun	Wed

Noon		JUL	AUG	SEP	OCT	NOV	DEC
☉	1	9♋17	8♌52	8♍42	7♎59	8♏46	9♐ 1
	9	16 54	16 32	16 28	15 52	16 48	17 9
	17	24 32	24 13	24 15	23 48	24 51	25 17
	25	2♌11	1♍56	2♎ 5	1♏46	2♐57	3♑26
☿	1	5♌ 8	3♌27	29♌51	23♎ 2	1♐43	19♏ 7
	7	9 48	1R 3	11♍29	2♏ 3	3 43	24 45
	13	12 4	2D24	22 45	10 34	0R29	2♐22
	19	11R34	7 55	3♎26	18 29	22♏53	10 52
	25	8 25	16 53	13 30	25 31	17 49	19 45
	31	4 6	27 55	...	1♐ 2	...	28 53
♀	1	24♌19	22♍49	6♎14	22♍49	26♍50	22♎15
	9	2♍22	28 26	4R39	20R27	2♎22	0♏32
	17	10 1	2 49	0 50	20D38	8 58	9 12
	25	17 9	5 33	26♍ 0	23 8	16 20	18 7
♂	1	22♊32	13♋21	3♌25	22♌ 8	10♍38	27♍25
	13	0♋41	21 12	10 59	29 25	17 31	3♎42
	25	8 43	28 57	18 27	6♍33	24 11	9 38
♃	1	26♎ 5	28♎11	2♏30	8♏ 6	14♏42	12♏17
	13	26 35	29 37	4 36	10 36	17 e1	23 50
	25	27 29	1♏22	6 54	13 11	19 59	26 16
♄	1	23♋51	27♋50	1♌36	4♌32	6♌17	6♌22
	13	25 23	29 21	2 53	5 23	6 31	5R57
	25	26 56	0♌48	4 1	6 1	6R29	5 17
♅	1	8♎28	9♎17	10♎46	12♎34	14♎29	16♎13
	13	8 41	9 47	11 27	13 19	15 10	16 32
	25	9 2	10 23	12 11	14 4	15 47	16 54
♆	1	29♉ 3	29♉48	0♊ 5	29♉52	29♉13	28♉22
	13	29 23	29 58	0R 4	29R39	28R53	28R 3
	25	29 40	0♊ 4	29♉57	29 23	28 33	27 46
Pl.	1	4♊14	4♊42	4♊53	4♊45	4♊21	3♊48
☊	1	20♌58	19♌20	17♌41	16♌ 6	14♌27	12♌52
	1st	Fri	Mon	Thu	Sat	Tue	Thu

d.		JAN	FEB	MAR	APR
☽	1	29♓49	14♉ 3	22♉42	10♋29
	3	23♈44	9♊32	18♊ 2	7♌50
	5	18♉40	6♋43	14♋53	6♍46
	7	15♊ 6	5♌35	13♌30	6♎54
	9	13♋ 6	5♍32	13♍33	7♏ 9
	11	12♌10	5♎29	14♎ 0	6♐16
	13	11♍28	4♏27	13♏35	3♐32
	15	10♎14	1♐58	11♐29	28 58
	17	8♏ 7	28 4	7♑36	23♒10
	19	5♐ 1	23♑ 3	2♒20	16♓48
	21	1♑ 1	17♒17	26 15	10♈26
	23	26 10	11♓ 4	19♓52	4♉27
	25	20♒32	4♈40	13♈31	29 4
	27	14♓20	28 25	7♉29	24♊23
	29	7♈55	...	2♊ 0	20♋32
	31	1♉48	...	27 22	...

d.		MAY	JUN	JUL	AUG
☽	1	17♌44	10♎54	20♏ 1	10♑54
	3	16♍10	9♏53	17♐53	6♒36
	5	15♎39	8♐38	14♑51	1♓23
	7	15♏25	6♑22	10♒40	25 29
	9	14♐23	2♒37	5♓22	19♈13
	11	11♑41	27 27	29 18	13♉ 4
	13	7♒15	21♓24	23♈ 2	7♊38
	15	1♓31	15♈ 6	17♉12	3♋28
	17	25 11	9♉13	12♊22	0♌54
	19	18♈55	4♊13	8♋52	29 47
	21	13♉13	0♋19	6♌39	29♍27
	23	8♊19	27 24	5♍17	28♎56
	25	4♋15	25♌10	4♎ 9	27♏27
	27	0♌57	23♍21	2♏43	24♐39
	29	28 22	21♎43	0♐38	20♑39
	31	26♍33	...	27 42	15♒41

d.		SEP	OCT	NOV	DEC
☽	1	27♒56	0♈50	15♉24	18♊50
	3	22♓ 1	24 33	9♊38	14♋ 7
	5	15♈47	18♉22	4♋24	10♌ 8
	7	9♉31	12♊33	29 58	7♍ 2
	9	3♊37	7♋29	26♌46	5♎ 1
	11	28 37	3♌42	25♍ 5	4♏ 1
	13	25♋ 4	1♍36	24♎50	3♐30
	15	23♌18	1♎15	25♏ 6	2♑28
	17	23♍ 5	1♏49	24♐34	0♒ 5
	19	23♎27	1♐56	22♑17	26 3
	21	23♏ 8	0♑25	18♒ 9	20♓40
	23	21♐15	26 57	12♓37	14♈31
	25	17♑40	21♒55	6♈24	8♉17
	27	12♒45	15♓58	0♉ 7	2♊31
	29	7♓ 0	9♈40	24 12	27 33
	31	...	3♉26	...	23♋29

STATIONS	☿	♀	♂	♃
	13Mar 6♈19	1Sep 6♎14	None	20Feb 5♏53
	5Apr 23♓33	12Oct 20♍13		25Jun 25♎59
	15Jul 12♌13	♄	♅	♆
	8Aug 0♌59	18Mar 15♋34	18Jan 12♎29	7Feb 25♉ 2
	8Nov 3♐35	19Nov 6♌32	18Jun 8♎22	1Sep 0♊ 5
	28Nov 17♏44	SIDER. TIME		1 Jan
		6h 41m 19s		Midn.
		18h 43m 17s		Noon.
		Common Year		1887

Noon		JAN	FEB	MAR	APR	MAY	JUN
☉	1	10♐34	12♒ 7	11♓23	12♈12	11♉30	11♊21
	9	18 43	20 14	19 23	20 4	19 15	19 1
	17	26 52	28 19	27 21	27 54	26 58	26 39
	25	5♒ 1	6♓22	5♈17	5♉41	4♊39	4♋17
☿	1	0♑25	21♒54	15♓54	14♓28	0♉47	2♋39
	7	9 48	2♓21	9R58	21 29	13 8	10 53
	13	19 25	11 42	5 55	29 44	26 9	17 10
	19	29 21	18 0	5D31	9♈ 3	9♊ 1	21 17
	25	9♒36	19R 6	8 19	19 24	20 50	22 51
	31	20 8	...	13 26	...	1♋ 7	...
♀	1	26♏ 6	2♑40	7♒48	15♓41	22♈25	0♊22
	9	5♐22	12 19	17 34	25 28	2♉12	10 10
	17	14 47	22 0	27 20	5♈16	12 0	19 59
	25	24 18	1♒43	7♓ 7	15 4	21 48	29 47
♂	1	12♎54	24♎54	0♏10	25♎19	14♎47	12♎36
	13	18 5	28 0	29♎42	20R56	12R27	14 52
	25	22 38	29 51	27R24	16 34	12D 0	18 29
♃	1	27♏37	2♐44	5♐42	6♐12	4♐ 0	0♐12
	13	29 47	4 13	6 14	5R36	2R36	28♏49
	25	1♐44	5 20	6R21	4 37	1 5	27R41
♄	1	4♌49	2♌21	0♌22	29♋36	0♌28	2♌51
	13	3R54	1R26	29♋52	29D45	1 14	4 4
	25	2 56	0 39	29R37	0♌10	2 12	5 25
♅	1	17♎ 3	17♎12	16♎34	15♎21	14♎ 7	13♎17
	13	17 13	17R 1	16R 8	14R50	13R43	13R 9
	25	17R15	16 43	15 39	14 21	13 25	13D 8
♆	1	27♉38	27♉17	27♉26	28♉ 5	29♉ 4	0♊13
	13	27R26	27D17	27 38	28 27	29 31	0 39
	25	27 19	27 22	27 54	28 51	29 58	1 4
Pl.	1	3♊17	2♊38	2♊58	3♊19	3♊52	4♊33
☊	1	11♌14	9♌35	8♌ 3	6♌24	4♌49	3♌11
	1st	Sun	Wed	Thu	Sun	Tue	Fri

Noon		JUL	AUG	SEP	OCT	NOV	DEC
☉	1	10♋ 0	9♌35	9♍26	8♎43	9♏31	9♐47
	9	17 38	17 16	17 12	16 37	17 33	17 55
	17	25 16	24 57	25 0	24 33	25 37	26 3
	25	2♌54	2♍39	2♎49	2♏31	3♐42	4♑12
☿	1	21♋43	20♋27	17♍12	2♏53	8♏21	25♏ 5
	7	18R29	29 9	27 40	9 42	2R31	4♐13
	13	14 51	10♌ 9	7♎27	15 1	2D56	13 29
	19	13 1	22 10	16 36	17 44	8 23	22 50
	25	14D23	4♍ 5	25 6	16R 8	16 16	2♑17
	31	19 18	15 23	...	9 39	...	11 54
♀	1	7♋ 9	15♌19	23♍37	0♏42	8♐55	15♑41
	9	17 0	25 12	3♎31	10 34	18 45	25 25
	17	26 50	5♍ 5	13 24	20 27	28 34	5♒ 6
	25	6♌42	14 58	23 17	0♐18	8♑21	14 42
♂	1	20♎42	5♏26	23♏55	14♐ 9	6♑43	29♑34
	13	25 49	12 14	1♐47	22 43	15 46	8♒52
	25	1♏42	19 30	9 58	1♑30	24 56	18 13
♃	1	27♏14	26♏37	28♏49	3♐ 7	9♐ 5	15♐40
	13	26R40	27 9	0♐19	5 17	11 39	18 23
	25	26D30	28 6	2 7	7 38	14 19	21 5
♄	1	6♌ 7	10♌ 1	13♌56	17♌13	19♌34	20♌21
	13	7 36	11 34	15 20	18 17	20 4	20R12
	25	9 7	13 4	16 37	19 9	20 20	19 48
♅	1	13♎11	13♎53	15♎18	17♎ 4	19♎ 0	20♎37
	13	13 22	14 22	15 58	17 49	19 42	21 8
	25	13 40	14 56	16 42	18 34	20 20	21 32
♆	1	1♊15	2♊ 1	2♊20	2♊ 8	1♊30	0♊40
	13	1 35	2 12	2R18	1R56	1R10	0R21
	25	1 53	2 18	2 13	1 40	0 50	0 3
Pl.	1	5♊11	5♊41	5♊51	5♊44	5♊20	4♊47
☊	1	1♌35	29♋57	28♋18	26♋43	25♋ 4	23♋29
	1st	Sun	Wed	Sat	Mon	Thu	Sat

	d.	JAN	FEB	MAR	APR
☽	1	6♌47	28♍13	22♎35	16♐ 5
	3	3♍56	26♎51	21♏48	13♑49
	5	1♎44	25♏14	19♐58	9♒59
	7	0♏ 2	23♐ 3	16♑57	5♓ 2
	9	28 35	20♑ 8	12♒53	29 23
	11	26♐57	16♒24	8♓ 1	23♈20
	13	24♑33	11♓45	2♈31	17♉ 5
	15	21♒ 0	6♈16	26 32	10♊51
	17	16♓12	0♉11	20♉16	4♋57
	19	10♈25	23 57	14♊ 7	29 55
	21	4♉12	18♊ 8	8♋36	26♌20
	23	28 9	13♋21	4♌24	24♍40
	25	22♊51	10♌ 5	1♍58	24♎42
	27	18♋42	8♍24	1♎20	25♏21
	29	15♌49	7♎47	1♏39	25♐10
	31	13♍56	...	1♐36	...

	d.	MAY	JUN	JUL	AUG
☽	1	23♑14	10♓56	13♈46	27♉35
	3	19♒29	5♈23	7♉38	21♊34
	5	14♓23	29 13	1♊25	16♋18
	7	8♈29	22♉57	25 34	12♌ 6
	9	2♉16	16♊54	20♋24	9♍ 2
	11	26 1	11♋18	16♌ 5	6♎52
	13	19♊55	6♌21	12♍40	5♏13
	15	14♋13	2♍18	10♎ 8	3♐40
	17	9♌17	29 26	8♏26	1♑53
	19	5♍37	27♎54	7♐15	29 36
	21	3♎37	27♏25	6♑ 7	26♒35
	23	3♏14	27♐ 9	4♒22	22♓35
	25	3♐40	26♑ 4	1♓27	17♈34
	27	3♋33	23♒27	27 12	11♉43
	29	1♒51	19♓14	21♈48	5♊29
	31	28 18	...	15♉42	29 27

	d.	SEP	OCT	NOV	DEC
☽	1	11♋44	15♌ 5	4♎34	12♏27
	3	7♌12	12♍16	4♏23	12♐57
	5	4♍ 8	11♎11	4♐54	13♑ 6
	7	2♎27	11♎ 5	4 42	11♒47
	9	1♏29	10♐44	2♒55	8♓39
	11	0♐25	9♑16	29 29	3♈59
	13	28 41	6♒28	24♓47	28 18
	15	26♑ 5	2♓30	19♈16	22♉ 6
	17	22♒40	27 43	13♉16	15♊47
	19	18♓29	22♈18	7♊ 0	9♋38
	21	13♈32	16♉22	0♋41	3♌54
	23	7♉52	10♊ 5	24 37	28 52
	25	1♊40	3♋45	19♌17	24♍52
	27	25 23	27 54	15♍13	22♎16
	29	19♋37	23♌18	12♎56	21♏ 8
	31	...	20♍17	...	21♐ 1

STATIONS	☿	♀	♂	♃
	24Feb 19♓20	None	5Mar 0♏14	23Mar 6♐22
	17Mar 5♓15		22May 11♎56	25Jul 26♏30
		♄	♅	♆
	26Jun 22♋51	28Mar 29♋36	23Jan 17♎15	7Feb 27♉16
	20Jul 13♋ 0	1Dec 20♌21	20Jun 13♎ 7	3Sep 2♊20
	20Oct 17♏49	SIDER. TIME		1 Jan
	11Dec 2♏ 5	6h 40m 22s		Midn.
		18h 42m 20s		Noon.
		LEAP YEAR		1888

1889

Noon		JAN	FEB	MAR	APR	MAY	JUN
☉	1	11♑20	12♒53	11♓ 8	11♈57	11♉16	11♊ 8
	9	19 30	21 0	19 9	19 49	19 1	18 47
	17	27 39	29 4	27 7	27 39	26 44	26 25
	25	5♒47	7♓ 7	5♈ 3	5♉27	4♊25	4♋ 3
☿	1	13♑31	1♓ 0	17♒52	20♓37	18♉35	1♋49
	7	23 23	2R39	20 29	0♈34	0♊52	2 56
	13	3♒26	28♒19	25 33	11 24	11 40	1R26
	19	13 28	21 46	2♓15	23 8	20 30	28♊16
	25	22 53	18 0	10 10	5♉42	27 8	25 13
	31	0♓ 9	...	19 3	...	1♋22	...
♀	1	23♒ 3	28♒41	27♈14	17♉49	10♉37	4♉31
	9	2♓29	7♈21	4♉ 9	19 8	5R59	8 10
	17	11 46	15 39	10 10	17R55	3 9	13 14
	25	20 53	23 31	14 58	14 17	2D51	19 21
♂	1	23♒41	17♓49	9♈16	2♉24	24♉ 4	15♊42
	13	3♓ 3	27 4	18 19	11 10	2♊32	23 53
	25	12 23	6♈14	27 15	19 48	10 52	1♋57
♃	1	22♐39	29♐ 9	3♑58	7♑26	8♑12	6♑11
	13	25 16	1♑22	5 35	8 4	7R44	4R49
	25	27 45	3 22	6 51	8 16	6 51	3 18
♄	1	19♌27	17♌14	15♌ 4	13♌35	13♌41	15♌23
	13	18R42	16R16	14R19	13R26	14 10	16 25
	25	17 48	15 21	13 47	13D32	14 53	17 35
♅	1	21♎43	21♎58	21♎28	20♎19	19♎ 3	18♎ 7
	13	21 55	21R50	21R 4	19R48	18R37	17R56
	25	21 59	21 34	20 36	19 18	18 16	17 52
♆	1	29♉54	29♉31	29♉39	0♊16	1♊13	2♊22
	13	29R42	29D31	29 50	0 37	1 40	2 48
	25	29 34	29 36	0♊ 5	1 1	2 6	3 13
Pl.	1	4♊17	3♊58	3♊57	4♊16	4♊48	5♊29
☊	1	21♋51	20♋12	18♋43	17♋ 5	15♋29	13♋51
		Tue	Fri	Fri	Mon	Wed	Sat

Noon		JUL	AUG	SEP	OCT	NOV	DEC
☉	1	9♋46	9♌22	9♍12	8♎29	9♏17	9♐32
	9	17 24	17 2	16 58	16 23	17 19	17 40
	17	25 2	24 43	24 45	24 19	25 22	25 48
	25	2♌40	2♍25	2♎35	2♏17	3♐28	3♑57
☿	1	24♊ 6	2♌18	29♍26	1♏25	20♎43	5♐56
	7	25 52	14 44	8♎ 8	0R58	28 27	15 21
	13	0♋38	26 44	16 0	25♎54	7♏31	24 48
	19	8 16	7♍57	22 51	18 55	16 59	4♑19
	25	18 23	18 20	28 16	16D11	26 29	13 55
	31	0♌14	27 55	...	19 41	...	23 32
♀	1	24♉27	25♊ 7	29♋43	5♍14	13♎13	20♏38
	9	1♊46	3♋46	9♌ 2	14 56	23 9	0♐40
	17	9 34	12 38	18 28	24 43	3♏ 7	10 43
	25	17 44	21 41	28 1	4♎33	13 7	20 46
♂	1	5♋58	26♋20	16♌15	5♍ 8	24♍16	12♎19
	13	13 55	4♌ 6	23 50	12 35	1♎33	19 23
	25	21 47	11 47	1♍23	19 59	8 45	26 18
♃	1	2♑32	29♐18	28♐31	0♑33	5♑ 2	10♑57
	13	1R 5	28R39	29 1	2 2	7 15	13 35
	25	29♐52	28 26	29 56	3 51	9 40	16 19
♄	1	18♌14	21♌55	25♌51	29♌24	2♍16	3♍46
	13	19 36	23 26	27 20	0♍38	3 3	3 55
	25	21 3	24 58	28 44	1 43	3 35	3R48
♅	1	17♎53	18♎28	19♎46	21♎29	23♎26	25♎ 7
	13	18 1	18 53	20 25	22 14	24 9	25 40
	25	18 16	19 25	21 7	23 0	24 48	26 6
♆	1	3♊24	4♊13	4♊34	4♊25	3♊48	2♊58
	13	3 46	4 25	4R34	4R13	3R29	2R39
	25	4 4	4 32	4 29	3 58	3 9	2 21
Pl.	1	6♊07	6♊36	6♊49	6♊42	6♊19	5♊47
☊	1	12♋16	10♋37	8♋59	7♋24	5♋45	4♋10
		Mon	Thu	Sun	Tue	Fri	Sun

d.	JAN	FEB	MAR	APR
☽ 1	6♑ 3	27♒33	5♓53	23♈52
3	5♒32	24♓44	2♈39	18♉35
5	3♓35	20♈26	28 14	12♊32
7	29 55	14♉53	22♉41	6♋ 9
9	24♈47	8♊38	16♊27	0♌ 5
11	18♉45	2♋22	10♋10	25 3
13	12♊25	26 40	4♌33	21♍37
15	6♋16	21♌56	0♍10	19♎52
17	0♌40	18♍18	27 14	19♏16
19	25 49	15♎36	25♎27	18♐46
21	21♍51	13♏31	24♏11	17♑31
23	18♎48	11♐44	22♐44	15♒12
25	16♏42	10♑ 2	20♑47	11♓52
27	15♐25	8♒12	18♒15	7♈40
29	14♑33	...	15♓ 5	2♉42
31	13♒27	...	11♈10	...

d.	MAY	JUN	JUL	AUG
☽ 1	27♉ 2	11♋15	14♌ 6	1♎18
3	20♊49	4♌59	8♍42	27 48
5	14♋23	29 21	4♎21	25♏25
7	8♌18	24♍55	1♏24	24♐ 8
9	3♍12	22♎10	0♐ 0	23♑37
11	29 43	21♏12	29 50	23♒ 6
13	28♎ 6	21♐26	0♒ 0	21♓39
15	27♏55	21♑42	29 22	18♈39
17	28♐ 5	20♒51	27♓ 9	14♉ 1
19	27♑27	18♓22	23♈11	8♊11
21	25♒24	14♈16	17♉50	1♋49
23	21♓56	8♉58	11♊40	25 33
25	17♈19	2♊54	5♋15	19♌55
27	11♉52	26 31	29 2	15♍10
29	5♊50	20♋ 9	23♌22	11♎22
31	29 28	...	18♍26	8♏22

d.	SEP	OCT	NOV	DEC
☽ 1	22♏ 8	1♑ 5	24♒ 3	1♈33
3	20♐ 7	29 16	21♓16	27 24
5	18♑39	27♒18	17♈44	22♉21
7	17♒27	24♓57	13♉20	16♊37
9	15♓57	21♈46	8♊ 3	10♋23
11	13♈26	17♉29	2♋ 1	3♌58
13	9♉29	12♊ 3	25 36	27 46
15	4♊11	5♋50	19♌23	22♍20
17	28 0	29 28	14♍ 3	18♎15
19	21♋39	23♌40	10♎11	15♏56
21	15♌49	19♍ 4	8♏ 4	15♐17
23	11♍ 0	15♎58	7♐21	15♑35
25	7♎26	14♏12	7♑ 8	15♒37
27	4♏52	13♐ 6	6♒26	14♓22
29	2♐53	11♑54	4♓37	11♈27
31	...	10♒10	...	7♉2

STATIONS	☿	♀	♂	♃
	7Feb 2♓39	10Apr 19♉ 7	None	26Apr 8♑16
	28Feb 17♒44	22May 2♉40		26Aug 28♐26
	8Jun 2♋51	♄	♅	♆
	1Jul 24♊ 6	15Apr 13♌26	26Jan 21♎59	10Feb 29♉51
	4Oct 1♏44	16Dec 3♍55	27Jun 17♌52	7Sep 4♊34
	25Oct 16♎11	SIDER. TIME 6h 43m 21s		1 Jan Midn.
		18h 45m 19s		Noon
		Common Year		1889

1890

Noon		JAN	FEB	MAR	APR	MAY	JUN
☉	1	11♑ 6	12♒38	10♓54	11♈43	11♉ 2	10♊54
	9	19 15	20 45	18 54	19 35	18 47	18 33
	17	27 24	28 49	26 52	27 25	26 30	26 11
	25	5♒32	6♓53	4♈48	5♉13	4♊11	3♋49
☿	1	25♑ 8	6♒29	14♒40	3♈41	1♊14	7♊27
	7	4♒20	1R31	22 26	15 38	7 58	4R53
	13	12 9	1D12	1♓ 6	28 10	11 53	4D31
	19	16 23	4 30	10 33	10♉38	12R52	6 50
	25	14R30	10 6	20 46	21 57	11 12	11 46
	31	7 40	...	1♈46	...	8 0	...
♀	1	29♐34	8♒31	13♓36	22♈10	29♉ 8	6♋54
	9	9♑38	18 33	23 35	2♉ 3	8♊55	16 33
	17	19 41	28 35	3♈32	11 56	18 41	26 10
	25	29 44	8♓36	13 29	21 46	28 24	5♌45
♂	1	0♏16	16♏58	0♐ 7	10♐33	12♐49	4♐46
	13	6 55	22 54	4 50	12 39	10R44	1R 0
	25	13 21	28 24	8 44	13R12	7 10	28♏33
♃	1	17♑57	25♑10	1♒19	7♒ 3	10♒50	12♒10
	13	20 45	27 52	3 42	8 48	11 41	11R53
	25	23 33	0♒28	5 53	10 15	12 7	11 9
♄	1	3♍37	1♍53	29♌40	27♌40	27♌ 1	28♌ 0
	13	3R 6	0R57	28R47	27R13	27 12	28 47
	25	2 23	29♌59	28 1	27 1	27 38	29 45
♅	1	26♎19	26♎43	26♎19	25♎14	23♎59	22♎57
	13	26 34	26R37	25R58	24R44	23R31	22R43
	25	26 42	26 25	25 32	24 14	23 8	22 36
♆	1	2♊12	1♊47	1♊52	2♊26	3♊22	4♊31
	13	1R58	1D46	2 2	2 47	3 48	4 58
	25	1 50	1 49	2 16	3 10	4 15	5 23
Pl.	1	5♊16	4♊57	5♊ 1	5♊14	5♊46	6♊26
☊	1	2♋31	0♋53	29♊24	27♊45	26♊10	24♊31
		Wed	Sat	Sat	Tue	Thu	Sun

Noon		JUL	AUG	SEP	OCT	NOV	DEC
☉	1	9♋32	9♌ 8	8♍58	8♎15	9♏ 2	9♐17
	9	17 10	16 48	16 43	16 8	17 4	17 25
	17	24 48	24 29	24 31	24 4	25 8	25 33
	25	2♌26	2♍12	2♎21	2♏ 2	3♐13	3♑42
☿	1	19♊ 6	19♌19	5♎52	4♎42	29♎23	17♐14
	7	28 39	0♍17	11 22	0R28	9♏14	26 33
	13	10♋ 6	10 19	14 47	2D13	18 57	5♑47
	19	22 40	19 27	15R 3	8 52	28 29	14 47
	25	5♌21	27 39	11 14	17 55	7♐54	22 58
	31	17 24	4♎48	...	27 44	...	28 57
♀	1	12♌53	19♍13	24♎ 0	24♏32	16♐58	13♐39
	9	22 22	28 23	2♏34	1♐38	19 21	8R54
	17	1♍47	7♎26	10 52	8 1	19R23	5 27
	25	11 7	16 21	18 50	13 24	16 52	4D24
♂	1	28♏ 3	2♐55	16♐49	5♑ 0	26♑25	18♒24
	13	28D31	7 30	23 41	13 4	5♒ 7	27 21
	25	0♐50	13 8	1♑ 7	21 26	13 57	6♓20
♃	1	10♒38	6♒59	3♒29	2♒21	4♒10	8♒26
	13	9R22	5R28	2R42	2 42	5 38	10 39
	25	7 53	4 8	2 20	3 31	7 25	13 6
♄	1	0♍18	3♍40	7♍31	11♍12	14♍28	16♍34
	13	1 31	5 7	9 1	12 34	15 28	17 0
	25	2 51	6 38	10 30	13 49	16 15	17 11
♅	1	22♎36	23♎ 2	24♎14	25♎54	27♎50	29♎34
	13	22 40	23 25	24 51	26 38	28 33	0♏ 9
	25	22 52	23 54	25 31	27 23	29 15	0 38
♆	1	5♊34	6♊24	6♊48	6♊41	6♊ 6	5♊18
	13	5♊56	6 37	6R49	6R31	5R48	4R58
	25	6 15	6 45	6 45	6 16	5 28	4 39
Pl.	1	7♊ 3	7♊33	7♊46	7♊41	7♊17	6♊46
☊	1	22♊56	21♊18	19♊39	18♊ 4	16♊25	14♊50
		Tue	Fri	Mon	Wed	Sat	Mon

	d.	JAN	FEB	MAR	APR
☽	1	19♉24	4♋12	12♋39	26♌27
	3	13♊32	27 47	6♌17	21♍11
	5	7♋16	21♌38	0♍22	16♎58
	7	0♌52	15♍59	25 11	13♏43
	9	24 39	11♎ 0	20♎47	11♐ 9
	11	18♍55	6♏52	17♏ 9	9♑ 3
	13	14♎ 4	3♐51	14♐17	7♒18
	15	10♏31	2♑11	12♑16	5♓43
	17	8♐37	1♒44	11♒ 6	3♈56
	19	8♑16	1♓44	10♓19	1♉24
	21	8♒41	1♈ 3	9♈ 6	27 41
	23	8♓38	28 44	6♉36	22♊41
	25	7♈ 1	24♉34	2♊28	16♋43
	27	3♉32	18♊59	26 58	10♌24
	29	28 27	...	20♋42	4♍23
	31	22♊24	...	14♌25	...
	d.	MAY	JUN	JUL	AUG
☽	1	29♍18	17♏21	24♐13	17♒51
	3	25♎29	15♐53	24♑10	18♓ 4
	5	22♏55	15♑15	24♒15	16♈50
	7	21♐13	14♒36	23♓23	13♉43
	9	19♑50	13♓13	20♈58	8♊59
	11	18♒19	10♈44	17♉ 2	3♋12
	13	16♓23	7♉ 8	11♊56	26 56
	15	13♈49	2♊32	6♋ 6	20♌36
	17	10♉26	27 8	29 52	14♍27
	19	6♊ 4	21♋ 9	23♌32	8♎43
	21	0♋44	14♌50	17♍22	3♏38
	23	24 41	8♍35	11♎43	29 35
	25	18♌22	2♎55	7♏ 4	26♐58
	27	12♍21	28 23	3♐54	25♑59
	29	7♎16	25♏27	2♑30	26♒13
	31	3♏36	...	2♒34	26♓28
	d.	SEP	OCT	NOV	DEC
☽	1	11♈11	17♉21	3♋56	6♌ 1
	3	9♉15	13♊35	28 14	29 48
	5	5♊23	8♋19	22♌ 0	23♍40
	7	0♋ 2	2♌12	15♍53	18♎13
	9	23 52	25 54	10♎27	14♏ 0
	11	17♌31	19♍58	6♏ 2	11♐12
	13	11♍24	14♎44	2♐43	9♑40
	15	5♎47	10♏18	0♑17	8♒44
	17	0♏45	6♐38	28 23	7♓40
	19	26 27	3♑42	26♒45	5♈54
	21	23♐ 6	1♒33	25♓ 3	3♉12
	23	20♑58	0♓ 7	23♈ 0	29 35
	25	20♒ 5	29 4	20♉16	25♊ 7
	27	19♓54	27♈41	16♊32	19♋54
	29	19♈19	25♉15	11♋44	14♌ 2
	31	...	21♊23	...	7♍48

STATIONS	☿	♀	♂	♃
	21Jan 16♒30	13Nov 9♐41	24Apr 13♐14	31May 12♒10
	10Feb 0♒49	24Dec 4♐23	5Jul 27♏59	29Sep 2♒20
	18May 12♊55	♄	♅	♆
	11Jun 4♊21	30Apr 27♌ 1	1Feb 26♎43	13Jan 1♊46
	17Sep 15♎23	29Dec 17♍11	1Jul 22♎36	11Sep 6♊49
	8Oct 0♎20	SIDER. TIME		1 Jan
		6h 42m 23s		Midn.
		18h 44m 21s		Noon
		Common Year		1890

Noon		JAN	FEB	MAR	APR	MAY	JUN
☉	1	19♑50	12♒23	10♓39	11♈29	10♉48	10♊40
	9	10 0	20 30	18 39	19 21	18 33	18 19
	17	27 9	28 35	26 38	27 11	26 16	25 58
	25	5♒17	6♓38	4♈34	4♉59	3♊57	3♑36
☿	1	29♑34	17♑22	22♒42	20♈21	23♉ 5	17♉29
	7	29 43	22 50	2♓31	2♉ 2	20R41	22 42
	13	23R37	29 49	13 0	11 54	17 9	29 59
	19	16 40	7♒48	24 11	18 57	14 36	9♊ 8
	25	14D23	16 31	6♈ 3	22 43	14D23	20 2
	31	16 40	...	18 19	...	16 50	...
♀	1	5♐35	26♐12	24♑36	29♒34	4♈48	11♉49
	9	8 57	3♑48	3♒24	8♓53	14 18	21 26
	17	13 56	11 52	12 23	18 16	23 51	1♊ 5
	25	20 6	20 17	21 30	27 41	3♉25	10 45
♂	1	11♓34	4♈37	25♈ 2	17♉ 3	7♊45	28♊33
	13	20 31	13 25	3♉38	25 24	15 52	6♋28
	25	29 26	22 9	12 8	3♊40	23 54	14 19
♃	1	14♒36	21♒45	28♒27	5♓33	11♓30	15♓53
	13	17 17	24 37	1♓17	8 5	13 28	17 5
	25	20 5	27 30	4 1	10 25	15 9	17 46
♄	1	17♍10	16♍ 4	14♍ 3	11♍43	10♍26	10♍39
	13	16R56	15R16	13R 5	11R 3	10D19	11 11
	25	16 27	14 22	12 12	10 35	10 28	11 55
♅	1	0♏52	1♏24	1♏ 8	0♏ 9	28♎53	27♎47
	13	1 11	1R22	0R49	29♎39	28R25	27R31
	25	1 22	1 13	0 25	29R 8	28 0	27 21
♆	1	4♊30	4♊ 2	4♊ 5	4♊37	5♊32	6♊40
	13	4R16	4R 0	4 14	4 57	5 58	7 6
	25	4 6	4D 3	4 27	5 19	6 24	7 32
Pl.	1	6♊15	5♊55	5♊53	6♊10	6♊41	7 21
☊	1	13♊11	11♊33	10♊ 4	8♊25	6♊50	5♊11
	1st	Thu	Sun	Sun	Wed	Fri	Mon

Noon		JUL	AUG	SEP	OCT	NOV	DEC
☉	1	9♑19	8♌54	8♍44	8♎ 1	8♏48	9♐ 3
	9	16 57	16 34	16 30	15 54	16 49	17 10
	17	24 34	24 15	24 17	23 50	24 53	25 18
	25	2♌12	1♍58	2♎ 7	1♏48	2♐58	3♑27
☿	1	2♋21	1♍45	28♍28	20♍33	11♏31	27♐10
	7	15 19	10 13	25R34	29 24	21 3	5♑12
	13	28 0	17 31	19 49	9♎34	0♐22	11 40
	19	9♌47	23 23	14 58	19 56	9 30	14 33
	25	20 32	27 20	15D 3	0♏ 4	18 29	11R16
	31	0♍14	28R35	...	9 55	...	3 31
♀	1	18♊ 1	25♋50	4♍ 5	11♎25	20♏10	27♐40
	9	27 44	5♌40	14 1	21 25	0♐10	7♑40
	17	7♋29	15 31	23 58	1♏24	10 10	17 39
	25	17 15	25 25	3♎56	11 24	20 10	27 38
♂	1	18♋13	8♌12	27♌59	17♍ 2	6♎41	25♎43
	13	25 59	15 53	5♍36	24 39	14 18	3♏19
	25	3♌43	23 32	13 13	2♎15	21 55	10 54
♃	1	17♓57	17♓ 2	13♓37	9♓55	8♓ 9	9♓27
	13	17R58	15R56	12R 2	8R53	8D18	10 45
	25	17 31	14 31	10 33	8 16	8 57	12 25
♄	1	12♍22	15♍18	18♍57	22♍40	26♍13	28♍48
	13	13 23	16 39	20 26	24 7	27 22	29 29
	25	14 33	18 5	21 56	25 28	28 22	29 57
♅	1	27♎18	27♎37	28♎41	0♏17	2♏12	3♏59
	13	27D19	27 57	29 17	1 1	2 57	4 36
	25	27 28	28 23	29 56	1 46	3 39	5 7
♆	1	7♊44	8♊36	9♊ 2	8♊58	8♊25	7♊36
	13	8 7	8 49	9 4	8R48	8R 6	7R16
	25	8 26	8 59	9R 1	8 34	7 47	6 57
Pl.	1	8♊ 0	8♊30	8♊44	8♊38	8♊16	7♊44
☊	1	3♊36	1♊58	0♊19	28♉44	27♉ 6	25♉30
	1st	Wed	Sat	Tue	Thu	Sun	Tue

	d.	JAN	FEB	MAR	APR
☽	1	19♍41	4♏25	13♏29	1♑50
	3	13♎43	29 50	8♐50	29 18
	5	8♏41	26♐56	5♑38	28♒14
	7	5♐ 9	25♑57	4♒16	28♓10
	9	3♑22	26♒21	4♓26	28♈ 1
	11	2♒59	26♓48	4♈59	26♉39
	13	3♓ 1	25♈58	4♉31	23♊32
	15	2♈17	23♉17	2♊10	18♋49
	17	0♉ 8	18♊58	28 0	13♌ 1
	19	26 34	13♋32	22♋32	6♍47
	21	21♊53	7♌32	16♌25	0♎38
	23	16♋28	1♍19	10♍ 8	24 56
	25	10♌35	25 6	4♎ 1	19♏53
	27	4♍24	19♎ 3	28 16	15♐37
	29	28 8	...	23♏ 2	12♑14
	31	22♎ 9	...	18♐37	...

	d.	MAY	JUN	JUL	AUG
☽	1	9♒48	3♈26	12♉ 8	1♋53
	3	8♓20	1♉47	9♊ 6	27 1
	5	7♈27	29 35	5♋15	21♌31
	7	6♉30	26♊28	0♌34	15♍30
	9	4♊40	22♋15	25 4	9♎11
	11	1♋27	16♌58	19♍ 0	3♏ 0
	13	26 48	10♍58	12♎44	27 30
	15	21♌ 6	4♎46	6♏54	23♐22
	17	14♍55	28 58	2♐ 6	21♑ 6
	19	8♎50	24♏ 9	28 53	20♒36
	21	3♏22	20♐39	27♑19	20♓57
	23	28 49	18♑26	26♒51	20♈49
	25	25♐17	17♒ 6	26♓26	19♉15
	27	22♑41	15♓57	25♈10	16♊ 4
	29	20♒45	14♈24	22♉40	11♋37
	31	19♓11	...	19♊ 3	6♌18

	d.	SEP	OCT	NOV	DEC
☽	1	18♌25	21♍17	5♏46	9♐10
	3	12♑22	14♎59	0♐12	5♑ 1
	5	6♎ 5	8♏51	25 20	1♒46
	7	29 47	3♐ 8	21♑22	29 18
	9	23♏52	28 16	18♒34	27♓28
	11	18♐53	24♑42	16♓58	26♈ 2
	13	15♑27	22♒48	16♈20	24♉39
	15	13♒57	22♓28	15♉54	22♊48
	17	14♓ 5	22♈48	14♊46	19♋57
	19	14♈41	22♉35	12♋11	15♌48
	21	14♉21	20♊48	8♌ 2	10♍26
	23	12♊17	17♋14	2♍35	4♎17
	25	8♋28	12♌13	26 25	28 0
	27	3♌22	6♍17	20♎ 8	22♏14
	29	27 30	29 59	14♏16	17♐31
	31	...	23♎46	...	14♑ 6

STATIONS	☿	♀	♂	♃
	5Jan 0♑25	None	None	10Jul 18♓ 0
	25Jan 14♑23			4Nov 8♓ 8
	30Apr 23♉15	♄	♅	♆
	22May 14♉ 9	13May 10♍19	4Feb 1♏22	14Feb 4♊ 0
	30Aug 28♍36	... ...	9Jul 27♎18	14Sep 9♊ 4
	23Sep 14♍22	SIDER. TIME 6h 41m 26s		1 Jan Midn.
	20Dec 14♐29	18h 43m 24s Common Year		Noon. 1891.

Noon		JAN	FEB	MAR	APR	MAY	JUN
☉	1	10♑35	12♒ 9	11♓24	12♈14	11♉33	11♊24
	9	18 45	20 15	19 25	20 6	19 17	19 3
	17	26 54	28 20	27 23	27 55	27 0	26 41
	25	5♒ 2	6♓23	5♈19	5♉43	4♊41	4♋19
☿	1	2♑19	20♑37	7♓15	1♉ 4	24♈ 9	21♉26
	7	28♐21	29 13	18 34	4 18	24D48	2♊ 6
	13	29D51	8♒21	0♈22	3R37	28 7	14 9
	19	4♑42	18 1	12 4	0 9	3♉36	27 7
	25	11 29	28 15	22 28	26♈14	10 54	10♋ 9
	31	19 16	...	0♉ 8	...	19 48	...
♀	1	6♒20	14♓40	19♈44	25♉34	27♊ 1	21♋21
	9	16 18	24 27	29 11	4♊21	4♋25	24 44
	17	26 13	4♈ 9	8♉31	12 55	11 12	26 8
	25	6♓ 3	13 46	17 41	21 7	17 7	25R 6
♂	1	15♏20	4♐47	22♐39	11♑ 2	27♑19	10♒50
	13	22 53	12 13	29 53	17 47	3♒ 5	14 26
	25	0♐26	19 36	6♑58	24 14	8 14	16 39
♃	1	13♓34	19♓37	26♓16	3♈45	10♈47	17♈13
	13	15 44	22 18	29 10	6 38	13 25	19 21
	25	18 8	25 6	2♈ 3	9 27	15 53	21 12
♄	1	0♎ 6	29♍40	27♍58	25♍33	23♍48	23♍22
	13	0R 8	29R 6	27R 3	24R45	23R27	23 38
	25	29♍56	28 20	26 6	24 3	23 19	24 8
♅	1	5♏24	6♏ 3	5♏53	4♏58	3♏44	2♏35
	13	5 45	6R 4	5R37	4R28	3R14	2R16
	25	5 59	5 58	5 14	3 59	2 48	2 4
♆	1	6♊48	6♊18	6♊19	6♊50	7♊44	8♊52
	13	6R33	6R15	6 27	7 9	8 9	9 18
	25	6 23	6D17	6 41	7 32	8 36	9 44
Pl.	1	7♊13	6♊54	6♊52	7♊ 8	7♊40	8♊20
☊	1	23♉52	22♉13	20♉41	19♉ 2	17♉27	15♉49
	1st	Fri	Mon	Tue	Fri	Sun	Wed

Noon		JUL	AUG	SEP	OCT	NOV	DEC
☉	1	10♋ 2	9♌38	9♍28	8♎46	9♏33	9♐49
	9	17 40	17 18	17 14	16 39	17 35	17 56
	17	25 18	24 59	25 2	24 35	25 39	26 5
	25	2♌56	2♍42	2♎52	2♏33	3♐44	4♑14
☿	1	22♋26	6♍34	28♌37	3♎32	24♏10	28♐39
	7	3♌36	10 13	28D28	14 9	2♐55	26R26
	13	13 34	11R 9	3♍26	24 21	11 19	18 54
	19	22 20	8 52	12 10	4♏ 9	19 2	13 4
	25	29 49	3 53	22 40	13 33	25 20	13D12
	31	5♍46	29♌ 8	...	22 42	...	17 38
♀	1	22♋43	9♋40	24♋45	23♌12	27♍52	3♏47
	9	18R 7	11 9	1♌33	1♍47	7♎18	13 34
	17	13 23	14 35	9 0	10 38	16 51	23 26
	25	10 21	19 31	16 57	19 46	26 30	3♐20
♂	1	17♒ 9	13♒ 0	7♒ 7	11♒56	25♒41	13♓ 8
	13	16R48	9R54	7D43	16 31	2♓21	20 41
	25	14 45	7 39	10 8	22 4	9 27	28 24
♃	1	22♈ 0	24♈37	24♈22	21♈22	17♈20	15♈ 6
	13	23 22	24 56	23R25	19R47	16R 8	15D 1
	25	24 19	24R43	22 8	18 12	15 20	15 25
♄	1	24♍28	26♍56	0♎18	3♎59	7♎40	10♎36
	13	25 17	28 10	1 45	5 27	8 58	11 30
	25	26 16	29 28	3 15	6 52	10 6	12 10
♅	1	2♏ 0	2♏11	3♏10	4♏44	6♏36	8♏26
	13	1R59	2 30	3 45	5 26	7 22	9 4
	25	2 5	2 55	4 23	6 11	8 5	9 37
♆	1	9♊56	10♊49	11♊17	11♊14	10♊42	9♊54
	13	10 19	11 3	11R19	11R 4	10R24	9R34
	25	10 39	11 13	11 17	10 51	10 4	9 15
Pl.	1	8♊58	9♊28	9♊41	9♊37	9♊14	8♊42
☊	1	14♉13	12♉35	10♉56	9♉21	7♉42	6♉ 7
	1st	Fri	Mon	Thu	Sat	Tue	Thu

	d.	JAN	FEB	MAR	APR
☽	1	27♑50	20♓12	14♈15	7♊ 9
	3	25♒54	19♈14	13♉36	4♋48
	5	24♓18	17♉28	11♊37	0♌55
	7	22♈36	14♊46	8♋18	25 50
	9	20♉34	11♋16	3♌55	19♍59
	11	18♊ 5	7♌ 2	28 45	13♎44
	13	15♋ 0	2♍ 4	22♍59	7♏22
	15	11♌ 2	26 22	16♎47	1♐10
	17	6♍ 4	20♎ 7	10♏23	25 29
	19	0♎13	13♏41	4♐12	20♑46
	21	23 53	7♐52	28 48	17♒30
	23	17♏44	3♑13	24♐49	15♓55
	25	12♑28	0♒20	22♒42	15♈45
	27	8♑41	29 16	22♓19	16♉ 3
	29	6♒32	29♓15	22♈45	15♊38
	31	5♓32	...	22♉41	...

	d.	MAY	JUN	JUL	AUG
☽	1	13♋40	1♍ 3	3♎32	17♏ 0
	3	9♌58	25 26	27 16	11♐ 2
	5	4♍52	19♎10	21♏ 0	6♑ 6
	7	28 52	12♏50	15♐21	2♒36
	9	22♎30	6♐56	10♑44	0♓25
	11	16♏12	1♑49	7♒16	29 0
	13	10♐17	27 36	4♓42	27♈41
	15	5♑ 1	24♒17	2♈41	26♉ 0
	17	0♒38	21♓48	0♉54	23♊47
	19	27 24	20♈ 4	29 12	20♋58
	21	25♓26	18♉55	27♊21	17♌25
	23	24♈38	17♊53	24♋59	12♍57
	25	24♉24	16♋17	21♌40	7♎31
	27	23♊47	13♌27	17♍ 7	1♏21
	29	21♋55	9♍ 7	11♎28	24 57
	31	18♌24	...	5♏10	18♐57

	d.	SEP	OCT	NOV	DEC
☽	1	1♑20	5♒17	25♓23	3♉20
	3	27 13	2♓50	25♈ 6	3♊27
	5	24♒48	2♈ 5	25♉32	3♋29
	7	23♓46	2♉13	25♊28	2♌17
	9	23♈18	2♊ 5	23♋55	29 14
	11	22♉27	0♋48	20♌35	24♍27
	13	20♊41	28 1	15♍43	18♎31
	15	17♋51	23♌52	9♎51	12♏ 5
	17	14♌ 3	18♍41	3♏30	5♐45
	19	9♍23	12♎48	27 5	29 53
	21	3♎56	6♏30	20♐54	24♑43
	23	27 51	0♐ 4	15♑14	20♒18
	25	21♏25	23 50	10♒21	16♓43
	27	15♐ 6	18♑16	6♓34	14♈ 7
	29	9♑31	13♒52	4♈12	12♉34
	31	...	11♓ 6	...	11♊55

STATIONS	☿	♀	♂	♃
	9Jan 28♑20	18Jun 26♋ 8	6Jul 17♒13	14Aug 24♈56
	10Apr 4♉26	31Jul 9♋39	3Sep 7♒ 5	10Dec 14♈59
		♄	♅	♆
	4May 24♈ 7	10Jan 0♎ 9	10Feb 6♏ 5	16Feb 6♊15
	11Aug 11♍11	27May 23♍19	10Jul 1♏59	13Sep 11♊19
	5Sep 27♌57	SIDER. TIME		1 Jan
	3Dec 28♐38	6h 40m 29s		Midn.
	23Dec 12♐33	18h 42m 27s		Noon.
		LEAP YEAR		1892

Noon		JAN	FEB	MAR	APR	MAY	JUN
☉	1	11♑22	12♒55	11♓10	11♈59	11♉18	11♊10
	9	19 31	21 1	19 10	19 51	19 3	18 49
	17	27 40	29 6	27 8	27 41	26 46	26 27
	25	5♒48	7♓ 9	5♈ 4	5♉29	4♊27	4♋ 5
☿	1	18♐39	2♒ 7	22♓14	11♈12	14♈41	6♊36
	7	25 36	12 4	2♈57	6R44	21 59	19 48
	13	3♑35	22 26	11 24	4 32	0♉43	2♋38
	19	12 7	3♓20	15 59	5D27	10 43	14 24
	25	21 8	14 39	15R52	9 0	22 0	24 54
	31	0♒33	...	12 4	...	4♊27	...
♀	1	11♐59	20♑34	25♒27	3♈59	11♉ 7	19♊13
	9	21 55	0♒30	5♓25	13 54	20 57	29 3
	17	1♑53	10 30	15 21	23 48	0♊46	8♋53
	25	11 51	20 28	25 18	3♉41	10 38	18 42
♂	1	2♈57	23♈28	12♉ 4	2♊25	21♊56	11♋48
	13	10 52	1♉26	19 58	10 16	29 39	19 26
	25	18 49	9 24	27 52	18 2	7 19	27 2
♃	1	15♈53	19♈36	24♈46	1♉38	8♉45	16♉ 1
	13	17 1	21 39	27 19	4 27	11 38	18 41
	25	18 33	23 57	0♉ 0	7 19	14 25	21 13
♄	1	12♎27	12♎42	11♎31	9♎15	7♎ 9	6♎ 3
	13	12 44	12R20	10R42	8R21	6R33	6D 2
	25	12R47	11 45	9 47	7 31	6 10	6 16
♅	1	9♏54	10♏40	10♏37	9♏48	8♏35	7♏23
	13	10 18	10 44	10R23	9R21	8R 6	7R 2
	25	10 34	10R40	10 2	8 51	7 38	6 47
♆	1	9♊ 5	8♊34	8♊33	9♊ 2	9♊54	11♊ 1
	13	8R50	8R30	8 40	9 20	10 19	11 28
	25	8 39	8D31	8 54	9 42	10 45	11 54
Pl.	1	8♊11	7♊49	7♊47	8♊ 3	8 35	9♊16
☊	1	4♉29	2♉50	1♉21	29♈43	28♈ 7	26♈29
		Sun	Wed	Wed	Sat	Mon	Thu

Noon		JUL	AUG	SEP	OCT	NOV	DEC
☉	1	9♋48	9♌24	9♍14	8♎31	9 19	9♐34
	9	17 26	17 4	17 0	16 25	17 21	17 42
	17	25 4	24 45	24 48	24 21	25 24	25 50
	25	2♌42	2♍28	2♎37	2♏19	3♐29	3♑59
☿	1	4♌ 0	21♌ 6	23♌ 6	16♎58	1♐58	28♏37
	7	11 39	16R47	3♍31	26 39	8 20	26D53
	13	17 39	12 28	14 51	5♏54	12 23	0♐35
	19	21 40	11D 7	26 2	14 40	12R 3	7 11
	25	23 7	14 13	6♎46	23 2	5 55	15 6
	31	21R37	21 33	...	0♐46	...	23 40
♀	1	26♋ 0	3♍53	11♎27	17♏21	23♐36	26♑47
	9	5♌48	13 38	21 5	26 49	2♑41	4♒56
	17	15 34	23 18	0♏41	6♐12	11 40	12 41
	25	25 21	3♎ 0	10 15	15 31	20 22	19 46
♂	1	0♌50	20♌29	10♍12	29♍25	19♎36	9♏26
	13	8 28	28 6	17 53	7♎13	27 29	17 28
	25	16 4	5♍44	25 34	15 0	5♏26	25 32
♃	1	22♉25	27♉44	0♊55	1♊14	28♉37	24♉39
	13	24 39	29 15	1 24	0R33	27R 2	23R15
	25	26 40	0♊25	1R24	29♉25	25 26	22 11
♄	1	6♎28	8♎24	11♎23	14♎54	18♎41	21♎54
	13	7 3	9 25	12 46	16 23	20 3	22 57
	25	7 50	10 38	14 11	17 50	21 19	23 51
♅	1	6♏42	6♏46	7♏37	9♏ 5	10♏57	12♏47
	13	6R38	7 1	8 8	9 47	11 42	13 27
	25	6D41	7 22	8 45	10 31	12 25	14 2
♆	1	12♊ 6	13♊ 0	13♊30	13♊30	13♊ 0	12♊13
	13	12 29	13 15	13 34	13R22	12R43	11R53
	25	12 50	13 26	13R32	13 9	12 23	11 34
Pl.	1	9♊54	10♊26	10♊41	10♊37	10♊14	9♊42
☊	1	24♈54	23♈15	21♈37	20♈ 2	18♈23	16♈48
		Sat	Tue	Fri	Sun	Wed	Fri

d.		JAN	FEB	MAR	APR
☽	1	26♊43	18♌ 9	26♌56	14♎13
	3	25♋57	14♍57	23♍ 5	8♏27
	5	23♌52	10♎17	18♎ 8	2♐13
	7	20♍ 4	4♏29	12♏16	25 54
	9	14♎44	28 7	5♐56	20♑ 3
	11	8♏30	21♐57	29 47	15♒16
	13	2♐ 6	16♑36	24♑27	12♓ 3
	15	26 9	12♒28	20♒29	10♈30
	17	21♑ 5	9♓31	18♓ 2	10♉ 9
	19	16♒57	7♈25	16♈44	10♊ 2
	21	13♓39	5♉39	15♉52	9♋11
	23	10♈58	3♊56	14♊44	7♌ 0
	25	8♉50	2♋ 2	12♋52	3♍25
	27	7♊11	29 48	10♌ 6	28 41
	29	5♋51	...	6♍24	23♎ 8
	31	4♌16	...	1♎49	...

d.		MAY	JUN	JUL	AUG
☽	1	17♏ 3	1♑28	4♒56	22♓56
	3	10♐44	25 34	0♓ 1	19♈43
	5	4♑28	20♒18	25 55	17♉22
	7	28 39	16♓ 2	22♈56	15♊55
	9	23♒47	13♈10	21♉17	15♋ 5
	11	20♓21	11♉57	20♊50	14♌ 6
	13	18♈39	12♊ 1	20♋48	12♍ 8
	15	18♉27	12♋22	19♌59	8♎37
	17	18♊51	11♌40	17♍31	3♏37
	19	18♋34	9♍ 8	13♎15	27 39
	21	16♌43	4♎48	7♏39	21♐22
	23	13♍ 6	29 10	1♐23	15♑25
	25	8♎ 5	22♏54	25 7	10♒15
	27	2♏11	16♐33	19♑18	6♓ 4
	29	25 54	10♑29	14♒12	2♈49
	31	19♐34	...	9♓50	0♉17

d.		SEP	OCT	NOV	DEC
☽	1	14♉14	23♊27	16♌24	23♍ 9
	3	12♊27	21♋47	13♍ 9	18♎25
	5	10♋54	19♌28	8♎51	12♏49
	7	9♌15	16♍20	3♏43	6♐46
	9	7♍ 1	12♎18	27 58	0♑30
	11	3♎43	7♏20	21♐49	24 15
	13	29 11	1♐35	15♑30	18♒15
	15	23♏35	25 21	9♒27	12♓54
	17	17♐24	19♑ 9	4♓11	8♈45
	19	11♑14	13♒32	0♈19	6♉19
	21	5♒42	9♓ 6	28 14	5♊46
	23	1♓16	6♈14	27♉52	6♋23
	25	28 9	4♉53	28♊16	6♌46
	27	26♈ 8	4♊27	28♋ 9	5♍37
	29	24♉46	3♋56	26♌31	2♎29
	31	...	2 33	...	27 42

STATIONS	☿	♀	♂	♃
	23Mar 16♓24	None	None	21Sep 1♊27
	15Apr 4♈31			...
				...
		♄	♅	♆
	26Jul 23♌ 5	25Jan 12♎47	15Feb 10♏44	17Feb 8♊30
	19Aug 11♌ 7	10Jun 6♎ 1	15Jul 6♏38	16Sep 13♊34
	16Nov 12♐56	SIDER. TIME		1 Jan
	6Dec 26♏43	6h 43m 28s		Midn.
		18h 45m 26s		Noon
		Common Year		1893

Noon		JAN	FEB	MAR	APR	MAY	JUN
☉	1	11♑ 7	12♒40	10♓55	11♈45	11♉ 4	10♊56
	9	19 17	20 46	11 56	19 37	18 49	18 35
	17	27 25	28 51	26 54	27 27	26 32	26 14
	25	5♒34	6♓54	4♈50	5♉15	4♊13	3♋51
☿	1	25♐ 7	14♒53	28♓13	16♓42	21♈33	24♊40
	7	4♑ 6	25 36	28R43	20 21	2♉21	5♋43
	13	13 21	6♓27	24 36	26 5	14 14	15 12
	19	22 53	16 44	19 8	3♈22	27 5	23 0
	25	2♒49	24 58	15 59	11 53	10♊10	29 0
	31	13 5	...	16D19	...	22 41	...
♀	1	25♒17	5♓ 0	21♒ 1	28♒56	24♓57	27♈56
	9	0♓30	1R48	19R54	4♓52	3♈ 7	6♉53
	17	4 9	27♒ 2	21D14	11 40	11 33	15 57
	25	5 43	22 32	24 40	19 5	20 11	25 7
♂	1	0♐19	21♐34	11♑ 2	2♒54	24♒ 4	15♓34
	13	8 30	29 52	19 29	11 22	2♓29	23 36
	25	16 44	8♑16	27 56	19 50	10 47	1♈25
♃	1	21♉47	21♉56	24♉40	29♉49	6♊ 5	13♊11
	13	21R26	22 50	26 27	2♊12	8 47	15 58
	25	21D36	24 7	28 31	4 46	11 34	18 45
♄	1	24♎17	25♎11	24♎34	22♎37	20♎21	18♎44
	13	24 49	25R 5	23R56	21R43	19R35	18R27
	25	25 7	24 44	23 9	20 47	19 0	18D25
♅	1	14♏21	15♏13	15♏17	14♏37	13♏26	12♏12
	13	14 46	15 20	15R 7	14R 9	12R57	11R49
	25	15 7	15R19	14 50	13 41	12 27	11 31
♆	1	11♊24	10♊51	10♊48	11♊13	12♊ 5	13♊10
	13	11R 8	10R46	10 54	11 31	12 30	13 37
	25	10 57	10D46	11 5	11 52	12 55	14 3
Pl.	1	9♊ 9	8♊49	8♊45	9♊ 1	9♊31	10♊13
☊	1	15♈ 9	13♈31	12♈ 2	10♈23	3♈48	7♈ 9
	1st	Mon	Thu	Thu	Sun	Tue	Fri

Noon		JUL	AUG	SEP	OCT	NOV	DEC
☉	1	9♋35	9♌10	9♍ 0	8♎17	9♏ 5	9♐20
	9	17 13	16 50	16 46	16 11	17 6	17 27
	17	24 50	24 31	24 34	24 7	25 10	25 35
	25	2♌29	2♍14	2♎24	2♏ 5	3♐15	3♑44
☿	1	2♌52	23♋36	7♍18	27♎51	26♏54	19♏47
	7	4R 9	26 10	18 40	5♏12	22R37	27 50
	13	2 43	2♌35	29 22	13 51	14 57	6♐34
	19	29♋ 9	12 8	9♎28	20 28	11 2	15 37
	25	25 17	23 32	18 56	25 21	13D28	24 49
	31	23 35	5♍20	...	27R 2	...	4♑12
♀	1	2♊ 5	8♋37	16♌ 6	23♍ 5	1♏50	9♐32
	9	11 24	18 11	25 54	3♎ 3	11 52	19 36
	17	20 47	27 49	5♍44	13 2	21 55	29 39
	25	0♋15	7♌33	15 39	23 3	2♐ 0	9♑44
♂	1	5♈10	22♈32	3♉36	3♉20	24♈ 2	21♈58
	13	12 23	27 50	5 0	29♈58	21R47	24 16
	25	19 0	1♉55	4R24	26R 3	21D28	27 53
♃	1	20♊ 4	26♊41	2♋ 6	5♋29	6♋14	4♋ 3
	13	22 44	28 57	3 43	6 8	5R41	2R34
	25	25 16	1♋ 1	4 59	6 21	4 41	0 56
♄	1	18♎29	19♎46	22♎21	25♎40	29♎23	2♏48
	13	18 51	20 38	23 36	27 5	0♏48	4 1
	25	19 22	21 41	24 57	28 33	2 10	5 3
♅	1	11♏24	11♏19	12♏ 5	13♏26	15♏16	17♏ 7
	13	11R17	11 32	12 34	14 5	16 1	17 48
	25	11D15	11 51	13 7	14 50	16 45	18 24
♆	1	14♊16	15♊12	15♊44	15♊46	15♊20	14♊32
	13	14 40	15 28	15 49	15R39	15R 2	14R12
	25	15 1	15 39	15R49	15 27	14 43	13 52
Pl.	1	10♊52	11♊24	11♊39	11♊35	11♊15	10♊43
☊	1	5♈34	3♈55	2♈17	0♈42	29♓ 3	27♓28
	1st	Sun	Wed	Sat	Mon	Thu	Sat

d.		JAN	FEB	MAR	APR
☽	1	9♏53	24♐17	2♑30	16♒22
	3	3♐48	18♑ 2	26 19	11♓17
	5	27 29	12♒10	20♒39	7♈23
	7	21♑17	6♓51	15♓48	4♉39
	9	15♒20	2♈11	11♈49	2♊49
	11	9♓51	28 20	8♉41	1♋22
	13	5♈ 6	25♉31	6♊19	29 50
	15	1♉33	23♊54	4♋34	27♌53
	17	29 36	23♋15	3♌13	25♍17
	19	29♊13	22♌48	1♍47	21♎52
	21	29♋37	21♍32	29 43	17♏33
	23	29♌26	18♎44	26♎32	12♐20
	25	27♍35	14♏19	22♏ 4	6♑24
	27	23♎49	8♐42	16♐32	0♒11
	29	18♏33	...	10♑24	24 14
	31	12♐27	...	4♒15	...

d.		MAY	JUN	JUL	AUG
☽	1	19♓11	7♉27	14♊51	8♌56
	3	15♈33	6♊29	15♋14	8♍56
	5	13♉27	6♋34	15♌36	7♎25
	7	12♊31	6♌27	14♍42	4♏ 5
	9	11♋54	5♍ 8	12♎ 0	29 14
	11	10♌44	2♎17	7♏45	23♐27
	13	8♍32	28 8	2♐25	17♑14
	15	5♎17	23♏ 4	26 29	11♒ 1
	17	1♏ 7	17♐25	20♑16	5♓ 2
	19	26 13	11♑22	14♒ 2	29 31
	21	20♐40	5♒ 7	7♓58	24♈44
	23	14♑38	28 55	2♈25	21♉ 1
	25	8♒22	3♓14	27 51	18♊39
	27	2♓22	18♈40	24♉49	17♋39
	29	27 14	15♉48	23♊33	17♌30
	31	23♈35	...	23♋41	17♍ 9

d.		SEP	OCT	NOV	DEC
☽	1	1♎34	7♏11	23♐35	25♐51
	3	29 14	3♐13	17♑52	19♒32
	5	25♏14	27 59	11♒37	13♓17
	7	19♐56	21♑56	5♓28	7♈48
	9	13♑52	15♒41	0♈ 5	3♉46
	11	7♒37	9♓51	26 0	1♊34
	13	1♓39	4♈51	23♉24	0♋52
	15	26 16	0♉58	21♊56	0♌43
	17	21♈41	28 7	20♋52	29 59
	19	17♉59	26♊ 1	19♌29	28♍ 1
	21	15♊12	24♋17	17♍24	24♎50
	23	13♋20	22♌38	14♎35	20♏41
	25	12♌10	20♍47	11♏ 3	15♐47
	27	11♍12	18♎27	6♐47	10♑15
	29	9♎45	15♏19	1♑42	4♒12
	31	...	11♐ 6	...	27 49

STATIONS	☿	♀	♂	♃
	6Mar 29♓ 0	27Jan 5♓43	16Sep 5♉ 3	17Jan 21♉26
	28Mar 15♓13	10Mar 19♒55	22Nov 21♈22	26Nov 6♋21
		♄	♅	♆
	7Jul 4♌ 9	6Feb 25♎10	19Feb 15R20	19Feb 10♊45
	1Aug 23♋36	23Jun 18♎25	21Jul 11♏15	20Sep 15♊40
	31Oct 27♏ 2	SIDER. TIME		1 Jan
	20Nov 11♏ 3	6h 42m 31s		Midn.
		18h 44m 29s		Noon.
		Common Year		1894

1895

Noon		JAN	FEB	MAR	APR	MAY	JUN
☉	1	10♑53	12♒25	10♓41	11♈31	10♉50	10♊42
	9	19 2	20 32	18 41	19 23	18 35	18 21
	17	27 10	28 36	26 39	27 12	26 18	25 60
	25	5♒19	6♓40	4♈36	5♉ 1	3♊59	3♋38
☿	1	5♑47	27♒35	2♓ 7	15♓ 7	6♉43	4♋ 2
	7	15 24	6♓24	28♒14	23 29	19 37	9 57
	13	25 13	11 45	28D15	2♈49	2♊29	13 32
	19	5♒23	11R29	1♓26	13 9	14 19	14R30
	25	15 46	6 12	6 52	24 28	24 30	12 53
	31	25 57	...	13 50	...	2♋51	...
♀	1	18♑31	27♒25	2♈18	10♉22	16♊21	22♋12
	9	28 36	7♓25	12 12	20 3	25 45	1♌ 8
	17	8♒39	17 23	22 1	29 40	5♋ 4	9 52
	25	18 39	27 19	1♉50	9♊13	14 18	18 22
♂	1	0♉28	14♉40	29♉47	17♊42	5♋36	24♋23
	13	5 31	20 58	6♊38	24 49	12 51	1♌44
	25	11 10	27 34	13 35	1♋59	20 7	9 8
♃	1	0♋ 1	26♊51	26♊26	28♊47	3♋19	9♋23
	13	28♊31	26R22	27 0	0♋23	5 32	11 56
	25	27R21	26D20	28 1	2 17	7 56	14 36
♄	1	5♏37	7♏ 6	7♏ 5	5♏37	3♏24	1♏24
	13	6 22	7 15	6R40	4R46	2R33	0R54
	25	6 54	7R11	6 3	3 52	1 46	0 37
♅	1	18♏44	19♏45	19♏56	19♏21	18♏14	16♏59
	13	19 13	19 55	19R48	18R58	17R45	16R34
	25	19 35	19R57	19 33	18 29	17 15	16 14
♆	1	13♊42	13♊ 9	13♊ 2	13♊25	14♊14	15♊20
	13	13R27	13R 2	13 6	13 42	14 39	15 47
	25	13 13	13D 2	13 16	14 2	15 4	16 14
Pl.	1	10♊10	9♊50	9♊44	10 0	10♊30	11♊ 9
☊	1	25♓49	24♓11	22♓42	21♓ 3	19♓28	17♓50
	1st	Tue	Fri	Fri	Mon	Wed	Sat

Noon		JUL	AUG	SEP	OCT	NOV	DEC
☉	1	9♋21	8♌57	8♍46	8♎ 3	8♏50	9♐ 5
	9	16 59	16 36	16 32	15 57	16 52	17 12
	17	24 36	24 17	24 20	23 52	24 55	25 21
	25	2♌15	2♍ 0	2♎10	1♏50	3♐ 0	3♑30
☿	1	9♋31	22♋36	21♍51	3♏39	25♎53	28♏34
	7	6R19	3♌43	1♎43	8 41	26D28	7♐53
	13	5D13	15 53	10 52	11 5	2♏ 8	17 16
	19	7 16	27 57	19 19	9R14	10 15	26 42
	25	12 36	9♍26	27 1	2 48	19 16	6♑16
	31	20 57	20 9	...	26♎27	...	15 58
♀	1	24♌32	22♍23	3♎46	19♍35	26♍ 3	22♎20
	9	2♍30	27 39	1R28	17R59	1♎55	0♏45
	17	10 0	1♎34	27♍ 8	18D53	8 47	9 29
	25	16 54	3 45	22 21	21 58	16 19	18 28
♂	1	12♌50	2♍ 8	21♍46	11♎17	1♏57	22♏32
	13	20 13	9 41	29 32	19 12	10 7	0♐56
	25	27 44	17 20	7 20	27 13	18 22	9 25
♃	1	15♋58	22♋52	29♋23	4♌39	8♌13	9♌ 6
	13	18 39	25 27	1♌37	6 17	8 55	8R38
	25	21 18	27 58	3 42	7 37	9 9	7 43
♄	1	0♏35	1♏12	3♏15	6♏15	9♏52	13♏26
	13	0D38	1 50	4 21	7 37	11 18	14 42
	25	0 55	2 41	5 36	9 1	12 44	15 54
♅	1	16♏ 5	15♏54	16♏31	17♏47	19♏33	21♏25
	13	15R56	16 2	16 57	18R25	20 18	22 6
	25	15D51	16 18	17 29	19 7	21 3	22 45
♆	1	16♊26	17♊25	17♊58	18♊ 3	17♊39	16♊52
	13	16 50	17 42	18 4	17 57	17R22	16R32
	25	17 13	17 54	18R 5	17 46	17 3	16 13
Pl.	1	11♊49	12♊20	12♊37	12♊34	12♊14	11 43
☊	1	16♓14	14♓36	12♓57	11♓22	9♓43	8♓ 8
	1st	Mon	Thu	Sun	Tue	Fri	Sun

d.		JAN	FEB	MAR	APR
☽	1	9♓37	24♈44	4♉14	23♊41
	3	3♈35	20♉22	29 58	21♋23
	5	28 35	17♊44	27♊ 5	20♌ 2
	7	25♉18	16♋56	25♋42	19♍16
	9	23♊59	17♌20	25♌30	18♎25
	11	24♋ 8	17♍40	25♍33	16♏41
	13	24♌31	16♎44	24♎46	13♐30
	15	23♍51	14♏ 2	22♏23	8♑49
	17	21♎34	9♐42	18♐17	2♒59
	19	17♏45	4♑12	12♑51	26 38
	21	12♐50	28 4	6♒39	20♓26
	23	7♑10	21♒42	0♓16	14♈56
	25	1♒ 4	15♓25	24♓10	10♉25
	27	24 43	9♈30	18♈40	6♊56
	29	18♓22	...	13♉59	4♋18
	31	12♈25	...	10♊12	...

d.		MAY	JUN	JUL	AUG
☽	1	2♌14	25♍32	3♏47	23♐ 1
	3	0♍32	23♎18	0♐20	17♑58
	5	28 59	20♏30	26 5	11♒56
	7	27♎17	16♐57	21♑ 0	5♓38
	9	24♏56	12♑25	15♒11	29 13
	11	21♐28	6♒53	8♓52	23♈ 6
	13	16♑42	0♓40	2♈30	17♉51
	15	10♒53	24 20	26 43	14♊ 0
	17	4♓34	18♈34	22♉11	11♋57
	19	28 25	14♉ 3	19♊23	11♌30
	21	23♈ 8	11♊ 9	18♋16	11♍49
	23	19♉ 7	9♋42	18♌10	11♎42
	25	16♊26	8♌57	17♍55	10♏14
	27	14♋38	8♍ 2	16♎41	7♐ 7
	29	13♌ 9	6♎22	14♏ 7	2♑33
	31	11♍30	...	10♐19	26 59

d.		SEP	OCT	NOV	DEC
☽	1	8♒57	11♎21	25♈50	29♉38
	3	2♓38	5♈ 5	20♉53	26♊19
	5	26 14	29 16	16♊47	23♋49
	7	20♈ 6	24♉ 7	13♋29	21♌44
	9	14♉31	19♊50	10♌53	19♍51
	11	9♊56	16♋34	9♍ 0	18♎ 2
	13	6♋44	14♌31	7♎45	16♏ 7
	15	5♌ 8	13♍38	6♏44	13♐42
	17	4♍54	13♎23	5♐ 9	10♑20
	19	5♎10	12♏51	2♑19	5♒43
	21	4♏46	11♐ 0	27 55	0♓ 0
	23	2♐48	7♑25	22♒15	23 40
	25	29 3	2♒17	15♓54	17♈24
	27	23♑51	26 9	9♈38	11♉55
	29	17♒46	19♓44	4♉ 5	7♊44
	31	...	13♈38	...	5♋ 1

STATIONS	☿	♀	♂	♃
	17Feb 12♓15	28Aug 3♎59	None	21Feb 26♊17
	11Mar 27♒51	11Oct 17♍59		27Nov 9♌ 9
		♄	♅	♆
	19Jun 14♋30	15Feb 7♏15	24Feb 19♏57	23Feb 13♊ 1
	13Jul 5♋13	6Jul 0♏34	25Jul 15♏51	22Sep 18♊ 5
	15Oct 11♏ 0	SIDER. TIME		1 Jan
	4Nov 25♎24	6h 41m 34s		Midn.
		18h 43m 32s		Noon
		Common Year		1895

1896

Noon		JAN	FEB	MAR	APR	MAY	JUN
☉	1	10♑38	12♒11	11♓27	12♈16	11♉35	11♊26
	9	18 47	20 17	19 27	20 8	19 19	19 5
	17	26 56	28 22	27 25	27 57	27 2	26 43
	25	5♒ 4	6♓26	5♈21	5♉45	4♊43	4♋21
☿	1	17♑35	25♒42	14♒34	26♓10	26♉13	24♊10
	7	27 26	20R59	20 12	7♈ 4	6♊36	21R48
	13	7♒16	14 16	27 18	18 51	14 52	18 31
	19	16 28	10 45	5♓29	1♉24	20 42	16 13
	25	23 30	11D31	14 33	14 9	23 56	16D17
	31	25 56	...	24 27	...	24R21	...
♀	1	26♏32	3♑14	8♒26	16♓19	23♈ 4	1♊ 4
	9	5♐50	12 52	18 11	26 6	2♉53	10 52
	17	15 17	22 34	27 58	5♈55	12 41	20 41
	25	24 48	2♒18	7♓45	15 43	22 29	0♋29
♂	1	14♐25	6♑59	28♑30	21♒57	14♓57	8♈ 4
	13	23 4	15 51	7♒36	1♓ 4	23 50	16 53
	25	1♑49	24 46	16 39	10 12	2♈52	25 36
♃	1	7♌ 1	3♌ 7	29♋58	29♋10	1♌13	5♌36
	13	5R35	1R36	29R18	29 40	2 41	7 40
	25	4 0	0 21	29 5	0♉36	4 25	9 58
♄	1	16♏33	18♏33	19♏ 6	18♏ 9	16♏ 9	13♏57
	13	17 30	18 58	18R55	17R26	15R15	13R17
	25	18 12	19 7	18 29	16 35	14 23	12 46
♅	1	23♏ 5	24♏11	24♏32	24♏ 1	23♏ 0	21♏42
	13	23 36	24 26	24R26	23R39	22R29	21R18
	25	24 0	24 32	24 12	23 14	21 59	20 55
♆	1	16♊ 0	15♊24	15♊16	15♊38	16♊26	17♊32
	13	15R44	15R18	15 21	15 57	16 50	17 58
	25	15 30	15D15	15 30	16 16	17 15	18 25
Pl.	1	11♊11	10♊50	10♊43	10♊58	11♊28	12♊ 8
☊	1	6♓30	4♓51	3♓19	1♓40	0♓ 5	28♒26
1st		Wed	Sat	Sun	Wed	Fri	Mon

Noon		JUL	AUG	SEP	OCT	NOV	DEC
☉	1	10♋ 4	9♌40	9♍30	8♎48	9♏35	9♐51
	9	17 42	17 20	17 16	16 42	17 38	17 59
	17	25 20	25 1	25 4	24 38	25 41	26 7
	25	2♌58	2♍44	2♎54	2♏35	3♐46	4♑16
☿	1	19♊12	10♌32	3♎40	23♎25	23♎47	11♐22
	7	24 55	22 33	11 17	17R40	3♏11	20 47
	13	3♋13	3♍45	17 45	11 15	12 49	0♑14
	19	13 45	14 6	22 34	9D49	22 26	9 43
	25	25 50	23 36	24 56	14 19	1♐57	19 6
	31	8♌28	2♎18	...	22 16	...	28 4
♀	1	7♋52	16♌ 2	24♍17	1♏22	9♐34	16♑17
	9	17 41	25 52	4♎10	11 15	19 23	25 58
	17	27 31	5♍44	14 5	21 7	29 10	5♒41
	25	7♌27	15 39	23 57	0♐59	8♑58	15 14
♂	1	29♈51	20♉53	9♊25	23♊10	29♊25	23♊31
	13	8♉13	28 28	15 33	26 51	28R30	18R54
	25	16 18	5♊32	20 54	29 0	25 33	14 47
♃	1	11♌11	17♌41	24♌26	0♍37	5♍57	9♍19
	13	13 38	20 18	27 0	2 51	7 34	9 59
	25	16 13	22 56	29 27	4 52	8 51	10 13
♄	1	12♏37	12♏41	14♏13	16♏52	20♏20	23♏52
	13	12R27	13 6	15 9	18 8	21 44	25 15
	25	12D31	13 45	16 16	19 31	23 12	26 33
♅	1	20♏47	20♏28	20♏58	22♏ 9	23♏51	25♏44
	13	20R34	20 34	21 22	22 48	24 37	26 28
	25	20 29	20 46	21 52	23 28	25 21	27 8
♆	1	18♊37	19♊36	20♊11	20♊18	19♊53	19♊10
	13	19 2	19 53	20 17	20R13	19R37	18R50
	25	19 24	20 6	20R19	20 2	19 19	18 30
Pl.	1	12♊47	13♊19	13♊35	13♊34	13♊13	12♊ 4
☊	1	26♒51	25♒13	23♒34	21♒59	20♒20	18♒45
1st		Wed	Sat	Tue	Thu	Sun	Tue

	d.	JAN	FEB	MAR	APR
☽	1	19♋ 6	11♏36	5♎ 9	28♏ 3
	3	17♌46	11♎ 1	4♎54	25♐53
	5	16♍32	9♏29	3♐12	21♑51
	7	14♎54	6♐44	29 50	16♒25
	9	12♏40	2♑50	25♑ 5	10♓13
	11	9♐46	28 0	19♒23	3♈47
	13	6♑ 4	22♒24	13♓10	27 32
	15	1♒28	16♓16	6♈47	21♉42
	17	25 58	9£53	0♊30	16♊29
	19	19♓47	3♉37	24 37	12♋ 5
	21	13♈22	27 59	19♊32	8♌50
	23	7♉22	10♊34	15♋40	6♍59
	25	2♊24	20♋50	13♌26	6♎29
	27	29 1	19♌50	12♍51	6♏39
	29	27♋18	19♍59	13♎16	6♐16
	31	26♌44	...	13♏27	...

	d.	MAY	JUN	JUL	AUG
☽	1	4♑17	20♒59	23♓ 4	6♉39
	3	0♒25	15♓ 9	16♈48	0♊55
	5	25 2	8♈50	10♉44	26 16
	7	18♓48	2♉41	5♊26	23♋ 3
	9	12♈25	27 12	1♋18	21♌13
	11	6♉21	22♊38	28 19	20♍18
	13	0♊55	18♋59	26♌14	19♎31
	15	26 12	16♌ 5	24♍38	18♏10
	17	22♋15	13♍48	23♎ 5	15♐53
	19	19♌ 9	12♎ 3	21♏20	12♑33
	21	17♍ 3	10♏40	19♐ 5	8♒16
	23	15♎57	9♐13	16♑ 2	3♓ 8
	25	15♏24	20♐31	11♒59	27 19
	27	14♐30	16♒25	6♓55	21♈ 6
	29	12♑20	11♓ 4	1♈ 1	14♉50
	31	8♒29	...	24 45	9♊ 3

	d.	SEP	OCT	NOV	DEC
☽	1	21♊30	25♋49	16♍11	24♎42
	3	17♋38	23♌14	15♎48	24♏35
	5	15♌ 7	22♍28	16♏19	24♐17
	7	14♍20	22♎55	16♐20	22♑40
	9	14♎22	23♏12	14♑42	19♒15
	11	14♏ 5	22♐10	11♒ 5	14♓14
	13	12♐35	19♑15	5♓56	8♈15
	15	9♐33	14♒43	29 53	1♉57
	17	5♒13	9♓ 6	23♈31	25 54
	19	29 55	2♈57	17♉24	20♊27
	21	24♓ 2	26 40	11♊37	15♋44
	23	17♈50	20♉29	6♋22	11♌47
	25	11♉33	14♊35	1♉46	8♍35
	27	5♊29	9♋16	28 6	6♎14
	29	0♋ 3	4♉54	25♍43	4♏42
	31	...	1♍59	...	3♐42

STATIONS	☿	♀	♂	♃
	1Feb 25♒42	None	2Nov 29♊25	26Mar 29♋ 5
	22Feb 10♒39		... ...	27Dec 10♍13
	30May 24♊28	♄ 28Feb 19♏ 7	♅ 28Feb 24♐32	♆ 25Feb 15♊15
	23Jun 15♊57	17Jul 12♏27	29Jul 20♏28	25Sep 20♊19
	27Sep 24♎54	SIDER TIME		1 Jan
	18Oct 9♎36	6h 40m 37s		Midn.
		18h 42m 35s		Noon.
		LEAP YEAR		1896

1897

Noon		JAN	FEB	MAR	APR	MAY	JUN
☉	1	11♑24	12♒57	11♓12	12♈ 1	11♉20	11♊12
	9	19 34	21 3	19 12	19 53	19 5	18 51
	17	27 42	29 8	27 11	27 43	26 48	26 29
	25	5♒50	7♓11	5♈ 6	5♉31	4♊29	4♋ 7
☿	1	29♑28	24♑ 8	17♒50	11♈21	1♊34	25♉59
	7	6♒40	24D50	26 39	23 46	4 23	26 45
	13	9 48	28 54	6♓13	6♉ 3	4R 8	0♊ 9
	19	6R34	5♒ 2	16 29	17 1	1 31	5D56
	25	29♑15	12 25	27 31	25 40	28♉12	13 56
	31	24 26	...	9♈19	...	26 6	...
♀	1	23♒32	28♓59	27♈ 6	16♉16	6♉58	3♉13
	9	2♓55	7♈35	3♉49	16R53	2R44	7 22
	17	12 11	5♒ 2	9 30	14 55	0 38	12 47
	25	21 14	23 30	13 54	10 44	1D 2	19 9
♂	1	13♊ 4	13♊ 7	21♊18	5♋ 1	20♋33	8♌ 1
	13	11R39	15 56	26 12	11 3	27 11	15 1
	25	12D 7	19 49	1♋38	17 21	4♌ 2	22 5
♃	1	10♍ 9	8♍ 1	4♍29	1♍ 9	0♍15	2♍ 6
	13	9R40	6R35	3R 0	0R28	0 39	3 30
	25	8 44	5 0	1 43	0 12	1 28	5 10
♄	1	27♏14	29♏42	0♐43	0♐22	28♏43	26♏27
	13	28 18	0♐18	0R46	29♏49	27 51	25R38
	25	29 13	0 39	0 35	29 7	26 58	24 58
♅	1	27♏28	28♏39	29♏ 3	28♏42	27♏43	26♏27
	13	28 0	28 56	29R 0	28R22	27R14	25R59
	25	28 27	29 2	28 51	27 57	26 44	25 35
♆	1	18♊19	17♊41	17♊31	17♊51	18♊37	19♊40
	13	18R 1	17R34	17 35	18 16	18 59	20 5
	25	17 48	17 31	17 44	18 26	19 25	20 32
Pl.	1	12♊ 9	11♊47	11♊43	11♊56	12♊25	13♊ 5
☊	1	17♒ 7	15♒29	14♒ 0	12♒21	10♒45	9♒ 7
		Fri	Mon	Mon	Thu	Sat	Tue

Noon		JUL	AUG	SEP	OCT	NOV	DEC
☉	1	9♋50	9♌26	9♍16	8♎34	9♏21	9♐37
	9	17 28	17 6	17 2	16 27	17 23	17 44
	17	25 6	24 47	24 50	24 23	25 27	25 52
	25	2♌44	2♍30	2♎40	2♏21	3♐32	4♑ 2
☿	1	23♊55	25♌59	5♎38	23♍37	5♏12	22♐23
	7	5♋40	5♍56	8 16	26 32	14 58	1♑27
	13	18 23	14 54	7R31	3♎57	24 32	10 8
	19	1♌ 8	22 53	2 56	13 26	3♐55	17 49
	25	13 11	29 40	26♍38	23 31	13 13	23 0
	31	24 14	4♎57	...	3♏32	...	22R58
♀	1	24♉24	25♊27	0♌14	5♍51	13♎53	21♏20
	9	1♊52	4♋12	9 36	15 33	23 49	1♐23
	17	9 46	13 7	19 2	25 20	3♏48	11 24
	25	18 1	22 11	28 36	5♎12	13 49	21 28
♂	1	25♌41	14♍40	4♎24	24♎10	15♏22	6♐42
	13	2♍57	22 13	12 14	2♏16	23 49	15 25
	25	10 20	29 54	20 10	10 31	2♐22	24 16
♃	1	6♍ 7	11♍42	4♎24	24♎10	0♎57	6♎ 3
	13	8 9	14 8	20 44	27 7	3 9	7 38
	25	10 21	16 38	23 19	29 35	5 9	8 54
♄	1	24♏42	24♏ 8	25♏ 7	27♏22	0♐34	4♐ 4
	13	24R19	24 21	25 52	28 29	1 56	5 28
	25	24 8	24 45	26 50	29 47	3 21	6 49
♅	1	25♏26	24♏59	25♏21	26♏27	28♏ 6	29♏57
	13	25R11	25 4	25 43	27 3	28 50	0♐40
	25	25 2	25 13	26 12	27 43	29 35	1 21
♆	1	20♊46	21♊46	22♊24	22♊34	22♊12	21♊27
	13	21 11	22 4	22 33	22R29	21R55	21R 8
	25	21 34	22 17	22 34	22 18	21 37	20 48
Pl.	1	13♊44	14♊16	14♊27	14♊28	14♊12	13♊41
☊	1	7♒32	5♒53	4♒15	2♒39	1♒ 1	29♑26
		Thu	Sun	Wed	Fri	Mon	Wed

d.	JAN	FEB	MAR	APR
☽ 1	18♐12	8♒46	17♒51	4♈26
3	16♑40	4♓49	13♓14	28 30
5	13♒54	29 47	7♈54	22♉16
7	9♓39	23♈56	1♉57	16♊ 1
9	4♈11	17♉42	25 41	10♋10
11	28 2	11♊41	19♊36	5♌20
13	21♉51	6♋30	14♋18	2♍ 8
15	16♊12	2♌36	10♌23	0♎50
17	11♋29	0♍ 8	8♍13	1♏ 3
19	7♌49	28 46	7♎35	1♐32
21	5♍ 7	27♎49	7♏33	0♑55
23	3♎ 4	26♏35	6♐59	28 33
25	1♏23	24♐33	5♑ 7	24♒32
27	29 44	8♑13	1♒51	19♓22
29	27♐51	4♒51	27 26	13♈31
31	25♑21	...	22♓15	...

d.	MAY	JUN	JUL	AUG
☽ 1	7♉22	22♊ 1	25♋36	14♍19
3	1♊ 6	16♋16	21♌ 1	11♎36
5	24 55	11♌10	17♍20	9♏44
7	19♋10	7♍ 3	14♎44	8♐16
9	14♌17	4♎22	13♏14	6♑49
11	10♍52	3♏15	12♐30	4♒58
13	9♎18	3♐15	11♑48	2♓14
15	9♏22	3♑17	10♒19	28 21
17	9♐58	2♒12	7♓25	23♈18
19	9♑42	29 22	3♈ 1	17♉23
21	7♒38	24♓54	27 28	11♊ 9
23	3♓45	19♈16	21♉ 9	5♋13
25	28 32	13♉ 4	15♊ 9	0♌ 9
27	22♈32	6♊50	9♋28	26 20
29	16♉16	0♋56	4♌36	23♍47
31	10♊ 3	...	0♍43	22♎ 7

d.	SEP	OCT	NOV	DEC
☽ 1	6♏27	15♐49	8♒ 0	13♓58
3	5♐ 2	14♑ 1	4♓22	9♈ 6
5	3♑14	11♒ 8	29 41	3♉24
7	0♒50	7♓19	24♈17	27 15
9	27 45	2♈46	18♉23	20♊57
11	23♓51	27 31	12♊ 9	14♋43
13	19♈ 3	21♉40	5♋47	8♌50
15	13♉24	15♊23	29 42	3♍42
17	7♊12	9♋ 5	24♌27	29 49
19	0♋59	3♌23	20♍43	27♎35
21	25 24	28 59	18♎54	27♏ 0
23	21♌ 5	26♍25	18♏49	27♐19
25	18♍24	25♎40	19♐25	27♑20
27	2♎40	25♏52	19♑16	25♒56
29	1♏55	25♐45	17♒29	22♓45
31	1♐20	24♑18	...	18♈ 0

STATIONS	☿	♀	♂	♃
	14Jan 9♒45	8Apr 16♉56	17Jan 11♊17	27Apr 0♍12
	4Feb 23♑57	21May 0♉32	... ...	... ...
	10Jan 4♊36	♄	♅	♆
	3Jul 25♊56	13Mar 0♐46	2Mar 29♐ 3	27Feb 17♊31
	10Sep 8♎22	29Jul 24♐ 7	1Aug 24♐59	30Sep 22♊34
	1Oct 23♍37	SIDER. TIME		1 Jan
	29Dec 23♑43	6h 43m 37s		Midn.
		18h 45m 35s		Noon.
		Common Year		1897.

Noon		JAN	FEB	MAR	APR	MAY	JUN
☉	1	11♑10	12♒42	10♓58	11♈47	11♉ 6	10♊58
	9	19 19	20 49	18 58	19 39	18 51	18 37
	17	27 28	28 53	26 56	27 29	26 34	26 15
	25	5♒36	6♓57	4♈52	5♉17	4♊15	3♋53
☿	1	22♑18	17♑49	28♒19	27♈12	11♉ 0	16♉51
	7	15R20	25 9	8♓48	6♉29	7R27	24 43
	13	8 58	3♒21	19 58	12 40	5 41	4♊19
	19	7D49	12 12	1♈45	15 14	6D35	15 30
	25	11 0	21 40	13 51	14R18	10 3	28 0
	31	16 42	...	25 25	...	15 43	...
♀	1	0♑16	9♒13	14♓17	22♈51	29♉49	7♋32
	9	10 19	19 15	24 16	2♉45	9♊35	17 11
	17	20 22	29 17	4♈14	12 37	19 21	26 47
	25	0♒26	9♓17	14 11	22 27	29 4	6♌21
♂	1	29♐30	22♑59	14♒38	8♓48	2♈ 3	25♈37
	13	8♑31	2♒13	23 59	18 8	11 15	4♉31
	25	17 37	11 31	3♓20	27 26	20 22	13 17
♃	1	9♎27	10♎11	8♎19	4♎33	1♎21	0♎23
	13	10 6	9R40	6R58	3R 6	0R38	0 46
	25	10R17	8 43	5 27	1 51	0 21	1 34
♄	1	7♐35	10♐25	11♐56	12♐11	10♐59	8♐50
	13	8 47	11 12	12 13	11R51	10R13	7R58
	25	9 51	11 47	12R16	11 19	9 21	7 10
♅	1	1♐43	3♐ 0	3♐32	3♐19	2♐24	1♐ 9
	13	2 18	3 19	3R32	3R 0	1R56	0R41
	25	2 47	3 30	3 26	2 37	1 26	0 15
♆	1	20♊36	19♊56	19♊44	20♊ 2	20♊46	21♊49
	13	20R18	19R49	19 47	20 16	21 9	22 16
	25	20 3	19 44	19 55	20 35	21 34	22 42
Pl.	1	13♊ 8	12♊45	12♊40	12♊53	12♊22	12♊ 2
☊	1	27♑47	26♑ 9	24♑40	23♑ 1	21♑26	19♑47
	1st	Sat	Tue	Tue	Fri	Sun	Wed

Noon		JUL	AUG	SEP	OCT	NOV	DEC
☉	1	9♋37	9♌12	9♍ 2	8♎19	9♏ 7	9♐22
	9	17 14	16 52	16 48	16 13	17 8	17 29
	17	24 52	24 33	24 36	24 9	25 12	25 38
	25	2♌31	2♍16	2♎26	2♏ 7	3♐17	3♑47
☿	1	11♋ 3	5♍20	17♍ 7	24♍48	17♏ 5	0♑15
	7	23 44	12 15	11R24	5♎16	26 21	6 1
	13	5♌28	17 36	7 39	15 48	5♐24	7R50
	19	16 7	20 49	9D 1	26 3	14 12	3 21
	25	25 39	21R 8	15 25	5♏56	22 37	25♐30
	31	4♍ 3	17 57	...	15 31	...	21 41
♀	1	13♌29	19♍44	24♎19	24♏24	15♐29	9♐43
	9	22 57	28 51	2♏47	1♐18	17 10	5R10
	17	2♍20	7♎52	10 59	7 23	16R25	2 23
	25	11 39	16 43	18 50	12 22	13 12	2D10
♂	1	17♉36	9♊10	29♊ 9	16♋21	0♌35	8♌14
	13	26 7	17 7	6♋20	22 24	4 36	8R35
	25	4♊25	24 48	13 8	27 49	7 24	6 59
♃	1	2♎ 6	6♎ 7	11♎42	17♎57	24♎39	0♏48
	13	3 25	8 8	14 7	20 32	27 11	3 0
	25	5 3	10 21	16 39	23 9	29 37	5 1
♄	1	6♐49	5♐42	6♐ 5	7♐49	10♐43	14♐ 8
	13	6R14	5D40	6 38	8 50	12 2	15 33
	25	5 50	5 52	7 22	9 59	13 25	16 57
♅	1	0♐ 5	29♏32	29♏45	0♐44	2♐20	4♐ 9
	13	29R47	29D31	0♐ 5	1 18	3 3	4 53
	25	29 35	29 38	0 30	1 56	3 47	5 35
♆	1	22♊56	23♊56	24♊36	24♊47	24♊28	23♊46
	13	23 21	24 14	24 44	24R43	24R13	23R25
	25	23 44	24 29	24 47	24 35	23 55	23 5
Pl.	1	14♊42	15♊15	15♊33	15♊33	15♊13	14♊42
☊	1	18♑12	16♑33	14♑55	13♑20	11♑41	10♑ 6
	1st	Fri	Mon	Thu	Sat	Tue	Thu

	d.	JAN	FEB	MAR	APR
☽	1	0♉12	14♊13	22♊ 8	5♌50
	3	24 6	7♋58	15♋54	0♍59
	5	17♊46	2♌15	10♌22	27 39
	7	11♋35	27 21	6♍ 0	25♎49
	9	5♌50	23♍25	2♎51	24♏51
	11	0♍45	20♎21	0♏40	23♐51
	13	26 32	18♏ 1	28 56	22♑14
	15	23♎26	16♐18	27♐14	19♒48
	17	21♏34	14♑58	25♑20	16♓36
	19	20♐47	13♒37	23♒ 6	12♈40
	21	20♑27	11♓40	20♓19	7♉56
	23	19♒37	8♈33	16♈40	2♊23
	25	17♓28	4♉ 4	11♉57	26 11
	27	13♈41	28 24	6♊14	19♋47
	29	8♉29	...	29 57	13♌48
	31	2♊24	...	23♋42	...

	d.	MAY	JUN	JUL	AUG
☽	1	8♍55	28♎ 4	5♐52	29♑35
	3	5♎44	27♏26	6♑ 3	29♒16
	5	4♏19	27♐43	6♒16	27♓43
	7	4♐ 2	27♑42	5♓22	24♈27
	9	3♑48	26♒26	2♈47	19♉35
	11	2♒40	23♓34	28 33	13♊38
	13	0♓17	19♈17	23♉ 4	7♋14
	15	26 43	13♉58	16♊53	0♌58
	17	22♈11	7♊58	10♋27	25 14
	19	16♉53	1♋38	4♌11	20♍16
	21	10♊58	25 13	28 21	16♎10
	23	4♋39	19♌ 5	23♍15	12♏58
	25	28 14	13♍39	19♎10	10♐40
	27	22♌14	9♎25	16♏21	9♑16
	29	17♍18	6♏48	14♐55	8♒27
	31	14♎ 0	...	14♑35	7♓35

	d.	SEP	OCT	NOV	DEC
☽	1	21♓52	27♈29	13♊35	15♋41
	3	19♈24	23♉14	7♋33	9♌16
	5	15♉20	17♊45	1♌ 8	0♍ 7
	7	9♊53	11♋30	25 1	27 52
	9	3♋38	5♌10	19♍54	24♎ 8
	11	27 17	29 29	16♎17	22♏11
	13	21♌28	24♍59	14♏17	21♐43
	15	16♍36	21♎50	13♐22	21♑49
	17	12♎47	19♏45	12♑40	21♒21
	19	9♏50	18♐10	11♒26	19♓35
	21	7♐30	16♑34	9♓19	16♈23
	23	5♑34	14♒41	6♈14	11♉55
	25	3♒56	12♓25	2♉16	6♊32
	27	2♓22	9♈36	27 28	0♋32
	29	0♈24	5♉57	21♊52	24 13
	31	...	1♊18	...	17♌50

STATIONS	☿	♀	♂	♃
	18Jan 7♑39	12Nov 17♐12	11Dec 8♌40	25Jan 10♎17
	21Apr 15♉17	23Dec 1♐58	... ...	29May 0♎21
	15May 5♉41	♄	♅	♆
	24Aug 21♍19	22Mar 12♐17	10Mar 3♐33	1Mar 19♊44
	16Sep 7♍38	11Aug 5♑39	9Aug 29♐31	29Sep 24♊47
	13Dec 7♑50	SIDER. TIME 6h 42m 40s 18h 44m 38s Common Year		1 Jan Midn. 1898

Noon		JAN	FEB	MAR	APR	MAY	JUN
☉	1	10♑55	12♒28	10 43	11♈33	10♉53	10♊44
	9	19 4	20 34	18 43	19 25	18 37	18 24
	17	27 13	28 39	26 42	27 15	26 20	26 2
	25	5♒21	6♓42	4♈38	5♉ 2	4♊ 1	3♋40
☿	1	21♐38	24♑57	12♓23	26♈49	17♈ 0	25♉38
	7	24 5	4♒10	23 58	25R23	20 49	7♊39
	13	29 37	13 53	5♈30	21 21	26 42	20 37
	19	6♑45	24 6	15 46	17 25	4♉15	3♋42
	25	14 48	4♓53	23 14	15 45	13 18	16 5
	31	23 27	...	26 40	...	23 46	...
♀	1	3♐58	26♐ 3	24 52	0♓ 3	5♈22	12♉27
	9	7 53	3♑49	3♒45	9 24	14 54	22 5
	17	13 17	12 0	12 47	18 48	24 48	1♊45
	25	19 45	20 31	21 57	28 15	4♉ 3	11 25
♂	1	5♌11	23♋42	19♋28	25♋ 8	6♌45	22♌ 2
	13	0R55	20R38	20 35	29 16	12 23	28 31
	25	26♋ 9	19 26	23 8	4♌ 7	18 23	5♍15
♃	1	6♏ 4	9♏26	10♏10	8♏13	4♏36	1♏19
	13	7 38	10 2	9R44	6R53	3R 9	0R37
	25	8 53	10 12	8 53	5 23	1 54	0 19
♄	1	17♐45	20♐53	22♐51	23♐41	23♐ 1	21♐ 8
	13	19 3	21 51	23 21	23R35	22R24	20R15
	25	20 14	22 38	23 38	23 15	21 37	19 23
♅	1	5♐58	7♐21	7♐58	7♐52	7♐ 4	5♐50
	13	6 34	7 41	8 2	7R36	6R37	5R21
	25	7 5	7 55	7R58	7 16	6 7	4 54
♆	1	22♊54	22♊13	21♊59	22♊13	22♊55	23♊57
	13	22R36	22R 4	22R 0	22 27	23 18	24 24
	25	22 21	21 59	22 7	22 45	23 42	24 51
Pl.	1	14♊ 8	13♊44	13♊39	13♊51	14♊26	15♊ 0
☊	1	8♑27	6♑49	5♑20	3♑41	2♑ 6	0♑28
	1st	Sun	Wed	Wed	Sat	Mon	Thu

Noon		JUL	AUG	SEP	OCT	NOV	DEC
☉	1	9♋23	8♌58	8♍48	8♎ 5	8♏52	9♐ 7
	9	17 1	16 38	16 34	15 59	16 54	17 15
	17	24 39	24 19	24 22	23 54	24 57	25 23
	25	2♌17	2♍ 1	2♎11	1♏52	3♐ 2	3♑32
☿	1	27♋19	3♍ 2	21♌42	8♎20	27♏14	19♐42
	7	7♌18	3R33	26 53	18 40	5♐28	12R10
	13	16 0	0 55	5♍45	28 31	12 58	6 23
	19	23 20	26♌ 2	16 27	7♏59	19 1	6D44
	25	29 1	21 47	27 32	17 4	22 3	11 27
	31	2♍40	21D18	...	25 49	...	18 22
♀	1	18♊41	26♋32	4♍47	12♎ 8	20♏51	28♐21
	9	28 25	6♌22	14 43	22 7	0♐51	8♑21
	17	8♋10	16 14	24 40	2♏ 6	10 51	18 20
	25	17 56	26 7	4♎38	12 6	20 51	28 18
♂	1	8♍41	27♍14	16♎56	7♏ 0	28♏45	20♐44
	13	15 44	4♎44	24 50	15 18	7♐26	29 45
	25	22 57	12 23	2♏54	23 45	16 16	8♑53
♃	1	0♏20	2♏ 5	6♏ 9	11♏37	18♏10	24♏47
	13	0 42	3 25	8 11	14 4	20 49	27 21
	25	1 27	5 4	10 26	16 38	23 28	29 51
♄	1	18♐58	17♐24	17♐10	18♐24	20♐55	24♐ 9
	13	18R14	17R 8	17 30	19 15	22 9	25 33
	25	17 39	17D 5	18 2	20 15	23 27	26 58
♅	1	4♐42	4♐ 3	4♐10	5♐ 2	6♐33	8♐20
	13	4R23	3D59	4 25	5 33	7 14	9 4
	25	4 8	4 4	4 48	6 10	7 58	9 47
♆	1	25♊ 4	26♊ 6	26♊48	27♊ 2	26♊44	26♊ 4
	13	25 30	26 25	26 57	26R59	26R30	25R44
	25	25 53	26 41	27 1	26 52	26 13	25 24
Pl.	1	15♊40	16♊15	16♊34	16♊34	16♊14	15♊43
☊	1	28♐52	27♐14	25♐35	24♐ 0	22♐21	20♐46
	1st	Sat	Tue	Fri	Sun	Wed	Fri

	d.	JAN	FEB	MAR	APR
☽	1	29♌44	15♎49	25♎39	15♐49
	3	23♍59	11♏44	21♏48	13♑34
	5	19♎17	9♐ 0	18♐56	11♒57
	7	16♏ 6	7♑50	17♑13	10♓45
	9	14♐41	7♒52	16♒32	9♈25
	11	14♑42	8♓ 6	16♓13	7♉11
	13	15♒ 8	7♈16	15♈13	3♊32
	15	14♓44	4♉37	12♉38	28 27
	17	12♈39	0♊ 9	8♊18	22♋25
	19	8♉49	24 23	2♋38	16♌ 5
	21	3♊36	18♋ 1	26 17	10♍ 8
	23	27 33	11♌38	19♌59	5♎ 7
	25	21♋10	5♍39	14♍16	1♏15
	27	14♌49	0♎18	9♎25	28 25
	29	8♍46	...	5♏26	26♐18
	31	3♎17	...	2♐11	...

	d.	MAY	JUN	JUL	AUG
☽	1	24♑31	17♓52	25♈47	13♊60
	3	22♒50	15♈23	21♉51	8♋14
	5	21♓ 2	11♉59	16♊53	2♌ 2
	7	18♈48	7♊39	11♋11	25 42
	9	15♉45	2♋26	5♌ 2	19♍29
	11	11♊36	26 31	28 42	13♎40
	13	6♋20	20♌13	22♍31	8♏36
	15	0♌16	14♍ 1	16♎58	4♐45
	17	23 58	8♎30	12♏33	2♑33
	19	18♍ 4	4♏14	9♐45	2♒ 1
	21	13♎ 9	1♐34	8♑42	2♓31
	23	9♏37	0♑25	8♒52	2♈42
	25	7♐26	0♒10	9♓ 9	1♉21
	27	6♑10	29 47	8♈18	28 4
	29	5♒ 9	28♓27	5♉45	23♊ 9
	31	3♓48	...	1♊34	17♋14

	d.	SEP	OCT	NOV	DEC
☽	1	29♋ 5	1♍21	16♎10	20♏ 0
	3	22♌44	25 23	11♏39	17♐ 7
	5	16♍34	20♎ 1	8♐ 2	15♑11
	7	10♎48	15♏19	5♑11	13♒45
	9	5♏35	11♐22	2♒57	12♓17
	11	1♐11	8♑16	1♓14	10♈26
	13	27 56	6♒13	29 48	7♉57
	15	26♑10	5♓10	28♈11	4♊40
	17	25♒48	4♈38	25♉51	0♋30
	19	26♓ 1	3♉38	22♊19	25 25
	21	25♈32	1♊18	17♋31	19♌35
	23	23♉22	27 19	11♌44	13♍20
	25	19♊20	21♋57	5♍30	7♎14
	27	13♋53	15♌48	29 26	1♏51
	29	7♌40	9♍33	24♎ 8	27 47
	31	...	3♎46	...	25♐18

STATIONS	☿	♀	♂	♃
	1Jan 21♐44 3Apr 26♈45 26Apr 15♈46 6Aug 3♍41 29Aug 20♌55 27Nov 21♐59 17Dec 6♐ 0	None	28Feb 19♋26	26Feb 10♏12 28Jun 0♏19
		♄	♅	♆
		4Apr 23♐41 23Aug 17♐ 5	14Mar 8♐ 2 13Aug 3♐59	5Mar 22♊ 0 29Sep 27♊ 2
		SIDER. TIME 6h 41m 43s 18h 43m 41s Common Year		1 Jan Midn. Noon. 1899

1900

Noon		JAN	FEB	MAR	APR	MAY	JUN
☉	1	10♑40	12♒13	10♓29	11♈19	10♉39	10♊30
	9	18 49	20 19	18 29	19 11	18 23	18 10
	17	26 58	28 24	26 27	27 1	26 6	25 48
	25	5♒ 6	6♓27	4♈24	4♉49	3♊48	3♋26
☿	1	19♐38	6♒15	26♓19	28♓20	15♈26	13♊15
	7	27 45	16 31	4♈38	26R32	24 16	26 8
	13	6♑24	27 15	8 52	27D55	4♉19	7♋59
	19	15 26	8♓21	8R 8	1♈55	15 35	18 28
	25	24 49	19 26	3 43	7 54	27 57	27 29
	31	4♒35	...	28♓56	...	11♊ 3	...
♀	1	7♒ 0	15♓17	19♈ 6	24♉51	26♊ 7	19♋52
	9	16 56	25 3	28 32	3♊37	3♋27	22 59
	17	26 50	4♈44	7♉51	12 7	10 6	24R 0
	25	6♓42	14 20	17 0	20 16	15 50	22 33
♂	1	14♑15	8♒24	0♓27	24♓48	17♈59	11♉15
	13	23 33	17 50	9 54	4♈ 8	27 5	20 2
	25	2♒54	27 18	19 20	13 23	6♉ 4	28 39
♃	1	1♐14	6♐36	9♐48	10♐50	9♐ 5	5♐24
	13	3 29	8 12	10 33	10R26	7R47	3R56
	25	5 31	9 28	10 52	9 38	6 18	2 40
♄	1	27♐47	1♑ 9	3♑30	4♑54	4♑48	3♑19
	13	29 9	2 16	4 13	5 2	4R22	2R30
	25	0♑27	3 13	4 43	4R56	3 45	1 37
♅	1	10♐10	11♐38	12♐22	12♐23	11♐41	10♐29
	13	10 48	12 1	12 28	12R11	11R15	10R 0
	25	11 21	12 18	12R27	11 52	10 46	9 32
♆	1	25♊12	24♊30	24♊13	24♊25	25♊ 4	26♊ 5
	13	24R54	24R19	24D14	24 38	25 26	26 32
	25	24 37	24 14	24 19	24 55	25 50	26 59
Pl.	1	15♊19	14♊45	14♊37	14♊45	15♊19	15♊58
☊	1	19♐ 8	17♐29	16♐ C	14♐22	12♐46	11♐ 8
	1st	Mon	Thu	Thu	Sun	Tue	Fri

Noon		JUL	AUG	SEP	OCT	NOV	DEC
☉	1	9♋ 9	8♉44	8♍34	7♎51	8♏37	8♐52
	9	16 47	16 24	16 19	15 44	16 39	16 60
	17	24 24	24 5	24 7	23 40	24 42	25 8
	25	2♌ 3	1♍48	1♎57	1♏37	2♐48	3♑17
☿	1	4♌57	8♌29	27♌ 7	20♎59	2♐ 5	20♏20
	7	10 40	4R44	8♍37	0♏14	5 51	24 16
	13	14 15	4D 1	20 2	8 59	5R18	1♐ 6
	19	15R13	7 30	0♎56	17 14	29♏ 9	9 13
	25	13 19	14 59	11 14	24 47	21 57	17 55
	31	9 15	25 14	...	1♐11	...	26 55
♀	1	19♋55	7♋36	23♋40	22♌24	27♍12	3♏10
	9	15R 8	9 26	0♌34	1♍ 2	6♎38	12 57
	17	10 35	13 9	8 6	9 56	16 12	22 49
	25	7 55	18 18	16 7	19 4	25 52	2♐42
♂	1	2♊55	24♊17	14♋32	2♌47	19♌46	3♍17
	13	11 19	2♋16	22 0	9 38	25 36	7 25
	25	19 34	10 4	29 15	16 8	0♍54	10 31
♃	1	2♐ 9	1♐ 2	2♐46	6♐44	12♐31	19♐ 2
	13	1R23	1 22	4 7	8 49	15 3	21 45
	25	1 2	2 8	5 48	11 6	17 41	24 29
♄	1	1♑11	29♐14	28♐26	29♐ 6	1♑11	4♑10
	13	0R20	28R45	28D32	29 46	2 17	5 32
	25	29♐36	28 29	28 51	0♑37	3 31	6 56
♅	1	9♐19	8♐34	8♐33	9♐18	10♐43	12♐29
	13	8R57	8R28	8 45	9 47	11 24	13 13
	25	8 41	8D29	9 5	10 21	12 7	13 56
♆	1	27♊12	28♊15	28♊59	29♊16	29♊ 1	28♊22
	13	27 38	28 35	29 9	29R14	28R48	28R 2
	25	28 2	28 52	29 15	29 7	28 31	27 42
Pl.	1	16♊38	17♊13	17♊33	17♊34	17♊15	16♊45
☊	1	9♐33	7♐54	6♐16	4♐40	3♐ 2	1♐26
	1st	Sun	Wed	Sat	Mon	Thu	Sat

d.		JAN	FEB	MAR	APR
☽	1	9♑37	2♓40	10♓50	4♉18
	3	8♒59	2♈42	11♈19	2♊45
	5	8♓28	1♉20	10♉28	29 19
	7	7♈14	28 18	7♊42	24♋20
	9	4♉50	23♊52	3♋15	18♌25
	11	1♊18	18♋30	27 40	12♍ 9
	13	26 48	12♌36	21♌34	5♎59
	15	21♋37	6♍27	15♍18	0♏12
	17	15♌50	0♎12	9♎ 8	24 57
	19	9♍41	24 6	3♏15	20♐26
	21	3♎25	18♏32	27 53	16♑52
	23	27 30	14♐ 4	23♐37	14♒31
	25	22♏32	11♑15	20♑24	13♓23
	27	19♐ 6	10♒22	19♒ 3	13♈ 1
	29	17♑32	...	19♓ 5	12♉27
	31	17♒28	...	19♈26	...

d.		MAY	JUN	JUL	AUG
☽	1	10♊44	28♋ 3	0♍39	14♎34
	3	7♋24	22♌41	24 34	8♏27
	5	2♌34	16♍38	18♎22	3♐ 9
	7	26 44	10♎27	12♏39	29 19
	9	20♍30	4♏44	8♐ 3	27♑17
	11	14♎26	29 57	4♑54	26♒46
	13	8♏56	26♐20	3♒12	26♓48
	15	4♐13	23♑48	2♓19	26♈11
	17	0♑23	22♒ 2	1♈26	24♉13
	19	27 25	20♓32	29 51	20♊52
	21	25♒17	18♈56	27♉18	16 27
	23	23♓48	16♉54	23♊51	11♋17
	25	2[illegible]♈37	14♊13	19♋36	5♍33
	27	21♉10	10♋39	14♌35	29 24
	29	18♊52	6♌ 7	8♍54	23♎ 4
	31	15♋19	...	2♎43	16♏54

d.		SEP	OCT	NOV	DEC
☽	1	29♏ 4	3♑15	23♒27	2♈11
	3	24♐18	29 58	22♓19	1♉13
	5	21♑15	28♒33	22♈13	0♊20
	7	20♒ 9	28♓40	22♉ 9	28 49
	9	20♓27	29♈12	21♊ 1	26♋ 0
	11	20♈52	28♉48	18♋12	21♌42
	13	20♉ 5	26♊38	13♌46	16♍11
	15	17♊36	22♋44	8♍ 8	9♎58
	17	13♋32	17♌30	1♎54	3♏43
	19	8♌23	11♍31	25 37	28 0
	21	2♍34	5♎14	19♏43	23♐14
	23	26 23	28 58	14♐27	19♑33
	25	20♎ 5	23♏ 0	9♑59	16♒50
	27	13♏51	17♐33	6♒26	14♓44
	29	8♐ 4	12♑57	3♓50	12♈57
	31	...	9♒35	...	11♉15

STATIONS	☿	♀	♂	♃
	16Mar 9♈ 6	17Jun 24♋ 0	None	29Mar 10♐52
	8Apr 26♓33	30Jul 7♋30		31Jul 1♐ 1
		♄	♅	♆
	19Jul 15♌13	15Apr 5♑ 2	18Mar 12♐29	6Mar 24♊13
	12Aug 3♌51	4Sep 28♐26	19Aug 8♐27	2Oct 29♊16
	10Nov 6♐16	SIDER. TIME		1 Jan
	29Nov 20♐ 8	6h 40m 46s		Midn.
		18h 42m 44s		Noon
		Common Year		1900

1901

Noon		JAN	FEB	MAR	APR	MAY	JUN
☉	1	10♑25	11♒58	10♓14	11♈ 4	10♉24	10♊16
	9	18 34	20 5	18 14	18 56	18 9	17 55
	17	26 43	28 10	26 13	26 47	25 52	25 34
	25	4♒52	6♓13	4♈ 9	3♉35	3♊34	3♋12
☿	1	28♐27	19♒27	21♓23	13♓29	26♈ 2	29♊11
	7	7♑43	0♓ 7	16R40	19 29	7♉50	8♋33
	13	17 14	10 14	11 4	26 57	20 32	16 9
	19	27 3	18 15	8 15	5♈35	3♊37	21 48
	25	7♒12	22 1	9D 1	15 17	16 11	25 11
	31	17 41	...	12 39	...	27 28	...
♀	1	11♐23	19♑59	24♒53	3♈25	10♉31	18♊40
	9	21 19	29 57	4♓50	13 20	20 23	28 30
	17	1♑17	9♒55	14 47	23 14	0♊14	8♋18
	25	11 15	19 54	24 44	3♉ 7	10 5	18 6
♂	1	11♍43	10♍ 7	0♍ 7	23♌ 7	27♌ 2	8♍21
	13	12 33	6R21	26♌ 6	23D34	0♍46	13 57
	25	11R34	1 40	23R40	25 33	5 22	20 0
♃	1	26♐ 5	2♑44	7♑50	11♑44	13♑ 3	11♑33
	13	28 44	5 4	9 36	12 35	12R48	10R18
	25	1♑18	7 11	11 3	13 1	12 7	8 50
♄	1	7♑46	11♑18	13♑58	15♑54	16♑22	15♑23
	13	9 11	12 32	14 53	16 16	16R 9	14R40
	25	10 33	13 39	15 35	16 24	15 43	13 51
♅	1	14♐21	15♐52	16♐43	16♐51	16♐15	15♐ 6
	13	15 0	16 18	16 52	16R42	15R51	14R37
	25	15 34	16 38	16R54	16 25	15 23	14 8
♆	1	27♊30	26♊45	26♊27	26♊37	27♊15	28♊14
	13	27R11	26R35	26D27	26 49	27 36	28 41
	25	26 55	26 29	26 32	27 5	28 0	29 8
Pl.	1	16♊13	15♊46	15♊38	15♊50	16♊17	16♊56
☊	1	29♏48	28♏ 9	26♏41	25♏ 2	23♏27	21♏48
		Tue	Fri	Fri	Mon	Wed	Sat

Noon		JUL	AUG	SEP	OCT	NOV	DEC
☉	1	8♋55	8♌30	8♍20	7♎36	8♏22	8♐37
	9	16 33	16 10	16 5	15 29	16 24	16 45
	17	24 11	23 51	23 53	23 25	24 28	24 53
	25	1♌49	1♍34	1♎43	1♏23	2♐32	3♑ 2
☿	1	25♋56	19♋17	12♍41	0♏25	15♏43	21♏52
	7	24R 0	25 58	23 33	7 55	8R11	0♐47
	13	20 21	5♌38	3♎43	14 20	4 27	9 57
	19	16 59	17 8	13 14	18 56	7D 3	19 13
	25	16D 1	29 9	22 8	20R20	13 36	28 36
	31	18 30	10♍48	...	16 48	...	8♑ 7
♀	1	25♋27	3♍17	10♎50	16♏41	22♐50	25♑49
	9	5♌14	13 1	20 27	26 7	1♑54	3♒56
	17	15 1	22 43	0♏ 2	5♐30	10 49	11 34
	25	24 46	2♎23	9 34	14 47	19 30	18 32
♂	1	23♍11	10♎57	0♏29	20♏48	13♐ 2	5♑34
	13	29 49	18 19	8 27	29 16	21 57	14 48
	25	6 46	25 56	16 39	7♐55	1♑ 0	24 8
♃	1	8♑ 4	4♑33	3♑14	4♑46	8♑53	14♑35
	13	6R34	3R42	3 31	6 6	11 0	17 11
	25	5 12	3 16	4 15	7 46	13 21	19 54
♄	1	13♑25	11♑15	9♑55	10♑ 1	11♑37	14♑17
	13	12R32	10R35	9R47	10 28	12 34	15 35
	25	11 41	10 6	9D53	11 8	13 41	16 57
♅	1	13♐55	13♐ 4	12♐55	13♐33	14♐54	16♐37
	13	13R31	12R55	13 5	14 0	15 33	17 20
	25	13 12	12D53	13 22	14 33	16 15	18 4
♆	1	29♊21	0♋25	1♋11	1♋29	1♋17	0♋40
	13	29 47	0 45	1 22	1R28	1R 5	0R20
	25	0♋11	1 3	1 28	1 23	0 49	0 0
Pl.	1	17♊37	18♊12	18 32	18♊33	18♊16	17♊46
☊	1	20♏13	18♏34	16♏56	15♏21	13♏42	12♏ 7
		Mon	Thu	Sun	Tue	Fri	Sun

d.		JAN	FEB	MAR	APR
☽	1	25♉23	16♋13	25♋59	12♍59
	3	23♊20	12♌17	21♌23	6♎59
	5	20 36	7♍30	16♍ 5	0♏41
	7	16♌48	1♎52	10♑10	24 19
	9	11♍49	25 37	3♏50	18♐15
	11	5♎54	19♏17	27 29	13♑ 2
	13	29 34	13♐34	21♐43	9♒14
	15	23♏32	9♑11	17♑12	7♓13
	17	18♐25	6♒32	14♒30	6♈51
	19	14♑42	5♓28	13♓39	7♉16
	21	12♒23	5♈ 7	13♈51	7♊12
	23	10♓58	4♉25	13♉51	5♋41
	25	9♈43	2♊41	12♊39	2♌28
	27	8♉ 3	29 49	9♋55	27 47
	29	5♊47	...	5♌51	22♍ 6
	31	2♋54	...	0♍47	

d.		MAY	JUN	JUL	AUG
☽	1	15♎52	0♐ 8	3♑24	21♒57
	3	9♏30	24 28	29 9	19♓51
	5	3♐16	19♑34	25♒50	18♈ 8
	7	27 30	15♒33	23♓17	16♉26
	9	22♑31	12♓34	21♈18	14♊33
	11	18♒43	10♈39	19♉46	12♋20
	13	16♓23	9♉40	18♊25	9♌31
	15	15♈30	9♊ 6	16♋46	5♍46
	17	15♉32	8♋10	14♌13	0♎55
	19	15♊25	6♌ 2	10♍20	25 5
	21	14♋ 9	2♍19	5♎ 7	18♏43
	23	11♌11	27 8	29 1	12♐31
	25	6♍35	21♎ 2	22♏40	7♑10
	27	0♎51	14♏40	16♐47	3♒14
	29	24 32	8♐39	11♑55	0♓50
	31	18♏12	...	8♒18	29 34

d.		SEP	OCT	NOV	DEC
☽	1	14♈ 6	28♉ 1	15♋35	21♌47
	3	13♉ 3	21♊53	12♌43	17♍29
	5	11♊25	19♋30	8♍21	11♎53
	7	9♋ 1	15♌54	2♎54	5♏35
	9	5♌50	11♍17	26 48	29 9
	11	1♍51	5♎52	20♏24	22♐57
	13	27 0	29 51	14♐ 2	17♑15
	15	21♎18	23♏27	7♑58	12♒14
	17	15♏ 1	17♐ 3	2♒35	8♓ 5
	19	8♐36	11♑ 7	28 19	5♈ 5
	21	2♑42	6♒16	25♓35	3♉23
	23	27 58	3♓ 1	24♈30	2♊54
	25	24♒55	1♈35	24♉40	2♋53
	27	23♓35	1♉33	25♊ 0	2♌13
	29	23♈17	1♊53	24♋17	29 58
	31	...	1♋23	...	25♍53

STATIONS	☿	♀	♂	♃
	27Feb 22♓ 1	None	14Jan 12♍32	1May 13♑ 3
	21Mar 8♓ 8		5Apr 23♌ 4	31Aug 3♑13
		♄	♅	♆
	1Jul 25♋56	26Apr 16♑24	23Mar 16♐54	8Mar 26♊27
	25Jul 16♋ 1	15Sep 9♑47	23Aug 12♐53	5Oct 1♋30
	25Oct 20♏20	SIDER. TIME		1 Jan
	14Nov 4♏29	6h 39m 48s		Midn.
		18h 41m 46s		Noon.
		Common Year		1901

Noon		JAN	FEB	MAR	APR	MAY	JUN
☉	1	10♑10	11♒43	9♓59	10♈50	10♉10	10♊ 2
	9	18 19	19 50	18 0	18 42	17 55	17 42
	17	26 28	27 55	25 58	26 32	25 38	25 20
	25	4♒37	5♓58	3♈55	4♉20	3♊20	2♋58
☿	1	9♑43	29♒48	20♒47	17♓17	13♉ 5	2♋36
	7	19 29	4♓57	21D11	26 40	25 53	5 37
	13	29 28	4R21	24 44	6♈57	7♊43	5R57
	19	9♒38	28♒39	0♓24	18 10	17 50	3R49
	25	19 36	22 45	7 33	0♉18	25 57	0 26
	31	28 33	...	15 49	...	1♋50	...
♀	1	23♒53	2♓13	18♒16	27♒34	24♓ 5	27♈12
	9	28 53	28♒39	17D36	3♓42	2♈17	6♉11
	17	2♓12	23R46	19 22	10 38	10 46	15 17
	25	3R21	19 35	23 6	18 8	19 28	24 29
♂	1	29♑37	24♒ 5	16♓11	10♈18	3♉ 2	25♉44
	13	9♒ 3	3♓34	25 34	19 29	11 55	4♊17
	25	18 32	13 2	4♈54	28 33	20 41	12 43
♃	1	21♑31	28♑47	5♒ 4	11♒ 6	15♒19	17♒13
	13	24 19	1♒32	7 33	13 1	16 23	17R10
	25	27 8	4 12	9 51	14 38	17 3	16 40
♄	1	17♑46	21♑24	24♑20	26♑43	27♑46	27♑20
	13	19 11	22 43	25 24	27 19	27R47	26R47
	25	20 36	23 57	26 17	27 40	27 34	26 5
♅	1	18♐29	20♐ 4	21♐ 0	21♐17	20♐47	19♐41
	13	19 9	20 33	21 12	21R10	20R24	19R12
	25	19 45	20 54	21 17	20 56	19 58	18 43
♆	1	29♊48	29♊ 3	28♊42	28♊49	29♊25	0♋23
	13	29R29	28R51	28D41	29 0	29 45	0 49
	25	29 11	28 43	28 44	29 16	0♋ 8	1 16
Pl.	1	17♊12	16♊48	16♊39	16♊49	17♊16	17♊55
☊	1	10♏28	8♏50	7♏21	5♏42	4♏ 7	2♏29
	1st	Wed	Sat	Sat	Tue	Thu	Sun

Noon		JUL	AUG	SEP	OCT	NOV	DEC
☉	1	8♋41	8♌17	8♍ 6	7♎22	8♏ 8	8♐22
	9	16 19	15 57	15 52	15 15	16 10	16 30
	17	23 57	23 38	23 39	23 11	24 13	24 38
	25	1♌35	1♍20	1♎28	1♏ 8	2♐18	2♑47
☿	1	27♊44	27♋12	25♍56	2♏17	19♎58	2♐16
	7	27D24	9♌29	5♎ 6	4 22	25 49	11 41
	13	0♋ 4	21 47	13 31	2R16	4♏10	21 7
	19	5 49	3♍26	21 4	25♎51	13 23	0♑36
	25	14 22	14 17	27 30	19 44	22 49	10 11
	31	25 14	24 20	...	19D24	...	19 52
♀	1	1♊26	8♋ 0	15♌31	22♍32	1♏16	8♐57
	9	10 46	17 36	25 19	2♎30	11 18	19 1
	17	20 11	27 15	5♍11	12 29	21 21	29 5
	25	29 39	6♌58	15 5	22 29	1♐24	9♑ 8
♂	1	16♊52	7♋52	28♋ 2	16♌41	4♍54	21♍ 3
	13	25 6	15 47	5♌36	23 53	11 35	26 57
	25	3♋12	23 32	13 1	0♍54	17 59	2♎21
♃	1	16♒15	12♒52	9♒ 7	7♒26	8♒41	12♒33
	13	15R 9	11R18	8R 8	7D33	9 57	14 38
	25	13 46	9 51	7 33	8 8	11 36	16 59
♄	1	25♑41	23♑27	21♑41	21♑12	22♑14	24♑34
	13	24R49	22R38	21R19	21 26	23 2	25 45
	25	23 56	21 59	21 11	21 53	24 0	27 3
♅	1	18♐29	17♐33	17♐17	17♐48	19♐ 2	20♐43
	13	18R 3	17R22	17 24	18 12	19 40	21 26
	25	17 43	17 17	17 38	18 42	20 21	22 9
♆	1	1♋29	2♋34	3♋22	3♋43	3♋33	2♋58
	13	1 55	2 55	3 34	3R43	3R22	2R39
	25	2 20	3 13	3 41	3 38	3 7	2 18
Pl.	1	18♊36	19♊10	19♊31	19♊34	19♊17	18♊47
☊	1	0♏53	29♎15	27♎36	26♎ 1	24♎22	22♎47
	1st	Tue	Fri	Mon	Wed	Sat	Mon

☽ d.	JAN	FEB	MAR	APR
1	8♎15	22♏ 0	29♏47	13♑26
3	2♏13	15♐40	23♐29	8♒14
5	25 47	9♑53	17♑47	4♓27
7	19♐32	5♒ 7	13♒15	2♈16
9	13♑56	1♓25	10♓ 5	1♉20
11	9♒ 8	28 34	8♈ 3	0♊52
13	5♓ 7	26♈16	6♉37	29 58
15	1♈51	24♉18	5♊13	28♋ 7
17	29 22	22♊34	3♋29	25♌ 6
19	27♉43	20♋52	1♌12	21♍ 1
21	26♊45	18♌46	28 14	16♎ 2
23	25♋51	15♍45	24 24	10♏20
25	24♌ 8	11♎29	19♎36	4♐ 9
27	20♍56	6♏ 0	13♏56	27 49
29	16♎ 8	...	7♐41	21♑45
31	10♏12	...	1♑24	...

☽ d.	MAY	JUN	JUL	AUG
1	16♒29	4♈48	12♉12	5♋50
3	12♓34	3♉11	11♊41	5♌28
5	10♈21	3♊ 4	11♋56	4♍18
7	9♉42	3♋31	11♌43	1♎31
9	9♊52	3♌15	9♍57	27 4
11	9♋41	1♍18	6♎16	21♏21
13	8♌13	27 30	1♏ 3	15♐ 5
15	5♍10	22♎17	24 56	8♑54
17	0♎41	16♏13	18♐35	3♒17
19	25 13	9♐52	12♑28	28 29
21	19♏ 9	3♑36	6♒52	24♓31
23	12♐50	27 40	1♓55	21♈18
25	6♑33	22♒16	27 41	18♉48
27	0♒36	17♓39	24♈21	16♊59
29	25 21	14♈11	22♉ 7	15♋43
31	21♓16	...	21♊ 3	14♌31

☽ d.	SEP	OCT	NOV	DEC
1	28♌43	4♎46	21♏12	23♐48
3	26♍16	0♏28	15♐17	17♑31
5	22♎25	25 8	9♑ 1	11♒10
7	17♏15	19♐ 5	2♒49	5♓39
9	11♐13	12♑50	27 16	1♈ 4
11	4♑58	6♒58	22♓56	28 9
13	29 7	2♓ 5	20♈16	27♉ 7
15	24♒10	28 35	19♉16	27♊30
17	20♓21	26♈29	19♊14	28♋ 1
19	17♈33	25♉21	19♋ 2	27♌16
21	15♉29	24♊29	17♌42	24♍40
23	13♊48	23♋10	14♍53	20♎22
25	12♋12	21♌23	10♎44	14♏55
27	10♌22	17♍53	5♏38	8♐52
29	8♍ 0	13♎50	29 55	2♑37
31	...	8♏56	...	26 22

STATIONS	☿	♀	♂	♃
	10Feb 5♓26	25Jan 3♓21	None	7Jun 17 15
	4Mar 20♒30	8Mar 17♒32		5Oct 7♒25
	12Jun 6♋ 5	♄	♅	♆
		9May 27♑48	28Mar 21♐17	11Jan 28♊41
	6Jul 27♊15	27Sep 21♑11	28Aug 17♐16	9Oct 3♋43
	8Oct 4♏21	SIDER. TIME		1 Jan
	29Oct 18♎46	6h 38m 51s		Midn.
		18h 40m 49s		Noon
		Common Year		1902

1903

Noon	JAN	FEB	MAR	APR	MAY	JUN
☉ 1	9♑55	11♒28	9♓44	10♈35	9♉56	9♊49
9	18 4	19 35	17 45	18 28	17 41	17 28
17	26 13	27 40	25 44	26 18	25 24	25 6
25	4♒21	5♓ 4	3♈40	4♉ 6	3♊ 6	2♋44
☿ 1	21♑29	13♒46	12♒49	29♓ 3	28♉19	13♊ 3
7	1♒ 5	6R54	19 52	10♈33	6♊45	9R47
13	10 1	3 35	27 58	22 49	12 36	7 43
19	16 52	4D41	6♓54	5♉28	15 39	8D 5
25	19R 5	8 53	16 40	17 40	15R49	11 11
31	14 56	...	27 13	...	13 34	...
♀ 1	17♑57	26♒50	1♈43	9♉45	15♊44	21♋31
9	28 0	6♓50	11 36	19 27	25 7	0♌25
17	8♒ 2	16 49	21 26	29 4	4♋25	9 6
25	18 4	26 45	1♉14	8♊37	13 36	17 33
♂ 1	5♎14	14♎37	15♎32	6♎12	27♍52	0♎26
13	9 37	16 8	12R57	1R51	27D32	3 58
25	13 7	15R59	8 55	28♍45	28 55	8 32
♃ 1	18♒27	25♒29	2♓13	9♓26	15♓38	20♓30
13	21 5	28 22	5 4	12 2	17 45	21 50
25	23 50	1♓15	7 51	14 28	19 35	22 45
♄ 1	27♑50	1♒30	4♒38	7♒27	9♒ 2	9♒13
13	29 15	2 54	5 51	8 14	9 17	8R52
25	0♒40	4 14	6 54	8 49	9R18	8 19
♅ 1	22♐34	24♐14	25♐15	25♐38	25♐15	24♐14
13	23 16	24 44	25 30	25R34	24R54	23R45
25	23 53	25 8	25 37	25 23	24 30	23 16
♆ 1	2♋ 6	1♋20	0♋57	1♋ 1	1♋34	2♋32
13	1R46	1R 7	0R54	1 11	1 54	2 57
25	1 29	0 59	0D58	1 26	2 17	3 24
Pl. 1	18♊14	17♊48	17♊39	17♊48	18♊15	18♊54
☊ 1	21♎ 9	19♎30	18♎ 1	16♎23	14♎47	13♎ 9
1st	Thu	Sun	Sun	Wed	Fri	Mon

Noon	JUL	AUG	SEP	OCT	NOV	DEC
☉ 1	8♋28	8♌ 3	7♍52	7♎ 8	7♏53	8♐ 8
9	16 5	15 43	15 37	15 1	15 55	16 15
17	23 43	23 23	23 25	22 56	23 58	24 23
25	1♌21	1♍ 6	1♎14	0♏54	2♐ 3	2♑32
☿ 1	16♊54	14♌26	4♎ 3	11♎39	25♎35	13♐38
7	25 2	25 57	10 34	5R12	5♏24	22 59
13	5♋19	6♍31	15 28	2D58	15 10	2♑19
19	17 17	16 12	17 57	6 48	24 46	11 33
25	29 59	25 0	16R51	14 33	4♐14	20 25
31	12♌26	2♎51	...	23 57	...	28 5
♀ 1	23♌42	21♍ 7	1♎17	16♍52	24♍40	21♎25
9	1♍35	26 12	28♍33	15R39	0♎43	29 53
17	9 0	29 51	24R 1	16D59	7 41	8♏40
25	15 48	1♎38	19 22	20 22	15 20	17 41
♂ 1	11♎ 7	27♎ 1	15♏55	6♐13	28♐43	21♑32
13	16 50	4♏ 2	23 50	14 45	7♑44	0♒51
25	23 7	11 26	2♐ 1	23 31	16 54	10 14
♃ 1	23♓ 3	22♓46	19♓43	15♓52	13♓32	14♓13
13	23 18	21R51	18R 8	2D43	13D26	15 19
25	23R 6	20 35	16 35	13 48	13 50	16 48
♄ 1	8♒ 0	5♒50	3♒45	2♒44	3♒11	5♒ 2
13	7R13	4R57	3R11	2D43	3 46	6 6
25	6 21	4 10	2 49	2 56	4 34	7 19
♅ 1	23♐ 1	22♐ 0	21♐38	22♐ 2	23♐10	24♐46
13	22R35	21R46	21D41	22 23	23 46	25 29
25	22 11	21 39	21 53	22 51	24 26	26 13
♆ 1	3♋37	4♋43	5♋33	5♋56	5♋49	5♋15
13	4 4	5 5	5 46	5R57	5R38	4R56
25	4 29	5 24	5 53	5 53	5 23	4 36
Pl. 1	19♊34	20♊10	20♊32	20♊35	20♊20	19♊50
☊ 1	11♎34	9♎55	8♎17	6♎41	5♎ 3	3♎27
1st	Wed	Sat	Tue	Thu	Sun	Tue

d.	JAN	FEB	MAR	APR
☽ 1	8♒18	24♓18	3♈53	23♉44
3	2♓27	19♈50	0♉ 0	21♊45
5	27 14	16♉29	26 60	20♋ 8
7	23♈11	14♊33	24♊56	18♌33
9	20♉48	14♋ 0	23♋43	16♍40
11	20♊13	14♋ 5	22♌52	14♎ 4
13	20 47	13♍34	21♍38	10♏27
15	21♌ 6	11♎29	19♎15	5♐45
17	19♍52	7♏36	15♏23	0♑ 6
19	16♎38	2♐17	10♐12	23 56
21	11♏45	26 10	4♑12	17♒50
23	5♐51	19♑53	27 58	12♓24
25	29 33	13♒55	22♒ 6	8♈ 8
27	23♑18	8♓32	17♓ 3	5♉14
29	17♒21	...	13♈ 0	3♊31
31	11♓51	...	9♉57	...

d.	MAY	JUN	JUL	AUG
☽ 1	2♋24	26♌ 2	3♎47	22♏ 4
3	1♌10	23♍41	0♏ 2	16♐35
5	29 21	20♎ 6	25 7	10♑32
7	26♍43	15♏36	19♐31	4♒17
9	23♎16	10♐23	13♑29	28 6
11	18♏59	4♑37	7♒15	22♓11
13	13♐55	28 29	1♓ 0	16♈52
15	8♑ 8	22♒12	25 6	12♉32
17	1♒57	16♓15	20♈ 3	9♊40
19	25 48	11♈14	16♉27	8♋26
21	20♓19	7♉47	14♊43	8♌27
23	16♈ 7	6♊14	14♋39	8♍37
25	13♉34	6♋12	15♌13	7♎44
27	12♊34	6♌33	15♍ 1	5♏ 8
29	12♋19	5♍58	13♎ 7	0♐52
31	11♌44	...	9♏27	25 23

d.	SEP	OCT	NOV	DEC
☽ 1	7♑22	9♒25	23♓29	26♈36
3	1♒ 7	3♓19	18♈46	23♉37
5	24 57	27 50	15♉20	22♊ 9
7	19♓ 9	23♈12	13♊ 1	21♋28
9	13♈56	19♉31	11♋22	20♌36
11	9♉30	16♊43	9♌50	18♍53
13	6♊ 6	14♋38	8♍ 2	16♎11
15	3♋52	13♌ 4	5♎48	12♏37
17	2♌45	11♍43	2♏59	8♐20
19	2♍16	10♎ 7	29 25	3♑10
21	1♎32	7♏44	24♐54	27 37
23	29 42	4♐11	19♑27	21♒22
25	26♏19	29 23	13♒17	14♓59
27	21♐29	23♑34	6♓59	9♈ 4
29	15♑39	17♒19	1♈11	4♉22
31	...	11♓15	...	1♊26

STATIONS	☿	♀	♂	♃
	25Jan 19♒ 5	28Aug 1♎43	19Feb 16♎17	15Jul 23♓18
	15Feb 3♒31	10Oct 15♍41	10May 27♍27	10Nov 13♓25
		♄	♅	♆
	23May 16♊ 4	21May 9♒19	1Apr 25♐38	14Mar 0♋54
	16Jun 7♊34	9Oct 2♒42	2Sep 21♐38	12Oct 5♋57
	21Sep 18♎ 3	SIDER. TIME 6h 37m 53s		1 Jan Midn.
	13Oct 2♎58	18h 39m 51s Common Year		Noon. 1903

Noon		JAN	FEB	MAR	APR	MAY	JUN
☉	1	9♑40	11♒13	10♓30	11♈20	10♉40	10♊32
	9	17 49	19 20	18 30	19 12	18 25	18 11
	17	25 58	27 25	26 29	27 3	26 8	25 50
	25	4♒ 7	5♓29	4♈25	4♉51	3♊49	3♋28
☿	1	29♑ 8	17♑45	20♒45	17♈17	26♉22	18♉50
	7	2♒58	21 40	0♓16	29 25	25R22	22 50
	13	0R39	27 43	10 28	10♉17	22 14	29 3
	19	23♑23	5♒ 4	21 23	18 47	18 58	7♊18
	25	17 52	13 19	3♈ 1	24 14	17 24	17 22
	31	17D24	...	15 13	...	18D24	...
♀	1	25♏45	2♑32	7♒47	15♓44	22♈30	0♊30
	9	5♐ 5	12 13	17 34	25 32	2♉19	10 18
	17	14 33	21 56	27 21	5♈21	12 7	20 7
	25	24 7	1♒40	7♓ 9	15 9	21 55	29 56
♂	1	15♒44	10♓ 5	2♈36	26♈ 6	18♉ 7	10♊ 5
	13	25 10	19 27	11 47	5♉ 0	26 42	18 22
	25	4♓35	28 45	20 51	13 46	5♊11	26 33
♃	1	17♓50	23♓35	0♈ 6	7♈33	14♈39	21♈18
	13	19 52	26 11	2 57	10 26	17 21	23 33
	25	22 9	28 55	5 51	13 16	19 54	25 33
♄	1	8♒ 4	11♒41	15♒ 5	18♒12	20♒16	21♒ 0
	13	9 26	13 6	16 23	19 10	20 44	20R53
	25	10 50	14 31	17 34	19 57	20 58	20 32
♅	1	26♐38	28♐20	29♐28	29♐57	29♐39	28♐42
	13	27 20	28 52	29 45	29R55	29R20	28R12
	25	27 59	29 19	29 55	29 46	28 57	27 43
♆	1	4♋23	3♋37	3♋12	3♋14	3♋46	4♋42
	13	4R 5	3R23	3R 8	3 23	4 5	5 8
	25	3 46	3 14	3D11	3 37	4 28	5 34
Pl.	1	19♊15	18♊49	18♊39	18♊47	19♊15	19♊54
☊	1	1♎49	0♎10	28♍38	27♍ 0	25♍24	23♍46
1st		Fri	Mon	Tue	Fri	Sun	Wed

Noon		JUL	AUG	SEP	OCT	NOV	DEC
☉	1	9♋11	8♌46	8♍35	7♎52	8♏39	8♐53
	9	16 48	16 26	16 21	15 46	16 40	17 1
	17	24 26	24 7	24 9	23 41	24 44	25 9
	25	2♌ 5	1♍49	1♎58	1♏39	2♐48	3♑18
☿	1	29♊ 7	29♌54	1♎16	20♍ 1	9♏19	25♐33
	7	11♋54	8♍52	0R11	27 34	18 56	4♑ 2
	13	24 46	16 45	25♍29	7♎16	28 20	11 28
	19	6♌58	23 22	19 30	17 33	7♐34	16 24
	25	18 9	28 22	16D53	27 45	16 40	16R13
	31	28 19	1♎ 6	...	7♏41	...	9 47
♀	1	7♋18	15♌28	23♍44	0♏46	8♐56	15♑37
	9	17 8	25 20	3♎37	10 38	18 45	25 19
	17	26 59	5♍12	13 30	20 29	28 33	4♒58
	25	6♌50	15 5	23 22	0♐20	8♑18	14 32
♂	1	0♋36	21♋ 9	11♌ 8	29♌58	18♍53	6♎31
	13	8 38	28 57	18 43	7♍21	26 2	13 19
	25	16 34	6 40	26 14	14 40	3♎ 3	19 55
♃	1	26♈27	29♈38	29♈58	27♈26	23♈22	20♈36
	13	27 59	0♉ 8	29R15	25R53	21R59	20R15
	25	29 9	0R10	28 8	24 16	20 57	20D24
♄	1	20♒16	18♒21	16♒ 6	14♒36	14♒20	15♒54
	13	19R38	17R27	15R22	14R23	14 53	16 49
	25	18 51	16 34	14 48	14D22	15 30	17 54
♅	1	27♐30	26♐26	25♐58	26♐15	27♐19	28♐53
	13	27R 2	26R10	26D 0	26 35	27 53	29 35
	25	26 38	26 0	26 8	27 1	28 32	0♑18
♆	1	5♋48	6♋54	7♋45	8♋ 9	8♋ 4	7♋31
	13	6 14	7 16	7 58	8R11	7R54	7R12
	25	6 40	7 35	8 6	8 8	7 39	6 52
Pl.	1	20♊35	21♊ 9	21♊33	21♊36	21♊20	20♊50
☊	1	22♍11	20♍32	18♍54	17♍18	15♍40	14♍ 5
1st		Fri	Mon	Thu	Sat	Tue	Thu

d.		JAN	FEB	MAR	APR
☽	1	15♊42	8♌31	1♍45	24♎34
	3	15♋21	9♍ 0	1♎57	22♏49
	5	15♌31	8♎25	0♏57	19♐25
	7	14♍58	6♏ 8	28 12	14♑30
	9	13♎ 1	2♐14	23♐47	8♒32
	11	9♏41	27 7	18♑11	2♓ 9
	13	5♐14	21♑16	11♒57	25 57
	15	0♑ 2	15♒ 1	5♓34	20♈22
	17	24 15	8♓39	29 24	15♉39
	19	18♒ 3	2♈25	23♈44	11♊51
	21	11♓39	26 39	18♉49	8♋55
	23	5♈25	21♉50	14♊52	6♌47
	25	29 56	18♊25	12♋ 9	5♍17
	27	25 50	16♋44	10♌42	4♎11
	29	23♊39	16♌33	10♍13	2♏55
	31	23♋17	...	9♎56	...

d.		MAY	JUN	JUL	AUG
☽	1	0♐48	18♑ 3	20♒36	4♈26
	3	27 21	12♒31	14♓18	28 22
	5	22♑29	6♓17	7♈59	23♉17
	7	16♒34	29 59	2♉21	19♊46
	9	10♓13	24♈21	28 3	18♋ 3
	11	4♈ 7	19♉58	25♊28	17♌47
	13	28 51	17♊ 3	24♋23	17♍57
	15	24♉44	15♋21	23♌59	17♎25
	17	21♊45	14♌11	23♍16	15♏30
	19	19♋34	12♍50	21♎37	12♐ 7
	21	17♌45	10♎57	18♏52	7♑30
	23	16♍ 1	8♏26	15♐ 6	2♒ 0
	25	14♎12	5♐15	10♑28	25 55
	27	12♏ 4	1♑15	5♒ 4	19♓33
	29	9♐16	26 22	29 2	13♈11
	31	5♑25	...	22♓39	7♉13

d.		SEP	OCT	NOV	DEC
☽	1	19♉32	24♊37	15♌31	24♍22
	3	15♊ 5	21♋31	13♍58	22♎51
	5	12♋13	19♌53	13♎13	21♏23
	7	11♌ 5	19♍30	12♏38	19♐22
	9	11♍12	19♎37	11♐15	16♑ 9
	11	11♎29	19♏ 5	8♑19	11♒31
	13	10♏46	17♐ 0	3♒44	5♓43
	15	8♐24	13♑ 7	27 55	29 22
	17	4♑22	7♒46	21♓32	23♈10
	19	29 2	1♓34	15♈17	17♉48
	21	22♒57	25 9	9♉44	13♊40
	23	16♓33	19♈ 1	5♊10	10♋48
	25	10♈14	13♉29	1♋31	8♌46
	27	4♉17	8♊42	28 37	7♍ 5
	29	28 58	4♋44	26♌15	5♎20
	31	...	1♌41	...	3♏23

STATIONS	☿	♀	♂	♃
	7Jan 2♒58	None	None	21Aug 0♉13
	29Jan 17♑ 1			16Dec 20♈14
	3May 26♉21	♄	♅	♆
	26May 17♉23	1Jun 21♒ 0	5Apr 29♐57	12Oct 8♋11
	3Sep 1♎19	20Oct 14♒21	5Sep 25♐27	... ...
	25Sep 16♍53	SIDER. TIME		1 Jan
	23Dec 17♐ 1	6h 36m 55s		Midn.
		18h 38m 53s		Noon.
		LEAP YEAR		1904

Noon		JAN	FEB	MAR	APR	MAY	JUN
☉	1	10♑26	11♒59	10♓16	11♈ 5	10♉26	10♊18
	9	18 35	20 6	18 16	18 58	18 11	17 57
	17	26 44	28 11	26 14	26 48	25 53	25 36
	25	4♒53	6♓14	4♈10	4♉36	3♊35	3♋13
☿	1	8♑26	19♑12	2♓48	29♈40	28♈28	18♉ 6
	7	2R 5	27 30	13 48	5♉30	27R13	27 47
	13	1D10	6♒23	25 25	7 27	28D43	9♊ 0
	19	4 37	15 49	7♈20	5R46	2♉43	21 28
	25	10 35	25 46	18 45	1 57	8 48	4♋34
	31	17 53	...	28 21	...	16 38	...
♀	1	22♒50	28♓ 9	26♈ 1	14♉17	3♉56	1♉36
	9	2♓12	6♈41	2♉34	14R29	29♈59	5 59
	17	11 26	14 49	8 6	12 6	28R18	11 34
	25	20 27	22 27	12 12	7 40	29D 7	18 5
♂	1	23♎39	8♏54	19♏38	25♏ 5	20♏ 5	10♏ 2
	13	29 51	13 58	22 47	24R23	15R50	8R25
	25	5♏41	18 21	24 41	21 55	11 49	8D46
♃	1	20♈43	23♈55	28♈45	5♉24	12♉27	19♉45
	13	21 38	25 48	1♉12	8 11	15 19	22 28
	25	22 58	27 58	3 49	11 1	18 8	25 3
♄	1	18♒37	22♒ 7	25♒28	28♒53	1♓25	2♓47
	13	19 54	23 33	26 52	0♓ 1	2 7	2 54
	25	21 17	25 0	28 10	1 0	2 36	2R47
♅	1	0♑44	2♑27	3♑37	4♑13	4♑ 2	1♑58
	13	1 26	3 1	3 57	4R14	3R45	2R41
	25	2 6	3 29	4 9	4 7	3 23	2 12
♆	1	6♋41	5♋53	5♋26	5♋26	5♋56	6♋51
	13	6R20	5R39	5R23	5 35	6 15	7 16
	25	6 2	5 29	5D24	5 48	6 37	7 43
Pl.	1	20♊16	19♊48	19♊38	19♊48	20♊30	20♊53
☊	1	12♍26	10♍48	9♍19	7♍40	6♍ 5	4♍26
	1st	Sun	Wed	Wed	Sat	Mon	Thu

Noon		JUL	AUG	SEP	OCT	NOV	DEC
☉	1	8♋57	8♌32	8♍21	7♎38	8♏24	8♐39
	9	16 35	16 12	16 7	15 31	16 26	16 46
	17	24 12	23 53	23 55	23 27	24 29	24 54
	25	1♌50	1♍35	1♎44	1♏24	2♐34	3♑ 3
☿	1	17♋22	5♍47	3♍55	29♍ 9	20♏45	29♐33
	7	29 13	10 51	0R40	9♎54	29 44	1♑ 9
	13	9♌55	13 42	2D22	20 18	8♐24	26♐34
	19	19 27	13R36	8 54	0♏18	16 39	18R41
	25	27 46	10 12	18 28	9 55	24 2	15 1
	31	4♍46	4 47	...	19 13	...	16D58
♀	1	23♉24	24♊43	29♋36	5♍14	13♎16	20♏43
	9	0♊58	3♋28	8♌57	14 57	23 13	0♐46
	17	8 56	12 25	18 25	24 45	3♏12	10 49
	25	17 14	21 31	28 0	4♎36	13 12	20 52
♂	1	9♏37	19♏44	6♐10	25♐30	17♑35	10♒ 4
	13	12 32	25 33	13 36	3♑52	26 30	19 14
	25	16 46	2♐ 4	21 27	12 28	5♒31	28 25
♃	1	26♉18	1♊54	5♊33	6♊27	4♊20	0♊27
	13	28 39	3 35	6 15	5R59	2R53	28♉56
	25	0♊46	4 56	6 30	5 4	1 16	27R42
♄	1	2♓38	1♓ 6	28♒50	26♒56	26♒12	27♒ 2
	13	2R11	0R15	27R59	26R28	26 21	27 46
	25	1 33	29 21	27 15	26 14	26 45	28 42
♅	1	1♑58	0♑51	0♑16	0♑27	1♑24	2♑54
	13	1R29	0R33	0D15	0 44	1 57	3 35
	25	1 4	0 20	0 21	1 7	2 34	4 18
♆	1	7♋56	9♋ 3	9♋55	10♋22	10♋19	9♋48
	13	8 23	9 26	10 10	10 25	10R10	9R30
	25	8 48	9 45	10 19	10R23	9 56	9 11
Pl.	1	21♊34	22♊12	22♊35	22♊39	22♊23	21♊54
☊	1	2♍51	1♍12	29♌34	27♌59	26♌20	24♌45
	1st	Sat	Tue	Fri	Sun	Wed	Fri

☽ d.	JAN	FEB	MAR	APR
1	17♏17	7♑40	17♑27	3♓27
3	14♐43	3♒ 4	12♒16	27 7
5	11♑22	27 40	6♓24	20♈44
7	6♒59	21♓36	0♈ 7	14♉35
9	1♓33	15♈13	23 44	8♊55
11	25 21	8♉58	17♉34	4♋ 1
13	18♈58	3♊30	12♊ 4	0♌17
15	13♉ 5	29 24	7♋46	28 5
17	8♊22	27 2	5♌ 5	27♍27
19	5♋12	26♌14	4♍ 9	27♎48
21	3♌29	26♍14	4♎25	27♏53
23	2♍35	25♎56	4♏44	26♐32
25	1♎43	24♏31	3♐54	23♑15
27	0♏15	21♐39	1♑18	18♒18
29	27 54	...	27 0	12♓17
31	24♐38	...	21♒30	...

☽ d.	MAY	JUN	JUL	AUG
1	5♈53	20♉18	23♊55	12♌51
3	29 34	15♊10	20♋13	11♍14
5	23♉42	10♋49	17♌23	10♎ 0
7	18♊26	7♌15	15♍12	8♏38
9	13♋53	4♍26	13♎24	6♐44
11	10♌15	2♎26	11♏49	4♑ 5
13	7♍47	1♏13	10♐ 8	0♒33
15	6♎36	0♐19	7♑54	26 4
17	6♏21	28 58	4♒40	20♓42
19	6♐ 6	26♑23	0♓13	14♈41
21	4♑42	22♒15	24 41	8♉24
23	1♒32	16♓48	18♈31	2♊23
25	26 40	10♈36	12♉18	27 14
27	20♓42	4♉21	6♊42	23♋28
29	14♈20	28 40	2♋11	21♌18
31	8♉10	...	28 59	20♍25

☽ d.	SEP	OCT	NOV	DEC
1	5♎14	14♏13	6♑41	12♒ 8
3	4♏46	13♐30	3♒39	7♓34
5	3♐30	11♑ 7	28 56	1♈48
7	1♑ 1	7♒ 8	23♓ 9	25 31
9	27 19	1♓58	16♈55	19♉17
11	22♒37	26 7	10♉38	13♊28
13	17♓ 9	19♈55	4♊34	8♋12
15	11♈10	13♉39	28 52	3♌35
17	4♉54	7♊30	23 45	29 44
19	28 41	1♋49	19♌34	26♍52
21	22♊57	27 1	16♍44	25♎10
23	18♋17	23♌38	15♎31	24♏27
25	15♌12	22♍ 3	15♏35	23♐59
27	13♍54	22♎ 6	15♐50	22♑44
29	13♎57	22♏43	14♑55	19♒58
31	...	22♐28	...	15♓33

STATIONS

☿	♀	♂	♃
12Jan 0♑57	7Apr 14♉40	4Apr 25♏ 6	26Sep 6♊30
14Apr 7♉24	19May 28♈17	18Jun 8♏20	...
8May 27♈16	♄	♅	♆
17Aug 14♍ 0	14Jun 2♓54	9Apr 4♑14	17Mar 5♋22
9Sep 0♍38	31Oct 26♒12	10Sep 0♑15	15Oct 10♋25
27Dec 15♐ 8			

SIDER. TIME	1 Jan
6h 39m 54s	Midn.
18h 41m 52s	Noon
Common Year	1905

Noon	JAN	FEB	MAR	APR	MAY	JUN
☉ 1	10♑11	11♒45	10♓ 0	10♈51	10♉11	10♊ 4
9	18 21	19 51	18 1	18 43	17 56	17 43
17	26 29	27 56	25 59	26 33	25 39	25 22
25	4♒38	6♓ 0	3♈56	4♉22	3♊21	3♋ 0
☿ 1	17♐43	28♑25	17♓36	17♈11	13♈38	1♊ 9
7	23 29	8♒ 4	28 57	12R38	19 51	14 5
13	0♑49	18 12	9♈ 4	8 46	27 39	27 13
19	9 0	28 50	16 18	7D34	6♉49	9♋40
25	17 43	9♓59	19 16	9 22	17 19	20 59
31	26 52	...	17R47	...	29 5	...
♀ 1	29♐40	8♒38	13♓43	22♈17	29♉14	6♋57
9	9♑44	18 40	23 42	2♉10	9♊ 1	16 36
17	19 47	28 42	3♈40	12 2	18 46	26 12
25	29 51	8♓43	13 36	21 53	28 29	5♌45
♂ 1	3♓47	27♓23	18♈18	10♉50	1♊57	23♊ 6
13	12 57	6♈24	27 6	19 21	10 13	1♋ 8
25	22 4	15 20	5♉48	27 47	18 23	9 5
♃ 1	27♉ 9	26♉40	28♉55	3♊40	9♊43	16♊42
13	26R34	27 21	0♊31	5 58	12 22	19 29
25	26D29	28 27	2 26	8 26	15 6	22 14
♄ 1	29♒20	2♓38	6♓ 0	9♓38	12♓34	14♓31
13	0♓31	4 3	7 27	10 54	13 29	14 54
25	1 49	5 31	8 51	12 3	14 12	15 2
♅ 1	4♑43	6♑29	7♑43	8♑26	8♑21	7♑34
13	5 26	7 4	8 5	8 30	8R 7	7R 7
25	6 7	7 34	8 20	8R26	7 48	6 39
♆ 1	8♋59	8♋10	7♋42	7♋39	8♋ 7	9♋ 0
13	8R39	7R55	7R37	7 47	8 25	9 25
25	8 20	7 45	7D37	7 59	8 46	9 51
Pl. 1	21♊18	20♊51	20♊39	20♊47	21♊13	21♊53
☊ 1	23♌ 6	21♌28	19♌59	18♌20	16♌45	15♌ 7
1st	Mon	Thu	Thu	Sun	Tue	Fri

Noon	JUL	AUG	SEP	OCT	NOV	DEC
☉ 1	8♋43	8♌18	8♍ 7	7♎24	8♏10	8♐24
9	16 20	15 58	15 53	15 17	16 11	16 31
17	23 58	23 39	23 40	23 12	24 14	24 39
25	1♌36	1♍21	1♎30	1♏10	2♐19	2♑48
☿ 1	0♌57	25♌42	20♌17	12♎55	29♏36	5♐24
7	9 33	22R46	29 17	22 52	6♐53	29♏43
13	16 42	18 2	10♍10	2♏21	12 40	0♐16
19	22 6	14 21	21 28	11 27	15 27	5D14
25	25 22	14D25	2♎28	20 7	12R57	12 23
31	25R55	19 6	...	28 17	...	20 32
♀ 1	12♌52	19♍ 3	23♎31	23♏18	13♐30	6♐19
9	22 19	28 9	1♏56	0♐ 3	14 44	1R59
17	1♍42	7♎ 8	10 3	5 57	13R30	29♏39
25	11 0	15 57	17 48	10 41	9 54	29D54
♂ 1	13♋ 2	3♌10	23♌ 0	12♍ 0	1♎27	20♎ 8
13	20 52	10 53	0♍37	19 33	8 57	27 33
25	28 39	18 33	8 13	27 5	16 25	4♏54
♃ 1	23♊36	0♋19	6♋ 0	9♋46	11♋ 3	9♋22
13	26 17	2 41	7 45	10 37	10R43	8R 0
25	28 52	4 50	9 11	11 2	9 55	6 26
♄ 1	15♓ 1	14♓ 1	11♓55	9♓44	8♓25	8♓37
13	14R48	13R17	11R 0	9R 4	8D18	9 8
25	14 22	12 26	10 8	8 35	8 27	9 53
♅ 1	6♑24	5♑15	4♑34	4♑38	5♑28	6♑53
13	5R56	4R55	4R30	4 52	5 59	7 34
25	5 29	4 40	4D33	5 13	6 34	8 17
♆ 1	10♋ 4	11♋12	12♋ 6	12♋35	12♋35	12♋ 6
13	10 31	11 35	12 21	12 39	12R26	11R48
25	10 57	11 56	12 32	12R38	12 14	11 29
Pl. 1	22♊34	23♊12	23♊36	23♊41	23♊26	22♊58
☊ 1	13♌31	11♌53	10♌14	8♌39	7♌ 0	5♌25
1st	Sun	Wed	Sat	Mon	Thu	Sat

d.	JAN	FEB	MAR	APR
☽ 1	27♓51	11♉31	19♉22	3♋22
3	21♈50	5♊22	13♊11	28 9
5	15♉33	29 49	7♋34	24♌23
7	9♊37	25♋20	3♌ 8	22♍27
9	4♋23	22♌ 5	0♍16	22♎ 8
11	0♌ 2	19♍54	28 52	22♏25
13	26 32	18♎21	28♎17	22♐ 0
15	23♍47	16♏55	27♏36	20♑ 6
17	21♎41	15♐11	26♐ 1	16♒37
19	20♏ 6	12♑54	23♑18	11♓56
21	18♐44	9♒52	19♒32	6♈28
23	17♑ 3	5♓59	14♓55	0♉32
25	14♒28	1♈10	9♈37	24 20
27	10♓38	25 32	3♉46	18♊ 4
29	5♈34	...	27 33	12♋ 2
31	29 38	...	21♊20	...

d.	MAY	JUN	JUL	AUG
☽ 1	6♌44	25♍35	3♏47	27♐36
3	2♍46	24♎ 7	3♐11	26♑28
5	0♎41	24♏ 8	3♑ 3	24♒32
7	0♏24	24♐35	2♒17	21♓19
9	1♐ 1	24♑ 7	0♓ 5	16♈45
11	1♑ 7	21♒53	26 13	11♉ 7
13	29 35	17♓53	21♈ 0	4♊56
15	26♒12	12♈33	14♉58	28 49
17	21♓23	6♉30	8♊43	23♋18
19	15♈40	0♊13	2♋43	18♌47
21	9♉31	24 4	27 19	15♍22
23	3♊15	18♋18	22♌43	12♎56
25	27 4	13♌ 6	19♍ 0	11♏ 7
27	21♋12	8♍46	16♎12	9♐32
29	16♌ 1	5♎35	14♏18	7♑52
31	12♍ 0	...	13♐ 5	5♒49

d.	SEP	OCT	NOV	DEC
☽ 1	19♒34	25♒14	11♉31	14♊13
3	16♓24	20♈33	5♊30	7♋53
5	12♈12	15♉ 5	29 10	1♌42
7	6♉57	8♊59	22♋53	26 6
9	0♊57	2♋40	17♌16	21♍41
11	24 42	26 42	12♍59	18♎58
13	18♋50	21♌49	10♎36	18♏ 7
15	13♌59	18♍34	10♏ 4	18♐31
17	10♍32	17♎ 6	10♐30	18♑53
19	8♎29	16♏47	10♑32	17♒58
21	7♏19	16♐31	9♒ 7	15♓15
23	6♐16	15♑18	6♓ 3	10♈55
25	4♑40	12♒47	1♈38	5♉26
27	2♒18	9♓ 7	26 19	29 19
29	29 9	4♈34	20♉26	23♊ 0
31	...	29 21	...	16♋46

STATIONS	☿	♀	♂	♃
	27Mar 19♈14	10Nov 14♐43	None	22Jan 26♉28
	19Apr 7♈34	21Dec 29♐28		30Oct 11♋ 4
	30Jul 26♌ 2	♄	♅	♆
	23Aug 13♌58	1Jul 15♓ 1	14Apr 8♑30	31Mar 7♋39
	21Nov 15♐18	13Nov 8♓18	15Sep 4♑30	17Oct 12♋30
	10Dec 29♒15	SIDER. TIME		1 Jan
		6h 38m 57s		Midn.
		18h 40m 55s		Noon
		Common Year		1906

1907

Noon		JAN	FEB	MAR	APR	MAY	JUN
☉	1	9♑56	11♒30	9♓46	10♈37	9♉57	9♊50
	9	18 6	19 36	17 46	18 29	17 42	17 29
	17	26 15	27 41	25 45	26 20	25 26	25 8
	25	4♒23	5♓45	3♈42	4♉ 8	3♊ 7	2♋46
☿	1	21♐57	10♒38	27♓51	18♓41	17♈53	19♊38
	7	0♑42	21 12	1♈46	20 33	27 57	1♋32
	13	9 46	2♓ 6	0R27	24 56	9♉11	12 0
	19	19 9	12 58	25♓30	1♈13	21 29	20 54
	25	28 51	22 47	20 39	8 57	4♊32	28 9
	31	8♒55	...	18 41	...	17 32	...
♀	1	2♐ 4	24♐58	24♑ 3	29♒21	4♈44	11♉51
	9	6 17	2♑49	2♒58	8♓43	14 17	21 30
	17	11 55	11 6	12 2	18 8	23 51	1♊ 9
	25	18 33	19 40	21 14	27 37	3♉27	10 50
♂	1	9♏10	27♏43	13♐44	29♐52	12♑24	18♑49
	13	16 26	4♐42	20 14	5♑23	15 56	18R28
	25	23 36	11 30	26 26	10 16	18 12	16 24
♃	1	5♋29	1♋59	1♋ 1	2♋53	7♋ 1	12♋51
	13	3R55	1R15	1 24	4 18	9 7	15 22
	25	2 36	1 0	2 13	6 2	11 26	17 59
♄	1	10♓24	13♓24	16♓42	20♓29	23♓46	26♓15
	13	11 27	11 5	18 11	21 52	24 52	26 53
	25	12 39	16 13	19 39	23 10	25 48	27 17
♅	1	8♑42	10♑29	11♑47	12♐36	12♑38	11♑56
	13	9 25	11 5	12 11	12 42	12R27	11R31
	25	10 6	11 37	12 29	12R41	12 9	11 4
♆	1	11♋17	10♋27	9♋58	9♋52	10♋18	11♋ 9
	13	10R57	10R12	9R52	9 59	10 35	11 34
	25	10 38	10 0	9D51	10 10	10 56	12 0
Pl.	1	22♊23	21♊56	21♊43	21♊50	22♊15	22♊54
☊	1	3♌47	2♌ 9	0♌39	29♋ 1	27♋25	25♋47
	1st	Tue	Fri	Fri	Mon	Wed	Sat

Noon		JUL	AUG	SEP	OCT	NOV	DEC
☉	1	8♋29	8♌ 4	7♍53	7♎ 9	7♏55	8♐ 9
	9	16 7	15 44	15 39	15 2	15 56	16 16
	17	23 45	23 25	23 26	22 58	23 59	24 24
	25	1♌23	1♍ 7	1♎16	0♏55	2♐ 4	2♑33
☿	1	3♌31	26♋54	2♍24	24♎35	29♏19	17♏58
	7	6 38	26D52	14 1	3♏18	28R31	25 2
	13	7R 5	0♌47	25 5	11 27	22 21	3♐21
	19	4 48	8 26	5♎31	18 49	15 16	12 11
	25	0 46	18 48	15 19	24 59	13D48	21 17
	31	27♋16	0♍26	...	28 58	...	0♑32
♀	1	18♊ 7	25♋58	4♍13	11♎33	20♏16	27♐45
	9	27 51	5♌48	14 9	21 32	0♐16	7♑44
	17	7♋36	15 40	24 6	1♏32	10 16	17 43
	25	17 23	25 33	4♎ 4	11 31	20 15	27 41
♂	1	14♑52	7♑24	10♑36	23♑18	11♒35	1♓35
	13	11R23	7D 7	14 50	29 57	19 25	9 54
	25	8 26	8 48	20 15	7♒10	27 29	18 17
♃	1	19♋18	26♋13	2♌48	8♌17	12♌14	13♌37
	13	21 59	28 50	5 8	10 4	13 7	13R22
	25	24 40	1♌23	7 17	11 32	13 34	12 38
♄	1	27♓24	27♓ 2	25♓17	23♓ 1	21♓10	20♓43
	13	27R27	26R30	24R23	22R11	20R48	20 59
	25	27 15	25 46	23 28	21 29	20 41	21 30
♅	1	10♑49	9♑38	8♑51	8♑48	9♑32	10♑52
	13	10R20	9R15	8R45	8 59	10 0	11 32
	25	9 52	8 59	8D45	9 18	10 34	12 13
♆	1	12♋13	13♋21	14♋16	14♋48	14♋50	14♋23
	13	12 40	13 44	14 32	14 53	14R42	14R 6
	25	13 6	14 5	14 44	14 52	14 31	13 47
Pl.	1	23♊35	24♊13	24♊36	24♊42	24♊26	24♊57
☊	1	24♋12	22♋33	20♋55	19♋19	17♋41	16♋ 5
	1st	Mon	Thu	Sun	Tue	Fri	Sun

d.		JAN	FEB	MAR	APR
☽	1	28♋46	15♍18	24♍43	15♏42
	3	23♌ 8	11♎29	21♎44	14♐20
	5	18♍17	8♏39	19♏27	12♑44
	7	14♎36	6♐48	17♐35	10♒40
	9	12♏25	5♑44	15♑56	8♓ 4
	11	11♐40	4♒58	14♒15	4♈49
	13	11♑43	3♓45	12♓12	0♉45
	15	11♒29	1♈20	9♈18	25 44
	17	9♓57	27 24	5♉13	19♊51
	19	6♈42	22♉ 6	29 55	13♋30
	21	1♉53	15♊58	23♊48	7♌18
	23	26 1	9♋38	17♋28	1♍58
	25	19♊41	3♌44	11♌38	28 7
	27	13♋26	28 41	6♍53	25♎57
	29	7♌38	...	3♎33	25♏ 4
	31	2♍32	...	1♏27	...

d.		MAY	JUN	JUL	AUG
☽	1	24♐32	17♒41	24♓50	12♉41
	3	23♑27	15♓14	21♈ 5	7♊ 3
	5	21♒23	11♈27	16♉ 2	0♋46
	7	18♓19	6♉38	10♊ 8	24 21
	9	14♈23	1♊ 3	3♋48	18♌14
	11	9♉40	24 57	27 24	12♍41
	13	4♊13	18♋32	21♌13	7♎56
	15	28 7	12♌11	15♍36	4♏ 7
	17	21♋42	6♍20	10♎56	1♐27
	19	15♌28	1♎35	7♏38	29 57
	21	10♍ 6	28 26	5♐55	29♑24
	23	6♎12	27♏ 7	5♑35	29♒ 4
	25	4♏10	27♐10	5♒49	27♓58
	27	3♐42	27♑30	5♓29	25♈23
	29	3♑49	26♒58	3♈40	21♉ 5
	31	3♒23	...	0♉ 4	15♊28

d.		SEP	OCT	NOV	DEC
☽	1	27♊22	28♋59	13♍ 9	16♎44
	3	20♋57	22♌57	8♎55	14♏11
	5	14♌48	17♍51	6♏ 9	13♐ 9
	7	9♍21	13♎55	4♐33	12♑50
	9	4♎47	11♏ 4	3♑22	12♒15
	11	1♏ 6	8♐52	2♒ 0	10♓42
	13	28 13	6♑59	0♓ 5	7♈57
	15	26♐ 2	5♒10	27 32	4♉ 5
	17	24 29	3♓19	24♈15	29 17
	19	23♒22	1♈11	20♉ 9	23♊44
	21	22♓ 6	28 21	15♊ 8	17♋37
	23	19♈58	24♉24	9♋17	11♌13
	25	16♉24	19♊15	2♌55	4♍56
	27	11♊24	13♋11	26 36	29 15
	29	5♋22	6♌47	20♍59	24♎48
	31	...	0♍47	...	22♏ 2

STATIONS	☿	♀	♂	♃
	9Mar 1♈54 1Apr 18♓41 12Jul 7♌12 5Aug 26♋27 4Ncv 29♏35 24Nov 13♏35	None	6Jun 18♑53 10Aug 7♑ 0	26Feb 1♋ 0 1Dec 13♌37
		♄	♅	♆
		10Jul 27♓28 26Nov 20♓41	18Apr 12♑43 19Sep 8♑44	22Mar 9♋51 1Nov 14♋50
		SIDER. TIME 6H 37m 59s 18h 39m 57s Common Year		1 Jan Midn. Noon. 1907

1908

Noon		JAN	FEB	MAR	APR	MAY	JUN
☉	1	9♑41	11♒15	10♓31	11♈22	10♉42	10♊34
	9	17 51	19 21	18 32	19 14	18 26	18 13
	17	26 0	27 27	26 30	27 4	26 9	25 51
	25	4♒ 8	5♓30	4♈26	4♉52	3♊51	3♋29
☿	1	2♑ 6	23♒47	7♓49	14♓ 9	3♉29	3♋14
	7	11 35	3♓41	2R29	21 58	16 12	10 14
	13	21 19	11 32	0 37	0♈51	29 13	15 6
	19	1♒20	15 2	2D21	10 44	11♊36	17 29
	25	11 38	12R44	6 44	21 37	22 37	17R12
	31	22 5	...	12 59	...	1♋52	...
♀	1	6♒23	14♓39	19♈37	25♉13	26♊ 7	18♋48
	9	16 19	24 24	29 2	3♊55	3♋18	21 22
	17	26 13	4♈ 5	8♉18	12 20	9 42	21R41
	25	6♓ 4	13 40	17 24	20 23	15 7	19 31
♂	1	23♓12	14♈57	5♉ 5	26♉12	16♊11	6♋27
	13	1♈38	23 19	13 19	4♊14	24 4	14 12
	25	10 3	1♉38	21 28	12 13	1♋54	21 54
♃	1	12♌ 2	8♌15	4♌53	3♌34	5♌ 7	9♌ 5
	13	10R43	6R42	4R 1	3 52	6 25	11 6
	25	9 11	5 21	3 36	4 36	8 1	13 18
♄	1	21♓55	24♓31	27♓47	1♈37	5♈ 8	8♈ 5
	13	22 47	25 48	29 15	3 4	6 23	8 56
	25	23 50	27 11	0♈45	4 28	7 30	9 35
♅	1	12♑38	14♑27	15♑51	16♑45	16♑52	16♑15
	13	13 21	15 4	16 17	16 53	16R42	15R51
	25	14 3	15 38	16 36	16R54	16 27	15 24
♆	1	13♋35	12♋45	12♋13	12♋ 6	12♋30	13♋20
	13	13 15	12R29	12R 6	12 12	12 47	13 44
	25	12 55	12 17	12D 5	12 23	13 7	14 10
Pl.	1	22♊27	22♊59	22♊47	22♊52	23♊17	23♊55
☊	1	14♋27	12♋48	11♋16	9♋38	8♋ 2	6♋24
	1st	Wed	Sat	Sun	Wed	Fri	Mon

Noon		JUL	AUG	SEP	OCT	NOV	DEC
☉	1	9♋12	8♌48	8♍37	7♎54	8♏41	8♐55
	9	16 50	16 28	16 23	15 47	16 42	17 3
	17	24 28	24 9	24 10	23 43	24 45	25 11
	25	2♌ 6	1♍51	2♎ 0	1♏41	2♐51	3♑20
☿	1	14♋32	20♋47	19♍27	3♏ 6	0♏25	26♏32
	7	10R55	0♌57	29 35	9 3	27D55	5♐49
	13	8 26	12 44	9♎ 2	12 56	1♏33	15 10
	19	8D44	24 54	17 49	13R19	8 45	24 34
	25	12 23	6♍39	25 54	8 48	17 23	4♑ 5
	31	19 21	17 40	...	1 26	...	13 45
♀	1	16♋28	5♋46	23♋26	22♌40	27♍40	3♏44
	9	11R34	8 11	0♌31	1♍22	7♎ 8	13 32
	17	7 25	12 21	8 12	10 20	16 44	23 24
	25	5 27	17 50	16 20	19 31	26 25	3♐18
♂	1	25♋45	15♌31	5♍15	24♍24	14♎21	3♏52
	13	3♌25	23 9	12 53	2♎ 6	22 8	11 44
	25	11 4	0♍47	20 33	9 50	29 57	19 38
♃	1	14♌28	20♌55	27♌40	3♍56	9♍29	13♍12
	13	16 54	23 32	0♍14	6 14	11 12	14 3
	25	19 25	26 9	2 44	8 21	12 37	14 29
♄	1	9♈49	10♈ 6	8♈50	6♈39	4♈27	3♈24
	13	10 7	9R47	8R 1	5R43	3R51	3D25
	25	10R11	9 14	7 7	4 52	3 29	3 41
♅	1	15♑10	13♑57	13♑ 7	12♑58	13♑37	14♑53
	13	14R41	13R34	12R58	13 7	14 3	15 32
	25	14 13	13 15	12D56	13 24	14 35	16 13
♆	1	14♋23	15♋31	16♋28	17♋ 1	17♋ 5	16♋39
	13	14 50	15 55	16 44	17 6	16R58	16R22
	25	15 17	16 17	16 57	17R 7	16 46	16 3
Pl.	1	24♊37	25♊14	25♊39	25♊45	25♊31	25♊ 3
☊	1	4♋49	3♋10	1♋32	29♊56	28♊18	26♊43
	1st	Wed	Sat	Tue	Thu	Sun	Tue

	d.	JAN	FEB	MAR	APR
☽	1	6♐20	29♑ 2	22♒25	15♈15
	3	6♑ 1	29♒29	22♓26	13♉ 9
	5	6♒20	29♓ 6	21♈24	9♊26
	7	6♓ 4	26♈59	18♉35	4♋12
	9	4♈23	23♉ 2	13♊59	28 3
	11	1♉ 3	17♊39	8♋ 8	21♌42
	13	26 20	11♋27	1♌44	15♍48
	15	20♊40	5♌ 2	25 26	10♎46
	17	14♋29	28 47	19♍40	6♏44
	19	8♌ 6	22♍57	14♎38	3♐35
	21	1♍48	17♎44	10♏21	1♑ 4
	23	25 54	13♏20	6♐51	29 2
	25	20♎46	10♐ 1	4♑10	27♒23
	27	16♏52	8♑ 3	2♒26	25♓54
	29	14♐34	7♒25	1♓30	24♈ 5
	31	13♑55	...	0♈48	...

	d.	MAY	JUN	JUL	AUG
☽	1	21♉21	7♋53	10♌18	24♍33
	3	17♊19	2♌ 0	3♍58	18♎44
	5	12♋ 2	25 42	27 50	13♏47
	7	5♌56	19♍35	22♎25	10♐15
	9	29 38	14♎14	18♏17	8♑27
	11	23♍49	10♏11	15♐49	8♒17
	13	19♎ 1	7♐40	14♑57	8♓40
	15	15♏30	6♑26	15♒ 0	8♈42
	17	13♐ 7	5♒47	14♓52	6♉56
	19	11♑26	4♓55	13♈33	3♊20
	21	9♒58	3♈14	10♉42	28 16
	23	8♓22	0♉29	6♊26	22♋19
	25	6♈20	26 40	1♋ 9	16♌ 1
	27	3♉40	21♊55	25 14	9♍42
	29	0♊ 7	16♋23	18♌58	3♎37
	31	25 33	...	12♍39	27 59

	d.	SEP	OCT	NOV	DEC
☽	1	10♏25	16♐ 1	7♒27	16♓46
	3	6♐ 4	12♑57	5♓53	15♈ 3
	5	3♑ 5	11♒12	4♈53	12♉56
	7	1♒47	10♓39	3♉45	10♊ 3
	9	1♓52	10♈34	♊43	6♋ 7
	11	2♈18	9♉46	28 14	1♌ 6
	13	1♉41	7♊21	23♋21	25 13
	15	29 12	3♋ 9	17♌27	18♍59
	17	24♊52	27 35	11♍11	12♎58
	19	19♋14	21♌21	5♎11	7♏47
	21	12♌58	15♍ 6	29 58	3♐53
	23	6♍39	9♎18	25♏48	1♑24
	25	0♎37	4♏13	22♐38	0♒ 0
	27	25 6	29 54	20♑17	29 1
	29	20♏10	26♐30	18♒25	27♓46
	31	...	23♑32	...	25♈46

STATIONS	☿	♀	♂	♃
	21Feb 14♓54	15Jun 21♋50	None	30Mar 3♌34
	14Mar 0♓41	28Jul 5♋21		31Dec 14♍31
		♄	♅	♆
	22Jun 17♋41	23Jul 10♈11	22Apr 16♑55	24Mar 12♋ 5
	16Jul 8♋11	7Dec 3♈22	23Sep 12♑56	21Oct 17♋ 7
	18Oct 13♏35	SIDER. TIME 6H 37m 2s		1 Jan Midn.
	7Nov 27♎55	18h 39m 0s		Noon.
		LEAP YEAR		1908

Noon		JAN	FEB	MAR	APR	MAY	JUN
☉	1	10♑28	12♒ 1	10♓17	11♈ 7	10♉28	10♊20
	9	18 37	20 7	18 17	19 0	18 12	17 59
	17	26 46	28 12	26 16	26 50	25 55	25 37
	25	4♒55	6♓16	4♈12	4♉38	3♊37	3♋15
☿	1	15♑23	28♒28	14♒42	22♓12	21♉23	27♊38
	7	25 15	26R29	18 59	2♈35	2♊55	26R51
	13	5♒12	20 0	25 10	13 51	12 36	24 2
	19	14 52	14 36	2♓39	25 59	20 4	20 49
	25	23 14	13D22	11 10	8♉43	25 7	19 4
	31	28 10	...	20 33	...	27 31	...
♀	1	12♐ 0	20♑37	25♒32	4♈ 5	11♉12	19♊21
	9	21 57	0♒36	5♓30	14 0	21 4	29 10
	17	1♑55	10 35	15 27	23 54	0♊55	8♋58
	25	11 53	20 33	25 24	3♉48	10 45	18 46
♂	1	24♏16	14♐53	3♑38	24♑26	14♒19	4♓ 3
	13	2♐13	22 54	11 41	2♒26	22 7	11 12
	25	10 13	0♑57	19 44	10 23	29 43	17 55
♃	1	14♍31	12♍50	9♍29	5♍54	4♍32	5♍56
	13	14R13	11R31	7R57	5R 2	4 45	7 10
	25	13 28	10 0	6 34	4 35	5 23	8 42
♄	1	3♈58	6♈ 7	9♈ 2	12♈49	16♈32	19♈53
	13	4 38	7 17	10 28	14 20	17 55	20 57
	25	5 31	8 35	11 57	15 49	19 12	21 50
♅	1	16♑37	18♑26	19♑50	20♑50	21♑ 4	20♑33
	13	17 20	19 5	20 18	21 1	20R57	20R11
	25	18 2	19 40	20 40	21 5	20 44	19 45
♆	1	15♋52	15♋ 1	14♋28	14♋19	14♋41	15♋29
	13	15 31	14R45	14R21	14 24	14 57	15 53
	25	15 12	14 32	14 19	14 34	15 16	16 19
Pl.	1	24♊29	24♊ 0	23♊48	23♊54	24♊18	24♊56
☊	1	25♊ 4	23♊26	21♊57	20♊18	18♊43	17♊ 4
	1st	Fri	Mon	Mon	Thu	Sat	Tue

Noon		JUL	AUG	SEP	OCT	NOV	DEC
☉	1	8♋59	8♌34	8♍23	7♎39	8♏26	8♐40
	9	16 36	16 13	16 9	15 33	16 27	16 48
	17	24 14	23 55	23 56	23 29	24 31	24 56
	25	1♌52	1♍37	1♎46	1♏26	2♐36	3♑ 5
☿	1	19♊57	5♌12	0♎44	27♎29	20♎49	7♐42
	7	23 44	17 35	8 57	24R22	29 37	17 7
	13	0♋20	29 16	16 13	17 39	9♏ 6	26 33
	19	9 29	10♍ 6	22 13	12 31	18 42	6♑ 3
	25	20 43	20 6	26 21	13D27	28 14	15 34
	31	3♌ 6	29 17	...	19 31	...	24 57
♀	1	26♋ 7	3♍56	11♎26	17♏12	23♐13	25♑55
	9	5♌53	13 38	21 2	26 37	2♑14	3♒54
	17	15 39	23 20	0♏35	5♐58	11 4	11 20
	25	25 25	3♎ 0	10 6	15 13	19 40	18 4
♂	1	21♓ 4	3♈40	6♈11	28♓44	25♓53	3♈43
	13	26 47	6 9	3R48	26R14	27 59	8 46
	25	1♈30	6R45	0 24	25D28	1♈31	14 32
♃	1	9♍35	14♍58	21♍18	27♍46	4♎12	9♎32
	13	11 30	17 20	23 53	0♎20	6 29	11 15
	25	13 38	19 49	26 29	2 48	8 34	12 40
♄	1	22♈12	23♈13	22♈37	20♈43	18♈19	16♈41
	13	22 47	23R10	21R58	19R47	17R32	16 25
	25	23 8	22 53	21 10	18 50	16 55	16D24
♅	1	19♑31	18♑18	17♑23	17♑ 7	17♑39	18♑50
	13	19 2	17R53	17R11	17 14	18 3	19 27
	25	18 34	17 32	17 7	17 28	18 33	20 7
♆	1	16♋32	17♋40	18♋38	19♋13	19♋19	18♋56
	13	16 58	18 4	18 55	19 19	19R13	18R40
	25	17 25	18 26	19 8	19R21	19 3	18 21
Pl.	1	25♊38	26♊17	26♊42	26♊49	26♊36	26♊ 8
☊	1	15♊29	13♊50	12♊12	10♊37	8♊58	7♊23
	1st	Thu	Sun	Wed	Fri	Mon	Wed

d.		JAN	FEB	MAR	APR
☽	1	9♉26	28♊41	8♋16	23♌39
	3	6♊ 6	23♋28	2♌41	17♍23
	5	1♋55	17♌44	26 38	11♎11
	7	26 56	11♍38	20♏25	5♏17
	9	21♌15	5♎22	14♎12	29 52
	11	15♍ 5	29 15	8♏13	25♐11
	13	8♎51	23♏48	2♐49	21♑36
	15	3♏ 4	19♐37	28 29	19♒30
	17	28 22	17♑14	25♑47	18♓51
	19	25♐16	16♒42	24♒55	18♈57
	21	23♑52	17♓14	25♓21	18♉37
	23	23♒39	17♈24	25♈46	16♊49
	25	23♓31	16♉ 4	24♉49	13♋14
	27	22♈24	12♊54	21♊57	8♌10
	29	19♉52	...	17♋23	2♍13
	31	16♊ 0	...	11♌42	...

d.		MAY	JUN	JUL	AUG
☽	1	25♍57	10♏25	13♐56	3♒23
	3	19♎52	5♐35	10♑44	2♓40
	5	14♏17	1♑44	8♒44	2♈14
	7	9♐29	28 50	7♓24	1♉ 9
	9	5♑14	26♒41	6♈ 7	28 56
	11	2♒ 2	25♓ 3	4♉24	25♊35
	13	29 52	23♈35	2♊ 0	21♋20
	15	28♓40	21♉55	28 50	16♌22
	17	27♈56	19♊36	24♋52	10♍46
	19	26♉55	16♋17	20♌ 1	4♎39
	21	24♊48	11♌49	14♍22	28 20
	23	21♋13	6♍19	8♎12	22♏15
	25	16♌15	0♎12	1♏59	17♐ 3
	27	10♍22	24 3	26 22	13♑24
	29	4♎ 9	18♏28	21♐57	11♒39
	31	28 10	...	19♑10	11♓29

d.		SEP	OCT	NOV	DEC
☽	1	26♓39	5♉31	27♊10	2♌ 3
	3	26♈40	4♊43	24♋ 0	27 31
	5	25♉25	2♋ 8	19♌17	21♍49
	7	22♊35	27 56	13♍30	15♎33
	9	18♋24	22♌36	7♎15	9♏19
	11	13♌18	16♍38	0♏58	3♐35
	13	7♍36	10♎22	24 8	28 40
	15	1♎29	4♏ 5	19♐30	24♑40
	17	25 10	27 59	14♑47	21♒34
	19	18♏54	22♐24	11♒ 3	19♓13
	21	13♐ 8	17♑47	8♓33	17♈31
	23	8♑31	14♒39	7♈17	16♉12
	25	5♒36	13♓14	6♉51	14♊51
	27	4♓38	13♈14	6♊25	12♋53
	29	5♈ 3	13♉36	5♋ 0	9♌47
	31	...	13♊ 3	...	5♍19

STATIONS	☿	♀	♂	♃
	3Feb 28♒32	None	24Aug 6♈47	1May 4♍32
	24Feb 13♒17		24Oct 25♒27	...
	3Jun 27♊40	♄	♅	♆
	27Jun 19♊ 2	6Aug 23♈14	26Apr 21♑ 5	26Mar 14♋19
	30Sep 27♎34	20Dec 16♈23	28Sep 17♑ 7	24Oct 19♋31
	22Oct 12♎11	SIDER. TIME		1 Jan
		6h 40m 1s		Midn.
		18h 41m 59s		Noon.
		Common Year		1909

Noon		JAN	FEB	MAR	APR	MAY	JUN
☉	1	10♑13	11♒46	10♓ 2	10♈53	10♉13	10♊ 6
	9	18 22	19 53	18 3	18 45	17 58	17 45
	17	26 31	27 58	26 1	26 36	25 41	25 24
	25	4♒40	6♓ 1	3♈58	4♉24	3♊23	3♋ 2
☿	1	26♑28	28♑46	15♒ 5	6♈16	0♊55	0♊10
	7	4♒56	26R32	23 24	18 29	5 51	29♉ 6
	13	11 1	28D35	2♓31	1♉ 1	7 44	0♊38
	19	11R59	3♒27	12 21	12 57	6R42	4D47
	25	6 39	10 2	22 56	23 10	3 42	11 18
	31	29♑38	...	4♈18	...	0 34	...
♀	1	23♒ 7	28♒56	15♒23	26♒58	24♓13	27♈37
	9	27 39	24R47	15D30	3♓23	2♈32	6♉39
	17	0♓23	19 55	17 56	10 31	11 5	15 47
	25	0R46	16 18	22 10	18 12	19 50	25 0
♂	1	18♈ 8	5♉27	22♉11	11♊12	29♊47	19♋ 2
	13	24 36	12 33	29 31	18 38	7♋14	26 30
	25	1♉24	19 46	6♊53	26 4	14 41	3♌58
♃	1	13♎19	14♎32	13♎ 6	9♎30	6♎ 3	4♎37
	13	14 8	14R12	11R51	7R58	5R10	4 49
	25	14 31	13 26	10 23	6 38	4 42	5 26
♄	1	16♈32	18♈ 4	20♈38	24♈17	28♈ 4	1♉45
	13	16 56	19 4	21 59	25 47	29 33	3 0
	25	17 35	20 13	23 25	27 19	0♉58	4 6
♅	1	20♑32	22♑21	23♑48	24♑53	25♑14	24♑49
	13	21 14	23 0	24 17	25 7	25R 9	24R29
	25	21 57	23 36	24 42	25 13	24 58	24 4
♆	1	18♋10	17♋19	16♋44	16♋33	16♋52	17♋38
	13	17R49	17R 2	16R36	16 37	17 7	18 1
	25	17 29	16 48	16 33	16 45	17 26	18 27
Pl.	1	25♊32	25♊ 2	24♊50	24♊55	25♊19	25♊57
☊	1	5♊44	4♊ 6	2♊37	0♊58	29♉23	27♉45
	1st	Sat	Tue	Tue	Fri	Sun	Wed

Noon		JUL	AUG	SEP	OCT	NOV	DEC
☉	1	8♋45	8♌20	8♍ 9	7♎25	8♏12	8♐26
	9	16 23	16 0	15 55	15 19	16 13	16 33
	17	24 0	23 41	23 42	23 14	24 16	24 41
	25	1♌39	1♍23	1♎32	1♏12	2♐21	2♑50
☿	1	20♊ 0	21♌42	5♎13	27♍31	1♏15	18♐54
	7	0♋42	2♍13	9 30	26D37	11 7	28 5
	13	12 54	11 47	11 7	1♎27	20 47	7♑ 6
	19	25 44	20 24	9R 0	9 49	0♐16	15 36
	25	8♌13	27 59	3 17	19 34	9 37	22 41
	31	19 51	4♎19	...	29 35	...	26 17
♀	1	1♊58	8♋37	16♌10	23♍12	1♏57	9♐39
	9	11 20	18 14	25 59	3♎10	12 0	19 43
	17	20 46	27 54	5♍51	13 10	22 3	29 46
	25	0♋15	7♌37	15 45	23 11	2♐ 6	9♑50
♂	1	7♌43	27♌ 9	16♍49	6♎11	26♎37	16♏54
	13	15 13	4♍44	24 31	14 2	4♏40	25 9
	25	22 44	12 21	2♎16	21 58	12 48	3♐29
♃	1	5♎54	9♎35	14♎57	21♎ 6	27♎49	4♏ 5
	13	7 4	11 30	17 20	23 41	0♏23	6 22
	25	8 34	13 38	19 49	26 18	2 53	8 29
♄	1	4♉35	6♉18	6♉26	5♉ 4	2♉42	0♉36
	13	5 25	6 33	6R 3	4R12	1R46	0R 3
	25	6 3	6R33	5 26	3 15	0 57	29 45
♅	1	23♑51	22♑37	21♑28	21♑16	21♑41	22♑47
	13	23R22	22R11	21R24	21 20	22 3	23 22
	25	22 53	21 49	21 17	21 31	22 31	24 1
♆	1	18♋40	19♋48	20♋48	21♋25	21♋34	21♋12
	13	19 7	20 13	21 6	21 32	21R29	20R57
	25	19 33	20 36	21 19	21 35	21 19	20 39
Pl.	1	26♊38	27♊18	27♊45	27♊52	27♊40	27♊12
☊	1	26♉ 9	24♉31	22♉52	21♉17	19♉39	18♉ 3
	1st	Fri	Mon	Thu	Sat	Tue	Thu

	d.	JAN	FEB	MAR	APR
☽	1	17♍37	1♏13	9♏13	23♐25
	3	11♎36	24 57	2♐54	18♑20
	5	5♏17	19♐24	27 17	14♒50
	7	29 19	15♑13	23♑ 4	13♓15
	9	24♐17	12♒38	20♒40	13♈11
	11	20♑29	11♓21	19♓56	13♉33
	13	17♒51	10♈32	19♈54	13♊ 7
	15	15♓58	9♉20	19♉26	11♋ 9
	17	14♈19	7♊19	17♊45	7♌36
	19	12♉32	4♋27	14♋45	2♍48
	21	10♊27	0♌50	10♌39	27 8
	23	7♋56	26 29	5♍43	20♎59
	25	4♌45	21♍23	0♎ 7	14♏36
	27	0♍36	15♎32	24 2	8♐19
	29	25 25	...	17♏39	2♑27
	31	19♎23	...	11♐21	...

	d.	MAY	JUN	JUL	AUG
☽	1	27♑27	17♓22	25♈58	19♊18
	3	23♒49	15♈47	24♉47	17♋28
	5	21♓52	15♉16	23♊53	15♌ 0
	7	21♈28	15♊ 6	22♋34	11♍26
	9	21♉47	14♋17	20♌ 7	6♎35
	11	21♊38	12♌ 0	16♍ 9	0♏43
	13	20♋ 4	8♍ 2	10♎49	24 21
	15	16♌45	2♎40	4♏38	18♐14
	17	11♍55	26 30	28 18	13♑ 1
	19	6♎ 6	20♏ 7	22♐27	9♒ 8
	21	29 47	14♐ 4	17♑32	6♓35
	23	23 25	8♑42	13♒43	4♈57
	25	17♐21	4♒11	10♓52	3♉33
	27	11♑52	0♓34	8♈40	1♊56
	29	7♒12	27 51	6♉48	29 52
	31	3♓39	...	5♊ 7	27♋17

	d.	SEP	OCT	NOV	DEC
☽	1	10♌45	16♍14	1♏53	4♐18
	3	7♍ 4	11♎ 1	25 32	28 2
	5	2♎24	5♏ 6	19♐ 7	22♑11
	7	26 46	28 43	13♑ 0	17♒ 2
	9	20♏30	22♐19	7♒40	12♓55
	11	14♐ 8	16♑30	3♓39	10♈12
	13	8♑22	11♒55	1♈22	9♉ 2
	15	3♒53	9♓ 2	0♉46	9♊ 3
	17	1♓ 3	7♈55	1♊ 9	9♋16
	19	29 42	7♉54	1♋19	8♌28
	21	29♈ 6	7♊52	0♌ 9	5♍53
	23	28♉19	6♋52	27 13	1♎28
	25	26♊44	4♌25	22♍40	25 44
	27	24♋10	0♍35	17♎ 0	19♏22
	29	20♌39	25 39	10♏44	12♐57
	31	...	19♎57	...	6♑56

STATIONS	☿	♀	♂	♃
	18Jan 12♒17	23Jan 0♓55	None	1Feb 14♎32
	8Feb 26♒37	5Mar 15♒ 7		1Jun 4♎37
	15May 7♊40	♄	♅	♆
		20Aug 6♉35	1May 25♑14	29Mar 16♋32
	8Jun 29♉10	...	1Oct 21♑16	26Oct 21♋35
	14Sep 11♎ 3	SIDER. TIME		1 Jan
	6Oct 26♍22	6h 39m 4s		Midn.
		18h 41m 2s		Noon
		Common Year		1910

1911

Noon		JAN	FEB	MAR	APR	MAY	JUN
☉	1	9♑58	11♒32	9♓48	10♈39	10♉ 0	9♊52
	9	18 8	18 38	17 48	18 31	17 44	17 31
	17	26 16	27 43	25 47	26 21	25 27	25 10
	25	4♒25	5♓46	3♈43	4♉10	3♊ 9	2♋48
☿	1	26♑22	16♑17	24♒22	22♈50	16♉33	15♉37
	7	22R45	22 48	4♓29	3♉36	13R 0	22 14
	13	15 7	0♒27	15 17	11 53	9 52	0♊41
	19	10 31	8 53	26 45	16 53	8D52	10 52
	25	11D 8	17 58	8♈48	18R19	10 33	22 37
	31	15 21	...	20 53	...	14 43	...
♀	1	18♑38	27♒31	2♈22	10♉23	16♊17	21♋57
	9	28 41	7♓30	12 15	20 3	25 40	0♌47
	17	8♒43	17 28	22 5	29 40	4♋56	9 25
	25	18 45	27 24	1♉52	9♊12	14 4	17 47
♂	1	8♐23	0♑27	20♑48	13♒43	6♓ 5	28♓59
	13	16 52	9 7	29 38	22 40	15 0	7♈40
	25	25 25	17 52	8♒31	1♓37	23 51	16 12
♃	1	9♏36	13♏22	14♏33	13♏ 5	9♏38	6♏ 6
	13	11 19	14 9	14R19	11R51	8R 8	5R14
	25	12 43	14 32	13 39	10 24	6 47	4 45
♄	1	29♈42	0♉33	2♉39	6♉ 1	9♉47	13♉41
	13	29 49	1 19	3 51	7 30	11 19	15 4
	25	0♉12	2 17	5 11	9 1	12 50	16 21
♅	1	24♑25	26♑14	27♑43	28♑54	29♑21	29♑ 3
	13	25 7	26 54	28 15	29 10	29R19	28R44
	25	25 50	27 32	28 41	29 19	29 11	28 21
♆	1	20♋27	19♋36	19♋ 0	18♋46	19♋ 2	19♋47
	13	20R 7	19R19	18R51	18 49	19 17	20 10
	25	19 47	19 4	18 47	18 57	19 35	20 35
Pl.	1	26♊35	26♊ 6	25♊52	25♊56	26♊19	26♊58
☊	1	16♉25	14♉46	13♉17	11♉39	10♉ 3	8♉25
	1st	Sun	Wed	Wed	Sat	Mon	Thu

Noon		JUL	AUG	SEP	OCT	NOV	DEC
☉	1	8♋31	8♌ 6	7♍55	7♎11	7♏57	8♐11
	9	16 9	15 46	15 41	15 4	15 58	16 18
	17	23 47	23 27	23 28	23 0	24 2	24 27
	25	1♌25	1♍ 9	1♎18	0♏57	2♐ 7	2♑36
☿	1	5♋26	2♍46	22♍43	21♍11	13♏22	27♐59
	7	18 24	10 33	17R56	1♎ 6	22 47	5♑10
	13	0♌43	16 59	12 18	11 36	1♐59	9 51
	19	12 1	21 42	10D 7	21 58	10 58	9R29
	25	22 15	24 3	13 28	2♏ 2	19 43	2 57
	31	1♍21	23R12	...	11 46	...	25 57
♀	1	23♌52	20♍32	28♍28	13♍57	24♍ 3	21♎34
	9	1♍37	25 13	25R 4	13D31	0♎24	0♏ 7
	17	8 52	28 22	20 17	15 30	7 35	8 59
	25	15 27	29R29	15 57	19 25	15 23	18 5
♂	1	20♐23	10♉50	28♉ 4	9♊ 0	9♊29	29♉32
	13	28 33	18 0	3♊21	10 47	6R 7	26R 5
	25	6♉25	24 35	7 28	10R35	1 42	24 25
♃	1	4♏40	5♏57	9♏40	14♏56	21♏24	28♏ 2
	13	4 50	7 8	11 37	17 21	24 3	0♐40
	25	5 25	8 39	13 47	19 53	26 43	3 12
♄	1	16♉57	19♉19	20♉14	19♉31	17♉26	15♉ 5
	13	18 1	19 52	20R 8	18R50	16R28	14R18
	25	18 54	20 10	19 47	17 59	15 31	13 44
♅	1	28♑ 8	26♑55	25♑53	25♑25	25♑42	26♑43
	13	27R41	26R28	25R37	25D26	26 2	27 16
	25	27 12	26 5	25 27	25 34	26 27	27 54
♆	1	20♋48	21♋56	22♋57	23♋36	23♋48	23♋29
	13	21 14	22 22	23 16	23 45	23R43	23R14
	25	21 41	22 45	23 30	23 48	23 35	22 56
Pl.	1	27♊40	28♊20	28♊48	28♊56	28♊44	28♊18
☊	1	6♉50	5♉11	3♉33	1♉57	0♉19	28♈43
	1st	Sat	Tue	Fri	Sun	Wed	Fri

d.		JAN	FEB	MAR	APR
☽	1	19♑ 9	6♓38	15♓49	7♉ 7
	3	14♒ 7	3♈25	13♈26	6♊ 9
	5	9♓50	0♉49	11♉33	4♋49
	7	6♈27	28 48	9♊48	2♌44
	9	4♉ 6	27♊20	7♋59	29 48
	11	2♊53	26♋ 6	5♌57	25♍57
	13	2♋27	24♌26	3♍21	21♎13
	15	1♌56	21♍37	29 50	15♏39
	17	0♍17	17♎20	25♎12	9♐31
	19	26 55	11♏45	19♏32	3♑11
	21	21♎54	5♐28	13♐17	27 11
	23	15♏49	29 12	7♑ 2	22♒ 7
	25	9♐23	23♑35	1♒27	18♓30
	27	3♑17	19♒ 6	27 7	16♈32
	29	27 56	...	24♓16	15♉55
	31	23♒31	...	22♈39	...

d.		MAY	JUN	JUL	AUG
☽	1	15♊46	8♌59	15♍42	2♏43
	3	15♋ 6	6♍37	11♎44	26 52
	5	13♌14	2♎35	6♏20	20♐33
	7	9♍59	27 18	0♐11	14♑21
	9	5♎33	21♏18	23 49	8♒41
	11	0♏13	14♐59	17♑39	3♓42
	13	24 17	8♑41	11♒55	29 27
	15	18♐ 1	2♒40	6♓46	25♈58
	17	11♑42	27 11	2♈25	23♉22
	19	5♒44	22♓37	29 7	21♊45
	21	0♓36	19♈24	27♉11	20♋54
	23	26 48	17♉50	26♊35	20♌ 9
	25	24♈42	17♊44	26♋38	18♍33
	27	24♉13	18♋11	26♌ 9	15♎27
	29	24♊34	17♌49	24♍ 7	10♏47
	31	24♋30	...	20♎15	4♐59

d.		SEP	OCT	NOV	DEC
☽	1	16♐52	18♑31	3♓ 3	6♈49
	3	10♑37	12♒46	28 59	4♉18
	5	4♒49	8♓ 2	26♈31	3♊33
	7	29 51	4♈33	25♉25	3♋52
	9	25♓51	2♉14	24♊59	3♌56
	11	22♈43	0♊39	24♋14	2♍40
	13	20♉15	29 18	22♌31	29 41
	15	18♊19	27♋43	19♍34	25♎16
	17	16♋45	25♌36	15♎33	19♏52
	19	15♌15	22♍45	10♏40	13♐56
	21	13♍18	19♎ 1	5♐ 6	7♑43
	23	10♎23	14♏21	29 3	1♒27
	25	6♏12	8♐48	22♑46	25 20
	27	0♐50	2♑40	16♒36	19♓45
	29	24 45	26 24	11♓ 5	15♈15
	31	...	20♒36	...	12♉23

STATIONS	☿	♀	♂	♃
	1Jan 26♑22	25Aug 29♍29	19Oct 10♊47	1Mar 14♏13
	22Jan 10♑15	7Oct 13♍23	30Dec 29♉12	3Jul 4♏40
	25Apr 18♉19	♄	♅	♆
	19May 8♉52	3Sep 20♉14	5May 29♑21	31Mar 18♋46
	27Aug 24♍10	...	6Oct 25♑24	28Oct 23♋48
	19Sep 10♍ 7	SIDER. TIME 6h 38m 7s / 18h 40m 5s / Common Year		1 Jan Midn. / Noon. / 1911
	16Dec 10♑29			

Noon		JAN	FEB	MAR	APR	MAY	JUN
☉	1	9♑44	11♒17	10♓34	11♈24	10♉44	10♊36
	9	17 53	19 24	18 34	19 16	18 28	18 15
	17	26 2	27 29	26 33	27 6	26 12	25 54
	25	4♒11	5♓32	4♈29	4♉54	3♊53	3♋32
☿	1	25♐16	21♑42	9♓36	28♈53	19♈ 7	23♉ 5
	7	24D35	0♒37	21 6	29R30	21 38	4♊32
	13	28 20	10 2	2♈48	26 35	26 29	17 8
	19	4♑31	19 57	13 53	22 20	3♉13	0♋17
	25	12 0	0♓25	22 53	19 23	11 32	13 2
	31	20 16	...	28 22		21 19	...
♀	1	26♏11	3♑ 5	8♒23	16♓22	23♈10	1♊10
	9	5♐34	12 47	18 10	26 11	2♉59	10 59
	17	15 4	22 31	27 59	6♈ 0	12 47	20 48
	25	24 39	2♒16	7♓47	15 49	22 35	0♋37
♂	1	24♉21	0♊32	12♊16	27♊52	14♋27	2♌28
	13	25 38	4 55	18 3	4♋23	21 20	9 36
	25	28 23	10 0	24 10	11 4	28 20	16 49
♃	1	4♐38	10♐16	13♐56	15♐24	14♐ 2	10♐31
	13	6 59	12 1	14 50	15R10	12R50	9R 1
	25	9 7	13 27	15 19	14 31	11 24	7 39
♄	1	13♉30	13♉34	15♉11	18♉11	21♉50	25♉49
	13	13R19	14 4	16 13	19 35	23 22	27 18
	25	13D24	14 49	17 25	21 4	24 55	28 43
♅	1	28♑17	0♒ 6	1♒40	2♒54	3♒26	3♒13
	13	28 59	0 47	2 13	3 12	3R27	2R57
	25	29 41	1 25	2 41	3 24	3 20	2 35
♆	1	22♋45	21♋53	21♋15	20♋59	21♋14	21♋58
	13	22R25	21R35	21R 5	21D 2	21 28	22 20
	25	22 4	21 20	21 0	21 9	21 46	22 45
Pl.	1	27♊50	27♊12	26♊56	26♊59	27♊23	28♊ 1
☊	1	27♈ 5	25♈26	23♈54	22♈16	20♈41	19♈ 2
1st		Mon	Thu	Fri	Mon	Wed	Sat

Noon		JUL	AUG	SEP	OCT	NOV	DEC
☉	1	9♋15	8♌50	8♍39	7♎56	8♏42	8♐57
	9	16 52	16 30	16 25	15 49	16 44	17 5
	17	24 30	24 11	24 13	23 45	24 47	25 13
	25	2♌ 8	1♍53	2♎ 2	1♏43	2♐52	3♑22
☿	1	24♋48	4♍34	23♌37	5♎46	25♏33	24♐ 9
	7	5♌21	6 33	26D31	16 16	4♐ 3	18R30
	13	14 39	5R29	3♍32	26 18	12 0	10 54
	19	22 39	1 26	13 54	5♏55	18 55	8D24
	25	29 13	26♌19	24 52	15 10	23 41	11 22
	31	3♍59	23 38	...	24 5	...	17 24
♀	1	7♋59	16♌ 9	24♍25	1♏26	9♐33	16♑11
	9	17 49	26 1	4♎17	11 17	19 21	25 52
	17	27 40	5♍53	14 10	21 8	29 8	5♒30
	25	7♌31	15 46	24 2	0♐58	8♑54	15 2
♂	1	20♌27	9♍34	29♍14	18♎52	9♏50	0♐51
	13	27 47	17 6	7♎ 0	26 54	18 9	9 27
	25	5♍12	24 44	14 53	5♏ 2	26 35	18 10
♃	1	7♐ 4	5♐33	6♐53	10♐35	16♐11	22♐39
	13	6R10	5D44	8 7	12 35	18 41	25 22
	25	5 39	6 20	9 41	14 48	21 18	28 7
♄	1	29♉23	2♊18	3♊55	3♊54	2♊19	29♉56
	13	0♊38	3 6	4 6	3R27	1R24	29R 1
	25	1 44	3 41	4R 2	2 47	0 25	28 13
♅	1	2♒23	1♒10	0♒ 5	29♑33	29♑45	0♒40
	13	1R56	0R43	29♑47	29D31	0♒ 2	1 13
	25	1 27	0 18	29R36	29 38	0 26	1 49
♆	1	22♋58	24♋ 6	25♋ 8	25♋48	26♋ 1	25♋43
	13	23 24	24 32	25 27	25 57	25R57	25R29
	25	23 51	24 55	25 42	26 1	25 49	25 12
Pl.	1	28♊43	29♊22	29♊51	0♋ 0	29♊49	29♊22
☊	1	17♈27	15♈48	14♈10	12♈34	10♈56	9♈21
1st		Mon	Thu	Sun	Tue	Fri	Sun

	d.	JAN	FEB	MAR	APR
☽	1	26♉41	19♋59	13♌48	6♎ 1
	3	26♊34	20♌24	13♍19	3♏12
	5	27♋17	19♍52	11♎44	29 4
	7	27♌20	17♎31	8♏31	23♐46
	9	25♍39	13♏18	3♐45	17♑44
	11	22♎ 2	7♐45	27 55	11♒32
	13	16♏56	1♑33	21♑40	5♓47
	15	10♐59	25 16	15♒34	0♈57
	17	4♑43	19♒15	10♓ 4	27 17
	19	28 27	13♓44	5♈21	24♉44
	21	22♒24	8♈50	1♉31	22♊57
	23	16♓44	4♉42	28 31	21♋29
	25	11♈44	1♊35	26♊17	19♌52
	27	7♉50	29 43	24♋41	17♍50
	29	5♊30	28♋57	23♌26	15♎ 8
	31	4♋51	...	22♍ 0	...

	d.	MAY	JUN	JUL	AUG
☽	1	11♏35	27♐50	0♒31	15♓ 6
	3	7♐ 5	21♑55	24 14	9♈21
	5	1♑40	15♒40	18♓ 7	4♉29
	7	25 38	9♓33	12♈39	1♊ 4
	9	19♒26	4♈10	8♉31	29 26
	11	13♓40	0♉ 8	6♊12	29♋23
	13	8♈56	27 53	5♋43	29♌52
	15	5♉40	27♊16	6♌13	29♍32
	17	3♊52	27♋21	6♍17	27♎30
	19	3♋ 1	26♌54	4♎52	23♏42
	21	2♌15	25♍ 8	1♏43	18♐33
	23	0♍47	21♎55	27 8	12♑37
	25	28 19	17♏32	21♐37	6♒23
	27	24♎53	12♐21	15♑37	0♓10
	29	20♏36	6♑38	9♒24	24 15
	31	15♐36	...	3♓ 9	18♈50

	d.	SEP	OCT	NOV	DEC
☽	1	1♉25	7♊43	0♌ 9	9♍28
	3	27 22	5♋ 8	28 29	7♎12
	5	24♊40	3♌29	26♍46	4♏16
	7	23♋25	2♍30	24♎41	0♐39
	9	23♌13	1♎34	21♏52	26 16
	11	23♍ 5	29 58	18♐ 0	21♑ 1
	13	21♎57	27♏ 6	13♑ 0	15♒ 1
	15	19♏10	22♐47	7♒ 6	8♓39
	17	14♐47	17♑18	0♓48	2♈32
	19	9♑13	11♒ 8	24 46	27 22
	21	3♒ 2	4♓56	19♈40	23♉47
	23	26 49	29 14	15♉56	22♊ 0
	25	20♓56	24♈29	13♊37	21♋29
	27	15♈42	20♉48	12♋14	21♌11
	29	11♉15	18♊ 5	11♌ 3	20♍ 6
	31	...	16♋ 2	...	17♎48

STATIONS	☿	☿	♀	♃
	5Jan 24♐12	cont'd 19Dec 8♐24	None	2Apr 15♐24
	6Apr 29♈40		♂ None	3Aug 5♐33
	29Apr 18♈58	♄ 16Jan 13♉18	♅ 8May 3♒28	♆ 2Apr 20♋59
	9Aug 6♍33	17Sep 4♊ 7	10Oct 29♑31	30Oct 26♋ 1
	2Sep 23♌45	SIDER. TIME 6h 37m 10s		1 Jan Midn.
	29Nov 24♐38 →	18h 39m 8s LEAP Year		Noon 1912

Noon		JAN	FEB	MAR	APR	MAY	JUN
☉	1	10♑30	12♒ 3	10♓19	11♈ 9	10♉30	10♊22
	9	18 39	20 10	18 20	19 2	18 15	18 1
	17	26 48	28 15	26 18	26 52	25 58	25 40
	25	4♒57	6♓18	4♈14	4♉40	3♊39	3♋17
☿	1	18♐34	3♒58	24♓13	3♈20	14♈23	9♊46
	7	26 16	14 5	3♈49	0R 2	22 36	22 53
	13	4♑40	24 39	10 12	29♓51	2♉ 4	5♋15
	19	13 30	5♓40	11R54	2♈34	12 47	16 22
	25	22 44	16 55	9 4	7D36	24 41	26 4
	31	2♒20	...	4 7	...	7♊34	...
♀	1	23♒18	28♓26	25♈47	12♉25	0♉22	0♉33
	9	2♓39	6♈51	2♉ 5	11R50	27♈ 2	5 20
	17	11 49	14 52	7 15	8 46	26D 6	11 14
	25	20 47	22 19	10 52	3 59	27 36	17 57
♂	1	23♐18	16♑27	7♒48	1♓45	24♓56	18♈29
	13	2♑11	25 33	17 3	11 3	4♈ 7	27 25
	25	11 10	4♒44	26 20	20 19	13 13	6♉12
♃	1	29♐42	6♑30	11♑48	16♑ 3	17♑48	16♑45
	13	2♑24	8 54	13 42	17 4	17R45	15R37
	25	5 1	11 7	15 17	17 40	17 14	14 14
♄	1	27♉51	27♉11	28♉ 6	0♊35	3♊57	7♊55
	13	27R23	27 24	28 54	1 51	5 28	9 28
	25	27 10	27 53	29 55	3 14	7 1	10 59
♅	1	2♒12	4♒ 0	5♒33	6♒52	7♒30	7♒23
	13	2 53	4 41	6 7	7 12	7R33	7R 9
	25	3 35	5 20	6 37	7 26	7 29	6 49
♆	1	25♋ 0	24♋ 9	23♋31	23♋13	23♋25	24♋ 7
	13	24R40	23R51	23R20	23D14	23 38	24 29
	25	24 20	23 35	23 14	23 20	23 55	24 53
Pl.	1	28♊36	28♊17	28♊ 2	28♊ 5	28♊27	29♊ 3
☊	1	7♈42	6♈ 4	4♈35	2♈56	1♈21	29♓42
	1st	Wed	Sat	Sat	Tue	Thu	Sun

Noon		JUL	AUG	SEP	OCT	NOV	DEC
☉	1	9♋ 1	8♌36	8♍25	7♎42	8♏28	8♐43
	9	16 39	16 16	16 11	15 35	16 30	16 50
	17	24 16	23 57	23 59	23 31	24 33	24 58
	25	1♌54	1♍39	1♎48	1♏28	2♐38	3♑ 7
☿	1	4♌18	13♌43	24♌35	18♎50	1♐52	22♏47
	7	10 57	9R16	5♍47	28 17	7 1	24D27
	13	15 41	6 41	17 16	7♏17	8R49	0♐ 9
	19	18 4	8D 1	28 21	15 48	5 9	7 44
	25	17R38	13 41	8♎52	23 44	27♏23	16 10
	31	14 27	22 50	...	0♐49	...	25 1
♀	1	23♉24	25♊ 5	0♌ 8	5♍50	13♎55	21♏23
	9	1♊ 6	3♋54	9 31	15 35	23 52	1♐26
	17	9 10	12 53	19 0	25 23	3♏51	11 29
	25	17 33	22 1	28 35	5♎15	13 52	21 32
♂	1	10♉31	2♊ 4	21♊48	8♋16	20♋39	24♋25
	13	19 2	9 57	28 46	13 46	23 24	22R38
	25	27 20	17 32	5♋14	18 25	24 33	19 0
♃	1	13♑28	9♑46	8♑ 1	9♑ 8	12♑55	18♑26
	13	11R56	8R46	8D 8	10 19	14 57	20 59
	25	10 30	8 10	8 41	11 52	17 14	23 40
♄	1	11♊43	15♊ 5	17♊24	18♊10	17♊17	15♊ 9
	13	13 7	16 8	17 54	18R 2	16R32	14R10
	25	14 24	16 59	18 9	17 38	15 38	13 14
♅	1	6♒37	5♒27	4♒19	3♒41	3♒45	4♒35
	13	6R11	4R58	3R59	3R37	4 0	5 6
	25	5 43	4 32	3 45	3D40	4 22	5 41
♆	1	25♋ 6	26♋14	27♋16	27♋59	28♋14	27♋59
	13	25 32	26 39	27 36	28 9	28R12	27R46
	25	25 59	27 3	27 52	28 14	28 4	27 29
Pl.	1	29♊45	0♋26	0♋54	1♋ 4	0♋53	0♋27
☊	1	28♓ 7	26♓29	24♓50	23♓15	21♓36	20♓ 1
	1st	Tue	Fri	Mon	Wed	Sat	Mon

	d.	JAN	FEB	MAR	APR
☽	1	1♏12	19♐42	29♐ 2	13♒56
	3	27 19	14♑14	23♑21	7♓32
	5	22♐39	8♒15	17♒ 7	1♈19
	7	17♑20	1♓57	10♓45	25 36
	9	11♒25	25 33	4♈30	20♉39
	11	5♓ 5	19♈27	28 41	16♊35
	13	28 42	14♉ 7	23♉36	13♋30
	15	22♈52	10♊10	19♊40	11♌29
	17	18♉16	8♋ 3	17♋11	10♍24
	19	15♊30	7♌40	16♌13	9♎47
	21	14♋38	8♍11	16♍14	8♏51
	23	14♌57	8♎16	16♎13	6♐50
	25	15♍ 6	6♏52	15♏ 4	3♑15
	27	13♎59	3♐43	12♐14	28 12
	29	11♏16	...	7♑44	22♒10
	31	7♐10	...	2♒ 3	...

	d.	MAY	JUN	JUL	AUG
☽	1	15♓48	0♉ 7	3♊59	24♋14
	3	9♈43	25 45	1♋28	23♌56
	5	4♉24	22♊42	0♌12	23♍44
	7	0♊ 6	20♋38	29 23	22♎43
	9	26 46	19♌ 2	28♍13	20♏27
	11	24♋13	17♍24	26♎18	16♐56
	13	22♌14	15♎30	23♏32	12♑24
	15	20♍38	13♏13	19♐57	7♒ 2
	17	19♎11	10♐22	15♑33	1♓ 3
	19	17♏29	6♑39	10♒19	24 42
	21	14♐57	1♒53	4♓21	18♈19
	23	11♑11	26 9	27 59	12♉21
	25	6♒ 7	19♓50	21♈42	7♊25
	27	0♓ 6	13♈35	16♉12	4♋ 3
	29	23 45	8♉ 6	12♊ 6	2♌29
	31	17♈47	...	9♋47	2♍21

	d.	SEP	OCT	NOV	DEC
☽	1	17♍31	25♎57	17♐23	22♑ 7
	3	17♎35	25♏12	14♑14	17♒21
	5	16♏26	22♐45	9♒25	11♓26
	7	13♐41	18♑34	3♓27	5♈ 2
	9	9♑26	13♒ 4	27 2	28 53
	11	4♒ 5	6♓50	20♈48	23♉35
	13	28 2	0♈25	15♉11	19♊22
	15	21♓41	24 13	10♊24	16♋12
	17	15♈19	18♉32	6♋26	13♌45
	19	9♉15	13♊31	3♌13	11♍40
	21	3♊52	9♋25	0♍46	9♎47
	23	29 35	6♌26	29 6	8♏ 2
	25	26♋48	4♍44	28♎ 3	6♐ 8
	27	25♌39	4♎10	27♏ 4	3♑37
	29	25♍42	4♏ 2	25♐18	29 59
	31	...	3♐18	...	25♒ 6

STATIONS	☿	♀	♂	♃
	19Mar	4Apr	27Nov	6May
	11♈54	12♉29	24♋34	17♑50
	11Apr	16May	...	4Sep
	29♓33	26♈ 5	...	8♑ 0
	22Jul	♄	♅	♆
	18♌13	29Jan	13May	4Apr
	14Aug	27♉10	7♒33	23♋13
	6♌36	1Oct	14Oct	1Nov
	13Nov	18♊10	3♒37	28♋14
	8♐49	SIDER. TIME		1 Jan
	3Dec	6h 40m 9s		Midn.
	22♏43	18h 42m 7s		Noon.
		Common Year		1913

Noon		JAN	FEB	MAR	APR	MAY	JUN
☉	1	10♑15	11♒49	10♓ 5	10♈55	10♉16	10♊ 8
	9	18 25	19 55	18 5	18 48	18 0	17 47
	17	26 33	28 0	26 4	26 38	25 43	25 26
	25	4♒42	6♓ 3	4♈ 0	4♉26	3♊25	3♋ 4
☿	1	26♐31	16♒57	24♓48	14♓ 3	23♈26	26♊53
	7	4♑ 7	27 40	22R 7	19 7	4♉47	7♋ 2
	13	15 4	8♓14	16 28	25 53	17 8	15 31
	19	24 46	17 32	12 4	3♈57	0♊11	22 12
	25	4♒48	23 35	11D 6	13 10	13 6	26 49
	31	15 11	...	13 24		25 2	...
♀	1	0♑21	9♒18	14♒23	22♈57	29♉53	7♋35
	9	10 24	19 21	24 22	2♉50	9♊40	17 13
	17	20 28	29 22	4♈20	12 42	19 24	26 48
	25	0♒31	9♓23	14 16	22 32	29 7	6♌20
♂	1	16♋19	6♋31	7♋14	16♋28	29♋50	16♌ 1
	13	11R38	5D40	10 2	21 27	5♌53	22 43
	25	7 55	6 35	13 51	26 56	12 13	29 36
♃	1	25♑17	2♒34	8♒57	15♒12	19♒45	22♒ 8
	13	28 5	5 21	11 31	17 14	21 0	22R18
	25	0♒55	8 4	13 54	19 0	21 51	21 59
♄	1	12♊44	11♊19	11♊30	13♊20	16♊19	20♊ 7
	13	12R 0	11D13	12 2	14 24	17 44	21 41
	25	11 30	11 23	12 47	15 38	19 13	23 14
♅	1	6♒ 3	7♒49	9♒24	10♒47	11♒31	11♒31
	13	6 43	8 31	9 59	11 9	11 37	11R19
	25	7 25	9 11	10 31	11 26	11R35	11 1
♆	1	27♋18	26♋26	25♋47	25♋26	25♋36	26♋15
	13	26R58	26R 8	25R35	25D27	25 48	26 37
	25	26 38	25 51	25 28	25 32	26 4	27 0
Pl.	1	29♊53	29♊22	29♊ 6	29♊ 8	29♊29	0♋ 6
☊	1	18♓23	16♓44	15♓15	13♓37	12♓ 1	10♓23
	1st	Thu	Sun	Sun	Wed	Fri	Mon

Noon		JUL	AUG	SEP	OCT	NOV	DEC
☉	1	8♋47	8♌22	8♍12	7♎28	8♏14	8♐28
	9	16 25	16 2	15 57	15 21	16 15	16 35
	17	24 2	23 43	23 44	23 16	24 18	24 43
	25	1♌41	1♍26	1♎34	1♏14	2♐23	2♑52
☿	1	29♋ 0	20♋ 8	9♍51	28♎59	21♏ 2	20♏20
	7	28R26	25 6	20 59	6♏54	14R13	28 57
	13	25 28	3♌27	1♎26	13 56	7 54	7♐59
	19	21 34	14 15	11 13	19 34	7D42	17 11
	25	19 4	26 7	20 23	22 45	12 44	26 30
	31	19D41	7♍56	...	21R44	...	5♑57
♀	1	13♌27	19♍31	23♎46	23♏ 4	11♐41	2♐23
	9	22 52	28 35	2♏ 6	29 34	12R11	28♏32
	17	2♍13	7♎31	10 7	5♐ 8	10 8	26R59
	25	11 30	16 16	17 43	9 23	6 0	28D 1
♂	1	3♍ 6	21♍49	11♎29	1♏24	22♏54	14♐36
	13	10 13	29 19	19 20	9 36	1♐29	23 30
	25	17 30	6♎57	27 20	17 58	10 11	2♑31
♃	1	21♒39	18♒34	14♒41	12♒33	13♒19	16♒48
	13	20R42	17R 1	13 32	12D28	14 26	18 48
	25	19 25	15 29	12 46	12 52	15 56	21 3
♄	1	24♊ 0	27♊43	0♋37	2♋ 9	2♋ 4	0♋26
	13	25 31	28 58	1 24	2 20	1R34	29R30
	25	26 56	0♋ 4	1 58	2R14	0 52	28 31
♅	1	10♒50	9♒42	8♒32	7♒48	7♒46	8♒30
	13	10R26	9R13	8R10	7R42	7 59	8 58
	25	9 58	8 46	7 54	7D42	8 18	9 32
♆	1	27♋13	28♋21	29♋25	0♌ 9	0♌27	0♌15
	13	27 39	28 47	29 45	0 20	0R26	0R 2
	25	28 6	29 12	0♌ 2	0 26	0 19	29♋46
Pl.	1	0♋48	1♋28	1♋58	2♋ 9	1♋59	1♋33
☊	1	8♓48	7♓ 9	5♓31	3♓55	2♓17	0♓41
	1st	Wed	Sat	Tue	Thu	Sun	Tue

	d.	JAN	FEB	MAR	APR
☽	1	7♓15	20♈41	28♈58	13♊53
	3	1♈ 1	14♉31	22♉48	9♋ 4
	5	24 40	9♊16	17♊27	5♌37
	7	18♉56	5♋27	13♋26	3♍52
	9	14♊23	3♌19	11♌10	3♎40
	11	11♋16	2♍28	10♍32	4♏10
	13	9♌20	2♎ 5	10♎47	4♐ 3
	15	8♍ 0	1♏15	10♏43	2♑18
	17	6♎37	29 24	9♐23	28 40
	19	4♏50	26♐22	6♑24	23♒31
	21	2♐29	22♑16	1♒58	17♓28
	23	29 28	17♒16	26 29	11♈ 3
	25	25♑38	11♓34	20♓23	4♉44
	27	20♒50	5♈21	14♈ 2	28 45
	29	15♓10	...	7♊42	23♊19
	31	8♈53	...	1♊40	...

	d.	MAY	JUN	JUL	AUG
☽	1	18♋40	9♍ 3	17♎56	11♐22
	3	15♌ 6	7♎15	16♏34	9♑ 1
	5	12♍56	6♏28	15♐17	5♒49
	7	12♎14	6♐ 1	13♑27	1♓33
	9	12♏25	4♑56	10♒25	26 16
	11	12♐18	2♒21	5♓59	20♈14
	13	10♑45	28 4	0♈23	13♉58
	15	7♒18	22♓28	24 10	8♊ 4
	17	2♓12	16♈11	18♉ 0	3♋ 7
	19	26 7	9♉56	12♊28	29 31
	21	19♈43	4♊15	8♋ 0	27♌20
	23	13♉31	29 25	4♌42	26♍11
	25	7♊53	25♋28	2♍20	25♎20
	27	2♋56	22♌17	0♎33	24♏ 7
	29	28 43	19♍48	28 58	22♐ 4
	31	25♌21	...	27♏19	19♑ 2

	d.	SEP	OCT	NOV	DEC
☽	1	2♒ 9	6♓55	22♈ 2	24♉35
	3	27 41	1♈12	15♉46	18♊40
	5	22♓25	25 5	9♊37	13♋12
	7	16♈31	18♉47	3♋48	8♌22
	9	10♉15	12♊37	28 38	4♍24
	11	4♊ 3	6♋59	24♌35	1♎40
	13	28 29	2♌24	22♍ 8	0♏23
	15	24♋ 6	29 24	21♎27	0♐13
	17	21♌20	28♍16	21♏55	0♑ 9
	19	20♍12	28♎31	22♐12	28 58
	21	20♎ 5	28♏58	21♑ 1	26♒ 0
	23	19♏54	28♐17	17♒51	21♓19
	25	18♐41	25♑47	13♓ 0	15♈31
	27	16♑ 1	21♒35	7♈ 6	9♉14
	29	11♒58	16♓11	0♉49	3♊ 4
	31	...	10♈ 9	...	27 25

STATIONS	☿	♀	♂	♃
	1Mar 24♓48	8Nov 12♐15	13Feb 5♋40	12Jun 22♒18
	24Mar 11♓ 1	18Dec 26♏59	... ...	10Oct 12♒27
		♄	♅	♆
	4Jul 29♋ 4	12Feb 11♊13	18May 11♒37	7Apr 25♋26
	27Jul 18♋32	16Oct 2♋20	19Oct 7♒41	4Nov 0♌27
	28Oct 22♏54	SIDER. TIME		1 Jan
	17Nov 7♏ 3	6h 39m 12s		Midn.
		18h 41m 10s		Noon
		Common Year		1914

Noon		JAN	FEB	MAR	APR	MAY	JUN
☉	1	10♑ 0	11♒34	9♓50	10♈41	10♉ 2	9♊54
	9	18 9	19 40	17 51	18 33	17 47	17 34
	17	26 19	27 45	25 49	26 24	25 30	25 13
	25	4♒27	5♓49	3♈46	4♉12	3♊12	2♋50
☿	1	7♑33	28♒40	24♒49	15♓44	9♉43	3♋ 8
	7	17 14	5♓47	23D18	24 40	22 40	7 31
	13	27 10	8R 4	25 25	4♈33	5♊ 3	9 18
	19	7 20	4 27	0♓ 8	15 22	16 1	8R25
	25	17 32	28♒ 3	6 35	27 7	25 8	5 28
	31	27 12	...	14 20	...	2♋11	...
♀	1	0♐43	24♐53	24♑21	29♒50	5♈19	12♉29
	9	5 25	2♑53	3♒20	9♓14	14 52	22 8
	17	11 24	11 16	12 27	18 41	24 27	1♊48
	25	18 18	19 56	21 41	28 10	4♉ 3	11 29
♂	1	7♑50	1♒45	23♒41	18♓ 1	11♈18	4♉45
	13	17 2	11 7	3♓ 7	27 23	20 28	13 37
	25	26 18	20 32	12 32	6♈41	29 32	22 19
♃	1	22♒29	29♒24	6♓ 7	13♓26	19♓49	25♓ 1
	13	25 3	2♓15	8 59	16 6	22 2	26 30
	25	27 46	5 9	11 49	18 37	24 0	27 36
♄	1	27♊57	25♊56	25♊23	26♊27	28♊54	2♋26
	13	27R 2	25 31	25 35	27 17	0♋11	3 56
	25	26 17	25 22	26 3	28 19	1 34	5 30
♅	1	9♒53	11♒38	13♒13	14♒40	15♒30	15♒37
	13	10 32	12 20	13 50	15 5	15 39	15R28
	25	11 13	13 0	14 23	15 24	15R40	15 12
♆	1	29♋35	28♋43	28♋ 3	27♋40	27♋47	28♋24
	13	29R15	28R24	27R51	27D39	27 58	28 45
	25	28 55	28 8	27 43	27 43	28 14	29 8
Pl.	1	0♋59	0♋27	0♋10	0♋12	0♋33	1♋ 9
☊	1	29♒ 3	27♒24	25♒55	24♒17	22♒42	21♒ 3
	1st	Fri	Mon	Mon	Thu	Sat	Tue

Noon		JUL	AUG	SEP	OCT	NOV	DEC
☉	1	8♋34	8♌ 9	7♍57	7♎13	7♏59	8♐13
	9	16 11	15 48	15 43	15 7	16 0	16 20
	17	23 49	23 29	23 31	23 2	24 4	24 28
	25	1♌27	1♍12	1♎20	0♏59	2♐ 8	2♑37
☿	1	2♋ 6	24♋26	23♍47	2♏48	21♎21	0♐11
	7	0R17	6♋20	3♎17	6 23	25 11	9 35
	13	1D18	18 40	12 3	6R29	2♏36	19 0
	19	5 29	0♍36	20 2	1 51	11 27	28 28
	25	12 43	11 46	27 6	24♎39	20 46	8♑ 2
	31	22 35	22 8	...	21D16	...	17 44
♀	1	18♊46	26♋38	4♍54	12♎14	20♏56	28♐24
	9	28 30	6♌28	14 50	22 13	0♐56	8♑23
	17	8♋16	16 20	24 47	2♏12	10 56	18 22
	25	18 3	26 14	4♎45	12 11	20 55	28 19
♂	1	26♉37	18♊ 9	8♋23	26♋25	12♌43	24♌42
	13	5♊ 5	26 9	15 49	3♌ 4	18 5	27 49
	25	13 23	3♋57	22 58	9 18	22 43	29 34
♃	1	28♓ 0	28♓14	25♓34	21♓41	18♓55	19♓ 5
	13	28 27	27R30	24R 2	20R20	18R37	19 59
	25	28R27	26 22	22 27	19 19	18D48	21 19
♄	1	6♋16	10♋12	13♋34	15♋46	16♋30	15♋33
	13	7 50	11 36	14 36	16 15	16R19	14R47
	25	9 21	12 53	15 26	16 29	15 52	13 52
♅	1	15♒ 2	13♒55	12♒44	11♒56	11♒47	12♒24
	13	14R38	13R27	12R21	11R47	11 56	12 50
	25	14 12	12 59	12 3	11D45	12 13	13 22
♆	1	29♋21	0♌29	1♌33	2♌19	2♌40	2♌30
	13	29 47	0 55	1 54	2 31	2R40	2R18
	25	0♌13	1 20	2 12	2 38	2 34	2 2
Pl.	1	1♋52	2♋34	3♋ 3	3♋14	3♋ 6	2♋41
☊	1	19♒28	17♒49	16♒11	14♒36	12♒57	11♒22
	1st	Thu	Sun	Wed	Fri	Mon	Wed

d.		JAN	FEB	MAR	APR
☽	1	9♋50	27♌39	6♍18	28♎15
	3	5♌15	25♍ 3	4♎38	28♏ 6
	5	1♍24	23♎ 3	3♏34	27♐10
	7	28 21	21♏23	2♐24	24♑55
	9	26♎12	19♐45	0♑35	21♒21
	11	24♏54	17♑49	27 56	16♓47
	13	24♐ 2	15♒12	24♒26	11♈30
	15	22♑48	11♓35	20♓ 6	5♉41
	17	20♒26	6♈51	14♈59	29 32
	19	16♓35	1♉11	9♉11	23♊15
	21	11♈23	25 0	2♊59	17♋15
	23	5♉21	18♊53	26 48	12♌ 7
	25	29 6	13♋26	21♋16	8♍30
	27	23♊15	9♌10	16♌58	6♎47
	29	18♋15	...	14♍22	6♏43
	31	14♌16	...	13♌21	...

d.		MAY	JUN	JUL	AUG
☽	1	7♐12	0♒ 6	6♓ 1	22♈31
	3	6♑53	27 30	1♈53	16♉45
	5	4♒54	23♓13	26 28	10♊31
	7	1♓14	17♈44	20♉22	4♋25
	9	26 20	11♉39	14♊ 6	28 54
	11	20♈39	5♊23	8♋ 4	24♌13
	13	14♉35	29 11	2♌31	20♍30
	15	8♊19	23♋17	27 40	17♎42
	17	2♋ 5	17♌56	23♍42	15♏38
	19	26 10	13♍32	20♎48	14♐ 6
	21	21♌ 1	10♎29	19♏ 4	12♑45
	23	17♍14	9♏ 4	18♐16	11♒ 8
	25	15♎16	8♐58	17♑45	8♓45
	27	15♏ 3	9♑10	16♒35	5♈13
	29	15♐41	8♒26	14♓ 5	0♉27
	31	15♑41	...	10♈ 3	24 42

d.		SEP	OCT	NOV	DEC
☽	1	6♊37	8♋15	22♌51	27♍ 7
	3	0♋24	2♌27	18♍53	24♎51
	5	24 38	27 47	16♎50	24♏26
	7	19♌50	24♍41	16♏25	24♐59
	9	16♍18	23♎ 7	16♐36	25♑ 6
	11	13♎57	22♏26	16♑ 7	23♒43
	13	12♏19	21♐39	14♒14	20♓35
	15	10♐53	20♑ 3	10♓55	16♈ 1
	17	9♑11	17♒25	6♈29	10♉30
	19	7♒ 0	13♓53	1♉17	4♊27
	21	4♓11	9♈34	25 32	28 9
	23	0♈35	4♉33	19♊22	21♋52
	25	26 4	28 52	13♋ 0	15♌50
	27	20♉38	22♊40	6♌47	10♍26
	29	14♊32	16♋19	1♍16	6♎12
	31	...	10♌25	...	3♏34

STATIONS	☿	♀	♂	♃
	13Feb 8♓ 4	None	None	20Jul 28♒31
	6Mar 23♒16			15Nov 18♓37
		♄	♅	♆
	14Jun 9♋20	27Feb 25♊22	21May 15♒40	10Apr 27♋39
	8Jul 0♋15	30Oct 16♋30	23Oct 11♒44	6Nov 2♌41
	10Oct 6♏58	SIDER. TIME		1Jan
	31Oct 21♏16	6h 38m 15s		Midn.
		18h 40m 13s		Noon.
		Common Year		1915

1916 (BST 21 May – 1 Oct.)

Noon		JAN	FEB	MAR	APR	MAY	JUN
☉	1	9♑45	11♒19	10♓35	11♈26	10♉46	10♊38
	9	17 55	19 25	18 36	19 18	18 31	18 17
	17	26 4	27 31	26 35	27 8	26 14	25 56
	25	4♒12	5♓34	4♈31	4♉56	3♊55	3♋34
☿	1	19♑22	19♒24	13♒29	28♓16	28♉ 2	17♊24
	7	29 7	12R37	20 7	9♈34	7♊13	14R12
	13	8♒33	7 16	27 54	21 41	13 58	11 28
	19	16 41	6D23	6♓37	4♉21	18 2	10D48
	25	21 26	9 13	16 8	16 49	19R16	12 53
	31	20R13	...	26 28	...	17 50	...
♀	1	7♒ 2	15♓15	20♈ 9	25♉35	26♊ 7	17♋37
	9	16 57	25 0	29 32	4♊13	3♋ 6	19 35
	17	26 51	4♈39	8♉46	12 33	9 16	19R12
	25	6♓41	14 13	17 50	20 29	14 20	16 20
♂	1	29♌49	23♌25	12♌55	11♌ 1	18♌34	1♍47
	13	28R46	18R41	10R44	13 11	23 13	7 48
	25	25 50	14 21	10 25	16 32	28 29	14 10
♃	1	22♓17	27♓44	4♈ 6	11♈30	18♈40	25♈28
	13	24 10	0♈16	6 56	14 24	21 24	27 48
	25	26 21	2 57	9 49	17 16	24 1	29 55
♄	1	13♋17	10♋54	9♋38	9♋57	11♋49	14♋57
	13	12R18	10R13	9D33	10 32	12 55	16 23
	25	11 23	9 45	9 43	11 20	14 10	17 53
♅	1	13♒43	15♒26	17♒ 5	18♒35	19♒29	19♒41
	13	14 21	16 8	17 43	19 1	19 39	19R33
	25	15 2	16 49	18 17	19 21	19R42	19 19
♆	1	1♌51	1♌ 0	0♌17	29♋53	29♋59	0♌35
	13	1R32	0R41	0R 5	29D52	0♌10	0 56
	25	1 12	0 24	29♋56	29 56	0 25	1 19
Pl	1	2♋ 5	1♋32	1♋16	1♋17	1♋37	2♋13
☊	1	9♒43	8♒ 5	6♒33	4♒54	3♒19	1♒40
	1st	Sat	Tue	Wed	Sat	Mon	Thu

Noon		JUL	AUG	SEP	OCT	NOV	DEC
☉	1	9♋17	8♌52	8♍42	7♎58	8♏45	8♐59
	9	16 55	16 32	16 27	15 52	16 46	17 7
	17	24 32	24 13	24 15	23 47	24 49	25 15
	25	2♌11	1♍55	2♎ 4	1♏44	2♐55	3♑24
☿	1	17♊41	13♌23	4♎17	16♎16	25♎ 9	13♐ 7
	7	25 2	25 6	11 14	9R33	4♏52	22 30
	13	4♋41	5♍54	16 45	5 33	14 36	1♑53
	19	16 14	15 49	20 8	7D41	24 13	11 14
	25	28 48	24 52	20R19	14 32	3♐43	20 20
	31	11♌21	3♎ 1	...	23 33	...	28 34
♀	1	12♋57	4♋ 8	23♋16	22♌59	28♍11	4♏20
	9	8R 5	7 6	0♌32	1♍45	7♎41	14 9
	17	4 28	11 41	8 21	10 46	17 18	24 2
	25	3D13	17 28	16 35	19 59	27 0	3♐57
♂	1	17♍28	5♎36	25♎14	15♏28	7♐31	29♐51
	13	24 18	13 2	3♏11	23 52	16 20	9♑ 0
	25	1♎22	20 41	11 19	2♐26	25 19	18 17
♃	1	0♉52	4♉29	5♉19	3♉13	29♈13	26♈ 4
	13	2 33	5 11	4R48	1R45	27R43	25R31
	25	3 53	5R24	3 50	0 9	26 32	25D28
♄	1	18♋39	22♋39	26♋19	29♋ 3	0♌30	0♌15
	13	20 12	24 8	27 32	29 48	0R36	29♋43
	25	21 45	25 33	28 35	0♌19	0 26	28R58
♅	1	19♒ 9	18♒ 5	16♒53	16♒ 1	15♒48	16♒20
	13	18R47	17R37	16 29	15R50	15 55	16 45
	25	18 21	17 9	16 9	15 47	16 10	17 15
♆	1	1♌31	2♌39	3♌44	4♌31	4♌53	4♌44
	13	1 57	3 5	4 5	4 43	4R53	4 32
	25	2 23	3 30	4 23	4 51	4 48	4 17
Pl.	1	2♋56	3♋38	4♋ 9	4♋22	4♋13	3♋47
☊	1	0♒ 5	28♑26	26♑48	25♑13	23♑34	21♑59
	1st	Sat	Tue	Fri	Sun	Wed	Fri

d.	JAN	FEB	MAR	APR
☽ 1	17♏54	11♑18	5♒14	26♒43
3	17♐42	11♒ 0	3♓53	23♈24
5	18♑ 6	9♓57	1♈44	18♉59
7	17♒50	7♈25	28 19	13♊20
9	15♓59	3♉14	23♉30	7♋18
11	12♈22	27 45	17♊38	0♌59
13	7♉18	21♊32	11♋18	25 16
15	1♊20	15♋12	5♌11	20♍46
17	25 1	9♌17	29 53	17♎50
19	18♋45	4♍ 7	25♍46	16♏13
21	12♌50	29 52	22♎50	15♐12
23	7♍30	26♎32	20♏43	14♑ 0
25	3♎ 0	23♏59	18♐59	12♒ 9
27	29 35	22♐ 9	17♑13	9♓35
29	27♏26	20♑49	15♒19	6♈17
31	26♐29	...	13♓ 4	...

d.	MAY	JUN	JUL	AUG
☽ 1	2♉14	18♊11	20♋42	5♍24
3	27 20	11♋57	14♌18	0♎ 3
5	21♊37	5♌31	8♍17	25 39
7	15♋19	29 22	3♎ 7	22♏31
9	8♌58	24♍ 8	29 17	20♐48
11	3♍13	20♎26	27♏10	20♑19
13	28 45	18♏35	26♐39	20♒22
15	26♎ 3	18♐18	26♑59	19♓51
17	24♏58	18♑35	26♒59	17♈53
19	24♐43	18♒14	25♓39	14♉ 9
21	24♑14	16♓30	22♈35	8♊55
23	22♒44	13♈13	17♉57	2♋47
25	20♓ 1	8♉39	12♊15	26 21
27	16♈14	3♊10	5♋57	20♌10
29	11♉33	27 5	29 32	14♍35
31	6♊ 8	...	23♌20	9♎46

d.	SEP	OCT	NOV	DEC
☽ 1	22♎41	29♏44	22♑26	1♓28
3	19♏12	27♐26	20♒37	29 6
5	16♐39	25♑35	18♓30	25♈51
7	15♑ 5	24♒ 3	15♈56	21♉44
9	14♒16	22♓32	12♉36	16♊46
11	13♓35	20♈29	8♊16	11♋ 2
13	12♈11	17♉18	2♋52	4♌46
15	9♉20	12♊44	26 41	28 22
17	4♊52	7♋ 0	20♌17	22♍23
19	29 8	0♌39	14♍22	17♎29
21	22♋46	24 20	9♎36	14♏12
23	16♌30	19♍ 0	6♏24	12♐41
25	10♍53	14♎49	4♐40	12♑25
27	6♎14	11♏55	3♑49	12♒24
29	2♏35	9♐55	2♒57	11♓36
31	...	8♑16	...	9♈27

STATIONS

☿	♀	♂	♃
27Jan 21♒46	12Jun 19♋44	1Jan 29♌49	25Aug 5♉24
18Feb 6♒14	25Jul 3♋13	22Mar 10♌20	21Dec 25♈25
	♄	♅	♆
25May 19♉16	12Mar 9♋33	25May 19♒42	10Apr 29♋52
18Jun 10♊44	12Nov 0♌36	26Oct 15♒47	7Nov 4♌54
23Sep 20♎42	SIDER. TIME		1 Jan
14Oct 5♎28	6h 37m 18s		Midn.
	18h 39m 16s		Noon.
	LEAP YEAR		1916

1917 (BST 8 Apr. – 17 Sep.)

Noon		JAN	FEB	MAR	APR	MAY	JUN
☉	1	10♑32	12♒ 5	10♓21	11♈11	10♉32	10♊24
	9	18 41	20 11	18 21	19 4	18 16	18 .3
	17	26 50	28 16	26 20	26 54	25 59	25 42
	25	4♒59	6♓20	4♈16	4♉42	3♊41	3♋20
☿	1	29♑46	19♑49	18♒57	14♈ 9	28♉44	20♉56
	7	4♒58	22 46	28 10	26 31	29R21	23 35
	13	4R39	28 13	8♓ 4	8♉ 9	27 13	28 39
	19	28♑19	5♒12	18 41	17 53	23 49	5♊54
	25	21 39	13 11	0♈ 3	24 52	21 10	15 6
	31	19D40	...	12 6	...	20D44	...
♀	1	12♐39	21♑17	26♒13	4♈46	11♉53	20♊ 2
	9	22 36	1♒16	6♓11	14 41	21 45	29 51
	17	2♑34	11 15	16 8	24 35	1♊36	9♋39
	25	12 33	21 14	26 5	4♉29	11 26	19 27
♂	1	23♑43	18♒ 6	10♓14	4♈29	27♈26	20♉23
	13	3♒ 7	27 35	19 40	13 44	6♉25	29 2
	25	12 34	7♓ 4	29 3	22 54	15 16	7♊33
♃	1	25♈39	28♈23	2♉56	9♉23	16♉22	23♉40
	13	26 22	0♉ 8	5 18	12 8	19 13	26 25
	25	27 32	2 11	7 50	14 56	22 3	29 3
♄	1	28♋27	25♋57	24♋12	23♋42	24♋50	27♋26
	13	27R30	25R 5	23R48	23 58	25 42	28 43
	25	26 30	24 23	23 39	24 29	26 45	0♌ 7
♅	1	17♒35	19♒16	20♒53	22♒25	23♒25	23♒43
	13	18 12	19 58	21 31	22 53	23 37	23R37
	25	18 52	20 39	22 7	23 16	23 43	23 25
♆	1	4♌ 7	3♌16	2♌34	2♌ 7	2♌11	2♌45
	13	3R48	2R56	2R20	2D 5	2 21	3 4
	25	3 27	2 39	2 11	2 8	2 35	3 27
Pl	1	3♋11	2♋39	2♋20	2♋21	2♋41	3♋17
☊	1	20♑20	18♑42	17♑13	15♑34	13♑59	12♑21
1st		Mon	Thu	Thu	Sun	Tue	Fri

Noon		JUL	AUG	SEP	OCT	NOV	DEC
☉	1	9♋ 3	8♌38	8♍27	7♎44	8♏30	8♐44
	9	16 40	16 18	16 13	15 37	16 31	16 52
	17	24 18	23 59	24 1	23 33	24 35	25 0
	25	1♌57	1♍42	1♎50	1♏30	2♐40	3♑ 9
☿	1	26♊ 8	27♌52	3♎14	20♍28	7♏ 5	23♐49
	7	8♋32	7♍17	3R55	26 14	16 48	2♑35
	13	21 28	15 41	0 52	5♎10	26 17	10 42
	19	3♌59	22 58	24♍54	15 13	5♐35	17 8
	25	15 36	28 51	20 4	25 26	14 46	19R42
	31	26 12	2♎49	...	5♏27	...	15 55
♀	1	26♋47	4♍34	12♎ 2	17♏44	23♐36	25♑59
	9	6♌34	14 17	21 36	27 7	2♑33	3♒48
	17	16 19	23 57	1♏ 9	6♐25	11 19	11 3
	25	26 4	3♎37	10 39	15 38	19 49	17 30
♂	1	11♊45	2♋55	23♋ 7	11♌39	29♌29	14♍49
	13	20 3	10 51	0♌40	18 44	5♍54	20 9
	25	28 13	18 38	8 2	25 36	11 57	24 51
♃	1	0♊19	6♊ 8	10♊ 9	11♊31	9♊52	6♊ 7
	13	2 44	7 57	11 2	11R15	8R31	4R32
	25	4 57	9 27	11 29	10 30	6 56	3 10
♄	1	0♌51	4♌48	8♌40	11♌50	13♌59	14♌31
	13	2 21	6 20	10 2	12 50	14 23	14R16
	25	3 54	7 50	11 16	13 37	14 32	13 45
♅	1	23♒17	22♒16	21♒ 4	20♒ 8	19♒48	20♒14
	13	22R57	21R48	20R38	19R55	19 53	20 36
	25	22 32	21 20	20 17	19 48	20 5	21 5
♆	1	3♌39	4♌46	5♌52	6♌41	7♌ 5	6♌59
	13	4 4	5 13	6 14	6 54	7R 6	6R48
	25	4 31	5 38	6 33	7 3	7 2	6 33
Pl.	1	4♋ 0	4♋42	5♋14	5♋27	5♋20	4♋45
☊	1	10♑45	9♑ 7	7♑28	5♑53	4♑15	2♑39
1st		Sun	Wed	Sat	Mon	Thu	Sat

☽ d.	JAN	FEB	MAR	APR
1	22♈51	10♊36	19♊28	3♌37
3	18♉41	4♋43	13♋29	27 15
5	13♊32	28 24	7♌ 4	21♍20
7	7♋42	22♌ 1	0♍45	16♎13
9	1♌27	15♍51	24 53	11♏57
11	25 3	10♎10	19♎39	8♐27
13	18♍52	5♏15	15♏ 8	5♑39
15	13♎19	1♐28	11♐29	3♒34
17	8♏58	29 10	8♑54	2♓ 9
19	6♐14	28♑25	7♒32	1♈ 6
21	5♑16	28♒40	7♓ 8	29 42
23	5♒31	28♓46	6♈49	27♉11
25	5♓49	27♈30	5♉30	23♊ 9
27	5♈ 1	24♉20	2♊28	17♋46
29	2♉27	...	27 43	11♌35
31	28 13	...	21♋48	...

☽ d.	MAY	JUN	JUL	AUG
1	5♍18	20♎ 4	24♏13	14♑37
3	29 33	16♏10	21♐59	14♒35
5	24♎47	13♐37	21♑ 5	14♓55
7	21♏ 9	12♑ 6	20♒49	14♈22
9	18♐26	10♒59	20♓11	12♉11
11	16♑20	9♓42	18♈28	8♊20
13	14♒33	7♈50	15♉28	3♋14
15	12♓53	5♉10	11♊16	27 21
17	11♈ 5	1♊36	6♋ 9	21♌ 6
19	8♉47	27 6	0♌21	14♍47
21	5♊33	21♋44	24 9	8♎38
23	1♋ 8	15♌41	17♍49	2♏56
25	25 38	9♍22	11♎45	28 8
27	19♌28	3♎18	6♏26	24♐41
29	13♍13	28 5	2♐25	22♑59
31	7♎31	...	0♑ 7	22♒53

☽ d.	SEP	OCT	NOV	DEC
1	8♓10	16♈47	7♊47	11♋57
3	8♈34	15♉57	4♋12	6♌53
5	7♉38	13♊17	29 8	0♍56
7	4♊46	8♋48	23♌ 7	24 41
9	0♋10	3♌ 4	16♍50	18♎46
11	24 26	26 47	10♎52	13♏43
13	18♌ 9	20♍31	5♏38	9♐51
15	11♍50	14♎40	1♐18	7♑10
17	5♎44	9♏24	27 48	5♒19
19	0♏ 2	4♐49	25♑ 2	3♓51
21	24 57	0♑59	22♒54	2♈18
23	20♐46	28 6	21♓18	0♉19
25	17♑54	26♒22	19♈56	27 43
27	16♒35	25♓36	18♉17	24♊19
29	16♓34	25♈ 8	15♊45	19♋58
31	...	23♉55	...	14♌43

STATIONS	☿	♀	♂	♃
	10Jan 5♒40	None	None	1Oct 11♊31
	31Jan 19♒40			...
				...
		♄	♅	♆
	6May 29♉28	26Mar 23♋39	29May 23♒43	13Apr 2♌ 5
	30May 20♉38	26Nov 14♌32	30Oct 19♒ 8	10Nov 7♌ 7
	6Sep 4♎ 3	SIDER. TIME		1 Jan
	28Sep 19♍31	6h 40m 18s		Midn.
	25Jan 19♐42	18h 42m 16s		Noon.
		Common Year		1917

1918 (BST 24 Mar.–30 Sep.)

Noon		JAN	FEB	MAR	APR	MAY	JUN
☉	1	10♑17	11♒50	10♓ 6	10♈57	10♉17	10♊10
	9	18 26	19 57	18 7	18 49	18 2	17 49
	17	26 35	28 2	26 5	26 40	25 46	25 28
	25	4♒44	6♓ 5	4♈ 2	4♉28	3♊27	3♋ 6
☿	1	14♑43	18♑ 1	0♓19	28♈27	3♉15	16♉47
	7	7R 3	25 56	11 5	5♉59	0R43	25 43
	13	3 30	4♒33	22 30	9 54	0D46	6♊14
	19	5D 9	13 44	4♈24	10R 1	3 29	18 12
	25	10 4	23 29	16 15	7 8	8 30	1♋ 8
	31	16 47	...	26 54	...	15 28	...
♀	1	22♒14	25♒27	12♒45	26♒29	24♓23	28♈ 4
	9	26 16	20R53	13D38	3♓ 9	2♈48	7♉ 7
	17	28 21	16 13	16 42	10 29	11 25	16 17
	25	27R57	13 17	21 23	18 17	20 14	25 32
♂	1	27♍13	3♎ 2	28♍55	17♍37	14♍ 3	20♍54
	13	0♎30	2R29	24R35	14R48	15 40	25 29
	25	2 32	0 5	19 57	13 51	18 39	0♎48
♃	1	2♊31	1♊32	3♊21	7♊46	13♊36	20♊29
	13	1R46	2 1	4 48	9 58	16 12	23 14
	25	1 28	2 57	6 36	12 21	18 53	26 0
♄	1	13♌22	11♌ 2	8♌56	7♌40	8♌ 3	10♌ 0
	13	12R33	10R 4	8R16	7D38	8 38	11 6
	25	11 37	9 11	7 49	7 51	9 26	12 21
♅	1	21♒24	23♒ 2	24♒39	26♒14	27♒18	27♒43
	13	21 59	23 44	25 18	26 44	27 33	27R40
	25	22 38	24 25	25 55	27 8	27 42	27 30
♆	1	6♌24	5♌33	4♌50	4♌22	4♌23	4♌54
	13	6R 5	5R13	4R36	4R19	4 31	5 13
	25	5 45	4 55	4 26	4D20	4 45	5 35
Pl.	1	4♋17	3♋47	3♋28	3♋27	3♋47	4♋23
☊	1	1♑ 1	29♐22	27♐53	26♐15	24♐39	23♐ 1
	1st	Tue	Fri	Fri	Mon	Wed	Sat

Noon		JUL	AUG	SEP	OCT	NOV	DEC
☉	1	8♋49	8♌24	8♍14	7♎30	8♏16	8♐30
	9	16 27	16 4	15 59	15 23	16 17	16 37
	17	24 5	23 45	23 47	23 18	24 20	24 45
	25	1♌43	1♍28	1♎36	1♏16	2♐25	2♑54
☿	1	14♋ 8	5♍24	9♍18	26♍40	18♏46	29♐50
	7	26 25	11 22	4R25	7♎23	27 53	3♑38
	13	7♌37	15 25	3D33	17 54	6♐45	2R 2
	19	17 41	16R54	7 58	28 2	15 17	24♐46
	25	26 35	15 5	16 23	7♏47	23 12	18 29
	31	4♍15	10 15	...	17 13	...	18D 2
♀	1	2♊32	9♋14	16♌50	23♍53	2♏38	10♐20
	9	11 55	18 52	26 39	3♎51	12 41	20 34
	17	21 22	28 32	6♍31	13 51	22 44	0♑27
	25	0♋52	8♌16	16 26	23 52	2♐47	10 31
♂	1	3♎41	20♎31	9♏47	0♐ 8	22♐34	15♑20
	13	9 51	27 44	17 44	8 40	1♑35	24 38
	25	16 29	5♏15	25 57	17 24	10 43	4♒ 1
♃	1	27♊22	4♋ 9	10♋ 1	14♋ 6	15♋49	14♋33
	13	0♋ 4	6 35	11 53	15 6	15R40	13R19
	25	2 41	8 49	13 27	15 42	15 2	11 48
♄	1	13♌ 1	16♌48	20♌44	24♌13	26♌55	28♌11
	13	14 25	18 20	22 12	25 24	27 37	28R14
	25	15 54	19 51	23 34	26 25	28 3	28 2
♅	1	27♒23	26♒26	25♒13	24♒14	23♒48	24♒ 7
	13	27R 5	25R58	24R47	23R59	23D50	24 27
	25	26 41	25 30	24 24	23 50	24 0	24 54
♆	1	5♌47	6♋54	8♌ 0	8♌51	9♌18	9♌13
	13	6 12	7 20	8 23	9 5	9R20	9R 4
	25	6 38	7 46	8 42	9 14	9 17	8 50
Pl.	1	5♋ 5	5♋47	6♋19	6♋33	6♋27	6♋ 3
☊	1	21♐26	19♐47	18♐ 9	16♐33	14♐55	13♐20
	1st	Mon	Thu	Sun	Tue	Fri	Sun

d.		JAN	FEB	MAR	APR
☽	1	26♌48	10♎39	19♎17	4♐44
	3	20♍38	4♏36	13♏16	0♑ 0
	5	14♎26	29 20	7♐55	26 36
	7	8♏49	25♐30	3♐50	24♒53
	9	4♐23	23♑28	1♒33	24♓44
	11	1♑29	23♒ 6	1♓ 8	25♈10
	13	0♒ 3	23♓24	1♈45	24♉50
	15	29 27	23♈ 5	1♉58	22♊47
	17	28♓45	21♉16	0♊36	18♋53
	19	27♈13	17♊50	27 20	13♌36
	21	24♉31	13♋ 8	22♋32	7♍33
	23	20♊46	7♌40	16♌48	1♎17
	25	16♋ 9	1♍43	10♍39	25 10
	27	10♌51	25 32	4♎24	19♏27
	29	5♍ 0	...	28 16	14♐19
	31	28 48	...	22♏27	...

d.		MAY	JUN	JUL	AUG
☽	1	9♑58	1♓14	10♈38	3♊32
	3	6♒41	29 38	8♉59	0♋21
	5	4♓41	28♈30	6♊53	26 22
	7	3♈54	27♉16	4♋ 5	21♌36
	9	3♉40	25♊18	0♌21	16♍ 7
	11	2♊56	22♋ 7	25 36	10♎ 2
	13	0♋50	17♌36	19♍57	3♏44
	15	27 5	12♍ 1	13♎47	27 46
	17	21♌56	5♎52	7♏39	22♐48
	19	15♍56	29 45	2♐11	19♑26
	21	9♎42	24♏13	27 55	17♒51
	23	3♏43	19♐41	25♑ 8	17♓33
	25	28 21	16♑17	23♒38	17♈25
	27	23♐48	13♒54	22♓44	16♉24
	29	20♑ 7	12♓ 9	21♈38	14♊ 2
	31	17♒18	...	19♉47	10♋24

d.		SEP	OCT	NOV	DEC
☽	1	23♋12	27♌35	12♎28	14♏ 6
	3	18♌15	21♍41	6♏10	8♐58
	5	12♍42	15♎28	0♐ 4	3♑50
	7	6♎39	9♏ 8	24 25	29 32
	9	0♏20	2♐57	19♑32	26♒ 9
	11	24 4	27 21	15♒48	23♓47
	13	18♐25	22♑52	13♓35	22♈23
	15	14♑ 4	20♒ 5	12♈50	21♉34
	17	11♒33	19♓10	12♉55	20♊42
	19	10♓56	19♈34	12♊43	18♋57
	21	11♈23	19♉59	11♋13	15♌48
	23	11♉32	19♊ 9	7♌58	11♍10
	25	10♊16	16♋29	3♍10	5♎24
	27	7♋18	12♌11	27 19	29 6
	29	2♌55	6♍43	21♎ 1	22♏55
	31	...	0♎37	...	17♐23

STATIONS

☿	♀	♂	♃
14Jan 3♑28	21Jan 28♒29	4Feb 3♎ 4	27Jan 1♊28
17Apr 10♈23	3Mar 12♒45	26Apr 13♍51	4Nov 15♋50
10May 0♉23	**♄**	**♅**	**♆**
19Aug 16♍54	9Apr 7♌37	1Jun 27♒43	15Apr 4♌18
12Sep 3♍19	10Dec 28♌15	4Nov 23♒47	12Nov 9♌20
9Dec 3♐50	SIDER. TIME		1 Jan
29Dec 17♐50	6h 39m 20s		Midn.
	18h 41m 18s		Noon.
	Common Year		1918.

1919 (BST 30 Mar.–29 Sep.)

Noon		JAN	FEB	MAR	APR	MAY	JUN
☉	1	10♑ 2	11♒35	9♓51	10♈43	10♉ 3	9♊56
	9	18 11	19 42	17 52	18 35	17 48	17 36
	17	26 20	27 47	25 51	26 25	25 31	25 14
	25	4♒29	5♓50	3♈47	4♉13	3♊13	2♋52
☿	1	18♐28	26♑25	14♓49	21♈36	14♈13	28♉ 4
	7	23 1	5♒53	26 21	18R 2	19 29	10♊38
	13	29 41	15 49	7♈16	13 33	26 30	23 48
	19	7♑29	26 15	16 5	10 53	5♉ 0	6♋38
	25	15 56	7♓14	21 14	11D10	14 52	18 28
	31	24 53	...	21R55	...	26 4	...
♀	1	19♑19	28♒11	3♈ 1	11♉ 0	16♊51	22♋22
	9	29 22	8♓10	12 54	20 40	26 12	1♌ 9
	17	9♒24	18 8	22 43	0♊15	5♋26	9 43
	25	19 25	28 4	2♉30	9 46	14 32	18 0
♂	1	9♒32	3♓58	25♓55	19♈43	12♉ 3	4♊20
	13	18 59	13 25	5♈12	28 44	20 46	12 44
	25	28 27	22 48	14 24	7♉38	29 22	21 1
♃	1	10♋52	7♋ 8	5♋46	7♋10	10♋58	16♋35
	13	9R16	6R15	5D57	8 27	12 59	19 3
	25	7 50	5 48	6 36	10 3	15 12	21 37
♄	1	27♌47	25♌52	23♌39	21♌47	21♌24	22♋38
	13	27R11	24R55	22R47	21R27	21 42	23 31
	25	26 24	23 57	22 6	21D21	22 14	24 34
♅	1	25♒12	26♒47	28♒23	0♓ 2	1♓10	1♓41
	13	25 46	27 28	29 4	0 33	1 28	1R41
	25	26 24	28 10	29 41	0 59	1 38	1 34
♆	1	8♌40	7♌50	7♌ 6	6♌36	6♌35	7♌ 4
	13	8R22	7R30	6R52	6R32	6 42	7 22
	25	8 2	7 12	6 41	6D33	6 55	7 43
Pl.	1	5♋27	4♋55	4♋36	4♋34	4♋53	5♋28
☊	1	11♐41	10♐ 3	8♐34	6♐55	5♐20	3♐41
	1st	Wed	Sat	Sat	Tue	Thu	Sun

Noon		JUL	AUG	SEP	OCT	NOV	DEC
☉	1	8♋35	8♌11	8♍ 0	7♎15	8♏ 1	8♐15
	9	16 13	15 50	15 45	15 9	16 2	16 22
	17	23 51	23 31	23 32	23 4	24 5	24 30
	25	1♌29	1♍14	1♎22	1♏ 1	2♐10	2♐39
☿	1	29♋ 3	29♌ 0	19♌53	10♎30	28♏16	11♐45
	7	8♌18	27R31	27 23	20 39	6♐ 2	4R11
	13	16 11	23 22	7♍35	0♏19	12 43	1D50
	19	22 31	18 39	18 44	9 34	17 12	5 3
	25	26 56	16D33	29 51	18 27	17R27	11 19
	31	28 57	19 0	...	26 54	...	19 3
♀	1	24♌ 0	19♍50	25♍26	11♍18	23♍32	21♎45
	9	1♍37	24 7	21R28	11D36	0♎ 9	0♏24
	17	8 41	26 42	16 36	14 12	7 32	9 20
	25	15 3	27R 7	12 44	18 35	15 29	18 29
♂	1	25♊ 7	15♋52	5♌55	24♌42	13♍24	0♎33
	13	3♋14	23 42	13 30	2♍ 2	20 23	7 3
	25	11 14	1♌27	21 0	9 15	27 13	13 17
♃	1	22♋56	29♋49	6♌28	12♌ 6	16♌21	18♌ 7
	13	25 35	2♌27	8 51	13 59	17 23	18R 2
	25	28 16	5 1	11 5	15 35	17 59	17 29
♄	1	25♌ 9	28♌38	2♍32	6♍12	9♍20	11♍15
	13	26 25	0♍ 7	4 2	7 31	10 16	11 36
	25	27 48	1 38	5 30	8 43	10 59	11R41
♅	1	1♓28	0♓35	29♒23	28♒20	27♒48	28♒ 1
	13	1R11	0R 8	28R55	28R 2	27D47	28 19
	25	0 49	29♒39	28 31	27 51	27 54	28 43
♆	1	7♌55	9♌ 1	10♌ 8	11♌ 0	11♌30	11♌28
	13	8 20	9 28	10 31	11 15	11 33	11R19
	25	8 46	9 54	10 52	11 26	11R31	11 6
Pl.	1	6♋11	6♋53	7♋26	7♋46	7♋40	7♋12
☊	1	2♐ 6	0♐27	28♏49	27♏14	25♏35	24♏ 0
	1st	Tue	Fri	Mon	Wed	Sat	Mon

d.	JAN	FEB	MAR	APR
☽ 1	29♐59	18♒30	26♒52	19♈30
3	25♑59	16♓50	26♓ 1	19♉35
5	22♒57	15♈31	25♈34	18♉40
7	20♓39	13♉56	24♉34	16♋17
9	18♈47	11♊50	22♊32	12♌32
11	17♉ 7	9♋11	19♋26	7♍43
13	15♊25	5♌54	15♌28	2♎ 9
15	13♋21	1♍51	10♍45	26 6
17	10♌27	26 53	5♎20	19♏44
19	6♍24	21♎ 3	29 18	13♐24
21	1♎ 9	14♏44	22♏55	7♑30
23	25 4	8♐30	16♐39	2♒36
25	18♏45	3♑ 4	11♑ 9	29 16
27	12♐52	29 6	7♒ 6	27♓45
29	8♑ 4	...	4♓54	27♈43
31	4♒41	...	4♈24	...

d.	MAY	JUN	JUL	AUG
☽ 1	28♉ 7	20♋24	26♌ 4	12♎20
3	27♊42	17♌50	21♍55	6♏23
5	25♋42	13♍35	16♎26	0♐ 1
7	22♌ 3	8♎ 4	10♏11	23 57
9	17♍ 4	1♏50	3♐51	18♑47
11	11♎14	25 27	27 59	14♒50
13	4♏57	19♐20	22♑57	12♓ 1
15	28 34	13♑48	18♒52	9♎58
17	22♐24	9♒ 3	15♓41	8♉12
19	16♑46	5♓15	13♈13	6♊26
21	12♒ 2	2♈32	11♉22	4♋32
23	8♓36	0♉55	9♊59	2♌18
25	6♈42	0♊11	8♋43	29 22
27	6♉12	29 43	6♌59	25♍25
29	6♊21	28♋35	4♍10	20 18
31	6♋ 3	...	29 57	14♎16

d.	SEP	OCT	NOV	DEC
☽ 1	26♏ 5	27♐46	13♒ 1	18♓ 4
3	19♐47	22♑ 7	9♓21	15♈47
5	14♑11	17♒48	7♈30	15♉ 8
7	9♒52	15♓13	7♉12	15♊29
9	7♓ 5	14♈12	7♊32	15♋41
11	5♈31	13♉57	7♋18	14♌31
13	4♉28	13♊26	5♌38	11♍31
15	3♊13	11♋56	2♍20	6♎49
17	1♋22	9♌13	27 40	0♏59
19	28 48	5♍23	22♎ 2	24 37
21	25♌30	0♎36	15♏50	18♐12
23	21♍22	25 3	9♐26	12♑ 5
25	16♎20	18♏56	3♑ 5	6♒30
27	10♏29	12♐30	27 8	1♓38
29	4♐ 7	6♑10	21♒59	27 43
31	...	0♒27	...	25♈ 2

STATIONS

☿	♀	♂	♃
29Mar 22♈11	23Aug 27♍14	None	3Mar 5♋46
22Apr 10♈39	4Oct 11♍ 7		5Dec 18♌ 9
2Aug 28♌58	♄	♅	♆
25Aug 16♌33	24Apr 21♌21	7Jun 1♓42	18Apr 6♌32
23Nov 18♐ 0	23Dec 11♍41	8Nov 27♒47	15Nov 11♌33
13Dec 1♐50	SIDER. TIME		1 Jan
	6h 38m 23s		Midn.
	18h 40m 21s		Noon.
	Common Year		1919

1920 (BST 28 Mar.–25 Oct.)

Noon		JAN	FEB	MAR	APR	MAY	JUN
☉	1	9♑47	11♒21	10♓37	11♈28	10♉48	10♊40
	9	17 57	10 27	18 38	19 20	18 32	18 19
	17	26 6	27 32	26 36	27 10	26 15	25 57
	25	4♒14	5♒36	4♈33	4♉58	3♊57	3♋35
☿	1	20♐25	8♒15	28♓27	21♓45	17♈40	18♊30
	7	28 55	18 40	3♈51	22D34	27 24	0♋44
	13	7♑50	29 30	4R12	26 10	8♉18	11 38
	19	17 4	10♓32	0 10	1♈50	20 20	21 2
	25	26 37	21 5	24♓58	9 6	3♊15	28 51
	31	6♒33	...	21 56	...	16 22	...
♀	1	26♏37	3♑38	8♒59	17♓ 1	23♈50	1♊51
	9	6 3	13 21	18 47	26 50	3♉39	11 39
	17	15 34	23 6	28 36	6♈39	13 27	21 29
	25	25 11	2♒52	8♓25	16 28	23 16	1♋18
♂	1	16♎45	0♏12	8♏ 2	7♏11	27♎11	21 15
	13	22 23	4 11	9 5	3R47	23R32	22 14
	25	27 30	7 9	8R25	29♎23	21 31	24 50
♃	1	16♌58	13♌23	9♌50	8♌ 7	9♌15	12♌54
	13	15R46	11R48	8R50	8D15	10 24	14 49
	25	14 18	10 21	8 15	8 49	11 54	16 57
♄	1	11♍36	10♍17	8♍ 6	5♍52	4♍50	5♍23
	13	11R16	9R26	7R 9	5R17	4D51	6 1
	25	10 42	8 30	6 18	4 56	5 7	6 51
♅	1	29♒ 0	0♓32	2♓11	3♓51	5♓ 3	5♓39
	13	29 32	1 12	2 51	4 23	5 22	5R40
	25	0♓ 9	1 54	3 30	4 51	5 35	5 35
♆	1	10♌57	10♌ 7	9♌21	8♌50	8♌47	9♌15
	13	10R39	9R47	9R 6	8R45	8 54	9 32
	25	10 19	9 29	8 55	8D45	9 6	9 54
Pl.	1	6♋37	6♋ 4	5♋44	5♋42	6♋ 0	6♋35
☊	1	22♏21	20♏43	19♏11	17♏32	15♏57	14♏18
1st		Thu	Sun	Mon	Thu	Sat	Tue

Noon		JUL	AUG	SEP	OCT	NOV	DEC
☉	1	9♋19	8♌54	8♍43	8♎ 0	8♏46	9♐ 1
	9	16 56	16 34	16 29	15 53	16 48	17 8
	17	24 34	24 15	24 17	23 49	24 51	25 17
	25	2♌12	1♍57	2♎ 6	1♏47	2♐56	3♑26
☿	1	4♌54	0♌38	1♍26	24♎11	1♐ 9	18♏50
	7	8 52	29D17	13 5	3♏ 4	1R55	25 12
	13	10 18	1 52	24 16	11 25	27♏12	3♐12
	19	8R55	8 26	4♎50	19 6	19 30	11 52
	25	5 14	18 8	14 47	25 45	16 5	20 51
	31	1 9	29 29	...	0♐37	...	0♑ 3
♀	1	8♋40	16♌50	25♍ 5	2♏ 5	10♐10	16♑45
	9	18 30	26 42	4♎57	11 55	19 58	26 25
	17	28 21	6♍34	14 49	21 46	29 44	6♒ 1
	25	8♌12	16 27	24 41	1♐35	9♑28	15 32
♂	1	26♎39	10♏ 0	27♏53	17♐51	10♑16	3♒ 2
	13	1♏ 7	16 30	5♐37	26 21	19 17	12 18
	25	6 30	23 34	13 42	5♑ 5	28 25	21 36
♃	1	18♌ 5	24♌26	1♍ 9	7♍29	13♍12	17♍12
	13	20 27	27 1	3 44	9 50	15 1	18 12
	25	22 56	29 38	6 16	12 1	16 33	18 46
♄	1	7♍20	10♍28	14♍12	17♍56	21♍22	23♍46
	13	8 27	11 52	15 43	19 21	22 28	24 22
	25	9 41	13 20	17 12	20 40	23 23	24 43
♅	1	5♓30	4♓40	3♓29	2♓24	1♓47	1♓56
	13	5R15	4R14	3R 1	2R 5	1D45	2 11
	25	4 54	3 46	2 35	1 52	1 50	2 34
♆	1	10♌ 5	11♌11	12♌18	13♌11	13♌42	13♌42
	13	10 30	11 38	12 42	13 27	13 46	13R33
	25	10 56	12 4	13 2	13 38	13R44	13 21
Pl.	1	7♋18	8♋ 1	8♋34	8♋48	8♋43	8♋20
☊	1	12♏44	11♏ 5	9♏26	7♏51	6♏12	4♏37
1st		Thu	Sun	Wed	Fri	Mon	Wed

	d.	JAN	FEB	MAR	APR
☽	1	9♉13	2♋30	26♋49	17♍58
	3	8♊32	1♌46	24♌59	13♎58
	5	8♋34	0♍24	22♍19	8♏58
	7	8♌14	27 38	18♎24	3♐ 8
	9	6♍26	23♎12	13♏12	26 50
	11	2♎46	17♏29	7♐ 7	20♑39
	13	27 31	11♐ 8	0♑47	15♒12
	15	21♏18	4♑52	24 53	11♓ 2
	17	14♐52	29 18	20♒ 1	8♈27
	19	8♑44	24♒45	16♓28	7♉12
	21	3♒17	21♓13	14♈ 7	6♊36
	23	28 37	18♈26	12♉29	5♋48
	25	24♓43	16♉10	11♊ 2	4♌11
	27	21♈31	14♊16	9♋23	1♍28
	29	19♉19	12♋37	7♌19	27 42
	31	17♊56	...	4♍37	...

	d.	MAY	JUN	JUL	AUG
☽	1	22♎58	8♐15	10♑49	26♒13
	3	17♏29	1♑56	4♒46	21♓22
	5	11♐25	25 42	29 10	17♈17
	7	5♑ 6	19♒52	24♓18	14♉12
	9	28 55	14♓52	20♈31	12♊19
	11	23♒25	11♈11	18♉12	11♋35
	13	19 9	9♉11	17♊26	11♌21
	15	16♈31	8♊48	17♋40	10♍31
	17	15♉32	9♋15	17♌43	8♎11
	19	15♊34	9♌13	16♍22	4♏ 6
	21	15♋30	7♍40	13♎ 6	28 37
	23	14♌21	4♎16	8♏11	22♐25
	25	11♍39	29 20	2♐13	16♑10
	27	7♎30	23♏26	25 52	10♒22
	29	2♏16	17♐ 8	19♑40	5♓18
	31	26 21	...	13♒53	1♈ 4

	d.	SEP	OCT	NOV	DEC
☽	1	14♈13	21♉30	14♋43	23♌42
	3	11♉ 6	19 41	13♌10	21♍14
	5	8♊44	18♋ 3	10♍47	17♎24
	7	7♋ 7	16♌20	7♎29	12♏33
	9	6♌ 1	14♍13	3♏16	7♐ 0
	11	4♍49	11♎19	28 14	1♑ 0
	13	2♎45	7♏21	22♐30	24 45
	15	29 18	2♐18	16♑18	18♒29
	17	24♏25	26 23	10♒ 3	12♓37
	19	18♐33	20♑ 8	4♓16	7♈43
	21	12♑17	14♒ 7	29 35	4♉22
	23	6♒17	8♓57	26♈30	2♊54
	25	1♓ 4	5♈ 4	25♉ 6	3♋ 3
	27	26 55	2♉36	24♊52	3♌37
	29	23♈49	1♊13	24♋45	3♍14
	31	...	0♋15	...	1♎ 4

STATIONS	☿	♀	♂	♃
	11Mar 4♈39	None	15Mar 9♏ 6	4Apr 8♌ 6
	3Apr 21♓49		31May 21♎15	...
		♄	♅	♆
	14Jul 10♌16	7May 4♍49	10Jun 5♓40	19Apr 8♌45
	7Aug 29♋17	...	11Nov 1♓45	16Nov 13♌46
	6Nov 2♐ 8	SIDER. TIME		1 Jan
	26Nov 16♏10	6h 37m 26s		Midn.
		18h 39m 24s		Noon.
		LEAP YEAR		1920

1921 (BST 3 Apr.–3 Oct.)

Noon		JAN	FEB	MAR	APR	MAY	JUN
☉	1	10♑33	12♒ 7	10♓23	11♈13	10♉33	10♊25
	9	18 43	20 13	18 23	19 5	18 18	18 5
	17	26 52	28 18	26 22	26 56	26 1	25 43
	25	5♒ 1	6♓22	4♈18	4♉44	3♊43	3♋21
☿	1	1♑36	23♒14	13♓34	13♓33	0♉25	1♋57
	7	11 2	3♓28	7R35	20 44	12 50	9 57
	13	20 43	12 11	3 54	29 7	25 51	15 57
	19	0♒41	17 15	3D57	8♈33	8♊39	19 42
	25	10 58	16R44	7 6	18 59	20 21	20R51
	31	21 28	...	12 29	...	0♋27	...
♀	1	23♒46	28♓39	25♈29	10♉16	26♈57	29♈37
	9	3♓ 4	6♈58	1♉29	8R58	24R16	4♉46
	17	12 11	14 51	6 15	5 15	24D 6	10 56
	25	21 5	22 7	9 21	0 18	26 14	17 52
♂	1	27♒ 3	21♓ 2	12♈20	5♉18	26♉48	18♊17
	13	6♓21	0♈13	21 19	13 59	5♊12	26 25
	25	15 38	9 20	0♉11	22 33	13 29	4♋27
♃	1	18♍54	17♍38	14♍27	10♍42	8♍58	9♍58
	13	18R46	16R25	12R53	9R42	9D 1	11 4
	25	18 10	14 58	11 26	9 6	9 30	12 29
♄	1	24♍48	24♍ 6	22♍17	19♍54	18♍17	18♍ 5
	13	24 44	23R26	21R21	19R 7	18R 1	18 27
	25	24 24	22 36	20 25	18 31	17D59	19 2
♅	1	2♓50	4♓19	5♓55	7♓36	8♓53	9♓34
	13	3 21	4 59	6 35	8 10	9 14	9 38
	25	3 57	5 41	7 14	8 40	9 29	9R35
♆	1	13♌12	12♌23	11♌38	11♌ 4	10♌59	11♌24
	13	12R54	12R 3	11R22	10R59	11 5	11 41
	25	12 35	11 44	11 10	10D58	11 16	12 2
Pl.	1	7♋46	7♋12	6♋52	6♋43	7♋ 5	7♋42
☊	1	2♏58	1♏20	29♎51	28♎13	26♎37	24♎59
	1st	Sat	Tue	Tue	Fri	Sun	Wed

Noon		JUL	AUG	SEP	OCT	NOV	DEC
☉	1	9♋ 4	8♌40	8♍29	7♎46	8♏32	8♐46
	9	16 42	16 20	16 15	15 39	16 34	16 54
	17	24 20	24 1	24 2	23 35	24 37	25 2
	25	1♌58	1♍43	1♎52	1♏32	2♐42	3♑11
☿	1	19♋20	19♋36	16♍54	2♏16	6♏ 7	24♏38
	7	15R56	28 35	27 20	8 55	0R47	3♐50
	13	12 31	9♌46	7♎ 4	13 58	1D48	13 7
	19	11D 9	21 51	16 10	16 17	7 38	22 29
	25	13 2	3♍47	24 35	14R 9	15 43	1♑57
	31	18 23	15 5	...	7 23	...	11 33
♀	1	23♉26	25♊28	0♌40	6♍28	14♎34	22♏ 4
	9	1♊15	4♋20	10 5	16 13	24 33	2♐ 7
	17	9 26	13 22	19 35	26 2	4♏32	12 10
	25	17 53	22 32	29 12	5♎54	14 33	22 14
♂	1	8♋26	28♋45	18♌38	7♍33	26♍49	15♎ 8
	13	16 21	6♌29	26 14	15 3	4♎11	22 19
	25	24 12	14 10	3♍48	22 30	11 29	29 25
♃	1	13♍19	18♍30	24♍45	1♎12	7♎42	13♎12
	13	15 9	20 50	27 19	3 47	10 2	15 1
	25	17 13	23 17	29 54	6 17	12 12	16 33
♄	1	19♍24	22♍ 3	25♍32	29♍15	2♎53	5♎43
	13	20 18	23 20	27 1	0♎42	4 8	6 33
	25	21 22	24 42	28 30	2 7	5 14	7 9
♅	1	9♓31	8♓47	7♓37	6♓30	5♓48	5♓50
	13	9R19	8R22	7R 9	6R 9	5R43	6 3
	25	9 0	7 54	6 42	5 54	5D45	6 23
♆	1	12♌13	13♌18	14♌36	15♌20	15♌53	15♌56
	13	12 37	13 45	14 50	15 37	15 58	15R48
	25	13 3	14 11	15 11	15 49	15R58	15 36
Pl.	1	8♋25	9♋ 9	9♋44	10♋ 2	9♋56	9♋33
☊	1	23♎23	21♎45	20♎ 6	18♎31	16♎53	15♎17
	1st	Fri	Mon	Thu	Sat	Tue	Thu

d.		JAN	FEB	MAR	APR
☽	1	14♎17	0♐59	9♐25	23♑23
	3	9♏39	24 56	3♑26	17♒12
	5	4♐ 2	18♑38	27 9	11♓29
	7	27 56	12♒26	21♒ 3	6♈38
	9	21♑41	6♓32	15♓28	2♉46
	11	15♒27	1♈ 7	10♈33	29 51
	13	9♓28	26 22	6♉24	27♊40
	15	4♈ 1	22♉41	3♊ 7	25♋58
	17	29 38	20♊26	0♋49	24♌27
	19	26♉50	19♋39	29 28	22♍46
	21	25♊53	19♌45	28♌42	20♎28
	23	26♋19	19♍33	27♍43	17♏12
	25	26♌50	17♎55	25♎43	12♐47
	27	26♍ 2	14♏27	22♎15	7♑21
	29	23♎16	...	17♐21	1♒16
	31	18♏44	...	11♑30	...

d.		MAY	JUN	JUL	AUG
☽	1	25♒ 6	9♈55	14♉15	5♋21
	3	19♓27	6♉ 7	12♊16	5♌37
	5	14♈50	4♊ 0	11♋57	6♍ 6
	7	11♉34	3♋13	12♌16	5♎28
	9	9♊31	2♌53	11♍56	3♏ 2
	11	8♋13	1♍58	10♎ 5	28 57
	13	7♌ 0	29 54	6♏40	23♐41
	15	5♍21	26♎38	2♐ 2	17♑45
	17	2♎58	22♏23	26 36	11♒32
	19	29 48	17♐24	20♑41	5♓17
	21	25♏49	11♑48	14♒30	29 15
	23	20♐59	5♒45	8♓13	23♈42
	25	15♑23	29 28	2♈10	19♉ 4
	27	9♒16	23♓23	26 51	15♊49
	29	3♓ 4	18♈ 6	22♉52	14♋15
	31	27 22	...	20♉43	14♌ 7

d.		SEP	OCT	NOV	DEC
☽	1	29♌18	7♎31	27♏42	1♑50
	3	29♍20	6♏ 3	23♐51	26 37
	5	28♎ 2	3♐ 5	18♑46	20♒36
	7	24♏57	28 35	12♒47	14♓16
	9	20♐18	22♑56	6♓30	8♈17
	11	14♑36	16♒43	0♈34	3♉20
	13	8♒24	10♓32	25 33	29 56
	15	2♓ 9	4♈50	21♉45	28♊ 5
	17	26 12	29 56	19♊ 6	27♋12
	19	20♈47	25♉56	17♋15	26♌22
	21	16♉ 4	22♊50	15♌40	24♍50
	23	12♊21	20♋32	13♍56	22♎23
	25	9♋49	18♌52	11♎51	19♏ 5
	27	8♌30	17♍33	9♏17	15♐ 2
	29	8♍ 1	16♎10	6♐ 1	10♑17
	31	...	14♏ 7	...	4♒47

STATIONS	☿	♀	♂	♃
	22Feb 17♓44	2Apr 10♉15	None.	4Jan 18♍55
	16Mar 3♓28	14May 23♈52		6May 8♍56
		♄	♅	♆
	25Jun 20♋51	4Jan 24♍48	14Jun 9♓38	22Apr 10♌58
	14Jul 11♋ 9	21May 17♍58	15Nov 5♓43	19Nov 15♌58
	20Oct 16–17	SIDER. TIME		1 Jan
	9Nov 0♏24	6h 40m 25s		Midn.
		18h 42m 23s		Noon.
		Common Year		1921

1922 (BST 26 Mar.- 8 Oct.)

Noon		JAN	FEB	MAR	APR	MAY	JUN
☉	1	10♑19	11♒52	10♓ 8	10♈59	10♉19	10♊12
	9	18 28	19 58	18 9	18 51	18 4	17 51
	17	26 37	28 3	26 7	26 41	25 47	25 29
	25	4♒45	6♓ 7	4♈ 3	4♉29	3♊29	3♋ 7
☿	1	13♑11	29♒51	16♒20	20♓ 7	18♉14	0♋ 8
	7	23 1	0♓52	19 19	0♈ 8	0♊25	0R48
	13	3♒ 1	26♒ 0	24 38	11 1	11 1	28♊56
	19	12 58	19R29	1♓31	22 49	19 36	25 40
	25	22 11	16 11	9 33	5♉23	25 55	22 53
	31	29 6	...	18 32	...	29 45	...
♀	1	1♑ 2	10♒ 0	15♓ 4	23♈38	0♊33	8♋13
	9	11 6	20 2	25 3	3♉31	10 19	17 50
	17	21 9	0♓ 4	5♈ 1	13 23	20 3	27 24
	25	1♒12	10 4	14 57	23 12	29 45	6♌55
♂	1	3♏31	20♏59	5♐21	18♐17	25♐ 0	21♐41
	13	10 25	27 21	10 50	21 53	25R 6	17R56
	25	17 9	3♐24	15 45	24 19	23 25	14 13
♃	1	17♎17	18♎54	17♎48	14♎24	10♎49	9♎ 0
	13	18 14	18R43	16R41	12R52	9R48	9D 3
	25	18 47	18 6	15 17	11 27	9 10	9 31
♄	1	7♎23	7♎24	6♎ 3	3♎43	1♎42	0♎49
	13	7 36	6R57	5R12	2R50	1R11	0D54
	25	7R33	6 18	4 16	2 2	0 53	1 13
♅	1	6♓38	8♓ 4	9♓38	11♓21	12♓41	13♓29
	13	7 8	8 43	10 19	11 56	13 4	13 35
	25	7 42	9 24	10 59	12 27	13 22	13R35
♆	1	15♌28	14♌40	13♌54	13♌19	13♌11	13♌34
	13	15R11	14R20	13R38	13R12	13 16	13 50
	25	14 51	14 0	13 25	13D10	13 26	14 10
Pl.	1	8♋57	8♋21	8♋ 0	7♋55	8♋13	8♋48
☊	1	13♎39	12♎ 0	10♎31	8♎53	7♎17	5♎39
1st		Sun	Wed	Wed	Sat	Mon	Thu

Noon		JUL	AUG	SEP	OCT	NOV	DEC
☉	1	8♋51	8♌26	8♍15	7♎31	8♏17	8♐31
	9	16 28	16 6	16 0	15 24	16 18	16 39
	17	24 6	23 47	23 48	23 20	24 22	24 47
	25	1♌44	1♍29	1♎38	1♏18	2♐26	2♑56
☿	1	22♊13	1♌58	29♍ 0	0♏ 1	19♎53	5♐35
	7	24 27	14 27	7 36	29R 4	27 52	15 1
	13	29 38	26 26	15 22	23 38	7♏ 4	24 27
	19	7♋34	7♍37	22 4	16 52	16 35	3♑57
	25	17 55	17 57	27 14	14D47	26 7	13 31
	31	29 54	27 29	...	18 47	...	23 4
♀	1	14♌ 1	19♍59	24♎ 0	22♏45	9♐39	28♏33
	9	23 25	29 0	2♏14	28 59	9R22	25R18
	17	2♍45	7♎53	10 7	4♈10	6 34	24D34
	25	11 59	16 34	17 33	7 56	2 2	26 20
♂	1	12♐46	12♐43	23♐46	10♑35	1♒12	22♒40
	13	11R12	15 57	29 59	18 17	9 40	1♓26
	25	11D35	20 34	6♑54	26 21	18 18	10 15
♃	1	9♎54	13♎18	18♎29	24♎32	1♏15	7♏35
	13	10 57	15 8	20 49	27 7	3 50	9 57
	25	12 21	17 11	23 16	29 43	6 22	12 8
♄	1	1♎28	3♎34	6♎42	10♎17	14♎ 2	17♎11
	13	2 8	4 41	8 6	11 46	15 23	18 12
	25	2 59	5 56	9 33	13 13	16 37	19 2
♅	1	13♓32	12♓53	11♓45	10♓36	9♓49	9♓44
	13	13R21	12R29	11R16	10R14	9R41	9 55
	25	13 5	12 2	10 49	9 56	9D41	10 13
♆	1	14♌21	15♌26	16♌33	17♌29	18♌ 5	18♌ 9
	13	14 45	15 52	16 58	17 46	18 10	18R 3
	25	15 10	16 19	17 20	17 59	18 11	17 52
Pl.	1	9♋31	10♋16	10♋52	11♋ 9	11♋ 5	10♋42
☊	1	4♎ 4	2♎25	0♎47	29♍11	27♍33	25♍58
1st		Sat	Tue	Fri	Sun	Wed	Fri

	d.	JAN	FEB	MAR	APR
☽	1	16♒47	0♈42	9♈33	25♉31
	3	10♓27	24 35	3♉37	21♊17
	5	4♈ 7	19♉24	28 30	18♋15
	7	28 27	15♊47	24♊43	16♌32
	9	24♉10	14♋ 7	22♋39	15♍57
	11	21♊44	14♌ 6	22♌12	15♎47
	13	21♋ 2	14♍37	22♍35	15♏ 2
	15	21♌ 7	14♎20	22♎34	12♐54
	17	20♍46	12♏27	21♏ 8	9♑ 4
	19	19♎ 9	8♐55	17♐54	3♒49
	21	16♏ 7	4♑ 5	13♑ 8	27 40
	23	11♐58	28 24	7♒20	21♓17
	25	6♑59	22♒14	1♓ 1	15♈11
	27	1♒22	15♓52	24 39	9♉45
	29	25 17	...	18♈33	5♊12
	31	18♓54	...	13♉ 0	...

	d.	MAY	JUN	JUL	AUG
☽	1	1♋34	23♌39	2♎54	25♏11
	3	28 48	21 54	0♏52	21♐42
	5	26♌51	20♎11	28 16	17♑20
	7	25♍33	18♏16	24♐58	12♒ 9
	9	24♎34	15♐46	20♑50	6♓17
	11	23♏14	12♑16	15♒44	29 57
	13	20♐52	7♒33	9♓49	23♈34
	15	17♑ 3	1♓47	3♈27	17♉42
	17	11♒51	25 28	27 15	12♊59
	19	5♓45	19♈17	21♉55	10♋ 0
	21	29 24	13♉55	18♊ 4	8♌42
	23	23♈28	9♊53	15♋53	8♍38
	25	18♉27	7♋17	15♌ 1	8♎39
	27	14♊35	5♌41	14♍31	7♏44
	29	11♋44	4♍25	13♎32	5♐24
	31	9♌35	...	11♏34	1♑40

	d.	SEP	OCT	NOV	DEC
☽	1	14♑22	18♒13	2♈25	4♉32
	3	9♒ 4	12♓ 0	26 10	29 11
	5	3♓ 8	5♈36	20♉26	24♊47
	7	26 49	29 20	15♊24	21♋16
	9	20♈24	23♉29	11♋10	18♌26
	11	14♉17	18♊21	7♌49	16♍ 9
	13	8♊56	14♋15	5♍30	14♎23
	15	4♋52	11♌32	4♎14	13♏ 0
	17	2♌29	10♍19	3♏43	11♐35
	19	1♍47	10♎13	3♐ 6	9♑23
	21	2♎ 4	10♏20	1♑25	5♒52
	23	2♏11	9♐30	28 4	0♓54
	25	1♐ 4	6♑56	23♒ 6	24 53
	27	28 13	2♒36	17♓ 3	18♈30
	29	23♑47	26 57	10♈38	12♉27
	31	...	20♓38	...	7♊22

STATIONS	☿	♀	♂	♃
	5Feb 1♓14	5Nov 9♐49	8May 25♐16	3Feb 18♎54
	27Feb 16♒ 2	16Dec 24♏31	17Jul 11♐ 6	6Jun 8♎58
		♄	♅	♆
	6Jun 0♋53	17Jan 7♎36	19Jun 13♓36	24Apr 13♌10
	30Jun 22♊ 8	3Jun 0♎49	20Nov 9♓41	21Nov 18♌11
	3Oct 0♏12	SIDER. TIME		1 Jan
	24Oct 14♎40	6h 39m 27s		Midn.
		18h 41m 25s		Noon.
		Common Year		1922

1923 (BST 22 Apr. – 16 Sep.)

Noon		JAN	FEB	MAR	APR	MAY	JUN
☉	1	10♑ 4	11♒37	9♓53	10♈44	10♉ 5	9♊58
	9	18 13	19 44	17 54	18 37	17 50	17 37
	17	26 22	27 49	25 53	26 27	25 33	25 16
	25	4♒31	5♓52	3♈49	4♉16	3♊15	2♋54
☿	1	24♑38	4♒11	13♒58	3♈21	0♊22	4♊52
	7	3♒42	29♑39	21 51	15 19	6 45	2R36
	13	11 14	29D49	0♓36	27 50	10 14	2D40
	19	14 57	3♒28	10 7	10♉13	10R45	5 25
	25	12R24	9 17	20 23	21 22	8 41	10 44
	31	5 20	...	1♈26	...	5 24	...
♀	1	29♏33	24♐51	24♑41	0♓20	5♈54	13♉ 7
	9	4 41	3♑ 0	3♒43	9 45	15 28	22 46
	17	10 59	11 29	12 53	19 13	25 4	2♊27
	25	18 7	20 14	22 9	28 44	4♉41	12 9
♂	1	15♓24	8♈ 5	28♈13	19♉58	10♊26	1♋ 4
	13	24 13	16 45	6♉42	28 13	18 29	8 56
	25	2♈59	25 22	15 6	6♊23	26 27	16 45
♃	1	13♏18	17♏22	18♏55	17♏51	14♏36	10♏55
	13	15 7	18 18	18R51	16R44	13R 4	9R54
	25	16 38	18 50	18 20	15 21	11 39	9 16
♄	1	19♎25	20♎ 6	19♎18	17♎15	15♎ 1	13♎33
	13	19 53	19R55	18R37	16R19	14R18	13R22
	25	20 6	19 30	17 46	15 26	13 46	13D25
♅	1	10♓27	11♓48	13♓21	15♓ 5	16♓29	17♓22
	13	10 54	12 26	14 2	15 41	16 54	17 31
	25	11 27	13 7	14 42	16 14	17 14	17R33
♆	1	17♌43	16♌56	16♌11	15♌33	15♌23	15♌44
	13	17R27	16R36	15R54	15R26	15 28	15 59
	25	17 8	16 17	15 40	15 23	15 36	16 18
Pl.	1	10♋ 7	9♋33	9♋11	9♋ 6	9♋22	9♋55
☊	1	24♍19	22♍41	21♍12	19♍33	17♍58	16♍19
1st		Mon	Thu	Thu	Sun	Tue	Fri

Noon		JUL	AUG	SEP	OCT	NOV	DEC
☉	1	8♋37	8♌12	8♍ 1	7♎16	8♏ 2	8♐16
	9	16 15	15 52	15 46	15 10	16 4	16 24
	17	23 53	23 33	23 34	23 5	24 7	24 32
	25	1♌31	1♍15	1♎23	1♏ 3	2♐12	2♑41
☿	1	18♊21	18♌59	5♎ 3	2♎30	28♎59	16♐53
	7	28 8	29 54	10 19	28♍50	8♏53	26 9
	13	9♋43	9♍52	13 24	1♎10	18 37	5♑20
	19	22 23	18 56	13R13	8D12	28 9	14 13
	25	5♌ 4	27 1	9 0	17 26	7♐33	22 11
	31	17 4	4♎ 1	...	27 20	...	27 48
♀	1	19♊26	27♋19	5♍35	12♎55	21♏37	29♐ 4
	9	29 10	7♌ 9	15 31	22 54	1♐36	9♑ 3
	17	8♋56	17 2	25 28	2♏53	11 36	19 1
	25	18 44	26 55	5♎26	12 52	21 35	28 58
♂	1	20♋38	10♌33	0♍18	19♍23	9♎ 9	28♎21
	13	28 22	18 12	7 56	27 2	16 49	6♏ 3
	25	6♌ 4	25 51	15 34	4♎41	24 30	13 45
♃	1	9♏ 7	10♏ 0	13♏25	18♏30	24♏53	1♐31
	13	9D 7	11 3	15 17	20 52	27 31	4 10
	25	9 33	12 28	17 23	23 22	0♐11	6 45
♄	1	13♎32	15♎ 2	17♎46	21♎ 7	24♎53	28♎16
	13	13 56	15 57	19 2	22 35	26 17	29 25
	25	14 34	17 3	20 25	24 2	27 38	0♏26
♅	1	17♓32	16♓58	15♓53	14♓43	13♓51	13♓40
	13	17R23	16R35	15R24	14R19	13R41	13 48
	25	17 9	16 9	14 56	13 59	13D38	14 3
♆	1	16♌29	17♌32	18♌41	19♌38	20♌15	20♌22
	13	16 52	17 59	19 5	19 55	20 22	20R17
	25	17 17	18 26	19 28	20 9	20R23	20 7
Pl.	1	10♋39	11♋23	12♋ 0	12♋18	12♋16	11♋11
☊	1	14♍44	13♍ 6	11♍27	9♍52	8♍13	6♍38
1st		Sun	Wed	Sat	Mon	Thu	Sat

☽ d.	JAN	FEB	MAR	APR
1	20♊17	9♌28	17♌26	10♎ 3
3	17♋ 3	8♍22	16♍53	10♏27
5	14♌46	7♎28	16♎51	9♐56
7	12♍57	6♏ 8	16♏16	7♑44
9	11♎11	4♐ 1	14♐27	3♒49
11	9♏19	1♑ 2	11♑14	28 34
13	7♐11	27 10	6♒48	22♓32
15	4♑33	22♒25	1♓27	16♈10
17	1♒ 2	16♓52	25 29	9♉49
19	26 25	10♈42	19♈11	3♊44
21	20♓46	4♉18	12♉49	28 12
23	14♈28	28 13	6♊46	23♋34
25	8♉ 9	23♊ 4	1♋32	20♌13
27	2♊31	19 23	27 37	18♍29
29	28 10	...	25♌26	18♎15
31	25♋21	...	24♍54	...

☽ d.	MAY	JUN	JUL	AUG
1	18♏41	11♑ 1	16♒18	1♈56
3	18♐29	8♒17	11♓47	25 52
5	16♑37	3♓46	6♈ 4	19♉37
7	12♒50	28 0	29 48	13♊48
9	7♓32	21♈39	23♉38	8♋59
11	1♈22	15♉24	18♊ 9	5♌26
13	24 57	9♊40	13♋38	3♍ 5
15	18♉44	4♋40	10♌ 5	1♎31
17	12♊58	0♌26	7♍21	0♏13
19	7♋49	26 59	5♎12	28 42
21	3♌26	24♍20	3♏28	26♐39
23	0♍ 3	22♎36	1♐57	23♑52
25	27 57	21♏36	0♑16	20♒10
27	27♎10	20♐47	27 55	15♓30
29	27♏ 7	19♑15	24♒26	9♈59
31	26♐43	...	19♓42	3♉51

☽ d.	SEP	OCT	NOV	DEC
1	15♉43	17♊52	3♌42	9♍13
3	9♊35	12♋21	29 56	6♎49
5	4♋11	8♌ 4	27♍57	6♏ 4
7	0♌ 3	5♍28	27♎42	6♐23
9	27 29	4♎35	28♏20	6♑29
11	26 18	4♏48	28♐24	5♒ 8
13	25♎49	4♐52	26♑47	1♓50
15	25♏ 8	3♑41	23♒14	26 53
17	23♐32	0♒50	18♓11	20♈56
19	20♑43	26 30	12♈15	14♉37
21	16♒47	21♓ 9	5♉59	8♊27
23	11♓55	15♈13	29 44	2♋43
25	6♈22	9♉ 0	23♊43	27 33
27	0♉19	2♊44	18♋ 6	23♌ 3
29	24 1	26 39	13♌ 8	19♍22
31	...	21♋ 7	...	16♎48

STATIONS	☿	♀	♂	♃
	20Jan 15♒ 0 / 10Feb 29♑12 / 10May 10♊51 / 10Jun 2♊18 / 16Sep 13♎47 / 8Oct 28♍48	None	None	6Mar 18♏56 / 7Jul 9♏ 4
		♄	♅	♆
		30Jan 20♎ 7 / 17Jun 13♎21	23Jun 17♓33 / 24Nov 13♓38	27Apr 15♌23 / 24Nov 20♌23
		SIDER. TIME 6h 38m 29s / 18h 40m 27s / Common Year		1 Jan / Midn. / Noon / 1923

1924 (BST 13 Apr. – 21 Sep.)

Noon		JAN	FEB	MAR	APR	MAY	JUN
☉	1	9♑49	11♒22	10♓39	11♈29	10♉49	10♊41
	9	17 58	19 29	18 40	19 22	18 34	18 21
	17	26 7	27 34	26 38	27 12	26 17	25 59
	25	4♒16	5♓38	4♈34	5♉ 0	3♊59	3♋37
☿	1	28♑20	16♑20	23♒52	21♈58	20♉35	16♉53
	7	27R51	22 3	3♓50	3♉16	17R32	22 47
	13	21 18	29 11	14 28	12 26	14 3	0♊38
	19	14 37	7♒16	25 47	18 33	12 9	10 17
	25	12D53	16 3	7♈45	21 15	12D50	21 36
	31	15 35	...	19 58	...	16 6	...
♀	1	7♒40	15♓51	20♈40	25♉55	26♊ 2	16♋15
	9	17 35	25 34	0♉ 1	4♊29	2♋49	17 35
	17	27 27	5♈13	9 12	12 43	8 42	16R28
	25	7♓17	14 45	18 13	20 31	13 25	12 58
♂	1	18♏15	8♐ 9	26♐39	16♑ 3	3♒58	20♒28
	13	25 58	15 50	4♑14	23 22	10 42	25 49
	25	3♐40	23 29	11 44	0♒30	17 1	0♓16
♃	1	8♐13	14♐ 2	18♐ 0	19♐52	18♐55	15♐36
	13	10 37	15 53	19 3	19R49	17R50	14R 5
	25	12 50	17 27	19 42	19 19	16 29	12 39
♄	1	0♏56	2♏15	2♏ 1	0♏21	28♎ 6	26♎13
	13	1 38	2R20	1R30	29♎28	27R16	25R49
	25	2 6	2 9	0 49	28R33	26 33	25 38
♅	1	14♓16	15♓33	17♓ 7	18♓52	20♓18	21♓16
	13	14 41	16 10	17 48	19 29	20 45	21 27
	25	15 13	16 50	18 29	20 3	21 6	21 31
♆	1	19♌59	19♌13	18♌25	17♌47	17♌36	17♌54
	13	19R43	18R53	18R 8	17R40	17 39	18 9
	25	19 24	18 33	17 54	17 36	17 47	18 28
Pl.	1	11♋19	10♋45	10♋23	10♋16	10♋32	11♋ 6
☊	1	4♍59	3♍21	1♍49	0♍10	28♌35	26♌56
	1st	Tue	Fri	Sat	Tue	Thu	Sun

Noon		JUL	AUG	SEP	OCT	NOV	DEC
☉	1	9♋20	8♌55	8♍45	8♎ 1	8♏48	9♐ 2
	9	16 58	16 35	16 30	15 55	16 49	17 10
	17	24 36	24 16	24 18	23 50	24 53	25 18
	25	2♌14	1♍59	2♎ 7	1♏48	2♐58	3♑27
☿	1	4♋11	2♍40	26♍20	21♍ 8	12♏48	28♐ 0
	7	17 11	10 50	22R28	0♎33	22 16	5♑41
	13	29 43	17 45	16 34	10 54	1♐32	11 24
	19	11♌17	23 6	12 51	21 17	10 37	12R51
	25	21 46	26 20	14D30	1♏24	19 29	7 53
	31	1♍12	26R38	...	11 12	...	0 10
♀	1	9♋22	2♋39	23♋ 9	23♌18	28♍41	4♏55
	9	4R41	6 8	0♌35	2♍ 8	8♎13	14 45
	17	1 41	11 6	8 30	11 12	17 51	24 39
	25	1D10	17 10	16 50	20 28	27 35	4♐34
♂	1	2♓ 3	4♓53	28♒ 0	25♒53	4♓43	19♓36
	13	4 32	2R50	25R51	28 11	10 10	26 28
	25	5R18	29♒47	25D24	1♓58	16 19	3♈39
♃	1	12♐ 1	10♐ 6	11♐ 2	14♐26	19♐50	26♐12
	13	10R58	10D 7	12 8	16 20	22 17	28 55
	25	10 18	10 34	13 35	18 29	24 52	1♑40
♄	1	25♎37	26♎32	28♎48	1♏55	5♏36	9♏ 6
	13	25 48	27 16	29 58	3 19	7 2	10 22
	25	26 12	28 11	1♏15	4 45	8 26	11 31
♅	1	21♓30	21♓ 1	19♓58	18♓47	17♓52	17♓36
	13	21R24	20R39	19R29	18R22	17R40	17 43
	25	21 11	20 14	19 1	18 1	17 36	17 56
♆	1	18♌38	19♌41	20♌50	21♌48	22♌26	22♌35
	13	19 1	20 8	21 15	22 6	22 33	22R30
	25	19 26	20 35	21 37	22 20	22R36	22 20
Pl.	1	11♋47	12♋33	13♋ 9	13♋27	13♋26	13♋ 5
☊	1	25♌21	23♌43	22♌ 4	20♌29	18♌50	17♌15
	1st	Tue	Fri	Mon	Wed	Sat	Mon

d.		JAN	FEB	MAR	APR
☽	1	0♏58	24♐35	19♑ 1	9♓ 1
	3	0♐ 7	23♑ 8	16♒16	4♈17
	5	29 47	20♒53	12♓41	28 53
	7	28♑52	17♓26	8♈ 9	22♉57
	9	26♒32	12♈41	2♉44	16♊42
	11	22♓31	6♉55	26 40	10♋32
	13	17♈ 7	0♊42	20♊27	5♌ 4
	15	10♉59	24 39	14♋38	0♍55
	17	4♊44	19♋19	9♌52	28 32
	19	28 56	15♌ 6	6♍34	27♎53
	21	23♋52	12♍ 4	4♎47	28♏ 4
	23	19♌40	10♎ 0	4♏ 1	27♐51
	25	16♍16	8♏27	3♐21	26♑16
	27	13♎38	6♐57	1♑59	23♒ 9
	29	11♏40	5♑ 7	29 34	18♓45
	31	10♐14	...	26♒ 5	...

d.		MAY	JUN	JUL	AUG
☽	1	13♈30	28♉37	1♋16	16♌46
	3	7♉43	22♊21	25 20	12♍18
	5	1♊35	16♋12	19♌56	8♎44
	7	25 18	10♌26	15♍18	6♏ 8
	9	19♋ 9	5♍29	11♎48	4♐28
	11	13♌37	1♎53	9♏42	3♑26
	13	9♍18	0♏ 2	8♐56	2♒29
	15	6♎47	29 49	8♑51	0♓53
	17	6♏ 9	0♑20	8♒24	28♉ 3
	19	6♐40	0♒11	6♓36	23♈49
	21	6♑58	28 23	3♈ 7	18♉23
	23	5♒49	24♓45	28 10	12♊16
	25	2♓50	19♈40	22♉16	6♋ 4
	27	28 19	13♉44	16♊ 1	0♌21
	29	22♈47	7♊29	9♋54	25 32
	31	16♉44	...	4♌18	21♍47

d.		SEP	OCT	NOV	DEC
☽	1	5♎18	13♏12	6♑53	15♒13
	3	2♏58	12♐ 5	5♒18	12♓31
	5	1♐11	10♑36	2♓27	8♈24
	7	29 36	8♒26	28 35	3♉18
	9	27♑55	5♓31	23♈55	27 34
	11	25♒50	1♈53	18♉36	21♊26
	13	22♓59	27 28	12♊43	15♋ 6
	15	19♈ 6	22♉14	6♋25	8♌49
	17	14♉ 8	16♊16	0♌ 5	3♍ 1
	19	8♊17	9♋57	24 14	28 14
	21	2♋ 1	3♌51	19♍34	25♎ 5
	23	26 0	28 38	16♎43	23♏5
	25	20♌50	24♍58	15♏48	24♐ 4
	27	17♍ 4	23♎ 4	16♐ 6	24♑34
	29	14♎36	22♏31	16♑17	24♒ 1
	31	...	22♐15	...	21♓44

STATIONS	☿	♀	♂	♃
	4Jan 28♑56	10Jun 17♋35	24Jul 5♓19	6Apr 19♐54
	24Jan 12♐49	23Jul 1♋ 4	22Sep 25♒20	7Aug 10♐ 3
	27Apr 21♉22	♄	♅	♆
	21May 12♉ 5	11Feb 2♏20	26Jun 21♓31	28Apr 17♌35
	29Aug 26♍55	29Jun 25♎37	27Nov 17♓36	25Nov 22♌36
	21Sep 13♍45	SIDER. TIME 6h 37m 32s		1 Jan Midn.
	18Dec 13♑ 1	18h 39m 30s		Noon
		LEAP YEAR		1924

1925 (BST 19 Apr. – 4 Oct.)

Noon		JAN	FEB	MAR	APR	MAY	JUN
☉	1	10♑35	12♒ 9	10♓24	11♈15	10♉35	10♊27
	9	18 44	20 15	18 25	19 7	18 20	18 7
	17	26 53	28 20	26 23	26 57	26 3	25 45
	25	5♒ 2	6♓23	4♈20	4♉45	3♊45	3♋23
☿	1	29♐11	21♑30	6♓53	29♈54	22♈ 2	20♉51
	7	26D47	0♒15	18 13	2♉37	23D 8	1♊39
	13	29 24	9 31	29 58	1R23	26 48	13 47
	19	4♑56	19 18	11♈33	27♈35	2♉35	26 48
	25	12 4	29 39	21 44	23 45	10 7	9♋49
	31	20 6	...	29 2	...	19 11	...
♀	1	13♐16	21♑56	26♒53	5♈26	12♉33	20♊42
	9	23 14	1♒55	6♓51	15 21	22 25	0♋31
	17	3♑13	11 54	16 48	25 16	2♊16	10 19
	25	13 12	21 53	26 45	5♉ 9	12 6	20 6
♂	1	7♈56	27♈29	15♉30	5♊27	24♊38	14♋18
	13	15 25	5♉11	23 14	13 9	2♋16	21 53
	25	23 1	12 55	0♊57	20 49	9 52	29 27
♃	1	3♑16	10♑10	15♑39	20♑13	22♑23	21♑46
	13	6 0	12 38	17 39	21 23	22R30	20R47
	25	8 40	14 56	19 22	22 10	22 10	19 29
♄	1	12♏ 7	13♏57	14♏16	13♏ 8	11♏ 2	8♏52
	13	12 59	14 15	14R 0	12R22	10R 8	8R16
	25	13 39	14R18	13 30	11 29	9 18	7 50
♅	1	18♓ 7	19♓21	20♓50	22♓36	24♓ 5	25♓ 8
	13	18 32	19 57	21 31	23 14	24 34	25 21
	25	19 1	20 37	22 12	23 49	24 57	25 28
♆	1	22♌13	21♌27	20♌41	20♌ 1	19♌48	20♌ 4
	13	21R57	21R 7	20R23	19R53	19R50	20 18
	25	21 39	20 47	20 9	19 48	19 57	20 36
Pl.	1	12♋31	11♋56	11♋33	11♋27	11♋42	12♋15
☊	1	15♌37	13♌58	12♌29	10♌51	9♌15	7♌37
	1st	Thu	Sun	Sun	Wed	Fri	Mon

Noon		JUL	AUG	SEP	OCT	NOV	DEC
☉	1	9♋ 6	8♌42	8♍31	7♎47	8♏33	8♐47
	9	16 44	16 21	16 16	15 40	16 34	16 55
	17	24 22	24 2	24 4	23 36	24 38	25 3
	25	2♌ 0	1 45	1♎53	1♏33	2♐43	3♑12
☿	1	22♋ 3	5 27	26♌44	3♎11	23♏45	27♐12
	7	3♌ 8	8 45	27D10	13 48	2♐28	24R22
	13	13 0	9R17	2♍36	24 0	10 45	16 38
	19	21 38	6 36	11 37	3♏47	18 19	11 18
	25	28 57	1 32	22 15	13 11	24 21	11D59
	31	4♍40	27♌ 8	...	22 16	...	16 48
♀	1	27♋26	5♍12	12♎36	18♏13	23♐56	25♑59
	9	7♌12	14 54	22 10	27 34	2♑50	3♒38
	17	16 58	24 34	1♏41	6♐51	11 31	10 40
	25	26 42	4♎12	11 9	16 1	19 55	16 49
♂	1	3♌14	22♌48	12♍29	1♎46	22♎ 1	12♏ 0
	13	10 48	0♍24	20 10	9 33	29 57	20 6
	25	18 23	8 2	27 53	17 24	7♏58	28 17
♃	1	18♑45	14♑56	12♑47	13♑28	16♑55	22♑13
	13	17R13	13R48	12D43	14 30	18 51	24 43
	25	15 44	13 2	13 6	15 56	21 2	27 22
♄	1	7♏43	7♏58	9♏43	12♏29	16♏ 1	19♏34
	13	7D38	8 29	10 43	13 48	17 27	20 55
	25	7 47	9 12	11 52	15 11	18 52	22 11
♅	1	25♓28	25♓ 5	24♓ 6	22♓55	21♓55	21♓33
	13	25R25	24R45	23R37	22R28	21R41	21D37
	25	25 14	24 21	23 9	22 6	21 34	21 48
♆	1	20♌46	21♌48	22♌56	23♌55	24♌36	24♌47
	13	21 8	22 15	23 22	24 14	24 44	24R43
	25	21 33	22 41	23 45	24 29	24 48	24 35
Pl.	1	12♋57	13♋42	14♋19	14♋39	14♋38	14♋18
☊	1	6♌ 1	4♌23	2♌44	1♌ 9	29♋31	27♋55
	1st	Wed	Sat	Tue	Thu	Sun	Tue

d.		JAN	FEB	MAR	APR
☽	1	4♈56	21♉10	29♉16	12♋58
	3	0♉15	15♊ 8	23♊17	6♌42
	5	24 34	8♋46	16♋56	1♍ 5
	7	18♊23	2♌35	10♌51	26 40
	9	12♋ 4	26 54	5♍32	23♎37
	11	5♌52	21♍57	1♎14	21♏39
	13	0♍ 3	17♎51	27 57	20♐10
	15	24 56	14♏44	25♏26	18♑37
	17	20♎55	12♐39	23♐28	16♒41
	19	18♏22	11♑29	21♑48	14♓18
	21	17♐20	10♒47	20♒14	11♈19
	23	17♑20	9♓50	18♓25	7♉34
	25	17♒20	7♈48	15♈51	2♊49
	27	16♓12	4♉16	12♉ 6	27 8
	29	13♈22	...	7♊ 6	20♋51
	31	8♉54	...	1♋ 8	...

d.		MAY	JUN	JUL	AUG
☽	1	14♌33	29♍44	4♏48	26♐27
	3	8♍57	26♎20	3♐ 5	26♑25
	5	4♎43	24♏46	2♑54	26♒39
	7	2♏ 8	24♐31	3♒16	25♓59
	9	0♐56	24♑30	2♓58	23♈41
	11	0♑18	23♒41	1♈13	19♉39
	13	29 19	21♓33	27 48	14♊15
	15	27♒28	18♈ 5	23♉ 2	8♋ 4
	17	24♓41	13♉32	17♊19	1♌38
	19	21♈ 2	8♊ 9	11♋ 4	25 23
	21	16♉34	2♋11	4♌39	19♍39
	23	11♊20	25 49	28 22	14♎37
	25	5♋24	19♌25	22♍33	10♏31
	27	29 2	13♍23	17♎36	7♐32
	29	22♌42	8♎20	13♏56	5♑48
	31	17♍ 4	...	11♐53	5♒ 8

d.		SEP	OCT	NOV	DEC
☽	1	20♒ 2	28♓ 9	18♉10	22♊ 8
	3	19♓41	26♈22	13♊57	16♋30
	5	18♈18	23♉13	8♋32	10♌14
	7	15♉15	18♊33	2♌20	3♍51
	9	10♊33	12♋41	25 58	28 0
	11	4♋40	6♌19	20♍11	23♎23
	13	28 17	0♍ 8	15♎35	20♏23
	15	22♌ 0	24 45	12♏26	19♐ 0
	17	16♍20	20♎30	10♐31	18♑31
	19	11♎29	17♏19	9♑12	18♒ 1
	21	7♏31	14♐54	7♒51	16♓41
	23	4♐22	12♑53	6♓ 3	14♈14
	25	1♑58	11♒ 2	3♈42	10♉39
	27	0♒18	9♓16	0♉41	6♊ 7
	29	29 12	7♈20	26 53	0♋47
	31	...	4♉48	...	24 50

STATIONS	☿	♀	♂	♃
	7Jan 26♐47	None	None	11May 22♑31
	8Apr 2♉40			9Sep 12♑41
	3May 22♈ 5	♄	♅	♆
	12Aug 9♍25	22Feb 14♏19	1Jul 25♓28	1May 19♌48
	4Sep 26♌18	12Jul 7♏18	2Dec 21♓33	27Nov 24♌48
	2Dec 27♐10	SIDER. TIME 6h 40m 31s		1 Jan Midn.
	22Dec 10♐58	18h 42m 29s		Noon
		Common Year		1925

1926 (BST 18 Apr. – 19 Sep.)

Noon		JAN	FEB	MAR	APR	MAY	JUN
☉	1	10♑20	11♒53	10♓ 9	11♈ 0	10♉21	10♊13
	9	18 29	20 0	18 10	18 53	18 6	17 53
	17	26 38	28 5	26 9	26 43	25 49	25 32
	25	4♒47	6♓ 8	4♈ 5	4♉31	3♊31	3♋10
☿	1	17♐50	1♒45	21♓46	8♈44	13♈42	6♊18
	7	24 58	11 41	2♈17	4R22	21 13	19 28
	13	3♑ 2	22 5	10 25	2 34	0♉ 5	2♋15
	19	11 40	2♓58	14 29	3D52	10 13	13 57
	25	20 42	14 15	13R46	7 47	21 37	24 18
	31	0♒ 8	...	9 34	...	4♊ 8	...
♀	1	21♒12	21♒46	10♒22	26♒ 4	24♓35	28♈30
	9	24 42	16R57	11 58	2♓58	3♈ 4	7♉36
	17	26 4	12 40	15 35	10 28	11 46	16 48
	25	24R52	10 29	20 42	18 24	20 38	26 4
♂	1	3♐ 5	24♐37	14♑27	6♒43	28♒25	20♓35
	13	11 22	3♑ 5	23 2	15 24	7♓ 3	28 57
	25	19 43	11 36	1♒40	24 5	15 37	7♈ 7
♃	1	28♑58	6♒14	12♒43	19♒ 9	24♒ 0	26♒49
	13	1♒45	9 3	15 20	21 18	25 24	27 9
	25	4 35	11 49	17 48	23 10	26 25	27R 2
♄	1	22♏51	25♏11	26♏ 4	25♏30	23♏44	21♏27
	13	23 54	25 43	26R 2	24R54	22R50	20R41
	25	24 46	26 1	25 46	24 9	21 57	20 4
♅	1	21♓58	23♓ 7	24♓34	26♓19	27♓52	29♓ 0
	13	22 20	23 42	25 14	26 58	28 22	29 15
	25	22 48	24 20	25 56	27 35	28 47	29 24
♆	1	24♌27	23♌44	22♌57	22♌16	22♌ 0	22♌13
	13	24R13	23R23	22R39	22R 6	22D 1	22 27
	25	23 55	23 3	22 23	22 1	22 8	22 44
Pl.	1	13♋43	13♋ 9	12♋45	12♋38	12♋51	13♋24
☊	1	26♋17	24♋38	23♋ 9	21♋31	19♋56	18♋17
	1st	Fri	Mon	Mon	Thu	Sat	Tue

Noon		JUL	AUG	SEP	OCT	NOV	DEC
☉	1	8♋53	8♌28	8♍17	7♎33	8♏19	8♐33
	9	16 30	16 8	16 3	15 26	16 20	16 40
	17	24 8	23 49	23 50	23 22	24 23	24 48
	25	1♌46	1♍31	1♎39	1♏19	2♐28	2♑57
☿	1	3♌15	18♌46	22♌27	16♎36	1♐14	26♏39
	7	10 43	14R22	3♍ 3	26 15	7 23	25D32
	13	16 29	10 23	14 28	5♏27	11 4	29 39
	19	20 9	9D35	25 42	14 12	10R10	6♐29
	25	21R13	13 11	6 26	22 28	3 37	14 33
	31	19 20	20 52	...	0♐ 3	...	23 11
♀	1	3♊ 4	9♋51	17♌29	24♍33	3♏19	11♐ 0
	9	12 29	19 29	27 19	4♎32	13 21	21 4
	17	21 57	29 10	7♍11	14 31	23 24	1♑ 7
	25	1♋28	8♌55	17 6	24 32	3♐28	11 11
♂	1	11♈ 6	0♉ 4	14♉21	19♉25	12♉14	4♉44
	13	18 48	6 21	17 43	17R57	8R13	4D48
	25	26 5	11 44	19 21	14 39	5 26	6 36
♃	1	26♒48	24♒ 3	20♒ 6	17♒35	17♒52	20♒59
	13	26R 1	22R31	18R49	17R19	18 49	22 52
	25	24 51	20 58	17 53	17D32	20 10	25 2
♄	1	19♏50	19♏28	20♏38	22♏59	26♏18	29♏50
	13	19R31	19 44	21 27	24 11	27 42	1♐14
	25	19D25	20 14	22 26	25 30	29 8	2 35
♅	1	29♓26	29♓ 9	28♓13	27♓ 3	25♓59	25♓32
	13	29R25	28R51	27R46	26R35	25R43	25D33
	25	29 17	28 28	27 17	26 11	25 34	25 42
♆	1	22♌54	23♌55	25♌ 3	26♌ 3	26♌46	27♌ 0
	13	23 16	24 21	25 28	26 23	26 55	26R56
	25	23 40	24 48	25 52	26 39	26 59	26 49
Pl.	1	14♋ 7	14♋52	15♋30	15♋51	15♋52	15♋31
☊	1	16♋42	15♋ 3	13♋25	11♋49	10♋11	8♋36
	1st	Thu	Sun	Wed	Fri	Mon	Wed

d.		JAN	FEB	MAR	APR
☽	1	6♌41	20♍54	29♍58	16♏55
	3	0♍17	15♎ 8	24♎33	13♐ 8
	5	24 5	10♏16	19♏53	10♑13
	7	18♎40	6♐45	16♐16	8♒17
	9	14♏37	4♑55	13♑59	7♓17
	11	12♐20	4♒39	13♒ 6	6♈43
	13	11♑41	5♓ 7	13♓10	5♉38
	15	11♒56	5♈ 1	13♈ 4	3♊ 9
	17	11♓52	3♉21	11♉37	29 0
	19	10♈32	29 48	8♊18	23♋28
	21	7♉35	24♊43	3♋18	17♌12
	23	3♊11	18♋41	27 15	10♍55
	25	27 44	12♌17	20♌50	5♎11
	27	21♋40	5♍57	14♍37	0♏22
	29	15♌19	...	8♎59	26 30
	31	8♍59	...	4♏ 5	...

d.		MAY	JUN	JUL	AUG
☽	1	23♐26	15♒50	25♓ 7	17♉ 8
	3	20♑59	14♓16	23♈10	13♊11
	5	19♒ 3	12♈24	20♉10	8♋ 9
	7	17♓32	10♉ 0	16♊10	2♌24
	9	16♈ 6	6♊46	11♋15	26 13
	11	14 13	2♋30	5♌36	19♍54
	13	11♊14	27 14	29 27	13♎42
	15	6♋53	21♌12	23♍ 7	8♏ 3
	17	1♌20	14♍54	17♎ 7	3♐26
	19	25 7	8♎56	12♏ 0	0♑21
	21	18♍53	3♏54	8♐18	29 4
	23	13♎18	0♐14	6♑17	29♒13
	25	8♏48	28 3	5♒43	29♓41
	27	5♐32	26♑57	5♓46	29♈10
	29	3♑16	26♒13	5♈19	26♉52
	31	1♒36	...	3♉35	22♊48

d.		SEP	OCT	NOV	DEC
☽	1	5♋15	8♌23	22♍21	24♎32
	3	29 29	2♍ 4	16♎24	19♏32
	5	23♌16	25 47	11♏ 5	15♐34
	7	16 56	19♎51	6♐30	12♑33
	9	10♎46	14♏24	2♑40	10♒15
	11	4♏57	9♐35	29 36	8♓24
	13	29 49	5♑38	27♒25	6♈46
	15	25♐45	2♒53	26♓ 5	5♉ 3
	17	23♑14	1♓32	25♈13	2♊52
	19	22♒25	1♈18	24♉ 1	29 49
	21	22♓47	1♉13	21♊42	25♋39
	23	23♈ 5	0♊ 6	17♋53	20♌25
	25	22♉ 1	27 12	12♌41	14♍25
	27	19♊ 0	22♋35	6♍38	8♎10
	29	14♋15	16♌47	0♎23	2♏18
	31	...	10♍29	...	27 24

STATIONS	☿	♀	♂	♃
	22Mar 14♈42	18Jan 26♒ 4	29Sep 19♉28	16Jun 27♒10
	14Apr 2♈35	28Feb 10♒29	7Dec 4♉32	14Oct 17♒19
		♄	♅	♆
	25Jul 21♌13	6Mar 26♐ 5	5Jul 29♓26	3May 22♌ 0
	18Aug 9♌25	24Jul 19♏25	6Dec 25♓31	30Nov 27♌ 0
	16Nov 11♐30	SIDER. TIME		1 Jan
	5Dec 25♏11	6h 39m 33s		Midn.
		18h 41m 31s		Noon
		Common Year		1926

1927 (BST 10 Apr. – 2 Oct)

Noon	JAN	FEB	MAR	APR	MAY	JUN
☉ 1	10♑ 5	11♒38	9♓55	10♈46	10♉ 7	10♊ 0
9	18 14	19 45	17 55	18 39	17 52	17 39
17	26 23	27 50	25 54	26 29	25 35	25 18
25	4♒32	5♓53	3♈51	4♉17	3♊17	2♋56
☿ 1	24♐39	14♒28	26♓54	15♓12	21♈ 4	24♊15
7	3♑41	25 10	26R45	19 12	1♉57	5♋ 9
13	12 58	5♓58	22 8	25 10	13 54	14 27
19	22 32	16 6	16 45	2♈37	26 44	22 3
25	2♒26	23 59	14 2	11 17	9♊50	27 46
31	12 43	...	14D47	...	22 17	...
♀ 1	19♑58	28♒50	3♈39	11♉36	17♊23	22♋46
9	0♒ 1	8♓49	13 32	21 15	26 42	1♌30
17	10 4	18 47	23 21	0♉50	5♋55	9 59
25	20 5	28 42	3♉ 7	10 19	14 58	18 11
♂ 1	8♉19	20♉ 0	3♊54	21♊ 2	8♋28	27♋ 0
13	12 11	25 42	10 23	27 56	15 36	4♌16
25	16 56	1♊48	17 4	4♋56	22 47	11 35
♃ 1	26♒24	3♓12	9♓53	17♓16	23♓48	29♓18
13	28 55	6 2	12 46	19 59	26 7	0♈55
25	1♓35	8 55	15 38	22 35	28 13	2 11
♄ 1	3♐19	6♐ 3	7♐26	7♐30	6♐ 9	3♐56
13	4 30	6 47	7 39	7R 6	5R20	3R 5
25	5 32	7 19	7D37	6 30	4 27	2 19
♅ 1	25♓50	26♓53	28♓18	0♈ 3	1♈38	2♈51
13	26 10	27 27	28 58	0 43	2 10	3 9
25	26 36	28 5	29 39	1 20	2 37	3 20
♆ 1	26♌42	25♌59	25♌13	24♌30	24♌12	24♌23
13	26R28	25R39	24R54	24R20	24D12	24 35
25	26 10	25 19	24 38	24 13	24 18	24 52
Pl. 1	14♋57	14♋21	13♋57	13♋49	14♋ 2	14♋35
☊ 1	6♋57	5♋19	3♋49	2♋11	0♋36	28♊57
1st	Sat	Tue	Tue	Fri	Sun	Wed

Noon	JUL	AUG	SEP	OCT	NOV	DEC
☉ 1	8♋39	8♌14	8♍ 3	7♎19	8♏ 4	8♐18
9	16 17	15 54	15 48	15 12	16 5	16 25
17	23 54	23 35	23 36	23 7	24 8	24 33
25	1♌32	1♍17	1♎25	1♏ 5	2♐13	2♑42
☿ 1	1♌17	21♋56	6♍58	27♎23	25♏10	19♏ 4
7	2R11	25 2	18 20	5♏39	20R22	27 16
13	0 21	1♌50	29 2	13 10	12 47	6♐ 6
19	26♋36	11 38	9♎ 5	19 37	9D30	15 12
25	23 0	23 8	18 31	24 12	12 27	24 26
31	21D48	5♍ 1	...	25R26	...	3♑50
♀ 1	24♌ 5	19♍ 2	22♍12	8♍52	23♍ 6	21♎56
9	1♍34	22 51	17R47	9D53	29 57	0♏41
17	8 26	24 50	13 1	13 3	7♎30	9 41
25	14 32	24R30	9 44	17 52	15 36	18 53
♂ 1	15♌16	4♍30	24♍ 9	13♎39	4♏24	25♏ 7
13	22 40	12 3	1♎53	21 37	12 37	3♐35
25	0♍ 7	19 40	9 43	29 40	20 55	12 9
♃ 1	2♈40	3♈25	1♈10	27♓19	24♓11	23♓51
13	3 19	2R52	29♓42	25R51	23R41	24 34
25	3R31	1 54	28R 6	24 41	23D40	25 44
♄ 1	1♐59	1♐ 2	1♐36	3♐30	6♐30	9♐58
13	1R27	1D 4	2 13	4 34	7 51	11 23
25	1 7	1 20	3 1	5 45	9 14	12 46
♅ 1	3♈23	3♈12	2♈21	1♈11	0♈ 5	29♓31
13	3R24	2R56	1R54	0R43	29R47	29D30
25	3 19	2 35	1 26	0 18	29 35	29 36
♆ 1	25♌ 1	26♌ 1	27♌ 9	28♌11	28♌55	29♌11
13	25 23	26 27	27 35	28 31	29 5	29R 9
25	25 46	26 54	27 58	28 47	29 11	29 2
Pl. 1	15♋23	16♋ 4	16♋43	17♋ 4	17♋ 6	16♋47
☊ 1	27♊22	25♊44	24♊ 5	22♊30	20♊51	19♊16
1st	Fri	Mon	Thu	Sat	Tue	Thu

d.	JAN	FEB	MAR	APR
☽ 1	10♐26	29♑47	7♒40	0♈57
3	7♑34	29♒18	7♓31	1♉31
5	5♒52	29♓11	8♈ 3	0♊57
7	4♓46	28♈19	7♉52	28 30
9	3♈35	26♉ 7	6♊ 0	24♋17
11	1♉47	22♊34	2♋25	18♌50
13	29 9	18♋ 0	27 31	12♍45
15	25♊40	12♌41	21♌49	6♎29
17	21♋21	6♍53	15♍44	0♏20
19	16♌14	0♎44	9♎30	24 30
21	10♍26	24 28	3♏18	19♐11
23	4♎14	18♏28	27 24	14♑42
25	28 3	13♐17	22♐12	11♒30
27	22♏29	9♑32	18♑16	9♓51
29	18♐ 9	...	16♒ 5	9♈34
31	15♑29	...	15♓42	...

d.	MAY	JUN	JUL	AUG
☽ 1	9♉44	1♋15	6♌ 3	21♍36
3	9♊ 6	28 2	1♍19	15♎32
5	6♋51	23♌23	25 37	9♏17
7	2♌49	17♍40	19♎26	3♐27
9	27 28	11♎28	13♏22	28 42
11	21♍22	5♏23	8♐ 0	25♑30
13	15♎ 7	29 52	3♑47	23♒53
15	9♏ 7	25♐13	0♒51	23♓15
17	3♐38	21♑32	28 59	22♈38
19	28 50	18♒46	27♓38	21♉13
21	24♑52	16♓43	26♈13	18♊41
23	21♒54	15♈10	24♉21	15♋ 9
25	20♓ 1	13♉45	21♊50	10♌46
27	19♈ 4	12♊ 4	18♋34	5♍41
29	18♉27	9♋37	14♌27	29 59
31	17♊17	...	9♍25	23♎48

d.	SEP	OCT	NOV	DEC
☽ 1	5♏37	8♐ 2	24♑23	0♓47
3	29 25	2♑29	20♒50	28 37
5	23♐57	28 16	19♓ 3	27♈40
7	19♑54	25♒54	18♈50	27♉25
9	17♒42	25♓25	19♉17	26♊53
11	17♓13	25♈59	19♊ 4	25♋ 9
13	17♈28	26♉12	17♋15	21♌47
15	17♉ 9	24♊55	13♌38	16♍54
17	15♊26	21♋51	8♍35	11♎ 0
19	12♋12	17♌18	2♎38	4♏40
21	7♌46	11♍47	26 20	28 30
23	2♍32	5♎43	20♏ 5	22♐55
25	26 45	29 26	14♐ 9	18♑10
27	20♎35	23♏ 9	8♑48	14♒20
29	14♏14	17♐ 7	4♒15	11♓22
31	...	11♑42	...	9♈10

STATIONS	☿	♀	♂	♃
	4Mar 27♓31	20Aug 25♍ 0	None	25Jul 3♈31
	27Mar 13♓55	3Oct 8♏54		20Nov 23♓37
	6Jul 2♌13	♄	♅	♆
	31Jul 21♋48	18Mar 7♐40	9Jul 3♈25	6May 4♌12
	30Oct 25♏33	6Aug 1♐ 1	10Dec 29♓30	2Dec 29♌11
	18Nov 9♏30	SIDER. TIME 6h 38m 36s 18h 40m 34s Common Year		1 Jan Midn. Noon 1927

1928 (BST 22Apr – 7 Oct)

Noon		JAN	FEB	MAR	APR	MAY	JUN
☉	1	9♑50	11♒24	10♓40	11♈31	10♉51	10♊43
	9	18 0	19 30	18 41	19 23	18 36	18 22
	17	26 8	27 35	26 39	27 13	26 19	26 1
	25	4♒17	5♓39	4♈36	5♉ 1	4♊ 1	3♋39
☿	1	5♑25	27♒ 1	28♒56	15♓45	8♉31	4♋ 8
	7	15 1	5♓32	26R 8	24 23	21 28	9 21
	13	24 52	10 23	27D10	4♈ 0	4♊ 8	12 7
	19	5♒ 0	9R29	1♓ 7	14 34	15 35	12R12
	25	15 18	3 50	7 3	26 5	25 17	9 52
	31	25 24	...	14 25	...	3♋ 2	...
♀	1	27♏ 3	4♑11	9♒35	17♓39	24♈29	2♊31
	9	6♐31	13 55	19 24	27 28	4♉18	12 20
	17	16 5	23 41	29 13	7♈18	14 7	22 9
	25	25 43	3♒28	9♓ 3	17 7	23 56	1♋58
♂	1	17♐11	9♑55	1♒42	25♒20	18♓18	11♈44
	13	25 55	18 53	10 49	4♓32	27 26	20 38
	25	4♑44	27 55	19 59	13 43	6♈30	29 22
♃	1	26♓36	1♈46	7♈59	15♈19	22♈31	29♈27
	13	28 22	4 13	10 46	18 13	25 17	1♉52
	25	0♈26	6 51	13 38	21 6	27 57	4 4
♄	1	13♐34	16♐37	18♐31	19♐ 7	18♐14	16♐14
	13	14 50	17 32	18 56	18R56	17R33	15R21
	25	16 0	18 16	19 7	18 31	16 44	14 29
♅	1	29♓43	0♈41	2♈ 6	3♈50	5♈27	6♈43
	13	0♈ 0	1 13	2 46	4 31	6 0	7 3
	25	0 24	1 50	3 27	5 9	6 29	7 16
♆	1	28♌56	28♌15	27♌27	26♌44	26♌24	26♌34
	13	28R43	27R55	27R 8	26R33	26D24	26 46
	25	28 26	27 35	26 52	26 26	26 29	27 2
Pl.	1	16♋12	15♋34	15♋ 9	15♋ 0	15♋13	15♋46
☊	1	17♊37	15♊59	14♊27	12♊48	11♊13	9♊34
	1st	Sun	Wed	Thu	Sun	Tue	Fri

Noon		JUL	AUG	SEP	OCT	NOV	DEC
☉	1	9♋22	8♌57	8♍47	8♎ 3	8♏49	9♐ 4
	9	17 0	16 37	16 32	15 56	16 51	17 11
	17	24 38	24 18	24 20	23 52	24 54	25 20
	25	2♌16	2♍ 1	2♎10	1♏50	2♐59	3♑29
☿	1	6♋22	23♋47	23♍11	3♏44	23♎52	29♏41
	7	3R43	5♌18	2♎52	8 8	26D 4	9♐ 4
	13	3D35	17 34	11 51	9R31	2♏39	18 28
	19	6 39	29 37	20 6	6 20	11 10	27 55
	25	12R55	10♍57	27 30	29♎16	20 20	7♑29
	31	22 2	21 30	...	24 8	...	17 11
♀	1	9♋21	17♌30	25♍45	2♏43	10♐46	17♑18
	9	19 11	27 22	5♎36	12 33	20 33	26 56
	17	29 1	7♍14	15 28	22 23	0♑18	6♒31
	25	8 53	17♍ 6	25 20	2♐12	10 2	16 0
♂	1	3♉41	25♉ 1	14♊11	29♊19	8♋31	6♋38
	13	12 8	2♊45	20 45	3♋53	9R17	2R38
	25	20 21	10 6	26 39	7 15	8 1	27♊57
♃	1	5♉ 5	9♉ 5	10♉25	8♉45	4♉53	1♉27
	13	6 54	9 57	10R 5	7R24	3R19	0R42
	25	8 23	10 23	9 18	5 50	1 59	0 26
♄	1	14♐ 6	12♐41	12♐42	14♐ 8	16♐49	20♐ 7
	13	13R25	12R31	13 7	15 3	18 5	21 32
	25	12 54	12 34	13 44	16 7	19 26	22 57
♅	1	7♈21	7♈14	6♈27	5♈18	4♈ 9	3♈32
	13	7R24	7R 0	6R 1	4R49	3R50	3D28
	25	7 20	6 41	5 32	4 23	3 36	3 32
♆	1	27♌11	28♌10	29♌18	0♍20	1♍ 6	1♍23
	13	27 32	28 36	29 44	0 40	1 16	1R22
	25	27 55	29 3	0♍ 8	0 57	1 22	1 15
Pl.	1	16♋30	17♋16	17♋56	18♋18	18♋19	18♋ 0
☊	1	7♊59	6♊21	4♊42	3♊ 7	1♊28	29♉53
	1st	Sun	Wed	Sat	Mon	Thu	Sat

	d.	JAN	FEB	MAR	APR
☽	1	23♈19	16♊28	10♋42	0♍ 3
	3	21♉59	14♋10	7♌21	25 0
	5	20♊47	11♌16	3♍17	19♎18
	7	19♋ 7	7♍26	28 25	13♏ 7
	9	16♌24	2♎32	22♎46	6♐43
	11	12♍18	26 41	16♏32	0♑32
	13	6♎56	20♏21	10♐10	25 10
	15	0♏46	14♐13	4♑19	21♒17
	17	24 28	8♑58	29 43	19♓15
	19	18♐41	5♒ 9	26♒52	18♈53
	21	13♑54	2♒54	25♓45	19♉14
	23	10♒22	1♈44	25♈35	19♊ 2
	25	7♓53	0♉47	25♉13	17♋25
	27	6♈ 0	29 20	23♊48	14♌13
	29	4♉18	27♊ 7	21♋ 7	9♍42
	31	2♊28	...	17♌18	...

	d.	MAY	JUN	JUL	AUG
☽	1	4♎15	18♏52	21♐14	7♒12
	3	28 12	12♐32	15♑39	3♓35
	5	21♏52	6♑33	10♒51	0♈50
	7	15♐31	1♒13	6♓57	28 39
	9	9♑29	26 47	3♈58	26♉50
	11	4♒13	23♓33	1♉53	25♊14
	13	0♓14	21♈41	0♊37	23♋35
	15	27 55	21♉ 2	29 48	21♌25
	17	27♈14	20♊57	28♋45	18♍13
	19	27♉31	20♋25	26♌41	13♎42
	21	27♊34	18♌32	23♍ 6	8♏ 2
	23	26♋22	14♍57	18♎ 2	1♐44
	25	23♌26	9♎52	12♏ 0	25 29
	27	18♍55	3♏49	5♐38	20♑ 0
	29	13♎18	27 26	29 36	15♒45
	31	7♏ 4	...	24♑24	12♓51

	d.	SEP	OCT	NOV	DEC
☽	1	26♓49	4♉54	28♊22	6♌16
	3	25♈11	4♊ 8	26♋58	3♍44
	5	23♉40	2♋44	24♌ 8	29 33
	7	21♊55	0♌24	20♍ 1	24♎ 6
	9	19♋46	27 8	14♎53	17♏57
	11	17♌ 7	23♍ 1	9♏ 3	11♐33
	13	13♍44	18♎ 3	2♐47	5♑12
	15	9♎23	12♏19	26 21	29 12
	17	4♏ 0	6♐ 1	20♑ 6	23♒48
	19	27 51	29 35	14♒31	19♓23
	21	21♐26	23♑34	10♓ 9	16♈18
	23	15♑29	18♒38	7♈26	14♉47
	25	10♒39	15♓20	6♉29	14♊38
	27	7♓24	13♈49	6♊44	14♋59
	29	5♈41	13♉35	7♋ 4	14♌33
	31	...	13♊36	...	12♍25

STATIONS	☿	♀	♂	♃
	16Feb 10♓42	None	12Nov 9♋17	30Aug 10♉25
	9Mar 26♒ 5		... ...	26Dec 0♉26
		♄	♅	♆
	17Jun 12♋29	29Mar 19♐ 8	13Jul 7♈24	7May 26♌23
	11Jul 3♋18	17Aug 12♐30	13Dec 3♈28	4Dec 1♍23
	13Oct 9♏31	SIDER. TIME		1 Jan
	2Nov 23♎49	6h 37m 39s		Midn.
		18h 39m 37s		Noon
		LEAP YEAR		1928

1929 (BST 21 Apr. - 6 Oct.)

Noon		JAN	FEB	MAR	APR	MAY	JUN
☉	1	10♑37	12♒10	10♓26	11♈16	10♉37	10♊29
	9	18 46	20 16	18 26	19 9	18 22	18 9
	17	26 55	28 21	26 25	26 59	26 5	25 47
	25	5♒ 3	6♓25	4♈21	4♉47	3♊46	3♋25
☿	1	18♑49	23♒23	13♒29	25♓45	25♉41	21♊50
	7	28 38	17R29	19 21	6♈42	5♊54	19R12
	13	8♒18	11 11	26 36	18 31	13 52	15 57
	19	17 4	8 54	4♓53	1♉ 3	19 21	14 0
	25	23 9	10D41	14 2	13 45	22 7	14D32
	31	23R54	...	24 1	...	22R 5	...
♀	1	24♒12	28♓51	25♈ 5	7♉56	23♈42	28♈48
	9	3♓27	7♈ 3	0♉46	5R52	21R44	4 17
	17	12 31	14 47	5 7	1 37	22D18	10 43
	25	21 22	21 51	7 38	26♈40	25 1	17 49
♂	1	25♊27	21♊ 9	26♊46	8♋58	23♋48	10♌47
	13	22R17	22 40	0♋57	14 39	0♌13	17 41
	25	21 1	25 33	5 51	20 41	6 51	24 42
♃	1	0♉30	2♉46	7♉ 1	13♉16	20♉ 9	27♉28
	13	1 2	4 23	9 17	15 58	22 59	0♊14
	25	2 0	6 18	11 45	18 44	25 50	2 55
♄	1	23♐46	27♐ 4	29♐17	0♑28	0♑ 8	28♐29
	13	25 7	28 7	29 55	0R30	29 37	27R37
	25	26 23	29 1	0♑20	0 19	28 56	26 44
♅	1	3♈38	4♈32	5♈51	7♈35	9♈13	10♈34
	13	3 54	5 3	6 30	8 15	9 48	28 55
	25	4 16	5 38	7 11	8 55	10 18	11 12
♆	1	1♍ 9	0♍29	29♌43	28♌58	28♌37	28♌44
	13	0R56	0R10	29R24	28R47	28D36	28 55
	25	0 40	29♌50	29 7	28 39	28 39	29 10
Pl.	1	17♋25	16♋48	16♋22	16♋12	16♋25	16♋56
☊	1	28♉15	26♉36	25♉ 7	23♉29	21♉53	20♉15
	1st	Tue	Fri	Fri	Mon	Wed	Sat

Noon		JUL	AUG	SEP	OCT	NOV	DEC
☉	1	9♋ 8	8♌44	8♍33	7♎49	8♏35	8♐50
	9	16 46	16 24	16 19	15 43	16 37	16 57
	17	24 24	24 5	24 6	23 38	24 40	25 5
	25	2♌ 2	1♍47	1♎55	1♏35	2♐45	3♐14
☿	1	17♊55	10♌13	3♎ 4	21♎23	23♎13	11♐ 1
	7	23 59	22 15	10 34	15R22	2♏44	20 25
	13	2♋33	3♍25	16 52	9 18	12 26	29 50
	19	13 18	13 43	21 26	8D30	22 4	9♑16
	25	25 31	23 8	23 21	13 29	1♐35	18 35
	31	8♌ 9	1♎44	...	21 42	...	27 25
♀	1	23♉30	25♊52	1♌13	7♍ 4	15♎14	22♏44
	9	1♊26	4♋47	10 38	16 50	25 12	2♐47
	17	9 42	13 51	20 10	26 40	5♏11	12 50
	25	18 13	23 3	29 48	6♎33	15 12	22 54
♂	1	28♌16	17♍ 9	6♎49	26♎37	17♏55	9♐21
	13	5♍29	24 40	14 39	4♏46	26 24	18 9
	25	12 49	2♎18	22 36	13 2	5♐ 0	27 3
♃	1	4♊12	10♊14	14♊34	16♊23	15♊12	11♊39
	13	6 41	12 9	15 37	16R18	13R58	10R 2
	25	8 59	13 47	16 15	15 44	12 28	8 34
♄	1	26♐18	24♐29	23♐54	24♐48	27♐ 3	0♑ 9
	13	25R30	24R 5	24 5	25 32	28 13	1 32
	25	24 49	23 54	24 30	26 27	29 29	2 57
♅	1	11♈17	11♈17	10♈35	9♈27	8♈16	7♈33
	13	11 23	11R 5	10R 9	8R58	7R55	7R27
	25	11R21	10 47	9 42	8 31	7 39	7D29
♆	1	29♌19	0♍17	1♍24	2♍27	3♍15	3♍35
	13	29 39	0 42	1 51	2 48	3 26	3R34
	25	0♍ 2	1 9	2 15	3 6	3 33	3 29
Pl.	1	17♋40	18♋24	19♋ 6	19♋30	19♋33	19♋15
☊	1	18♉39	17♉ 1	15♉22	13♉47	12♉ 9	10♉33
	1st	Mon	Thu	Sun	Tue	Fri	Sun

	d.	JAN	FEB	MAR	APR
☽	1	25♍37	11♏10	18♏59	2♑27
	3	20♎48	4♐55	12♐49	26 19
	5	14♏51	28 31	6♑28	21♒ 1
	7	8♐25	22♑33	0♒39	17♓ 2
	9	2♑ 4	17♒24	25 50	14♈29
	11	26 9	13♓ 8	22♓11	13♉ 0
	13	20♒53	9♈39	19♈32	11♊56
	15	16♓21	6♉50	17♉28	10♋41
	17	12♈40	4♊40	15♊39	8♌48
	19	10♉ 3	3♋ 8	13♋53	6♍ 8
	21	8♊37	2♌ 0	12♌ 0	2♎35
	23	8♋ 8	0♍36	9♍41	28 8
	25	7♌49	28 11	6♎30	22♏49
	27	6♍35	24 17	2♏11	16♐49
	29	3♎40	...	26 46	10♑29
	31	29 0	...	20♐37	...

	d.	MAY	JUN	JUL	AUG
☽	1	4♒22	20♓13	25♈43	17♊34
	3	29 1	16♈52	23♉48	17♋19
	5	25♓ 2	15♉15	23♊28	17♌25
	7	22♈40	15♊ 5	23♋55	16♍38
	9	21♉44	15♋24	23♌51	14♎ 7
	11	21♊30	15♌ 0	22♍10	9♏46
	13	20♋57	13♍ 1	18♎35	4♐ 8
	15	19♌22	9♎20	13♏27	27 52
	17	16♍27	4♏20	7♐26	21♑35
	19	12♎20	28 29	1♑ 5	15♒45
	21	7♏14	22♐14	24 51	10♓32
	23	1♐28	15♑55	18♒58	6♈ 1
	25	25 17	9♒47	13♓36	2♉16
	27	18♑57	4♓ 7	8♈58	29 24
	29	12♒52	29 16	5♉22	27♊34
	31	7♓29	...	3♊ 8	26♋40

	d.	SEP	OCT	NOV	DEC
☽	1	11♌23	19♍29	8♏35	12♐11
	3	10♍36	16♎56	3♐43	6♑16
	5	8♎43	13♏ 6	28 2	0♒ 1
	7	5♏12	8♐ 2	21♑50	23 46
	9	0♐11	2♑ 4	15♒37	18♓ 2
	11	24 12	25 49	0♓ 1	13♈25
	13	17♑55	19♒54	5♈36	10♉27
	15	11♒57	14♓52	2♉43	9♊19
	17	6♓44	11♈ 2	1♊17	9♋26
	19	2♈27	8♉23	0♋41	9♌38
	21	29 1	6♊34	0♌ 1	8♍42
	23	26♉18	5♋ 7	28 32	6♎ 6
	25	24♊12	3♌35	25♍54	2♏ 1
	27	22♋35	1♍39	22♎10	26 51
	29	21♌10	29 4	17♏32	21♐ 3
	31	...	25♎39	...	14♑55

STATIONS	☿	♀	♂	♃
	29Jan 24♒23	30Mar 8♉ 2	27Jan 20♉59	5Oct 16♊24
	20Feb 8♒56	12May 21♈40	...	...
	29May 22♊27	♄	♅	♆
	21Jun 13♊52	10Apr 0♑31	17Jul 11♈23	10May 28♌35
	26Sep 23♎20	29Aug 23♐54	17Dec 7♈27	6Dec 3♍35
	17Oct 8♎ 2	SIDER. TIME 6h 40m 38s 18h 42m 36s Common Year		1 Jan Midn. Noon 1929

1930 (BST 13 Apr. - 5 Oct.)

Noon		JAN	FEB	MAR	APR	MAY	JUN
☉	1	10♑22	11♒55	10♓11	11♈ 2	10♉23	10♊15
	9	18 31	20 2	18 12	18 54	18 7	17 55
	17	26 40	28 7	26 10	26 44	25 50	25 33
	25	4♒48	6♓10	4♈ 7	4♉33	3♊32	3♋11
☿	1	28♑47	22♑22	17♒17	11♈ 0	0♊11	23♉48
	7	5♒37	23D34	26 11	23 25	2 31	25D 1
	13	8R14	27 57	5♓47	5♉34	1R47	28 50
	19	4 22	4♒15	16 6	16 19	28♉52	4♊58
	25	26♑59	11 46	27 10	24 42	25 36	13 13
	31	22 36	...	8♈58	...	23 51	...
♀	1	1♑42	10♒40	15♓45	24♈18	1♊12	8♋50
	9	11 46	20 43	25 44	4♉11	10 58	18 26
	17	21 49	0♓44	5♈41	14 2	20 42	28 0
	25	1♒53	10 45	15 37	23 51	0♋23	7♌30
♂	1	2♑18	25♑57	17♒42	11♓57	5♈14	28♈47
	13	11 23	5♒14	27 5	21 18	14 26	7♉41
	25	20 33	14 34	6♓28	0♈36	23 32	16 27
♃	1	7♊50	6♊21	7♊45	11♊48	17♊26	24♊11
	13	6R54	6 39	9 3	13 54	19 58	26 55
	25	6 25	7 24	10 42	16 12	22 37	29 41
♄	1	3♑47	7♑16	9♑50	11♑33	11♑48	10♑36
	13	5 11	8 27	10 40	11 50	11R30	9R51
	25	6 31	9 31	11 17	11R52	10 59	8 59
♅	1	7♈33	8♈21	9♈37	11♈19	12♈59	14♈24
	13	7 46	8 50	10 15	12 0	13 35	14 48
	25	8 6	9 24	10 55	12 40	14 7	15 6
♆	1	3♍24	2♍45	1♍59	1♍13	0♍49	0♍54
	13	3R11	2R26	1R40	1R 1	0D48	1 4
	25	2 56	2 6	1 22	0 52	0 50	1 19
Pl.	1	18♋41	18♋ 6	17♋39	17♋28	17♋39	18♋ 9
☊	1	8♉55	7♉16	5♉47	4♉ 9	2♉34	0♉55
	1st	Wed	Sat	Sat	Tue	Thu	Sat

Noon		JUL	AUG	SEP	OCT	NOV	DEC
☉	1	8♋55	8♌30	8♍19	7♎35	8♏21	8♐35
	9	16 32	16 10	16 4	15 28	16 22	16 42
	17	24 10	23 50	23 52	23 23	24 25	24 50
	25	1♌48	1♍33	1♎41	1♏21	2♐30	2♑59
☿	1	23♊25	25♌36	4♎28	22♍ 7	4♏49	21♐57
	7	5♋16	5♍28	6 43	25 35	14 36	0♑56
	13	18 4	14 21	5R33	3♎19	24 10	9 30
	19	0♌49	22 11	0 37	12 58	3♐33	16 58
	25	12 50	28 48	24♍31	23 6	12 48	21 44
	31	23 52	3♎50	...	3♏10	...	21R 4
♀	1	14♌35	20♍26	24♎12	22♏22	7♐23	24♏51
	9	23 58	29 25	2♏20	28 18	6R18	22R19
	17	3♍16	8♎13	10 5	3♐ 4	2 49	22D23
	25	12 28	16 51	17 20	6 17	28♏ 5	24 50
♂	1	20♉46	12♊22	2♋31	20♋ 9	5♌22	15♌ 2
	13	29 17	20 22	9 50	26 29	10 1	16 39
	25	7♊36	28 7	16 49	2♌18	13 40	16R29
♃	1	1♋ 3	7♋55	13♋56	18♋18	20♋27	19♋37
	13	3 46	10 23	15 54	19 28	20R28	18R31
	25	6 25	12 41	17 35	20 13	20 1	17 5
♄	1	8♑33	6♑27	5♑19	5♑38	7♑26	10♑14
	13	7R40	5R51	5D16	6 10	8 27	11 34
	25	6 52	5 27	5 27	6 54	9 37	12 57
♅	1	15♈13	15♈20	14♈42	13♈37	12♈25	11♈37
	13	15 21	15R10	14R19	13R 8	12R 1	11R28
	25	15R22	14 54	13 51	12 40	11 43	11D27
♆	1	1♍27	2♍23	3♍31	4♍34	5♍24	5♍46
	13	1 47	2 49	3 57	4 56	5 36	5R47
	25	2 9	3 15	4 22	5 15	5 44	5 42
Pl.	1	18♋53	19♋40	20♋21	20♋45	20♋49	20♋32
☊	1	29♈20	27♈41	26♈ 3	24♈27	22♈49	21♈14
	1st	Tue	Fri	Mon	Wed	Sat	Mon

d.		JAN	FEB	MAR	APR
☽	1	26♑48	11♓33	20♓41	7♉58
	3	20♒32	5♈58	15♈32	4♊41
	5	14♓29	1♉10	11♉ 8	2♋13
	7	9♈ 7	27 39	7♊44	0♌30
	9	4♉59	25♊48	5♋34	29 17
	11	2♊38	25♋34	4♌39	28♍ 3
	13	2♋ 9	26♌ 3	4♍24	26♎ 8
	15	2♌48	25♍53	3♎47	23♏ 3
	17	3♍ 8	23♎59	1♏50	18♐37
	19	1♎54	20♏10	28 12	13♑ 5
	21	28 42	14♐54	23♐ 6	6♒57
	23	23♏54	8♑48	17♑ 6	0♓48
	25	18♐ 8	2♒30	10♒50	25 14
	27	11♑56	26 23	4♓51	20♈39
	29	5♒39	...	29 29	17♉13
	31	29 31	...	24♈55	...

d.		MAY	JUN	JUL	AUG
☽	1	14♊48	8♌ 2	17♍12	8♏16
	3	13♋ 4	6♍44	15♎ 0	3♐59
	5	11♌33	4♎32	11♏28	28 42
	7	9♍54	1♏22	6♐54	22♑49
	9	7♎47	27 22	1♑37	16♒38
	11	4♏58	22♐36	25 49	10♓22
	13	1♐16	17♑ 8	19♒39	4♈14
	15	26 34	11♒ 7	13♓22	28 38
	17	20♑59	4♓51	7♈20	24♉ 5
	19	14♒51	28 51	2♉10	21♊ 8
	21	8♓42	23♈46	28 29	20♋ 2
	23	3♈ 9	20♉12	26♊43	20♌18
	25	28 46	18♊25	26♋38	20♍43
	27	25♉51	18♋ 3	27♌ 7	19♎58
	29	24♊18	18♌ 1	26♍49	17♏25
	31	23♋28	...	24♎53	13♐12

d.		SEP	OCT	NOV	DEC
☽	1	25♐37	28♑26	12♓11	14♈ 7
	3	19♑50	22♒11	6♈18	9♉19
	5	13♒38	16♓ 0	1♉15	5♊55
	7	7♓23	10♈14	27 15	3♋49
	9	1♈20	5♉ 7	24♊14	2♌28
	11	25 43	0♊49	21♋57	1♍ 9
	13	20♉51	27 27	20♌ 8	29 22
	15	17♊ 5	25♋ 6	18♍31	26♎59
	17	14♋47	23♌42	16♎48	23♏58
	19	13♌56	22♍52	14♏40	20♐15
	21	13♍57	21♎56	11♐42	15♑42
	23	13♎42	20♏ 7	7♑35	10♒17
	25	12♏11	16♐55	2♒20	4♓ 9
	27	8♐58	12♑17	26 17	27 47
	29	4♑13	6♒33	19♓59	21♈50
	31	...	0♓18	...	17♉ 2

STATIONS	☿	♀	♂	♃
	13Jan 8♒14	2Nov 7♐23	19Dec 16♌48	31Jan 6♊21
	3Feb 22♑19	13Dec 22♏ 2	... ...	8Nov 20♋31
	9May 2♊35	♄	♅	♆
	3Jun 23♉54	22Apr 11♑53	22Jul 15♈23	12May 0♍48
	9Sep 6♎45	10Sep 5♑15	21Dec 11♈27	9Dec 5♍47
	30Sep 22♍ 7	SIDER. TIME 6h 39m 41s		1 Jan Midn.
	28Dec 22♑15	18h 41m 39s		Noon
		Common Year		1930

1931

(BST 19 Apr. – 4 Oct.)

Noon		JAN	FEB	MAR	APR	MAY	JUN
☉	1	10♑ 7	11♒41	9♓57	10♈48	10♉ 9	10♊ 2
	9	16 14	19 47	17 58	18 41	17 54	17 41
	17	26 25	27 52	25 57	26 31	25 37	25 20
	25	4♒34	5♓56	3♈53	4♉20	3♊19	2♋58
☿	1	20♑17	17♑ 4	27♒55	26♈36	8♉24	15♉54
	7	13R 1	24 32	8♓26	5♉36	4R58	24 0
	13	7 2	2♒49	19 36	11 21	3 35	3♊46
	19	6D25	11 45	1♈23	13 24	4D54	15 6
	25	9 59	21 15	13 26	11R58	8 45	27 41
	31	15 56	...	24 51	...	14 43	...
♀	1	28♏31	24♐52	25♑ 1	0♓50	6♈28	13♉44
	9	4♐ 3	3♑ 8	4♒ 6	10 17	16 3	23 24
	17	10 38	11 43	13 19	19 46	25 40	3♊ 5
	25	17 59	20 32	22 38	29 18	5♉18	12 48
♂	1	15♌30	5♌ 2	27♋45	0♌33	10♌43	25♌15
	13	12R19	0R51	27D35	3 59	15 59	1♍33
	25	7 49	28♋13	29 3	8 17	21 43	8 8
♃	1	16♋10	12♋16	10♋30	11♋27	14♋55	20♋18
	13	14R33	11R14	10D31	12 35	16 50	22 43
	25	13 2	10 36	10 59	14 4	18 58	25 14
♄	1	13♑46	17♑23	20♑14	22♑27	23♑16	22♑37
	13	15 12	18 41	21 14	22 57	23R12	22R 0
	25	16 36	19 52	22 4	23 14	22 54	21 14
♅	1	11♈30	12♈11	13♈23	15♈ 4	16♈45	18♈14
	13	11 40	12 39	14 1	15 46	17 23	18 40
	25	11 58	13 11	14 41	16 26	17 56	19 0
♆	1	5♍38	5♍ 1	4♍15	3♍29	3♍ 3	3♍ 5
	13	5R26	4R42	3R56	3R15	3R 0	3 14
	25	5 11	4 22	3 38	3 6	3D 2	3 27
Pl.	1	19♋59	19♋22	18♋54	18♋43	18♋53	19♋16
☊	1	19♈34	17♈57	16♈28	14♈49	13♈14	11♈35
	1st	Thu	Sun	Sun	Wed	Fri	Mon

Noon		JUL	AUG	SEP	OCT	NOV	DEC
☉	1	8♋41	8♌16	8♍ 5	7♎21	8♏ 6	8♐20
	9	16 19	15 56	15 51	15 14	16 8	16 28
	17	23 57	23 37	23 38	23 10	24 11	24 36
	25	1♌35	1♍19	1♎28	1♏ 7	2♐16	2♑45
☿	1	10♋45	4♍36	14♍48	24♍18	16♏43	29♐27
	7	23 24	11 21	9R11	4♎52	25 57	4♑54
	13	5♌ 5	16 27	5 57	15 27	4♐57	6R10
	19	15 38	19 19	7D54	25 42	13 42	1 6
	25	25 4	19R13	14 41	5♏35	22 1	23♐20
	31	3♍21	15 41	...	15 9	...	20 6
♀	1	20♊ 5	27♋59	6♍17	13♎36	22♏17	29♐44
	9	29 50	7♌50	16 13	23 35	2♐16	9 42
	17	9♋36	17 42	26 10	3♏34	12 16	19 40
	25	19 24	27 36	6♎ 7	13 33	22 15	29 37
♂	1	11♍31	29♍53	19♎31	9♏36	1♐26	23♐30
	13	18 28	7♎21	27 26	17 56	10 9	2♑34
	25	25 38	14 59	5♏30	26 24	19 1	11 45
♃	1	26♋32	3♌23	10♌ 5	15♌52	20♌23	22♌32
	13	29 10	6 2	12 31	17 50	21 33	22R37
	25	1♌49	8 37	14 48	19 32	22 19	22 14
♄	1	20♑49	18♑35	16♑59	16♑43	17♑59	20♑27
	13	19R57	17R50	16R42	17 2	18 51	21 41
	25	19 4	17 14	16D39	17 34	19 53	23 1
♅	1	19♈ 8	19♈22	18♈50	17♈47	16♈34	15♈41
	13	19 19	19R14	18R28	17R18	16R 9	15 30
	25	19 23	19 1	18 1	16 50	15 49	15 26
♆	1	3♍36	4♍30	5♍38	6♍42	7♍33	7♍58
	13	3 55	4 56	6 4	7 4	7 46	7R59
	25	4 16	5 22	6 30	7 23	7 55	7 56
Pl.	1	20♋ 6	20♋53	21♋35	22♋ 1	22♋ 5	21♋49
☊	1	10♈ 0	8♈22	6♈43	5♈ 8	3♈29	1♈54
	1st	Wed	Sat	Tue	Thu	Sun	Tue

	d.	JAN	FEB	MAR	APR
☽	1	0♊14	20♋26	28♋31	21♍55
	3	28 0	20♌32	28♌30	22♎ 3
	5	27♋12	20♍47	29♍ 2	21♏16
	7	26♌52	19♎59	28♎46	18♐51
	9	25♍58	17♏38	26♏53	14♑43
	11	23♎56	13♐51	23♐17	9♒15
	13	20♏48	8♑59	18♑19	3♓ 3
	15	16♐46	3♒24	12♒28	26 39
	17	11♑59	27 20	6♓11	20♈30
	19	6♒33	20♓59	29 48	14♉55
	21	0♓32	14♈37	23♈37	10♊ 7
	23	24 9	8♉38	17♉55	6♋14
	25	17♈51	3♊36	13♊ 4	3♌25
	27	12♉16	0♋ 7	9♋29	1♍42
	29	8♊ 6	...	7♌27	0♎52
	31	5♋51	...	6♍52	...

	d.	MAY	JUN	JUL	AUG
☽	1	0♏21	21♐28	26♑19	11♓38
	3	29 16	18♑ 4	21♒19	5♈19
	5	26♐53	13♒18	15♓23	28 58
	7	22♑54	7♓27	9♈ 1	23♉13
	9	17♒31	1♉ 7	2♉55	18♊46
	11	11♓20	24 59	27 45	16♋ 1
	13	4♈58	19♉42	24♊ 2	14♌54
	15	29 2	15♊38	21♋51	14♍40
	17	23♉55	12♋48	20♌41	14♎15
	19	19♊48	10♌48	19♍44	12♏52
	21	16♋37	9♍ 8	18♎20	10♐15
	23	14♌10	7♎25	16♏11	6♑28
	25	12♍18	5♏29	13♐ 6	1♒45
	27	10♎49	3♐11	9♑34	26 15
	29	9♏27	0♑14	5♒ 1	20♓10
	31	7♐41	...	29 37	13♈47

	d.	SEP	OCT	NOV	DEC
☽	1	25♈34	28♉27	15♋53	22♌59
	3	19♉27	23♊17	12♌35	20♍43
	5	14♊13	19♋21	10♍35	19♎17
	7	10♋27	17♌ 1	9♎50	18♏25
	9	8♌29	16♍18	9♏47	17♐25
	11	8♍ 6	16♎33	9♐21	15♑24
	13	8♎23	16♏40	7♑32	11♒49
	15	8♏ 9	15♐31	3♒55	6♓42
	17	6♐34	12♑34	28 43	0♈35
	19	3♑23	7♒58	22♓34	24 11
	21	28 49	2♓13	16♈ 8	18♉12
	23	23♒16	25 54	10♉ 1	13♊ 7
	25	17♓ 7	19♈30	4♊34	9♋ 8
	27	10♈44	13♉23	29 55	6♌ 5
	29	4♉24	7♊48	26♋ 4	3♍39
	31	...	2♋57	...	1♎35

STATIONS	☿	♀	♂	♃
	17Jan 6♑ 4	None	9Mar 27♋26	7Mar 10♋27
	20Apr 13♉23		... ...	10Dec 22♌38
	14May 3♉37	♄	♅	♆
	22Aug 19♍41	4May 23♑17	26Jul 19♈23	15May 3♍ 0
	14Sep 5♍53	22Sep 16♑39	26Dec 15♈26	11Dec 7♍59
	12Dec 6♑22	SIDER. TIME 6h 38m 44s		1 Jan Midn.
		18h 40m 42s Common Year		Noon 1931

1932 (BST 17 Apr. - 2 Oct)

Noon		JAN	FEB	MAR	APR	MAY	JUN
☉	1	9♑53	11♒26	10♓43	11♈33	10♉53	10♊45
	9	18 2	19 33	18 43	19 26	18 38	18 25
	17	26 11	27 38	26 42	27 16	26 21	26 3
	25	4♒19	5♓41	4♈38	5♉ 4	4♊ 3	3♋41
☿	1	20♐ 8	24♑30	13♓55	24♈59	15♈57	27♉ 7
	7	23D 2	3♒46	25 30	22R27	20 28	9♊25
	13	28 50	13 29	6♈47	18 3	26 55	21 30
	19	6♑ 8	23 44	16 27	14 36	4♉56	5♋30
	25	14 17	4♓31	22 53	13D50	14 22	17 38
	31	23 0	...	25R 3	...	25 11	...
♀	1	8♒18	16♓26	21♈10	26♉15	25♊55	14♋43
	9	18 12	26 8	0♉29	4♊43	2♋28	15R23
	17	28 4	5♈46	9 38	12 51	8 3	13 32
	25	7♓53	15 17	18 36	20 32	12 21	9 29
♂	1	17♑ 9	11♒23	4♓16	28♓37	21♈44	14♉54
	13	26 29	20 51	13 44	7♈56	0♉48	23 38
	25	5♒52	0♓19	23 9	17 9	9 44	2♊13
♃	1	21♌48	18♌27	14♌48	12♌41	13♌24	16♌43
	13	20R44	16R52	13R40	12D38	14 25	18 33
	25	19 21	15 22	12 55	13 3	15 47	20 36
♄	1	23♑49	27♑29	0♒40	3♒17	4♒37	4♒30
	13	25 14	28 51	1 48	3 59	4 46	4R 4
	25	26 40	0♒ 9	2 47	4 28	4R40	3 26
♅	1	15♈28	16♈ 3	17♈14	18♈53	20♈35	22♈ 6
	13	15 36	16 29	17 50	19 34	21 13	22 34
	25	15 51	16 59	18 30	20 15	21 48	22 56
♆	1	7♍52	7♍17	6♍30	5♍43	5♍15	5♍16
	13	7R41	6R58	6R10	5R29	5R12	5 25
	25	7 26	6 38	5 52	5 19	5D13	5 38
Pl.	1	21♋17	20♋39	20♋10	19♋59	20♋ 9	20♋39
☊	1	0♈16	28♓37	27♓ 5	25♓26	23♓51	22♓13
1st		Fri	Mon	Tue	Fri	Sun	Wed

Noon		JUL	AUG	SEP	OCT	NOV	DEC
☉	1	9♋24	9♌ 0	8♍49	8♎ 6	8♏52	9♐ 7
	9	17 2	16 40	16 35	15 59	16 54	17 14
	17	24 40	24 21	24 22	23 55	24 57	25 22
	25	2♌18	2♍ 3	2♎12	1♏52	3♐ 2	3♑31
☿	1	28♋34	1♍42	21♌ 2	9♎45	28♏ 9	16♐32
	7	8♌14	1R17	27 23	20 0	6♐11	8R39
	13	16 33	27 50	6♍57	29 46	13 20	4 24
	19	23 26	22 52	17 54	9♏ 8	18 43	6D11
	25	28 34	19 30	29 0	18 8	20R32	11 42
	31	1♍28	20D25	...	26 45	...	19 2
♀	1	5♋46	1♋20	23♋ 5	23♌38	29♍13	5♏31
	9	1R26	5 18	0♌40	2♍33	8♎46	15 22
	17	29♊ 8	10 36	8 43	11 40	18 26	25 16
	25	29D19	16 56	17 8	20 57	28 10	5♐12
♂	1	6♊28	27♊47	18♋ 1	6♌24	23♌44	8♍ 0
	13	14 50	5♋45	25 31	13 21	29 48	12 39
	25	23 3	13 33	2♌50	20 0	5♍25	16 25
♃	1	21♌42	27♌55	4♍37	10♍59	16♍51	21♍ 7
	13	24 0	0♍29	7 12	13 23	18 46	22 15
	25	26 27	3 5	9 45	15 38	20 25	22 58
♄	1	3♒ 4	0♒50	28♑53	28♑ 7	28♑51	0♒56
	13	2R14	0R 0	28R25	28D13	29 32	2 4
	25	1 21	29♑15	28 9	28 33	0♒26	3 19
♅	1	23♈ 5	23♈23	22♈56	21♈56	20♈41	19♈45
	13	23 17	23R18	22R35	21R27	20R16	19R33
	25	23 23	23 6	22 10	20 58	19 54	19 27
♆	1	5♍46	6♍39	7♍46	8♍51	9♍43	10♍ 9
	13	6 4	7 5	8 13	9 13	9 57	10R11
	25	6 26	7 31	8 39	9 33	10 6	10 8
Pl.	1	21♋21	22♋ 9	22♋52	23♋18	23♋24	23♋ 8
☊	1	20♓37	18♓59	17♓20	15♓45	14♓ 7	12♓31
1st		Fri	Mon	Thu	Sat	Tue	Thu

	d.	JAN	FEB	MAR	APR
☽	1	15♎39	8♐35	2♑44	21♒15
	3	13♏55	5♑49	28 56	15♓37
	5	12♐11	2♒17	24♒12	9♈27
	7	9♑58	27 47	18♓41	3♉ 5
	9	6♒43	22♓21	12♈36	26 47
	11	2♓10	16♈12	6♉14	20♊54
	13	26 28	9♉49	29 59	15♋48
	15	20♈ 8	3♊50	24♊23	12♌ 0
	17	13♉53	28 54	20♋ 0	9♍52
	19	8♊24	25♋31	17♌19	9♎22
	21	4♋11	23♌43	16♍19	9♏50
	23	1♌21	23♍ 0	16♎25	9♐57
	25	29 32	22♎30	16♏28	8♑37
	27	28♍ 8	21♏23	15♐27	5♒23
	29	26♎38	19♐14	12♑51	0♓33
	31	24♏43	...	8♒45	...

	d.	MAY	JUN	JUL	AUG
☽	1	24♓40	8♉50	11♊21	27♋50
	3	18♈19	2♊45	6♋15	24♌43
	5	11♉57	27 14	2♌ 1	22♍26
	7	5♊51	22♋24	28 34	20♎39
	9	0♋13	18♌19	25♍51	19♏ 3
	11	25 19	15♍10	23♎49	17♐21
	13	21♌26	13♎ 9	22♏25	15♑15
	15	18♍57	12♏14	21♐16	12♒22
	17	18♎ 0	11♐54	19♑44	8♓27
	19	18♏ 8	11♑ 8	17♒ 5	3♈26
	21	18♐15	8♒59	13♓ 1	27 33
	23	17♑ 7	5♓ 4	7♈39	21♉18
	25	14♒ 5	29 43	1♉32	15♊15
	27	9♓19	23♈32	25 17	10♋ 1
	29	3♈24	17♉13	19♊33	6♌ 4
	31	27 1	...	14♋47	3♍31

	d.	SEP	OCT	NOV	DEC
☽	1	17♍42	25♎48	19♐39	27♑12
	3	16♎36	25♏40	18♑29	24♒29
	5	15♏38	24♐42	15♒29	19♓59
	7	14♐11	22♑21	10♓55	14♈17
	9	11♑54	18♒38	5♈20	8♉ 3
	11	8♒40	13♓50	29 14	1♊46
	13	4♓30	8♈18	22♉58	25 44
	15	29 29	2♉17	16♊45	20♋ 6
	17	23♈44	26 2	10♋48	15♌ 2
	19	17♉33	19♊47	5♌24	10♍46
	21	11♊17	13♋57	1♍ 1	7♎42
	23	5♋31	9♌ 4	28 10	6♏ 7
	25	0♌48	5♍40	27♎ 7	5♐49
	27	27 37	4♎ 6	27♏28	5♑55
	29	26♍ 7	4♏ 7	27♐57	5♒ 8
	31	...	4♐38	...	2♓38

STATIONS	☿	♀	♂	♃
	31Mar 25♈ 3	8Jun 15♋26	None	9Apr 12♌36
	24Apr 13♈45	21Jul 28♊55		3
	4Aug 1♍53	♄	♅	♆
	27Aug 19♌16	15May 4♒46	29Jul 23♈24	16May 5♍12
	25Nov 20♐32	29Dec	29Dec 19♈27	12Dec 10♍11
	14Dec 4♐19	SIDER. TIME 6h 37m 47s		1 Jan Midn.
		18h 39m 45s		Noon
		LEAP YEAR		1932

1933 (BST 9 Apr. – 8 Oct.)

Noon		JAN	FEB	MAR	APR	MAY	JUN
☉	1	10♑39	12♒12	10♓28	11♈19	10♉39	10♊31
	9	18 48	20 19	18 29	19 11	18 24	18 11
	17	26 57	28 23	26 27	27 1	26 7	25 49
	25	5♒ 6	6♓27	4♈24	4♉49	3♊48	3♋27
☿	1	20♐21	7♒35	27♓13	25♓34	16♈ 6	15♊ 8
	7	28 40	17 55	4♈35	24D44	25 17	27 49
	13	7♑27	28 42	7 27	27 0	5♉39	9♋21
	19	16 35	9♓48	5R21	1♈40	17 12	19 27
	25	26 3	20 40	0 21	8 10	29 48	28 3
	31	5♒54	...	26♓ 1	...	12♊57	...
♀	1	13♐55	22♑36	27♒33	6♈ 7	13♉14	21♊23
	9	23 53	2♒35	7♓31	16 2	23 6	1♋11
	17	3♑52	12 34	17 29	25 56	2♊57	10 59
	25	13 51	22 34	27 25	5♉50	12 47	20 46
♂	1	18♍ 6	19♍26	10♍58	1♍34	2♍59	12♍56
	13	19 56	16R43	6R23	0D52	6 4	18 12
	25	20R 9	12 32	2 51	1 54	10 9	24 2
♃	1	23♍12	22♍19	19♍21	15♍30	13♍25	14♍ 1
	13	23R13	21R14	17R48	14R23	13D18	14 59
	25	22 47	19 51	16 18	13 38	13 38	16 17
♄	1	4♒ 6	7♒45	10♒59	13♒59	15♒51	16♒21
	13	5 29	9 10	12 15	14 52	16 14	16R 8
	25	6 55	10 32	13 23	15 35	16 23	15 42
♅	1	19♈27	19♈58	21♈ 2	22♈40	24♈22	25♈56
	13	19 33	20 22	21 37	23 21	25 1	26 26
	25	19 47	20 51	22 16	24 2	25 37	26 50
♆	1	10♍ 5	9♍31	8♍46	7♍58	7♍29	7♍27
	13	9R54	9R12	8R26	7R43	7R24	7 35
	25	9 40	8 53	8 8	7 33	7D25	7 47
Pl.	1	22♋35	22♋ 0	21♋29	21♋15	21♋25	21♋55
☊	1	10♓53	9♓14	7♓45	6♓ 7	4♓31	2♓53
	1st	Sun	Wed	Wed	Sat	Mon	Thu

Noon		JUL	AUG	SEP	OCT	NOV	DEC
☉	1	9♋10	8♌46	8♍35	7♎51	8♏37	8♐52
	9	16 48	16 25	16 20	15 44	16 39	16 59
	17	24 26	24 6	24 8	23 40	24 42	25 7
	25	2♌ 4	1♍49	1♎58	1♏38	2♐47	3♑16
☿	1	5♌ 1	5♌21	28♌36	22♎11	1♐55	19♏28
	7	10 7	2R22	10 13	1♏18	4 43	24 26
	13	12 56	2D52	21 35	9 55	2R40	1♐46
	19	13R 1	7 33	2♎22	17 59	25♏31	10 8
	25	10 20	15 56	12 34	25 14	19 22	18 58
	31	6 3	26 41	...	1♐ 8	...	28 3
♀	1	28♋ 6	5♍50	13♎11	18♏44	24♐17	25♑57
	9	7♌52	15 31	22 44	28 3	3♑ 6	3♒26
	17	17 37	25 10	2♏14	7♐17	11 42	10 13
	25	27 20	4♎48	11 41	16 25	20 0	16 2
♂	1	27♍ 7	14♎36	4♏ 3	24♏23	16♐42	9♑18
	13	3♎37	21 55	12 1	2♐52	25 38	18 34
	25	10 27	29 31	20 13	11 33	4♑43	27 56
♃	1	17♍ 3	22♍ 2	28♍10	4♎36	11♎ 9	16♎48
	13	18 48	24 18	0♎43	7 11	13 32	18 43
	25	20 47	26 43	3 18	9 43	15 46	20 21
♄	1	15♒24	13♒22	11♒10	9♒52	9♒59	11♒35
	13	14R42	12R28	10R30	9R43	10 28	12 35
	25	13 52	11 37	10 1	9D49	11 10	13 43
♅	1	27♈ 0	27♈25	27♈ 4	26♈ 7	24♈53	23♈53
	13	27 15	27R22	26R45	25R39	24R26	23R38
	25	27 23	27 13	26 21	25 9	24 2	23 29
♆	1	7♍54	8♍47	9♍53	10♍58	11♍52	12♍20
	13	8 12	9 11	10 19	11 21	12 7	12 23
	25	8 33	9 37	10 45	11 42	12 17	12R21
Pl.	1	22♋33	23♋26	24♋10	23♋34	24♋41	24♋27
☊	1	1♓18	29♒39	28♒ 1	26♒25	24♒47	23♒11
	1st	Sat	Tue	Fri	Sun	Wed	Fri

	d.	JAN	FEB	MAR	APR
☽	1	15♓41	0♉40	8♉26	22♊ 9
	3	10♈39	24 31	2♊20	16♋ 5
	5	4♉39	18♊20	26 8	10♌49
	7	28 21	12♋39	20♋28	6♍56
	9	22♊17	7♌50	15♌51	4♎45
	11	16♋45	4♍ 2	12♍36	4♏ 0
	13	11♌55	1♎ 9	10♎36	3♐48
	15	7♍48	28 58	9♏21	3♑ 4
	17	4♎29	27♏13	8♐12	1♒ 7
	19	2♏ 6	25♐38	6♑34	27 53
	21	0♐39	23♑54	4♒11	23♓35
	23	29 49	21♒34	0♓57	18♈31
	25	28♑50	18♓17	26 54	12♉52
	27	26♒52	13♈52	22♈ 2	6♊48
	29	23♓25	...	16♉25	0♋31
	31	18♈31	...	10♊17	...

	d.	MAY	JUN	JUL	AUG
☽	1	24♋24	10♍35	16♎42	9♐23
	3	19♌ 0	7♎16	14♏57	8♑50
	5	15♍ 0	5♏51	14♐41	8♒19
	7	12♎50	6♐ 2	14♑59	6♓55
	9	12♏26	6♑37	14♒35	4♈ 2
	11	12♐53	6♒13	12♓36	29 37
	13	12♑47	4♓ 2	8♈49	24♉ 2
	15	11♒10	0♈ 5	3♉39	17♊52
	17	7♓52	24 51	27 39	11♋40
	19	3♈15	18♉53	21♊23	5♌56
	21	27 46	12♊38	15♋14	1♍ 0
	23	21♉48	6♋23	9♌31	26 58
	25	15♊35	0♌22	4♍25	23♎52
	27	9♋18	24 48	0♎ 9	21♏35
	29	3♌15	20♍ 6	26 56	19♐56
	31	27 51	...	24♏57	18♑38

	d.	SEP	OCT	NOV	DEC
☽	1	2♒58	10♓32	29♈ 1	2♊39
	3	1♓19	7♈14	23♉53	26 36
	5	28 45	3♉ 1	18♊ 4	20♋15
	7	24♈56	27 49	11♋47	13♌56
	9	19♉53	21♊51	5♌29	8♍11
	11	13♊58	15♋33	29 48	3♎39
	13	7♋43	9♌34	25♍26	0♏55
	15	1♌46	4♍34	22♎55	0♐ 7
	17	26 41	1♎ 4	22♏ 9	0♑33
	19	22♍48	29 8	22♐15	0♒51
	21	20♎ 6	28♏14	21♑57	29 51
	23	18♏15	27♐27	20♒23	27♓ 7
	25	16♐44	26♑ 1	17♓23	22♈52
	27	15♑ 6	23♒38	13♈13	17♉33
	29	13♒ 6	20♓22	8♉14	11♊37
	31	...	16♈19	...	5♋22

STATIONS	☿	♀	♂	♃
	14Mar 7♈25	None	21Jan 20♍17	8Jan 23♍16
	6Apr 24♓39		12Apr 0♍52	10May 13♍17
	17Jul 13♌19	♄	♅	♆
	10Aug 2♌ 6	27May 16♒23	3Aug 27♈25	19May 7♍24
	8Nov 4♐46	15Oct 9♒43	...	15Dec 12♍23
	28Nov 18♐38	SIDER. TIME 6h 40m 47s 18h 42m 45s Common Year		1 Jan Midn. Noon 1933

1934 (BST 22 Apr. - 7 Oct)

Noon		JAN	FEB	MAR	APR	MAY	JUN
☉	1	10♑24	11♒57	10♓13	11♈ 4	10♉25	10♊18
	9	18 33	20 4	18 14	18 57	18 10	17 57
	17	26 42	28 9	26 13	26 47	25 53	25 36
	25	4♒51	6♓12	4♈ 9	4♉35	3♊35	3♋14
☿	1	29♐35	20♒49	18♓45	13♓19	27♈32	0♋15
	7	8♑55	1♓21	13R13	19 48	9♉33	9 9
	13	18 29	11 3	8 6	27 37	22 24	16 11
	19	28 21	18 9	6D20	6♈33	5♊26	21 9
	25	8♒33	20R25	8 3	16 32	17 44	23 43
	31	19 3	...	12 24	...	28 36	...
♀	1	20♒ 2	17♒57	8♒13	25♒44	24♓49	28♈57
	9	22 56	13R 4	10 30	2♓50	3♈23	8♉ 6
	17	23R33	9 19	14 38	10 30	12 8	17 19
	25	21 33	7 56	20 7	18 34	21 3	26 37
♂	1	3♒25	27♒54	19♓58	13♈59	6♉36	29♉10
	13	12 52	7♓23	29 20	23 7	15 26	7♊40
	25	22 22	16 49	8♈37	2♉ 8	24 9	16 3
♃	1	21♎ 9	23♎ 9	22♎25	19♎15	15♎34	13♎24
	13	22 15	23R 8	21R25	17R43	14R26	13D17
	25	22 56	22 40	20 6	16 14	13 40	13 36
♄	1	14♒27	18♒ 0	21♒21	24♒40	27♒ 1	28♒ 9
	13	15 46	19 27	22 42	25 44	27 38	28R10
	25	17 10	20 53	23 59	26 38	28 1	27 57
♅	1	23♈28	23♈52	24♈52	26♈27	28♈ 9	29♈46
	13	23D31	24 14	25 26	27 7	28 49	0♉18
	25	23 42	24 41	26 3	27 49	29 26	0 44
♆	1	12♍18	11♍46	11♍ 2	10♍13	9♍42	9♍38
	13	12R 9	11R28	10R42	9R58	9R37	9 45
	25	11 55	11 9	10 23	9 46	9D36	9 56
Pl.	1	23♋55	23♋17	22♋45	22♋30	22♋37	23♋ 8
☊	1	21♒33	19♒54	18♒25	16♒47	15♒12	13♒33
1st		Mon	Thu	Thu	Sun	Tue	Fri

Noon		JUL	AUG	SEP	OCT	NOV	DEC
☉	1	8♋57	8♌32	8♍21	7♎37	8♏23	8♐37
	9	16 34	16 12	16 7	15 30	16 24	16 44
	17	24 12	23 53	23 54	23 26	24 28	24 53
	25	1♌51	1♍35	1♎43	1♏23	2♐32	3♑ 1
☿	1	23♋35	19♋ 7	14♍14	1♏ 9	12♏16	22♏49
	7	21R 0	26 42	24 57	8 22	5R 6	1♐52
	13	17 14	7♌ 0	4♎58	14 21	3D 5	11 6
	19	14 30	18 47	14 21	18 12	7 2	20 24
	25	14D34	0♍49	23 5	18R24	14 15	29 49
	31	18 10	12 22	...	13 30	...	9♑22
♀	1	3♊38	10♋29	18♌ 8	25♍14	4♏ 0	11♐42
	9	13 4	20 7	27 59	5♎13	14 3	21 45
	17	22 33	29 49	7♍52	15 13	24 6	1♑49
	25	2♋ 5	9♌34	17 47	25 14	4♐ 9	11 52
♂	1	20♊12	11♋ 7	1♌14	19♌57	8♍22	24♍55
	13	28 23	19 0	8 49	27 12	15 10	1♎ 3
	25	6♋27	26 46	16 16	4♍18	21 44	6 48
♃	1	13♎55	17♎ 0	21♎59	27♎56	4♏38	11♏ 3
	13	14 50	18 45	24 16	0♏30	7 15	13 28
	25	16 7	20 44	26 41	3 7	9 48	15 43
♄	1	27♒46	26♒ 4	23♒46	22♒ 1	21♒32	22♒35
	13	27R14	25R11	22R58	21R39	21 46	23 24
	25	26 32	24 17	22 18	21 30	22 15	24 24
♅	1	0♉55	1♉27	1♉12	0♉19	29♈ 5	28♈ 2
	13	1 13	1R26	0R55	29♈51	28R37	27R44
	25	1 24	1 19	0 32	29R22	28 12	27 33
♆	1	10♍ 3	10♍54	11♍59	13♍ 5	14♍ 0	14♏31
	13	10 20	11 18	12 26	13 28	14 16	14 35
	25	10 40	11 44	12 52	13 49	14 27	14R34
Pl.	1	23♋51	24♋39	25♋25	25♋53	26♋ 2	25♋47
☊	1	11♒58	10♒19	8♒41	7♒ 6	5♒27	3♒52
1st		Sun	Wed	Sat	Mon	Thu	Sat

	d.	JAN	FEB	MAR	APR
☽	1	17♋12	2♍ 2	10♍59	29♎ 6
	3	10♌55	26 51	6♎26	26♏44
	5	4♍59	22♎33	2♏48	24♐51
	7	29 49	19♏26	0♐ 1	23♑ 7
	9	25♎57	17♐39	28 1	21♒18
	11	23♏48	16♑59	26♑38	19♓15
	13	23♐19	16♒48	25♒32	16♈40
	15	23♑43	16♓ 3	24♓ 9	13♉ 9
	17	23♒44	13♈56	21♈46	8♊29
	19	22♓19	10♉ 9	18♉ 0	2♋46
	21	19♈ 6	4♊56	12♊53	26 28
	23	14♉20	28 50	6♋49	20♌15
	25	8♊33	22♋28	0♌28	14♍48
	27	2♋16	16♌23	24 31	10♎41
	29	25 56	...	19♍28	8♏ 4
	31	19♌53	...	15♎36	...

	d.	MAY	JUN	JUL	AUG
☽	1	6♐35	0♒ 3	8♓37	29♈13
	3	5♑29	28 46	6♈26	24♉55
	5	4♒ 5	26♓20	2♉48	19♊25
	7	2♓ 3	22♈50	27 59	13♋14
	9	29 21	18♉25	22♊20	6♌49
	11	25♈58	13♊14	16♋10	0♍30
	13	21♉47	7♋22	9♌45	24 37
	15	16♊43	1♌ 2	3♍25	19♎27
	17	10♋49	24 38	27 33	15♏19
	19	4♌28	18♍40	22♎40	12♐33
	21	28 12	13♎48	19♏18	11♑15
	23	22♍45	10♏36	17♐40	11♒ 5
	25	18♎44	9♐14	17♑31	11♓ 9
	27	16♏28	9♑11	17♒53	10♈21
	29	15♐39	9♒21	17♓36	7♉54
	31	15♑20		15♈47	3♊42

	d.	SEP	OCT	NOV	DEC
☽	1	16♊ 4	18♋19	1♍41	3♎48
	3	10♋ 5	11♌55	26 1	29 24
	5	3♌40	5♍46	21♎28	26♏34
	7	27 22	0♎21	18♏13	25♐ 4
	9	21♍35	25 54	15♐57	24♑12
	11	16♎31	22♏23	14♑10	23♒ 9
	13	12♏17	19♐36	12♒26	21♓25
	15	8♐58	17♑23	10♓33	18♈51
	17	6♑41	15♒38	8♈25	15♉26
	19	5♒23	14♓13	5♉46	11♊10
	21	4♓47	12♈45	2♊17	6♋ 3
	23	4♈ 6	10♉33	27 43	0♌11
	25	2♉26	7♊ 4	22♋ 6	23 51
	27	29 10	2♋10	15♌49	17♍30
	29	24♊18	26 12	9♍28	11♎44
	31	...	19♌42	...	7♏13

STATIONS	☿	♀	♂	♃
	25Feb 20♓25	15Jan 23♒38	None	7Feb 23♎12
	19Mar 6♓20	26Feb 7♒57		11Jun 13♎17
	28Jun 24♋ 0	♄	♅	♆
	22Jul 14♋ 7	9Jun 28♒11	3Jan 23♈28	21May 9♍36
	23Oct 18♏51	27Oct 21♒30	7Aug 1♉27	17Dec 14♍35
	12Nov 2♏57	SIDER. TIME		1 Jan
		6h 39m 50s		Midn.
		18h 41m 48s		Noon
		Common Year		1934

1935 (BST 14 Apr. - 6 Oct)

Noon		JAN	FEB	MAR	APR	MAY	JUN
☉	1	10♑ 9	11♒43	9♓59	10♈50	10♉11	10♊ 4
	9	18 19	19 49	18 0	18 43	17 56	17 43
	17	26 28	27 54	25 58	26 33	25 39	25 22
	25	4♒36	5♓58	3♈55	4♉21	3♊21	3♋ 0
☿	1	10♑59	0♓ 2	18♒48	18♓14	14♉56	1♋50
	7	20 46	3 49	20D15	27 51	27 34	3 59
	13	0♒46	1R32	24 31	8♈21	8♊59	3R26
	19	10 51	25♒ 8	0♓40	19 47	18 34	0 43
	25	20 37	19 59	8 11	2♉ 5	26 3	27♊22
	31	28 56	...	16 43	...	1♋13	...
♀	1	20♑40	29♒31	4♈19	12♉13	17♊56	23♋10
	9	0♒42	9♓30	14 10	21 51	27 13	1♌50
	17	10 44	19 27	23 59	1♊25	6♋23	10 14
	25	20 46	29 22	3♉44	10 53	15 24	18 20
♂	1	9♎55	20♎59	24♎35	17♎58	7♎50	7♎20
	13	14 49	23 29	23R22	13R24	6R11	10 6
	25	18 59	24 36	20 22	9 21	6D25	14 3
♃	1	16♏56	21♏17	23♏11	22♏31	19♏30	15♏43
	13	18 51	22 22	23R17	21R32	17R59	14R36
	25	20 29	23 3	22 56	20 14	16 30	13 49
♄	1	25♒ 3	28♒26	1♓49	5♓23	8♓10	9♓54
	13	26 17	29 52	3 15	6 36	9 0	10 10
	25	27 37	1♓20	4 37	7 41	9 38	10R13
♅	1	27♈30	27♈48	28♈43	0♉15	1♉57	3♉37
	13	27 31	28 7	29 15	0 55	2 37	4 10
	25	27 40	28 33	29 52	1 36	3 16	4 38
♆	1	14♍31	14♍ 1	13♍18	12♍28	11♍57	11♍49
	13	14R23	13R44	12R58	12R13	11R49	11 55
	25	14 10	13 25	12 39	12 0	11D48	12 5
Pl.	1	25♋17	24♋36	24♋ 6	23♋51	23♋58	24♋25
☊	1	2♒13	0♒35	29♑ 6	27♑27	25♑52	24♑13
1st		Tue	Fri	Fri	Mon	Wed	Sat

Noon		JUL	AUG	SEP	OCT	NOV	DEC
☉	1	8♋43	8♌18	8♍ 7	7♎23	8♏ 8	8♐22
	9	16 21	15 58	15 52	15 16	16 10	16 29
	17	23 58	23 39	23 40	23 11	24 13	24 38
	25	1♌37	1♍21	1♎29	1♏ 9	2♐18	2♑47
☿	1	25♊21	28♋51	27♍ 5	1♏39	19♎38	3♐29
	7	25D59	11♌15	6♎ 4	2R42	26 25	12 55
	13	29 38	23 28	14 15	29♎19	5♏ 9	22 21
	19	6♋13	4♍59	21 31	22 22	14 32	1♑50
	25	15 29	15 39	27 32	17 29	24 1	11 25
	31	26 49	25 31	...	18D51	...	21 3
♀	1	24♌ 8	18♍ 6	18♍47	6♍40	22♍45	22♎11
	9	1♍28	21 26	14R 4	8 22	29 50	1♏ 0
	17	8 8	22 46	9 34	12 3	7♎33	10 4
	25	13 57	21R41	6 58	17 16	15 46	19 19
♂	1	16♎24	1♏31	20♏ 6	10♐18	2♑47	25♑36
	13	21 44	8 23	27 58	18 50	11 49	4♒55
	25	27 45	15 41	6♐ 7	27 36	20 59	14 17
♃	1	13♏35	14♏ 4	17♏11	22♏ 4	28♏21	4♐59
	13	13D26	15 0	18 57	24 24	0♐58	7 39
	25	13 43	16 17	20 59	26 51	3 38	10 16
♄	1	10♓ 8	8♓55	6♓44	4♓39	3♓32	4♓ 0
	13	9R50	8R 8	5R50	4R 3	3D32	4 36
	25	9 19	7 16	5 1	3 40	3 47	5 25
♅	1	4♉50	5♉28	5♉20	4♉32	3♉19	2♉12
	13	5 10	5R31	5R 5	4R 5	2R50	1R53
	25	5 24	5 26	4 44	3 36	2 24	1 40
♆	1	12♍12	13♍ 0	14♍ 5	15♍11	16♍ 8	16♍41
	13	12 28	13 24	14 32	15 35	16 25	16 46
	25	12 48	13 50	14 58	15 57	16 37	16R46
Pl.	1	25♋ 8	25♋58	26♋43	27♋14	27♋24	27♋11
☊	1	22♑38	21♑ 0	19♑21	17♑46	16♑ 7	14♑32
1st		Mon	Thu.	Sun	Tue	Fri	Sun

d.		JAN	FEB	MAR	APR
☽	1	20♏35	11♑ 4	19♑29	12♓51
	3	18♐38	11♒ 6	19♒ 8	12♈42
	5	18♑ 6	11♓30	19♓30	11♉45
	7	18♒ 4	11♈ 1	19♈21	9♊10
	9	17♓28	8♉52	17♉36	4♋47
	11	15♈39	5♊ 0	13♊56	29 4
	13	12♉27	29 48	8♋42	22♌44
	15	8♊ 2	23♋47	2♌34	16♍26
	17	2♋44	17♌26	26 8	10♎41
	19	26 48	11♍ 5	19♍54	5♏44
	21	20♌30	5♎ 0	14♎ 9	1♐35
	23	14♍ 7	29 27	9♏ 2	28 11
	25	8♎ 2	24♏46	4♐39	25♑32
	27	2♏45	21♐20	1♑14	23♒39
	29	28 47	...	29 0	22♓28
	31	26♐32	...	28♒ 0	...

d.		MAY	JUN	JUL	AUG
☽	1	21♈30	12♊11	16♋33	1♍26
	3	19♉58	8♋ 7	11♌ 0	25 6
	5	17♊ 6	2♌53	4♍52	18♎56
	7	12♋42	26 50	28 34	13♏23
	9	7♌ 3	20♍32	22♎41	9♐ 2
	11	0♍46	14♎40	17♏47	6♑19
	13	24 34	9♏47	14♐20	5♒20
	15	19♎ 2	6♐12	12♑27	5♓30
	17	14♏31	3♑54	11♒46	5♈39
	19	11♐ 3	2♒26	11♓24	4♉39
	21	8♑26	1♓14	10♈28	1♊59
	23	6♒21	29 48	8♉24	27 46
	25	4♓36	27♈46	5♊ 5	22♋26
	27	2♈58	24♉57	0♋40	16♌28
	29	1♉11	21♊13	25 24	10♍12
	31	28♉46	...	19♌32	3♎53

d.		SEP	OCT	NOV	DEC
☽	1	15♎48	19♏18	7♑21	14♒53
	3	9♏56	14♐22	4♒11	12♓53
	5	4♐51	10♑28	2♓11	11♈25
	7	1♑ 3	8♒ 0	1♈17	10♉ 7
	9	28 57	7♓ 9	0♉56	8♊23
	11	28♒35	7♈23	0♊ 5	5♋37
	13	29♓ 9	7♉31	27 48	1♌31
	15	29♈17	6♊15	23♋49	26 12
	17	27♉50	3♋ 4	18♌26	20♍ 8
	19	24♊26	28 10	12♍17	13♎54
	21	19♋28	22♌14	6♎ 1	8♏ 9
	23	13♌33	15♍54	0♏12	3♐21
	25	7♍14	9♎42	25 9	29 45
	27	0♎57	3♏57	20♐57	27♑14
	29	24 55	28 48	17♑34	25♒26
	31	...	24♐18	...	23♓55

STATIONS

☿	♀	♂	♃
8Feb 3♓52	18Aug 22♍46	27Feb 24♎37	10Mar 23♏18
2Mar 18♒48	30Sep 6♍37	18May 6♎ 3	12Jul 13♐25
9Jun 4♋ 5	♄	♅	♆
3Jul 25♊14	22Jun 10♓13	12Aug 5♉31	24May 11♍48
6Oct 2♏49	8Nov 3♓31	...	20Dec 16♍47
27Oct 17♎14			

SIDER. TIME	1 Jan
6h 38m 52s	Midn.
18h 40m 50s	Noon
Common Year	1935

1936 (BST 19 Apr. – 4 Oct)

Noon		JAN	FEB	MAR	APR	MAY	JUN
☉	1	9♑55	11♒28	10♓45	11♈35	10♉56	10♊48
	9	18 4	19 35	18 45	19 27	18 40	18 27
	17	26 13	27 40	26 44	27 18	26 23	26 5
	25	4♒22	5♓44	4♈40	5♉ 6	4♊ 5	3♋43
☿	1	22♑39	10♒14	14♒17	2♈26	0♊38	9♊19
	7	2♒ 6	3R54	21 51	14 14	7 55	6R27
	13	10 36	1D53	0♓20	26 42	12 27	5D31
	19	16 29	4 2	9 38	9♉15	14 3	7 16
	25	17R 2	8 53	19 42	20 54	12R53	11 40
	31	11 28	...	0♈33	...	9 53	...
♀	1	27♏32	4♑46	10♒13	18♓18	25♈10	3♊12
	9	7 2	14 30	20 2	28 8	4♉59	13 1
	17	16 37	24 17	29 52	7♈58	14 48	22 50
	25	26 16	4♒ 5	9♓42	17 48	24 37	2♋40
♂	1	19♒46	14♓ 0	6♈24	29♈43	21♉34	13♊22
	13	29 10	23 19	15 30	8♉33	0♊ 5	21 36
	25	8♓33	2♈34	24 31	17 15	8 30	29 44
♃	1	11♐46	17♐47	22♐ 1	24♐18	23♐46	20♐43
	13	14 13	19 44	23 13	24R25	22R49	19R12
	25	16 32	21 25	24 2	24 6	21 33	17 43
♄	1	5♓59	9♓ 7	12♓34	16♓18	19♓26	21♓41
	13	7 5	10 30	14 2	17 38	20 27	22 11
	25	8 20	11 58	15 29	18 52	21 17	22 28
♅	1	1♉35	1♉46	2♉38	4♉ 7	5♉49	7♉31
	13	1D33	2 3	3 9	4 47	6 30	8 5
	25	1 39	2 26	3 45	5 29	7 9	8 35
♆	1	16♍44	16♍ 6	15♍32	14♍42	14♍ 8	14♍ 0
	13	16R36	15R59	15R12	14R26	14R 2	14 5
	25	16 25	15 40	14 53	14 13	13D59	14 15
Pl.	1	26♋39	26♋ 9	25♋18	25♋10	25♋16	25♋44
☊	1	12♑54	11♑15	9♑43	8♑ 4	6♑29	4♑51
	1st	Wed	Sat	Sun	Wed	Fri	Mon

Noon		JUL	AUG	SEP	OCT	NOV	DEC
☉	1	9♋27	9♌ 2	8♍51	8♎ 7	8♏53	9♐ 8
	9	17 4	16 41	16 36	16 0	16 55	17 15
	17	24 42	24 22	24 24	23 56	24 58	25 24
	25	2♌20	2♍ 5	2♎14	1♏54	3♐ 3	3♑33
☿	1	18♊31	18♌ 3	5♎37	7♎ 5	28♎26	16♐23
	7	27 39	29 12	11 27	1R56	8♏18	25 43
	13	8♋45	9♍25	15 22	2D26	18 2	4♑59
	19	21 11	18 43	16R23	8 19	27 36	14 3
	25	3♌55	27 8	13 24	17 3	7♐ 2	22 29
	31	16 6	4♎30	...	26 47	...	29 6
♀	1	10♋ 2	18♌11	26♍25	3♏22	11♐23	17♑51
	9	19 52	28 3	6♎17	13 11	21 9	27 28
	17	29 43	7♍55	16 8	23 1	0♑53	7♒ 1
	25	9♌34	17 47	25 59	2♐49	10 36	16 29
♂	1	3♋46	24♋14	14♌11	3♍ 3	22♍ 6	10♎ 0
	13	11 45	2♌ 1	21 47	10 29	29 20	16 57
	25	19 40	9 43	29 19	17 51	6♎28	23 45
♃	1	17♐ 2	14♐45	15♐16	18♐21	23♐33	29♐49
	13	15R52	14D36	16 13	20 9	25 57	2♑31
	25	15 2	14 53	17 33	22 14	28 30	5 16
♄	1	22♓32	21♓52	19♓55	17♓40	16♓ 3	15♓55
	13	22R27	21R13	19R 0	16R54	15R49	16 18
	25	22 8	20 26	18 6	16 19	15D49	16 56
♅	1	8♉48	9♉31	9♉28	8♉44	7♉32	6♉23
	13	9 10	9 35	9R15	8R18	7R 2	6R 2
	25	9 25	9R33	8 55	7 49	6 35	5 47
♆	1	14♍21	15♍ 9	16♍14	17♍20	18♍17	18♍52
	13	14 37	15 33	16 40	17 44	18 34	18 57
	25	14 57	15 58	17 7	18 6	18 47	18R58
Pl.	1	26♋27	27♋17	28♋ 3	28♋35	28♋45	28♋32
☊	1	3♑15	1♑37	29♐58	28♐23	26♐44	25♐ 9
	1st	Wed	Sat	Tue	Thu	Sun	Tue

d.	JAN	FEB	MAR	APR
☽ 1	8♈ 8	0♊46	24♊20	11♌47
3	6♉19	27 18	19♋57	5♍56
5	3♊57	22♋58	14♌41	29 45
7	0♋50	17♌53	8♍53	23♎30
9	26 48	12♍11	2♎46	17♏24
11	21♌49	6♎ 4	26 30	11♐40
13	16♍ 1	29 48	20♏23	6♑40
15	9♎48	23♏53	14♐48	2♒54
17	3♏42	18♐56	10♑22	0♓49
19	28 19	15♑33	7♒39	0♈25
21	24♐14	13♒59	6♓51	0♉53
23	21♑42	13♓52	7♈20	0♊51
25	20♒29	14♈ 4	7♉45	29 13
27	19♓52	13♉21	6♊46	25♋43
29	18♈57	11♊ 4	3♋55	20♌43
31	17♉ 6	...	29 27	...

d.	MAY	JUN	JUL	AUG
☽ 1	14♍48	28♎55	1♐18	17♑53
3	8♎33	23♏ 3	26 28	15♒25
5	2♏21	17♐49	22♑44	14♓ 4
7	26 30	13♑24	20♒ 2	13♈ 5
9	21♐ 8	9♒52	18♓ 5	11♉45
11	16♑31	7♓15	16♈30	9♊41
13	12♒55	5♈29	14♉56	6♋46
15	10♓38	4♉21	13♊ 2	3♌ 4
17	9♈40	3♊18	10♋32	28 34
19	9♉28	1♋40	7♌ 7	23♍17
21	9♊ 1	28 51	2♍40	17♎21
23	7♋19	24♌39	27 14	11♏ 3
25	3♌57	19♍17	21♎ 9	4♐57
27	29 5	13♎13	14 57	29 41
29	23♍14	7♏ 2	9♐15	25♑55
31	17♎ 0	...	4♑39	23♒54

d.	SEP	OCT	NOV	DEC
☽ 1	8♓29	17♈ 2	10♊40	17♋29
3	8♈17	17♉19	9♋21	14♌40
5	7♉54	16♊24	6♌13	10♍12
7	6♊29	13♋47	1♍33	4♎32
9	3♋45	9♌43	25 53	28 18
11	29 53	4♍36	19♎42	21♏59
13	25♌10	28 50	13♏23	16♐ 1
15	19♍48	22♎42	7♐11	10♑39
17	13♎54	16♏22	1♑21	6♒ 3
19	7♏37	10♐ 6	26 12	2♓23
21	1♐17	4♑16	22♒ 8	29 45
23	25 26	29 28	19♓32	28♈ 8
25	20♑43	26♒15	18♈31	27♉18
27	17♒45	24♓57	18♉33	26♊37
29	16♓44	25♈10	18♊35	25♋13
31	...	25♉43	...	22♌29

STATIONS	☿	♀	♂	♃
	23Jan 17♒35	None	None	11Apr 24♐26
	13Feb 1♒53			12Aug 14♐35
		♄	♅	♆
	20May 14♊ 2	4Jul 22♓32	11Jan 11♉33	25May 13♍59
	13Jun 5♊31	19Nov 15♓47	15Aug 9♉36	21Dec 18♍58
	18Sep 16♎28	SIDER TIME		1 Jan
	10Oct 1♎24	6h 37m 55s		Midn.
		18h 39m 53s		Noon
		LEAP YEAR		1936

1937

(BST 18 Apr. – 3 Oct.)

Noon		JAN	FEB	MAR	APR	MAY	JUN
☉	1	10♑41	12♒14	10♓30	11♈21	10♉41	10♊33
	9	18 50	20 21	18 31	19 13	18 26	18 13
	17	26 59	28 26	26 29	27 3	26 9	25 51
	25	5♒ 8	6♓29	4♈26	4♉51	3♊51	3♋29
☿	1	29♑52	17♑36	21♒51	18♈58	24♉24	17♉48
	7	1♒18	22 38	1♓32	0♉52	22R29	22 34
	13	26♑14	29 22	11 53	11 11	19 1	29 26
	19	18R50	7♒10	22 56	18 52	16 7	8♊13
	25	15 29	15 45	4♈41	23 20	15D21	18 47
	31	16D59	...	16 56	24R27	17 14	...
♀	1	24♒39	29♓ 2	24♈38	5♉23	20♈39	28♈ 6
	9	3♓51	7♈ 7	29 58	2R35	19D27	3♉54
	17	12 52	14 40	3♉50	27♈57	20 42	10 33
	25	21 37	21 32	5 44	23 11	23 58	17 50
♂	1	27♎37	13♏45	25♏59	4♐32	3♐45	23♏59
	13	4♏ 6	19 22	0♐ 7	5 32	0R29	20R52
	25	10 18	24 26	3 15	4R48	26♏20	19 33
♃	1	6♑53	13♑52	19♑33	24♑25	27♑ 0	26♑52
	13	9 38	16 25	21 39	25 45	27 19	26R 2
	25	12 20	18 48	23 29	26 41	27R10	24 51
♄	1	17♓23	20♓12	23♓26	27♓14	0♈40	3♈26
	13	18 21	21 32	24 54	28 40	1 52	4 12
	25	19 28	22 56	26 23	0♈ 2	2 54	4 44
♅	1	5♉41	5♉46	6♉32	7♉58	9♉39	11♉23
	13	5R37	6 2	7 2	8 37	10 20	11 58
	25	5D41	6 24	7 36	9 18	11 0	12 30
♆	1	18♍56	18♍29	17♍47	16♍57	16♍22	16♍11
	13	18R49	18R13	17R27	16R40	16R14	16 15
	25	18 38	17 54	17 8	16 27	16 11	16 24
Pl.	1	27♋59	27♋19	26♋47	26♋29	26♋34	27♋ 2
☊	1	23♐31	21♐52	20♐23	18♐45	17♐ 9	15♐31
	1st	Fri	Mon	Mon	Thu	Sat	Tue

Noon		JUL	AUG	SEP	OCT	NOV	DEC
☉	1	9♋12	4♌48	8♍37	7♎53	8♏39	8♐53
	9	16 50	16 28	16 23	15 46	16 41	17 1
	17	24 28	24 9	24 10	23 42	24 44	25 9
	25	2♌ 6	1♍51	1♎59	1♏39	2♐49	3♑18
☿	1	0♋52	0♍58	29♍41	20♍ 9	10♏37	26♐30
	7	13 47	9 39	27R32	28 32	20 11	4♑43
	13	26 34	17 12	22 9	8♎33	29 32	11 38
	19	8♌34	23 24	16 43	18 54	8♐43	15 28
	25	19 31	27 48	15D37	29 6	17 44	13R31
	31	29 25	29 40	...	8♏59	...	6 8
♀	1	23♉37	26♊17	1♌46	7♍42	15♎54	23♏25
	9	1♊39	5♋14	11 13	17 28	25 52	3♐28
	17	10 0	14 21	20 46	27 19	5♏52	13 31
	25	18 36	23 35	0♍25	7♎12	15 53	23 35
♂	1	19♏39	26♏56	12♐ 2	0♑45	22♑29	14♒43
	13	21 13	2♐ 5	19 9	8 57	1♒17	23 46
	25	24 26	8 9	26 47	17 26	10 13	2♓51
♃	1	24♑ 9	20♑16	17♑44	17♑58	21♑ 3	26♑ 8
	13	22R39	19R 1	17R29	18 51	22 53	28 35
	25	21 7	18 5	17D42	20 8	25 0	1♒11
♄	1	4♈56	4♈56	3♈27	1♈13	29♓ 9	28♓21
	13	5 7	4R31	2R36	0R19	28R39	28D28
	25	5R 4	3 54	1 41	29♓32	28 23	28 51
♅	1	12♉44	13♉34	13♉37	12♉58	11♉48	10♉37
	13	13 8	13 41	13R26	12R33	11R18	10R14
	25	13 26	13R40	13 9	12 5	10 50	9 57
♆	1	16♍30	17♍16	18♍19	19♍26	20♍25	21♍ 1
	13	16 45	17 39	18 46	19 50	20 42	21 8
	25	17 3	18 4	19 13	20 13	20 56	21R 9
Pl.	1	27♋44	28♋35	29♋22	29♋54	0♌ 6	29♋55
☊	1	13♐56	12♐17	10♐39	9♐ 3	7♐25	5♐49
	1st	Thu	Sun	Wed	Fri	Mon	Wed

	d.	JAN	FEB	MAR	APR
☽	1	5♍31	20♎27	28♎19	12♐ 1
	3	0♎33	14♏14	22♏ 4	5♑54
	5	24 35	7♐57	15♐45	0♒43
	7	18♏15	2♑17	10♑ 4	27 9
	9	12♐10	27 49	5♒42	25♓26
	11	6♑50	24♒43	3♓ 1	25♈11
	13	2♒30	22♓46	1♈50	25♉18
	15	29 10	21♈19	1♉17	24♊37
	17	26♓38	19♉48	0♊25	22♋34
	19	24♈38	17♊51	28 36	19♌ 8
	21	22♉58	15♋24	25♋47	14♍36
	23	21♊22	12♌22	22♌ 5	9♎15
	25	19♋32	8♍37	17♍37	3♏19
	27	16♌58	3♎55	12♎25	27 1
	29	13♍16	...	6♏33	20♐37
	31	8♎19	...	0♐14	...

	d.	MAY	JUN	JUL	AUG
☽	1	14♑34	1♓39	8♈39	1♊30
	3	9♒22	28 38	6♉48	0♋16
	5	5♓39	27♈11	5♊59	29 3
	7	3♈44	27♉ 0	5♋37	27♌12
	9	3♉27	27 11	4♌48	24♍ 4
	11	3♊50	26♋35	2♍41	19♎29
	13	3♋40	24♌25	28 54	13♏43
	15	2♌ 2	20♍31	23♎40	7♐23
	17	28 45	15♎15	17♏32	1♑12
	19	24♍ 4	9♏ 8	11♐10	25 45
	21	18♎24	2♐45	5♑ 7	21♒28
	23	12♏12	26 31	29 50	18♓19
	25	5♐49	20♑47	25♒27	16♈ 1
	27	29 33	15♒46	21♓58	14♉ 7
	29	23♑44	11♓40	19♈17	12♊20
	31	18♒43	...	17♉16	10♋32

	d.	SEP	OCT	NOV	DEC
☽	1	24♋33	1♍57	19♎53	23♏ 3
	3	22♌17	28 7	14♏13	16♐41
	5	19♍13	23♎22	8♐ 0	10♑17
	7	15♎ 0	17♏43	1♑33	4♒11
	9	9♏38	11♐27	25 19	28 46
	11	3♐27	5♑ 3	19♒52	24♓30
	13	27 6	29 10	15♓48	21♈49
	15	21♑16	24♒30	13♈31	20♉49
	17	16♒36	21♓29	12♉54	21♊ 4
	19	13♓25	20♈ 6	13♊10	21♋26
	21	11♈32	19♉41	13♋ 8	20♌40
	23	10♉20	19♊14	11♌49	18♍ 6
	25	9♊ 5	17♋58	8♍53	13♎46
	27	7♋22	15♌32	4♎31	8♏ 9
	29	5♌ 0	11♍59	29 7	1♐52
	31	...	7♎27	...	25 26

STATIONS

☿	♀	♂	♃
6Jan 1♒30	28Mar 5♉49	15Apr 5♐32	16May 27♑19
26Jan 15♑27	9May 19♈27	27Jun 19♏32	14Sep 17♑29
30Apr 24♉27			
24May 15♉18			
2Sep 29♍35			
24Sep 15♍24			
21Dec 15♑34			

♄	♅	♆
17Jul 5♈ 8	14Jan 5♉37	29May 16♍11
2Dec 28♓21	19Aug 13♉41	24Dec 21♍ 9

SIDER. TIME	1 Jan
6h 40m 55s	Midn.
18h 42m 53s	Noon
Common Year	1937

1938 (BST 10 Apr. – 2 Oct)

Noon		JAN	FEB	MAR	APR	MAY	JUN
☉	1	10♑26	11♒59	10♓15	11♈ 6	10♉27	10♊20
	9	18 35	20 6	18 16	18 59	18 12	17 59
	17	26 44	28 11	26 15	26 49	25 55	25 37
	25	4♒52	6♓14	4♈11	4♉37	3♊37	3♋15
☿	1	4♑50	20♑ 0	4♓15	29♈56	25♈45	18♉57
	7	29♐45	28 28	15 22	4♉41	25D22	29 4
	13	0♑15	7♒30	27 2	5R25	27 43	10♊38
	19	4D35	17 3	8♈53	2 46	2♉26	23 21
	25	11 1	27 10	19 56	28♈43	9 5	6♋28
	31	18 38	...	28 47	...	17 25	...
♀	1	2♑23	11♒21	16♓26	24♈58	1♊52	9♋27
	9	12 27	21 24	26 25	4♉52	11 37	19 3
	17	22 31	1♓25	6♈22	14 42	21 21	28 36
	25	2♒34	11 20	10 18	24 32	1♋ 1	8♌ 4
♂	1	8♓ 9	1♈29	22♈ 9	14♉26	5♊20	26♊18
	13	17 13	10 24	0♉51	22 52	13 31	4♋17
	25	26 15	19 14	9 27	1♊12	21 37	12 10
♃	1	2♒46	10♒ 2	16♒35	23♒13	28♒22	1♓37
	13	5 32	12 52	19 16	25 28	29 55	2 9
	25	8 22	15 40	21 48	27 28	1♓ 6	2R14
♄	1	29♓11	1♈32	4♈33	8♈22	12♈ 1	15♈13
	13	29 56	2 45	6 0	9 52	13 21	16 12
	25	0♈53	4 5	7 30	11 19	14 34	17 0
♅	1	9♉50	9♉48	10♉29	11♉50	13♉30	15♉15
	13	9R43	10 1	10 57	12 29	14 12	15 52
	25	9D44	10 21	11 29	13 10	14 53	16 26
♆	1	21♍ 8	20♍44	20♍ 3	19♍12	18♍35	18♍22
	13	21R 2	20R28	19R43	18R55	18R26	18 25
	25	20 51	20 9	19 23	18 41	18 22	18 33
Pl.	1	29♋23	28♋43	28♋10	27♋52	27♋58	28♋27
☊	1	4♐11	2♐32	1♐ 4	29♏25	27♏50	26♏11
	1st	Sat	Tue	Tue	Fri	Sun	Wed

Noon		JUL	AUG	SEP	OCT	NOV	DEC
☉	1	8♋59	8♌34	8♍23	7♎39	8♏25	8♐39
	9	16 36	16 14	16 8	15 32	16 26	16 46
	17	24 14	23 55	23 56	23 27	24 29	24 54
	25	1♌52	1♍37	1♎45	1♏25	2♐34	3♑ 3
☿	1	19♋ 5	5♍46	0♍59	0♎36	21♏53	28♐59
	7	0♌41	10 14	29 0	11 20	0♐46	29R 4
	13	11 5	12 16	2♍ 8	21 40	9 19	22 59
	19	20 18	11R12	9 42	1♏35	17 20	15 36
	25	28 17	7 0	19D46	11 8	24 18	13D33
	31	4♍50	1 42	...	20 22	...	16 42
♀	1	15♌ 9	20♍52	24♎23	21♏54	4♐52	21♏21
	9	24 30	29 48	2♏24	27 30	3R 0	19R36
	17	3♍46	8♎33	10 0	1♐49	28♏56	20D26
	25	12 57	17 7	17 4	4 25	24 12	23 31
♂	1	16♋ 6	6♌10	25♌59	15♍ 0	4♎34	23♎27
	13	23 54	13 52	3♍36	22 35	12 8	0♏58
	25	1♌40	21 31	11 12	0♎10	19 41	8 27
♃	1	2♓ 6	29♒44	25♒48	22♒ 5	22♒41	25♒24
	13	1R30	28R16	24R25	22R27	23 27	27 9
	25	0 29	26 42	23 19	23D28	24 39	29 13
♄	1	17♈19	18♈ 3	17♈10	15♈ 9	12♈48	11♈23
	13	17 47	17R53	16R28	14R12	12R 5	11R14
	25	18 1	17 30	15 37	13 18	11 34	11D20
♅	1	16♉41	17♉36	17♉47	17♉14	16♉ 6	14♉54
	13	17 7	17 46	17R39	16R50	15R36	14R29
	25	17 28	17R49	17 23	16 23	15 7	14 10
♆	1	18♍38	19♍22	20♍25	21♍31	22♍32	23♍10
	13	18 53	19 45	20 52	21 56	22 50	23 18
	25	19 11	20 10	21 18	22 20	23 4	23 20
Pl.	1	29♋10	0♌ 1	0♌49	1♌21	1♌32	1♌20
☊	1	24♏36	22♏57	21♏19	19♏44	18♏ 5	16♏30
	1st	Fri	Mon	Thu	Sat	Tue	Thu

d.	JAN	FEB	MAR	APR
☽ 1	7♑16	22♒40	1♓29	20♈16
3	1♒15	18♓ 8	27 38	18♉25
5	25 47	14♈21	24♈36	16♊53
7	21♓ 5	11♉23	22♉ 8	15♋17
9	17♈26	9♊21	20♊ 8	13♌22
11	15♉ 7	8♋15	18♋29	10♍55
13	14♊12	7♌37	16♌59	7♎42
15	14♋14	6♍35	15♍ 5	3♏31
17	14♌ 9	4♎14	12♎12	28 19
19	12♍47	0♏12	7♏58	22♐20
21	9♎34	24 44	2♐30	16♑ 1
23	4♏38	18♐28	26 18	9♒58
25	28 36	12♑ 7	20♑ 1	4♓49
27	22♐ 9	6♒20	14♒20	1♈ 3
29	15♑54	...	9♓46	28 48
31	10♒13	...	6♈29	...

d.	MAY	JUN	JUL	AUG
☽ 1	27♉43	21♋18	29♌46	19♎51
3	27♊ 3	20♌24	27♍41	15♏15
5	26♋ 1	18♍ 3	23♎48	9♐28
7	24♌ 7	14♎14	18♏34	3♑10
9	21♍10	9♏16	12♐33	26 53
11	17♎12	3♐32	6♑14	20♒58
13	12♏19	27 22	29 57	15♓35
15	6♐42	21♑ 2	23♒58	10♈50
17	0♑34	14♒52	18♓29	6♉56
19	24 15	9♓11	13♈50	4♊ 8
21	18♒12	4♈29	10♉24	2♋38
23	12♓58	1♉15	8♊33	2♌13
25	9♈ 7	29 45	8♋12	2♍ 2
27	6♉57	29♊43	8♌35	0♎55
29	6♊17	0♌ 9	8♍23	28 7
31	6♋21	...	6♎31	23♏37

d.	SEP	OCT	NOV	DEC
☽ 1	5♐51	7♑46	21♒20	23♓42
3	29 45	1♒31	15♓54	19♈23
5	23♑27	25 40	11♈40	16♉43
7	17♒30	20♓41	8♉49	15♊40
9	12♓12	16♈45	7♊ 8	15♋31
11	7♈41	13♉47	6♋ 3	15♌11
13	3♉56	11♊32	4♌53	13♍44
15	0♊55	9♋43	3♍ 7	10♎53
17	28 44	8♌ 5	0♎32	6♏48
19	27♋20	6♍22	27 3	1♐47
21	26♌22	4♎10	22♏42	26 10
23	25♍ 7	1♏ 6	17♐32	20♑ 7
25	22♎47	26 54	11♑41	13♒50
27	18♏59	21♐38	5♒27	7♓37
29	13♐48	15♑36	29 15	1♈56
31	...	9♒21	...	27 23

STATIONS

☿	♀	♂	♃
10Jan 29♐23	31Oct 4♐55	None	22Jun 2♓15
12Apr 5♉34	11Dec 19♏34		19Oct 22♒24
6May 25♈14	♄	♅	♆
15Aug 12♑17	31Jul 18♈ 3	18Jan 9♉43	30May 18♍22
7Sep 29♌ 0	15Dec 11♈14	24Aug 17♉49	26Dec 23♍20
5Dec 29♐43	SIDER. TIME 6h 39m 57s		1 Jan Midn.
24Dec 13♐28	18h 41m 55s Common Year		Noon 1938

1939 (BST 16 Apr. - 19 Nov)

Noon	JAN	FEB	MAR	APR	MAY	JUN
☉ 1	10♑11	11♒44	10♓ 1	10♈52	10♉13	10♊ 6
9	18 20	19 51	18 1	18 45	17 58	17 45
17	26 29	27 56	26 0	26 35	25 41	25 24
25	4♒38	6♓ 0	3♈57	4♉23	3♊23	3♋ 2
☿ 1	17♐34	29♑39	19♓ 7	14♈ 8	13♈27	2♊56
7	23 55	9♒22	0♈13	9R23	20·11	15 59
13	1♑34	29 35	9 43	6 9	28 24	29 3
19	9 56	0♓18	15 54	5D54	7♉56	11♋16
25	18 47	11 30	17R32	8 31	18 46	22 14
31	28 2	...	14 52	...	0♊49	...
♀ 1	27♍38	24♐55	25♑23	1♓21	7♈ 4	14♉22
9	3♐31	3♑18	4♒31	10 49	16 40	24 3
17	10 22	11 59	13 46	20 20	26 17	3♊44
25	17 55	20 52	23 7	29 53	5♉56	13 27
♂ 1	12♏49	1♐53	18♐38	6♑ 9	21♑ 4	2♒ 2
13	20 14	9 8	25 35	12 27	26 2	4 10
25	27 37	16 17	2♑20	18 19	0♒ 9	4R40
♃ 1	0♓32	7♓11	13♓50	21♓16	27♓58	3♈44
13	2 58	10 0	16 44	24 2	0♈23	5 30
25	5 36	12 52	19 37	26 42	2 34	6 56
♄ 1	11♈31	13♈18	16♈ 1	19♈43	23♈29	27♈ 3
13	12 1	14 22	17 23	21 14	24 56	28 13
25	12 46	15 35	18 51	22 45	26 18	29 15
♅ 1	14♉ 1	13♉53	14♉27	15♉45	17♉23	19♉ 9
13	13R52	14 3	14 53	16 22	18 4	19 48
25	13D50	14 20	15 24	17 2	18 46	20 23
♆ 1	23♍19	22♍57	22♍18	21♍27	20♍48	20♍33
13	23R14	22R42	21R58	21R 9	20R39	20D35
25	23 5	22 24	21 38	20 54	20 34	20 42
Pl. 1	0♌50	0♌ 9	29♋37	29♋18	29♋21	29♋46
☊ 1	14♏51	13♏13	11♏44	10♏ 5	8♏30	6♏52
1st	Sun	Wed	Wed	Sat	Mon	Thu

Noon	JUL	AUG	SEP	OCT	NOV	DEC
☉ 1	8♋45	8♌20	8♍ 9	7♎24	8♏10	8♐23
9	16 23	16 0	15 54	15 18	16 11	16 31
17	24 1	23 41	23 42	23 13	24 14	24 39
25	1♌39	1♍23	1♎31	1♏10	2♐19	2♑48
☿ 1	1♌51	23♋17	20♌50	14♎17	0♐16	1♐55
7	10 4	19R38	0♍32	24 8	7 11	27♏47
13	16 43	14 58	11 41	3♏31	12 18	29D47
19	21 31	12 14	23 0	12 29	13R52	5♐53
25	24 0	13D37	3♎55	21 1	9 46	13 6
31	23R38	19 29	...	29 0	...	21 28
♀ 1	20♊45	28♋40	6♍58	14♎17	22♏58	0♑23
9	0♋30	8♌31	16 54	24 15	2♐57	10 21
17	10 16	18 23	26 51	4♏14	12 56	20 18
25	20 5	28 17	6♎48	14 13	22 54	0♒15
♂ 1	4♒14	27♈ 7	24♑25	2♒57	18♒55	7♓37
13	2R 9	24R40	26 41	8 32	26 9	15 31
25	28♑59	23D56	0♒32	12 55	3♓44	23 35
♃ 1	7♈31	8♈47	7♈ 0	3♈16	29♓48	28♓57
13	8 22	8R26	5R38	1R44	29R 6	29 28
25	8 46	7 39	4 4	0 24	28D52	0♈27
♄ 1	29♈41	1♉ 8	0♉58	29♈23	26♈59	25♈ 3
13	0♉26	1 16	0R29	28R29	26R 6	24R36
25	0 56	1R 9	29♈47	27 32	25 21	24 25
♅ 1	20♉38	21♉40	21♉58	21♉30	20♉26	19♉13
13	21 7	21 52	21R52	21R 8	19R56	18R47
25	21 30	21 58	21 39	20 43	19 27	18 25
♆ 1	20♍47	21♍29	22♍31	23♍37	24♍38	25♍19
13	21 0	21 51	22 57	24 2	24 58	25 27
25	21 17	22 16	23 24	24 26	25 13	25 31
Pl. 1	0♌28	1♌19	2♌ 7	2♌43	2♌56	2♌47
☊ 1	5♏16	3♏38	1♏59	0♏24	28♎45	27♎10
1st	Sat	Tue	Fri	Sun	Wed	Fri

d.	JAN	FEB	MAR	APR
☽ 1	10♉42	1♋37	10♋41	4♍30
3	8♊48	1♌51	10♌18	3♎44
5	8♋38	2♍30	10♍31	2♏ 6
7	9♌13	2♎ 6	10♎ 3	29 2
9	9♍ 7	29 48	7♏57	24♐28
11	7♎22	25♏38	4♐ 2	18♑47
13	3♏49	20♐10	28 42	12♒35
15	28 54	14♑ 2	22♑35	6♓28
17	23♐ 9	7♒43	16♒18	0♈55
19	17♑ 1	1♓34	10♓17	26 15
21	10♒45	25 44	4♈49	22♉34
23	4♓33	20♈24	0♉ 1	19♊46
25	28 38	15♉51	26 0	17♋41
27	23♈23	12♊31	22♊55	16♌ 4
29	19♉21	...	20♋54	14♍36
31	17♊ 3	...	19♌50	...

d.	MAY	JUN	JUL	AUG
☽ 1	12♎53	2♐34	6♑44	21♒45
3	10♏27	28 0	1♒ 3	15♓27
5	6♐58	22♑37	24 55	9♈18
7	2♑18	16♒36	18♓38	3♉44
9	26 40	10♓22	12♈42	29 24
11	20♒30	4♈30	7♉44	26♊49
13	14♓25	29 37	4♊23	26♋ 8
15	8♈58	26♉15	2♋53	26♌37
17	4♉40	24♊29	2♌50	26♍53
19	1♊40	23♋51	3♍ 2	25♎45
21	29 47	23♌22	2♎17	22♏50
23	28♋28	22♍ 7	29 58	18♐23
25	27♌ 8	19♎43	26♏11	12♑54
27	25♍19	16♏13	21♐21	6♒53
29	22♎48	11♐50	15♑49	0♓38
31	19♏31	...	9♒51	24 24

d.	SEP	OCT	NOV	DEC
☽ 1	6♈22	10♉ 7	29♊ 3	7♌20
3	0♉37	5♊35	26♋30	5♍41
5	25 41	2♋ 6	24♌41	3♎53
7	22♊ 4	29 54	23♍22	1♏46
9	20♋ 9	28♋55	22♎ 8	29 8
11	19♌48	28♍36	20♏24	25♐44
13	20♍10	28♎ 1	17♐36	21♑20
15	19♎58	26♏15	13♑28	15♒55
17	18♏12	22♐52	8♒ 6	9♓46
19	14♐40	18♑ 1	1♓59	3♈27
21	9♑40	12♒ 9	25 43	27 40
23	5♒47	5♓53	19♈57	23♉ 4
25	27 32	29 46	15♉11	20♊ 3
27	21♓19	24♈13	11♊38	18♋27
29	15♈27	19♉28	9♋10	17♌35
31	...	15♊38	...	16♍32

STATIONS	☿	♀	♂	♃
	25Mar 17♈32	None	23Jun 4♒42	30Jul 8♈48
	17Apr 5♈38		24Aug 23♑55	25Nov 28♓52
	28Jul 24♌12	♄	♅	♆
	21Aug 12♌11	14Aug 1♉16	22Dec 13♉50	2Jun 20♍33
	19Nov 13♐52	28Dec 24♈25	29Aug 21♉58	28Dec 25♍31
	8Dec 27♐44	SIDER. TIME 6h 39m 0s 18h 40m 58s Common Year		1 Jan Midn. Noon 1939

1940 (BST 25 Feb. onwards)

Noon		JAN	FEB	MAR	APR	MAY	JUN
☉	1	9♑56	11♒29	10♓46	11♈37	10♉57	10♊49
	9	18 5	19 36	18 47	19 29	18 42	18 29
	17	26 14	27 41	26 45	27 19	26 25	26 7
	25	4♒23	5♓45	4♈42	5♉ 7	4♊ 6	3♋45
☿	1	22♐54	12♒ 1	28♓32	17♓21	20♈35	23♎21
	7	1♑46	22 37	0♈ 8	20 31	1♉ 9	4♋40
	13	10 55	3♓30	26♓44	25 51	12 49	14 28
	19	20 22	14 10	21R14	2♈51	25 28	22 38
	25	0♒ 8	23 23	17 28	11 8	8♊36	29 2
	31	10 17	...	17D 6	...	21 20	...
♀	1	8♒56	17♓ 1	21♈40	26♉33	25♊44	13♋ 1
	9	18 49	26 42	0♉57	4♊57	2♋ 3	12R58
	17	28 41	6♈18	10 3	12 58	7 19	10 26
	25	8♓29	15 48	18 58	20 30	11 10	5 56
♂	1	28♓18	19♈25	9♉ 5	29♉49	19♊33	9♋36
	13	6♈28	27 35	17 9	7♊45	27 21	17 18
	25	14 39	5♉42	25 10	15 38	5♋ 6	24 57
♃	1	1♈13	6♈ 3	12♈ 5	19♈20	26♈33	3♉36
	13	2 50	8 25	14 50	22 14	29 22	6 6
	25	4 47	10 58	17 40	25 7	2♉ 4	8 24
♄	1	24♈26	25♈33	27♈57	1♉27	5♉15	9♉ 3
	13	24 40	26 25	29 13	2 57	6 45	10 22
	25	25 9	27 28	0♉36	4 29	8 13	11 35
♅	1	18♉15	18♉ 0	18♉30	19♉44	21♉20	23♉ 8
	13	18R 3	18 7	18 54	20 20	22 2	23 47
	25	17 59	18 22	19 24	21 0	22 44	24 23
♆	1	25♍31	25♍11	24♍31	23♍40	23♍ 0	22♍44
	13	25R27	24R56	24R 1	23R22	22R50	22D45
	25	25 18	24 39	23 51	23 7	22 45	22 51
Pl.	1	2♌14	1♌34	0♌59	0♌39	1♌ 6	1♌50
☊	1	25♎32	23♎53	22♎21	20♎42	19♎ 7	17♎29
1st		Mon	Thu	Fri	Mon	Wed	Sat

Noon		JUL	AUG	SEP	OCT	NOV	DEC
☉	1	9♋28	9♌ 3	8♍53	8♎ 9	8♏55	9♐10
	9	17 6	16 43	16 38	16 2	16 57	17 17
	17	24 44	24 24	24 26	23 58	25 0	25 25
	25	2♌22	2♍ 7	2♎15	1♏55	3♐ 5	3♑34
☿	1	3♌23	24♋39	5♍59	27♎ 7	28♏ 6	19♏20
	7	5 16	26D25	17 27	5♏35	24R56	27 9
	13	4R22	2♌ 5	28 18	13 23	17 26	5♐47
	19	1 5	11 5	8♎29	20 16	12 18	14 47
	25	27♋ 3	22 13	18 5	25 35	13D35	23 58
	31	24 43	4♍ 1	...	28 6	...	3♑18
♀	1	2♋15	0♋11	23♋ 4	24♌ 0	29♍44	6♏ 7
	9	28♊24	4 35	0♌47	2♍58	9♎19	15 59
	17	26R48	10 12	8 56	12 7	19 0	25 54
	25	27D41	16 45	17 26	21 27	28 45	5♐50
♂	1	28♋46	18♌28	8♍11	27♍22	17♎26	7♏ 7
	13	6♌24	26 6	15 50	5♎ 6	25 16	15 5
	25	14 2	3♍43	23 31	12 53	3♏ 9	23 5
♃	1	9♉28	13♉50	15♉40	14♉29	10♉50	7♉ 9
	13	11 24	14 53	15R33	13R16	9R13	6R12
	25	13 2	15 31	14 57	11 46	7 46	5 44
♄	1	12♉ 7	14♉12	14♉45	13♉44	11♉29	9♉14
	13	13 5	14 37	14R31	12R57	10R32	8R33
	25	13 51	14 47	14 3	12 3	9 38	8 6
♅	1	24♉40	25♉46	26♉ 9	25♉46	24♉45	23♉31
	13	25 10	26 0	26R 5	25R26	24R15	23R 4
	25	25 34	26 8	25 54	25 1	23 45	22 41
♆	1	22♍56	23♍37	24♍38	25♍44	26♍47	27♍28
	13	23 9	23 59	25 5	26 10	27 6	27 37
	25	23 26	24 23	25 31	26 34	27 22	27 42
Pl.	1	2♌40	3♌55	4♌ 0	4♌ 4	4♌19	4♌12
☊	1	15♎53	14♎15	12♎36	11♎ 1	9♎23	7♎47
1st		Mon	Thu	Sun	Tue	Fri	Sun

d.		JAN	FEB	MAR	APR
☽	1	0♎45	22♏30	15♐31	2♒26
	3	28 31	18♐37	10♑59	26 27
	5	25♍28	13♑52	5♒30	20♓ 5
	7	21♐41	8♒27	29 27	13♈44
	9	17♑11	2♓30	23♓ 7	7♉44
	11	11♒54	26 10	16♈44	2♊19
	13	5♓56	19♈46	10♉39	27 48
	15	29 33	13♉50	5♊17	24♋26
	17	23♈19	9♊ 0	1♋ 8	22♌26
	19	17♉57	5♋54	28 40	21♍42
	21	14♊ 7	4♌44	27♌55	21♎35
	23	12♋ 9	4♍58	28♍14	21♏ 7
	25	11♌43	5♎21	28♎25	19♐23
	27	11♍44	4♏38	27♏22	15♑57
	29	11♎ 1	2♐18	24♐33	10♒58
	31	9♏ 0	...	20♑ 7	...

d.		MAY	JUN	JUL	AUG
☽	1	4♓59	18♈37	20♉57	8♋11
	3	28 36	12♉52	16♊34	6♌23
	5	22♈22	8♊ 6	13♋35	5♍37
	7	16♉43	4♋27	11♌42	4♎58
	9	11♊52	1♌43	10♍18	3♏41
	11	7♋56	29 36	8♎48	1♐26
	13	4♌55	27♍48	6♏55	28 13
	15	2♍46	26♎ 9	4♐31	24♑ 7
	17	1♎24	24♏25	1♑30	19♒12
	19	0♏29	22♐12	27 40	13♓31
	21	29 24	19♑ 3	22♒51	7♈16
	23	27♐24	14♒39	17♓ 7	0♉51
	25	23♑58	9♓ 6	10♈48	24 48
	27	19♒ 4	2♈51	4♉31	19♊46
	29	13♓ 6	26 34	28 55	16♋19
	31	6♈45	...	24♊41	14♌40

d.		SEP	OCT	NOV	DEC
☽	1	29♌25	7♎45	1♐ 1	7♑44
	3	29♍26	8♏ 0	29 47	4♒50
	5	29♎13	7♐13	26♑44	0♓13
	7	27♏54	4♑46	21♒59	24 21
	9	25♐10	0♒40	16♓ 6	17♈57
	11	21♑ 8	25 20	9♈42	11♉42
	13	16♒ 5	19♓15	3♉22	6♊ 7
	15	10♓19	12♈52	27 27	1♋26
	17	4♈ 5	6♉31	22♊11	27 38
	19	27 40	0♊31	17♋41	24♌33
	21	21♉25	25 8	14♌ 3	22♍ 5
	23	15♊49	20♋43	11♍27	20♎12
	25	11♋24	17♌39	9♎59	18♏50
	27	8♌37	16♍ 6	9♏25	17♐35
	29	7♍35	15♎52	9♐ 1	15♑44
	31	...	16♏ 6	...	12♒37

STATIONS

☿	♀	♂	♃
6Mar 0♈15	5Jun 13♋ 1	None	5Sep 15♉41
29Mar 16♓51	19Jul 26♊48		31Dec 5♉41
9Jul 5♌16	♄	♅	♆
2Aug 24♋40	28Aug 14♉47	27Jan 17♉59	3Jun 22♍44
1Nov 28♏ 6	... ...	1Sep 26♉ 9	30Dec 27♍42
21Nov 12♏ 3	SIDER. TIME 6h 38m 2s / 18h 40m 0s LEAP YEAR		1 Jan Midn. Noon 1940

(BST throughout, but-) 1941 (DST 4 May - 10 Aug.)

Noon		JAN	FEB	MAR	APR	MAY	JUN
☉	1	10♑42	12♒16	10♓31	11♈22	10♉43	10♊35
	9	18 52	20 22	18 32	19 15	18 28	18 14
	17	27 0	28 27	26 30	27 5	26 10	25 53
	25	5♒ 9	6♓30	4♈27	4♉53	3♊52	3♋31
☿	1	4♑52	26♒41	4♓23	14♓37	5♉14	3♋39
	7	14 26	5♓53	29♒48	22 45	18 4	10 1
	13	24 15	12 8	29D 3	1♈55	1♊ 0	14 8
	19	4♒21	13R 5	1♓40	12 2	13 6	15 40
	25	14 41	8 36	6 41	23 9	23 39	14R32
	31	25 0	...	13 22	...	2♋23	...
♀	1	14♐33	23♑15	28♒13	6♈47	13♉55	22♊ 3
	9	24 32	3♒15	8♓11	16 43	23 47	1♋51
	17	4♑31	13 14	18 9	26 37	3♊37	11 39
	25	14 30	23 14	28 6	6♉30	13 27	21 26
♂	1	27♏47	18♐45	7♑55	29♑19	20♒ 0	10♓51
	13	5♐51	26 56	16 11	7♒37	28 10	18 36
	25	13 59	5♑10	24 29	15 53	6♓14	26 2
♃	1	5♉41	7♉26	11♉20	17♉21	24♉ 7	1♊25
	13	6 0	8 53	13 30	19 59	26 56	4 12
	25	6 46	10 40	15 53	22 43	29 46	6 54
♄	1	7♉57	8♉23	10♉12	13♉21	17♉ 4	21♉ 1
	13	7D54	9 1	11 18	14 48	18 36	22 28
	25	8 8	9 52	12 34	16 18	20 8	23 50
♅	1	22♉30	22♉ 9	23♉33	23♉42	25♉16	27♉ 4
	13	22R16	22 14	22 55	24 17	25 58	27 44
	25	22 10	22 27	23 23	24 56	26 40	28 21
♆	1	27♍42	27♍23	26♍45	25♍55	25♍14	24♍55
	13	27R38	27R 9	26R26	25R36	25R 3	24 56
	25	27 30	26 52	26 6	25 21	24 57	25 1
Pl.	1	3♌41	3♌ 0	2♌26	2♌ 4	2♌ 5	2♌30
☊	1	6♎ 9	4♎30	3♎ 1	1♎23	29♍47	28♍ 9
	1st	Wed	Sat	Sat	Tue	Thu	Sun

Noon		JUL	AUG	SEP	OCT	NOV	DEC
☉	1	9♋14	8♌50	8♍39	7♎55	8♏41	8♐55
	9	16 52	16 29	16 24	15 48	16 42	17 2
	17	24 30	24 10	24 11	23 43	24 45	25 10
	25	2♌ 8	1♍53	2♎ 1	1♏41	2♐50	3♑19
☿	1	11♋24	21♋41	20♍50	3♏26	27♎36	27♏40
	7	7R 8	2♌24	0♎49	8 52	26D52	7♐ 0
	13	8 18	14 26	10 6	11 56	1♏45	16 23
	19	7D38	26 37	18 42	11R 4	9 32	25 48
	25	12 18	8♍14	26 33	5 21	18 25	5♑20
	31	20 6	19 6	...	28♎23	...	15 0
♀	1	28♋46	6♍28	13♎46	19♏12	24♐35	25♑52
	9	6♌ 5	16 8	23 17	28 30	3♑20	3♒ 8
	17	18 16	25 47	2♏46	7♐41	11 50	9 39
	25	27 59	5♎23	12 11	16 46	20 1	15 6
♂	1	29♓35	15♈24	23♈32	19♈37	11♈36	13♈50
	13	6♈18	19 46	23R24	15R54	11D 8	17 24
	25	12 19	22 40	21 15	12 43	12 32	22 1
♃	1	8♊13	14♊25	19♊ 5	21♊19	20♊37	17♊21
	13	10 45	16 27	20 17	21R26	19R33	15R44
	25	13 8	18 12	21 5	21 3	18 9	14 10
♄	1	24♉28	27♉ 9	28♉28	28♉10	26♉21	23♉58
	13	25 38	27 51	28R33	27R37	25R25	23R 6
	25	26 39	28 19	28 21	26 52	24 26	22 23
♅	1	28♉39	29♉51	0♊21	0♊ 5	29♉ 8	27♉54
	13	29 11	0♊ 8	0R20	29R47	28R39	27R26
	25	29 38	0 18	0 10	29 23	28 9	27 1
♆	1	25♍ 5	25♍44	26♍44	27♍50	28♍53	29♍37
	13	25 17	26 5	27 10	28 16	29 13	29 47
	25	25 33	26 29	27 37	28 40	29 30	29 52
Pl.	1	3♌12	4♌ 3	4♌52	5♌29	5♌47	5♌40
☊	1	26♍34	24♍55	23♍17	21♍41	20♍ 3	18♍28
	1st	Tue	Fri	Mon	Wed	Sat	Mon

	d.	JAN	FEB	MAR	APR
☽	1	25♒29	9♈57	17♈59	1♊56
	3	20♓13	3♉36	11♉36	26 3
	5	14♈ 2	27 24	5♊24	21♋ 6
	7	7♉40	22♊ 3	29 58	17♌38
	9	1♊49	18♋ 4	25♋54	15♍55
	11	27 0	15♌35	23♌32	15♎44
	13	23♋25	14♍12	22♍39	16♏ 8
	15	20♌51	13♎14	22♎31	15♐53
	17	18♍51	12♏ 0	22♏ 5	14♑ 5
	19	17♎ 2	10♐ 5	20♐34	10♒33
	21	15♏13	7♑22	17♑42	5♓35
	23	13♐14	3♒47	13♒34	29 43
	25	10♑51	29 19	8♓28	23♈25
	27	7♒40	24♓ 0	2♈40	17♉ 3
	29	3♓23	...	26 27	10♊52
	31	27 59	...	20♉ 4	...

	d.	MAY	JUN	JUL	AUG
☽	1	5♋ 9	23♌ 2	0♎25	23♏34
	3	0♌14	19♍58	28 29	22♐ 7
	5	26 33	18♎17	27♏26	20♑25
	7	24♍28	17♏51	26♐45	17♒54
	9	23♎59	17♐55	25♑33	14♓ 8
	11	24♏24	17♑15	23♒ 1	9♈ 8
	13	24♐28	14♒57	18♓51	3♉13
	15	23♑ 2	10♓48	13♈22	26 57
	17	19♒39	5♈16	7♉ 9	20♊59
	19	14♓39	29 0	0♊55	15♋53
	21	8♈38	22♉40	25 13	11♌59
	23	2♉15	16♊45	20♋25	9♍18
	25	25 56	11♋31	16♌34	7♎29
	27	20♊ 1	7♌ 2	13♍33	6♏ 5
	29	14♋39	3♍18	11♎12	4♐36
	31	10♌ 0	...	9♏21	2♑44

	d.	SEP	OCT	NOV	DEC
☽	1	16♑34	23♒24	10♈19	13♉12
	3	13♒38	18♓49	4♉19	6♊56
	5	9♓46	13♈28	28 5	0♋49
	7	4♈55	7♉33	21♊50	25 2
	9	29 14	1♊18	15♋50	19♌50
	11	23♉ 2	25 4	10♌29	15♍36
	13	16♊50	19♋21	6♍21	12♎49
	15	11♋12	14♌43	3♎56	11♏44
	17	6♌44	11♍41	3♏21	11♐57
	19	3♍46	10♎26	3♐55	12♑17
	21	2♎15	10♏27	4♑14	11♒22
	23	1♏36	10♐37	3♒ 3	8♓32
	25	0♐58	9♑45	29 55	3♈56
	27	29 34	7♒16	25♓10	28 9
	29	27♑ 3	3♓16	19♈25	21♉53
	31	...	28 9	...	15♊38

STATIONS	☿	♀	♂	♃
	17Feb 13♓27	None	7Sep 23♈43	10Oct 21♊27
	12Mar 28♒55		10Nov 11♈ 5	... ...
	20Jun 15♋39	♄	♅	♆
	14Jul 6♋18	9Jan 7♉54	30Jan 22♉ 9	1Jun 24♍55
	15Oct 12♏10	12Sep 28♉33	6Sep 0♊21	... ...
	5Nov 26♎22	SIDER. TIME 6h 41m 1s 18h 42m 59s Common Year		1 Jan Midn. Noon 1941

(BST throughout, but–) 1942 (DST 5 Apr. – 9 Aug)

Noon		JAN	FEB	MAR	APR	MAY	JUN
☉	1	10♑27	12♒ 0	10♓17	11♈ 8	10♉28	10♊21
	9	18 36	20 7	18 17	19 0	18 13	18 0
	17	26 46	28 12	26 16	26 50	25 57	25 39
	25	4♒54	6♓16	4♈12	4♉39	3♊38	3♋17
☿	1	16♑38	27♒ 0	14♒ 2	23♓25	22♉58	25♊37
	7	26 29	23R22	18 57	4♈ 0	4♊ 4	24R 2
	13	6♒21	16 33	25 34	15 28	13 10	20 52
	19	15 45	12 9	3♓23	27 45	19 56	17 59
	25	23 25	12D 6	12 8	10♉32	24 10	17D 3
	31	26 59	...	21 44	...	25 38	...
♀	1	18♒41	14♒ 1	6♒16	25♒28	25♓ 4	29♈25
	9	20 56	9R17	9 11	2♓46	3♈42	8♉35
	17	20R46	6 12	13 47	10 34	12 31	17 50
	25	18 1	5D37	19 37	18 45	21 29	27 10
♂	1	25♈ 4	10♉44	26♉35	15♊ 0	2♋12	22♋12
	13	0♉47	17 24	3♊39	22 15	10 32	29 35
	25	6 58	24 16	10 48	29 33	17 54	7♌ 1
♃	1	13♊22	11♊25	12♊21	16♊ 1	21♊23	28♊ 0
	13	12R16	11D30	13 29	17 59	23 51	0♋42
	25	11 35	12 4	14 59	20 12	26 27	3 26
♄	1	22♉ 4	21♉43	22♉54	25♉36	29♉ 5	3♊ 4
	13	21R43	22 3	23 48	26 55	0♊36	4 36
	25	21D38	22 39	24 53	28 21	2 10	6 4
♅	1	26♉49	26♉21	26♉39	27♉42	29♉13	1♊ 1
	13	26R32	26D24	26 58	28 16	29 55	1 42
	25	26 23	26 34	27 24	28 54	0♊37	2 21
♆	1	29♍53	29♍37	29♍ 0	28♍10	27♍28	27♍ 6
	13	29R50	29R23	28R41	27R51	27R16	27D 6
	25	29 43	29 6	28 21	27 35	27 9	27 10
Pl.	1	5♌10	4♌29	3♌54	3♌31	3♌31	3♌54
☊	1	16♍49	15♍11	13♍42	12♍ 3	10♍28	8♍49
	1st	Thu	Sun	Sun	Wed	Fri	Mon

Noon		JUL	AUG	SEP	OCT	NOV	DEC
☉	1	9♋ 0	8♌36	8♍25	7♎40	8♏26	8♐40
	9	16 38	16 16	16 10	15 34	16 27	16 47
	17	24 16	23 57	23 58	23 29	24 31	24 55
	25	1♌54	1♍39	1♎47	1♏27	2♐35	3♑ 4
☿	1	18♊53	6♌59	1♎38	25♎32	21♎33	8♐55
	7	23 34	19 17	9 36	21R13	0♏41	18 20
	13	0♋56	0♍48	16 33	14 20	10 17	27 45
	19	10 42	11 27	22 5	10 37	19 55	7♑13
	25	22 21	21 15	25 28	13D 9	29 27	16 41
	31	4♌53	0♎13	...	20 9	...	25 53
♀	1	4♊12	11♋ 6	18♌48	25♍55	4♏41	12♐22
	9	13 38	20 45	28 39	5♎53	14 43	22 25
	17	23 8	0♌28	8♍32	15 53	24 46	2♑29
	25	2♋42	10 13	18 27	25 54	4♐49	12 32
♂	1	10♌45	0♍ 6	19♍46	9♎10	29♎43	20♏ 8
	13	18 12	7 40	27 28	17 4	7♏49	28 28
	25	25 43	15 18	5♎15	25 2	16 1	6♐54
♃	1	4♋48	11♋42	17♋53	22♋30	25♋ 2	24♋39
	13	7 32	14 13	19 56	23 48	25R14	23R42
	25	10 11	16 35	21 43	24 42	24 58	22 23
♄	1	6♊47	9♊59	12♊ 1	12♊29	11♊19	9♊ 4
	13	8 7	10 56	12 24	12R13	10R29	8R 5
	25	9 20	11 41	12R31	11 43	9 33	7 12
♅	1	2♊39	3♊56	4♊33	4♊24	3♊32	2♊19
	13	3 13	4 16	4R35	4R 8	3R 4	1R49
	25	3 42	4 29	4 29	3 46	2 34	1 23
♆	1	27♍14	27♍51	28♍50	29♍56	1♎ 0	1♎45
	13	27 25	28 12	29 16	0♎22	1 21	1 56
	25	27 41	28 35	29 42	0 46	1 38	2 2
Pl.	1	4♌35	5♌30	6♌17	6♌55	7♌14	7♌ 8
☊	1	7♍14	3♍36	3♍57	2♍22	0♍43	29♌ 8
	1st	Wed	Sat	Tue	Thu	Sun	Tue

d.	JAN	FEB	MAR	APR
☽ 1	27♊38	13♌22	21♌45	10♎50
3	22♋ 0	9♍18	18♍22	9♏48
5	16♌55	6♎ 2	16♎ 1	9♐ 6
7	12♍32	3♏31	14♏18	7♑54
9	9♎ 5	1♐43	12♐47	5♒45
11	6♏49	0♑25	11♑ 5	2♓34
13	5♐48	29 8	8♒55	28 30
15	5♑31	27♒14	6♓ 4	23♈40
17	4♒55	24♓ 9	2♈19	18♉10
19	3♓ 1	19♈43	27 36	12♊ 8
21	29 24	14♉11	22♉ 1	5♋51
23	24♈18	8♊ 1	15♊52	29 49
25	18♉17	1♋52	9♋41	24♌38
27	12♊ 0	26 19	4♌ 6	20♍56
29	6♋ 2	...	29 40	19♎ 2
31	0♌43	...	26♍44	...

d.	MAY	JUN	JUL	AUG
☽ 1	18♏40	12♑46	20♒42	9♈56
3	18♐47	11♒58	18♓22	5♉17
5	18♑12	9♓22	14♈18	29 33
7	16♒11	5♈10	8♉56	23♊20
9	12♓42	29 52	2♊53	17♋ 8
11	8♈ 6	23♉56	26 37	11♌20
13	2♉44	17♊44	20♋26	6♍13
15	26 53	11♋27	14♌34	1♎54
17	20♊42	5♌20	9♍17	28 31
19	14♋25	29 43	4♎52	26♏ 8
21	8♌22	25♍ 3	1♏42	24♐42
23	3♍ 5	21♎55	0♐ 1	23♑51
25	29 14	20♏36	29 36	22♒54
27	27♎15	20♐46	29♑37	21♓ 5
29	27♏ 3	21♑15	28♒55	17♈56
31	27♐38	...	26♓42	13♉21

d.	SEP	OCT	NOV	DEC
☽ 1	25♉37	27♊30	11♌ 3	13♍36
3	19♊37	21♋14	5♍33	9♎22
5	13♋22	15♌22	1♎28	7♏ 3
7	7♌28	10♍31	29 8	6♐32
9	2♍22	7♎ 1	28♏17	6♑54
11	28 18	4♏51	27♐58	6♒47
13	25♎15	3♐30	27♑ 8	5♓15
15	23♏ 0	2♑15	25♒11	2♈ 9
17	21♐14	0♒34	22♓ 4	27 46
19	19♑40	28 15	18♈ 2	22♉31
21	18♒ 0	25♓14	13♉15	16♊41
23	15♓50	21♈30	7♊50	10♋30
25	12♈50	16♉56	1♋51	4♌ 8
27	8♉44	11♊32	25 30	27 55
29	3♊31	5♋26	19♌13	22♍18
31	...	29 6	...	17♎54

STATIONS	☿	♀	♂	♃
	2Feb 26♒49	13Jan 21♒11	None	5Feb 11♊23
	23Feb 11♒40	23Feb 5♒31		13Nov 25♋14
	1Jun 25♊37			
	25Jun 17♊ 3			
	29Sep 25♎58			
	20Oct 10♎37			

	♄	♅	♆
	23Jan 21♉38	4Feb 26♉21	2Jan 29♍53
	25Sep 12♊31	10Sep 4♊35	8Jun 27♍ 6

SIDER. TIME	1 Jan
6h 40M 3s	Midn.
18h 42m 1s	Noon
Common Year	1942

(BST throughout, but-) 1943 (DST 4 Apr.– 15 Aug.)

Noon		JAN	FEB	MAR	APR	MAY	JUN
☉	1	10♑12	11♒45	10♓ 2	10♈53	10♉14	10♊ 7
	9	18 22	19 52	18 3	18 46	17 59	17 47
	17	26 31	27 57	26 1	26 36	25 42	25 25
	25	4♒39	6♓ 1	3♈58	4♉24	3♊24	3♋ 3
☿	1	27♑22	26♑ 3	15♒48	7♈55	0♊48	27♉28
	7	5♒21	25D 8	24 22	20 13	4 47	27D14
	13	10 20	28 9	3♓39	2♉40	5R40	29 40
	19	9R34	3♒36	13 39	14 14	3 48	4♊36
	25	3 3	10 34	24 24	23 50	0 30	11 48
	31	26♑42	...	5♈56	...	27♉45	...
♀	1	21♑20	0♓10	4♈57	12♉49	18♊27	23♋31
	9	1♒22	10 9	14 48	22 26	27 43	2♌ 8
	17	11 24	20 6	24 36	1♊59	6♋51	10 27
	25	21 25	0♈ 0	4♉21	11 26	15 49	18 26
♂	1	11♐51	4♑ 9	24♑46	17♒59	10♓37	3♈47
	13	20 25	12 56	3 43	27 2	19 38	12 35
	25	29 4	21 48	12 43	6♓ 6	28 36	21 14
♃	1	21♋39	17♋30	15♋21	15♋50	18♋56	24♋ 4
	13	19R54	16R19	15D11	16 48	20 44	26 24
	25	18 20	15 31	15 28	18 9	22 46	28 52
♄	1	6♊44	5♊37	6♊ 5	8♊11	11♊20	15♊13
	13	6R 7	5D38	6 44	9 20	12 47	16 46
	25	5 43	5 56	7 35	10 38	14 18	18 19
♅	1	1♊10	0♊36	0♊46	1♊44	3♊12	5♊ 0
	13	0R51	0D35	1 4	2 16	3 53	5 41
	25	0 39	0 43	1 28	2 53	4 35	6 21
♆	1	2♎ 4	1♎50	1♎15	0♎24	29♍41	29♍18
	13	2R 2	1R37	0R56	0R 6	29R29	29D17
	25	1 56	1 21	0 36	29♍49	29 21	29 20
Pl.	1	6♌40	6♌ 0	5♌23	4♌59	4♌58	5♌21
☊	1	27♌29	25♌51	24♌22	22♌43	21♌ 8	19♌28
1st		Fri	Mon	Mon	Thu	Sat	Tue

Noon		JUL	AUG	SEP	OCT	NOV	DEC
☉	1	8♋46	8♌22	8♍11	7♎26	8♏12	8♐25
	9	16 24	16 2	15 56	15 19	16 13	16 33
	17	24 2	23 42	23 43	23 14	24 16	24 41
	25	1♌40	1♍25	1♎33	1♏12	2♐21	2♑49
☿	1	21♊ 4	23♌ 9	5♎ 4	25♍ 8	2♏32	20♐ 1
	7	2♋13	3♍26	8 40	25D52	12 23	29 9
	13	14 42	12 46	9R18	1♎55	22 1	8♑ 1
	19	27 33	21 7	6 5	10 51	1♐28	16 12
	25	9♌54	28 22	29♍54	20 48	10 48	22 34
	31	21 20	4♎15	...	0♏52	...	24R48
♀	1	24♌ 9	17♍ 3	15♍15	4♍41	22♍29	22♎26
	9	1♍18	19 50	10R24	7 1	29 45	1♏20
	17	7 45	20R29	6 19	11 11	7♎37	10 27
	25	13 15	18 40	4 25	16 45	15 57	19 45
♂	1	25♈29	16♈25	4♊38	17♊38	22♊ 6	14♊24
	13	3♉49	23 52	10 33	20 45	20R18	9R55
	25	11 52	0♊51	15 33	22 11	16 39	6 31
♃	1	0♌ 8	6♌56	13♌40	19♌34	24♌19	26♌49
	13	2 44	9 34	16 7	21 37	25 37	27 4
	25	5 23	12 11	18 28	23 24	26 31	26R51
♄	1	19♊ 4	22♊40	25♊20	26♊34	26♊10	24♊19
	13	20 32	23 50	26 0	26R37	25R33	23R21
	25	21 55	24 50	26 27	26 24	24 46	22 22
♅	1	6♊40	8♊ 2	8♊46	8♊44	7♊57	6♊45
	13	7 16	8 25	8 51	8R30	7R30	6R15
	25	7 46	8 40	8R48	8 11	7 0	5 48
♆	1	29♍24	29♍58	0♎56	2♎ 1	3♎ 6	3♎54
	13	29 34	0♎18	1 21	2 28	3 28	4 5
	25	29 48	0 41	1 48	2 53	3 46	4 13
Pl.	1	6♌ 3	6♌53	7♌44	8♌23	8♌43	8♌39
☊	1	17♌54	16♌16	14♌37	13♌ 2	11♌23	9♌48
1st		Thu	Sun	Wed	Fri	Mon	Wed

d.	JAN	FEB	MAR	APR
☽ 1	1♏20	23♐ 5	2♑48	26♒10
3	29 40	22♑58	1♒52	24♓34
5	29♐38	23♒ 6	1♓17	22♈19
7	0♒12	22♓21	0♈11	18♉56
9	29 58	19♈57	27 50	14♊14
11	28♓ 7	15♉50	23♉54	8♋27
13	24♈30	10♊25	18♊35	2♌ 8
15	19♉32	4♋14	12♋26	25 58
17	13♊42	27 52	6♌ 5	20♍37
19	7♋27	21♌46	0♍ 9	16♎31
21	1♌ 7	16♍12	25 2	13♏43
23	24 58	11♎23	20♎56	11♐50
25	19♍15	7♏29	17♏47	10♑17
27	14♎21	4♐36	15♐22	8♒37
29	10♏41	...	13♑28	6♓37
31	8♐33	...	11♒54	...

d.	MAY	JUN	JUL	AUG
☽ 1	4♈11	23♉25	27♊23	11♌55
3	1♉ 8	18♊25	21♋18	5♍34
5	27 12	12♋40	14♌54	29 34
7	22♊14	6♌22	8♍32	24♎21
9	16♋22	29 58	2♎42	20♏21
11	10♌ 1	24♍ 8	28 0	17♐56
13	3♍50	19♎30	24♏58	17♑ 6
15	28 33	16♏37	23♐45	17♒18
17	24♎44	15♐27	23♑49	17♓25
19	22♏31	15♑19	24♒ 5	16♈22
21	21♐28	15♒ 5	23♓25	13♉34
23	20♑42	13♓53	21♈11	9♊ 6
25	19♒27	11♈22	17♉22	3♋26
27	17♓21	7♉37	12♊19	27 9
29	14♈23	2♊53	6♋27	20♌43
31	10♉36	...	0♌ 8	14♍34

d.	SEP	OCT	NOV	DEC
☽ 1	26♍40	1♏ 2	21♐ 0	29♑24
3	21♎24	27 12	18♑49	27♒53
5	17♏ 0	24♐11	16♒54	25♓57
7	13♐42	21♑57	15♓10	23♈30
9	11♑41	20♒30	13♈24	20♉23
11	10♒53	19♓34	11♉10	16♊25
13	10♓44	18♈31	7♊57	11♋29
15	10♈16	16♉30	3♋27	5♌40
17	8♉30	12♉58	27 47	29 20
19	5♊ 0	7♋56	21♌28	23♍27
21	29 55	1♌52	15♍11	17♎27
23	23♋49	25 28	9♎39	13♏12
25	17♌24	19♍27	5♏24	10♐38
27	11♍14	14♎18	2♐33	9♑30
29	5♎43	10♏17	0♑46	9♒ 2
31	...	7♐15	...	8♓18

STATIONS	☿	♀	♂	♃
	16Jan 10♒48	16Aug 20♍32	28Oct 22♊14	12Mar 13♋10
	6Feb 24♑58	27Sep 4♍21	... ...	14Dec 27♌ 4
	13May 5♊40	♄	♅	♆
	5Jun 27♉ 1	8Feb 5♊36	8Feb 0♊34	5Jan 2♎ 4
	12Sep 9♎27	10Oct 26♊38	15Sep 8♊51	11Jun 29♍17
	4Oct 24♍44	SIDER. TIME		1 Jan
	31Dec 24♑48	6h 39m 6s Midn	18h 41m 4s Noon	Common Year 1943

(BST throughout, but–) 1944 (DST 2 Apr. – 17 Sept.)

Noon		JAN	FEB	MAR	APR	MAY	JUN
☉	1	9♑58	11♒31	10♓48	11♈38	10♉59	10♊51
	9	18 7	19 38	18 48	19 30	18 43	18 30
	17	26 16	27 43	26 47	27 21	26 26	26 8
	25	4♒24	5♓46	4♈43	5♉ 9	4♊ 8	3♋47
☿	1	24♑33	16♑26	27♒17	26♈ 5	12♉55	16♉33
	7	19R19	23 21	7♓39	5♉54	9R14	24 3
	13	11 50	1♒15	18 41	12 46	6 59	3♊18
	19	8 40	9 53	0♈22	16 6	7D18	14 11
	25	10D28	19 8	12 28	15R52	10 15	26 28
	31	15 25	...	24 14	...	15 29	...
♀	1	27♏59	5♑19	10♒49	18♓56	25♈49	3♊52
	9	7♐31	15 5	20 39	28 46	5♉38	13 41
	17	17 8	24 52	0♓29	8♈37	15 27	23 30
	25	26 49	4♒41	10 20	18 27	25 16	3♋20
♂	1	5♊22	7♊43	17♊33	2♋ 4	18♋ 5	5♌45
	13	4D56	11 10	22 50	8 18	24 49	12 48
	25	6 15	15 31	28 33	14 46	1♌41	19 57
♃	1	26♌30	23♌26	19♌43	17♌15	17♌33	20♌31
	13	25R35	21R52	18R28	17D 2	18 25	22 15
	25	24 18	20 19	17 34	17 16	19 39	24 12
♄	1	21♊49	20♊ 1	19♊47	21♊12	23♊55	27♊35
	13	20R58	19R44	20 8	22 9	25 16	29 7
	25	20 18	19D42	20 44	23 17	26 42	0♋41
♅	1	5♊33	4♊53	4♊58	5♊51	7♊16	9♊ 3
	13	5R12	4D50	5 13	6 22	7 57	9 45
	25	4 58	4 54	5 35	6 57	8 38	10 26
♆	1	4♎14	4♎ 3	3♎28	2♎38	1♎54	1♎30
	13	4R14	3R51	3R 9	2R19	1R42	1D28
	25	4 9	3 36	2 50	2 2	1 33	1 31
Pl.	1	8♌12	7♌31	6♌53	6♌28	6♌26	6♌47
☊	1	8♌10	6♌31	4♌59	3♌20	1♌45	0♌ 7
	1st	Sat	Tue	Wed	Sat	Mon	Thu

Noon		JUL	AUG	SEP	OCT	NOV	DEC
☉	1	9♋30	9♌ 5	8♍54	8♎11	8♏57	9♐11
	9	17 7	16 45	16 40	16 4	16 58	17 19
	17	24 45	24 26	24 27	23 59	25 2	25 27
	25	2♌23	2♍ 8	2♎17	1♏57	3♐ 7	3♑36
☿	1	9♋29	♍49	19♍12	23♍48	16 11	29♐50
	7	22 17	12 1	13R37	4♎10	25 29	6♑ 7
	13	4♌14	17 43	9 7	14 43	4♐35	8 58
	19	15 6	21 26	9D20	25 1	13 27	5R46
	25	24 51	22R25	14 51	4♏59	21 59	27♐59
	31	3♍29	19 57	...	14 36	...	22 59
♀	1	10♋42	18♌52	27♍ 4	4♏ 0	11♐59	12♑23
	9	20 32	28 43	6♎55	13 49	21 43	27 59
	17	0♌23	8♍35	16 47	23 37	1♑27	7♒30
	25	10 14	18 27	26 37	3♐25	11 9	10 55
♂	1	23♌34	12♍35	2♎15	21♎56	13♏ 1	4♐11
	13	0♍51	20 7	10 3	0♏ 0	21 24	12 51
	25	8 14	27 45	17 57	8 12	29 53	21 38
♃	1	25♌16	1♍21	7♍59	14♍24	20♍24	24♍53
	13	27 31	3 53	10 35	16 50	22 23	26 8
	25	29 54	6 28	13 9	19 8	24 7	27 0
♄	1	1♋28	5♋18	8♋27	10♋21	10♋43	9♋25
	13	3 0	6 38	9 23	10 42	10R22	8R34
	25	4 28	7 50	10 5	10R47	9 48	7 36
♅	1	10♊45	12♊11	13♊ 1	13♊14	12♊21	11♊11
	13	11 22	12 36	13 8	12R53	11R55	10R41
	25	11 55	12 54	13R 7	12 34	11 26	10 12
♆	1	1♎34	2♎ 7	3♎ 4	4♎ 9	5♎15	6♎ 3
	13	1 44	2 27	3 29	4 36	5 37	6 15
	25	1 57	2 49	3 56	5 1	5 55	6 23
Pl.	1	7♌38	8♌19	9♌13	9♌53	10♌13	10♌ 9
☊	1	28♋31	26♋53	25♋14	23♋39	22♋ 1	20♋25
	1st	Sat	Tue	Fri	Sun	Wed	Fri

☽ d.	JAN	FEB	MAR	APR
1	22♓37	14♉ 1	6♊30	22♋33
3	20♈26	9♊57	1♋44	16♌21
5	17♉ 9	4♋45	25 53	9♍56
7	12♊54	28 51	19♌32	3♎50
9	7♋48	22♌33	13♍ 9	28 21
11	2♌ 1	16♍11	7♎ 3	23♏34
13	25 45	10♎ 2	1♏26	19♐32
15	19♍21	4♏26	26 32	16♑21
17	13♎19	29 51	22♐36	14♒12
19	8♏12	26♐47	20♑ 0	13♓ 4
21	4♐35	25♑25	18♒52	12♈34
23	2♑45	25♒28	18♓51	11♉47
25	2♒25	25♓55	18♈57	9♊44
27	2♓39	25♈28	17♉55	5♋58
29	2♈17	23♉17	15♊ 2	0♌42
31	0♉31	...	10♋23	...

☽ d.	MAY	JUN	JUL	AUG
1	24♌33	8♎13	10♏51	28♐27
3	18♍13	2♏52	6♐50	26♑51
5	12♎18	28 39	4♑16	26♒31
7	7♏12	25♐36	2♒53	26♓28
9	3♐ 2	23♑25	2♓ 2	25♈40
11	29 42	21♒44	1♈ 1	23♉29
13	27♑ 1	20♓ 9	29 16	19♊52
15	24♒57	18♈25	26♉33	15♋ 6
17	23♓24	16♉15	22♊51	9♌32
19	22♈ 6	13♊20	18♋13	3♍28
21	20♓29	9♋24	12♌47	27 10
23	17♉52	4♌24	6♍45	20♎54
25	13♋53	28 32	0♎26	15♏ 4
27	8♌35	22♍15	24 18	10♐ 9
29	2♍29	16♎ 9	18♏56	6♑41
31	26 12	...	14♐52	5♒ 0

☽ d.	SEP	OCT	NOV	DEC
1	19♒48	28♓27	21♉50	28♊ 8
3	20♓10	28♈54	20♊19	24♋43
5	20♈28	28♉14	16♋57	19♌50
7	19♉28	25♊39	11♌57	13♍57
9	16♊38	21♋15	5♍57	7♎41
11	12♋11	15♌35	29 38	1♏40
13	6♌37	9♍20	23♎32	26 24
15	0♍29	3♎ 1	18♏ 1	22♐ 7
17	24 11	26 57	13♐11	18♑48
19	17♎56	21♏20	9♑ 5	16♒15
21	11♏59	16♐16	5♒45	14♓16
23	6♐36	12♑ 2	3♓19	12♈36
25	2♑14	8♒57	1♈50	10♉59
27	29 19	7♓18	1♉ 0	9♊ 2
29	28♒10	6♈56	0♊ 3	6♋19
31	...	7♉ 1	...	2♌30

STATIONS	☿	♀	♂	♃
	20Jan 8♑40	None	10Jan 4♊51	13Apr 17♌ 2
	22Apr 16♉24		...	...
	16May 6♉48		...	...
	24Aug 22♍28			
	16Sep 8♍31			
	14Dec 8♑54			

	♄	♅	♆
	21Feb 19♊41	13Feb 4♊50	7Jan 4♎15
	23Oct 10♋47	19Sep 13♊ 8	13Jun 1♎28

SIDER. TIME	1 Jan
6h 38m 8s	Midn.
18h 40m 6s	Noon
LEAP YEAR	1944

(BST throughout, but –) 1945 (DST, 2 Apr. – 15 July)

Noon		JAN	FEB	MAR	APR	MAY	JUN
☉	1	10♑44	12♒17	10♓33	11♈24	10♉44	10♊36
	9	18 53	20 23	18 33	19 16	18 29	18 16
	17	27 2	28 29	26 32	27 6	26 12	25 55
	25	5♒10	6♓32	4♈29	4♉54	3♊54	3♋32
☿	1	22♐45	24♑ 9	11♓ 7	27♈41	17♈37	24♉25
	7	24D18	3♒17	22 39	27R 4	20 56	6♊11
	13	29 21	12 53	4♈16	23 22	26 25	19 0
	19	6♑14	23 0	14 55	19 12	3♉39	2♋ 9
	25	14 8	3♓41	23 4	16 58	12 24	14 43
	31	22 40	...	27 23	...	22 35	...
♀	1	25♒ 3	29♓ 9	24♈ 3	2♉34	17♈46	27♈29
	9	4♓13	7♈ 6	29 0	29♈ 5	17D20	3♉34
	17	13 9	14 29	2♉21	24R13	19 14	10 26
	25	21 50	21 6	3R35	19 48	23 1	17 52
♂	1	26♐48	20♑ 8	11♒39	5♓43	28♓58	22♈33
	13	5♑45	29 18	20 57	15 3	8♈10	1♉30
	25	14 48	8♒33	0♓17	24 20	17 17	10 17
♃	1	27♍19	26♍50	24♍ 6	20♍12	17♍48	18♍ 0
	13	27R30	25R53	22R34	18R58	17R32	18 49
	25	27 13	24 35	21 2	18 5	17D42	20 0
♄	1	7♋ 2	4♋47	3♋51	4♋29	6♋37	9♋55
	13	6R 4	4R13	3D53	5 11	7 47	11 23
	25	5 12	3 54	4 11	6 5	9 6	12 55
♅	1	9♊57	9♊12	9♊11	9♊57	11♊19	13♊ 4
	13	9R35	9R 6	9 24	10 26	11 58	13 47
	25	9 18	9D 9	9 43	11 0	12 40	14 28
♆	1	6♎25	6♎16	5♎43	4♎53	4♎ 9	3♎42
	13	6R26	6R 4	5R25	4R34	3R55	3R39
	25	6 21	5 49	5 5	4 17	3 46	3D41
Pl.	1	9♌42	9♌ 1	8♌49	8♌25	7♌56	8♌17
☊	1	18♋47	17♋ 8	15♋39	14♋ 1	12♋26	10♋47
1st		Mon	Thu	Thu	Sun	Tue	Fri

Noon		JUL	AUG	SEP	OCT	NOV	DEC
☉	1	9♋16	8♌51	8♍40	7♎56	8♏42	8♐57
	9	16 53	16 31	16 26	15 50	16 44	17 4
	17	24 31	24 12	24 13	23 45	24 47	25 12
	25	2♌ 9	1♍54	2♎ 3	1♏43	2♐52	3♑21
☿	1	26♋12	3♍39	22♌17	7♎12	26♏32	21♐44
	7	6♌27	4R47	26 32	17 38	4♐51	14R51
	13	15 24	2 47	4♍49	27 35	12 34	8 6
	19	23 1	28♋11	15 16	7♏ 6	19 0	7D15
	25	29 4	23 29	26 20	16 16	22 50	11 18
	31	3♍12	22D 4	...	35 5	...	17 53
♀	1	23♉44	26♊42	2♌18	8♍18	16♎32	24♏ 5
	9	1♊53	5♋42	11 47	18 6	26 31	4♐ 8
	17	10 18	14 50	21 21	27 57	6♏31	14 11
	25	18 58	24 6	1♍ 1	7♎51	16 33	24 15
♂	1	14♉37	6♊13	26♊10	13♋10	26♋49	3♌ 9
	13	23 8	14 10	3♋18	19 3	0♌25	2R43
	25	1♊28	21 50	10 0	24 13	2 39	0 19
♃	1	20♍43	25♍29	1♎29	7♎53	14♎29	20♎16
	13	22 22	27 42	4 1	10 28	16 55	22 16
	25	24 16	0♎ 3	6 35	13 2	19 12	24 0
♄	1	13♋41	17♋40	21♋13	23♋44	24♋53	24♋20
	13	15 15	19 7	22 21	24 22	24R51	23R41
	25	16 47	20 29	23 19	24 46	24 34	22 51
♅	1	14♊48	16♊19	17♊15	17♊25	16♊49	15♊41
	13	15 27	16 46	17 25	17R17	16R25	15R11
	25	16 1	17 6	17R27	17 1	15 56	14 41
♆	1	3♎44	4♎15	5♎10	6♎15	7♎21	8♎11
	13	3 52	4 34	5 35	6 42	7 44	8 25
	25	4 6	4 56	6 2	7 7	8 3	8 33
Pl.	1	8♌57	9♌50	10♌43	11♌23	11♌45	11♌43
☊	1	9♋12	7♋33	5♋55	4♋19	2♋41	1♋ 6
1st		Sun	Wed	Sat	Mon	Thu	Sat

	d.	JAN	FEB	MAR	APR
☽	1	15♌ 9	29♍37	7♎58	22♏26
	3	9♍42	23♎23	1♏43	16♐38
	5	3♎36	17♏18	25 36	11♑42
	7	27 24	11♐59	20♐ 9	8♒12
	9	21♏43	8♑ 3	16♑ 1	6♓34
	11	17♐ 6	5♒48	13♒42	6♈35
	13	13♑50	5♓ 1	13♓12	7♉13
	15	11♒49	4♈50	13♈39	6♊59
	17	10♓33	4♉10	13♉41	4♋58
	19	9♓22	2♊17	12♊13	1♌ 8
	21	7♉44	29 4	9♋ 1	25 56
	23	5♊22	24♋46	4♌24	19♍58
	25	2♋ 9	19♌41	28 54	13♎44
	27	28 7	14♍ 2	22♍55	7♏31
	29	23♌15	...	16♎43	1♐33
	31	17♍39	...	10♏29	...

	d.	MAY	JUN	JUL	AUG
☽	1	26♐ 2	14♒33	22♓41	16♉17
	3	21♑17	11♓11	21♈ 1	14♊18
	5	17♒44	10♈17	19♉40	11♋41
	7	15♓46	9♉35	18♊11	8♌18
	9	15♈16	9♊ 0	16♋ 3	4♍ 1
	11	15♉30	7♋36	12♌51	28 49
	13	15♊12	4♌48	8♍25	22♎52
	15	13♋21	0♍28	2♎55	16♏36
	17	9♌43	24 57	26 48	10♐37
	19	4♍37	18♎49	20♏38	5♑34
	21	28 39	12♏38	15♐ 3	1♒58
	23	22♎24	6♐55	10♑30	29 57
	25	16♏17	2♑ 0	7♒12	29♓ 5
	27	10♐37	28 0	5♓ 2	28♈27
	29	5♑34	24♒56	3♈30	27♉12
	31	1♒19	...	2♉ 5	24♊55

	d.	SEP	OCT	NOV	DEC
☽	1	8♋24	14♌32	0♎56	3♏35
	3	4♌41	9♍31	24 49	27 17
	5	0♍12	3♎53	18♏30	21♐13
	7	25 1	27 49	12♐14	15♑39
	9	19♎11	21♏29	6♑16	10♒49
	11	12♏56	15♐11	1♒ 4	7♓ 2
	13	6♐38	9♑25	27 9	4♈32
	15	0♑56	4♒50	24♓57	3♉22
	17	26 30	2♓ 1	24♈27	3♊ 5
	19	23♒52	1♈ 9	24♉54	2♋47
	21	23♓ 2	1♉36	24♊58	1♌27
	23	23♈10	1♊59	23♋35	28 31
	25	23♉ 0	1♋ 4	20♌23	23♍58
	27	21♊35	28 24	15♍38	18♎15
	29	18♋41	24♌10	9♎51	11♏58
	31	...	18♍51	...	5♐42

STATIONS

☿	♀	♂	♃
3Jan 22♐44	24Mat 3♉35	5Dec 3♌14	12Jan 27♍30
4Apr 27♈52	7May 17♈12	... ...	15May 17♍32
27Apr 16♈52			
7Aug 4♍47			
30Aug 21♌58			
27Nov 23♐ 9			
17Dec 6♐52			

♄	♅	♆
6Mar 3♋50	16Feb 9♊ 6	8Jan 6♎26
7Nov 24♋54	23Sep 17♊27	15Jun 3♎39

SIDER. TIME	1 Jan
6h 41m 7s	Midn.
18h 43m 5s	Noon
Common Year	1945

(No DST.) 1946 (BST 14 Apr. – 6 Oct)

Noon		JAN	FEB	MAR	APR	MAY	JUN
☉	1	10♑29	12♒ 2	10♓18	11♈ 9	10♉30	10♊23
	9	18 38	20 9	18 19	19 2	18 15	18 2
	17	26 47	28 14	26 18	26 52	25 58	25 41
	25	4♒56	6♓17	4♈14	4♉40	3♊40	3♋19
☿	1	19♐ 8	5♒15	25♓22	0♈10	14♈51	11♊39
	7	27 5	15 26	4♈17	27♓43	23 26	24 39
	13	5♑38	26 5	9 28	28D28	3♉15	6♋45
	19	14 36	7♓ 8	9R44	1♈59	14 16	17 31
	25	23 55	18 17	5 51	7 36	26 26	26 50
	31	3♒36	...	0 52	...	9♊27	...
♀	1	3♑ 3	12♒ 2	17♓ 6	25♈38	2♊30	10♋ 4
	9	13 7	22 4	27 5	5♉31	12 15	19 38
	17	23 11	2♓ 5	7♈ 2	15 21	21 58	29 10
	25	3♒14	12 6	16 58	25 10	1♋38	8♌38
♂	1	28♋ 6	16♋48	14♋27	21♋36	3♌56	19♌35
	13	23R28	14 33	16 16	26 5	9 44	26 9
	25	18 56	14D11	19 21	1♌12	15 52	2♍56
♃	1	24♎52	27♎13	26♎51	23♎56	20♎12	17♎43
	13	26 6	27R22	25 59	22 25	18 58	17 27
	25	26 56	27 3	24 46	20 55	18 4	17D37
♄	1	22♋18	19♋50	18♋16	18♋ 5	19♋32	22♋21
	13	21 20	19 2	18 0	18 29	20 29	23 41
	25	20 21	18 25	17D58	19 7	21 37	25 8
♅	1	14♊25	13♊34	13♊27	14♊ 6	15♊24	17♊ 8
	13	14R 1	13 26	13 36	14 33	16 2	17 50
	25	13 42	13D25	13 53	15 6	16 43	18 32
♆	1	8♎36	8♎29	7♎58	7♎ 9	6♎23	5♎54
	13	8R37	8 18	7 40	6 49	6 9	5 51
	25	8 33	8 3	7 20	6 31	5 59	5D52
Pl.	1	11♌17	10♌36	9♌59	9♌31	9♌26	9♌46
☊	1	29♊27	27♊49	26♊20	24♊41	23♊ 6	21♊27
	1st	Tue	Fri	Fri	Mon	Wed	Sat

Noon		JUL	AUG	SEP	OCT	NOV	DEC
☉	1	9♋ 2	8♌37	8♍26	7♎42	8♏28	8♐42
	9	16 40	16 17	16 12	15 35	16 29	16 49
	17	24 17	23 58	23 59	23 31	24 32	24 57
	25	1♌56	1♍[illegible]	1♎49	1♏28	2♐37	3♑ 6
☿	1	4♌38	10♌31	25♌55	20♎ 5	2♐ 1	21♏10
	7	10 44	6 24	7♍20	29 25	6 25	24D12
	13	14 48	4D54	18 49	8♏17	6R55	0♐37
	19	16 21	7 31	29 49	16 38	1 46	8 33
	25	15R 2	14 16	10♎14	24 21	24♏ 6	17 9
	31	11 16	24 5	...	1♐ 3	...	26 6
♀	1	15♌41	21♍17	24♎31	21♏20	2♐ 8	18♏ 6
	9	25 1	0♎10	2♏25	26 35	29♏29	17D 8
	17	4♍16	8 51	9 51	0♐24	25 1	18 43
	25	13 24	17 20	16 42	2 21	20 27	22 22
♂	1	6♍24	25♍ 0	14♎39	4♏38	26♏14	18♐ 4
	13	13 28	2♎29	22 32	12 53	4♐52	27 2
	25	20 42	10 8	0♏33	21 16	13 38	6♑ 7
♃	1	17♎52	20♎38	25♎24	1♏16	7♏56	14♏25
	13	18 39	22 17	27 38	3 48	10 34	16 52
	25	19 48	24 12	0♏ 1	6 24	13 9	19 11
♄	1	25♋53	29♋52	3♌40	6♌40	8♌33	8♌47
	13	27 25	1♌23	4 59	7 34	8 50	8 24
	25	28 58	2 51	6 9	8 16	8 52	7 48
♅	1	18♊53	20♊27	21♊30	21♊48	21♊18	20♊13
	13	19 32	20 56	21 43	21 42	20 55	19 43
	25	20 8	21 20	21 48	21 28	20 28	19 12
♆	1	5♎54	6♎23	7♎16	8♎21	9♎28	10♎19
	13	6 2	6 41	7 41	8 47	9 50	10 32
	25	6 14	7 2	8 7	9 13	10 10	10 43
Pl.	1	10♌26	11♌18	12♌12	28♌55	13♌18	13♌17
☊	1	19♊52	18♊14	16♊35	15♊ 0	13♊21	11♊46
	1st	Mon	Thu	Sun	Tue	Fri	Sun

d.	JAN	FEB	MAR	APR
☽ 1	17♐43	3♒35	14♒42	1♈40
3	12♑17	0♓16	9♓ 2	1♉17
5	7♒42	27 53	7♈35	0♊58
7	4♓ 1	26♈ 1	6♉33	29 48
9	1♈11	24♉16	5♊13	27♋24
11	29 10	22♊25	3♋11	23♌53
13	27♉46	20♋19	0♌26	19♍28
15	26♊40	17♌42	26 59	14♎17
17	25♋17	14♍12	22♍48	8♏29
19	22♌55	9♎36	17♎47	2♐13
21	19♍12	3♏58	11♏58	25 49
23	14♎ 7	27 42	5♐39	19♑47
25	8♏ 5	21♐26	29 21	14♒46
27	1♐45	15♑55	23♑47	11♓22
29	25 46	...	19♒37	9♓50
31	20♑41	...	17♓14	...

d.	MAY	JUN	JUL	AUG
☽ 1	9♉45	3♋26	10♌56	29♍58
3	10♊ 1	2♌34	8♍36	25♎13
5	9♋26	0♍ 2	4♎34	19♏20
7	7♌22	25 51	29 9	12♐59
9	3♍48	20♎27	22♏57	6♑49
11	29 2	14♏20	16♐34	1♒22
13	23♎25	7♐57	10♑29	26 54
15	17♏18	1♑40	5♒ 2	23♓27
17	10♐56	25 47	0♓24	20♈46
19	4♑37	20♒36	26 40	18♉38
21	28 43	16♓26	23♈52	16♊54
23	23♒44	13♈33	22♉ 2	15♋23
25	20♓11	12♉ 6	21♊ 1	13♌46
27	18♈21	11♊45	20♋19	11♍29
29	18♉ 3	11♋43	19♌10	8♎ 0
31	18♊24	...	16♍46	3♏10

d.	SEP	OCT	NOV	DEC
☽ 1	15♏19	16♐59	0♒42	3♓56
3	9♐ 6	10♑38	25 27	29 57
5	2♑47	4♒55	21♓44	27♈43
7	27 3	0♓28	19♈47	27♉11
9	22♒28	27 37	19♉18	27 34
11	19♓12	26♈10	19♊18	27♋41
13	17♈ 1	25 22	18♋45	26♌27
15	15♉21	24♊24	16♌57	23♍27
17	13♊43	22♋43	13♍45	18♎53
19	11♋52	20♌10	9♎23	13♏14
21	9♌41	16♍44	4♏ 5	6♐59
23	6♍58	12♎28	28 9	0♑34
25	3♎26	7♏20	21♐50	24 17
27	28 52	1♐28	15♑24	18♒22
29	23♏16	25 6	9♒16	13♓10
31	...	18♑43	...	9♈ 2

STATIONS

☿	♀	♂	♃
17Mar 10♈11	28Oct 2♐30	22Feb 14♋ 7	11Feb 27♎22
9Apr 27♓38	8Dec 17♏ 7	...	15Jun 17♎27
20Jul 16♌20	♄	♅	♆
13Aug 4♌54	20Mar 17♋57	20Feb 13♊25	10Jan 8♎36
11Nov 7♐19	21Nov 8♌53	28Sep 21♊48	17Jun 5♎51
1Dec 21♏10	SIDER. TIME 6h 40m 10s		1 Jan Midn.
	18h 42m 8s		Noon
	Common Year		1946

(BST 16 Mar. – 2 Nov. but –) 1947 (DST 13 Apr. – 10 Aug.)

Noon		JAN	FEB	MAR	APR	MAY	JUN
☉	1	10♑14	11♒48	10♓ 4	10♈55	10♉16	10♊ 9
	9	18 23	19 54	18 5	18 48	18 1	17 48
	17	26 32	27 59	26 3	26 38	25 44	25 27
	25	4♒41	6♓13	4♈ 0	4♉27	3♊26	3♋ 5
☿	1	27♐37	18♒20	22♓54	13♓33	24♈50	28♊ 9
	7	6♑50	29 1	18R55	19 12	6♉25	7♋52
	13	16 18	9♓20	13 8	26 23	18 59	15 51
	19	26 3	17 57	9 36	4♈48	2♊ 3	21 55
	25	6♒ 8	22 45	9D40	14 17	14 48	25 48
	31	16 34	...	12 48	...	26 22	...
♀	1	26♏52	25♐ 1	25♑46	1♓52	7♈39	15♉ 0
	9	3♐ 5	3♑30	4♒56	11 21	17 15	24 41
	17	10 10	12 15	14 14	20 53	26 53	4♊23
	25	17 53	21 13	23 36	0♈27	6♉32	14 6
♂	1	11♑27	5♒29	27♒29	21♓51	15♈ 6	8♉28
	13	20 42	14 54	6♓56	1♈12	24 14	17 18
	25	0♒ 1	24 19	16 22	10 29	3♉16	25 58
♃	1	20♏27	25♏ 4	27♏18	27♏ 4	24♏18	20♏28
	13	22 27	26 17	27 34	26R12	22R48	19R14
	25	24 12	27 7	27R22	25 0	21 18	18 19
♄	1	7♌21	4♌55	2♌55	1♌57	2♌38	4♌51
	13	6R28	3R59	2R22	2D 2	3 20	6 2
	25	5 30	3 10	2 2	2 22	4 15	7 21
♅	1	18♊56	17♊59	17♊45	18♊18	19♊30	21♊12
	13	18R30	17R48	17 52	18 43	20 8	21 55
	25	18 8	17D45	18 6	19 13	20 48	22 37
♆	1	10♎46	10♎42	10♎12	9♎24	8♎38	8♎ 7
	13	10R48	10R32	9R55	9R 4	8R23	8R 2
	25	10 46	10 18	9 35	8 46	8 12	8D 2
Pl.	1	12♌52	12♌12	11♌34	11♌ 5	10♌59	11♌17
☊	1	10♊ 7	8♊29	7♊ 1	5♊21	3♊46	2♊ 8
	1st	Wed	Sat	Sat	Tue	Thu	Sun

Noon		JUL	AUG	SEP	OCT	NOV	DEC
☉	1	8♋48	8♌23	8♍12	7♎28	8♏13	8♐27
	9	16 26	16 3	15 57	15 21	16 14	16 34
	17	24 4	23 44	23 45	23 16	24 18	24 42
	25	1♌42	1♍26	1♎34	1♏14	2♐22	2♑51
☿	1	27♋ 8	19♋26	11♍27	29♎49	18♏ 4	21♏ 9
	7	25R43	25 25	22 26	7♏30	10R40	29 59
	13	22 18	4♌33	2♎44	14 11	5 42	9♐ 6
	19	18 40	15 48	12 23	19 14	7D 9	18 21
	25	17 3	27 47	21 25	21 27	13 7	27 42
	31	18D47	9♍32	...	19R 0	...	7♑12
♀	1	21♊24	29♋20	7♍38	14♎57	23♏37	1♑ 2
	9	1♋ 9	9♌11	17 34	24 56	3♐36	11 0
	17	10 56	19 4	27 31	4♏54	13 35	20 56
	25	20 44	28 58	7♎29	14 53	23 33	0♒53
♂	1	0♊16	21♊44	12♋ 1	0♌14	17♌ 0	0♍ 0
	13	8 42	29 45	19 30	7 2	22 42	3 48
	25	17 0	7♋34	26 43	13 27	27 46	6 25
♃	1	18♏ 0	18♏ 6	20♏54	25♏36	1♐46	8♐24
	13	17R42	18 54	22 35	27 52	4 23	11 5
	25	17D50	20 4	24 32	0♐18	7 3	13 44
♄	1	8♌ 2	11♌54	15♌50	19♌12	21♌41	22♌40
	13	9 30	13 26	17 15	20 18	22 16	22R36
	25	11 0	14 58	18 35	21 14	22 36	22 16
♅	1	22♊58	24♊37	25♊46	26♊10	25♊48	24♊47
	13	23 39	25 8	26 1	26R 7	25R27	24R17
	25	24 16	25 33	26 9	25 57	25 1	23 46
♆	1	8♎ 4	8♎31	9♎32	10♎26	11♎34	12♎27
	13	8 11	8 48	9 47	10 53	11 57	12 42
	25	8 22	9 9	10 13	11 19	12 18	12 52
Pl.	1	11♌56	12♌49	13♌44	14♌27	14♌53	14♌53
☊	1	0♊32	28♉54	17♉15	25♉40	24♉ 2	22♉26
	1st	Tue	Fri	Mon	Wed	Sat	Mon

☽ d.	JAN	FEB	MAR	APR
1	22♈29	14♊24	24♊41	18♌ 1
3	20♉37	13♋49	23♋22	15♍56
5	20♊15	13♌39	22♌20	13♎ 5
7	20♋37	12♍46	20♍50	9♏ 7
9	20♌30	10♎18	18♎ 6	3♐58
11	18♍50	6♏ 2	13♏50	27 57
13	15♎14	0♐22	8♐15	21♑38
15	10♏ 3	24 1	1♑58	15♒40
17	3♐55	17♑40	25 42	10♓41
19	27 28	11♒52	20♒ 5	7♈ 3
21	21♑11	6♓53	15♓32	4♉44
23	15♒23	2♈45	12♈ 5	3♊20
25	10♓15	29 22	9♉31	2♋11
27	5♈51	26♉40	7♊27	0♌45
29	2♉23	...	5♋38	28 42
31	0♊ 5	...	3♌54	...

☽ d.	MAY	JUN	JUL	AUG
1	25♍53	14♏13	17♐36	2♒ 4
3	22♎11	8♐38	11♑20	26 3
5	17♏34	2♑33	5♒ 2	20♓30
7	12♐ 5	26 14	28 58	15♈37
9	5♑59	20♒ 3	23♓27	11♉43
11	29 40	14♓27	18♈53	9♊ 9
13	23♒42	9♈58	15♉46	8♋ 5
15	18♓40	7♉ 5	14♊20	8♌ 8
17	15♈ 6	5♊55	14♋22	8♍11
19	13♉ 7	5♋59	14♌50	7♎ 0
21	12♊24	6♌10	14♍24	3♏57
23	12♋ 5	5♍21	12♎10	29 12
25	11♌15	2♎52	8♏ 6	23♐19
27	9♍13	28 48	2♐41	17♑ 0
29	6♎ 5	23♏33	26 32	10♒48
31	1♏44	...	20♑12	5♓ 5

☽ d.	SEP	OCT	NOV	DEC
1	17♓27	22♈10	12♊33	21♋ 8
3	12♈41	18♉50	10♋58	20♋15
5	8♉39	16♊12	9♌27	18♍27
7	5♊30	14♋12	7♍39	15♎32
9	3♋26	12♌42	5♎18	11♏37
11	2♌25	11♍22	2♏11	6♐51
13	1♍56	9♎36	28 7	1♑24
15	1♎ 2	6♏49	23♐ 5	25 25
17	28 47	2♐42	17♑14	19♒ 8
19	24♏51	27 22	11♒ 0	12♓58
21	19♐31	21♑17	4♓53	7♓27
23	13♑23	15♒ 3	29 32	3♉12
25	7♒ 8	9♓19	25♈28	0♊43
27	1♓19	4♈33	22♉57	29 58
29	26 18	0♉58	21♊45	0♌12
31	...	28 29	...	0♍ 8

STATIONS	☿	♀	♂	♃
	28Feb 23♓ 6 22Mar 9♓12 2Jul 27♋ 5 26Jul 17♋ 5 26Oct 21♏24 15Nov 5♏30	None	None	14Mar 27♐34 16Jul 17♏42
		♄	♅	♆
		4Apr 1♌57 4Dec 22♌41	25Feb 17♊45 3Oct 26♊10	13Jan 10♎48 20Jun 8♎ 2
		SIDER. TIME		1 Jan
		6h 39m 13s		Midn.
		18h 41m 11s		Noon
		Common Year		1947

1948 (BST, 14 Mar. – 31 Oct)

Noon		JAN	FEB	MAR	APR	MAY	JUN
☉	1	9♑59	11♒33	10♓50	11♈40	11♉ 0	10♊53
	9	18 9	19 39	18 50	19 32	18 45	18 32
	17	26 18	27 45	26 49	27 23	26 28	26 11
	25	4♒26	5♓48	4♈45	5♉11	4♊10	3♋48
☿	1	8♑48	29♒19	21♒54	18♓ 1	13♉43	3♋32
	7	18 31	5♓22	22D10	27 22	26 32	6 40
	13	28 28	6R 1	25 37	7♈37	8♊24	7R 7
	19	8♒37	1 4	1♓13	18 49	18 35	5 4
	25	18 42	24♒47	8 19	0♉55	26 46	1 42
	31	27 57	...	16 33	...	2♋46	...
♀	1	9♒33	17♓36	22♈ 9	26♉49	25♊29	11♋ 6
	9	19 26	27 16	1♉24	5♊ 7	1♋32	10R20
	17	29 17	6♈50	10 27	13 1	6 26	7 7
	25	9♓ 4	16 18	19 18	20 24	9 48	2 20
♂	1	7♍18	3♍52	23♌ 4	18♌ 9	23♌44	5♍56
	13	7R27	29♌35	19R44	19 23	27 53	11 42
	25	5 43	24R52	18 12	22 0	2♍48	17 54
♃	1	15♐15	21♐27	25♐58	28♐39	28♐32	25♐47
	13	17 46	23 30	27 18	28 56	27R44	24R18
	25	20 9	25 18	28 16	28R47	26 35	22 47
♄	1	21♌58	19♌51	17♌34	15♌58	15♌56	17♌31
	13	21R16	18R53	16R48	15R46	16 22	18 30
	25	20 24	17 56	16 13	15D49	17 2	19 39
♅	1	23♊29	22♊27	22♊ 7	22♊34	23♊42	25♊22
	13	23R 1	22R13	22D11	22 57	24 18	26 4
	25	22 38	22 7	22 23	23 26	24 58	26 47
♆	1	12♎57	12♎54	12♎26	11♎38	10♎51	10♎19
	13	13 0	12R45	12R 8	11R18	10R36	10R14
	25	12R58	12 32	11 49	10 59	10 24	10D13
Pl.	1	14♌29	13♌49	13♌ 9	12♌40	12♌33	12♌51
☊	1	20♉48	19♉ 9	17♉37	15♉59	14♉23	12♉45
	1st	Thu	Sun	Mon	Thu	Sat	Tue

Noon		JUL	AUG	SEP	OCT	NOV	DEC
☉	1	9♋32	9♌ 7	8♍56	8♎12	8♏59	9♐13
	9	17 9	16 47	16 42	16 6	17 0	17 21
	17	24 47	24 28	24 29	24 1	25 3	25 29
	25	2♌25	2♍10	2♎19	1♏59	3♐ 8	3♑38
☿	1	28♊56	27♋52	26♍37	3♏12	20♎52	2♐57
	7	28D27	10♌ 7	5♎49	5 24	26 37	12 22
	13	1♋ 0	22 24	14 15	3R29	4♏54	21 48
	19	6 38	4♍ 5	21 51	27♎ 9	14 5	1♑17
	25	15 6	14 57	28 20	20 54	23 30	10 52
	31	25 54	25 1	...	20D20	...	20 34
♀	1	28♊47	29♊ 9	23♋ 5	24♌23	0♎16	6♏43
	9	25R31	3♋57	0♌56	3♍23	9 52	16 36
	17	24D40	9 52	9 11	12 36	19 34	26 31
	25	26 12	16 38	17 46	21 58	29 21	6♐28
♂	1	21♍ 8	9♎ 4	28♎38	18♏54	11♐ 3	3♑30
	13	27 52	16 28	6♏36	27 21	19 56	12 42
	25	4♎52	24 6	14 45	5♐57	28 56	22 0
♃	1	22♐ 3	19♐26	19♐31	22♐16	27♐16	3♑26
	13	20R46	19R 7	20 20	23 59	29 37	6 7
	25	19 49	19D14	21 32	25 59	2♑ 8	8 52
♄	1	20♌16	23♌54	27♌50	1♍25	4♍22	5♍59
	13	21 37	25 25	29 19	2 41	5 12	6 12
	25	23 2	26 57	0♍45	3 48	5 47	6R 8
♅	1	27♊ 8	28♊50	0♋ 4	0♋34	0♋17	29♊20
	13	27 50	29 22	0 21	0R33	29♊58	28R50
	25	28 29	29 50	0 32	0 25	29R34	28 19
♆	1	10♎15	10♎40	11♎30	12♎34	13♎42	14♎36
	13	10 21	10 57	11 55	13 1	14 6	14 51
	25	10 32	11 17	12 21	13 27	14 27	15 3
Pl.	1	13♌31	14♌25	15♌18	16♌ 3	16♌29	16♌30
☊	1	11♉ 9	9♉31	7♉52	6♉17	4♉39	3♉ 3
	1st	Thu	Sun	Wed	Fri	Mon	Wed

☽ d.	JAN	FEB	MAR	APR
1	14♍39	5♏16	26♏53	12♑24
3	12♎26	0♐49	21♐59	6♒17
5	8♏41	25 15	16♑ 3	0♓ 2
7	3♐46	19♑ 8	9♒45	24 9
9	28 9	12♒51	3♓33	18♈56
11	22♑ 7	6♓39	27 41	14♉30
13	15♒52	0♈42	22♈20	10♊56
15	9♓37	25 14	17♉41	8♋14
17	3♈41	20♉42	13♊58	6♌21
19	28 34	17♊36	11♋31	5♍ 7
21	24♉51	16♋15	10♌23	4♎ 2
23	23♊ 2	16♌23	10♍ 9	2♏26
25	22♋59	16♍52	9♎47	29 43
27	23♌41	16♎19	8♏14	25♐37
29	23♍40	13♏53	5♐ 1	20♑20
31	21♎53	...	0♑14	...

☽ d.	MAY	JUN	JUL	AUG
1	14♒17	28♓ 1	0♉42	18♊38
3	8♓ 5	22♈43	26 44	17♋24
5	2♈19	18♉41	24♊32	17♌35
7	27 26	16♊ 7	23♋51	17♍56
9	23♉39	14♋44	23♌46	17♎11
11	20♊56	13♌50	23♍ 8	14♏45
13	18♋59	12♍38	21♎14	10♐47
15	17♌24	10♎40	18♏ 1	5♑43
17	15♍50	7♏47	13♐43	29 59
19	13♎55	4♐ 4	8♑39	23♒52
21	11♏24	29 33	3♒ 0	17♓36
23	8♐ 1	24♑18	26 56	11♈23
25	3♑36	18♒24	20♓38	5♉35
27	28 14	12♓10	14♈29	0♊43
29	22♒12	6♈ 3	9♉ 3	27 32
31	16♓ 0	...	4♊59	25♋53

☽ d.	SEP	OCT	NOV	DEC
1	10♌47	19♍38	12♏17	18♐13
3	11♍16	19♎37	10♐13	14♑28
5	11♎28	18♏30	6♑39	9♒30
7	10♏15	15♐42	1♒41	3♓36
9	7♐13	11♑16	25 46	27 17
11	2♑37	5♒40	19♓29	21♈15
13	27 1	29 29	13♈26	16♉ 8
15	20♒53	23♓14	8♉ 7	12♊20
17	14♓37	17♈18	3♊47	9♋53
19	8♈28	11♉57	0♋28	8♌19
21	2♉40	7♊22	27 57	6♍58
23	27 32	3♋42	26♌ 0	5♎17
25	23♊27	1♌ 4	24♍21	3♏ 4
27	20♋47	29 28	22♎45	0♐18
29	19♌40	28♍37	20♏51	26 51
31	...	27♎53	...	22♑36

STATIONS	☿	♀	♂	♃
	11Feb 6♓30	3Jun 11♋ 9	9Jan 7♍36	15Apr 28♐56
	4Mar 21♒34	16Jul 24♊38	30Mar 18♌ 7	16Aug 19♐ 6
	11Jun 7♓16	♄	♅	♆
	6Jul 28♊20	17Apr 15♌45	2Mar 22♊ 7	15Jan 13♎ 0
	8Oct 5♏24	17Dec 6♍12	6Oct 0♋35	21Jun 10♎13
	29Oct 19♎47	SIDER. TIME 6h 38m 16s		1 Jan Midn.
		18h 40m 14s LEAP YEAR		Noon 1948

1949 (BST, 3 Apr. – 30 Oct.)

Noon		JAN	FEB	MAR	APR	MAY	JUN
☉	1	10♑46	12♒19	10♓35	11♈26	10♉46	10♊39
	9	18 55	20 26	18 36	19 18	18 31	18 18
	17	27 4	28 31	26 34	27 8	26 14	25 57
	25	5♒12	6♓34	4♈31	4♉57	3♊56	3♋35
☿	1	22♑11	15♒ 5	13♒38	29♓42	29♉ 3	14♊18
	7	1♒48	8R10	20 38	11♈11	7♊34	11R 3
	13	10 47	4 41	28 42	23 26	13 32	8 54
	19	17 45	5D39	7♓38	6♉ 6	16 42	9D 8
	25	20R10	9 45	17 21	18 19	17R 0	12 7
	31	16 13	...	27 52	...	14 50	...
♀	1	15♐11	23♑55	28♒53	7♈28	14♉35	22♊43
	9	25 10	3♒55	8♓52	17 24	24 27	2♋31
	17	5♑10	13 54	18 50	27 17	4♊18	12 19
	25	15 10	23 54	28 46	7♉11	14 8	22 6
♂	1	27♑28	21♒54	14♓ 1	8♈13	1♉ 3	23♉52
	13	6♒54	1♓23	23 26	17 26	9 59	2♊29
	25	16 22	10 52	2♈48	26 33	18 48	10 57
♃	1	10♑30	17♑35	23♑25	28♑36	1♒36	1♒57
	13	13 16	20 11	25 38	0♒ 5	2 6	1R17
	25	16 1	22 38	27 35	1 12	2R 8	0 14
♄	1	5♍59	4♍22	2♍10	0♍ 5	29♌19	0♍ 9
	13	5R31	3R27	1R15	29♌36	29D26	0 53
	25	4 50	2 29	0 28	29R20	29 49	1 50
♅	1	28♊ 1	26♊56	26♊31	26♊50	27♊53	29♊30
	13	27R33	26R41	26D32	27 11	28 28	0♋12
	25	27 8	26 32	26 42	27 38	29 6	0 55
♆	1	15♎ 7	15♎ 6	14♎40	13♎52	13♎ 5	12♎32
	13	15 10	14R58	14R23	13R33	12R50	12R26
	25	15R 9	14 45	14 4	13 14	12 37	12D24
Pl.	1	16♌ 6	15♌25	14♌47	14♌16	14♌ 8	14♌26
☊	1	1♉25	29♈46	28♈17	26♈39	25♈ 4	23♈25
1st		Sat	Tue	Tue	Fri	Sun	Wed

Noon		JUL	AUG	SEP	OCT	NOV	DEC
☉	1	9♋18	8♌53	8♍42	7♎58	8♏44	8♐58
	9	16 55	16 33	16 28	15 51	16 45	17 6
	17	24 33	24 14	24 15	23 47	24 49	25 14
	25	2♌11	1♍56	2♎ 5	1♏45	2♐54	3♑[illegible]
☿	1	17♊44	15♌ 4	4♎50	12♎57	26♎16	14♐19
	7	25 46	26 36	11 24	6R26	6♏ 5	23 41
	13	5♋59	7♍12	16 23	3D59	15 51	3♑ 1
	19	17 55	16 54	18 58	7 38	25 27	12 17
	25	0♌36	25 44	18R 2	15 18	4♐56	21 10
	31	13 4	3♎37	...	24 39	...	28 54
♀	1	29♋25	7♍ 5	14♎20	19♏41	24♐53	25♑43
	9	9♌10	16 45	23 50	28 56	3♑33	2♒47
	17	18 54	26 22	3♏18	8♐ 5	11 57	9 0
	25	28 36	5♎58	12 41	17 7	20 0	14 3
♂	1	15♊ 8	6♋13	26♋24	15♌ 1	3♍ 5	18♍55
	13	23 24	14 8	3♌58	22 10	9 39	24 35
	25	1♋32	21 55	11 22	29 8	15 55	29 43
♃	1	29♑35	25♑43	22♑49	22♑36	25♑18	0♒ 8
	13	28R 8	24R21	22R23	23 19	27 1	2 30
	25	26 36	23 16	22D25	24 27	29 2	5 4
♄	1	2♍21	5♍39	9♍28	13♍10	16♍30	18♍42
	13	3 32	7 5	10 58	14 33	17 32	19 11
	25	4 50	8 35	12 27	15 50	18 22	19 25
♅	1	1♋17	3♋ 1	4♋21	4♋59	4♋49	3♋57
	13	1 59	3 36	4 41	5R 1	4R32	3R28
	25	2 39	4 6	4 55	4 56	4 10	2 58
♆	1	12♎25	12♎48	13♎37	14♎40	15♎48	16♎43
	13	12 30	13 4	14 1	15 6	16 12	17 0
	25	12 40	13 24	14 26	15 33	16 34	17 12
Pl.	1	15♌14	15♌55	16♌51	12♌39	18♌ 6	18♌ 9
☊	1	21♈50	20♈11	18♈33	16♈57	15♈19	13♈44
1st		Fri	Mon	Thu	Sat	Tue	Thu

d.		JAN	FEB	MAR	APR
☽	1	5♒ 8	19♓38	28♓14	12♉44
	3	29 31	13♈13	21♈50	7♊11
	5	23♓17	7♉ 2	15♉42	2♋37
	7	16♈57	1♊46	10♊23	29 26
	9	11♉14	28 5	6♋30	27♌51
	11	6♊49	26♋ 8	4♌28	27♍37
	13	4♋ 7	26♌ 9	4♍10	27♎50
	15	2♌59	26♍25	4♎40	27♏22
	17	2♍33	25♎53	4♏39	25♐22
	19	1♎46	23♏54	3♐10	21♑36
	21	0♏ 0	20♐27	29 58	16♒25
	23	27 9	15♑51	25♑17	10♓20
	25	23♐22	10♒28	19♒38	3♈56
	27	18♑51	4♓32	13♓26	27 40
	29	13♒38	...	7♈ 2	21♉53
	31	7♓46	...	0♉45	...

d.		MAY	JUN	JUL	AUG
☽	1	16♊49	6♌28	15♍ 3	8♏22
	3	12♋39	4♍ 8	13♎20	6♐ 3
	5	9♌33	2♎24	11♏30	3♑ 0
	7	7♍36	1♏ 4	9♐24	29 10
	9	6♎40	29 46	6♑45	24♒27
	11	6♏14	27♐54	3♒10	18♓53
	13	5♐26	24♑52	28 27	12♈40
	15	3♑27	20♒25	22♓42	6♉16
	17	29 50	14♓47	16♈24	0♊19
	19	24♒44	8♈30	10♉10	25 31
	21	18♓40	2♉15	4♊43	22♋21
	23	12♈17	26 42	0♋38	20♌52
	25	6♉11	22♊17	28 3	20♍27
	27	0♊49	19♋ 6	26♌38	20♎ 5
	29	26 23	16♌51	25♍36	18♏54
	31	22♋54	...	24♎16	16♐34

d.		SEP	OCT	NOV	DEC
☽	1	29♐57	5♒40	21♓20	23♈26
	3	25♑58	0♓21	14♈57	17♉11
	5	21♒ 4	24 20	8♉35	11♊30
	7	15♓27	18♈ 0	2♊34	6♋36
	9	9♈17	11♉36	27 6	2♌29
	11	2♉51	5♊30	22♋26	29 9
	13	26 36	0♋ 5	18♌48	26♍39
	15	21♊ 6	25 48	16♍29	25♎ 3
	17	16♋57	23♌ 5	15♎32	24♏11
	19	14♌34	22♍ 3	15♏28	23♐24
	21	13♍52	22♎12	15♐18	21♑46
	23	14♎ 5	22♏29	13♑55	18♒37
	25	14♏ 2	21♐42	10♒43	13♓50
	27	12♐47	19♑10	5♓51	7♈54
	29	9♑56	14♒55	29 51	1♉30
	31	...	9♓23	...	25 21

STATIONS	☿	♀	♂	♃
	25Jan 20♒10	None	None	21May 2♒10
	15Feb 4♒35			19Sep 22♑20
	23May 17♊13	♄	♅	♆
	16Jun 8♊40	2May 29♌19	5Mar 26♊30	16Jan 15♎11
	21Sep 19♎ 7	... ...	11Oct 5♋ 1	24Jun 12♎24
	13Oct 3♎59	SIDER. TIME		1 Jan
		6h 41m 15s		Midn.
		18h 43m 13s		Noon
		Common Year		1949

Noon	JAN	FEB	MAR	APR	MAY	JUN
☉ 1	10♑31	12♒ 4	10♓20	11♈12	10♉33	10♊25
9	18 40	20 11	18 21	19 4	18 17	18 4
17	26 49	28 16	26 20	26 54	26 1	25 43
25	4♒58	6♓19	4♈16	4♉43	3♊42	3♋21
☿ 1	29♑59	18♑43	19♒56	15♈51	27♉19	19♉27
7	3♒59	22 32	29 20	28 6	26R55	22 55
13	1R53	28 31	9♓24	9♉20	24 7	28 43
19	24♑41	5♒50	20 10	18 22	20 42	6♊33
25	19 1	14 3	1♈40	24 29	18 39	16 16
31	18D23	...	13 48	...	19D 6	...
♀ 1	17♒ 9	10♒ 4	4♒33	25♒16	25♓21	29♈54
9	18 43	5R40	8 2	2♓45	4♈ 3	9♉ 6
17	17R45	3 19	13 4	10 41	12 55	18 22
25	14 17	3D33	19 13	18 58	21 56	27 43
♂ 1	2♎24	10♎22	9♎ 8	28♍29	22♍ 2	26♍35
13	6 21	11R 2	5R40	24R38	22D35	0♎37
25	9 15	9 55	1 9	22 26	24 43	5 32
♃ 1	6♒38	13♒53	20♒30	27♒19	2♓45	6♓26
13	9 23	16 44	23 14	29 40	4 27	7 10
25	12 13	19 34	25 51	1♓47	5 49	7 27
♄ 1	19♍26	18♍28	16♍30	14♍ 9	12♍45	12♍50
13	19R15	17R42	15R33	13R26	12R35	13 18
25	18 49	16 49	14 38	12 55	12D40	14 0
♅ 1	2♋39	1♋30	0♋58	1♋10	2♋ 7	3♋40
13	2R10	1R12	0D57	1 28	2 40	4 22
25	1 43	1 0	1 3	1 53	3 17	5 5
♆ 1	17♎16	17♎18	16♎54	16♎ 7	15♎20	14♎44
13	17 21	17R10	16R37	15R48	15R 3	14R37
25	17R21	16 58	16 19	15 28	14 50	14 35
Pl. 1	17♌47	17♌ 7	16♌ 9	15♌56	15♌46	16♌ 2
☊ 1	12♈ 5	10♈27	8♈58	7♈19	5♈44	4♈ 5
1st	Sun	Wed	Wed	Sat	Mon	Thu

Noon	JUL	AUG	SEP	OCT	NOV	DEC
☉ 1	9♋ 4	8♋40	8♍28	7♎44	8♏30	8♐44
9	16 42	16 19	16 14	15 37	16 31	16 51
17	24 20	24 0	24 1	23 33	24 34	24 59
25	1♌58	1♍43	1♎51	1♏30	2♐39	3♑ 8
☿ 1	27♊43	29♌ 2	2♎ 7	20♍ 0	8♏22	24♐49
7	10♋22	8♍11	1R48	26 52	18 2	3♑25
13	23 17	16 18	27♍45	6♎18	27 28	11 9
19	5♌39	23 12	21 40	16 31	6♐44	16 46
25	17 3	28 35	18 2	26 45	15 52	17R50
31	27 24	1♎51	...	6♏44	...	12 27
♀ 1	4♊46	11♋44	19♌28	26♍36	5♏22	13♐ 3
9	14 14	21 24	29 19	6♎34	15 24	23 6
17	23 45	1♌ 7	9♍12	16 34	25 27	3♑10
25	3♋19	10 53	19 8	26 36	5♐30	13 13
♂ 1	8♎16	24♎35	13♏39	3♐58	26♐26	19♑14
13	14 11	1♏42	21 35	12 30	5♑27	28 33
25	20 38	9 9	29 47	21 15	14 36	7♒56
♃ 1	7♓25	5♓30	1♓40	28♒27	27♒42	29♒58
13	7R 1	4R 8	0R11	27R47	28 16	1♓35
25	6 10	2 35	28♒56	27D36	29 18	3 32
♄ 1	14♍25	17♍16	20♍52	24♍36	28♍11	0♎51
13	15 24	18 36	22 22	26 3	29 22	1 35
25	16 32	20 1	23 52	27 25	0♎24	2 5
♅ 1	5♋27	7♋14	8♋39	9♋24	9♋22	8♋36
13	6 10	7 50	9 2	9 29	9R 8	8R 8
25	6 51	8 22	9 18	9R27	8 48	7 38
♆ 1	14♎35	14♎56	15♎43	16♎45	17♎54	18♎50
13	14 40	15 11	16 6	17 12	18 18	19 7
25	14 48	15 30	16 32	17 38	18 40	19 20
Pl. 1	16♋10	17♌30	18♌29	19♌16	19♌45	19♌50
☊ 1	2♈30	0♈52	29♓13	27♓38	25♓59	24♓24
1st	Sat	Tue	Fri	Sun	Wed	Fri

d.	JAN	FEB	MAR	APR
☽ 1	7♊33	24♋25	1♌57	22♍12
3	2♋42	21♌28	29 46	22♎ 5
5	28 55	19♍43	28♍47	22♏12
7	25♌57	18♎14	28♎13	21♐27
9	23♍32	16♏37	27♏15	19♑13
11	21♎31	14♐37	25♐21	15♒28
13	19♏47	12♑ 6	22♑23	10♓30
15	18♐10	8♒51	18♒24	4♈44
17	16♑14	4♓40	13♓30	28 32
19	13♒21	29 29	7♓53	22♉ 9
21	9♓ 9	23♈30	1♉43	15♊55
23	3♈42	17♉ 7	25 20	10♋11
25	27 29	10♊59	19♊12	5♌23
27	21♉ 9	5♋46	13♋52	2♍ 0
29	15♊25	...	9♌55	0♎21
31	10♋51	...	7♍41	...

d.	MAY	JUN	JUL	AUG
☽ 1	0♏14	24♐ 8	1♒35	19♓58
3	0♐44	23♑22	28 59	14♈53
5	0♑32	20♒47	24♓38	8♉53
7	28 40	16♓22	18♈59	2♊37
9	24♒57	10♈39	12♉42	26 42
11	19♓48	4♉19	6♊27	21♋40
13	13♈45	27 59	0♋44	17♌41
15	7♉23	22♊ 0	25 49	14♍44
17	1♊ 3	16♋36	21♌42	12♎30
19	25 2	11♌53	18♍21	10♏43
21	19♋31	7♍58	15♎45	9♐ 7
23	14♌49	5♎ 5	13♏55	7♑25
25	11♍17	3♏25	12♐42	5♒14
27	9♎15	2♐50	11♑38	2♓11
29	8♏43	2♑35	9♒58	28 2
31	9♐ 2	...	7♓ 0	22♈47

d.	SEP	OCT	NOV	DEC
☽ 1	4♉51	6♊42	21♋ 1	24♌46
3	28 38	0♋31	15♌49	20♍43
5	22♊29	24 57	12♍ 2	18♎21
7	17♋ 1	20♌36	10♎ 2	17♏47
9	12♌43	17♍52	9♏46	18♐21
11	9♍48	16♎43	10♐16	18♑39
13	8♎ 4	16♏29	10♑11	17♒24
15	6♏59	16♐10	8♒31	14♓10
17	5♐52	14♑49	5♓ 3	9♈17
19	4♑12	12♒ 4	0♈11	3♉24
21	1♒42	8♓ 4	24 27	27 8
23	28 17	3♈ 6	18♉18	20♊53
25	23♓58	27 28	12♊ 3	14♋55
27	18♈48	21♉24	5♋52	9♌21
29	12♉56	15♊ 8	29 59	4♍24
31	...	8♋56	...	0♎22

STATIONS

☿	♀	♂	♃
8Jan 4♒ 7	10Jan 18♒44	12Feb 11♎ 2	26Jun 7♓27
29Jan 18♑14	20Feb 3♒ 6	3May 22♍ 0	24Oct 27♒35

☿	♄	♅	♆
3May 27♉31	1Jan 19♍26	9Mar 0♋56	18Jan 17♎22
27May 18♉30	15May 12♍35	15Oct 9♋29	26Jun 14♎35
4Sep 2♎24	SIDER. TIME		1 Jan
26Sep 17♍57	6h.40m 18s		Midn.
23Dec 18♑10	18h 42m 16s		Noon
	Common Year		1950

Noon	JAN	FEB	MAR	APR	MAY	JUN
☉ 1	10♑16	11♒49	10♓ 6	10♈57	10♉18	10♊11
9	18 25	19 56	18 7	18 50	18 4	17 51
17	26 34	28 1	26 5	26 40	25 47	25 29
25	4♒43	6♓ 4	4♈ 2	4♉28	3♊28	3♋ 7
☿ 1	11♑ 7	18♑39	1♓42	29♈ 8	0♉12	17♉24
7	4R 0	26 48	12 35	5♉43	28♈23	26 47
13	1D58	5♒34	24 6	8 28	29D19	7♊42
19	4 43	14 54	6♈ 0	7R28	2♉50	19 58
25	10 17	24 47	17 38	3 56	8 30	3♋ 0
31	17 22	...	27 42	...	16 0	...
♀ 1	22♑ 0	0♓50	5♈36	13♉25	18♊59	23♋53
9	2♒ 2	10 48	15 26	23 2	28 12	2♌25
17	12 4	20 45	25 14	2♊33	7♋18	10 39
25	22 5	0♈39	4♉58	11 59	16 14	18 31
♂ 1	13♒26	7♓50	29♓41	23♈21	15♉32	7♊40
13	22 53	17 15	8♈56	2♉19	24 12	16 1
25	2♓20	26 35	18 4	11 10	2♊44	24 15
♃ 1	4♓48	11♓16	17♓52	25♓20	2♈11	8♈13
13	7 9	14 3	20 46	28 9	4 41	10 7
25	9 42	16 54	23 40	0♈52	6 59	11 43
♄ 1	2♎16	2♎ 0	0♎26	28♍ 3	26♍10	25♍33
13	2R22	1R27	29♍32	27R12	25R45	25 45
25	2 12	0 43	28R36	26 28	25 33	26 10
♅ 1	7♋20	6♋ 6	5♋29	5♋33	6♋24	7♋53
13	6R49	5R46	5D24	5 48	6 55	8 34
25	6 21	5 32	5 27	6 10	7 30	9 17
♆ 1	19♎26	19♎30	19♎ 7	18♎22	17♎34	16♎57
13	19 31	19R23	18R52	18R 2	17R17	16R49
25	19R32	19 12	18 33	17 43	17 3	16 46
Pl. 1	19♌29	18♌58	18♌ 9	17♌36	17♌25	17♌40
☊ 1	22♓45	21♓ 7	19♓38	18♓ 0	16♓24	14♓46
1st	Mon	Thu	Thu	Sun	Tue	Fri

Noon	JUL	AUG	SEP	OCT	NOV	DEC
☉ 1	8♋51	8♌26	8♍14	7♎30	8♏15	8♐29
9	16 28	16 6	16 0	15 23	16 17	16 36
17	24 6	23 46	23 47	23 18	24 20	24 44
25	1♌44	1♍29	1♎36	1♏16	2♐24	2♑53
☿ 1	15♋55	5♍37	6♍ 3	28♍ 2	19♏55	29♐44
7	27 59	11 4	2R 3	0♎48	28 58	2♑20
13	8♌55	14 25	2D39	19 16	7♐43	29♐ 1
19	18 40	14R59	8 20	29 20	16 5	21R10
25	27 15	12 13	17 28	9♏ 1	23 42	16 17
31	4♍32	6 58	...	18 23	...	17D17
♀ 1	24♌ 7	15♍51	11♍37	2♍54	22♍16	22♎44
9	1♍ 5	18 4	6R48	5 49	29 44	1♏41
17	7 17	17R59	3 15	10 26	7♎44	10 52
25	12 27	15 26	2D 7	16 20	16 11	20 12
♂ 1	28♊20	18♋59	9♌ 1	27♌50	16♍41	4♎ 8
13	6♋24	26 48	16 36	5♍13	23 46	10 49
25	14 22	4♌32	24 7	12 29	0♎43	17 17
♃ 1	12♑23	14♈10	12♈54	9♈22	5♈38	4♈15
13	13 25	14R 2	11R40	7R46	4R44	4 33
25	14 1	13 27	10 10	6 20	4 17	6 20
♄ 1	26♍28	28♍48	2♎ 6	5♎44	9♎28	12♎30
13	27 14	29 59	3 32	7 13	10 46	13 26
25	28 10	1♎17	5 0	8 39	11 57	14 10
♅ 1	9♋38	11♋27	12♋58	13♋50	13♋56	13♋16
13	10 22	12 6	13 23	13 58	13R45	12R50
25	11 4	12 40	13 43	13R59	13 27	12 20
♆ 1	16♎46	17♎ 4	17♎49	18♎50	19♎59	20♎57
13	16 49	17 18	18 12	19 17	20 24	21 15
25	15 47	17 37	18 37	19 44	20 46	21 28
Pl. 1	18♌16	19♌ 9	22♌ 5	22♌54	21♌55	21♌32
☊ 1	3♓10	11♓32	9♓53	8♓18	6♓40	5♓ 4
1st	Sun	Wed	Sat	Mon	Thu	Sat

d.	JAN	FEB	MAR	APR
☽ 1	13♎50	6♐26	17♐15	10♒20
3	11♏55	5♑35	15♑43	7♓24
5	11♐26	4♒48	13♒57	3♈38
7	11♑37	3♓12	11♓31	29 2
9	11♒12	0♈10	8♈ 1	23♉37
11	9♓ 9	25 36	3♉21	17♊36
13	5♈15	19♉55	27 42	11♋21
15	29 55	13♊42	21♊32	5♌26
17	23♉47	7♋35	15♋25	0♍28
19	17♊30	2♌ 4	9♌58	27 1
21	11♋31	27 27	5♍39	25♎13
23	6♌ 7	23♍49	2♎41	24♏38
25	1♍22	21♎ 3	0♏50	24♐18
27	27 22	18♏56	29 36	23♑14
29	24♎15	...	28♐19	20♒55
31	22♏ 7	...	26♑30	...

d.	MAY	JUN	JUL	AUG
☽ 1	17♓25	4♉49	8♊ 1	22♋27
3	12♈59	28 59	1♋45	16♌34
5	7♉49	22♊49	25 31	11♍14
7	2♊ 5	16♋32	19♌33	6♎41
9	25 57	10♌22	14♍ 8	3♏ 9
11	19♋39	4♍45	9♎42	0♐53
13	13♌40	0♎16	6♏44	29 49
15	8♍35	27 29	5♐29	29♑27
17	5♎ 3	26♏36	5♑33	28♒52
19	3♏25	27♐ 3	5♒50	27♓10
21	3♐20	27♑28	5♓ 5	23♈52
23	3♑42	26♒36	2♈35	19♉ 6
25	3♒11	23♓53	28 23	13♊17
27	1♓ 5	19♈32	22♉56	7♋ 3
29	27 24	14♉ 4	16♊49	0♌55
31	22♈32	...	10♋32	25 20

d.	SEP	OCT	NOV	DEC
☽ 1	7♍50	12♎43	4♐ 3	12♑53
3	3♎31	10♏12	3♑14	12♒15
5	0♏ 6	8♐23	1♒56	10♓16
7	27 34	6♑49	29 47	6♈57
9	25♐47	5♒ 6	26♓45	2♉36
11	24♑29	3♓ 1	22♈58	27 30
13	23♒15	0♈23	18♉27	21♊49
15	21♓30	26 57	13♊10	15♋41
17	18♈41	22♉32	7♋14	9♌18
19	14♉34	17♊ 9	0♌53	3♍ 4
21	9♊15	11♋ 2	24 40	27 33
23	3♋11	4♌45	19♍16	23♎27
25	26 57	28 58	15♎22	21♏15
27	21♌10	24♍18	13♏19	20♐53
29	16♍20	21♎11	12♐51	21♑24
31	...	19♏32	...	21♒24

STATIONS	☿	♀	♂	♃
	12Jan 1♑55	12Aug 18♍19	None	3Aug 14♈11
	14Apr 8♉33	24Sep 2♍ 7		29Nov 4♈15
	8May 28♈21	♄	♅	♆
	18Aug 15♍ 7	11Jan 2♎22	13Mar 5♋24	20Jan 19♎32
	9Sep 1♍39	28May 25♍32	20Oct 14♋ 0	28Jun 16♎45
	7Dec 2♑20	SIDER. TIME		1 Jan
		6h 39m 21s		Midn.
	27Dec 16♐ 2	18h 41m 19s		Noon
		Common Year		1951

Noon		JAN	FEB	MAR	APR	MAY	JUN
☉	1	10♑ 1	11♒35	10♓52	11♈42	11♉ 3	10♊55
	9	18 11	19 41	18 52	19 35	18 47	18 34
	17	26 19	27 46	26 51	27 25	26 30	26 13
	25	4♒28	5♓50	4♈47	5♉13	4♊12	3♋51
☿	1	17♐53	27♑33	18♓16	18♈26	14♈32	1♊47
	7	23 12	7♒ 7	29 37	13R57	20 41	14 42
	13	0♑17	17 9	9♈49	10 0	28 25	27 50
	19	8 19	27 41	17 12	8D41	7♉32	10♋20
	25	16 56	8♓45	20 21	10 22	17 59	21 40
	31	26 0	...	19R 1	...	29 43	...
♀	1	28♏29	5♑54	11♒26	19♓35	26♈29	4♊33
	9	8♐ 2	15 40	21 17	29 26	6♉18	14 22
	17	17 40	25 28	1♓ 7	9♈16	16 8	24 11
	25	27 22	5♒18	10 58	19 6	25 57	4♋ 1
♂	1	20♎55	5♏29	15♏20	18♏10	10♏28	1♏40
	13	26 54	10 9	17 38	16R12	6R 9	1D14
	25	2♏28	14 1	18R28	12 37	2 49	2 40
♃	1	6♈ 0	10♈28	16♈17	23♈26	0♉38	7♉47
	13	7 28	12 44	18 58	26 19	3 28	10 21
	25	9 16	15 12	21 46	29 12	6 14	12 44
♄	1	14♎30	14♎55	13♎50	11♎37	9♎28	8♎16
	13	14 52	14 38	13R 3	10R42	8R50	8D12
	25	14R59	14 7	12 10	9 51	8 24	8 23
♅	1	12♋ 2	10♋46	10♋ 1	10♋ 0	10♋45	12♋11
	13	11R31	10R23	9R55	10 13	11 15	12 51
	25	11 2	10 6	9D56	10 33	11 49	13 34
♆	1	21♎35	21♎42	21♎20	20♎35	19♎47	19♎ 9
	13	21 41	21R35	21R 4	20R15	19R30	19R 0
	25	21R43	21 25	20 46	19 56	19 15	18 56
Pl.	1	21♌12	20♌33	19♌51	19♌17	19♌ 5	19♌19
☊	1	3♓26	1♓47	0♓15	28♒37	27♒ 1	25♒23
	1st	Tue	Fri	Sat	Tue	Thu	Sun

Noon		JUL	AUG	SEP	OCT	NOV	DEC
☉	1	9♋34	9♌ 9	8♍58	8♎15	9♏ 1	9♐15
	9	17 12	16 49	16 44	16 8	17 2	17 22
	17	24 49	24 30	24 31	24 3	25 6	24 31
	25	2♌28	2♍13	2♎21	2♏ 1	3♐11	3♑40
☿	1	1♌41	26♌52	21♌ 6	13♎36	0♐21	6♐45
	7	10 21	24R 2	0♍ 0	23 34	7 41	0R51
	13	17 32	19 19	10 50	3♏ 4	13 32	1D12
	19	23 2	15 31	22 7	12 9	16 28	6 3
	25	26 23	15D24	3♎ 7	20 50	14R11	13 8
	31	27R 3	19 56	...	29 3	...	21 16
♀	1	11♋23	19♌33	27♍44	4♏38	12♐35	18♑55
	9	21 14	29 24	7♎35	14 27	22 19	28 30
	17	1♌ 4	9♍15	17 26	24 15	2♑ 2	7♒59
	25	10 55	19 7	27 16	4♐ 2	11 42	17 22
♂	1	3♏59	15♏42	2♐51	22♐30	14♑45	7♒23
	13	7 40	21 51	10 26	0♑56	23 43	16 36
	25	12 28	28 39	18 24	9 36	2♒48	25 51
♃	1	13♉51	18♉34	20♉53	20♉12	16♉50	12♉59
	13	15 54	19 47	20R58	19R 9	15R13	11R52
	25	17 40	20 36	20 34	17 45	13 40	11 11
♄	1	8♎34	10♎21	13♎17	16♎46	20♎31	23♎48
	13	9 5	11 22	14 37	18 14	21 54	24 54
	25	9 50	12 32	16 2	19 41	23 12	25 49
♅	1	13♋55	15♋46	17♋20	18♋18	18♋30	17♋55
	13	14 39	16 25	17 48	18 29	18R21	17R30
	25	15 22	17 1	18 10	18R32	18 5	17 2
♆	1	18♎56	19♎13	19♎57	20♎58	22♎ 6	23♎ 5
	13	18 59	19 27	20 20	21 24	22 31	23 23
	25	19 6	19 45	20 45	21 51	22 54	23 38
Pl.	1	19♌56	20♌48	21♌46	22♌36	23♌10	23♌15
☊	1	23♒48	22♒ 9	20♒31	18♒55	17♒17	15♒41
	1st	Tue	Fri	Mon	Wed	Sun	Mon

d.	JAN	FEB	MAR	APR
☽ 1	5♓53	25♈43	16♉59	2♋11
3	3♈32	21♉18	12♊ 4	25 59
5	29 37	15♊43	6♋ 7	19♌40
7	24♉33	9♋31	29 45	13♍53
9	18♊46	3♌ 9	23♌33	9♎ 6
11	12♋35	26 59	17♍54	5♏28
13	6♌15	21♍15	13♎ 5	2♐49
15	30 0	16♎13	9♏ 9	0♑46
17	24♍11	12♏11	6♐ 7	28 59
19	19♎17	9♐24	3♑55	27♒15
21	15♏50	7♑58	2♒27	25♓23
23	14♐11	7♒35	1♓25	23♈ 4
25	14♑ 4	7♓25	0♈16	19♉53
27	14♒31	6♈25	28 15	15♊32
29	14♓14	3♉53	24♉52	10♋ 3
31	12♈21	...	20♊ 2	...

d.	MAY	JUN	JUL	AUG
☽ 1	3♌50	17♍30	20♎38	9♐27
3	27 32	12♎23	17♏ 1	8♑18
5	21♍50	8♏50	15♐15	8♒26
7	17♎21	6♐59	14♑58	8♓44
9	14♏20	6♑18	15♒ 7	8♈ 4
11	12♐33	5♒51	14♓37	5♉46
13	11♑19	4♓45	12♈45	1♊48
15	9♒58	2♈35	9♉26	26 32
17	8♓ 6	29 21	4♊54	20♋29
19	5♈37	25♉13	29 27	14♌ 5
21	2♉30	20♊16	22♋25	7♍43
23	28 36	14♋35	17♌ 2	1♎40
25	23♊48	8♌21	10♍38	26 15
27	18♋ 6	1♍55	4♎36	21♏49
29	11♌49	25 48	29 26	18♐42
31	5♍29	...	25♏41	17♑ 7

d.	SEP	OCT	NOV	DEC
☽ 1	1♒50	10♓33	2♉57	8♊54
3	1♓54	10♈ 4	0♊33	4♋40
5	1♈53	8♉47	26 43	29 18
7	0♉42	5♊56	21♋31	23♌ 9
9	27 46	1♋25	15♌22	16♍45
11	23♊ 9	25 38	8♍59	10♎52
13	17♋21	19♌15	3♎ 5	6♏ 6
15	10♌59	12♍58	28 13	2♐52
17	4♍36	7♎19	24♏37	1♑ 2
19	28 38	2♏35	22♐ 3	29 59
21	23♎20	28 47	20♑ 6	28♒57
23	18♏49	25♐45	18♒18	27♓23
25	15♐13	23♑20	16♓28	25♈ 2
27	12♑39	21♒28	14♈28	21♉53
29	11♒10	20♓ 4	12♉ 4	17♊54
31	...	18♈46	...	13♋ 3

STATIONS	☿	♀	♂	♃
	27Mar 20♈22	None	25Mar 18♏28	10Sep 20♉59
	19Apr 8♈41		10Jun 1♏10	... ...
	30Jul 27♌ 9	♄	♅	♆
	23Aug 14♌56	25Jan 14♎59	18Mar 9♋54	24Jan 21♎43
	20Nov 16♐31	11Jun 8♎12	25Oct 18♋32	30Jun 18♎56
	10Dec 0♐17	SIDER. TIME		1 Jan
		6h 38m 24s		Midn.
		18h 40m 22s		Noon
		LEAF YEAR		1952

Noon		JAN	FEB	MAR	APR	MAY	JUN
☉	1	10♑48	12♒21	10♓37	11♈28	10♉48	10♊41
	9	18 57	20 27	18 37	19 20	18 33	18 20
	17	27 6	28 33	26 36	27 10	26 16	25 59
	25	5♒14	6♓36	4♈33	4♉59	3♊58	3♋37
☿	1	22♐40	11♒18	28♓41	19♓47	18♈35	20♊15
	7	1♑24	21 51	2♈47	21D31	28 38	2♋11
	13	10 27	2♓45	1R41	25 50	9♉49	12 42
	19	19 49	13 38	26♓48	2♈ 2	22 5	21 41
	25	29 30	23 32	21 54	9 42	5♊ 7	29 0
	31	9♒35	...	19 48	...	18 9	...
♀	1	25♒28	29♓15	23♈24	29♈33	15♈ 9	26♈59
	9	4♓34	7♈ 3	27 56	25R29	15D27	3♉19
	17	13 26	14 15	0♉43	20 32	17 58	10 23
	25	22 2	20 37	1R14	16 37	22 13	17 58
♂	1	1♓14	25♓ 1	16♈ 8	8♉52	0♊10	21♊29
	13	10 28	4♈ 8	25 1	17 28	8 30	29 34
	25	19 41	13 9	3♉48	25 58	16 44	7♋33
♃	1	11♉ 0	12♉13	15♉45	21♉30	28♉ 7	5♊21
	13	11D 6	13 29	17 48	24 3	0♊54	8 9
	25	11 40	15 8	20 5	26 44	3 43	10 53
♄	1	26♎16	27♎17	26♎47	24♎56	22♎41	20♎57
	13	26 51	27R14	26R12	24R 1	21R53	20R38
	25	27 12	26 56	25 26	23 7	21 14	20D33
♅	1	16♋44	15♋27	14♋38	14♋29	15♋ 7	16♋28
	13	16R13	15R 2	14R28	14 39	15 34	17 7
	25	15 43	14 43	14D26	14 56	16 7	17 49
♆	1	23♎44	23♎52	23♎33	22♎50	22♎ 1	21♎22
	13	23 51	23R47	23R18	22 30	21R44	21R13
	25	23R53	23 37	23 1	22 11	21 29	21 7
Pl.	1	22♌53	22♌14	21♌33	20♌58	20♌45	20♌57
☊	1	14♒ 3	12♒24	10♒55	9♒17	7♒42	6♒ 3
	1st	Thu	Sun	Sun	Wed	Fri	Mon

Noon		JUL	AUG	SEP	OCT	NOV	DEC
☉	1	9♋20	8♌55	8♍44	8♎ 1	8♏46	9♐ 1
	9	16 58	16 35	16 30	15 54	16 48	17 8
	17	24 36	24 16	24 18	23 49	24 51	25 16
	25	2♌14	1♍59	2♎ 7	1♏47	2♐56	3♑25
☿	1	4♌27	28♋ 5	3♍ 2	25♎17	0♐18	18♏48
	7	7 40	27D52	14 39	4♏ 1	29♏42	25 48
	13	8R15	1♌38	25 44	12 11	23R41	4♐ 4
	19	6 4	9 10	6♎10	19 36	16 29	12 52
	25	2 4	19 28	16 0	25 50	14D48	21 58
	31	28♋28	1♍ 4	...	29 56	...	1♑13
♀	1	23♉55	27♊ 8	2♌52	8♍56	17♎12	24♏45
	9	2♊ 9	6♋10	12 22	18 44	27 11	4♐48
	17	10 39	15 21	21 57	28 35	7♏11	14 51
	25	19 22	24 39	1♍38	8♎30	17 13	24 55
♂	1	11♋31	1♌44	21♌36	10♍34	29♍56	18♎27
	13	19 24	9 28	29 13	18 5	7 23	25 47
	25	27 13	17 8	6♍47	25 35	14 47	3♏ 2
♃	1	12♊13	18♊35	23♊31	26♊10	25♊58	23♊ 2
	13	14 48	20 42	24 52	26 28	25R 4	21R26
	25	17 14	22 34	25 51	26R18	23 47	19 49
♄	1	20♎36	21♎46	24♎14	27♎28	1♏11	4♏39
	13	20 52	22 35	25 27	28 54	2 37	5 53
	25	21 22	23 35	26 47	0♏21	4 0	6 58
♅	1	18♋10	20♋ 2	21♋40	22♋45	23♋ 6	22♋38
	13	18 54	20 43	22 11	22 59	23R 0	22R15
	25	19 37	21 20	22 35	23 6	22 47	21 48
♆	1	21♑ 7	21♎21	22♎ 3	23♎ 2	24♎11	25♎11
	13	21D 9	21 34	22 25	23 29	24 37	25 30
	25	21 15	21 51	22 49	23 56	25 0	25 46
Pl.	1	21♌32	22♌25	23♌23	24♌14	24♌48	24♌57
☊	1	4♒28	2♒49	1♒11	29♑36	27♑57	26♑22
	1st	Wed	Sat	Tue	Thu	Sun	Tue

d.		JAN	FEB	MAR	APR
☽	1	25♋19	9♍33	18♍17	3♏26
	3	19♌19	3♎12	12♎ 6	28 26
	5	12♍56	27 16	6♏22	24♐14
	7	6♎40	22♏16	1♐25	21♑ 5
	9	1♏11	18♐44	27 39	19♒13
	11	27 5	16♑57	25♑26	18♓35
	13	24♐41	16♒44	24♒49	18♈32
	15	23♑50	17♓ 8	25♓ 9	17♉55
	17	23♒43	16♈55	25♈16	15♊46
	19	23♓17	15♉11	23♉56	11♋46
	21	21♈45	11♊42	20♊42	6♌19
	23	18♉53	6♋47	15♋47	0♍ 4
	25	14♊47	0♌57	9♌48	23 42
	27	9♋43	24 40	3♍24	17♎46
	29	3♌57	...	27 5	12♏34
	31	27 44	...	21♍10	...

d.		MAY	JUN	JUL	AUG
☽	1	8♐ 9	28♑25	7♓ 6	0♉37
	3	4♑30	26♒22	5♈42	28 13
	5	1♒36	24♓40	3♉51	24♊38
	7	29 33	23♈ 6	1♊18	20♋ 2
	9	28♓18	21♉18	27 53	14♌39
	11	27♈27	18♊44	23♋30	8♍41
	13	26♉13	15♋ 1	18♌12	2♎24
	15	23♊46	10♌ 4	12♍12	26 9
	17	19♋44	4♍10	5♎54	20♏24
	19	14♌19	27 53	29 52	15♐43
	21	8♍ 8	21♎52	24♏41	12♑36
	23	1♎52	16♏42	20♐52	11♒15
	25	26 7	12♐46	18♑36	11♓13
	27	21♏18	10♑ 7	17♒38	11♈26
	29	17♐31	8♒24	17♓11	10♉43
	31	14♑37	...	16♈23	8♊25

d.		SEP	OCT	NOV	DEC
☽	1	21♊39	26♋28	11♍21	13♎18
	3	17♋ 1	20♌44	5♎ 1	7♏19
	5	11♌37	14♍29	28 54	2♐ 1
	7	5♍34	8♎10	23♏15	27 32
	9	29 17	2♏ 2	18♐11	23♑52
	11	23♎ 0	26 16	13♑49	20♒57
	13	17♏ 0	21♐ 5	10♒21	18♓45
	15	11♐40	16♑51	8♓ 3	17♈12
	17	7♑30	14♒ 2	6♈59	15♉59
	19	5♒ 0	12♓52	6♉40	14♊31
	21	4♓18	13♈ 1	6♊ 7	12♋ 7
	23	4♈47	13♉21	4♋17	8♌24
	25	5♉ 9	12♊31	0♌43	3♍22
	27	4♊ 6	9♋46	25 37	27 26
	29	1♋ 7	5♌14	19♍35	21♎11
	31	...	29 28	...	15♏15

STATIONS

☿	♀	♂	♃
9Mar 2♈59	23Mar 1♉21	None	5Jan 10♉59
2Apr 19♓52	4May 14♈58		15Oct 26♊29
11Jul 8♌22	♄	♅	♆
5Aug 27♋31	4Feb 27♎18	22Mar 14♋26	24Jan 23♎53
3Nov 0♐41	24Jun 20♎33	29Oct 23♋ 6	2Jul 21♎ 7
23Nov 14♏36			

SIDER. TIME	1 Jan
6h 41m 24s	Midn
18h 43m 22s	Noon
Common Year	1953

Noon		JAN	FEB	MAR	APR	MAY	JUN
☉	1	10♑33	12♒ 7	10♓22	11♈13	10♉34	10♊27
	9	18 43	20 13	18 23	19 6	18 19	18 7
	17	26 52	28 18	26 21	26 56	26 2	25 45
	25	5♒59	6♓22	4♈28	4♉44	3♊44	3♋23
☿	1	2♑17	24♒29	10♓10	13♓17	2♉ 4	2♋ 9
	7	12 16	4♓25	4R26	21 22	14 39	10 4
	13	21 59	12 22	1 46	29 45	27 41	15 24
	19	2♒ 0	16 2	2D51	9♈44	10♊ 0	18 20
	25	12 18	14R21	6 45	20 4	21 36	18R35
	31	22 46	...	12♓39	...	1♋13	...
♀	1	3♑44	12♒42	17♓48	26♈19	3♊19	10♋41
	9	13 48	22 46	27 45	24♉ 8	13 1	19 45
	17	23 51	2♓49	7♈43	16 1	22 43	29 45
	25	3♒54	12 48	17 38	25 49	2♋23	8♌ 1
♂	1	7♏13	25♏19	10♐39	25♐33	5♑48	8♑ 0
	13	14 19	2♐ 3	16 46	0♑18	7 56	5R49
	25	21 18	8 33	22 27	4 13	8R32	2 23
♃	1	18♊57	16♊33	17♊ 2	20♊16	25♊21	1♋49
	13	17 42	16D26	17 58	22 7	27 45	4 29
	25	16 51	16 48	19 20	24 13	0♋17	7 11
♄	1	7♏31	9♏ 8	9♏15	7♏51	5♏40	3♏37
	13	8 19	9 19	8R51	7R 2	4R47	3R 5
	25	8 53	9R17	8 16	6 7	4 1	2 44
♅	1	21♋29	20♋11	18♋19	19♋ 1	19♋32	20♋47
	13	20R58	19R46	19R 6	19D 7	19 56	21 25
	25	20 28	19 26	18 59	19 22	20 27	22 6
♆	1	25♎49	25♎59	25♎46	25♎ 5	24♎15	23♎35
	13	25 55	25R57	25R33	24R45	23R58	23R25
	25	25 58	25 50	25 16	24 24	23 43	23 20
Pl.	1	25♌	24♌	23♌	23♌	23♌	23♌
☊	1	24♑43	23♑ 5	21♑26	19♑57	18♑22	16♑43
	1st	Fri	Mon	Mon	Thu	Sat	Tue

Noon		JUL	AUG	SEP	OCT	NOV	DEC
☉	1	9♋ 6	8♌42	8♍31	7♎45	8♏32	8♐46
	9	16 44	16 22	16 16	15 40	16 33	16 53
	17	24 22	24 2	24 3	23 35	24 36	25 1
	25	2♌ 0	1♍53	1♎53	1♏32	2♐41	3♑ 1
☿	1	16♋23	20♋ 8	13♍24	20♏45	2♏43	25♏42
	7	12R47	29 47	28 38	8 56	28♎57	4♐58
	13	9 54	10♌52	8♎12	13 25	1♏31	14 17
	19	9D31	11 22	17 7	14R40	8D11	23 42
	25	12 28	5♍24	25 23	11 9	16 37	3♑10
	31	18 46	16 34	...	3 53	...	12 48
♀	1	16♌14	21♍41	24♎38	2♏43	29♏ 8	15♏ 4
	9	25 31	0♎32	2♏23	25 31	25R48	8♐ 4
	17	4♍44	9 10	9 39	28 48	21 4	20D33
	25	13 50	17 32	16 16	0♐ 4	16 51	3♑10
♂	1	0♑33	25♐39	2♑51	17♑44	7♒12	27♒59
	13	27♐22	27D 8	8 7	24 56	15 22	6♓32
	25	25R43	0♑18	14 21	2♒34	24 15	15 8
♃	1	8♋34	15♋28	21♋46	26♋38	29♋32	29♋38
	13	11 17	18 2	23 54	28 3	29 55	28R47
	25	13 44	20 27	25 47	29 7	29R49	27 35
♄	1	2♏40	3♏11	5♏ 9	8♏ 4	11♏40	15♏12
	13	2D41	3 48	6 13	9 24	13 6	16 32
	25	2 56	4 36	7 25	10 49	14 30	17 45
♅	1	22♋27	24♋20	26♋ 2	27♋13	27♋42	27♋22
	13	23 11	25 1	26 35	27 30	27R40	27R 1
	25	23 55	25 41	27 2	27 40	27 31	26 35
♆	1	23♎18	23♎30	24♎10	25♎ 8	26♎16	27♎17
	13	23D18	23 42	24 31	25 35	26 42	27 37
	25	23 25	23 58	24 56	26 1	27 6	27 53
Pl.	1	24♌	24♌	25♌	26♌	27♌	27♌
☊	1	15♑ 8	13♑29	11♑51	10♑16	8♑37	7♑ 2
	1st	Thu	Sun	Wed	Fri	Mon	Wed

d.	JAN	FEB	MAR	APR
☽ 1	27♍24	14♑10	22♑ 5	12♓40
3	22♐58	11♒58	19♒57	12♈57
5	19♑39	10♓54	19♓31	13♉33
7	17♒17	10♈13	19♈42	12♊43
9	15♓31	9♉ 3	19♉17	10♋24
11	13♈57	6♊46	17♊18	6♌17
13	12♉13	3♋46	13♋52	1♍ 6
15	10♊ 6	29 56	9♌16	25 3
17	7♋17	24♌56	3♍53	17♎51
19	3♌33	19♍20	28 2	13♏38
21	28 51	13♎18	21♎53	6♐34
23	23♍15	7♏ 4	15♏38	0♑46
25	18♎ 7	0♐56	9♐38	26 12
27	10♍55	25 46	4♑14	22♒54
29	5♐23	...	0♒13	21♓17
31	0♑30	...	28 1	...

d.	MAY	JUN	JUL	AUG
☽ 1	21♈18	15♊ 1	21♋53	0♍41
3	21♉52	13♋41	18♌43	4♎28
5	21♊22	10♌44	14♍13	28 30
7	19♋ 6	6♍11	8♎38	22♏16
9	15♌17	1♎37	2♏27	16♐23
11	9♍56	24 19	26 20	11♑27
13	2♎59	18♏ 9	20♐47	7♒34
15	27 41	14♐24	16♑11	5♓54
17	21♏32	7♑19	12♒38	4♈20
19	15♐41	3♒ 2	10♓ 5	3♉20
21	10♑30	29 38	8♈10	1♊47
23	5♒49	26♓14	6♉ 5	29 30
25	2♓45	25♈42	5♊ 1	26♋27
27	0♈41	24♉43	3♋ 5	22♌40
29	0♉17	23♊41	0♌28	18♍ 1
31	0♊11	...	26 52	12♎36

d.	SEP	OCT	NOV	DEC
☽ 1	4♎38	26♍43	11♑16	15♒37
3	18♏23	20♐27	6♒ 7	11♓52
5	12♐10	14♑48	2♓39	9♈48
7	6♑52	10♒32	0♈48	9♉ 7
9	2♒29	8♓ 5	0♉15	9♊16
11	0♓ 5	7♈31	1♊20	9♋11
13	29 11	7♉54	1♋13	7♌42
15	28♈56	8♊ 1	29 24	4♍ 3
17	27♉15	6♋28	25♌49	29 35
19	26♊16	3♌29	20♍49	23♎43
21	23♋23	29 6	15♎ 1	17♏21
23	19♌20	23♍48	8♏47	11♐ 6
25	14♍28	17♎58	2♐28	5♑14
27	9♒ 2	11♏47	26 19	0♒ 0
29	3♏ 2	5♐26	20♑34	25 36
31	...	29 14	...	22♓ 4

STATIONS	☿	♀	♂	♃
	20Feb 15♓ 5	26Oct 0♐ 4	23May 8♑31	10Feb 16♊25
	15Mar 1♓42	6Dec 14♏40	30Jul 25♐36	17Nov 29♋57
		♄	♅	♆
	23Jun 18♋39	16Feb 9♏20	27Mar 18♋59	30Jan 25♎59
	17Jul 9♋18	5Jul 2♏37	3Nov 27♋43	3Jul 23♎18
	18Oct 14♏46	SIDER. TIME		1 Jan
	9Nov 28♏58	6h 40m 27s		Midn.
		18h 42m 25s		Noon
		Common Year		1954

1955

Noon		JAN	FEB	MAR	APR	MAY	JUN
☉	1	10♑18	11♒52	10♓ 9	10♈59	10♉21	10♊13
	9	18 27	19 58	18 59	18 52	18 5	17 35
	17	26 36	28 3	26 7	26 42	25 49	25 31
	25	4♒46	6♓ 7	4♈ 4	4♉31	3♊31	3♋10
☿	1	14♑26	29♒ 7	15♒14	21♓25	19♉57	28♊36
	7	24 16	28R25	19 0	1♈28	1♊47	28R22
	13	4♒20	22 29	24 50	12 33	11 53	25 48
	19	13 55	16 24	2♓ 6	24 32	19 50	22 36
	25	22 45	14D22	10 25	7♉12	25 24	20 23
	31	28 35	...	19 38	...	28 23	...
♀	1	26♏12	25♐10	26♑ 8	2♓24	8♈15	12♉38
	9	2♐45	3♑43	5♒23	11 55	17 52	25 19
	17	10 2	12 34	14 43	21 28	27 31	5♊ 2
	25	17 55	21 36	24 7	1♈ 3	7♉10	14 45
♂	1	20♓10	12♈22	2♉ 9	23♉34	13♊48	4♋14
	13	28 47	20 53	10 31	1♊43	21 46	12 1
	25	7♈22	29 21	18 47	9 7	29 39	19 48
♃	1	26♋46	22♋44	20♋16	20♋16	22♋59	27♋50
	13	25R14	21 26	19 55	21 4	24 40	0♌ 8
	25	23 37	20 30	20D 1	22 16	26 36	2 26
♄	1	18♏23	20♏31	21♏11	20♏22	18♏27	16♏13
	13	19 22	20 58	21R 4	19R42	17R34	15R30
	25	20 9	21 10	20 41	18 53	16 41	14 56
♅	1	26♋18	24♋59	24♋ 1	23♋36	24♋ 0	25♋ 9
	13	25R47	24R31	23R46	23D40	24 22	25 43
	25	25 16	24 8	23 38	23 52	24 50	26 25
♆	1	28♎ 0	28♎15	28♎ 0	27♎18	26♎31	25♎48
	13	28 10	28R11	27R46	26R59	26R13	25R37
	25	28 14	28 3	27 29	26 40	25 56	25 31
Pl.	1	27♌	26♌	25♌	25♌	24♌	24♌
☊	1	5♑24	3♑45	2♑16	0♑37	28♐ 2	27♐24
	1st	Sat	Tue	Tue	Fri	Sun	Wed

Noon		JUL	AUG	SEP	OCT	NOV	DEC
☉	1	8♋23	8♌28	8♍17	7♎32	8♏17	8♐31
	9	16 30	16 7	16 2	15 25	16 13	16 38
	17	24 8	23 48	23 49	23 20	24 22	24 46
	25	1♌46	1♍30	1♎39	1♏18	2♐27	2♑55
☿	1	20♊40	3♌44	0♎ 0	28♎36	18♎18	6♐48
	7	23D51	16 11	8 23	26R25	28 47	16 14
	13	29 52	28 2	15 47	20 10	8♏12	25 40
	19	8♋ 2	9♍ 2	22 10	14 12	17 47	5♑ 9
	25	19 23	19 11	26 45	13D51	27 10	14 41
	31	1♌ 8	28 31	...	19 4	...	24 7
♀	1	22♊ 3	0♌ 2	8♍19	15♎38	24♏18	1♑41
	9	1♋49	9 53	18 15	25 36	4♐16	11 38
	17	11 37	19 45	28 12	5♏35	14 13	21 35
	25	21 25	29 38	8♎ 9	15 34	24 13	1♒30
♂	1	23♋39	13♌30	3♍14	22♍21	12♎12	1♏35
	13	1♌21	21 8	10 53	0♎ 1	19 51	9 23
	25	9 2	28 47	18 31	7 42	27 42	17 11
♃	1	3♌45	10♌29	17♌14	23♌15	28♌14	1♍ 3
	13	6 19	13 8	19 44	25 23	29 39	1 27
	25	8 57	15 44	22 7	27 15	0♍41	1R25
♄	1	14♏45	14♏38	16♏ 3	18♏35	21♏58	25♏32
	13	14R32	15 1	16 55	19 49	23 24	26 35
	25	14D32	15 37	18 0	21 9	24 50	28 13
♅	1	26♋46	28♋39	0♌24	1♌42	2♌19	2♌ 5
	13	27D29	29 21	0 59	2 2	2R19	2R47
	25	28 13	0♌ 2	1 29	2 15	2 12	1 24
♆	1	25♎28	25♎37	26♎16	27♎14	28♎22	29♎24
	13	25D28	25 49	26 37	27 40	28 49	29 45
	25	25 33	26 4	27 1	28 7	29 13	0♏ 1
Pl.	1	25♌	26♌	27♌	28♌	28♌	28♌
☊	1	25♐48	24♐11	22♐31	20♐56	19♐17	17♐42
	1st	Fri	Mon	Thu	Sat	Tue	Thu

d.	JAN	FEB	MAR	APR
☽ 1	5♈46	28♉48	9♊44	2♌ 0
3	3♉58	27♊16	7♋50	28 38
5	3♊ 1	25♋38	5♌14	24♍26
7	2♋27	23♌20	2♍ 8	19♎27
9	1♌23	20♍ 2	28 14	13♏47
11	28 34	15♎25	23♎50	7♐33
13	25♍ 8	9♏40	17♏32	1♑ 9
15	19♎52	3♐24	23♐ 1	25 13
17	14♏46	29 14	14♑59	20♒23
19	7♐24	21♑38	29 33	17♓22
21	1♑30	17♒35	25♒42	16♈10
23	26 22	13♓47	23♓21	16♉ 5
25	22♒14	12♈55	22♈21	15♊46
27	19♓ 2	11♉25	21♉41	14♋37
29	16♈ 2	...	20♊32	12♌25
31	14♉37	...	18♋40	...

d.	MAY	JUN	JUL	AUG
☽ 1	8♍10	25♌32	28♏15	12♑13
3	3♎46	19♍30	21♐52	6♒46
5	28 27	13♐ 6	15♑42	1♓37
7	22♏25	12♑42	10♒ 5	28 21
9	16♐ 7	0♒47	5♓ 4	25♈43
11	9♑45	25 21	2♈ 6	23♉12
13	3♒51	21♓23	28 39	21♊42
15	28 29	18♈47	27♉20	20♋37
17	25♓45	17♉13	26♊36	19♌25
19	24♈20	17♊50	26♋17	17♍17
21	24♉20	17♋58	25♌17	13♎51
23	24♊40	16♌59	22♍42	8♏55
25	24♋ 7	14♍21	18♎30	2♐56
27	22♌ 2	10♎ 3	12♏47	26 36
29	18♍24	4♏29	6♐29	20♑31
31	13♎18	...	0♑27	15♒20

d.	SEP	OCT	NOV	DEC
☽ 1	28♒11	3♈ 5	28♉20	3♋56
3	24♓44	1♉53	25♊ 1	3♌34
5	22♈ 9	0♊36	23♋55	1♍49
7	20♉ 4	29 10	21♌45	28 30
9	18♊14	27♋15	18♍29	23♎50
11	16♋28	24♌48	14♎10	18♏15
13	14♌37	21♍40	9♏ 9	12♐ 6
15	12♍17	17♎41	3♐24	5♑52
17	9♎ 1	12♏43	27 4	26 22
19	2♏32	6♐55	20♑39	23♒22
21	28 55	0♑34	14♒32	18♓16
23	22♐18	24 14	9♓29	14♈16
25	16♑20	18♒37	5♈51	13♉ 3
27	10♒51	14♓21	3♉57	11♊23
29	6♓27	11♈47	3♊40	11♋54
31	...	10♉41	...	12♌ 6

STATIONS	☿	♀	♂	♃
	4Feb 29♒39	None	None	17Mar 19♋54
	26Feb 14♒22			18Dec 1♍30
	4Jun 28♊50	♄	♅	♆
	28Jun 20♊ 9	1Mar 21♏11	1Apr 23♋26	29Jan 28♎15
	2Oct 28♎27	19Jul 14♏30	8Nov 2♌20	7Jul 25♎26
	23Oct 13♎11	SIDER TIME		1Jan
		6h 39m 29s		Midn.
		18h 41m 27s		Noon
		Common Year		1955

Noon	JAN	FEB	MAR	APR	MAY	JUN
☉ 1	10♑ 3	11♒37	10♓53	11♈44	11♉ 5	10♊56
9	16 10	19 43	18 54	19 37	18 49	18 36
17	26 22	27 49	26 53	27 27	26 32	26 15
25	4♒30	5♓52	4♈49	5♉15	4♊14	3♋53
☿ 1	25♑40	0♒54	15♒51	6♈55	1♊46	1♊26
7	4♒23	27♑40	24 8	19 6	7 4	0R15
13	11 8	28D55	3♓14	1♉40	8 50	1D38
19	13R26	3♒22	13 3	13 38	7R57	5 40
25	9 18	9 38	23 36	23 55	5 1	12 7
31	1 54	...	4♈57	...	1 51	...
♀ 1	10♒11	18♓10	22♈38	27♉ 6	25♊12	9♋ 0
9	20 3	27 49	1♉50	5♊17	0♋17	7R32
17	2♓20	7♈22	10 50	13 3	5 27	3 42
25	9 40	16 48	19 38	20 15	8 16	29♊ 2
♂ 1	21♏47	12♐ 4	1♑ 6	20♑48	10♒26	28♑58
13	0♐ 7	19 56	8 58	29 3	17 50	5♓29
25	4 12	27 49	16 56	6♒40	24 58	11 25
♃ 1	1♍10	28♌26	24♌43	21♌52	21♌47	24♌29
13	0R25	26R53	23R21	21R31	22 30	25 1
25	29 15	25 20	22 20	21D35	23 37	27 52
♄ 1	28♏56	1♐31	2♐44	2♐29	0♐53	28♏38
13	0♐ 5	2 10	2R50	1R58	0R 3	27R51
25	1 3	2 36	2 41	1 17	29♏ 8	27 6
♅ 1	1♌ 8	29♋48	28♋45	28♋14	28♋32	29♋36
13	0R35	29R20	28R28	28D15	28 52	0♌12
25	0 6	28 54	26 16	28 24	29 18	0 50
♆ 1	0♏ 9	0♏25	0♏10	29♎31	28♎43	28♎ 0
13	0 17	0R22	29♎58	29R13	28R24	27R49
25	0R25	0 14	29 42	28 54	28 8	27 41
Pl. 1	28♌	28♌	27♌	26♌	26♌	26♌
☊ 1	16♐ 4	14♐26	12♐53	11♐15	9♐39	8♐ 1
1st	Sun	Wed	Thu	Sun	Tue	Fri

Noon	JUL	AUG	SEP	OCT	NOV	DEC
☉ 1	9♋36	9♌11	9♍ 0	8♎17	9♏ 3	9♐17
9	17 14	16 51	16 46	16 10	17 5	17 25
17	24 51	24 32	24 34	24 6	25 8	25 33
25	2♌29	2♍14	2♎32	2♏ 3	3♐13	3♑42
☿ 1	20♊43	22♌22	6♎ 0	28♏44	1♏55	19♐35
7	1♋22	2♍54	10 26	27R37	11 48	28 48
13	13 31	13 0	12 9	2♎17	21 23	7♑45
19	26 20	21 9	10R10	10D33	0♐57	17 21
25	8♌50	28 46	4 35	20 15	10 18	23 31
31	20 31	5♎10	...	1♏ 5	...	27 19
♀ 1	25♊30	28♊16	23♋10	24♌48	0♎49	7♏20
9	22R53	3♋25	1♌ 8	3♍51	10 28	17 13
17	22D45	9 37	9 28	13 6	20 9	27 9
25	24 53	16 35	18 8	22 29	2♏57	7♐ 7
♂ 1	14♓ 5	23♓ 5	20♓41	13♓40	16♓12	27♓37
13	18 38	23R37	17R24	13R13	20 0	3♈34
25	21 54	22 14	14 35	14D37	24 51	10 3
♃ 1	28♌54	4♍49	11♍24	17♍50	23♍57	28♍40
13	1♍ 4	7 20	14 0	20 19	25 2	0♎ 3
25	3 24	9 53	16 35	22 39	27 51	1 3
♄ 1	26♏49	26♏10	27♏ 2	29♏ 9	2♐19	5♐49
13	26 24	26D18	27 45	0♐17	3 41	7 13
25	26 13	26 41	28 38	1 33	5 7	8 35
♅ 1	1♌11	3♌ 4	4♌51	6♌13	6♌56	6♌50
13	1 54	3 46	5 27	6 35	6 59	6R35
25	2 38	4 28	5 59	6 50	6R55	6 13
♆ 1	27♎40	27♎48	28♎25	29♎20	0♏30	1♏32
13	27D39	27 59	28 45	29 48	0 56	1 53
25	27 44	28 14	29 8	0♏14	1 23	2 10
Pl. 1	27♌	27♌	29♌	0♍	0♍	1♍
☊ 1	6♐25	4♐47	3♐ 8	1♐33	29♏55	28♏19
1st	Sun	Wed	Sat	Mon	Thu	Sat

d.	JAN	FEB	MAR	APR
☽ 1	26♌42	16♎12	7♏ 7	21♐46
3	24♍35	11♏42	1♐56	15♑28
5	26♎38	6♐51	26 48	9♒16
7	15♏15	29 27	19♑27	3♓51
9	9♐ 7	23♑ 6	13♒26	29 34
11	2♑44	17♒14	8♓18	25♈16
13	26 22	12♓10	4♈ 8	24♉24
15	20♒16	7♈39	0♉49	22♊45
17	15♓ 6	4♉ 0	28 24	21♋ 9
19	10♈36	1♊15	26♊ 2	19♌22
21	7♉21	29 29	24♋21	17♍11
23	5♊18	28♋40	22♌56	14♎14
25	4♋48	27♌38	21♍18	10♏22
27	4♌58	26♍58	18♎16	5♐27
29	4♍42	24♎ 7	14♏54	29 37
31	2♎52	...	9♐43	...

d.	MAY	JUN	JUL	AUG
☽ 1	23♑23	7♓32	11♈14	0♊26
3	17♒12	2♈24	7♉38	29 4
5	21♓47	29 13	5♊45	29♋ 5
7	7♈39	27♉29	5♋28	29♌32
9	5♉ 0	26♊58	5♌54	28♍54
11	3♊38	27♋ 4	5♍46	26♎30
13	2♋40	26♌24	4♎ 4	22♏15
15	1♌53	24♍22	0♏34	16♐41
17	0♍12	20♎54	25 37	10♑28
19	27 32	16♏12	19♐46	4♒ 9
21	23♎53	10♐40	13♑29	28 6
23	19♏16	4♑36	7♒10	22♓25
25	15♐52	28 19	1♓ 4	17♈33
27	7♑51	22♒ 4	25 25	13♉22
29	1♒28	16♓12	20♈30	10♊19
31	25 23	...	16♉44	8♋29

d.	SEP	OCT	NOV	DEC
☽ 1	23♋ 5	2♍12	24♎ 7	29♍29
3	22♌56	1♎11	24♏50	24♐34
5	22♍40	28 46	16♐25	18♑54
7	21♎12	25♏51	10♑57	12♒44
9	17♏55	20♐58	4♒44	6♓31
11	13♐ 0	15♑ 5	28 25	0♈43
13	7♑ 4	8♒50	22♓55	26 2
15	0♒54	2♓49	19♈21	22♉57
17	24 37	27 35	15♉ 7	21♊31
19	19♓15	23♈20	13♊ 7	21♋10
21	14♈24	20♉ 4	12♋21	20♌53
23	10♉22	17♊35	10♌42	19♍44
25	7♊ 6	15♋36	9♍ 5	17♎13
27	4♋42	13♌57	6♎44	13♏26
29	3♌ 8	12♍19	3♏32	8♐40
31	...	10♎21	...	3♑16

STATIONS

☿	♀	♂	♃
19Jan 13♒26	1Jun 9♋ 0	11Aug 23♍39	18Apr 21♌29
9Feb 27♑38	14Jul 22♊30	11Oct 13♓ 9	...
15May 8♊52	♄	♅	♆
8Jun 10♊14	12Mar 2♐50	6Apr 28♋13	30Jun 0♏25
14Sep 12♎ 9	1Aug 26♏10	12Nov 6♌59	9Jul 27♎39
6Oct 27♏17	SIDER. TIME		1 Jan
	6h 38m 32s		Midn.
	18h 40m 30s		Noon
	LEAP YEAR		1956

Noon	JAN	FEB	MAR	APR	MAY	JUN
☉ 1	10♑50	12♒23	10♓39	11♈31	10♉50	10♊43
9	18 59	20 29	18 40	19 22	18 35	18 22
17	27 8	28 34	26 38	27 12	26 18	26 1
25	5♒16	6♓38	4♈34	4♉ 1	4♊ 0	3♋39
☿ 1	27♑25	17♑10	25♒ 4	23♈29	17♉48	16♉31
7	24R 2	23 35	5♓11	15 35	14R18	23 3
13	16 26	1♒11	15 56	23 1	11 7	1♊21
19	11 40	9 37	27 24	29♉56	10 1	11 33
25	12D 6	18 41	9♈26	7 52	11D34	23 15
31	16 13	...	21 31	...	15 37	...
♀ 1	15♐50	24♑34	29♒33	8♈ 9	15♉16	23♊24
9	25 49	4♒34	9♓32	18 4	25 7	3♋12
17	5♑49	14 34	19 30	27 58	5♊21	12 59
25	15 49	24 34	29♈27	7♉52	14 48	22 45
♂ 1	13♈59	2♉22	19♉43	9♊11	28♊ 2	17♋29
13	20 57	9 46	27 15	16 43	5♋34	25 0
25	28 8	17 13	4♊47	24 15	13 15	2♌31
♃ 1	1♎27	1♎24	28♍58	25♍ 1	22♍18	22♍ 6
13	1 46	0R33	27R26	23R42	21R54	22 47
25	1R39	29♍22	25 54	22 40	21D54	23 51
♄ 1	9♐21	12♐15	13♐53	1♐15	13♐ 9	11♐ 3
13	10 36	13 6	14 12	13R57	12R25	10 11
25	11 41	13 43	14R18	13 29	11 34	9 21
♅ 1	5♌57	4♌38	3♌34	2♌55	3♌ 4	4♌ 2
13	5R28	4R 8	3R13	2D52	3 21	4 35
25	4 57	3 41	2 59	2 58	3 46	5 12
♆ 1	2♏18	2♏36	2♏24	1♏47	1♏ 0	0♏15
13	2 29	2R34	2R13	1R28	0R40	0R 2
25	2 35	2 28	1 57	1 9	0 23	29♎54
Pl. 1	0♍	0♍	29♌	28♌	28♌	28♌
☊ 1	26♏41	25♏ 2	23♏33	21♏55	20♏20	18♏41
1st	Tue	Fri	Fri	Mon	Wed	Sat

Noon	JUL	AUG	SEP	OCT	NOV	DEC
☉ 1	9♋22	8♌57	8♍46	8♎ 2	8♏48	9♐ 2
9	17 0	16 37	16 32	15 56	16 49	17 10
17	26 32	24 58	24 19	23 51	24 53	25 18
25	2♌16	2♍ 0	2♎ 9	1♏49	2♐58	3♑27
☿ 1	6♋ 1	3♍30	23♍54	21♍56	14♏ 3	28♐44
7	18 59	11 19	19R13	1♎47	23 27	5♑59
13	1♌22	17 50	13 32	12 16	2♐40	10 47
19	12 41	22 37	11 11	22 39	11 40	10R37
25	22 55	25 5	14D14	2♏42	20 25	4 16
31	2♍ 5	24R22	...	12 28	...	27♐12
♀ 1	1♋ 4	7♍41	14♎59	19♏53	25♐ 8	25♑31
9	9♌48	17 21	24 23	29 7	3♑33	2♒21
17	19 32	26 58	3♏49	8♐29	11 46	8 14
25	29 13	6♎34	13 11	17 26	19 55	12 50
♂ 1	6♌27	25♌46	15♍26	4♎45	25♎ 6	15♏14
13	13 45	3♍21	23 7	12 34	3♏ 6	23 25
25	21 21	10 58	0♎47	20 28	11 10	1♐41
♃ 1	24♍30	29♍ 3	4♎54	11♎14	17♎54	23♎48
13	26 4	1♎11	7 23	13 50	20 22	25 53
25	27 52	3 30	9 56	16 25	22 41	27 42
♄ 1	8♐59	7♐46	8♐ 2	9♐40	12♐30	15♐52
13	8R20	7D41	8 31	10 40	13 48	17 17
25	7 55	7 50	9 15	11 47	15 10	18 41
♅ 1	5♌32	7♌24	9♌15	10♌41	11♌32	11♌34
13	6 15	8 8	9 52	11 6	11 39	11R22
25	6 58	8 51	10 26	11 24	11R37	11 0
♆ 1	29♎52	29♎57	0♏32	1♏27	2♏36	3♏39
13	29D50	0♏ 7	0 52	1 53	3 2	4 0
25	29 53	0 21	1 15	2 19	3 27	4 17
Pl. 1	29♌	29♌	1♍	1♍	2♍	2♍
☊ 1	17♏ 6	15♏27	13♏39	12♏14	10♏35	9♏ 0
1st	Mon	Thu	Sun	Tue	Fri	Sun

d.	JAN	FEB	MAR	APR
☽ 1	15♑20	0♓50	8♓45	24♈10
3	9♒14	23 39	2♈46	19♉29
5	2♓56	17♈50	27 14	15♊35
7	26 48	12♉28	22♉26	12♋48
9	21♈21	9♊14	18♊57	11♌ 5
11	17♉10	7♋ 9	16♋36	10♍18
13	14♊46	7♌26	15♌58	9♎42
15	14♋16	8♍ 8	16♍11	8♏28
17	14♌46	8♎ 9	16♎12	5♐43
19	15♍ 3	6♏12	14♏23	1♑28
21	13♎ 4	2♐26	10♐53	26 2
23	10♏24	27 15	5♑50	20♒25
25	5♐51	21♑14	0♒51	13♓44
27	0♑14	14♒57	24 35	7♈59
29	24 11	...	17♓27	3♉ 1
31	18♒58	...	11♈49	...

d.	MAY	JUN	JUL	AUG
☽ 1	29♉ 2	20♋ 2	29♌10	22♎28
3	25♊47	18♌40	28♍ 1	19♏43
5	23♋38	17♍13	25♎52	15♐38
7	21♌57	15♎16	22♏43	10♑39
9	20♍27	12♏38	18♐36	5♒ 0
11	18♎59	9♐14	13♑45	28 59
13	16♏53	5♑16	8♒15	22♓43
15	14♐43	29 48	2♓13	16♈26
17	9♑52	24♒54	26 55	10♉39
19	3♒55	17♓42	1 ♈54	6♊ 0
21	28 51	11♈46	14♉36	3♋ 9
23	21♓41	6♉30	10♊58	2♌ 2
25	16♈ 2	2♊44	9♋ 3	2♍17
27	11♉24	0♋35	8♌37	2♎43
29	8♊ 5	29 42	8♍48	1♏55
31	5♋49	...	8♎16	29 17

d.	SEP	OCT	NOV	DEC
☽ 1	12♐29	16♑42	1♓20	2♈59
3	7♑44	11♒ 0	25 10	27 3
5	2♒ 5	4♓48	18♈59	22♉ 0
7	26 0	28 32	13♉36	18♊ 4
9	19♓45	22♈31	9♊ 1	15♋17
11	13♈31	16♉59	5♋20	13♌16
13	7♉35	12♊14	2♌47	11♍30
15	2♊25	8♋23	0♍31	9♎45
17	28 26	5♌51	29 40	7♏47
19	26♋ 7	5♍ 9	28♎ 2	5♐23
21	25♌30	4♎20	26♏33	2♑20
23	25♍50	3♏52	24♐ 9	28 17
25	25♎49	2♐29	20♑17	23♒ 4
27	24♏ 2	29 38	15♒18	17♓ 4
29	8♐10	25♑ 5	9♓17	10♈46
31	...	19♒25	...	4♉ 8

STATIONS	☿	♀	♂	♃
	1Jan 27♑25 22Jan 11♑16 25Apr 19♉27 19May 10♉ 1 27Aug 25♍14 19Sep 11♍11 16Dec 11♑31	None	None	16Jan 1♎47 18May 21♍51
		♄	♅	♆
		24Mar 14♐18 11Aug 7♐41	10Apr 2♌52 17Nov 11♌30	3Feb 2♏36 12Jul 29♎50
		SIDER. TIME 6h 41m 31s 18h 43m 29s Common Year		1 Jan Midn. Noon 1957

Noon		JAN	FEB	MAR	APR	MAY	JUN
☉	1	10♐35	12♒ 8	10♓25	11♈15	10♉36	10♊29
	9	18 44	20 14	18 25	19 8	18 21	18 8
	17	26 53	28 20	26 23	26 58	26 4	25 47
	25	5♑ 1	6♓23	4♈20	4♉47	3♊46	3♋25
☿	1	26♐29	22♑25	8♓23	29♈19	20♈ 5	21♉52
	7	25D32	1♒20	19 48	0♉50	22D 2	3♊11
	13	29 11	10 43	1♈31	28♈12	26 23	15 37
	19	5♑17	22 20	12 50	24R18	2♉47	28 42
	25	12 14	1♓ 5	22 32	20 55	10 48	11♋37
	31	20 59	...	28 40	...	20 18	...
♀	1	15♒27	6♒10	3♒ 2	25♒ 8	25♓39	0♉ 8
	9	16R15	2R16	7 3	2♓47	4♈25	9 37
	17	14 29	0 42	12 27	10 50	13 20	18 55
	25	10 26	1D42	18 53	19 13	22 23	28 17
♂	1	6♐33	28♐23	18♑31	11♒10	3♓15	25♓52
	13	14 56	6♑58	27 15	19 59	12 3	4♈27
	25	23 25	15 37	6♒ 4	28 50	20 49	13 6
♃	1	28♎39	1♏21	1♏22	28♎46	25♎ 0	22♎14
	13	0♏ 0	1 39	0R38	27R17	23R41	21R50
	25	0 58	1R31	29♎32	25 46	22 40	21D49
♄	1	19♐29	22♐42	24♐45	25♐43	25♐ 8	23♐20
	13	20 49	23 42	25 18	25R40	24R33	22R27
	25	22 3	24 31	25 38	25 22	23 49	21 34
♅	1	10♌47	9♌31	8♌23	7♌38	7♌39	8♌30
	13	10R20	9R 0	8R 0	7 33	7 53	9 0
	25	9 49	8 43	7 44	7D35	8 15	9 37
♆	1	4♏27	4♏47	4♏36	4♏ 1	3♏13	2♏29
	13	4 38	4R45	4 26	3R33	2R54	2R16
	25	4 45	4 39	4 11	3 23	2 37	2 7
Pl.	1	2♍	2♍	1♍	0♍	0♍	0♍
☊	1	7♏21	5♏43	4♏14	2♏35	1♏ 0	29♎21
	1st	Wed	Sat	Sat	Tue	Thu	Sun

Noon		JUL	AUG	SEP	OCT	NOV	DEC
☉	1	9♋ 8	8♌44	8♍52	7♎48	8♏34	8♐48
	9	16 46	16 23	16 19	15 41	16 35	16 55
	17	23 24	24 4	24 6	23 37	24 38	25 3
	25	2♌ 2	1♍47	1♎55	1♏34	2♐43	3♑12
☿	1	23♋35	4♍56	24♌45	4♎38	24♏48	25♐34
	7	4♌23	7 29	26D35	15 13	3♐23	21R37
	13	13 56	6R56	3♍10	25 20	11 29	13 14
	19	22 13	3 33	12 49	5♏ 2	18 44	9 25
	25	29 4	28♌23	23 42	14 20	24 2	11D28
	31	4♍16	24 44	...	23 32	...	17 3
♀	1	5♊20	12♋22	19♌37	27♍16	6♏ 3	13♐44
	9	14 50	22 0	29 58	7♎15	16 5	23 47
	17	24 22	1♌46	9♍52	17 14	26 9	3♑51
	25	3♋56	11 31	19 48	27 15	6♐12	13 54
♂	1	16♈59	6♉54	23♉ 7	1♊58	29♉ 0	19♉ 2
	13	24 59	13 45	27 45	2R28	24R52	16 54
	25	2♉38	19 56	0♊59	0 52	20 42	16D36
♃	1	22♎ 0	24♎26	28♎58	4♏42	11♏21	17♏55
	13	22 39	25 59	1♏ 9	7 12	13 59	20 23
	25	23 12	27 48	3 29	9 49	16 36	22 46
♄	1	21♐ 9	19♐30	19♐ 9	20♐16	22♐43	25♐54
	13	20R24	19R12	19 26	21 5	23 55	27 18
	25	19 46	19D 5	19 57	22 4	25 13	28 43
♅	1	9♌56	11♌46	13♌39	15♌11	16♌11	16♌20
	13	10 37	12 31	14 3	15 39	16 20	16R10
	25	11 20	13 14	14 54	16 1	16R22	15 51
♆	1	2♏ 4	2♏ 6	2♏40	3♏33	4♏41	5♏44
	13	2R 1	2 15	2 58	3 58	5 7	6 7
	25	2D 3	2 30	3 21	4 24	5 32	6 26
Pl.	1	0♍	1♍	2♍	3♍	4♍	4♍
☊	1	27♎46	26♎ 8	24♎29	22♎54	21♎15	19♎40
	1st	Tue	Fri	Mon	Wed	Sat	Mon

d.	JAN	FEB	MAR	APR
☽ 1	18♉ 7	4♋17	12♋ 9	3♍39
3	12♊54	2♌36	10♌33	3♎51
5	10♋14	2♍22	10♍35	4♏14
7	8♌52	2♎12	11♎ 1	3♐36
9	7♍53	1♏12	10♏38	0♑39
11	7♎ 5	28 49	8♐40	26 34
13	4♏ 5	25♐14	5♑ 7	21♒42
15	1♐47	20♑44	0♒18	15♓34
17	28 15	15♒32	24 41	9♈10
19	24♑ 1	9♓45	18♓31	3♉51
21	18♒59	3♈27	18♈11	27 0
23	13♓11	27 2	6♉48	21♊39
25	7♈51	20♉53	29 49	17♋22
27	0♉32	15♊42	24♊42	14♌21
29	24 52	...	20♋56	12♍43
31	20♊35	...	18♌59	...

d.	MAY	JUN	JUL	AUG
☽ 1	12♎19	5♐30	12♑18	29♒57
3	12♏20	3♑53	8♒55	24♓25
5	11♐40	0♒50	4♓12	18♈11
7	9♑31	26 15	28 24	11♉53
9	5♒39	20♓ 9	22♈ 3	5♊59
11	0♓20	14♈ 7	15♉52	1♋12
13	24 9	7♉51	10♊29	28 23
15	18♈43	2♊19	6♋27	26♌53
17	11♉34	27 54	3♌12	26♍ 9
19	6♊ 3	24♋18	1♍57	25♎19
21	1♋23	21♌40	0♎26	23♏46
23	27 37	19♍39	28 52	21♐16
25	24♌47	17♎52	26♏53	17♑53
27	22♍52	16♏17	21♐19	13♒38
29	21♎44	14♐36	21♑25	8♓33
31	20♏58	...	17♒19	2♈43

d.	SEP	OCT	NOV	DEC
☽ 1	13♈31	16♉43	8♋ 8	7♌11
3	8♉10	10♊31	27 15	3♍46
5	1♊56	5♋12	23♌48	1♎26
7	26 36	1♌ 9	21♍54	0♏20
9	22♋44	28 51	21♎29	29 58
11	20♌46	27♍59	21♏47	29♐33
13	20♍ 8	28♎36	21♐39	27♑29
15	20♎11	28♏42	20♑ 0	24♒37
17	19♏33	27♐31	16♒27	19♓39
19	17♐59	24♑35	11♓20	14♈31
21	14♑54	20♒ 6	5♈13	7♉ 4
23	10♒36	14♓32	28 47	0♊55
25	5♓22	8♈19	22♉32	25 37
27	29 28	1♉55	16♊41	21♋ 2
29	23♈ 9	25 37	11♋33	17♋19
31	...	19♊42	...	14♍19

STATIONS	☿	♀	♂	♃
	5Jan 25♐14	8Jan 16♒16	11Oct 2♊32	15Feb 1♏40
	7Apr 0♉50	18Feb 0♒42	21Dec 16♉36	19Jun 21♎46
	30Apr 20♈ 1			
	10Aug 7♍42			
	30Nov 25♐41			
	20Dec 9♐27			

♄	♅	♆
5Apr 25♐43	15Apr 7♌ 2	4Feb 4♏47
24Aug 19♐ 5	22Nov 16♌22	14Jul 2♏ 1

SIDER. TIME	1 Jan
6h 40m 34s	Midn.
18h 42m 32s	Noon
Common Year	1958

Noon		JAN	FEB	MAR	APR	MAY	JUN
☉	1	10♑20	11♒53	10♓ 9	11♈ 1	10♉22	10♊15
	9	18 29	20 0	18 10	18 54	18 7	17 55
	17	26 38	28 5	26 9	26 44	25 51	25 33
	25	4♒46	6♓ 8	4♈ 6	4♉32	3♊31	3♋11
☿	1	18♐11	3♒19	23♓ 6	5♈24	13♈56	8♊10
	7	25 41	13 2	3♈ 8	1R34	21 53	21 20
	13	3♑56	23 32	10 21	0D41	2♉46	3♋54
	19	12 43	4♓27	13 0	2 54	11 4	15 17
	25	21 52	15 40	11R11	7 29	23 16	25 17
	31	1♒52	...	6 14	...	5♊59	2♌30
♀	1	22♑44	1♓31	6♈14	14♉ 1	19♊29	24♋13
	9	2♒43	11 28	16 4	23 36	28 41	2♌40
	17	12 45	21 24	25 50	3♊ 7	7♋45	10 48
	25	22 46	1♈18	5♉34	12 37	16 36	18 37
♂	1	17♉32	26♉18	8♊48	25♊ 3	12♋ 2	0♌15
	13	20 1	1♊18	14 53	1♋45	19 1	7 27
	25	23 43	6 51	21 15	8 34	26 6	14 42
♃	1	24♏ 0	18♏57	1♐31	1♐42	29♏15	25♏25
	13	26 10	9♐18	1 57	0R58	27R48	24R 5
	25	28 0	1 17	1R56	29♏53	26 17	23 3
♄	1	29♐33	2♑57	5♑23	6♑52	6♑52	5♑29
	13	0♑54	4 6	6 8	7 3	6R29	4R41
	25	2 14	5 5	6 40	7R 0	5 54	3 48
♅	1	15♌35	14♌25	13♌15	12♌23	12♌17	13♌ 0
	13	15R13	13R24	12R50	12R16	12 28	13 29
	25	14 43	13 29	12 31	12D15	12 46	14 2
♆	1	6♏35	6♏57	6♏50	6♏15	5♏28	4♏42
	13	6 47	6R58	6R40	5R57	5R 9	4R28
	25	6 54	6 53	6 25	5 38	4 51	4 20
Pl.	1	4♍	3♍	3♍	2♍	2♍	2♍
☊	1	18♎ 1	16♎23	14♎54	13♎16	11♎40	10♎ 2
	1st	Thu	Sun	Sun	Wed	Fri	Mon

Noon		JUL	AUG	SEP	OCT	NOV	DEC
☉	1	8♑54	8♌29	8♍18	7♎34	8♏19	8♐33
	9	16 32	16 9	16 5	15 27	16 20	16 40
	17	24 10	23 50	23 51	23 22	26 24	26 48
	25	1♌48	1♍32	1♎40	1♏19	2♐28	2♑57
☿	1	3♌54	15♌43	23♌32	17♎54	1♎38	24♏12
	7	10 49	11R13	4♍34	22 27	7 12	24♐42
	13	15 59	8 2	16 1	6♏31	9 53	29 50
	19	19 5	8D27	29 1	15 10	7R26	7♐ 8
	25	19R 8	13 17	7♎50	23 13	29♏59	15 27
	31	16 6	21 20	...	0♐32	...	25 43
♀	1	24♌ 3	14♍30	7♍56	1♍18	22♍ 8	23♎ 2
	9	0♍48	16 4	3R19	4 47	27 48	2♏ 4
	17	6 45	15R18	0 18	9 48	7♎53	11 17
	25	11 32	12 3	0D 2	15 59	16 27	24 41
♂	1	18♌22	7♍30	27♍10	16♎43	7♏34	28♏25
	13	25 43	15 3	4♎55	24 41	15 49	6♐57
	25	3♍ 8	22 40	12 45	2♏48	24 11	15 25
♃	1	22♏40	22♏21	24♏49	29♏17	5♐20	11♐57
	13	22R12	23 1	26 24	1♐30	7 55	14 38
	25	22D 9	24 2	28 16	3 52	10 35	17 19
♄	1	3♑22	1♑22	0♑28	1♑ 3	3♑ 2	5♑57
	13	2R31	0R52	0D30	1 40	4 6	7 18
	25	1 45	0 33	0 48	2 28	5 18	8 42
♅	1	14♌21	16♌10	18♌ 5	19♌41	20♌46	21♌ 3
	13	15 2	16 54	18 47	20 12	21 0	20R58
	25	15 44	17 40	19 24	20 35	21 4	20 43
♆	1	4♏16	4♏17	4♏47	5♏39	6♏46	7♏46
	13	4R13	4 24	5 5	6 4	7 13	8 13
	25	4D14	4 38	5 27	6 31	7 38	8 33
Pl.	1	2♍	3♍	4♍	5♍	6♍	6♍
☊	1	8♎26	6♎48	5♎ 9	3♎34	1♎56	0♎20
	1st	Wed	Sat	Tue	Thu	Sun	Tue

d.	JAN	FEB	MAR	APR
☽ 1	28♍ 3	21♏ 6	2♐ 4	24♑ 6
3	26♎ 1	19♐15	29 58	20♒17
5	24♏37	17♑ 5	26♑36	15♓28
7	23♐31	14♒14	23♒23	9♈51
9	22♑ 0	10♓18	18♓45	3♉43
11	19♒19	5♈13	13♈16	27 21
13	15♓23	29 9	7♉ 7	21♊ 5
15	9♈30	22♉45	0♊45	15♋22
17	3♉12	16♊43	24 40	10♌46
19	26 53	11♋38	19♋31	7♍45
21	21♊12	8♌ 0	15♌51	6♎29
23	16♋40	5♍47	13♍53	6♏35
25	13♌17	4♎32	13♎20	6♐56
27	10♍48	3♍28	13♏ 6	6♑19
29	8♎50	...	12♐24	4♒ 2
31	7♏ 0	...	10♑33	...

d.	MAY	JUN	JUL	AUG
☽ 1	0♓ 4	15♈54	18♉ 8	2♊20
3	24 50	9♉32	11♊52	27 14
5	18♈50	3♊10	6♋ 1	21♋ 6
7	12♉30	27 7	0♌58	17♍48
9	6♊ 8	21♋32	26 35	17♎14
11	0♋ 1	16♌39	20♍59	15♏13
13	24 26	12♍40	20♎19	14♐41
15	17♌47	9♎58	18♏40	12♑20
17	16♍30	9♏42	17♐53	10♒36
19	14♎53	8♐37	17♑18	7♓52
21	13♏47	8♑43	15♒55	3♈49
23	15♐20	7♒44	13♓ 0	28 31
25	15♑ 7	4♋26	8♈26	22♉28
27	13♒ 9	0♓19	2♉40	16♊11
29	7♓17	24 30	16 21	10♋23
31	3♈55	...	20♉11	5♌33

d.	SEP	OCT	NOV	DEC
☽ 1	18♌34	23♍59	16♏ 5	24♐48
3	15♍33	22♎43	16♐19	24♑51
5	13♎30	22♏ 6	15♑51	23♒ 9
7	11♏57	21♐17	13♒39	19♓32
9	10♐30	19♑35	9♓59	14♈27
11	8♑45	16♒47	5♈ 7	9♉ 2
13	6♒28	12♓56	29 29	2♊17
15	3♓24	8♈11	23♉27	26 2
17	29 22	2♉44	17♊11	19♋57
19	24♈20	26 43	10♋56	14♌15
21	18♉30	20♊26	5♌ 2	9♍11
23	12♊14	14♋15	29 54	5♎15
25	6♋ 6	8♌45	26♍10	2♏54
27	0♌43	2♍27	24♎15	2♐17
29	24 35	1♎54	24♏ 6	2♑46
31	...	1♏ 3	...	2♒58

STATIONS	☿	♀	♂	♃
	20Mar 13♈ 1	11Aug 16♍ 8	None	19Mar 1♐59
	12Apr 0♈38	23Sep 29♌53		20Jul 22♏ 7
		♄	♅	♆
	23Jul 19♌22	16Apr 7♑ 4	20Apr 12♌14	8Feb 6♏58
	16Aug 7♌41	5Sep 0♑27	27Nov 21♌ 4	15Jul 4♏13
	4Nov 9♐55	SIDEREAL TIME		1 Jan
	4Dec 23♏41	6h 39m 36s		Midn.
		18h 41m 34s		Noon
		Common Year		1959

1960

Noon		JAN	FEB	MAR	APR	MAY	JUN
☉	1	10♑ 5	11♒39	10♓55	11♈46	11♉ 6	10♊59
	9	18 14	19 46	18 56	19 38	18 52	18 38
	17	26 23	27 50	26 54	27 28	26 34	26 16
	25	4♒32	5♓54	4♈51	5♉17	4♊16	3♋54
☿	1	25♐43	15♒52	25♓51	14♓59	24♈ 7	27♊34
	7	4♑49	26 35	23R29	19 0	5♉26	7♋46
	13	14 9	7♓13	17 48	26 41	17 46	16 19
	19	23 49	17 8	13 19	5♈43	0♊48	23 4
	25	3♒47	23 48	12D11	13 52	13 44	27 47
	31	14 6	...	14 22	...	25 42	...
♀	1	28♏58	6♑29	12♒ 3	20♓13	27♈ 9	5♊14
	9	8♐34	16 16	21 54	0♈ 5	6♉57	15 3
	17	18 14	26 5	1♓45	9 56	16 48	24 53
	25	27 57	5♒54	11 36	19 32	26 37	28 34
♂	1	20♐40	13♑39	5♒36	29♒25	22♓30	16♈ 2
	13	29 29	22 41	14 48	8♓40	1♈41	25 3
	25	8♑24	1♒47	24 2	14 3	10 47	3♉44
♃	1	18♐52	25♐14	0♑ 0	3♑ 5	3♑25	1♑ 1
	13	20 22	27 23	1 30	3 33	2R46	29♐35
	25	23 52	29 18	2 36	3R35	1 45	28R 3
♄	1	9♑32	13♑ 5	15♑54	17♑52	18♑25	17♑29
	13	10 56	14 20	16 48	18 17	18R13	16R47
	25	12 19	15 29	17 33	18 26	18 0	15 59
♅	1	20♌31	19♌21	18♌ 7	17♌10	16♌57	17♌35
	13	20R 7	18R50	17R41	17R 0	17 5	18 2
	25	19 39	18 19	17 20	16D56	17 22	18 34
♆	1	8♏43	9♏ 7	9♏ 2	8♏28	7♏41	6♏55
	13	8 56	9R 8	8R51	8R11	7R21	6R42
	25	9 4	9 4	8 37	7 52	7 3	6 31
Pl.	1	6♍	6♍	5♍	4♍	4♍	4♍
☊	1	28♍42	27♍ 4	25♍31	23♍53	22♍17	20♍39
	1st	Fri	Mon	Tue	Fri	Sun	Wed

Noon		JUL	AUG	SEP	OCT	NOV	DEC
☉	1	9♋38	9♌13	9♍ 2	8♎18	9♏ 4	9♐19
	9	17 15	16 52	16 47	16 11	17 5	17 26
	17	24 53	24 34	24 35	24 7	25 9	25 34
	25	2♌31	2♍16	2♎25	2♏ 5	3♐14	3♑43
☿	1	0♌ 6	21♋ 5	10♍30	29♎42	22♏13	21♏ 4
	7	29R40	25 57	21 39	7♏39	16R 2	29 40
	13	27 44	5♌50	2♎ 6	14 44	9 6	8♐42
	19	22 50	14 55	11 56	20 26	8D39	17 52
	25	20 11	26 46	21 7	23 43	13 33	27 11
	31	20D40	8♍34	...	22R54	...	6♑38
♀	1	12♋ 4	20♌13	28♍24	5♏16	13♐10	19♑56
	9	21 54	0♍ 4	8♎15	15 4	22 53	28 59
	17	1♌45	9 55	18 5	24 52	2♑35	8♒27
	25	11 36	19 47	27 54	4♐37	12 4	17 46
♂	1	8♉ 3	29♉33	19♊ 5	5♋ 5	16♋23	17♋49
	13	16 33	7♊24	25 54	10 16	18 18	15R 1
	25	24 51	14 54	2♋11	14 26	18R27	10 43
♃	1	27♐19	24♐22	24♐ 1	26♐25	1♑ 8	7♑12
	13	26R 3	12R42	24 40	28 1	3 25	9 52
	25	24 50	23D49	25 44	29 55	5 54	12 35
♄	1	15♑33	13♑22	11♑58	12♑ 2	13♑33	16♑11
	13	14R40	12R42	11R50	12 27	14 29	17 28
	25	13 49	12 11	11D54	13 5	15 35	18 50
♅	1	18♌52	20♌37	22♌33	24♌13	25♌24	25♌48
	13	19 30	21 22	23 12	24 45	25 40	25 44
	25	20 12	22 8	23 54	25 12	25 48	25 32
♆	1	6♏27	6♏26	6♏55	7♑46	8♏54	9♏58
	13	6R23	6 33	7 13	8 12	9 20	10 22
	25	6D23	6 46	7 34	8 39	9 46	10 41
Pl.	1	4♍	5♍	6♍	7♍	8♍	8♍
☊	1	19♍ 4	17♍45	15♍47	14♍11	12♍43	13♍ 7
	1st	Fri	Mon	Thu	Sat	Tue	Thu

d.		JAN	FEB	MAR	APR
☽	1	17♒19	6♈10	26♈41	11♊14
	3	15♓ 4	1♉25	21♉23	5♋ 3
	5	10♈45	26 31	15♊20	28 59
	7	5♉21	19♊17	9♋15	23♌39
	9	29 8	13♋10	3♌25	19♍32
	11	22♊51	7♌38	26 41	10♎ 6
	13	16♋56	2♍54	25♍46	15♏38
	15	14♌15	28 56	22♎ 7	14♐51
	17	6♍14	25♎47	20♏11	13♑46
	19	2♎ 3	23♏26	18♐36	11♒51
	21	28 53	21♐49	16♑55	6♓57
	23	26♏59	20♑36	15♒ 5	5♈ 1
	25	26♐18	19♒12	13♓ 8	1♉ 2
	27	26♑ 6	17♓ 3	9♈ 2	25 12
	29	25♒18	13♈34	4♉36	19♊20
	31	20♓59	...	29 13	...

d.		MAY	JUN	JUL	AUG
☽	1	13♋ 8	27♌38	29♍43	21♏46
	3	7♌ 2	22♍41	28♎13	20♐32
	5	1♍35	19♎20	26♏31	20♑22
	7	27 29	17♏54	26♐34	20♒37
	9	25♎10	18♐ 2	27♑ 2	19♓32
	11	24♏26	18♑23	26♒48	16♈40
	13	24♐27	18♒ 1	24♓52	12♉20
	15	14♑ 5	13♓49	21♈ 9	6♊48
	17	22♒21	11♈57	16♉ 3	0♋39
	19	18♓47	6♉55	10♊ 8	24 25
	21	14♈55	1♊ 6	3♋54	18♌26
	23	9♉50	24 58	27 40	13♍ 5
	25	4♊ 4	18♋45	21♌38	8♎22
	27	27 58	12♌39	16♍ 8	4♏48
	29	21♋42	6♍40	11♎26	1♐52
	31	15♌22	...	7♏55	0♑30

d.		SEP	OCT	NOV	DEC
☽	1	15♑ 7	23♒58	14♈57	20♉ 6
	3	14♒18	22♓ 4	11♉ 6	14♊53
	5	13♓18	19♈24	6♊22	9♋ 4
	7	11♈14	15♉ 8	0♋47	2♌47
	9	7♉43	10♊41	24 36	26 25
	11	2♊49	4♋48	18♌17	20♍42
	13	26 55	28 34	12♍34	16♎ 0
	15	20♋42	22♌26	7♎55	13♏10
	17	14♌38	17♍22	5♏ 9	12♐16
	19	10♍16	13♎30	4♐11	12♑29
	21	4♎54	10♏58	3♑51	12♒33
	23	1♏39	9♐23	2♒58	11♓21
	25	29 1	8♑ 4	1♓15	8♈35
	27	27♐ 6	6♒29	28 26	4♉31
	29	25♑32	4♓33	24♈39	29 29
	31	...	1♈44	...	23♊45

STATIONS	☿	♀	♂	♃
	2Mar 25♓51 24Mar 12♓ 6 3Jul 0♌14 28Jul 20♌ 0 28Oct 24♏ 0 17Nov 8♏ 2	None	21Nov 18♋37	20Apr 3♑37 21Aug 23♐47
		♄	♅	♆
		27Apr 18♑26 16Sep 11♑50	24Apr 16♌56 2Dec 25♌48	9Feb 9♏ 8 18Jul 6♏23
		SIDER. TIME 6h 38m 38s 18h 40m 36s LEAP YEAR		1 Jan Midn. Noon 1960

1961 (BST 31 Mar - 27 Oct)

	Noon	JAN	FEB	MAR	APR	MAY	JUN
☉	1	10♑51	12♒24	10♓41	11♈31	10♉52	10♊44
	9	19 0	20 31	18 41	19 24	18 37	18 24
	17	27 9	28 36	26 40	27 14	26 20	26 3
	25	5♒18	6♓40	4♈36	5♉ 2	4♊ 2	3♋41
☿	1	8♑14	29♒26	26♒ 1	16♓28	10♉20	4♋ 1
	7	17 55	6♓39	24D21	25 23	23 17	8 30
	13	27 50	9R 9	26 22	5♈14	5♊42	10 24
	19	8♒ 0	5 43	0♓59	16 1	16 44	9R38
	25	18 14	29♒20	7 23	27 45	25 54	6 44
	31	27 56	...	15 5	...	3♋ 2	...
♀	1	25♒52	29♓19	22♈37	26♈19	12♈45	26♈33
	9	4♓54	6♈58	26 42	21R48	13D45	3♉ 8
	17	13 42	13 56	28 52	16 58	16 51	10 22
	25	22 12	20 1	28R39	13 38	21 30	18 5
♂	1	7♋56	0♋ 8	3♋ 3	13♋39	27♋41	14♒14
	13	3R39	0D20	6 29	18 56	3♌54	21 1
	25	0 52	2 8	10 48	24 41	10 22	27 57
♃	1	14♑13	21♑22	27♑22	2♒50	6♒14	7♒ 5
	13	17 0	24 2	29 40	4 28	6 55	6R36
	25	19 47	26 34	1♒45	5 44	7 9	5 42
♄	1	19♑39	23♑17	26♑15	28♑42	29♑48	29♑26
	13	21 4	24 37	27 20	29 18	29R50	28R55
	25	22 29	25 52	28 15	29 42	29 39	28 13
♅	1	25♌22	24♌16	23♌ 2	22♌59	21♌39	22♌ 8
	13	24R59	24R43	22R34	21R46	21D45	22 33
	25	24 32	23 12	22 10	21 40	21 58	23 3
♆	1	10♏51	11♏17	11♏14	10♏42	9♏55	9♏ 8
	13	11 5	11R19	11R 4	10R24	9R36	8R54
	25	11 14	11 16	10 51	10 5	9 18	8 42
Pl.	1	8♍ 0	7♍29	6♍45	6♍ 1	5♍36	5♍35
☊	1	9♍19	7♍41	6♍12	4♍33	2♍58	1♍19
	1st	SUN	WED	WED	SAT	MON	THU

	Noon	JUL	AUG	SEP	OCT	NOV	DEC
☉	1	9♋24	8♌59	8♍48	8♎ 4	8♏50	9♐ 4
	9	17 1	16 39	16 34	15 57	16 51	17 11
	17	24 39	24 20	24 21	23 53	24 54	25 19
	25	2♌17	2♍ 2	2♎10	1♏50	2♐59	3♑28
☿	1	3♋20	25♋ 6	24♍28	3♏40	22♎22	0♐52
	7	1R25	6♌58	3♎59	7 21	26D 1	10 16
	13	2D18	19 18	12 46	7R36	3♏20	19 41
	19	6 21	1♍14	20 48	3 8	12 10	29 9
	25	13 28	12 25	27 54	25♎55	21 28	8♑43
	31	23 16	22 49	...	22 19	...	18 25
♀	1	24♉ 7	27♊35	3♌28	9♍34	17♎52	25♏25
	9	2♊26	6♋40	12 57	19 22	27 51	5♐29
	17	11 0	15 52	22 34	29 14	7♏52	15 32
	25	19 46	25 12	2♍15	9♎ 9	17 53	25 36
♂	1	1♍29	20♍16	9♎56	29♎47	21♏11	12♐45
	13	8 39	27 46	17 46	7♏58	29 43	21 36
	25	15 57	5♎25	25 45	16 16	8♐23	0♑35
♃	1	5♒ 7	1♒19	28♑ 6	27♑25	27♑41	4♒14
	13	3R45	29♑52	27R29	27 57	1♒16	6 33
	25	2 14	28R39	27D19	28 56	3 11	9 3
♄	1	27♑50	25♑35	23♑47	23♑15	24♑13	26♑29
	13	26R59	24R47	23R24	23D26	24 59	27 40
	25	26 6	24 6	23 14	23 52	25 57	28 57
♅	1	23♌20	25♌ 3	26♌58	28♌42	0♍ 0	0♍32
	13	23 57	25 47	27 42	29 16	0 19	0R31
	25	24 38	26 37	28 23	29 46	0 30	0 22
♆	1	8♏38	8♏35	9♏ 2	9♏52	10♏58	12♏ 4
	13	8R33	8 42	9 19	10 16	11 25	12 27
	25	8D33	8 53	9 40	10 43	11 51	12 48
Pl.	1	6♍ 2	6♍50	7♍53	8♍54	9♍40	10♍ 5
☊	1	29♌44	28♌ 5	26♌27	24♌52	23♌13	21♌38
	1st	SAT	TUE	FRI	SUN	WED	FRI

☽ d.	JAN	FEB	MAR	APR
1	5♋48	20♌11	28♌54	14♎34
3	29 33	14♍ 5	23♍ 8	10♏39
5	23♌11	8♎30	18♎ 4	7♐38
7	17♍ 2	3♏51	13♏53	5♑19
9	11♎40	0♐33	10♐33	3♒31
11	7♏41	28 53	8♑40	2♓ 4
13	5♐34	28♑35	7♒39	0♈38
15	5♑14	28♒49	7♓ 6	28 41
17	5♒46	28♓23	6♈17	25♉40
19	5♓50	26♈25	4♉19	21♊19
21	4♈22	22♉42	0♊47	15♋45
23	1♉ 9	17♊32	25 46	9♌30
25	26 29	11♋30	19♋45	3♍14
27	20♊50	5♌ 8	13♌23	27 37
29	14♋40	...	7♍17	23♎ 9
31	8♌20	...	1♎54	...

☽ d.	MAY	JUN	JUL	AUG
1	19♏59	11♑56	20♒53	13♈42
3	17♐50	11♒ 1	19♓54	11♉ 0
5	16♑10	9♓30	17♈40	6♊50
7	14♒30	7♈11	14♉13	1♋33
9	12♓38	4♉ 4	9♊45	25 33
11	10♈24	0♊10	4♋30	19 12
13	7♉38	25 26	28 32	12 47
15	4♊ 1	19♋53	22♌12	6♎39
17	29 30	13♌41	15♍46	1♏10
19	23♋40	7♍17	19♎45	26 50
21	17♌22	1♎15	4♏45	24♐ 3
23	11♍ 6	26 18	1♐19	22♑55
25	5♎31	22♏59	29 42	23♒ 0
27	1♏20	21♐26	29♑34	23♓17
29	28 43	21♑ 5	29♒52	22♈34
31	27♐22	...	29♓26	20♉10

☽ d.	SEP	OCT	NOV	DEC
1	3♊18	7♋ 3	21♌ 1	22♍27
3	28 28	1♌ 7	14♍39	16♎41
5	22♋35	24 43	8♎47	12♏ 4
7	16♌12	18♍25	3♏54	8♐50
9	9♍49	12♎42	0♐ 5	6♑45
11	3♎44	7♏45	27 9	5♒14
13	28 15	3♐38	24♑47	3♓44
15	23♏34	0♑20	22♒46	1♈54
17	19♐57	27 53	21♓ 2	29 38
19	17♑38	26♒17	19♈23	26♉46
21	16♒37	25♓22	17♉25	23♊ 7
23	16♓29	24♈31	14♊34	18♋29
25	16♈15	22♉53	10♋25	12♌54
27	14♉54	19♊47	5♌ 1	6♍39
29	11♊49	15♋ 5	28 48	0♎16
31	...	9♌12	...	24 28

STATIONS	☿	♀	♂	♃
	12Feb	20Mar	6Feb	25May
	9♓ 9	29♈ 6	0♋ 0	7♒ 9
	6Mar	2May		23Sep
	24♒21	12♈44		27♑19
	14Jun	♄	♅	♆
	10♋27	9May	29Apr	11Feb
	8Jul	29♑51	21♌39	11♏19
	1♋21	27Sep	6Dec	20Jul
	10Oct	23♑14	0♍33	8♏33
	8♏ 1	Sider pl. Time		1Jan
	31Oct	6h 41m 37s		Midn
	22♎19	18h 43m 35s		Noon
		Common Year		1961

1962 (BST 25 Mar - 28 Oct)

Noon		JAN	FEB	MAR	APR	MAY	JUN
☉	1	10♑36	12♒ 9	10♓25	11♈17	10♉38	10♊30
	9	18 45	20 16	18 26	19 9	18 23	18 10
	17	26 54	28 21	26 25	27 0	26 6	25 49
	25	5♒ 3	6♓24	4♈21	4♉48	3♊48	3♋26
☿	1	20♑ 2	20♒38	13♒22	27♓ 7	26♉58	19♊ 4
	7	29 48	13R55	19 42	8♈15	6♊36	16R 1
	13	9♒16	8 27	27 17	20 4	13 52	13 2
	19	17 29	7D24	5♓49	2♉50	18 32	11D50
	25	22 24	10 7	15 10	15 25	20 22	13 19
	31	21R26	...	25 20	...	19R27	...
♀	1	4♑24	13♒23	18♓27	26♈58	3♊48	11♋17
	9	14 28	23 25	28 26	6♉51	13 32	20 50
	17	24 32	3♓27	8♈23	16 41	23 14	0♌20
	25	4♒36	13 27	18 18	26 29	2♋53	9 45
♂	1	5♑52	29♑39	21♒31	15♓49	9♈ 7	2♉38
	13	15 0	8♒59	0♓56	25 11	18 18	11 31
	25	24 14	18 22	10 20	4♈30	27 23	20 15
♃	1	10♒35	17♒47	24♒27	1♓25	7♓ 7	11♓12
	13	13 18	20 39	27 14	3 51	8 57	12 7
	25	16 7	23 31	29 55	6 5	10 29	12 37
♄	1	29♑44	3♒24	6♒34	9♒25	11♒ 4	11♒18
	13	1♒ 8	4 48	7 46	10 13	11 20	10R59
	25	2 33	6 8	8 51	10 50	11R23	10 28
♅	1	0♍14	29♌11	27♌59	26♌52	26♌24	26♌45
	13	29♌54	28R41	27R29	26R35	26D26	27 6
	25	29R28	28 9	27 4	26 26	26 36	27 34
♆	1	12♏58	13♏27	13♏25	12♏56	12♏10	11♏22
	13	13 13	13R30	13R17	12R38	11R50	11R 7
	25	13 23	13 27	13 4	12 20	11 32	10 55
Pl.	1	10♍ 1	9♍31	8♍48	8♍ 3	7♍36	7♍34
☊	1	19♌59	18♌21	16♌52	15♌13	13♌38	12♌ 0
	1st	MON	THU	THU	SUN	TUE	FRI

Noon		JUL	AUG	SEP	OCT	NOV	DEC
☉	1	9♋10	8♌45	8♍34	7♎50	8♏35	8♐49
	9	16 48	16 25	16 19	15 43	16 36	16 56
	17	26 20	24 6	24 7	23 38	24 39	25 4
	25	2♌ 3	1♍48	1♎56	1♏35	2♐44	3♑13
☿	1	17♊34	11♌58	3♎46	18♎29	24♎15	12♐14
	7	24 24	23 50	10 57	11R56	3♏55	21 37
	13	3♋37	4♍49	16 48	6 56	13 40	1♑ 0
	19	14 51	14 54	20 43	7D50	23 18	10 22
	25	27 18	24 8	21R40	13 57	2♐48	19 33
	31	9♌54	2♎28	...	22 40	...	28 3
♀	1	16♌46	22♍ 5	24♎42	19♏54	25♏54	12♏18
	9	26 3	0♎51	2♏20	24 19	21R58	12D56
	17	5♍13	9 25	9 24	27 1	17 11	15 50
	25	14 17	17 42	15 45	27R31	13 31	20 30
♂	1	24♉34	16♊ 9	6♋23	24♋16	10♌10	21♌16
	13	3♊ 4	24 9	13 46	0♌48	15 15	23 48
	25	11 23	1♋57	20 51	6 52	19 31	24 48
♃	1	12♓41	11♓16	7♓36	4♓ 6	2♓50	4♓37
	13	12R29	10R 0	6R 2	3R15	3D12	6 5
	25	11 50	8 31	4 40	2 51	4 2	7 54
♄	1	10♒ 9	8♒ 1	5♒54	4♒49	5♒12	7♒ 0
	13	9R23	7R 8	5R19	4D46	5 46	8 3
	25	8 32	6 19	4 56	4 58	6 33	9 15
♅	1	27♌50	29♌29	1♍24	3♍11	4♍35	5♍16
	13	28 25	0♍13	2 8	3 48	4 57	5R18
	25	29 5	0 58	2 51	4 19	5 11	5 11
♆	1	10♏50	10♏44	11♏ 9	11♏58	13♏ 3	14♏ 9
	13	10R44	10 50	11 26	12 22	13 30	14 33
	25	10D43	11 1	11 46	12 48	13 57	14 55
Pl.	1	7♍59	8♍48	9♍49	10♍50	11♍41	12♍ 7
☊	1	10♌24	8♌46	7♌ 7	5♌32	3♌53	2♌18
	1st	SUN	WED	SAT	MON	THU	SAT

	d.	JAN	FEB	MAR	APR
☽	1	6♏58	24♐40	3♑ 2	24♒39
	3	3♐ 9	23♑16	1♒17	24♓31
	5	0♑57	23♒ 9	1♓ 5	24♈45
	7	29 59	23♓17	1♈33	24♉ 6
	9	29♒27	22♈23	1♉25	21♊40
	11	28♓28	20♉21	29 40	17♋23
	13	26♈33	16♊38	26♊ 4	11♌45
	15	23♉34	11♋43	20♋58	5♍25
	17	19♊36	5♌59	14♌57	29 3
	19	14♋15	29 47	8♍34	23♎ 5
	21	9♌ 9	23♍25	2♎14	17♏43
	23	3♍ 1	17♎10	26 13	13♐ 3
	25	26 37	11♏23	20♏43	9♑10
	27	20♎26	6♐31	16♐ 0	6♒13
	29	15♏ 3	...	12♑23	4♓22
	31	11♐ 2	...	10♒11	...

	d.	MAY	JUN	JUL	AUG
☽	1	3♈34	26♉39	3♋ 8	19♌54
	3	3♉11	24♊25	28 59	14♍ 1
	5	2♊12	20♋48	23♌45	7♎45
	7	29 44	15♌48	17♍45	1♏32
	9	25♋32	9♍50	11♎28	25 56
	11	19♌58	3♎32	5♏32	21♐31
	13	13♍42	27 35	0♐32	18♑42
	15	7♎25	22♏29	26 52	17♒29
	17	1♏41	18♐32	24♑36	17♓16
	19	26 46	15♑39	23♒20	17♈ 2
	21	22♐45	13♒32	22♓25	15♉51
	23	19♑30	11♓49	21♈11	13♊15
	25	16♒55	10♈13	19♉12	9♋20
	27	14♓59	8♉27	16♊16	4♌22
	29	13♈37	6♊12	12♋23	28 42
	31	12♉24	...	7♌36	22♍35

	d.	SEP	OCT	NOV	DEC
☽	1	4♎26	7♏ 3	23♐ 2	28♑40
	3	28 8	1♐11	18♑30	25♒30
	5	22♏ 8	25 59	15♒ 5	23♓18
	7	16♐56	21♑56	13♓ 6	22♈ 5
	9	13♑ 6	19♒30	12♈34	21♉24
	11	11♒ 1	18♓50	12♉44	20♊22
	13	10♓37	19♈20	12♊22	18♋ 9
	15	11♈ 6	19♉40	10♋24	14♌22
	17	11♉ 6	18♊31	6♌33	9♍10
	19	9♊36	15♋24	1♍14	3♎ 7
	21	6♋16	10♌35	25 5	26 52
	23	1♌29	4♍43	18♎46	20♏59
	25	25 45	28 24	12♏47	15♐55
	27	19♍34	22♎ 8	7♐23	11♑49
	29	13♎15	16♏ 8	2♑39	8♒38
	31	...	10♐35	...	6♓10

STATIONS	☿	♀	♂	♃
	27Jan	23Oct	26Dec	2Jul
	22♒29	27♏38	24♌48	12♓41
	17Feb	3Dec	...	29Oct
	7♒16	12♏13	...	2♓49
	26May	♄	♅	♆
	20♊24	22May	4May	13Feb
	19Jun	11♒24	26♌24	13♏30
	11♊50	9Oct	11Dec	22Jul
	24Sep	4♒46	5♍18	10♏43
	21♎46	Sider pl. Time		1Jan
	15Oct	6h 40m 40s		Midn
	6♎31	18h 42m 38s		Noon
		Common Year		1962

1963 (BST 31 Mar - 27 Oct)

Noon		JAN	FEB	MAR	APR	MAY	JUN
☉	1	11♑21	11♒54	10♓11	11♈ 3	10♉24	10♊17
	9	18 30	20 1	18 12	18 55	18 9	17 56
	17	26 39	28 6	26 10	26 46	25 52	25 35
	25	4♒48	6♓10	4♈ 7	4♉34	3♊34	3♋13
☿	1	29♑20	20♑42	15♒11	12♈43	29♉19	21♉50
	7	5♒18	22D57	27 16	25 6	0♊36	23 56
	13	6R18	28 0	7♓ 2	6♉59	28♉59	28 32
	19	0 54	4♒43	17 31	17 10	25R41	5♊20
	25	23♑44	12 31	28 44	24 47	22 43	14 9
	31	20 42	...	10♈40	...	21D45	...
♀	1	25♏39	25♐19	26♑34	2♓56	8♈50	16♉16
	9	2♐27	3♑59	5♒50	12 28	18 29	25 58
	17	9 57	12 53	15 11	22 2	28 8	5♊41
	25	17 58	21 58	24 37	1♈38	7♉48	15 25
♂	1	24♌32	16♌ 9	6♌49	6♌45	15♌23	29♌ 7
	13	22R34	11R27	5 24	9 27	20 16	5♍15
	25	18 51	7 42	5D47	13 11	25 44	11 42
♃	1	9♓ 6	15♓23	21♓53	29♓23	6♈19	12♈35
	13	11 22	18 6	24 47	2♈13	8 54	14 37
	25	13 51	20 56	27 42	4 59	11 17	16 21
♄	1	10♒ 0	13♒36	16♒54	20♒ 5	22♒14	23♒ 6
	13	11 21	15 2	18 13	21 5	22 45	23R 2
	25	12 45	16 26	19 26	21 54	23 3	22 43
♅	1	5♍ 6	4♍19	2♍57	1♍46	1♍10	1♍23
	13	4R48	3R39	2R26	1R26	1D 9	1 42
	25	4 25	3 7	1 59	1 14	1 16	2 6
♆	1	15♏ 5	15♏36	15♏37	15♏ 9	14♏24	13♏36
	13	15 21	15 40	15R29	14R53	14R 5	13R20
	25	15 32	15R38	15 18	14 34	13 46	13 7
Pl.	1	12♍ 4	11♍35	10♍53	10♍ 7	9♍38	9♍34
☊	1	0♌40	29♋ 1	27♋32	25♋54	24♋18	22♋40
	1st	TUE	FRI	FRI	MON	WED	SAT

Noon		JUL	AUG	SEP	OCT	NOV	DEC
☉	1	8♋56	8♌31	8♍20	7♎35	8♏20	8♐34
	9	16 34	16 11	16 5	15 28	16 21	16 41
	17	24 12	23 52	23 52	23 23	24 25	26 51
	25	1♌50	1♍34	1♎42	1♏21	2♐30	2♑58
☿	1	24♊50	26♌52	3♎46	20♍57	6♏ 6	23♐ 1
	7	7♋ 1	6♍30	5R 7	25D57	15 52	1♑52
	13	19 55	15 6	2 52	4♎16	25 23	10 11
	19	2♌34	22 38	27♍15	14 12	4♐43	17 5
	25	14 22	28 50	21 45	24 24	13 56	20 40
	31	25 10	3♎15	...	4♏27	...	18R14
♀	1	22♊44	0♌42	9♍ 0	16♎19	24♏57	2♑19
	9	2♋29	10 33	18 56	26 17	4♐55	12 16
	17	14 44	20 26	28 53	8♏45	17 23	24 42
	25	22 6	0♍20	8♎51	16 14	24 51	2♒ 8
♂	1	15♍ 2	3♎14	22♎50	12♏58	4♐53	27♐ 5
	13	21 54	10 40	0♏45	21 19	13 39	6♑11
	25	29 0	18 18	8 51	29 51	22 34	15 25
♃	1	17♈ 6	19♈22	18♈38	15♈22	11♈36	9♈34
	13	18 18	19R27	17R33	13R46	10R21	9D39
	25	19 7	19 4	16 9	12 14	9 42	10 14
♄	1	22♒29	20♒37	18♒21	16♒17	16♒33	17♒50
	13	21R53	19R44	17R36	16R30	16 53	18 43
	25	21 7	18 51	17 1	16D28	17 28	19 47
♅	1	2♍21	3♍57	5♍51	7♍40	9♍10	9♍58
	13	2 55	4 40	6 36	8 18	9 35	10 4
	25	3 33	5 24	7 19	8 52	9 52	10R 2
♆	1	13♏ 2	12♏54	13♏ 6	14♏ 3	15♏ 8	16♏15
	13	12R56	12D59	13 32	14 27	15 35	16 39
	25	12 53	13 9	13 52	14 53	16 2	17 1
Pl.	1	9♍57	10♍45	11♍47	12♍49	13♍41	14♍ 9
☊	1	21♋ 5	19♋26	17♋48	16♋12	14♋34	12♋58
	1st	MON	THU	SUN	TUE	FRI	SUN

	d.	JAN	FEB	MAR	APR
☽	1	20♓ 9	13♉38	24♉19	15♋31
	3	18♈24	11♊29	22♊ 4	11♌13
	5	16♉51	8♋33	18♋35	5♍56
	7	15♊ 7	4♌48	14♌ 7	0♎ 5
	9	12♋43	0♍12	8♍56	23 57
	11	9♌15	24 48	3♎13	17♏42
	13	4♍36	18♎48	27 6	11♐34
	15	28 57	12♏33	20♏50	5♑56
	17	22♎46	6♐36	14♐50	1♒19
	19	16♏39	1♑36	9♑40	28 19
	21	11♐11	28 4	5♒59	27♓12
	23	6♑52	26♒12	4♓11	27♈32
	25	3♒53	25♓36	4♈ 1	28♉ 3
	27	2♓ 2	25♈19	4♉27	27♊22
	29	0♈45	...	4♊ 6	24♋49
	31	29 27	...	2♋ 8	...

	d.	MAY	JUN	JUL	AUG
☽	1	20♌34	5♎54	8♏ 1	22♐ 9
	3	15♍ 8	29 41	1♐55	17♑18
	5	9♎ 5	23♏29	26 21	13♒38
	7	2♏50	17♐39	21♑35	11♓ 8
	9	26 39	12♐23	17♒46	9♈25
	11	20♐44	7♒51	14♓50	7♉57
	13	15♑20	4♓17	12♈42	6♊19
	15	10♒50	1♈53	11♉10	4♋14
	17	7♓41	0♉40	9♊54	1♌31
	19	6♈11	0♊10	8♋24	28 0
	21	6♉ 4	29 32	6♌ 7	23♍33
	23	6♊20	27♋51	2♍38	18♎ 9
	25	5♋42	24♌39	27 55	12♏ 5
	27	3♌22	19♍57	22♎13	5♐49
	29	29 17	14♎13	16♏ 1	0♑ 1
	31	23♍54	...	9♐57	25 18

	d.	SEP	OCT	NOV	DEC
☽	1	8♒30	14♓18	7♉11	15♊43
	3	6♓ 5	13♈47	7♊41	15♋30
	5	4♈56	13♉54	7♋ 7	13♌38
	7	4♉14	13♊24	4♌50	9♍59
	9	3♊ 6	11♋32	0♍56	4♎55
	11	1♋ 4	8♌16	25 51	28 58
	13	28 4	3♍54	20♎ 4	22♏40
	15	24♌13	28 46	13♏53	16♐22
	17	19♍38	23♎ 4	7♐33	10♑22
	19	14♎19	16♏55	1♑18	4♒55
	21	8♏22	10♐33	25 27	0♓17
	23	2♐ 3	4♑19	20♒31	26 46
	25	25 51	28 47	17♓ 0	24♈38
	27	20♑25	24♒37	15♈19	23♉49
	29	16♒26	22♓21	15♉13	23♊42
	31	...	21♈57	...	23♋17

STATIONS	☿	♀	♂	♃
	11Jan	None	16Mar	9Aug
	6♒42		5♌20	19♈29
	1Feb		...	5Dec
	20♑42		...	9♈32
	6May	♄	♅	♆
	0♊37	3Jun	9May	16Feb
	30May	23♒ 7	1♍ 9	15♏40
	21♉44	21Oct	16Dec	25Jul
	7Sep	16♒27	10♍ 4	12♏53
	5♎ 8	Sider Pl. Time		1Jan
	29Sep	6h 39m 42s		Midn
	20♍33	18h 41m 40s		Noon
	26Dec	Common Year		1963
	20♑44			

1964 (BST 22 Mar - 25 Oct

Noon		JAN	FEB	MAR	APR	MAY	JUN
☉	1	10♑ 6	11♒39	10♓56	11♈47	11♉ 8	11♊ 0
	9	18 15	19 46	18 57	19 39	18 53	18 40
	17	26 24	27 51	26 56	27 30	26 36	26 18
	25	4♒33	5♓55	4♈52	5♉18	4♊17	3♋56
☿	1	17♑11	17♑32	0♓58	29♈11	4♉32	17♉34
	7	9R27	25 17	11 43	6♉51	1R54	26 26
	13	4 47	3♒46	23 7	10 55	1D50	6♊54
	19	5D32	12 50	5♈ 1	11R12	4 26	18 49
	25	9 55	22 29	16 54	8 25	9 22	1♋43
	31	16 20	...	27 37	...	16 15	...
♀	1	10♒47	18♓44	23♈ 6	27♉18	24♊47	6♋41
	9	20 39	28 21	2♉15	5♊24	0♋13	4R47
	17	0♓28	7♈53	11 12	13 1	5 4	0 10
	25	10 14	17 17	19 55	20 3	6 35	25♊16
♂	1	20♑50	15♒ 9	8♓ 3	2♈22	25♈24	18♉28
	13	0♒12	24 37	17 30	11 39	4♉26	27 9
	25	9 38	4♓ 6	26 55	20 51	13 20	5♊42
♃	1	10♈47	14♈51	20♈25	27♈26	4♉37	11♉50
	13	12 4	17 0	23 3	0♉18	7 28	14 27
	25	13 44	19 22	25 48	3 11	10 15	16 54
♄	1	20♒28	23♒56	27♒25	0♓52	3♓27	4♓53
	13	21 45	25 23	28 49	2 1	4 10	5 2
	25	23 7	26 50	0♓ 9	3 1	4 41	4R57
♅	1	9♍57	9♍ 6	7♍54	6♍39	5♍59	6♍ 5
	13	9R42	8R38	7R23	6R18	5D55	6 20
	25	9 21	8 7	6 54	6 3	5 59	6 43
♆	1	17♏12	17♏45	17♏48	17♏21	16♏37	15♏48
	13	17 28	17 50	17R41	17R 5	16R17	15R32
	25	17 40	17R49	17 30	16 47	15 58	15 19
Pl.	1	14♍10	13♍42	12♍59	12♍13	11♍43	11♍35
☊	1	11♋20	9♋42	8♋ 9	6♋31	4♋56	3♋17
	1st	WED	SAT	SUN	WED	FRI	MON

Noon		JUL	AUG	SEP	OCT	NOV	DEC
☉	1	9♋39	9♌14	9♍ 4	8♎20	9♏ 6	9♐20
	9	17 17	16 54	16 49	16 13	17 7	17 28
	17	24 55	24 35	24 37	24 9	25 11	25 36
	25	2♌33	2♍18	2♎26	2♏ 6	3♐15	3♑44
☿	1	14♋14	6♍11	10♍35	27♍20	19♏26	0♑40
	7	27 3	12 14	5R36	8♎ 2	28 34	4 37
	13	8♌17	16 22	4D32	18 33	7♐27	3R14
	19	18 23	17R58	8 47	28 42	16 0	26♐ 5
	25	27 19	16 17	17 5	8♏27	23 58	19 39
	31	5♍ 2	11 32	...	17 54	...	19D 0
♀	1	22♊20	27♊29	23♋16	25♌11	1♎22	7♏57
	9	20R26	2♋58	1♌20	4♍18	11 1	17 51
	17	21D 1	9 24	9 46	13 34	20 45	27 47
	25	23 44	16 33	18 29	23 0	0♏33	7♐44
♂	1	9♊56	1♋10	21♋24	9♌53	27♌32	12♍27
	13	18 16	9 8	28 56	16 56	3♍49	17 31
	25	26 28	16 56	6♌17	23 42	9 42	21 51
♃	1	18♉ 4	23♉ 5	25♉50	25♉40	22♉38	18♉41
	13	20 13	24 28	26 8	24R47	22R 1	17R25
	25	22 7	25 27	25R56	23 30	19 26	16 32
♄	1	4♓49	3♓21	1♓ 5	29♒ 9	28♒21	29♒ 6
	13	4R24	2R30	0R13	28R39	28D28	29 49
	25	3 47	1 37	29♒28	28 23	28 50	0♓44
♅	1	6♍57	8♍29	10♍22	12♍12	12♍47	14♍41
	13	7 29	9 11	11 7	12 52	14 14	14 50
	25	8 6	9 55	11 51	13 28	14 34	14R50
♆	1	15♏14	15♏ 4	15♏25	16♏11	17♏15	18♏22
	13	15R 7	15D 9	15 40	16 34	17 42	18 47
	25	15 4	15 18	16 0	17 0	18 9	19 9
Pl.	1	11♍59	12♍47	13♍48	14♍51	15♍43	16♍14
☊	1	1♋42	0♋ 3	28♊25	26♊49	25♊11	23♊36
	1st	WED	SAT	TUE	THU	SUN	TUE

d.	JAN	FEB	MAR	APR
☽ 1	7♌38	26♍ 0	16♎36	1♐ 9
3	5♍ 8	21♎14	11♏12	24 46
5	0♎57	15♏23	5♐ 2	18♑36
7	25 28	9♐ 4	28 43	13♒21
9	19♏15	2♑55	22♑56	9♓38
11	12♐55	27 33	18♒21	7♈40
13	6♑57	23♒18	15♓16	7♉ 2
15	1♒40	20♓10	13♈30	6♊42
17	27 15	17♈52	12♉20	5♋43
19	23♓43	16♉ 0	11♊ 3	3♌37
21	21♈ 3	14♊14	9♋11	0♍23
23	19♉13	12♋24	6♌40	26 13
25	18♊ 0	10♌18	3♍29	21♎17
27	16♋59	7♍35	29 34	15♏40
29	15♌29	3♎53	24♎49	9♐30
31	12♍52	...	19♏13	...

d.	MAY	JUN	JUL	AUG
☽ 1	3♑ 5	18♒ 0	22♓57	13♉50
3	26 55	13♓21	19♈45	12♊17
5	21♒37	10♈16	17♉59	11♋29
7	17♓48	8♉56	17♊31	10♌52
9	15♈51	8♊56	17♋34	9♍31
11	15♉29	9♋15	17♌ 4	6♎43
13	15♊44	8♌41	15♍ 9	2♏19
15	15♋22	6♍32	11♎29	26 39
17	13♌38	2♎42	6♏20	20♐20
19	10♍24	27 33	0♐16	14♑ 3
21	5♎55	21♏34	23 52	8♒22
23	0♏31	15♐13	17♑39	3♓37
25	24 32	8♑52	11♓59	29 ·51
27	18♐12	2♒50	7♓ 5	26♈55
29	11♑49	27 25	3♈ 4	24♉36
31	5♒46	...	29 59	22♊46

d.	SEP	OCT	NOV	DEC
☽ 1	6♋59	15♌45	6♎18	11♏ 4
3	5♌36	13♍17	1♏53	5♐18
5	3♍58	10♎ 5	26 36	29 4
7	1♎30	5♏50	20♐35	22♑38
9	27 42	0♐29	14♑11	16♒23
11	22♏33	24 20	7♒53	10♓48
13	16♐28	17♑56	2♓21	6♈27
15	10♑ 6	12♒ 0	28 14	3♉47
17	4♒10	7♓12	25♈51	2♊53
19	29 16	3♈57	25♉ 3	3♋ 9
21	25♓38	2♉ 9	24♊58	3♌25
23	23♈ 8	1♊11	24♋34	2♍33
25	21♉17	0♋13	23♌ 4	29 57
27	19♊36	28 41	20♍12	25♎44
29	17♋48	26♌21	16♎ 7	20♏19
31	...	23♍12	...	14♐12

STATIONS	☿	♀	♂	♃
	15Jan	29May	None	15Sep
	4♑30	6♋52		26R 8
	16Apr	11Jul		...
	11♉31	20♊22		...
	10May	♄	♅	♆
	1249	15Jun	13May	18Feb
	19Aug	5♓ 2	5♍55	17♏50
	17♍58	1Nov	20Dec	27Jul
	11Sep	28♒21	14♍51	15♏ 4
	4♍18	Sider Pl. Time		1Jan
	9Dec	6h 38m 45s		Midn
	4♑53	18h 40m 43s		Noon
	29Dec	Leap Year		1964
	18♐35			

1965 (BST 21 Mar. - 24 Oct)

Noon		JAN	FEB	MAR	APR	MAY	JUN
☉	1	10♑53	12♒26	10♓42	11♈33	10♉53	10♊46
	9	19 2	20 32	18 42	19 25	18 38	18 26
	17	27 11	28 37	26 41	27 15	26 21	26 4
	25	5♒19	6♓41	4♈37	5♉ 3	4♊ 3	3♋42
☿	1	19♐24	27♑ 6	15♓27	22♈46	15♈ 9	28♉41
	7	23 50	6♒33	26 59	19R18	20 20	11♊14
	13	0♑27	16 28	7♈58	14 49	27 17	24 23
	19	8 12	26 54	16 53	12 3	5♉43	7♋15
	25	16 38	7♓52	22 12	12D 3	15 33	19 7
	31	25 34	...	23R 3	...	26 42	...
♀	1	16♐29	25♑14	0♓13	8♈49	15♉56	24♊ 3
	9	26 28	5♒14	10 12	18 45	25 48	3♋51
	17	6♑28	15 14	20 10	28 39	5♊39	13 38
	25	16 28	25 14	0♈ 7	8♉32	15 28	23 24
♂	1	23♍57	27♍58	21♍49	10♍54	9♍31	17♍48
	13	26 40	26R29	17R10	8R59	11 49	22 42
	25	27 58	23 13	12 51	8D55	15 19	28 15
♃	1	16♉15	16♉56	20♉ 5	25♉33	2♊ 0	9♊11
	13	16D 7	18 2	22 0	28 2	4 45	11 58
	25	16 30	19 31	24 10	0♊39	7 33	14 43
♄	1	1♓20	4♓37	7♓59	11♓38	14♓37	16♓38
	13	2 31	6 2	9 26	12 55	15 33	17 3
	25	3 49	7 29	10 51	14 5	16 18	17 13
♅	1	14♍47	14♍ 2	12♍53	11♍37	10♍49	10♍47
	13	14R35	13R34	12R22	11R13	10R42	11 0
	25	14 16	13 4	11 52	10 56	10D43	11 20
♆	1	19♏20	19♏55	19♏59	19♏35	18♏51	18♏ 2
	13	19 37	20 0	19R53	19R19	18R32	17R45
	25	19 50	20R 0	19 42	19 1	18 13	17 32
Pl.	1	16♍16	15♍49	15♍ 9	14♍21	13♍49	13♍41
☊	1	21♊57	20♊19	18♊50	17♊11	15♊36	13♊57
	1st	FRI	MON	MON	THU	SAT	TUE

Noon		JUL	AUG	SEP	OCT	NOV	DEC
☉	1	9♋25	9♌ 1	8♍50	8♎ 6	8♏51	9♐ 5
	9	17 3	16 40	16 35	15 59	16 53	17 13
	17	24 41	24 21	24 22	23 54	24 56	25 21
	25	2♌19	2♍ 4	2♎12	1♏52	3♐ 1	3♑30
☿	1	29♋44	0♍ 5	20♌44	11♎ 9	28♏59	13♐ 3
	7	9♌ 3	28♌44	28 7	21 18	6♐47	5R25
	13	16 59	24R38	8♍14	0♏59	13 32	2D50
	19	23 22	19 52	19 23	10 15	18 8	5 54
	25	27 53	17D37	0♎29	19 9	18R35	12 6
	31	0♍ 0	19 53	...	27 38	...	19 46
♀	1	0♌43	8♍20	15♎27	20♏36	25♐23	25♑14
	9	10 28	17 58	24 55	29 47	3♑53	1♒48
	17	20 10	27 34	4♏19	8♐50	12 3	7 20
	25	29 52	7♎ 7	13 39	17 45	19 48	11 27
♂	1	1♎14	18♎22	7♏43	28♏ 3	20♐26	13♑ 7
	13	7 33	25 38	15 40	6♐34	29 24	22 25
	25	14 17	3♏11	23 52	15 16	8♑31	1♒47
♃	1	16♊ 4	22♊33	27♊45	0♋46	1♋ 3	28♊27
	13	18 41	24 46	29 14	1 15	0R18	26R54
	25	21 11	26 44	0♋22	1R16	29♊ 9	25 17
♄	1	17♓13	16♓17	14♓13	12♓ 1	10♓38	10♓45
	13	17R 2	15R34	13R18	11R19	10R29	11 15
	25	16 37	14 44	12 25	10 49	10D36	11 58
♅	1	11♍32	12♍58	14♍49	16♍41	18♍21	19♍22
	13	12 1	13 40	15 35	17 23	18 50	19 34
	25	12 36	14 23	16 19	18 1	19 13	19R38
♆	1	17♏26	17♏14	17♏32	18♏16	19♏20	20♏27
	13	17R18	17D18	17 47	18 40	19 47	20 52
	25	17 14	17 26	18 6	19 5	20 14	21 15
Pl.	1	14♍ 2	14♍49	15♍50	16♍54	17♍49	18♍21
☊	1	12♊22	10♊44	9♊ 5	7♊30	5♊51	4♊16
	1st	THU	SUN	WED	FRI	MON	WED

	d.	JAN	FEB	MAR	APR
☽	1	26♐ 1	10♒19	18♒56	5♈16
	3	19♑36	4♓38	13♓42	1♉59
	5	13♒22	29 37	9♈17	29 28
	7	7♓35	25♈23	5♉39	27♊25
	9	2♈35	22♉11	2♊43	25♋38
	11	28 46	20♊13	0♋33	23♌58
	13	26♉32	19♋29	29 10	22♍ 6
	15	25♊52	19♌24	28♌13	19♎34
	17	26♋13	18♍51	27♍ 1	15♏57
	19	22♌22	16♎50	24♎41	11♐ 6
	21	25♍ 7	12♏58	20♏48	5♑16
	23	21♎58	7♐35	15♐29	28 59
	25	17♏ 7	1♑20	9♑19	22♒53
	27	11♐ 9	24 55	2♒59	17♓36
	29	4♑43	...	27 9	13♈36
	31	28 22	...	22♓17	...

	d.	MAY	JUN	JUL	AUG
☽	1	10♉29	3♋ 1	11♌56	4♎47
	3	9♊15	2♌35	11♍23	2♏ 0
	5	8♋ 0	1♍26	9♎16	27 31
	7	6♌37	29 9	5♏33	21♐51
	9	4♍46	25♎39	0♐34	15♑38
	11	2♎13	21♏ 6	24 46	9♒18
	13	28 49	15♐44	18♑35	3♓11
	15	24♏29	9♑48	12♒16	27 28
	17	19♐58	3♒31	6♓ 7	22♈21
	19	13♑17	27 16	0♈24	18♉ 8
	21	6♒59	21♓29	25 33	15♊13
	23	0♓53	16♈42	22♉ 4	13♋52
	25	25 36	13♉25	20♊17	13♌49
	27	21♈38	11♊52	20♊ 5	14♍ 3
	29	19♉16	11♋43	20♌35	13♎16
	31	18♊15	...	20♍27	10♏40

	d.	SEP	OCT	NOV	DEC
☽	1	23♏39	26♐43	10♒28	12♓ 6
	3	18♐31	20♑43	4♓18	6♈30
	5	12♑28	14♒25	28 46	2♉ 5
	7	6♒ 8	8♓27	24♈16	29 9
	9	0♓ 1	3♈11	20♉56	27♊36
	11	24 25	28 46	18♊34	26♋51
	13	19♈25	25♉ 9	16♋49	26♌ 2
	15	15♈ 7	22♊16	15♌16	24♍27
	17	11♊41	20♋ 5	13♍34	21♎50
	19	9♋20	18♌30	11♎26	18♏12
	21	8♌ 9	17♍15	8♏37	13♐42
	23	7♍43	15♎45	4♐52	8♑28
	25	7♎ 6	13♏20	0♑ 7	2♒37
	27	5♏17	9♐36	24 29	26 24
	29	1♐46	4♑33	18♒18	20♓ 9
	31	...	28 36	...	14♈25

STATIONS	☿	♀	♂	♃
	29Mar	None	29Jan	10Jan
	23♈15		28♍ 3	16♉ 6
	22Apr		20Apr	19Oct
	11♈45		8♍43	1♋19
	1Aug	♄	♅	♆
	0♍ 5	28Jun	18May	20Feb
	25Aug	17♓13	10♍42	20♏ 1
	17♍37	14Nov	25Dec	30Jul
	23Nov	10♓29	19♍38	17♏14
	19♐ 3	Sider Pl. Time		1Jan
	12Dec	6h 41m 44s		Midn
	2♐49	18h 43m 42s		Noon
		Common Year		1965

1966 (BST 20 Mar - 23 Oct)

Noon		JAN	FEB	MAR	APR	MAY	JUN
☉	1	10♑38	12♒11	10♓27	11♈18	10♉40	10♊32
	9	18 47	20 17	18 28	19 11	18 24	18 12
	17	26 56	28 23	26 26	27 1	26 8	25 50
	25	5♒ 4	6♓26	4♈23	4♉50	3♊49	3♋29
☿	1	21♐ 8	8♒54	27♓54	23♓ 4	16♈52	16♊58
	7	29 37	19 19	4♈11	23D14	26 23	29 25
	13	8♑31	0♓ 9	5R36	26 18	7♉ 3	10 36
	19	17 44	11 11	2 17	1♈36	18 52	20 19
	25	27 17	21 47	27♓ 1	8 34	1♊39	28 28
	31	17♒12	...	23 22	...	14 48	...
♀	1	13♒29	2♒20	1♒39	25♒ 2	25♓58	0♉52
	9	13R32	29♑ 3	6 9	2♓49	4♈47	10 8
	17	10 58	28D18	11 56	11 0	13 45	19 27
	25	6 29	0♒ 1	18 38	19 28	22 50	28 51
♂	1	7♒17	1♓45	23♓45	17♈40	10♉ 8	2♊33
	13	16 45	11 13	3 5	26 44	18 55	11 0
	25	26 13	20 38	12 19	5 42	27 34	19 20
♃	1	24♊22	21♊34	21♊35	24♊25	29♊14	5♋30
	13	23R 0	21R15	22 22	26 9	1♋33	8 8
	25	21 58	21D25	23 33	28 9	4 1	10 49
♄	1	12♓28	15♓26	18♓43	22♓31	25 49	28♓23
	13	13 30	16 48	20 12	23 54	26 57	29 2
	25	14 41	18 14	21 40	25 13	27 54	29 28
♅	1	19♍36	18♍59	17♍54	16♍35	15♍42	15♍31
	13	19R28	18R33	17R22	16R10	15R32	15 41
	25	19 11	18 4	16 52	15 50	15D29	15 58
♆	1	21♏27	22♏ 3	22♏10	21♏48	21♏ 6	20♏16
	13	21 44	22 10	22R 5	21R33	20R46	19R59
	25	21 58	22R11	21 55	21 15	20 27	19 45
Pl.	1	18♍26	18♍ 0	17♍19	16♍32	15♍58	15♍48
☊	1	2♊37	0♊59	29♉30	27♉51	26♉16	24♉38
	1st	SAT	TUE	TUE	FRI	SUN	WED

Noon		JUL	AUG	SEP	OCT	NOV	DEC
☉	1	9♋12	8♌47	8♍36	7♎51	8♏37	8♐51
	9	16 49	16 27	16 21	15 45	16 38	16 58
	17	24 27	24 8	24 9	23 40	24 41	25 6
	25	2♌ 6	1♍50	1♎58	1♏37	2♐46	3♑15
☿	1	4♌54	2♌24	0♍ 8	23♎21	1♐31	18♏56
	7	9 21	0D21	11 48	2♏20	3R12	24D46
	13	11 21	2 5	23 6	10 48	29♏37	2♐32
	19	10R33	7 53	3♎46	18 38	21 58	11 6
	25	7 14	17 3	13 50	25 33	17 16	20 2
	31	3 0	28 11	...	0♐52	...	29 11
♀	1	5♊56	12♋59	20♌47	27♍57	6♏44	14♐24
	9	15 25	22 40	0♍39	7♎56	16 46	24 27
	17	24 58	2♌24	10 33	17 56	26 49	4♑30
	25	4♋33	12 11	20 29	27 57	6♐52	14 33
♂	1	23♊27	14♋17	4♌23	23♌ 8	11♍43	28♍38
	13	1♋36	22 9	11 58	0♍27	18 38	5♎ 0
	25	9 39	29 54	19 27	7 37	25 22	11 1
♃	1	12♋11	19♋ 7	25♋31	0♌35	3♌50	4♌19
	13	14 53	21 41	27 43	2 8	4 23	3R41
	25	17 34	24 9	29 42	3 19	4 27	2 38
♄	1	29♓36	29♓19	27♓38	25♓21	23♓28	22♓56
	13	29R41	28R48	26R44	24R30	23R 4	23 10
	25	29 31	28 6	25 48	23 48	22 55	23 39
♅	1	16♍ 9	17♍29	19♍18	21♍10	22♍54	23♍ 2
	13	16 35	18 9	20 3	21 53	23 26	24 18
	25	17 8	18 52	20 48	22 33	23 52	24 25
♆	1	19♏39	19♏24	19♏40	20♏22	21♏25	22♏32
	13	19R30	19D27	19 54	20 45	21 52	22 58
	25	19 25	19 34	20 12	21 10	22 19	23 21
Pl.	1	16♍ 7	16♍53	17♍54	18♍58	19♍55	20♍36
☊	1	23♉ 2	21♉24	19♉45	18♉10	16♉32	14♉56
	1st	FRI	MON	THU	SAT	TUE	THU

d.	JAN	FEB	MAR	APR
☽ 1	26♈56	14♊53	23♊48	16♌ 9
3	23♉ 7	13♋35	22♋ 4	15♍51
5	21♊ 6	13♌52	21♌58	15♎41
7	20♋40	14♍30	22♍32	14♏32
9	20♌53	14♎ 3	22♎20	11♐44
11	20♍30	11♏44	20♏22	7♑17
13	18♎39	7♐38	16♐31	1♒39
15	15♏15	2♑18	11♑14	25 26
17	10♐38	26 19	5♒ 9	19♓14
19	5♑12	20♒ 4	28 51	13♈28
21	29 17	13♓49	22♓42	8♉23
23	23♒ 5	7♈45	16♈55	4♊ 6
25	16♓49	2♉ 6	11♉40	0♋40
27	10♈45	27 17	7♊ 9	28 9
29	5♉21	...	3♋14	26♌30
31	1♊16	...	1♌40	...

d.	MAY	JUN	JUL	AUG
☽ 1	25♍27	17♏44	23♐39	10♒ 8
3	24♎24	14♐40	19♑ 1	4♓11
5	22♏38	10♑34	13♒37	27 54
7	19♐36	5♒26	7♓37	21♈40
9	15♑11	29 32	1♈21	16♉ 0
11	9♒39	23♓19	25 23	11♊34
13	3♓30	17♈24	20♉21	8♋56
15	27 22	12♉22	16♊50	8♌10
17	21♈46	8♊41	15♋ 3	8♍31
19	17♉ 6	6♋25	14♌35	8♎37
21	13♊32	5♌ 8	14♍22	7♏23
23	10♋57	4♍ 8	13♎22	4♐29
25	9♌ 3	2♎43	11♏ 5	0♑12
27	7♍29	0♏32	7♐34	24 57
29	5♎54	27 30	3♑ 6	19♒ 8
31	3♏57	...	27 56	12♓59

d.	SEP	OCT	NOV	DEC
☽ 1	24♓50	27♈36	14♊ 0	20♋17
3	18♈33	21♉54	10♋ 2	17♌52
5	12♉35	16♊56	7♌ 6	15♍59
7	7♊26	13♋10	5♍16	14♎24
9	3♋41	10♌57	4♎20	12♏50
11	1♌48	10♍15	3♏44	10♐54
13	1♍37	10♎24	2♐36	8♑ 5
15	2♎11	10♏14	0♑13	4♒ 4
17	2♏ 5	8♐43	26 17	28 50
19	0♐22	5♑28	21♒ 1	22♒46
21	26 52	0♒40	14♓56	16♈27
23	21♑57	24 52	8♈39	10♉35
25	16♒10	18♓36	2♉44	5♊45
27	9♓59	12♈23	27 36	2♋16
29	3♈43	6♉33	23♊23	0♌ 1
31	...	1♊19	...	28 29

STATIONS	☿	♀	♂	♃
	12Mar	5Jan	None	15Feb
	5♈44	13♒50		21♊15
	4Apr	15Feb		21Nov
	22♓44	28♑14		4♌29
	14Jul	♄	♅	♆
	11♌25	11Jul	24May	22Feb
	7Aug	29♓41	15♍29	22♏11
	0♌21	26Nov	30Dec	1Aug
	6Nov	22♓55	24♍26	19♏24
	3♐14	Sider'l Time		1Jan
	26Nov	6h 40m 47s		Midn
	17♏ 7	18h 42m 45s		Noon
		Common Year		1966

1967 (BST 19 Mar - 29 Oct)

Noon		JAN	FEB	MAR	APR	MAY	JUN
☉	1	10♑23	11♒56	10♓12	11♈ 4	10♉25	10♊18
	9	18 36	20 3	18 13	18 56	18 10	17 58
	17	26 41	28 8	26 12	26 47	25 54	25 37
	25	4♒49	6♓11	4♈ 9	4♉35	3♊35	3♋15
☿	1	0♑42	22♒ 8	15♓46	13♓18	29♈ 5	1♋11
	7	10 6	2♓30	9R48	20 13	11♉19	9 33
	13	19 43	11 41	5 25	28 23	24 16	16 0
	19	29 38	17 41	4D43	7♈36	1♊11	20 14
	25	9♒52	18R22	7 19	17 50	19 10	21 58
	31	20 17	...	12 18	...	29 36	...
♀	1	23♑20	2♓ 9	6♈52	14♉36	19♊59	24♋32
	9	3♒22	12 7	16 42	24 10	29 9	2♌54
	17	13 24	22 3	26 28	3♊39	8♋10	10 56
	25	23 24	1♈56	6♉10	13 2	16 59	18 33
♂	1	14♎21	26♎51	2♏53	29♎39	19♎ 2	15♎13
	13	19 41	0♏14	3R 3	25R33	16R 5	16D58
	25	24 26	2 27	1 25	21 4	16 59	20 10
♃	1	1♌52	27♋50	25♋ 4	24♋37	26♋58	1♌32
	13	0R21	26R25	24 32	25 16	28 31	3 43
	25	28♋45	25 20	24D27	26 18	0♌21	6 4
♄	1	24♓ 2	26♓36	29♓43	3♈33	7♈ 7	10♈ 9
	13	24 53	27 52	1♈11	5 1	8 24	11 2
	25	25 55	29 14	2 40	6 26	9 33	11 43
♅	1	24♍26	23♍56	22♍54	21♍35	20♍36	20♍17
	13	24R20	23R32	22R23	21R 8	20R23	20D23
	25	24 7	23 4	21 52	20 45	20 17	20 37
♆	1	23♏33	24♏12	24♏21	24♏ 1	23♏20	22♏30
	13	23 51	24 19	24R17	23R46	23R 1	22R13
	25	24 5	24R21	24 8	23 29	22 41	21 58
Pl.	1	20♍37	20♍14	19♍34	18♍46	18♍10	17♍58
☊	1	13♉18	11♉39	10♉10	8♉32	6♉56	5♉18
	1st	SUN	WED	WED	SAT	MON	THU

Noon		JUL	AUG	SEP	OCT	NOV	DEC
☉	1	8♋58	8♌33	8♍22	7♎37	8♏22	8♐36
	9	16 36	16 13	16 7	15 30	16 24	16 43
	17	24 13	23 54	23 54	23 26	24 27	24 51
	25	1♌52	1♍36	1♎44	1♏23	2♐31	3♑ 0
☿	1	20♋59	19♋12	15♍44	1♏48	8♏42	23♏49
	7	17R51	27 37	26 18	8 42	2R25	2♐58
	13	14 15	8♌27	6♎11	14 10	2D 9	12 15
	19	12 18	20 27	15 24	17 9	7 15	21 36
	25	13D27	2♍27	23 57	16R 3	15 1	1♑ 2
	31	18 6	13 54	...	10 0	...	10 36
♀	1	23♌54	12♍59	4♍15	29♌54	22♍ 2	23♎22
	9	0♍27	13R53	0♌ 0	3♍52	29 49	2♏27
	17	6 5	12 21	27R48	9 16	8♎ 4	11 43
	25	10 28	8 31	28D 8	15 43	16 42	21 8
♂	1	22♎13	6♏19	24♏29	14♐31	6♑58	29♑45
	13	27 3	12 58	2♐16	23 2	15 59	9♒ 2
	25	2♏42	20 7	10 22	1♑46	25 8	18 22
♃	1	7♌17	13♌56	20♌42	26♌49	2♍ 0	5♍ 9
	13	9 49	16 34	23 14	29 0	3 32	5 43
	25	12 24	19 12	25 39	0♍58	4 42	5R50
♄	1	11♈59	12♈25	11♈16	9♈ 7	6♈52	5♈42
	13	12 21	12R 9	10R29	8R11	6R14	5D40
	25	12R28	11 39	9 36	7 19	5 59	5 53
♅	1	20♍47	22♍ 1	23♍46	25♍39	27♍26	28♍41
	13	21 11	22 39	24 31	26 23	28 1	29 0
	25	21 41	23 21	25 16	27 4	28 29	29 10
♆	1	21♏52	21♏35	21♏48	22♏29	23♏30	24♏38
	13	21R42	21D36	22 2	22 51	23 57	25 3
	25	21 36	21 43	22 19	23 15	24 24	25 27
Pl.	1	18♍15	18♍59	20♍ 0	21♍ 4	22♍ 3	22♍42
☊	1	3♉43	2♉ 4	0♉26	28♈50	27♈12	25♈37
	1st	SAT	TUE	FRI	SUN	WED	FRI

d.		JAN	FEB	MAR	APR
☽	1	12♍46	6♏ 0	16♏ 5	6♑32
	3	11♎ 9	3♐25	13♐41	2♒11
	5	9♏ 6	29 54	9♑56	26 44
	7	6♐32	25♑38	5♒ 9	20♓39
	9	3♑22	20 38	29 39	14♈17
	11	29 25	14♓57	23♓38	7♉56
	13	24♒31	8♈43	17♈17	1♊53
	15	18♓43	2♉18	10♉53	26 31
	17	12♈24	26 17	4♊54	22♋16
	19	6♉ 9	21♊23	29 54	19♌31
	21	0♊43	18♋12	26♋30	18♍23
	23	26 42	16♌55	24♌59	18♎26
	25	24♋25	15♍56	25♍ 1	18♏37
	27	23♌29	17♎ 1	25♎29	17♐48
	29	22♍57	...	25♏ 7	15♑19
	31	21♎54	...	23♐ 9	...

d.		MAY	JUN	JUL	AUG
☽	1	11♒ 7	25♓59	27♈40	11♊46
	3	5♓38	19♈39	21♉33	7♋19
	5	29 25	13♉23	16♊15	4♌21
	7	23♈ 1	7♊46	12♋ 7	2♍37
	9	16♉49	3♋ 3	9♌ 7	1♎27
	11	11♊10	29 16	6♍55	0♏ 9
	13	16♋15	26♌20	5♎ 6	28 20
	15	2♌19	24♍ 8	3♏21	25♐52
	17	29 30	22♎34	1♐32	22♑42
	19	27♍52	21♏23	29 26	18♒44
	21	27♎13	20♐ 6	26♑40	13♓51
	23	26♏52	18♑ 4	22♒52	8♈ 6
	25	25♐53	14♒42	17♓53	1♉47
	27	23♑30	9♓54	11♈56	25 26
	29	19♒28	4♈ 1	5♉34	19♊45
	31	14♓ 2	....	29 29	15♋21

d.		SEP	OCT	NOV	DEC
☽	1	28♋47	5♍ 1	27♎49	6♐10
	3	26♌54	4♌39	28♏12	5♑50
	5	26♍15	4♏52	27♐46	4♒ 1
	7	25♎52	4♐32	25♑40	0♓21
	9	24♏52	2♑50	21♒47	25 7
	11	22♐48	29 35	16♓30	18♈56
	13	19♑36	25♒ 1	10♈24	12♉30
	15	15♒24	19♓30	3♉59	6♊21
	17	10♓22	13♈24	27 41	0♋50
	19	4♈37	7♉ 2	21♊44	26 4
	21	28 21	0♊40	16♋25	22♌ 4
	23	21♉55	24 41	12♌ 0	18♍53
	25	15♊48	19♋29	8♍36	16♎36
	27	10♋36	15♌35	6♎40	15♏17
	29	6♌55	13♍19	6♏ 4	14♐36
	31	...	12♎42	...	13♑47

STATIONS	☿	♀	♂	♃
	23Feb	8Aug	8Mar	21Mar
	18♓48	13♍54	3♏12	24♋26
	17Mar	20Sep	26May	22Dec
	4♓33	27♌38	14♎59	5♍50
	26Jun	♄	♅	♆
	21♋59	25Jul	28May	24Feb
	20Jul	12♈28	20♍17	24♏21
	12♋15	9Dec	...	3Aug
	21Oct	5♈39	...	21♏35
	17♏20	Sider Pl. Time		1Jan
	10Nov	6h 39m 50s		Midn
	1♏27	18h 41m 48s		Noon
		Common Year		1967

(Feb B.STD.T. adopted, 1 hour ahead of G.M.T.)

1968

Noon		JAN	FEB	MAR	APR	MAY	JUN
☉	1	10♑ 8	11♒42	10♓59	11♈49	11♉10	11♊ 2
	9	18 18	19 48	18 59	19 42	18 55	18 42
	17	26 26	27 53	26 58	27 31	26 38	26 10
	25	4♒35	5♓57	4♈54	5♉20	4♊19	3♋58
☿	1	12♑12	29♒57	17♒20	20♓48	18♉50	1♋10
	7	22 0	2♓12	20D13	0R47	1♊ 3	1R58
	13	2♒ 0	28R21	25 27	11 39	11 44	0 12
	19	12 0	21♒43	2♓17	23 25	20 23	26♊57
	25	21 28	17 4	10 16	6♉ 0	26 49	24 5
	31	29 1	...	19 14	...	0♋45	...
♀	1	29♏28	7♑ 3	12♒40	20♓52	27♈48	5♊53
	9	9♐ 5	16 51	22 32	0♈44	7♉38	15 43
	17	18 45	26 41	2♓23	10 35	17 28	25 32
	25	28 29	6♒31	12 15	20 25	27 17	5♋22
♂	1	23♒52	17♓57	10♈11	3♉19	24♉59	16♊37
	13	3♓12	27 13	19 14	12 5	3♊27	24 48
	25	12 32	6♈23	28 10	20 43	11 48	2♋53
♃	1	5♍41	3♍17	29♌34	26♌29	25♌58	28♌13
	13	5R 4	1R48	28R 8	25R57	26 32	29 42
	25	4 2	0 13	26 59	25D51	27 29	1♍29
♄	1	6♈ 8	8♈10	11♈ 7	14♈54	18♈38	22♈ 2
	13	6 44	9 18	12 33	16 25	20 2	23 7
	25	7 34	10 34	14 2	17 54	21 20	24 2
♅	1	29♍13	28♍52	27♍52	26♍33	25♍30	25♍ 5
	13	29R11	28R30	27 22	26R 5	25R14	25D 8
	25	29 0	28 4	26 51	25 41	25 6	25 19
♆	1	25♏39	26♏20	26♏32	26♏14	25♏33	24♏43
	13	25 58	26 29	26R28	26R 0	25R14	24R26
	25	26 13	26 32	26 20	25 43	24 55	24 10
Pl.	1	22♍51	22♍30	21♍50	21♍ 0	20♍24	20♍10
☊	1	23♈59	22♈20	20♈48	19♈10	17♈34	15♈56
	1st	MON	THU	FRI	MON	WED	SAT

Noon		JUL	AUG	SEP	OCT	NOV	DEC
☉	1	9♋41	9♌17	9♍ 6	8♎22	9♏ 8	9♐22
	9	17 19	16 56	16 51	16 15	17 9	17 29
	17	24 57	24 37	24 39	24 11	25 13	25 38
	25	2♌35	2♍20	2♎28	2♏ 8	3♐18	3♑47
☿	1	23♊20	2♌34	29♍41	1♏ 1	20♎40	6♐15
	7	25D25	15 3	8♎20	0R15	28 35	15 40
	13	0♋28	27 3	16 7	24♎56	7♏45	25 7
	19	8 18	8♍14	22 51	18 7	17 15	4 36
	25	18 34	18 36	28 7	15D47	26 46	14 11
	31	0♌30	28 10	...	19 36	...	23 45
♀	1	12♋44	20♌53	29♍ 3	5♏53	13♐45	19♑57
	9	22 34	0♍43	8♎53	15 41	23 28	29 30
	17	2♌25	10 35	18 43	25 28	3♑ 8	8♒54
	25	12 15	20 26	28 32	5♐14	12 46	18 13
♂	1	6♋53	27 17	17♌11	6♍ 6	25♍17	13♎24
	13	14 51	5♌ 2	24 47	13 34	2♎35	20 30
	25	22 43	12 43	2♍21	20 59	9 49	27 28
♃	1	2♍27	8♍14	14♍45	21♍13	27♍27	2♎22
	13	4 33	10 42	17 21	23 43	29 35	3 51
	25	6 50	13 15	19 57	26 7	1♎31	5 0
♄	1	24♈25	25♈31	25♈ 1	23♈10	20♈46	19♈ 3
	13	25 2	25R31	24 24	22R15	19R56	18R46
	25	25 25	25 16	23 37	21 18	19 18	18D43
♅	1	25♍28	26♍36	28♍18	0♎11	2♎ 1	3♎21
	13	25 49	27 13	29 3	0 56	2 35	3 41
	25	26 18	27 54	29 48	1 38	3 8	3 55
♆	1	24♏ 4	23♏46	23♏57	24♏37	25♏38	26♏45
	13	23R54	23D47	24 10	24 58	26 4	27 11
	25	23 47	23 52	24 27	25 23	26 31	27 35
Pl.	1	20♍25	21♍ 8	22♍ 9	23♍15	24♍16	24♍55
☊	1	14♈20	12♈42	11♈ 3	9♈28	7♈50	6♈14
	1st	MON	THU	SUN	TUE	FRI	SUN

	d.	JAN	FEB	MAR	APR
☽	1	28♑ 1	16♓ 3	6♈32	20♉48
	3	25♒17	10♈54	0♉44	14♊38
	5	20♓49	4♉48	24 27	8♋29
	7	15♈11	28 27	18♊14	3♌30
	9	8♉49	22♊31	12♋43	0♍ 0
	11	2♊33	17♋37	8♌33	28 11
	13	27 2	14♌ 1	5♍53	27♎48
	15	22♋20	11♍35	4♎37	27♏53
	17	18♌41	9♎51	3♏57	27♐22
	19	15♍47	8♏17	3♐ 5	25♑29
	21	13♎25	6♐35	1♑24	22♒ 6
	23	11♏28	4♑30	28♑44	17♓26
	25	9♐51	1♒55	25♒33	11♈51
	27	8♑18	28 32	20♓25	5♉46
	29	6♒16	24♓ 9	15♈ 1	29 26
	31	3♓ 8	...	8♉58	...

	d.	MAY	JUN	JUL	AUG
☽	1	23♊ 8	8♌53	14♍24	5♏12
	3	17♋13	4♍26	11♎14	4♐ 5
	5	12♌ 9	1♎17	9♏19	3♑ 3
	7	8♍23	29 42	8♐36	2♒ 2
	9	6♎22	29♏34	8♑27	0♓ 8
	11	5♏58	29♐56	7♒47	26 51
	13	6♐26	29♑32	5♓37	22♈ 4
	15	6♑27	27♒20	1♈39	16♉13
	17	4♒59	23♓19	26 15	9♊58
	19	1♓41	17♈52	20♉ 3	3♋55
	21	26 49	11♉38	13♊45	28 36
	23	20♈47	5♊15	7♋51	24♌21
	25	14♉39	29 9	2♌41	21♍ 3
	27	8♊18	23♋33	28 17	18♎35
	29	2♋ 9	18♌35	24♍40	16♏38
	31	26 29	...	21♎50	15♐ 0

	d.	SEP	OCT	NOV	DEC
☽	1	29♐12	7♒55	27♓28	1♉32
	3	27♑28	4♓47	22♈21	25 30
	5	25♒12	0♈45	16♉28	19♊16
	7	21♓50	25 51	10♊31	13♋ 2
	9	17♈34	20♉10	4♋14	7♌ 1
	11	12♉ 7	14♊ 0	28 7	1♍34
	13	5♊59	7♋46	22♌43	27 11
	15	29 46	1♌59	18♍30	24♎24
	17	24♋ 5	27 18	16♎ 5	23♏28
	19	19♌27	24♍ 9	15♏27	23♐53
	21	16♍10	22♎40	15♐52	24♑23
	23	14♎ 7	22♏12	16♑ 0	23♒34
	25	13♏ 0	21♐55	14♒41	20♓47
	27	11♐42	20♑49	11♓38	16♈15
	29	10♑11	18♒24	7♈ 4	10♉34
	31	...	14♓42	...	4♊22

STATIONS	☿	♀	♂	♃
	7Feb	None	None	22Apr
	2♓ 7			25♌50
	28Feb			
	17♒ 6			
	6Jun	♄	♅	♆
	2♋ 1	7Aug	4Jan	27Feb
	30Jun	25♈33	29♍13	26♏32
	23♊15	21Dec	2Jun	5Aug
	3Oct	18♈42	25♍ 5	23♏46
	1♏14	Sider Pl Time		1Jan
	24Oct	6h 38m 53s		Midn
	15♎43	18h 40m 51s		Noon
		Leap Year		1968

1969 (B.STD.T.)

Noon		JAN	FEB	MAR	APR	MAY	JUN
☉	1	10♑55	12♒28	10♓44	11♈35	10♉56	10♊48
	9	19 4	20 34	18 45	19 28	18 40	18 27
	17	27 13	28 39	26 43	27 18	26 24	26 6
	25	5♒20	6♓43	4♈40	5♉ 6	4♊ 5	3♋44
☿	1	25♑19	5♒29	14♒43	3♈58	1♊ 9	6♊ 8
	7	4♒26	0R47	22 34	15 54	7 38	3R47
	13	12 2	0D48	1♓17	28 25	11 15	3D43
	19	15 56	4 20	10 47	10♉50	11R53	6 22
	25	13R36	10 5	21 1	22 3	9 56	11 34
	31	6♒39	...	2♈ 3	...	6 40	...
♀	1	26♒14	29♓19	21♈43	22♈52	10♈33	26♈12
	9	5♓12	6♈48	25 18	18R 4	12D14	2♉59
	17	13 56	13 32	26 49	13 30	15 50	10 23
	25	22 19	19 19	25R49	10 52	20 54	18 13
♂	1	1♏28	18♏23	1♐53	13♐ 4	16♐40	9♐43
	13	8 11	24 27	6 50	15 38	15R 9	5R45
	25	14 43	0♐ 7	11 3	16 44	12 1	2 49
♃	1	5♎29	5♎50	3♎39	29♍48	26♍49	26♍14
	13	5 58	5R 9	2R14	28R24	26R15	26 46
	25	6R 1	4 6	0 41	27 16	26D 7	27 42
♄	1	18♈48	20♈16	22♈47	26♈24	0♉12	3♉55
	13	19 11	21 14	24 6	27 55	1 42	5 10
	25	19 48	22 22	25 32	29 26	3 7	6 17
♅	1	3♎59	3♎44	2♎52	1♎33	0♎26	29♍53
	13	4R 0	3R26	2R23	1R 4	0R 8	29D53
	25	3 52	3 1	1 52	0 38	29♍56	0♎ 1
♆	1	27♏48	28♏30	28♏43	28♏27	27♏48	26♏58
	13	28 7	28 39	28R40	28R13	27R29	26R40
	25	28 23	28 43	28 33	27 57	27 9	26 24
Pl.	1	25♍ 6	24♍46	24♍ 8	23♍18	22♍41	22♍24
☊	1	4R36	2♈57	1♈28	29♓50	28♓15	26♓36
	1st	WED	SAT	SAT	TUE	THU	SUN

Noon		JUL	AUG	SEP	OCT	NOV	DEC
☉	1	9♋27	9♌ 3	8♍52	8♎ 8	8♏54	9♐ 8
	9	17 5	16 42	16 37	16 1	16 55	17 15
	17	25 42	24 23	24 25	23 57	24 58	25 23
	25	2♌21	2♍ 6	2♎14	1♏54	3♐ 3	3♑32
☿	1	19♊ 7	19♌36	5♎52	3♎47	29♎40	17♐33
	7	28 48	0♍33	11 12	29♍56	9♏33	26 50
	13	10♋20	10 34	14 23	2D 3	19 17	6♐ 1
	19	22 58	19 38	14R22	8 56	28 49	14 56
	25	5♌39	27 46	10 17	18 7	8♐14	22 58
	31	17 41	4♎49	...	28 0	...	28 42
♀	1	24♉20	28♊ 3	4♌ 1	10♍11	18♎30	26♏ 5
	9	2♊44	7♋10	13 32	20 0	28 30	6♐ 8
	17	11 22	16 23	23 10	29 53	8♏31	16 12
	25	20 11	25 44	2♍47	9♎48	18 33	26 16
♂	1	2♐ 1	5♐30	18♐40	6♑27	27♑39	19♒31
	13	1D53	9 44	25 20	14 25	6♒17	28 26
	25	3 41	15 5	2♑37	22 42	15 5	7♓23
♃	1	28♍17	2♎34	8♎13	14♎35	21♎16	27♎20
	13	29 43	4 39	10 45	17 12	23 47	29 28
	25	1♎26	6 55	13 18	19 45	26 10	1♏23
♄	1	6♉48	8♉36	8♉50	7♉32	5♉12	3♉ 3
	13	7 40	8 54	8R29	6R42	4R15	2 29
	25	8 20	8R56	7 54	5 46	3 24	2 9
♅	1	0♎ 8	1♎ 9	2♎48	4♎39	6♎31	7♎57
	13	0 27	1 44	3 31	5 24	7 9	8 21
	25	0 52	2 23	4 16	6 7	7 42	8 37
♆	1	26♏18	25♏57	26♏ 6	26♏43	27♏43	28♏50
	13	26R 6	25D57	26 18	27 4	28 10	29 17
	25	25 59	26 1	26 34	27 28	28 37	29 41
Pl.	1	22♍47	23♍19	24♍19	25♍25	26♍26	27♍ 8
☊	1	25♓ 1	23♓22	21♓44	20♓ 8	18♓30	16♓55
	1st	TUE	FRI	MON	WED	SAT	MON

	d.	JAN	FEB	MAR	APR
☽	1	16♊12	0♌47	9♌ 6	25♍31
	3	10♋ 1	25 28	4♍12	22♎48
	5	4♌ 5	20♍51	0♎15	21♏ 4
	7	28 37	17♎59	27 11	19♐47
	9	23♍48	14♏ 3	24♏52	18♑22
	11	20♎ 5	12♐12	23♐ 6	16♒25
	13	17♏49	11♑19	21♑36	13♓45
	15	17♐ 4	10♒39	20♒ 1	10♈17
	17	17♑16	9♓40	17♓52	5♉57
	19	17♒ 8	6♈48	14♈43	0♊47
	21	15♓33	2♉37	10♉22	24 54
	23	12♈ 5	27 9	4♊57	18♋40
	25	7♉ 2	21♊ 1	28 52	12♌27
	27	1♊ 3	14♋49	22♋41	7♍23
	29	24 46	...	17♌ 1	3♎32
	31	18♋39	...	12♍22	17 13

	d.	MAY	JUN	JUL	AUG
☽	1	1♏18	24♐14	3♒15	25♓24
	3	0♐25	24♑25	2♓43	22♈25
	5	0♑ 2	23♒26	0♈24	17♉48
	7	29♑ 8	20♓52	26 23	12♊ 0
	9	27♒ 7	16♈51	21♉10	5♋58
	11	23♓54	11♉49	15♊15	29♋41
	13	19♈45	6♊ 8	9♋ 1	23♌40
	15	14♉49	0♋ 4	2♌44	18♍ 8
	17	9♊16	23 47	26 37	13♎18
	19	3♋13	17♌33	21♍ 1	9♏28
	21	26 56	11♍44	16♎17	6♐53
	23	20♌50	6♎56	12♏59	5♑36
	25	15♍29	3♏44	11♐21	5♒13
	27	11♎34	2♐29	11♑15	4♓51
	29	9♏29	3♑43	11♒38	3♈32
	31	9♐ 5	...	11♓13	0♉34

	d.	SEP	OCT	NOV	DEC
☽	1	13♉46	16♊27	0♌13	1♍53
	3	8♊29	10♋31	23 59	26 13
	5	2♋30	4♌16	18♍25	21♎54
	7	26 14	28 18	14♎ 7	19♏25
	9	20♌12	23♍11	11♏22	18♐35
	11	14♍46	19♎12	9♐56	18♑32
	13	10♎ 9	16♏22	9♑00	18♒ 4
	15	6♏26	14♐20	7♒48	16♓24
	17	3♐38	12♑40	5♓51	13♈24
	19	1♑38	11♒ 0	3♈ 4	9♉19
	21	0♒18	9♓ 4	29 32	4♊25
	23	29♒10	6♈41	25♉16	28 55
	25	27♓42	3♉34	20♊14	22♋55
	27	25♈16	29♊28	14♋28	16♌34
	29	21♉30	24♋20	8♌12	10♍13
	31	...	19♌22	...	4♎28

STATIONS	☿	♀	♂	♃
	20Jan	18Mar	27Apr	20Jan
	16♒ 1	26♈50	16♐46	6♎ 3
	10Feb	29Apr	8Jul	23May
	0♒15	10♈30	1♐43	26♍ 6
	18May	♄	♅	♆
	12♊ 0	21Aug	9Jan	1Mar
	10Jun	8♉57	4♎ 0	28♏43
	3♊25		6Jun	7Aug
	16Sep		29♏52	25♏56
	14♎51	Sider Pl. Time		1Jan
	7Oct	6h 41m 52s		Midn
	29♍52	18h 43m 50s		Noon
		Common Year		1969

1970 (B.STD.T.)

Noon	JAN	FEB	MAR	APR	MAY	JUN
☉ 1	10♑39	12♒13	10♓29	11♈20	10♉42	10♊35
9	18 49	20 20	18 30	19 13	18 27	18 14
17	26 58	28 25	26 29	27 3	26 10	25 52
25	5♒ 7	6♓28	4♈25	4♉51	3♊51	3♋31
☿ 1	29♑16	17♑13	22♏56	20♈35	22♉ 4	17♉ 2
7	29R29	22 51	2♓47	2♉10	19R23	22 29
13	22 37	29 56	13 17	11 51	15 50	29 57
19	15 51	7♒59	24 28	18 38	13 29	9♊15
25	13D55	16 44	6♈20	22 4	13D35	20 14
31	16 29	...	18 33	...	16 20	...
♀ 1	5♑ 5	14♒ 3	19♓ 7	27♈38	4♊26	11♋53
9	15 8	24 5	29 5	7♉30	14 10	21 30
17	25 12	4♓ 6	9♈ 2	17 20	23 49	0♌53
25	5♒16	14 7	18 58	27 5	3♋29	10 17
♂ 1	12♓36	5♈36	26 1	18♉ 1	8♊41	29♊29
13	21 33	14 24	4♉36	26 21	16 48	7 24
25	0♈26	23 7	13 6	4♊36	24 50	15 15
♃ 1	2♏24	5♏26	5♏49	3♏33	29♎51	26♎47
13	3 53	5 54	5R15	2R 8	28R27	26R13
25	4 59	5R56	4 16	0 36	27 18	26D 5
♄ 1	2♉ 4	2♉48	4♉51	8♉11	11♉56	15♉51
13	2D 8	3 33	6 2	9 39	13 28	17 15
25	2 29	4 30	7 22	11 10	14 59	18 33
♅ 1	8♎43	8♎38	7♎50	6♎34	5♎23	4♎42
13	8 47	8 21	7R22	6R 3	5R 2	4D39
25	8R43	7 59	6 52	5 35	4 48	4 44
♆ 1	29♏54	0♐38	0♐53	0♐40	0♐ 2	29♏13
13	0♐14	0 48	0R51	0R27	29♏43	28R55
25	0 31	0 53	0 45	0 11	29R24	28 38
Pl. 1	27♍23	27♍ 6	26♍28	25♍38	24♍59	24♍41
☊ 1	15♓16	13♓38	12♓ 9	10♓30	8♓55	7♓16
1st	THU	SUN	SUN	WED	FRI	MON

Noon	JUL	AUG	SEP	OCT	NOV	DEC
☉ 1	9♋14	8♌49	8♍38	7♎53	8♏39	8♐53
9	16 52	16 29	16 23	15 46	16 40	17 0
17	24 29	24 9	24 10	23 42	24 43	25 8
25	2♌ 7	1♍52	2♎ 0	1♏39	2♐48	3♑17
☿ 1	2♋38	1♍55	27♍46	20♍34	11♏22	27 21
7	15 37	10 18	24R36	29 44	21 23	5♑16
13	28 17	17 30	18 48	9♎50	0♐41	11 31
19	10♌ 3	23 13	14 18	20 14	9 48	14R 4
25	20 46	26 57	14D47	0♏24	18 44	10 22
31	0♍24	27R56	...	10 15	...	2 33
♀ 1	17♌18	22♍28	24♎45	19♏ 1	22♏27	9♏47
9	26 33	1♎10	2♏12	22 57	18R 4	11D 9
17	5♍41	9 39	9 5	25 0	13 27	14 39
25	14 42	17 51	15 9	24R45	10 25	19 46
♂ 1	9♋ 9	9♌ 8	28♌55	17♍58	7♎39	26♎42
13	26 55	16 49	6♍32	25 35	15 16	4♏19
25	4♌38	24 28	14 10	3♎12	22 53	11 56
♃ 1	26♎10	28♎15	2♏33	8♏ 9	14♏45	21♏20
13	26 40	29 42	4 40	10 39	17 25	23 53
25	27 34	1♏25	6 57	13 14	20 2	26 19
♄ 1	19♉ 9	21♉36	22♉36	22♉ 0	19♉58	17♉35
13	20 15	22 11	22R33	21R20	19R 0	16R48
25	21 10	22 31	22 14	20 31	18 3	16 11
♅ 1	4♎48	5♎43	7♎16	9♎ 6	11♎ 0	12♎32
13	5 4	6 16	7 59	9 52	11 40	12 58
25	5 27	6 52	8 43	10 36	12 16	13 18
♆ 1	28♏31	28♏ 9	28♏15	28♏50	29♏49	0♐55
13	28R19	28D 8	28 26	29 11	0♐15	1 22
25	28 11	28 11	28 41	29 34	0 42	1 47
Pl. 1	24♍52	25♍31	26♍31	27♍37	28♍41	29♍25
☊ 1	5♓41	4♓ 3	2♓24	0♓49	29♒10	27♒35
1st	WED	SAT	TUE	THU	SUN	TUE

d.	JAN	FEB	MAR	APR
☽ 1	17♎ 2	5♐54	15♐30	8♒18
3	13♏24	4♑44	13♑47	7♓17
5	11♐43	4♒43	13♒16	6♈18
7	11♑41	5♓15	13♓12	4♈38
9	12♒10	4♈36	12♈31	1♊38
11	11♓49	2♉14	10♉25	27 9
13	9♈51	28 10	6♊37	21♋27
15	6♉17	22♊50	1♋23	15♌ 8
17	1♊29	16♋55	25 15	8♍54
19	25 53	10♌24	18♌53	3♎19
21	19♋48	4♍ 6	12♍45	28 47
23	13♌31	28 14	7♎16	25♏20
25	7♍10	24♎58	2♏36	22♐47
27	1♎10	18♏37	28 50	20♑47
29	26 0	...	25♐58	19♒ 1
31	22♏ 9	...	23♑59	...

d.	MAY	JUN	JUL	AUG
☽ 1	17♓20	8♉56	14♊41	0♌38
3	15♈29	5♊20	9♋35	24 19
5	13♉ 4	0♋50	3♌47	17♍57
7	9♊40	25 21	27 28	11♎42
9	5♋ 9	19♌11	21♍ 3	6♏17
11	29 20	12♍48	15♎ 7	2♐11
13	23♌ 1	6♎53	10♏20	29 46
15	16♍49	2♏11	7♐14	29♑ 3
17	11♎23	29 3	5♑55	29♒21
19	7♏15	27♐32	5♒49	29♓28
21	4♐32	26♑55	5♓49	28♈23
23	2♑51	26♒16	4♈56	25♉36
25	1♒32	24♓50	2♉40	21♊14
27	0♓ 1	22♈23	29 0	15♋44
29	28 8	18♉59	24♊13	9♌34
31	25♈27	...	18♋38	3♍ 9

d.	SEP	OCT	NOV	DEC
☽ 1	14♍57	17♎54	6♐15	12♑ 5
3	8♎47	12♏43	1♑57	10♒ 7
5	3♏ 8	8♐23	29 19	8♓16
7	28 24	4♑59	27♒19	6♈25
9	24♐57	2♒41	25♓53	4♉25
11	23♑ 1	1♓32	24♈43	1♊57
13	22♒31	1♈ 7	23♉10	28 38
15	22♓43	0♈33	20♊29	24♋ 8
17	22♈31	29 1	16♋18	18♌33
19	20♉55	25♊43	10♌47	12♍16
21	17♊30	20♊48	4♍31	5♎58
23	12♋30	14♌48	28 11	0♏17
25	6♌29	8♍23	22♎30	25 54
27	0♍ 3	2♎13	17♏55	23♐ 3
29	23 45	26 45	14♐33	20♑26
31	...	22♏12	...	19♒ 2

STATIONS

☿	♀	♂	♃
4Jan	21Oct	None	20Feb
29♑59	25♏13		5♏58
24Jan	1Dec		23Jun
13♑52	9♏46		26♎ 4
28Apr	♄	♅	♆
22♉28	4Jan	13 Jan	3Mar
22May	2♉ 3	8♎47	0♐54
13♉12	4Sep	12Jun	9Aug
30Aug	22♉37	4♎39	28♏ 7
28♍ 0	Sider Pl.Time		1Jan
21Sep	6h 40m 55s		Midn
13♍46	18h 42m 53s		Noon
19Dec	Common Year		1970
14♑ 5			

(B.STD.T. until G.M.T. readopted Oct)

1971

Noon		JAN	FEB	MAR	APR	MAY	JUN
☉	1	10♑25	11♒59	10♓15	11♈ 7	10♉28	10♊21
	9	18 35	20 5	18 16	18 59	18 13	18 0
	17	26 43	28 10	26 15	26 50	25 56	25 39
	25	4♒52	6♓14	4♈11	4♉38	3♊38	3♋17
☿	1	1♑27	20♑49	5♓41	29♈55	23♈18	19♉54
	7	27♐51	29 27	16 55	3♉30	23D48	0♊24
	13	29D37	8♒37	28 37	3R 2	26 58	12 18
	19	4♑42	18 18	10♈20	29♈36	2♉20	25 12
	25	11 33	28 32	20 56	25 34	9 32	8♋11
	31	19 26	...	28 56	...	18 18	...
♀	1	25♏12	25♐31	26♑59	3♓28	9♈27	16♉55
	9	2♐14	4♑16	6♒18	13 1	19 5	26 37
	17	9 55	13 14	15 41	22 36	28 45	6♊20
	25	18 5	22 22	25 9	2♈13	8♉26	16 4
♂	1	16♏23	5♐56	23♐20	11♑59	28♑46	13♒15
	13	23 58	13 26	0♑39	18 54	4♒51	17 27
	25	1♐32	20 52	7 51	25 33	10 22	20 26
♃	1	27♏41	2♐49	5♐43	6♐20	4♐13	0♐26
	13	29 51	4 18	6 18	5R46	2R50	29♏ 2
	25	1♐48	5 25	6R27	4 49	1 19	27R52
♄	1	15♉56	15♉55	17♉22	20♉17	23♉53	27♉52
	13	15R43	16 22	18 22	21 39	25 25	29 22
	25	15 45	17 5	19 32	23 7	26 58	0♊48
♅	1	13♎26	13♎28	12♎47	11♎33	10♎20	9♎33
	13	13 33	13R15	12R21	11R 2	9R57	9R26
	25	13R32	12 55	11 51	10 33	9 40	9D28
♆	1	2♐ 1	2♐47	3♐ 4	2♐53	2♐17	1♐28
	13	2 21	2 58	3R 3	2R41	1R59	1R 9
	25	2 39	3 3	2 58	2 26	1 39	0 52
Pl.	1	29♍42	29♍27	28♍51	28♍ 1	27♍20	26♍59
☊	1	25♒56	24♒17	22♒48	21♒10	19♒35	17♒56
	1st	FRI	MON	MON	THU	SAT	TUE

Noon		JUL	AUG	SEP	OCT	NOV	DEC
☉	1	9♋ 0	8♌35	8♍24	7♎39	8♏24	8♐38
	9	16 38	16 15	16 9	15 32	16 25	16 45
	17	24 16	23 56	23 56	23 27	24 29	24 53
	25	1♌54	1♍38	1♎46	1♏25	2♐34	3♑ 2
☿	1	20♋43	5♍34	28♌20	2♎ 1	22♏57	28♐ 3
	7	2♌ 2	9 22	27D44	12 43	1♐45	26R31
	13	12 9	10R32	2♍13	23 0	10 9	19 19
	19	21 3	8 30	10 40	2♏51	17 54	12 56
	25	28 38	3 45	21 6	12 19	24 22	12D29
	31	4♍44	28♌53	...	21 28	...	16 39
♀	1	23♊23	1♌22	9♍41	16♎59	25♏37	2♑58
	9	3♋ 9	11 14	19 37	26 57	5♐35	12 55
	17	12 57	21 7	29 34	6♏55	15 33	22 51
	25	22 46	1♍ 1	9♎31	16 53	25 30	2♒45
♂	1	21♒22	19♒14	12♒19	14♒59	27♒25	14♓13
	13	21R56	16R 9	12D 0	18 56	3♓46	21 36
	25	20 41	13 21	13 33	24 2	10 38	29 12
♃	1	27♏25	26♏41	28♏47	3♐ 0	8♐55	15♐29
	13	26R47	27 11	0♐15	5 9	11 29	18 11
	25	26D36	28 5	2 1	7 29	14 8	20 54
♄	1	1♊29	4♊30	6♊15	6♊23	4♊55	2♊34
	13	2 46	5 21	6 30	6R 0	4R 2	1R38
	25	3 55	5 59	6R29	5 23	3 4	0 48
♅	1	9♎31	10♎18	11♎45	13♎33	15♎29	17♎ 4
	13	9 44	10 48	12 27	14 18	16 10	17 34
	25	10 3	11 23	13 11	15 3	16 47	17 56
♆	1	0♐45	0♐20	0♐25	0♐58	1♐55	3♐ 1
	13	0R32	0R18	0 35	1 17	2 21	3 28
	25	0 24	0D21	0 49	1 40	2 48	3 53
Pl.	1	27♍ 1	27♍45	28♍45	29♍52	0♎57	1♎43
☊	1	16♒21	14♒42	13♒ 4	11♒28	9♒50	8♒15
	1st	THU	SUN	WED	FRI	MON	WED

☽ d.	JAN	FEB	MAR	APR
1	4♓43	27♈46	7♉16	27♊21
3	3♈16	25♉14	5♊ 3	22♋47
5	1♉ 8	21♊26	1♋10	17♌ 1
7	28 15	16♋38	25 59	10♍40
9	24♊33	11♌ 4	20♌ 1	4♎18
11	19♋58	4♍58	13♍42	28 15
13	14♌32	28 36	7♎21	22♏43
15	8♍25	22♎19	1♏14	17♐51
17	2♎ 1	16♏34	25 39	13♑52
19	25 54	11♐54	20♐57	11♒ 3
21	20♏43	8♑49	17♑34	9♓35
23	17♐ 2	7♒29	15♒49	9♈16
25	15♑ 4	7♓31	15♓34	9♉15
27	14♒26	7♈51	16♈ 1	8♊20
29	14♓15	...	15♉50	5♋41
31	13♈33	...	13♊59	...

☽ d.	MAY	JUN	JUL	AUG
1	1♌15	15♍28	17♎ 7	1♐39
3	25 31	9♎10	11♏17	27 29
5	19♍10	3♏15	6♐24	24♑50
7	12♎53	28 9	2♑46	23♒33
9	7♏ 6	24♐ 4	0♒19	22♓58
11	2♐ 2	20♑52	28 40	22♈14
13	27 44	18♒22	27♓17	20♉40
15	24♑12	16♓22	25♈46	17♊58
17	21♒29	14♈45	23♉47	14♋ 9
19	19♓41	13♉16	21♊ 7	9♌23
21	18♈41	11♊25	17♋32	3♍53
23	17♉56	8♋40	12♌58	27 50
25	16♊32	4♌40	7♍30	21♎31
27	13♋42	29 26	1♎23	15♏21
29	9♌16	23♍23	25 6	9♐50
31	3♍35	...	19♏14	5♑32

☽ d.	SEP	OCT	NOV	DEC
1	18♑59	25♒23	18♈36	27♉16
3	17♒13	25♓ 7	19♉ 4	26♊31
5	16♓56	25♈44	18♊38	24♋17
7	17♈10	25♉48	16♋22	20♌17
9	16♉41	24♊13	12♌12	14♍59
11	14♊44	20♋44	6♍40	8♎44
13	11♋12	15♌44	0♎27	2♏28
15	6♌24	9♍50	24 8	26 37
17	0♍45	3♎33	18♏ 6	21♐28
19	24 40	27 16	12♐32	17♑ 7
21	18♎22	21♏11	7♑34	13♒34
23	12♏ 7	15♐29	3♒20	10♓46
25	6♐13	10♑28	0♓ 7	8♈43
27	1♑ 7	6♒32	28 10	7♉21
29	27 22	4♓10	27♈26	6♊13
31	....	3♈28	...	4♋40

STATIONS ☿	♀	♂	♃
9 JAN	NONE	11JUL	24MAR
27♐51		21♒57	6♐27
10APR		10SEP	25JUL
3♉46		11♒53	26♏36
4 MAY	♄	♅	♆
23♈10	18JAN	19JAN	6 MAR
13AUG	15♉42	13♎34	3♐ 4
10♍33	20SEP	18JUN	13AUG
6 SEP	6♊32	9♎26	0♐18
27♌24	SIDER. TIME		1JAN
3 DEC	6h 39m 58s		Midn
28♐16	18h 41m 56s		noon
23DEC	Common Year		1971
11♐58			

1972

(As from Oct 1971 G.M.T. readopted)

Noon		JAN	FEB	MAR	APR	MAY	JUN
☉	1	10♑11	11♒44	11♓01	11♈52	11♉12	11♊05
	9	18 20	19 51	19 01	19 44	18 57	18 44
	17	26 29	27 56	27 00	27 35	26 40	26 23
	25	4♒38	6♓00	4♈57	5♉23	4♊22	4♋01
☿	1	17♐38	0♒49	22♓25	10♈03	14♈32	6♊54
	7	24 28	10 40	3♈00	5R38	21 59	20 04
	13	2♑23	20 58	11 15	3 43	0♉49	2♋52
	19	10 54	1♓46	15 29	4D53	10 54	14 37
	25	19 52	13 00	14R58	8 42	22 15	25 01
	31	29 13	...	10 53	...	4♊44	...
♀	1	11♒24	19♓18	23♈34	27♉31	24♊20	4♋10
	9	21 16	28 54	2♉40	5♊29	29 25	1R14
	17	1♓04	8♈24	11 34	12 58	3♋02	26♊35
	25	10 50	17 47	20 13	19 47	4 41	21 53
♂	1	3♈43	24♈00	13♉09	3♊29	22♊54	12♋45
	13	11 31	1♉56	21 02	11 17	0♋37	20 23
	25	19 24	9 51	28 54	19 02	8 17	27 59
♃	1	22♐28	28♐59	4♑01	7♑28	8♑16	6♑15
	13	25 05	1♑14	5 38	8 07	7R48	4R53
	25	27 35	3 15	6 54	8R19	6 55	3 22
♄	1	0♊24	29♉35	0♊25	2♊49	6♊10	10♊07
	13	29R53	29D45	1 11	4 04	7 39	11 40
	25	29♉36	0♊10	2 10	5 26	9 12	13 11
♅	1	18♎06	18♎17	17♎41	16♎29	15♎15	14♎23
	13	18 17	18R07	17R16	15R58	14R50	14R14
	25	18R19	17 50	16 47	15 29	14 31	14D12
♆	1	4♐07	4♐56	5♐15	5♐05	4♐30	3♐41
	13	4 29	5 07	5R15	4R54	4R12	3R23
	25	4 47	5 14	5 10	4 39	3 53	3 06
Pl.	1	2♎03	1♎50	1♎14	0♎24	29♍42	29♍19
☊	1	6♒36	4♒57	3♒25	1♒47	0♒11	28♑35
	1st	SAT	TUE	WED	SAT	MON	THU

Noon		JUL	AUG	SEP	OCT	NOV	DEC
☉	1	9♋44	9♌19	9♍08	8♎24	9♏10	9♐25
	9	17 22	16 58	16 54	16 18	17 12	17 32
	17	25 00	24 40	24 41	24 13	25 14	25 40
	25	2♌38	2♍22	2♎31	2♏10	3♐19	3♑49
☿	1	4♌01	19♌46	23♌10	17♎16	2♐00	27♏53
	7	11 33	15R39	3♍43	26 56	8 15	26D32
	13	17 23	11 36	15 06	6♏08	12 03	29 35
	19	21 09	10D38	26 21	14 55	11R21	7♐16
	25	22R20	14 04	7♎05	23 12	4 58	15 16
	31	20 34	21 36	...	0♐50	...	23 53
♀	1	19♊24	26♊50	23♋24	25♌37	1♎55	8♏34
	9	18R14	2♋37	1♌35	4♍46	11 36	18 29
	17	19D29	9 16	10 06	14 05	21 21	28 25
	25	22 43	16 35	18 53	23 33	1♏10	8♐23
♂	1	1♌47	21♌25	11♍06	0♎21	20♎30	10♏21
	13	9 23	29 01	18 47	8 07	28 24	18 23
	25	16 59	6♍39	26 29	15 55	6♏21	26 30
♃	1	2♑36	29♐22	28♐34	0♑35	5♑03	10♑57
	13	1R10	28R43	29D04	2 04	7 16	13 35
	25	29♐56	28 29	29 59	3 52	9 41	16 19
♄	1	13♊55	17♊21	19♊44	20♊36	19♊48	17♊44
	13	15 20	18 25	20 16	20R30	19R05	16R44
	25	16 39	19 18	20 33	20 08	18 12	15 47
♅	1	14♎14	14♎55	16♎18	18♎03	19♎59	21♎38
	13	14 25	15 23	16 58	18 48	20 42	22 09
	25	14 41	15 56	17 41	19 33	21 21	22 34
♆	1	2♐58	2♐32	2♐35	3♐07	4♐03	5♐09
	13	2R45	2R29	2 45	3 26	4 29	5 36
	25	2 36	2D32	2 58	3 48	4 55	6 01
Pl.	1	29♍27	0♎03	1♎02	2♎10	3♎16	4♎04
☊	1	26♑57	25♑19	23♑39	22♑05	20♑27	18♑51
	1st	SAT	TUE	FRI	SUN	WED	FRI

	d.	JAN	FEB	MAR	APR
☽	1	18♋28	5♍47	26♍26	10♏59
	3	15♌08	0♎26	20♎33	4♐45
	5	10♍26	24 24	14♏20	28 50
	7	4♎42	18♏12	8♐12	23♑48
	9	28 30	12♐24	2♑44	20♒16
	11	22♏26	7♑37	28 33	18♓37
	13	17♐05	4♒15	26♒05	18♈36
	15	12♑48	2♓18	25♓17	19♉07
	17	9♒37	1♈19	25♈19	18♊47
	19	7♓19	0♉26	24♉59	16♋45
	21	5♈34	29 02	23♊24	13♌00
	23	3♉58	26♊39	20♋20	7♍59
	25	2♊11	23♋19	16♌01	20 12
	27	29 58	19♌07	10♍52	26♎04
	29	27♋00	14♍10	5♎10	19♏50
	31	23♌06	...	29 06	...

	d.	MAY	JUN	JUL	AUG
☽	1	13♐42	29♑54	5♓58	28♈16
	3	7♑55	25♒47	3♈17	26♉42
	5	2♒55	22♓46	1♉34	25♊06
	7	29 13	21♈19	0♊34	23♋07
	9	27♓17	20♉59	29 41	20♌21
	11	26♈59	20♊54	28♋10	16♍32
	13	27♉29	19♋56	25♌24	11♎37
	15	27♊21	17♌23	21♍14	5♏49
	17	25♋37	13♍10	15♎51	29 36
	19	22♌06	7♎44	9♏47	23♐36
	21	17♍03	1♏37	3♐37	18♑25
	23	11♎10	25 24	27 53	14♒30
	25	4♏56	19♐30	23♑00	11♓55
	27	28 44	14♑12	19♒08	10♈22
	29	22♐48	9♒38	16♓15	9♉10
	31	17♑21	...	14♈08	7♊42

	d.	SEP	OCT	NOV	DEC
☽	1	21♊45	29♋44	18♍23	22♎09
	3	19♋19	25♌57	13♎00	16♏00
	5	16♌09	21♍22	7♏05	9♐40
	7	12♍13	16♎06	0♐50	3♑26
	9	7♎26	10♏16	24 29	27 32
	11	1♏51	4♐00	18♑21	22♒19
	13	25 42	27 40	12♒58	18♓15
	15	19♐27	21♑50	8♓56	15♈43
	17	13♑44	17♒11	6♈46	14♉46
	19	9♒12	14♓19	6♉24	14♊53
	21	6♓20	13♈20	6♊57	14♋58
	23	5♈04	13♉33	7♋02	13♌51
	25	4♉40	13♊39	5♌38	11♍01
	27	4♊04	12♋34	2♍27	6♎33
	29	2♋30	9♌53	27 47	0♏54
	31	...	5♍49	...	24 39

STATIONS	☿	♀	♂	♃
	22MAR	27MAY	NONE	25APR
	15♈51	4♋45		8♑19
	14APR	10JUL		26AUG
	3♈41	18♊14		28♐29
	25JUL	♄	♅	♆
	22♌21	31JAN	23JAN	7 MAR
	18AUG	29♉35	18♎19	5♐15
	10♌28	3 OCT	22JUN	14AUG
	16NOV	20♊36	14♎12	2♐29
	12♐27	SIDER. TIME		1 JAN
	6 DEC	6h 39m 1s		MIDN
	26♏15	18h 40m 59s		NOON
		LEAP YEAR		1972

	Noon	JAN	FEB	MAR	APR	MAY	JUN
☉	1	10♑57	12♒30	10♓46	11♈37	10♉58	10♊51
	9	19 6	20 37	18 47	19 30	18 43	18 30
	17	27 15	28 42	26 45	27 20	26 26	26 8
	25	5♒23	6♓45	4♈42	5♉ 8	4♊ 7	3♋46
☿	1	25♐22	15♒ 8	27♓51	16♓13	21♈46	24♊54
	7	4♑22	25 49	27R58	20 6	2♉35	5♋50
	13	13 39	6♓39	22 26	26 0	14 30	15 12
	19	23 12	16 50	18 3	3♈23	27 20	22 52
	25	3♒ 6	24 49	15 12	12 1	10♊25	28 40
	31	13 22	...	15D48	...	22 55	...
♀	1	17♐08	25♑54	0♓54	9♈30	16♉37	24♊44
	9	27 08	5♒55	10 53	19 25	26 29	4♋32
	17	7♑08	15 55	20 51	29 20	6♊19	14 18
	25	17 09	25 55	0♈48	9♉13	16 09	24 04
♂	1	1♐15	22♐32	12♑05	4♒00	25♒17	16♓58
	13	9 27	0♑53	20 32	12 31	3♓45	25 07
	25	17 42	9 16	29 02	21 02	12 08	3♈02
♃	1	17♑56	25♑09	1♒17	7♒01	10♒48	12♒08
	13	20 44	27 51	3 40	8 46	11 39	11R50
	25	23 32	0♒27	5 51	10 13	12 05	11 07
♄	1	15♊16	13♊47	13♊52	15♊37	18♊32	22♊19
	13	14R31	13D38	14 22	16 40	19 57	23 52
	25	13 58	13 46	15 05	17 53	21 26	25 26
♅	1	22♎46	23♎03	22♎34	21♎27	20♎11	19♎13
	13	22 59	22R56	22R11	20R56	19R44	19R01
	25	23 04	22 41	21 44	20 26	19 23	18 56
♆	1	6♐15	7♐05	7♐25	7♐18	6♐45	5♐56
	13	6 37	7 17	7R26	7R08	6R27	5R37
	25	6 56	7 24	7 22	6 53	6 08	5 20
Pl.	1	4♎25	4♎14	3♎40	2♎50	2♎07	1♎42
☊	1	17♑13	15♑34	14♑05	12♑27	10♑52	9♑13
	1st	MON	THU	THU	SUN	TUE	FRI

	Noon	JUL	AUG	SEP	OCT	NOV	DEC
☉	1	9♋30	9♌ 5	8 54	8♎10	8♏56	9♐10
	9	17 8	16 45	16 40	16 3	16 57	17 17
	17	24 45	23 26	24 27	23 58	25 0	25 25
	25	2♌23	2♍ 8	2♎16	1♏56	3♐ 5	3♑34
☿	1	2♌17	23♋ 0	7♍36	28♎05	26♏17	19♏50
	7	3R19	25 56	18 59	6♏23	21R40	28 00
	13	1 35	2♌36	29 41	13 57	14 04	6♐48
	19	27 55	12 19	9♎45	20 27	10D35	15 53
	25	24 14	23 46	19 12	25 07	13 20	25 07
	31	22D53	5♍38	...	25R31	...	4♑30
♀	1	1♌23	8♍57	16♎00	21♏03	25♐36	24♑54
	9	11 07	18 34	25 27	0♐11	4♑00	1♒11
	17	20 49	28 09	4♏49	9 12	12 01	6 19
	25	0♍30	7♎42	14 08	18 02	19 37	9 53
♂	1	6♈51	24♈45	6♉54	8♉17	29♈13	25♈31
	13	14 13	0♉23	8 58	5R23	26R22	27D13
	25	21 05	4 55	9R03	1 27	25 19	0♉22
♃	1	10♒36	6♒57	3♒28	2♒19	4♒08	8♒22
	13	9R21	5R26	2R40	2D40	5 34	10 35
	25	7 51	4 06	2 19	3 28	7 22	13 01
♄	1	26♊12	29♊57	2♋55	4♋32	4♋32	2♋59
	13	27 43	1♋13	3 44	4 45	4R05	2R04
	25	29 10	2 21	4 19	4R41	3 23	1 05
♅	1	18♎57	19♎29	20♎46	22♎28	24♎25	26♎07
	13	19D04	19 54	21 24	23 13	25 08	26 40
	25	19 18	20 26	22 06	23 58	25 48	27 08
♆	1	5♐12	4♐44	4♐44	5♐14	6♐08	7♐14
	13	4R58	4R40	4 53	5 32	6 34	7 41
	25	4 48	4D42	5 06	5 54	7 01	8 07
Pl.	1	1♎47	2♎21	3♎19	4♎26	5♎34	6♎25
☊	1	7♑38	5♑59	4♑21	2♑45	1♑07	29♐32
	1st	SUN	WED	SAT	MON	THU	SAT

☽ d.	JAN	FEB	MAR	APR
1	6♐28	20♑47	28♑49	15♓44
3	0♑16	15♒51	24♒17	13♈46
5	24 29	11♓53	21♓04	12♉49
7	19♒23	8♈49	18♈54	11♊59
9	15♓08	6♉28	17♉16	10♋32
11	11♈54	4♊38	15♊37	8♌14
13	9♉48	3♋08	13♋42	5♍04
15	8♊44	1♌39	11♌24	1♎08
17	8♋13	29 40	8♍34	26 26
19	7♌23	26♍41	4♎57	20♏57
21	5♍27	22♎24	0♏21	14♐50
23	1♎57	16♏56	24 46	8♑27
25	27 00	10♐44	18♐33	2♒23
27	21♏01	4♐28	12♑16	27 17
29	14♐41	...	6♒38	23♓47
31	8♑36	...	2♓18	...

☽ d.	MAY	JUN	JUL	AUG
1	22♈05	15♊15	23♋48	15♍33
3	21♉43	15♋22	23♌08	12♎34
5	21♊36	14♌23	20♍52	7♏57
7	20♋45	11♍50	16♎55	2♐10
9	18♌37	7♎47	11♏37	25 49
11	15♍13	2♏36	5♐31	19♑33
13	10♎46	26 40	29 08	13♒49
15	5♏30	20♐21	22♑53	8♓53
17	29 38	13♑59	17♒06	4♈49
19	23♐22	7♒52	12♓00	1♉35
21	16♑59	2♓23	7♈50	29 11
23	10♒56	27 57	4♉48	27♊33
25	5♓48	25♈01	3♊03	26♋29
27	2♈11	23♉42	2♋23	25♌28
29	0♉22	23♊36	2♌10	23♍43
31	0♊06	...	1♍24	20♎38

☽ d.	SEP	OCT	NOV	DEC
1	3♏31	6♐08	19♑41	21♒41
3	28 16	29 59	13♒29	16♓16
5	22♐07	23♑38	8♓11	12♈16
7	15♑47	17♒52	4♈21	10♉00
9	9♒55	13♓13	2♉10	9♊22
11	5♓00	9♈58	1♊14	9♋31
13	1♈11	7♉55	0♋44	9♌21
15	28 19	6♊29	29 46	7♍56
17	26♉03	5♋02	27♌51	4♎58
19	24♊07	3♌15	24♍53	0♏38
21	22♋22	0♍57	20♎55	25 16
23	20♌43	28 02	16♏05	19♐17
25	18♍33	24♎21	10♐29	12♑56
27	15♎38	19♏43	4♑20	6♒33
29	11♏29	14♐08	27 54	0♓26
31	...	7♑53	...	25 01

STATIONS	☿	♀	♂	♃
	5 MAR	NONE	20SEP	31MAY
	28♓55		9♉16	12♒ 8
	28MAR		26NOV	29SEP
	15♓ 2		25♈18	2♒17
	7 JUL	♄	♅	♆
	3♌21	13FEB	27JAN	9 MAR
	31JUL	13♊38	23♎ 4	7♐26
	22♋52	17OCT	27JUN	16AUG
	31OCT	4♋45	18♎56	4♐40
	26♏35	SIDERPl. TIME		1 JAN
	19NOV	6h 42m 1s		MIDN
	10♏34	18h 43m59s		NOON
		COMMON YEAR		1973

Noon		JAN	FEB	MAR	APR	MAY	JUN
☉	1	10♑42	12♒16	10♓31	11♈23	10♉44	10♊37
	9	18 51	20 22	18 32	19 15	18 29	18 17
	17	22 56	24 25	22 32	23 11	22 20	22 06
	25	5♒09	6♓31	4♈27	4♉54	3♊54	3♋34
☿	1	6♑05	27♒43	1♓04	15♓11	7♉00	3♋52
	7	15 42	6♓20	27♒28	23 37	19 54	9 35
	13	25 32	11 21	27D47	3♈02	2♊42	12 53
	19	5♒40	10R40	1♓13	13 24	14 27	13R33
	25	15 58	5 10	6 47	24 44	24 33	11 40
	31	26 06	...	13 53	...	2♋43	...
♀	1	11♒18	28♑39	0♒28	25♒00	26♓18	1♉23
	9	10R33	26R07	5 25	2♓56	5♈11	10 40
	17	7 16	26D10	11 31	11 13	14 12	20 01
	25	2 31	28 34	18 26	19 46	23 20	29 56
♂	1	2♉44	16♉19	1♊09	18♊53	6♋40	25♋24
	13	7 29	22 34	7 54	25 56	13 53	2♌44
	25	12 55	29 02	14 48	3♋04	21 09	10 06
♃	1	14♒32	21♒40	28♒21	5♓27	11♓23	15♓50
	13	17 13	24 32	1♓10	7 58	13 21	16 57
	25	20 00	27 24	3 55	10 18	15 01	17 38
♄	1	0♋30	28♊25	27♊47	28♊46	1♋09	4♋38
	13	29♊35	27R58	27 58	29 34	2 24	6 08
	25	28R47	27 47	28 24	0♋35	3 47	7 41
♅	1	27♎21	27♎47	27♎25	26♎22	25♎06	24♎03
	13	27 38	27R42	27R05	25R52	24R38	23R49
	25	27 46	27 30	26 39	25 21	24 14	23 41
♆	1	8♐21	9♐13	9♐35	9♐30	8♐59	8♐11
	13	8 44	9 26	9R37	9R20	8R41	7R52
	25	9 03	9 34	9 34	9 07	8 22	7 34
Pl.	1	6♎49	6♎40	6♎08	5♎18	4♎33	4♎06
☊	1	27♐53	26♐15	24♐43	23♐05	21♐29	19♐51
	1st	TUE	FRI	FRI	MON	WED	SAT

Noon		JUL	AUG	SEP	OCT	NOV	DEC
☉	1	9♋17	8♌52	8♍40	7♎56	9♏11	8♐55
	9	16 54	16 31	16 25	15 49	17 12	17 02
	17	24 32	24 12	24 13	24 44	24 46	25 10
	25	2♌10	1♍55	2♎03	1♏42	2♐51	3♑19
☿	1	8♋15	22♋45	22♍10	3♏37	25♎17	29♏19
	7	5R15	3♌57	2♎00	8 29	26D15	8♐11
	13	4D30	16 09	11 07	10 37	2♏10	17 34
	19	6 52	28 16	19 31	8R26	10 24	27 01
	25	12 29	9♍46	27 07	1♎50	19 34	6♑33
	31	21 04	20 28	...	25 47	...	16 14
♀	1	6♊31	13♋38	21♌27	28♍37	7♏25	15♐05
	9	16 01	23 19	1♍19	8♎37	17 27	25 08
	17	25 35	3♌04	11 13	18 37	27 30	5♑11
	25	5♋11	12 51	21 10	28 37	7♐33	15 14
♂	1	13♌48	3♍05	22♍44	12♎11	2♏50	23♏25
	13	21 14	10 38	0♎28	20 12	11 00	1♐49
	25	28 42	18 15	8 16	28 07	19 15	10 19
♃	1	17♓49	16♓53	13♓27	9♓45	8♓00	9♓18
	13	17R49	15R46	11R53	8R44	8D09	10 36
	25	17 21	14 22	10 24	8 08	8 48	12 17
♄	1	8♋28	12♋44	15♋48	18♋05	18♋54	18♋03
	13	10 01	13 49	16 52	18 36	18R45	17R18
	25	11 32	15 07	17 44	18 52	18 21	16 24
♅	1	23♎40	24♎04	25♎14	26♎53	28♎48	0♏34
	13	23D43	24 26	25 51	27 37	29 37	1 09
	25	23 54	24 55	26 31	28 22	0♏14	1 39
♆	1	7♐26	6♐56	6♐54	7♐21	8♐14	9♐20
	13	7R12	6R51	7 02	7 39	8 39	9 47
	25	7 01	6D52	7 14	8 00	9 06	10 13
Pl.	1	4♎09	4♎41	5♎38	6♎45	7♎54	8♎46
☊	1	18♐16	16♐37	14♐59	13♐23	11♐45	10♐09
	1st	MON	THU	SUN	TUE	FRI	SUN

☽ d.	JAN	FEB	MAR	APR
1	7♈43	27♉13	7♊20	0♌12
3	4♉13	25♊42	5♋22	28 50
5	2♊28	25♋28	4♌24	27♍23
7	2♋15	25♌40	3♍56	25♎12
9	2♌42	25♍ 5	3♎ 0	21♏43
11	2♍34	22♎47	0♏41	16♐51
13	0♎52	18♏37	26 39	10♑57
15	27 20	13♐ 2	21♐11	4♒39
17	22♏17	6♑44	14♑55	28 38
19	16♐18	0♒20	8♒36	23♓28
21	9♑55	24 19	2♓48	19♈28
23	3♒33	18♓55	27 52	16♉36
25	27 29	14♈14	23♈51	14♊31
27	21♓57	10♉21	20♉37	12♋49
29	17♈12	...	18♊ 2	11♌10
31	13♉32	...	16♋ 1	...

☽ d.	MAY	JUN	JUL	AUG
1	9♍20	0♏25	5♐28	20♑43
3	7♎ 2	26 6	29 49	14♒25
5	3♏59	20♐57	23♑43	8♓15
7	29 54	15♑ 6	17♒25	2♈26
9	24♐47	8♒51	11♓15	27 16
11	18♑50	2♓38	5♈35	23♉12
13	14♒33	26 59	0♉56	20♊38
15	6♓33	22♈28	27 47	19♋44
17	1♈27	19♉29	26♊23	20♌ 0
19	27 41	18♊ 7	26♋22	20♍15
21	25♉21	17♋49	26♌43	19♎12
23	24♊ 5	17♌38	26♍11	16♏16
25	23♋12	16♍34	23♎58	11♐37
27	22♌ 1	14♎ 9	20♏ 2	5♑50
29	20♍ 6	10♏21	14♐49	29 34
31	17♎13	...	8♑51	23♒17

☽ d.	SEP	OCT	NOV	DEC
1	5♓15	8♈36	26♉26	3♋21
3	29 31	3♉56	23♊40	2♌ 5
5	24♈19	0♊ 1	21♋30	0♍46
7	19♉52	26 53	19♌45	28 59
9	16♊27	24♋41	18♍11	26♎28
11	14♋22	23♌22	16♎25	23♏ 7
13	13♌39	22♍34	13♏59	18♐55
15	13♍38	21♎29	10♐30	13♑52
17	13♎12	19♏14	5♑49	8♒ 5
19	11♏17	15♐28	0♒ 9	1♓52
21	7♐33	10♑18	23 58	25 42
23	2♑19	4♒17	17♓52	20♈10
25	26 13	28 3	12♈26	15♉53
27	19♒56	22♓12	8♉10	13♊12
29	13♓57	17♈10	5♊13	12♋ 3
31	...	13♉ 7	...	11♌44

STATIONS	☿	♀	♂	♃
	16FEB	4 JAN	NONE	8 JUL
	11♓50	11♒22		17♓52
	10MAR	14FEB		4 NOV
	27♒ 8	25♑49		7♓59
	18JUN	♄	♅	♆
	13♋39	28FEB	2 FEB	12MAR
	12JUL	27♊47	27♎47	9♐37
	4♋24	2 NOV	2 JUL	19AUG
	14OCT	18♋54	23♎40	6♐51
	10♏38	SIDER Pl. TIME		1 JAN
	4 NOV	6H 41m 4s		MIDN
	24♎53	18h 43m 2s		NOON
		COMMON YEAR		1974

Noon		JAN	FEB	MAR	APR	MAY	JUN
☉	1	10♑26	11♒59	10♓16	♈	10♉ 0	10♊23
	9	9 0	20 6	18 17	19 0	18 15	18 2
	17	26 45	28 12	26 16	26 51	25 58	25 41
	25	4♒53	6♓15	4♈13	4♉40	6♊10	3♋19
☿	1	17♑51	25♒ 1	13♒35	24♓41	24♉27	23♊17
	7	27 41	19R58	19 5	5♈28	5♊ 4	21R 1
	13	7♒25	13 17	26 5	17 6	13 31	17 45
	19	16 28	10 4	4♓10	29 61	19 33	15 23
	25	23 17	11D 7	13 10	12♉16	22 54	15D20
	31	25R19	...	22 58	...	23R28	...
♀	1	24♑ 0	2♓18	7♈30	15♉12	20♊29	24♋50
	9	4♒ 2	12 45	17 19	24 44	29 37	3♌ 6
	17	14 3	22 41	27 4	4♊12	8♋35	26 3
	25	24 3	2♈35	6♉46	13 33	17 21	18 31
♂	1	15♐19	7♑51	28♑41	22♒ 9	14♓59	8♈21
	13	23 58	16 44	7♒44	1♓17	24 5	17 13
	25	2♑43	25 41	16 50	10 26	3♈ 7	25 56
♃	1	13♓24	19♓26	25♓51	3♈20	10♈22	16♈50
	13	15 33	22 7	28 44	6 12	13	18 58
	25	17 57	24 55	1♈39	9 0	15 29	20 50
♄	1	15♋50	13♋25	12♋ 6	12♋15	13♋59	17♋ 1
	13	14R50	12R41	11R57	12 46	15 2	18 25
	25	13 54	12 12	12D 3	13 32	16 15	19 55
♅	1	1♏54	2♏28	2♏13	1♏16	0♏ 1	28♎53
	13	2 13	2R27	1R50	0R16	29R31	10R 6
	25	2 24	2 18	1 32	0 16	29♎ 6	28 25
♆	1	10♐27	11♐20	11♐45	11♐42	11♐13	10♐25
	13	10 50	11 33	11 48	11R33	10R56	10R 6
	25	11 10	11 43	11R46	11 20	10 37	9 48
Pl.	1	9♎13	9♎ 7	8♎37	7♎48	7♎ 2	6♎33
☊	1	8♐33	6♐55	5♐26	3♐48	2♐12	0♐34
1st		WED	SAT	SAT	TUE	THU	SUN

Noon		JUL	AUG	SEP	OCT	NOV	DEC
☉	1	9♋ 2	8♌37	8♍26	7♎41	8♏26	8♐40
	9	16 40	16 17	16 11	15 34	16 28	16 47
	17	24 18	23 58	23 58	23 29	24 0	24 55
	25	1♌56	1♍40	1♎47	1♏27	2♐35	3♑ 3
☿	1	18♊ 7	8♌44	2♎27	23♎11	22♎25	10♐ 7
	7	23 38	20 55	10 10	17R51	1♏48	19 32
	13	1♋42	2♍16	16 44	11 17	11 29	28 56
	19	12 3	12 44	21 43	9D13	21 8	8♑22
	25	24 2	22 19	24 17	13 11	0♐40	17 44
	31	7♌21	1♎ 5	...	20 56	...	26 44
♀	1	23♌44	11♍17	0♍39	28♌40	21♍59	23♎43
	9	0♍ 1	11R30	26R54	3♍ 5	29 55	2♏51
	17	5 20	9 13	25♌26	8 49	8♎17	12 10
	25	9 17	4 55	26D28	15 31	17 0	21 37
♂	1	0♉14	21♉29	10♊23	24♊51	2♋29	28♊15
	13	8 40	29 9	25 51	28 57	2R19	23R47
	25	16 51	6♊23	22 23	1♋40	0 4	19 20
♃	1	21♈40	24♈24	24♈11	21♈16	17♈13	14♈53
	13	23 3	24 42	23R17	19R40	15R59	14D45
	25	24 2	24R31	22 0	18 5	15 8	15 8
♄	1	20♋41	24♋41	28♋23	1♌13	2♌48	2♌43
	13	22 14	26 11	29 39	2 1	2 58	2R13
	25	23 47	27 36	0♌44	2 35	2R52	1 31
♅	1	28♎22	28♎38	29♎41	1♏15	3♏10	4♏58
	13	28D22	28 57	0♏15	1 59	3 55	5 35
	25	28 30	29 23	0 25	2 44	4 38	6 8
♆	1	9♐39	9♐ 8	9♐ 3	9♐28	10♐20	11♐24
	13	9R24	9R 2	9 10	9 45	10 45	11 51
	25	9 12	9D 2	9 21	10 6	11 11	12 18
Pl.	1	6♎32	7♎ 2	7♎57	9♎ 5	10♎15	11♎ 9
☊	1	28♏58	27♏22	25♏41	24♏ 6	22♏28	20♏52
1st		TUE	FRI	MON	WED	SAT	MON

d.	JAN	FEB	MAR	APR
☽ 1	26♌34	19♎34	28♎25	17♐35
3	25♍36	16♏50	26♏ 1	12♑52
5	23♎24	12♐33	21♐50	7♒ 5
7	19♏56	7♑15	16♑24	0♓50
9	15♐27	1♒20	10♒19	24 39
11	10♑14	25 10	4♓ 2	18♈48
13	4♒28	18♓54	27 51	13♉33
15	28 19	12♈46	21♈57	9♊ 0
17	22♓ 2	7♉ 7	16♉32	5♋21
19	16♈ 1	2♊26	11♊57	2♌48
21	10♉51	29 17	8♋39	1♍24
23	7♊ 7	28♋ 3	6♌58	0♎47
25	5♋16	28♌20	6♍42	0♏10
27	5♌ 4	28♍50	6♎59	28 36
29	5♍32	...	6♏30	25♐32
31	5♎16	...	4♐21	...

d.	MAY	JUN	JUL	AUG
☽ 1	20♑58	5♓11	6♈56	21♉35
3	15♒17	29 0	1♉ 6	17♊27
5	9♓ 6	23♈11	26 16	15♋ 6
7	2♈59	18♉15	22♊54	14♌25
9	27 24	14♊30	21♋ 4	14♍30
11	22♉38	11♋57	20♌14	14♎ 7
13	18♊47	10♌14	19♍31	12♏27
15	15♋49	8♍34	18♎ 7	9♐19
17	13♌38	7♎14	15♏42	5♑ 1
19	12♍ 2	5♏10	12♐18	29 54
21	10♎42	2♐27	8♑ 4	24♒12
23	9♏ 9	28 55	3♒ 6	18♓ 6
25	6♐53	24♑28	27 29	11♈48
27	3♑28	19♒ 8	21♓22	5♉37
29	28 51	13♓ 9	15♈ 6	0♊ 5
31	23♒14	...	9♉11	25 49

d.	SEP	OCT	NOV	DEC
☽ 1	9♋21	16♌31	9♎59	18♏17
3	7♌22	16♍17	9♏47	16♐43
5	7♍57	16♎42	8♐45	14♑ 1
7	8♎25	16♏27	6♑13	9♒56
9	7♏56	14♐37	1♒63	4♓35
11	5♐46	11♑ 2	26 37	28 27
13	1♑59	6♒ 1	20♓28	22♈12
15	26 59	0♓ 9	14♈12	16♉25
17	21♒14	23 54	8♉17	11♊36
19	15♓ 6	17♈40	3♊ 2	7♋55
21	8♈55	11♉43	28 36	5♌16
23	2♉38	6♊18	25♋ 4	3♍15
25	26 50	1♋40	22♌25	1♎29
27	21♊53	28 9	20♍35	29 43
29	18♋19	25♌59	19♎21	27♏43
31	...	25♍ 6	...	25♐18

STATIONS	☿	♀	♂	♃
	31JAN	6 AUG	7 NOV	15AUG
	25♒25	11♍43	2♋40	24♈42
	21FEB	18SEP		11DEC
	9♒58	25♍26		14♈45
	30MAY	♄	♅	♆
	23♊36	15MAR	6 FEB	14MAR
	23JUN	11♋57	2♏28	11♐48
	15♊ 1	15NOV	9 JUL	21AUG
	27SEP	2♌59	28♎21	9♐ 1
	24♎25	SIDER Pl. TIME		1 JAN
	19OCT	6h 40m 6s		MIDN
	9♎ 6	18h 42m 4s		NOON
		COMMON YEAR		1975

Noon		JAN	FEB	MAR	APR	MAY	JUN
☉	1	10♑12	11♒46	11♓02	11♈53	11♉14	11♊07
	9	18 22	19 58	19 03	19 46	18 59	18 46
	17	26 31	27 57	27 02	27 35	26 42	26 25
	25	4♒38	6♓01	4♈58	5♉24	4♊23	4♋02
☿	1	28♑ 9	23♑45	18♒00	11♈37	1♊08	24♉58
	7	5♒31	24D05	26 53	24 02	3 36	26D04
	13	9 41	27 56	6♓28	6♉13	3R06	29 46
	19	6R40	3♒53	16 46	17 02	0♊10	5♊47
	25	28♑29	11 12	27 50	27 32	26♉53	13 58
	31	24 10	...	9♈35	...	25 02	...
♀	1	29♏59	7♑38	13♒18	21♓32	28♈28	6♊34
	9	7 19	17 58	23 10	1♈23	8♉19	16 23
	17	19 16	27 17	3♓02	11 14	18 08	26 13
	25	29 4	7♒ 8	12 54	21 05	27 58	6♋03
♂	1	17♊14	15♊33	23♊08	6♋25	23♋08	9♌05
	13	15R05	17 53	27 50	12 21	27 50	16 02
	25	14D52	21 24	3♋07	18 35	3♌07	23 07
♃	1	15♈34	19♈13	24♈32	1♉24	8♉42	15♉48
	13	16 34	21 15	27 05	4 14	11 23	18 28
	25	18 02	23 31	29 47	7 06	14 12	20 59
♄	1	1♌02	28♋32	26♋39	26♋03	27♋ 6	29♋37
	13	0R05	27R39	26R13	26D17	27 55	0♌54
	25	29♋11	26 54	26 02	26 47	28 57	2 17
♅	1	6♏24	7♏06	6♏59	6♏05	4♏56	3♏41
	13	6 46	7R08	6R43	5R37	4R22	3R22
	25	7 02	7 03	6 20	5 07	3 55	3 09
♆	1	12♐33	13♐28	13♐55	13♐54	13♐24	12♐39
	13	12 56	13 42	13 58	13R46	13R 8	12R19
	25	13 15	13 52	13R57	13 33	12 50	12 01
Pl.	1	11♎40	11♎37	11♎07	10♎18	9♎31	9♎00
☊	1	19♏14	17♏35	16♏ 3	14♏25	12♏49	11♏11
	1st	THU	SUN	MON	THU	SAT	TUE

Noon		JUL	AUG	SEP	OCT	NOV	DEC
☉	1	9♋46	9♌21	9♍10	8♎26	9♏12	9♐26
	9	17 23	17 06	16 55	16 19	17 13	17 34
	17	25 01	24 41	24 43	24 14	25 17	25 41
	25	2♌40	2♍24	2♎32	2♏12	3♐21	3♑50
☿	1	24♊05	26♌16	5♎23	23♍11	5♏29	22♐38
	7	5♋53	6♍09	7 45	26D26	15 16	1♑38
	13	18 40	15 04	6R43	4♎02	24 50	10 14
	19	1♌26	22 57	1♎55	13 38	4♐13	17 46
	25	13 28	14 38	25♍47	23 46	13 29	22 40
	31	24 31	4♎44	...	3♏50	14 18	22R14
♀	1	13♋25	21 33	29♍42	6♏31	14♐20	20♑28
	9	23 15	1♍24	9♎32	16 18	24 02	29 58
	17	3♌06	11 15	19 22	26 05	3♑41	9♒21
	25	12 56	21 06	29 10	5♐50	13 18	18 37
♂	1	26♌42	15♍39	5♎19	25♎03	16♏15	7♐33
	13	3♍57	23 10	13 07	3♏10	24 41	16 17
	25	11 19	0♎48	21 02	11 23	3♐14	25 08
♃	1	22♉12	27♉29	0♊40	0♊59	28♉20	24♉22
	13	24 26	29 07	1 09	0R17	26 47	22 59
	25	26 27	0♊11	1R10	29♉09	25 09	21 55
♄	1	2♌59	6♌56	10♌49	14♌02	16♌15	16♌52
	13	4 30	8 28	12 12	15 03	16 41	16R39
	25	6 02	9 58	13 27	15 52	16 52	16 11
♅	1	3♏05	3♏14	4♏11	5♏42	7♏35	9♏24
	13	3D02	3 31	4 44	6 25	8 20	10 03
	25	3 08	3 54	5 22	7 09	9 04	10 37
♆	1	11♐52	11♐20	11♐14	11♐37	12♐27	13♐32
	13	11R37	11R14	11 20	11 54	12 52	13 59
	25	11 25	11D12	11 30	12 14	13 18	14 26
Pl.	1	8♎58	9♎27	10♎21	11♎29	12♎39	13♎36
☊	1	9♏36	7♏57	6♏19	4♏43	3♏ 5	1♏29
	1st	THU	SUN	WED	FRI	MON	WED

d.		JAN	FEB	MAR	APR
☽	1	8♑44	25♒57	16♓49	1♉12
	3	5♒02	20♓22	10♈41	24 54
	5	0♓11	14♈09	4♉16	19♊06
	7	24 21	7♉47	28 03	14♋19
	9	18♈04	1♊56	22♊38	11♌04
	11	11♉56	27 20	18♋41	9♍35
	13	6♊41	24♋26	16♌39	9♏33
	15	2♋50	23♌15	16♍16	9♏56
	17	0♌28	23♍00	16♎37	9♐30
	19	29 08	22♎34	16♏24	7♑30
	21	28♍05	21♏07	14♐47	3♒48
	23	26♎35	18♐26	11♑37	28 43
	25	24♏22	14♑40	7♒08	22♓46
	27	21♐26	10♒02	1♓43	16♈25
	29	17♑54	4♓43	25 43	10♉03
	31	13♒27	...	14♈24	...

d.		MAY	JUN	JUL	AUG
☽	1	3♊59	20♋59	27♌51	20♎35
	3	28 31	17♌23	25♍35	18♏50
	5	23♋57	14♍47	23♎46	16♐47
	7	20♌38	13♎08	22♏13	14♑17
	9	18♍44	12♏13	20♐40	11♒02
	11	18♎08	11♐29	18♑38	6♓50
	13	18♏07	10♑08	15♒35	1♈35
	15	17♐41	7♒28	11♓13	25 31
	17	15♑53	3♓14	5♈40	19♉08
	19	12♒25	27 43	28 55	13♊10
	21	7♓25	21♈27	23♉10	8♋15
	23	1♈25	15♉10	17♊35	5♌22
	25	25 01	9♊02	13♋11	2♍59
	27	18♉47	4♋35	10♌05	2♎01
	29	13♊05	0♌46	8♍00	1♏08
	31	8♋08	...	6♎23	29 42

d.		SEP	OCT	NOV	DEC
☽	1	13♐40	21♑16	9♓20	12♈25
	3	10♑58	17♒16	3♈35	6♉02
	5	7♒25	12♓17	27 20	29 42
	7	3♓02	6♈35	20♉58	23♊44
	9	27 47	0♉23	14♊43	18♋23
	11	21♈50	23 59	8♋56	13♌46
	13	15♉28	17♊44	3♌57	10♍03
	15	9♊11	12♋08	0♍10	7♎27
	17	1♋18	7♌46	27 55	6♏04
	19	29 23	5♍04	27♎12	5♐40
	21	26♌55	4♎05	27♏26	5♑23
	23	26♍01	4♏15	27♐27	4♒09
	25	25♎54	4♐26	26♑11	1♓15
	27	25♏31	4♑04	23♒05	26 38
	29	24♐03	1♒00	18♓19	20♈45
	31	...	26 53	...	14♉23

STATIONS	☿	♀	♂	♃
	15JAN	NONE	21JAN	20SEP
	9♒15		14♊44	1♊12
	4 FEB			
	23♑20			
	10MAY	♄	♅	♆
	3♊43	28MAR	11FEB	16MAR
	2 JUN	26♋02	7♏ 9	13♐58
	24♉57	28NOV	11JUL	23AUG
	9 SEP	16♌53	3♏ 2	11♐12
	7 ♎51	SIDERL. TIME		1 JAN
	1 OCT	6h 39m 9s		MIDN
	23♍ 9	18h 41m 7s		NOON
	28DEC	LEAP YEAR		1976
	23♑19			

Noon		JAN	FEB	MAR	APR	MAY	JUN
☉	1	10♑58	12♒31	10♓48	11♈38	10♉59	10♊52
	9	19 7	20 37	20 37	19 30	18 44	18 31
	17	27 16	28 43	26 47	27 21	26 27	26 10
	25	5♒54	6♓46	4♈43	5♉ 9	4♊ 9	3♋48
☿	1	21♑30	17♑50	28♒34	27♈17	9♉41	16♉43
	7	14R21	25 16	9♓ 4	6♉22	6R13	24 44
	13	8 13	3♒32	20 13	12 16	4 43	4♊26
	19	7D25	27 26	2♈ 0	14 29	5D55	15 44
	25	10 51	21 55	14 3	13R11	9 39	28 16
	31	16 43	...	25 31	...	15 33	...
♀	1	26♒35	29♓17	20♈41	19♈17	8♈34	25♈55
	9	5♓29	6♈35	23 42	14R20	10D52	2♉54
	17	14 7	13 4	24R31	10 13	15 8	10 27
	25	22 25	18 29	22 45	8 19	20 23	18 24
♂	1	0♑21	23♑51	15♒30	9♓40	2♈58	26♈32
	13	9 22	3♒ 5	26 12	19 1	12 10	5♉28
	25	18 29	12 23	4♓13	28 20	21 17	14 15
♃	1	21♉60	21♉40	24♉25	29♉35	5♊52	26♊32
	13	21R11	22 35	26 12	1♊59	8 34	10 46
	25	21D21	23 54	28 16	4 32	11 21	18 31
♄	1	15♌48	13♌30	11♌22	10♌ 2	10♌19	12♌11
	13	15R 0	12R32	10R40	9D57	10 51	13 16
	25	14 4	11 39	10 12	10 8	11 39	14 29
♅	1	10♏54	11♏42	11♏41	10♏55	9♏43	8♏30
	13	11 18	11 47	11R28	10R28	9R12	8R 8
	25	11 35	11R44	11 9	9 58	8 44	7 52
♆	1	14♐40	15♐35	16♐ 4	16♐ 5	15♐39	14♐53
	13	15 4	15 50	16 8	15R57	15R22	14R33
	25	11 25	16 1	16R 8	15 46	15 4	14 15
Pl.	1	14♎ 7	14♎ 6	13♎39	12♎51	12♎ 3	11♎30
☊	1	29♎51	28♎12	26♎43	25♎ 5	23♎30	21♎51
	1st	SAT	TUE	TUE	FRI	SUN	WED

Noon		JUL	AUG	SEP	OCT	NOV	DEC
☉	1	9♋31	9♌ 7	8♍56	7♎56	8♏57	9♐11
	9	17 9	16 46	16 42	16 4	16 59	17 18
	17	24 47	24 28	24 29	24 0	25 2	25 26
	25	2♌25	2♍10	2♎18	1♏58	3♐ 6	3♑37
☿	1	11♋20	5♍22	16♍ 5	24♍58	17♏23	0♑15
	7	24 0	12 10	10R27	5♎31	26 38	5 48
	13	5♌43	17 21	7 4	16 5	5♐39	7R15
	19	16 19	20 20	8D48	26 21	14 25	2 24
	25	25 47	20R21	15 27	6♏15	22 45	24♐37
	31	4♍ 6	16 57	...	15 49	...	21 10
♀	1	24♉35	28♊31	4♌35	10♍49	19♎10	26♏45
	9	3♊ 4	7♋39	14 8	20 39	29 10	6♐49
	17	11 46	16 56	23 47	0♎33	9♏11	16 53
	25	20 37	26 18	3♍29	10 27	19 13	26 57
♂	1	13♉34	10♊12	15♊18	17♋42	2♌20	10♌45
	13	27 6	18 11	7♋33	23 53	6 36	11R33
	25	5♊26	25 55	14 25	29 27	9 43	10 27
♃	1	19♊52	26♊29	1♋54	5♋17	6♋ 2	3♋50
	13	22 31	28 45	3 30	5 57	5R28	2R21
	25	25 4	0♋39	4 47	6R 8	4 28	0 44
♄	1	15♌ 8	18♌53	22♌50	26♌20	29♌ 6	0♍27
	13	16 32	20 25	24 18	27 33	29 49	0R33
	25	18 0	21 57	25 41	28 35	0♍18	0 22
♅	1	7♏47	7♏48	8♏38	10♏ 3	11♏55	13♏45
	13	7R41	8 1	9 8	10 45	12 40	11 25
	25	7D43	8 23	9 44	11 29	13 24	15 1
♆	1	14♐ 6	13♐31	13♐23	13♐44	14♐33	15♐37
	13	13R50	13R25	13D28	14 0	14 57	16 4
	25	13 37	13 22	13 37	14 20	15 23	16 31
Pl.	1	11♎25	11♎51	12♎45	13♎51	15♎ 1	16♎ 1
☊	1	20♎16	18♎37	16♎59	15♎24	13♎45	12♎10
	1st	FRI	MON	THU	SAT	TUE	THU

	d.	JAN	FEB	MAR	APR
☽	1	26♉11	10♋45	18♋37	6♍ 5
	3	20♊12	6♌27	14♌36	4♎28
	5	14♋59	3♍15	11♍58	3♏55
	7	10♌37	0♎49	10♎24	3♐33
	9	7♍ 1	28 47	9♏14	2♑31
	11	4♎ 7	26♏57	7♐52	0♒18
	13	1♏55	25♐ 9	5♑53	26 49
	15	0♐25	23♑11	3♒21	22♓16
	17	29 21	20♒65	29 55	16♈53
	19	28♑ 4	17♓ 1	25♓35	10♉55
	21	25♒44	12♈12	20♈20	4♊36
	23	21♓55	6♉24	14♉12	28 18
	25	16♈39	0♊ 5	8♊ 2	22♋27
	27	10♉30	23 56	1♋43	17♌35
	29	4♊ 9	...	26 31	19♍11
	31	28 19	...	22♌29	...

	d.	MAY	JUN	JUL	AUG
☽	1	12♎32	5♐47	14♑31	6♓ 3
	3	12♏19	6♑10	13♒51	2♈41
	5	12♐36	5♒27	11♓59	27 46
	7	12♑11	2♓56	7♈16	21♉50
	9	10♒16	28 37	1♉41	15♊33
	11	6♓41	23♈ 2	25 26	9♋32
	13	1♈46	16♉49	19♊ 8	4♌13
	15	25 58	10♊25	13♋12	29 47
	17	19♉44	4♋16	7♌52	26♍12
	19	13♊23	28 32	3♍14	23♎21
	21	7♋10	23♌25	29 22	21♏10
	23	1♌26	19♍11	26♎26	19♐33
	25	26 56	16♎10	24♏35	18♑14
	27	22♍55	14♏38	23♐42	16♒43
	29	20♎57	14♐22	23♑12	14♓19
	31	20♏35	...	22♒ 6	10♈38

	d.	SEP	OCT	NOV	DEC
☽	1	23♈18	25♉42	9♋33	12♌ 6
	3	17♉47	19♊32	3♌31	6♍45
	5	11♊38	13♋21	28 18	2♎39
	7	5♋28	7♌46	24♍28	0♏19
	9	29 54	3♍19	22♎22	29 48
	11	25♌21	0♎19	21♏49	0♑20
	13	21♍59	28 42	21♐57	0♒33
	15	19♎36	27♏53	21♑33	29 16
	17	17♏51	27♐ 3	19♒47	26♓35
	19	16♐19	25♑32	16♓28	21♈20
	21	14♑40	20♒30	11♈54	15♉37
	23	12♒35	19♓27	6♉29	9♊28
	25	9♓47	14♈59	0♊35	3♋13
	27	6♈ 4	9♉45	24 24	27 4
	29	1♉19	3♊54	18♋ 8	21♌13
	31	...	27 41	...	17♍58

STATIONS	☿	♀	♂	♃
	18JAN	17MAR	13DEC	16JAN
	7♑ 8	24♈33	11♌34	21♉10
	20APR	28APR		25OCT
	14♉31	8♈15		6♋ 8
	14MAY	♄	♅	♆
	4♉43	11APR	15FEB	19MAR
	23AUG	9♌57	11♏47	16♐ 9
	20♍46	12DEC	17JUL	26AUG
	15SEP	0♍33	7♏41	13♐22
	6♍58	SIDER. TIME (Pl.)		1 JAN
	12DEC	6h 42m	8s	MIDN
	7♑27	18h 44m	6s	NOON
		COMMON YEAR		1977

Noon		JAN	FEB	MAR	APR	MAY	JUN
☉	1	10♑43	12♒16	10♓33	11♈23	10♉45	10♊38
	9	18 52	18 21	18 34	19 17	18 30	18 17
	17	27 2	28 28	26 32	27 7	26 13	25 55
	25	5♒10	6♓31	4♈28	4♉55	3♊55	3♋34
☿	1	21♐12	25♑11	12♓38	26♈07	16♈25	25♉50
	7	23D55	4♒26	24 12	24R19	20D28	7♊54
	13	29 33	14 09	5♈38	20 05	26 33	20 53
	19	6♑53	24 23	15 45	16 15	4♉15	3♋58
	25	15 00	5♓09	22 57	14 53	13 24	16 19
	31	23 41	...	26 02	...	23 57	...
♀	1	5♑46	14♒44	19♓48	28♈17	5♊05	12♋29
	9	15 50	24 47	29 46	8♉19	14 48	22 00
	17	25 54	4♓48	9♈43	17 59	24 29	1♌28
	25	5♒57	14 48	19 38	27 46	4♋06	10 50
♂	1	8♌55	27♋37	22♋17	27♋03	8♌13	23♌15
	13	4R59	24R08	26D49	0♌58	13 43	29 40
	25	0♋14	22 26	27 51	5 39	19 38	6♍20
♃	1	29♊48	26♊39	26♊13	28♊38	3♋09	9♋14
	13	28R20	26D09	26R49	0♋13	5 22	11 49
	25	27 10	26 08	27 51	2 06	7 46	14 28
♄	1	0♍09	28♌18	26♌05	24♌10	23♌41	24♌50
	13	29R35	27R21	25R12	23R47	23D56	25 41
	25	28♌49	26 23	24 30	23 39	24 27	26 42
♅	1	15♏20	16♏16	16♏22	15♏42	14♏33	13♏18
	13	15 47	16 24	16R12	15R17	14R03	12R54
	25	17 32	16R24	15 55	14 48	13 34	12 36
♆	1	16♐46	17♐43	18♐13	18♐17	17♐53	17♐08
	13	17 10	17 59	18 19	18R11	17R37	16R48
	25	17 32	18 11	18R19	18 00	17 19	16 29
Pl.	1	16♎36	16♎39	16♎14	15♎26	14♎37	14♎03
☊	1	10♎33	8♎53	7♎24	5♎45	4♎10	2♎31
	1st	SUN	WED	WED	SAT	MON	THU

Noon		JUL	AUG	SEP	OCT	NOV	DEC
☉	1	9♋17	8♌53	8♍42	7♎57	8♏42	8♐56
	9	16 55	16 33	16 27	15 50	16 44	17 4
	17	24 33	24 13	24 14	23 45	24 47	25 12
	25	2♌11	1♍55	2♎ 4	1♏43	2♐52	3♑20
☿	1	27♋31	2♍30	21♌23	8♎38	27♏27	18♐52
	7	7♌26	2R43	26 51	18 59	5♐37	11R14
	13	16 02	29♌51	5♍54	28 50	13 00	5 48
	19	23 13	24 58	16 41	8♏16	18 52	6D29
	25	28 45	21 00	27 49	17 21	21 36	11 26
	31	2♍10	20D55	...	25 53	...	18 29
♀	1	17♌49	22♍50	24♎44	18♏00	18♏50	7♏31
	9	27 02	1♎28	2♏02	21 25	14R09	9D36
	17	6♍09	9 52	8 41	22 48	9 50	13 38
	25	15 07	17 58	14 26	21R44	7 32	19 08
♂	1	9♍46	28♍14	17♎52	7♏53	29♏37	21♐34
	13	16 46	5♎42	25 45	16 10	8♐17	0♑35
	25	23 57	13 20	3♏48	24 37	17 06	9 43
♃	1	15♋49	22♋45	29♋15	4♌31	8♌07	9♌01
	13	18 31	25 21	1♌31	6 11	8 48	8R33
	25	21 12	27 51	3 35	7 31	9 04	7 39
♄	1	27♌16	0♍43	4♍36	8♍17	11♍28	13♍26
	13	28 32	2 12	6 06	9 37	12 25	13 49
	25	29 53	3 43	7 34	10 50	13 10	13R56
♅	1	12♏30	12♏22	13♏04	14♏25	16♏14	18♏05
	13	12R21	12 33	13 33	15 05	16 58	18 46
	25	12D19	12 51	14 06	15 48	17 43	19 24
♆	1	16♐20	15♐44	15♐33	15♐53	16♐39	17♐42
	13	16R04	15R36	15D38	16 08	17 03	18 09
	25	15 51	15 33	15 46	16 27	17 29	18 36
Pl.	1	13♎55	14♎18	15♎09	16♎16	17♎28	18♎28
☊	1	0♎56	29♍18	27♍39	26♍ 4	24♍25	22♍50
	1st	SAT	TUE	FRI	SUN	WED	FRI

	d.	JAN	FEB	MAR	APR
☽	1	28♍41	18♏47	29♏25	22♑51
	3	25♎ 8	17♐16	27♐39	21♒ 3
	5	23♏18	16♑51	26♑27	18♓44
	7	23♐ 5	16♒39	25♒20	15♈37
	9	23♑35	15♓33	23♓34	11♉30
	11	23♒24	12♈49	20♈34	6♊22
	13	21♓30	8♉24	16♉11	0♋29
	15	17♈42	2♊46	10♊40	24 17
	17	12♉26	26 34	4♋57	18♌22
	19	6♊22	20♋23	28 24	13♍18
	21	0♋ 5	14♌40	22♌49	9♎34
	23	23 57	9♍39	18♍12	7♏17
	25	18♌14	5♎25	14♎40	6♐ 3
	27	13♍ 2	2♏ 0	12♏ 7	5♑ 9
	29	8♎33	...	10♐14	3♒49
	31	5♏ 3	...	8♑39	...

	d.	MAY	JUN	JUL	AUG
☽	1	1♓41	21♈36	26♉ 6	11♋ 8
	3	28 37	16♉42	20♊15	4♌51
	5	24♈42	11♊11	14♋ 5	28 46
	7	20♉ 0	0♋12	7♌47	23♍ 4
	9	14♊35	28 57	1♍38	18♎ 6
	11	8♋35	22♌43	25 59	14♏16
	13	2♌20	17♍ 1	21♎22	11♐56
	15	26 20	12♎27	18♏21	11♑ 6
	17	21♍13	9♏37	17♐11	11♒ 9
	19	17♎34	8♐41	17♑26	11♓ 0
	21	15♏41	8♑59	17♒52	9♈ 5
	23	15♐12	9♒15	17♓12	6♉27
	25	15♑ 6	8♓15	14♈46	1♊45
	27	14♒19	5♈34	10♉37	26
	29	12♓12	1♉21	5♊17	19♋47
	31	8♈44	...	29 15	13♌34

	d.	SEP	OCT	NOV	DEC
☽	1	25♌35	27♍49	17♏11	24♐38
	3	20♍ 1	24♎38	15♐19	24♑ 7
	5	15♎10	21♏24	13♑54	23♒ 6
	7	11♏10	18♐59	11♒21	21♓ 4
	9	8♐13	17♑ 8	10♓21	18♈
	11	6♑22	15♒37	7♈48	14♉ 5
	13	5♒25	14♓ 4	4♉37	9♊27
	15	4♓16	12♈ 6	0♊38	4♋ 8
	17	3♈36	9♉15	25 44	28 11
	19	1♉14	5♊43	19♋59	21♌51
	21	27 24	0♋ 1	13♌43	15♍34
	23	22♊ 9	24 1	7♍31	10♎ 0
	25	16♋ 8	17♌46	2♎ 4	5♏50
	27	9♌53	11♍55	28 0	3♐33
	29	2♍59	7♎ 2	25♏38	2♑59
	31	...	3♏29	...	3♒11

STATIONS	☿	♀	♂	♃
	1 JAN	19OCT	3 MAR	20FEB
	21♐ 9	22♏48	22♋17	26♊ 4
	26APR	29NOV		26NOV
	14♈53	7♏20		9♌ 4
	5 AUG	♄	♅	♆
	3♍ 1	26APR	20FEB	21MAR
	29AUG	23♌39	16♏24	18♐19
	20♌21	25DEC	21JUL	28AUG
	26NOV	13♍56	12♏19	15♐33
	21♐38	SIDER TIME		1 JAN
	16DEC	6h 41m 10s		MIDN
	5♐22	18h 43m 8s		NOON
		COMMON YEAR		1978

Noon	JAN	FEB	MAR	APR	MAY	JUN
☉ 1	10♑28	12♒ 2	10♓18	11♈10	10♉21	10♉24
9	18 37	20 9	18 19	19 3	18 16	18 4
17	26 47	28 13	26 18	26 53	25 59	25 42
25	4♒55	6♓17	4♈14	4♉41	3♊41	3♋20
☿ 1	19♐46	6♒33	26♓22	27♓15	15♈26	13 32
7	27 57	16 48	4♈27	25D44	24 23	26 23
13	6♑38	27 31	8 20	27 24	4♉31	8♋10
19	15 42	8♓35	7R12	1♈37	15 50	18 34
25	25 7	19 36	2 32	7 47	28 14	27 29
31	4♒53	...	27♓49	...	11♊20	...
♀ 1	24♏48	25♐45	27♑25	4♓ 0	10♈ 2	17♉32
9	2♐ 5	4♑36	6♒45	13 35	19 42	27 15
17	9 56	13 36	16 10	23 11	29 22	6♊58
25	18 13	22 46	25 40	2♈48	9♉ 4	16 44
♂ 1	14♑55	9♒14	1♓18	25♓41	18♈52	12♉ 8
13	24 23	18 41	10 46	5♈ 0	27 59	20 57
25	3♒41	28 9	20 12	14 16	6♉59	29 36
♃ 1	6♌56	3♌ 0	29♋57	29♋ 5	1♌ 1	5♌18
13	5R30	1R30	29R16	29 33	2 27	7 23
25	3 55	0 17	29D 0	0♌25	4 11	9 41
♄ 1	13♍53	12♍39	10♍33	8♍17	7♍ 8	7♍32
13	13R35	11R49	9R37	7R40	7D 6	8 7
25	13 3	10 53	8 44	7 15	7 18	8 54
♅ 1	19♏44	20♏45	20♏59	20♏27	19♏21	18♏ 5
13	20 13	20 56	20R53	20R 3	18R51	17 40
25	20 36	21R 0	20 38	19 36	18 21	17 19
♆ 1	18♐51	19♐49	20♐22	20♐29	20♐ 6	19♐22
13	19 16	20 6	20 28	20R23	19R50	19R 3
25	19 38	20 18	20 30	20 13	19 33	18 44
Pl. 1	19♎ 6	19♎12	18♎49	18♎ 2	17♎15	16♎35
☊ 1	21♍12	19♍33	18♍ 4	16♍26	14♍50	13♍12
1st	MON	THU	THU	SUN	TUE	FRI

Noon	JUL	AUG	SEP	OCT	NOV	DEC
☉ 1	9♋ 4	8♌39	8♍27	7♎43	8♏28	9♐41
9	14 47	16 18	16 12	15 36	16 29	16 48
17	20 31	23 59	23 59	23 31	24 32	24 56
25	1♌57	1♍41	1♎49	1♏28	2♐37	3♑ 5
☿ 1	4♌49	7♌21	27♌20	21♎17	1♐59	20♏ 0
7	10 20	3R51	8♍54	0♏30	5 30	24D12
13	13 40	3D31	20 21	9 14	4R34	1♐17
19	14R21	7 21	1♎15	17 25	28♏11	9 24
25	12 12	15 3	11 33	24 52	21 13	18 10
31	8 5	25 27	...	1♐ 7	...	27 11
♀ 1	24♊ 3	2♌ 3	10♍22	17♎40	26♏16	3♑37
9	3♋49	11 54	20 18	27 37	6♐14	14 33
17	13 37	21 47	0♎15	7♏35	16 12	23 27
25	23 26	1♍41	10 12	17 33	26 9	3♒22
♂ 1	3♊51	25♊16	15♋34	3♌55	21♌ 5	4♍56
13	12 16	3♋16	23 5	10 49	27 2	9 17
25	20 32	11 6	0♌22	17 24	2♍27	12 39
♃ 1	10♌52	17♌26	24♌12	0♍24	5♍48	9♍15
13	13 21	20 4	26 45	2 39	7 26	9 58
25	15 55	22 42	29 13	4 42	8 44	10 15
♄ 1	9♍23	12♍25	16♍ 7	19♍51	23♍20	25♍50
13	10 26	13 47	17 37	21 17	24 28	26 28
25	11 39	15 15	19 7	22 37	25 26	26 52
♅ 1	17♏11	16♏56	17♏30	18♏46	20♏31	22♏22
13	17R 0	17D 3	17 56	19 23	21 15	23 5
25	16 55	17 18	18 27	20 5	22 0	23 44
♆ 1	18 35	17♐57	17♐44	18♐ 0	18♐45	19♐47
13	18R18	17R48	17D47	18 14	19 8	20 14
25	18 4	17 44	17 54	18 33	19 34	20 41
Pl. 1	16♎26	16♎46	17♎36	18♎41	19♎55	20♎56
☊ 1	11♍36	9♍58	8♍19	6♍44	5♍ 6	3♍30
1st	SUN	WED	SAT	MON	THU	SAT

d.	JAN	FEB	MAR	APR
☽ 1	18♒12	10♈29	18♈43	7♊31
3	17♓18	7♉40	16♉17	2♋50
5	14♈48	3♊19	12♊10	27 2
7	11♉ 8	27 55	6♋44	20♌42
9	6♊21	21♋52	0♌35	14♍28
11	0♋52	15♌33	24 13	8♎53
13	24 53	9♍15	18♍ 4	4♏10
15	18♌36	3♎14	12♎25	0♐24
17	12♍16	27 50	7♏31	27 30
19	6♎14	23♏ 0	3♐32	25♑18
21	1♏11	20♐37	0♑38	23♒38
23	27 41	19♑22	28 54	22♓18
25	26♐ 5	19♒20	28♒ 6	20♈52
27	26♑ 4	19♓ 0	27♓39	18♉46
29	25♒32	...	26♈38	15♊27
31	26♓14	...	24♉18	...

d.	MAY	JUN	JUL	AUG
☽ 1	10♋46	24♌44	26♍28	11♏37
3	4♌29	18♍25	20♎41	7♐49
5	28 40	12♎45	16♏10	5♑48
7	22♍32	8♏ 6	13♐20	5♒21
9	17♎26	5♐ 4	12♑ 7	5♓35
11	13♏ 1	3♑22	11♒48	5♈21
13	10♐ 3	2♒20	11♓22	3♉47
15	7♑57	1♓12	9♈59	0♊40
17	6♒14	29 27	7♉26	26 11
19	4♓31	26♈59	3♊45	20♋43
21	2♈36	23♉44	29 6	14♌37
23	0♉21	19♊42	23♋40	8♍14
25	27 28	14♋49	17♌39	1♎52
27	23♊39	9♌ 6	11♍16	25 51
29	18♋45	2♍49	4♎54	20♏38
31	12♌53	...	29 7	16♐40

d.	SEP	OCT	NOV	DEC
☽ 1	0♑18	7♒53	1♈ 8	9♉29
3	28 49	7♓12	0♉25	7♊26
5	28♒42	7♈12	29 7	4♋19
7	29♓ 2	6♉48	26♊25	29 52
9	28♈37	5♊ 1	23♋ 6	24♌14
11	26♉37	1♋27	16♌28	17♍56
13	22♊52	26 20	10♍ 8	11♎42
15	17♋42	20♌14	3♎21	6♏11
17	11♌40	13♍19	28 13	1♐54
19	5♍15	7♎38	23♏34	28 55
21	28 55	2♏ 4	19♐54	26♑56
23	22♎57	27 16	17♑ 2	25♒21
25	17♏35	23♐16	14♒41	23♓42
27	13♐ 8	20♑ 8	12♓44	21♈47
29	9♑49	17♒53	11♈ 5	19♉26
31	...	16♓33	...	16♊29

STATIONS	☿	♀	♂	♃
	15MAR			25MAR
	8♈31	NONE	NONE	29♋ 0
	7 APR			27DEC
	25♓45			10♍15
	18JUL	♄	♅	♆
	14♌27	10MAY	25FEB	24MAR
	11AUG	7♍ 5	21♏ 0	21♐ 0
	3♌10		27JUL	31AUG
	10NOV		16♏55	17♐43
	5♐48	SIDER. TIME		1 JAN
	30NOV	6h 40m 12s		MIDN
	19♏41	18h 42m 10s		NOON
		COMMON YEAR		1979

Noon		JAN	FEB	MAR	APR	MAY	JUN
☉	1	10♑13	11♒47	11♓ 4	11♈55	11♉15	11♊ 8
	9	18 22	19 53	19 4	19 47	19 0	18 47
	17	26 32	27 58	27 3	27 37	27 41	26 26
	25	4♒40	6♓ 3	4♈59	5♉25	4♊24	4♋ 4
☿	1	28♐43	19♒41	19♓57	14♓10	28♈ 9	0♋57
	7	8♑ 0	0♓16	14 32	20 35	10♉10	9 54
	13	17 32	10 16	9 20	28 21	22 59	17 2
	19	27 20	18 04	7 25	7♈15	6♊ 2	22 6
	25	7♒28	21 28	9 0	17 11	18 21	24 46
	31	17 56	...	13 15	...	29 17	...
♀	1	12♒ 1	19♓51	24♈ 0	27♉40	23♊46	1♋24
	9	21 51	29 25	3♉ 3	5♊51	28 28	27♊50
	17	1♓39	8♈53	11 53	12 50	1♋34	22 58
	25	11 23	18 14	20 28	19 26	2R35	18 37
♂	1	14♍ 3	13♍38	3♍42	26♌ 1	29♌18	10♍18
	13	15 18	10R14	29♌30	26D10	2♍53	15 48
	25	14R48	5 40	26 45	27 56	7 21	21 47
♃	1	10♍12	8♍ 9	4♍32	1♍11	0♍16	2♍ 9
	13	9R44	6R45	3R 3	0 30	0 41	3 31
	25	8 51	5 11	1 46	0D14	1 29	5 12
♄	1	27♍ 0	26♍27	24♍38	22♍14	20♍34	20♍16
	13	26R59	25R48	23R42	21R26	20R16	20 36
	25	26 42	25 0	22 45	20 49	20D12	21 9
♅	1	24♏ 5	25♏13	25♏34	25♏ 7	24♏ 5	22♏49
	13	24 36	25 28	25R29	24R46	23R35	22R22
	25	25 2	25 34	25 17	24 19	23 5	22 0
♆	1	20♐56	21♐56	22♐31	22♐40	22♐19	21♐36
	13	21 22	22 14	22 39	22R34	22R 4	21R16
	25	21 44	22 27	22R41	22 25	21 46	20 57
Pl.	1	21♎36	21♎46	21♎24	20♎38	19♎49	19♎11
☊	1	1♍52	0♍13	28♌41	27♌ 3	25♌27	23♌49
	1st	TUE	FRI	SAT	TUE	THU	SUN

Noon		JUL	AUG	SEP	OCT	NOV	DEC
☉	1	9♋47	9♌22	9♍11	8♎27	9♏13	9♐27
	9	17 24	17 2	16 57	16 20	17 15	17 35
	17	25 02	24 43	24 45	24 16	25 18	25 43
	25	2♌40	2♍25	2♎34	2♏14	3♐23	3♑52
☿	1	24♋45	19♋58	14♍50	1♏53	13♏34	23♏31
	7	22R15	27 26	25 35	9 8	5R21	2♐31
	13	18 31	7♌39	5♎35	15 11	4D 1	11 46
	19	15 40	19 24	14 56	19 8	7 53	21 3
	25	15D36	1♍25	23 47	19R30	15 0	0♑28
	31	19 3	12 59	...	14 37	...	10 3
♀	1	16♊38	26♊14	23♋33	26♌ 5	2♎28	9♏10
	9	16D11	2♋19	1♌50	5♍14	12 9	19 6
	17	18 4	9 10	10 25	14 35	21 56	29 2
	25	21 48	16 38	19 15	24 5	1♏46	9♐ 1
♂	1	24♍57	12♎37	2♏ 8	22♏25	14♐38	7♑10
	13	1♎32	19 58	10 5	0♐53	23 32	16 24
	25	8 27	27 33	18 15	9 31	2♑36	25 45
♃	1	6♍ 8	11♍49	18♍10	24♍39	0♎59	6♎ 6
	13	8 9	14 10	20 46	27 11	3 11	7 43
	25	10 22	16 41	23 22	29 36	5 12	8 59
♄	1	21♍31	24♍ 6	27♍34	1♎14	4♎54	7♎47
	13	22 23	25 22	29 1	2 43	6 10	8 38
	25	23 25	26 43	0♎30	4 8	7 17	9 16
♅	1	21♏50	21♏30	21♏58	23♏ 7	24♏50	26 41
	13	21R37	21D35	22 21	23 44	25 34	27 24
	25	21 31	21 48	22 51	24 25	26 19	28 4
♆	1	20♐48	20♐ 9	19♐54	20♐ 9	20♐53	21♐55
	13	20R31	20R 0	19D57	20 23	21 16	22 22
	25	20 16	19 55	20 4	20 41	21 41	22 49
Pl.	1	18♎58	19♎17	20♎ 5	21♎10	22♎24	23♎26
☊	1	22♌14	20♌35	18♌57	17♌21	15♌43	14♌ 7
	1st	TUE	FRI	MON	WED	SAT	MON

d.		JAN	FEB	MAR	APR
☽	1	29♊44	16♌15	6♍58	21♎21
	3	25♋25	10♍14	0♎39	15♏25
	5	20♌ 4	3♎53	24 21	10♐ 6
	7	13♍57	27 37	18♏23	5♑42
	9	7♎34	22♏ 1	13♐17	2♒22
	11	1♏34	17♐37	9♑25	0♓36
	13	26 38	14♑54	7♒21	0♈15
	15	23♐11	13♒52	6♓47	0♉28
	17	21♑19	13♓52	7♈11	0♊ 5
	19	20♒28	13♈49	7♉ 6	28 10
	21	19♓48	12♉42	5♊54	24♋21
	23	18♈33	7♊ 6	4♋45	18♌56
	25	16♉22	6♋ 3	27 58	12♍43
	27	13♊10	0♌56	22♌ 8	6♎19
	29	9♋ 2	25 4	15♍54	0♏12
	31	4♌ 2	...	9♎27	...

d.		MAY	JUN	JUL	AUG
☽	1	24♏39	12♑28	19♒36	12♈42
	3	19♐44	9♒18	17♓44	11♉16
	5	15♐35	6♓51	16♈ 6	9♊ 4
	7	12♒22	5♈ 7	14♉26	5♋58
	9	10♓17	3♉55	12♊26	1♌54
	11	9♈18	2♊45	9♋40	26 58
	13	9♉ 3	0♋51	5♌52	21♍16
	15	8♊20	27 37	0♍55	15♎ 4
	17	6♋19	29♌19	25 5	8♏48
	19	2♌29	17♍10	18♎49	3♐ 0
	21	27 13	10♎54	12♏45	28 16
	23	21♍ 3	4♏49	7♐28	25♑ 3
	25	14♎44	29 28	3♑28	23♒28
	27	8♏48	25♐11	0♒50	23♓ 2
	29	3♐38	22♑ 0	29 17	22♈49
	31	29 19	...	28♓15	21♉51

d.		SEP	OCT	NOV	DEC
☽	1	5♊53	12♋51	29♌49	2♎21
	3	2♋56	8♌23	23♍48	26♏ 3
	5	28 45	2♍52	17♎29	19♏56
	7	23♌39	26 47	11♏16	14♐19
	9	17♍52	20♎29	5♐20	9♑22
	11	11♎42	14♏14	29 52	5♒ 5
	13	5♏22	8♐14	25♑ 5	1♓39
	15	29 16	2♑48	21♒21	29 12
	17	23♐49	28 25	19♓ 1	27♈49
	19	19♑38	25♒35	18♈13	27♉ 8
	21	17♒ 7	24♓34	18♉22	26♊22
	23	16♓23	24♈46	18♊18	24♋33
	25	16♈45	25♉26	16♋46	21♌11
	27	16♉55	24♊42	13♌23	16♍17
	29	15♊46	22♋ 2	8♍21	10♎25
	31	...	17♌33	...	4♏ 8

STATIONS	☿	♀	♂	♃
	26FEB	25MAY	17JAN	27APR
	21♓30	2♋35	15♍21	0♍14
	20MAR	7 JUL	7 APR	
	7♓25	16♊ 3	25♌52	
	29JUN	♄	♅	♆
	25♋ 6	7 JAN	29FEB	25MAR
	23JUL	27♍ 1	25♏34	22♐41
	15♋13	23MAY	31JUL	2 SEP
	23OCT	20♍12	21♏30	19♐54
	19♏55	SIDER. TIME		1 JAN
	13NOV	6h 39m 15s		MIDN
	4♏ 1	18h 41m 13s		NOON
		LEAP YEAR		1980

Noon		JAN	FEB	MAR	APR	MAY	JUN
☉	1	11♑ 0	12♒33	10♓49	11♈40	11♉ 1	10♊54
	9	19 9	20 40	18 50	19 33	18 46	18 33
	17	27 18	28 45	26 49	27 23	26 29	26 12
	25	5♒26	6♓48	4♈45	5♉11	4♊11	3♋50
☿	1	11♑38	0♓51	19♒54	18♓57	15♉32	2♋47
	7	21 26	4 48	21D12	28 32	28 11	4 63
	13	1♒25	2R45	25 22	9♈ 0	9♊40	4R37
	19	11 31	26♒26	1♓28	20 24	19 19	1 58
	25	21 21	21 11	8 55	2♉41	26 53	28♊37
	31	29 43	. . .	17 26	. . .	2♋ 9	. . .
♀	1	17♐46	26♑34	1♓34	10♈10	17♉18	25♊24
	9	27 46	6♒34	11 30	20 6	27 9	3♋58
	17	7♑47	16 35	21 28	0 0	6♊59	14 58
	25	17 45	26 35	1♈29	9♉53	16 49	24 43
♂	1	1♒14	25♒42	17♓48	11♈55	4♉39	27♉20
	13	10 41	5♓11	27 12	21 5	13 32	5♊54
	25	20 9	14 39	1♈29	0 9	22 17	14 19
♃	1	9♎32	10♎17	8♎27	4♎41	1♎28	0♎28
	13	10 11	9R46	7R 6	3R13	0R45	0 52
	25	10R23	8 50	5 34	1 58	0 27	1 39
♄	1	9♎31	9♎37	8♎19	6♎ 1	3♎58	3♎ 0
	13	9 46	9R12	7 28	5R 7	3R25	3D 3
	25	9R44	8 34	6 33	4 19	3 5	3 21
♅	1	28♏27	29♏40	0♐ 6	29♏47	28♏49	27♏33
	13	28 59	29 56	0R 5	29R28	28R23	27R 5
	25	29 27	0♐ 5	29 56	29 3	27 50	26 41
♆	1	23♐ 4	24♐ 5	24♐40	24♐51	24♐32	23♐50
	13	23 30	24 22	24 48	24R46	24R18	23R31
	25	23 54	24 37	24 52	24 39	24 1	23R11
Pl.	1	24♎10	24♎20	24♎ 1	23♎17	22♎27	21♎46
☊	1	12♌29	10♌51	9♌22	7♌43	6♌ 8	4♌29
		THUR	SUN	SUN	WED	FRI	MON

Noon		JUL	AUG	SEP	OCT	NOV	DEC
☉	1	9♋33	9♌ 9	8♍57	8♎13	8♏59	9♐13
	9	17 11	16 48	16 43	16 6	17 0	17 20
	17	24 49	24 29	24 30	24 2	25 3	25 28
	25	2♌27	2♍11	2♎20	1♏59	3♐ 8	3♑37
☿	1	26♊30	29♋28	27♍46	2♏35	20♎31	4♐ 9
	7	27D 0	11♌52	6♎46	3R46	27 10	13 35
	13	0♋31	24 5	14 59	0 33	5♏51	23 1
	19	7 0	5♍36	22 17	23♎40	15 12	2♑30
	25	16 10	16 23	28 22	18 37	24 42	12 5
	31	27 27	26 7		19D45		21 44
♀	1	2♌ 1	9♍33	16♎33	21♏28	25♐47	24♑27
	9	11 45	19 10	25 58	0♐34	4♑ 5	0♒26
	17	21 27	28 44	5♏19	9 31	11 59	5 8
	25	1♍ 7	8♎15	14 35	18 17	19 22	8 7
♂	1	18♊28	9♋29	29♋38	18♌19	6♍36	22♍52
	13	26 42	17 23	7♌13	25 32	13 18	28 49
	25	4♋48	25 10	14 39	2♍35	19 46	4♎19
♃	1	2♎11	6♎12	11♎46	18♎ 1	24♎43	0♏52
	13	3 30	8 13	14 12	20 36	27 15	3 5
	25	5 8	10 25	16 43	23 13	29 41	5 5
♄	1	3♎35	5♎36	8♎42	12♎16	16♎ 1	19♎12
	13	4 13	6 42	10 5	13 44	17 23	20 14
	25	5 2	7 56	11 32	15 12	18 38	21 5
♅	1	26♏31	26♏ 3	26♏23	27♏27	29♏ 6	0♐56
	13	26R15	26D 5	26 44	28 2	29 49	1 40
	25	26 5	26 14	27 11	28 41	0♐34	2 21
♆	1	23♐ 2	22♐21	22♐ 5	22♐18	23♐ 0	24♐ 1
	13	22R45	22R12	22D 7	22 31	23 23	24 28
	25	22 29	22 6	22 13	22 48	23 48	24 55
Pl.	1	21♎32	21♎48	22♎34	23♎38	24♎52	25♎57
☊	1	2♌54	1♌16	29♋37	28♋ 2	26♋23	24♋48
		WED	SAT	TUES	THURS	SUN	TUES

d.		JAN	FEB	MAR	APR
☽	1	16♏ 5	0♑41	8♑31	26♒10
	3	10♐22	26 44	4♒35	24♓50
	5	5♑31	24♒ 0	20 17	24♈53
	7	1♒34	22♓14	1♓22	25♉ 7
	9	28 29	20♈55	0♉49	25♊ 2
	11	26♓ 6	19♉28	0♊ 8	21♋53
	13	24♈14	17♊31	28 11	17♌56
	15	22♉41	14♋51	25♋ 2	12♍54
	17	21♊ 5	11♌23	20♌51	7♎13
	19	18♋58	7♍34	15♍54	4♏42
	21	15♌52	1♎55	10♎21	24 56
	23	11♍33	26 3	4♏20	18♐44
	25	6♎ 9	19♏51	28 6	12♑56
	27	0♏ 4	13♐48	22♐ 0	8♒ 3
	29	23 54	• • •	16♑36	4♓39
	31	18♐14	• • •	12♒32	• • •

d.		MAY	JUN	JUL	AUG
☽	1	3♈ 7	26♉57	5♋30	26♌ 6
	3	3♉12	27♊ 5	4♌10	22♍20
	5	3♊45	25♋31	1♍21	17♎21
	7	3♋22	23♌12	27♎ 0	11♏28
	9	1♌14	18♍43	21♎29	5♐16
	11	27 22	13♎ 7	15♏21	29 20
	13	22♍11	6♏58	9♐10	24♑13
	15	16♎17	0♐44	3♑26	20♒13
	17	10♏ 5	24 46	28 25	17♓22
	19	3♐51	19♑18	24♒47	15♈23
	21	27 50	14♒30	21♓ 3	13♉48
	23	22♑15	10♓39	18♈41	12♊16
	25	7♒28	7♈57	17♉ 2	10♋18
	27	13♓59	6♉30	15♊47	7♌50
	29	12♈ 9	5♊58	14♋28	4♍38
	31	11♉13	• • •	12♌29	0♎28

d.		SEP	OCT	NOV	DEC
☽	1	13♎ 1	15♏36	29♐37	2♒28
	3	7♏26	9♐21	23♑31	27 15
	5	1♐17	3♑ 5	18♒17	23♓22
	7	25 6	27 26	14♓36	21♈15
	9	19♑32	23♒ 4	12♈53	20♉50
	11	15♒11	20♓29	12♉49	21♊18
	13	12♓22	19♈36	13♊19	21♋21
	15	10♈53	19♉34	13♋ 1	19♌54
	17	10♉ 2	19♊12	10♌37	16♍40
	19	8♊57	17♋38	7♍35	11♎54
	21	7♋ 7	14♌41	2♎47	6♏ 9
	23	4♌22	10♍36	27 10	5♐49
	25	0♍48	5♎41	21♏ 5	23 34
	27	26 28	0♏13	14♐47	17♑27
	29	21♎23	24 9	8♑28	11♒49
	31	• • •	17♐49	• • •	6♓54

STATIONS	☿	♀	♂	♃
	9 FEB	NONE	NONE	25JAN
	4♓54			10♎23
	3 MAR			27MAY
	19♒52			0♎27
	10JUN	♄	♅	♆
	5♋12	19JAN	5MAR	29MAR
	4JUL	9♎47	0♐ 7	24♏52
	26♊20	5JUN	3AUG	5SEPT
	6OCT	3♎ 0	26♏ 3	22♐ 5
	3♏51	SIDER. TIME		1JAN
	27OCT	6HR 42M 14S		MIDN
	18♎16	18HR 44M 11S		NOON
		COMMON YEAR		1981

Noon		JAN	FEB	MAR	APR	MAY	JUN
☉	1	10♑45	12♒18	10♓35	11♈26	10♉47	10♊40
	9	18 54	20 25	18 36	19 19	18 32	18 20
	17	27 3	20 30	26 34	27 9	26 15	25 58
	25	5♒12	6♓34	4♈31	4♉57	3♊57	3♋36
☿	1	23♑20	11♒32	13♒55	1♈11	29♉54	11♊ 9
	7	2♒48	5R 7	21 15	12 50	7♊43	8R 4
	13	11 22	2 56	29 34	25 12	12 50	6 38
	19	17 22	4D56	8♓43	7♉48	15 4	7D47
	25	18R 8	9 43	18 37	19 43	14R27	11 39
	31	12 45	• • •	29 19	• • •	11 43	• • •
♀	1	8♒53	25♑10	29♑25	25♒ 0	26♓39	1♉53
	9	7R19	23R24	4♒46	3♓ 3	5♈35	11 6
	17	3 25	24D13	11 9	11 26	14 37	20 34
	25	28♑35	27 15	18 18	20 3	23 48	29 54
♂	1	7♎16	17♎ 5	18♎42	9♎57	1♎ 4	2♎53
	13	11 47	18 52	16R27	5R29	0D24	6 14
	25	15 27	19R 2	12 37	2 7	1 30	10 39
♃	1	6♏ 9	9♏32	10♏17	8♏22	4♏45	1♏27
	13	7 44	10 9	9R52	7R 1	3R18	0R44
	25	8 59	10R19	9 1	5 31	2 3	0 26
♄	1	21♎28	22♎15	21♎31	19♎29	17♎16	15♎44
	13	21 58	22R 5	20R50	18R34	16R31	15R31
	25	22 13	21 42	20 1	17 41	15 58	15D32
♅	1	2♐43	4♐ 2	4♐35	4♐24	3♐31	2♐16
	13	3 18	4 22	4R37	4R 7	3R 3	1R47
	25	3 48	4 33	4 31	3 44	2 33	1 22
♆	1	25♐10	26♐12	26♐49	27♐ 3	26♐45	26♐ 5
	13	25 36	26 31	26 58	26R59	26R32	25R46
	25	26 0	26 45	27 2	26 51	26 15	25 26
Pl.	1	26♎41	26♎56	26♎39	25♎56	25♎ 6	24♎24
☊	1	23♋ 9	21♋31	20♋ 2	18♋23	16♋48	15♋10
		FRI	MON	MON	THUR	SAT	TUES

Noon		JUL	AUG	SEP	OCT	NOV	DEC
☉	1	9♋20	8♌55	8♍43	7♎59	8♏44	8♐58
	9	16 57	16 34	16 29	15 52	16 45	17 5
	17	24 35	24 15	24 16	23 47	24 49	25 14
	25	2♌13	1♍57	2♎ 6	1♏45	2♐54	3♑22
☿	1	18♊ 1	16♌43	5♎17	9♎31	27♎28	15♐30
	7	26 41	28 3	11 26	3R40	7♏20	24 50
	13	7♋26	8♍27	15 48	2D54	17 6	4♑ 8
	19	19 39	17 57	17 30	7 52	26 41	13 16
	25	2♌25	26 32	15R23	16 13	6♐ 8	21 54
	31	14 45	4♎ 8	• • •	25 49	• • •	29 1
♀	1	7♊ 6	14♋16	22♌ 7	29♍18	8♏ 5	15♐45
	9	16 37	23 58	1♍59	9♎17	18 8	25 48
	17	26 11	3♌43	11 54	19 18	28 10	5♑51
	25	5♋48	13 31	21 50	29 19	8♐13	15 54
♂	1	13♎11	28♎53	17♏41	7♐55	0♑24	23♑13
	13	18 48	5♏51	25 34	16 28	9 26	2♒32
	25	25 1	13 13	3♐45	25 13	18 35	11 55
♃	1	0♏27	2♏11	6♏13	11♏40	18♏13	24♏49
	13	0D48	3 30	8 16	14 8	20 51	27 24
	25	1 34	5 9	10 30	16 42	23 30	29 53
♄	1	15♎38	17♎ 4	19♎44	23♎ 4	26♎49	0♏13
	13	16 1	17 58	21 0	24 31	28 14	1 24
	25	16 37	19 2	22 21	25 59	29 35	2 25
♅	1	1♐11	0♐36	0♐48	1♐45	3♐20	5♐ 8
	13	0R52	0D35	1 6	2 18	4 2	5 52
	25	0 40	0 41	1 31	2 56	4 46	6 34
♆	1	25♐17	24♐35	24♐16	24♐28	25♐ 7	26♐ 6
	13	24R59	24R25	24D17	24 39	25 29	26 33
	25	24 43	24 18	24 23	24 56	25 53	27 0
Pl.	1	24♎ 7	24♎20	25♎ 4	26♎ 6	27♎21	28♎26
☊	1	13♋34	11♋56	10♋17	8♋42	7♋ 3	5♋28
		THURS	SUN	WED	FRI	MON	WED

☽	d.	JAN	FEB	MAR	APR
☽	1	19♓50	10♉59	21♉53	15♋ 8
	3	16♈39	9♊21	20♊ 6	12♌48
	5	14♉54	8♋18	18♋21	9♍53
	7	14♊23	7♌18	16♌25	6♎15
	9	14♋19	5♍37	13♍59	1♏46
	11	13♌40	2♎40	10♎36	26 26
	13	11♍35	28 15	6♏ 4	20♐18
	15	7♎49	22♏39	0♐27	13♑56
	17	2♏37	16♐23	24 12	7♒58
	19	26 32	10♑ 9	17♑58	3♓ 5
	21	20♐11	4♒32	12♒28	29 49
	23	14♑ 4	29 42	8♓14	28♈13
	25	8♒34	26♓28	5♈27	27♉39
	27	3♓51	23♈54	3♉47	27♊ 6
	29	0♈ 2	• • •	2♊32	25♋46
	31	27 7	• • •	1♋ 4	• • •

☽	d.	MAY	JUN	JUL	AUG
☽	1	23♌22	12♎42	16♏46	1♑10
	3	19♍56	7♏33	10♐40	24 53
	5	15♎39	1♐43	4♑18	19♒ 2
	7	10♏35	25 28	1♒54	13♓53
	9	4♐50	19♑ 4	22 4	9♈34
	11	28 36	12♒54	16♓50	6♉13
	13	22♑13	7♓25	12♈39	3♊58
	15	16♒14	3♈10	9♉50	2♋38
	17	11♓18	0♉34	8♊30	2♌ 2
	19	7♈59	29 40	8♋17	1♍22
	21	6♉30	29♊51	8♌19	29 44
	23	6♊20	27♋59	7♍31	26♎31
	25	6♋25	29♌ 0	5♎ 7	21♏45
	27	5♌40	26♍22	1♏ 1	15♐51
	29	3♍30	22♎ 9	25 34	9♑29
	31	29 56	• • •	19♐22	3♒20

☽	d.	SEP	OCT	NOV	DEC
☽	1	15♒29	19♓ 1	8♉14	15♊42
	3	10♓27	15♈39	7♊ 1	15♋32
	5	6♈22	13♉15	6♋ 0	14♌50
	7	3♉ 9	10♊52	4♌35	12♍57
	9	0♊37	9♋36	2♍27	9♎16
	11	28 39	7♌45	29 33	5♏27
	13	27♋ 9	5♍41	25♎49	0♐15
	15	25♌50	3♎ 9	21♏15	24 23
	17	24♍ 9	29 46	15♐49	18♑ 6
	19	21♎24	25♏17	9♑41	10♒42
	21	17♏17	19♐43	3♒16	5♓37
	23	11♐51	13♑28	27 11	0♈16
	25	5♑38	7♒ 9	21♓56	26 20
	27	29 20	1♓29	18♈15	24♉ 8
	29	23♒38	27♈ 4	16♉18	23♊36
	31	• • •	24♈10	• • •	23♋56

STATIONS	☿	♀	♂	♃
	23JAN	11FEB	21FEB	24FEB
	18♒38	3♒15	19♎11	10♏20
	13FEB		12MAY	27JUN
	2♒55		0♎23	0♏26
	21MAY	♄	♅	♆
	15♊10	2FEB	9MAR	2APR
	14JUN	22♎15	4♐37	27♐ 2
	13♓40	18JUN	9AUG	4SEPT
	19SEPT	15♎30	0♐34	24♐16
	17♎31	SIDER Pl. TIME		1JAN
	11OCT	6H 41m 16s		MIDN
	2♎25	18h 43m 14s		NOON
		COMMON YEAR		1982

Noon		JAN	FEB	MAR	APR	MAY	JUN
☉	1	10♑30	12♒ 4	10♓20	11♈12	10♉33	10♊26
	9	18 39	20 10	18 21	19 4	18 18	18 6
	17	26 49	28 15	26 20	26 55	26 1	25 45
	25	4♒57	6♓19	4♈16	4♉43	3♊43	3♋23
☿	1	29♑56	17♑55	20♒59	17♈31	25♉32	18♉14
	7	2♒32	22 29	0♓32	29 36	24R11	22 30
	13	28♑42	28 56	10 45	10♉20	20 54	28 57
	19	21R12	6♒32	21 40	18 37	17 43	7♊21
	25	16 47	14 58	3♈18	23 46	16 26	17 34
	31	17D25	• • •	15 28	• • •	17D45	• • •
♀	1	24♑41	3♓28	8♈ 8	15♉47	25♊32	25♋ 6
	9	4♒43	13 25	17 56	25 18	0♋ 3	3 ♌17
	17	14 44	23 20	27 41	4♊44	8 58	11 7
	25	24 44	3♈13	7♉22	14 4	17 41	17 34
♂	1	17♒24	11♓44	3♈28	26♈58	18♉59	10♊57
	13	26 48	21 5	12 39	5♉52	27 35	19 15
	25	6♓15	0♈23	21 43	14 39	6♊ 4	27 27
♃	1	1♐17	6♐38	9♐51	10♐53	9♐ 8	5♐28
	13	3 32	8 15	10 36	10R30	7R51	4R 0
	25	5 34	9 31	10 55	9 41	6 22	2 44
♄	1	2♏56	4♏20	4♏11	2♏37	0♏23	28♎26
	13	3 40	4R26	3R43	1R45	29♎31	27R59
	25	4 9	4 17	3 4	0 50	28 47	27 45
♅	1	6♐58	8♐22	9♐ 2	8♐58	8♐11	6♐57
	13	7 35	8 44	9 6	8R44	7R44	6R28
	25	8 6	8 59	9R 3	8 23	7 15	6 1
♆	1	27♐16	28♐19	28♐59	29♐14	28♐59	28♐20
	13	27 42	28 39	29♐ 8	29R11	28R46	28R 1
	25	28 6	28 54	29 13	29 4	28 30	27 42
Pl.	1	29♎15	29♎32	29♎28	28♎37	27♎47	27♎ 3
☊	1	3♋50	2♋11	0♋42	29♊ 4	27♊28	25♊50
		SAT	TUES	TUES	FRI	SUN	WED

Noon		JUL	AUG	SEP	OCT	NOV	DEC
☉	1	9♋ 6	8♌41	8♍29	7♎45	8♏30	8♐43
	9	16 44	16 20	16 15	15 38	16 32	16 41
	17	24 21	24 2	24 2	23 33	24 34	24 58
	25	1♌59	1♍43	1♎51	1♏30	2♐39	3♑ 7
☿	1	29♊23	0♌ 7	0♎42	19♍54	9♏39	25♐46
	7	12♋12	9♍ 0	29♍20	27 41	19 16	4♑ 9
	13	25 5	16 48	24R27	7♎30	28 40	11 26
	19	7♌15	23 18	18 39	17 50	7♐52	16 5
	25	18 25	28 7	16D26	28 4	16 56	15R29
	31	28 32	0♎35	• • •	8♏ 1	• • •	8 48
♀	1	23♌28	9♍23	27♌ 7	27♌34	21♍59	24♎ 4
	9	29 30	8R52	23R58	2♍24	0♎ 3	3♏16
	17	4♍27	5 53	23D16	8 26	8 31	12 38
	25	7 56	1 14	24 58	15 22	17 19	22 7
♂	1	1♋30	22♋ 4	12♌ 4	0♍56	19♍54	7♎38
	13	9 32	29 52	19 40	8 21	27 5	14 29
	25	17 29	7♌36	27 12	15 40	4♎ 9	21 9
♃	1	2♐13	1♐ 5	2♐48	6♐45	12♐31	19♐1
	13	1R27	1D25	4 9	8 50	15 2	21 44
	25	1 5	2 11	5 49	11 6	17 40	24 27
♄	1	27♎43	28♎30	0♏41	3♏44	7♏24	10♏55
	13	27D50	29 12	1 49	5 7	8 50	12 12
	25	28 12	0♏ 5	3 4	6 33	10 14	13 22
♅	1	5♐49	5♐ 8	5♐13	6♐ 3	7♐32	9♐19
	13	5R29	5 4	5 28	6 34	8 14	10 4
	25	5 13	5D 7	5 49	7 10	8 57	10 46
♆	1	27♐32	26♐50	26♐28	26♐36	27♐15	28♐13
	13	27R14	26R38	26D28	26 48	27 36	28 39
	25	26 58	26 31	26 33	27 4	28 0	29 6
Pl.	1	26♎43	26♎53	27♎34	28♎36	29♎50	0♏57
☊	1	24♊15	22♊36	20♊58	19♊22	17♊44	16♊ 8
		FRI	MON	THUR	SAT	TUES	THUR

	d.	JAN	FEB	MAR	APR
☽	1	9♌ 3	1♎14	9♎13	27♏38
	3	8♍29	28 33	6♏43	22♐39
	5	6♎18	24♏ 4	2♐25	16♑38
	7	2♏28	18♐20	26 45	10♒18
	9	27 19	11♑59	20♑25	4♓19
	11	21♐22	5♒35	14♒ 5	29 10
	13	15♑ 2	29 30	8♓15	25♉ 4
	15	8♒39	23♓56	3♈10	21♉54
	17	2♓29	19♈ 3	28 53	19♊25
	19	26 51	15♉ 1	25♉21	17♋24
	21	22♈ 7	12♊ 7	22♊35	15♌41
	23	18♉42	10♋32	20♋38	14♍ 4
	25	16♊54	10♌ 6	19♌29	12♎10
	27	16♋36	10♍ 3	18♍38	9♏28
	29	16♌ 1	• • •	17♎15	5♐34
	31	16♏52	• • •	14♏35	• • •

	d.	MAY	JUN	JUL	AUG
☽	1	0♑28	14♒19	16♓29	2♉21
	3	24 29	8♓ 9	10♈56	28 31
	5	18♒12	2♈38	6♉32	26♊21
	7	12♓17	28 20	3♊43	25♋51
	9	7♈19	25♉34	2♋35	26♌17
	11	3♉37	24♊12	2♌35	26♍21
	13	1♊ 9	23♋37	2♍37	24♎56
	15	29 31	22♌57	1♎37	21♏39
	17	28♋11	21♍29	29 2	16♐48
	19	26♌40	18♎53	24♏58	10♑58
	21	24♍41	15♏ 9	19♐46	4♒43
	23	22♎ 0	10♐26	13♑54	28 26
	25	18♏27	4♑57	7♒41	22♓23
	27	13♐56	28 56	1♓23	16♈45
	29	8♑32	22♒39	25 18	11♉48
	31	2♒28	• • •	19♈46	7♊53

	d.	SEP	OCT	NOV	DEC
☽	1	21♊26	29♋29	23♍ 4	1♏18
	3	19♋46	28♌37	21♎46	28 20
	5	19♌31	28♍19	19♏42	24♐25
	7	19♍49	27♎30	16♐21	19♑28
	9	19♎22	25♏17	11♑38	13♒41
	11	17♏13	21♐21	5♒53	7♓28
	13	13♐11	16♑ 0	29 40	1♈23
	15	7♑45	9♒53	23♓37	28 27
	17	1♒35	3♓38	18♈19	21♉59
	19	25 17	27 49	14♉ 4	19♊23
	21	19♓17	22♈43	10♊55	18♋ 1
	23	13♈46	18♉26	8♋39	17♌13
	25	8♉52	14♊55	6♌54	16♍11
	27	4♊43	12♋ 8	5♍17	14♎19
	29	1♋30	10♌ 5	3♎31	11♏28
	31	• • •	10♍39	• • •	7♐40

STATIONS

☿	♀	♂	♃
7 JAN	4 AUG	NONE	28MAR
2♒34	9♍30		10♐55
28JAN	16SEPT		29JUL
16♑29	23♌12		1♐ 4
2 MAY	♄	♅	♆
25♉33	13FEB	15MAR	2 APR
26MAY	4♏26	9♐ 7	29♐14
16♉26	2 JUL	15AUG	10SEPT
2SEPT	27♎43	5♐ 4	26♐28
0♎45	Pl.		
25SEPT			
16♍23			
22DEC			
16♑39			

1 JAN
6HRS 40M 19S MIDN
18HRS 42M 17S NOON
COMMON YEAR 1983

1984

Noon		JAN	FEB	MAR	APR	MAY	JUN
☉	1	10♑15	11♒49	11♓ 6	11♈57	11♉18	11♊10
	9	18 25	19 55	19 7	19 49	19 2	18 49
	17	26 34	28 1	27 5	27 39	26 45	26 28
	25	4♒42	6♓ 4	5♈ 2	5♉28	4♊27	4♋ 6
☿	1	7♑27	19♑23	4♓54	0♉45	26♈58	19♉41
	7	1R22	27 43	16 0	5 38	26D27	29 44
	13	0D49	6♒39	27 40	6R32	28 42	11♊15
	19	4 32	16 6	9♈31	4 1	3♉19	23 56
	25	10 38	26 6	20 37	0 0	9 53	7♋ 3
	31	18 3	• • •	29 34	• • •	18 9	• • •
♀	1	0♐31	8♑14	13♒56	22♓11	29♈ 9	7♊15
	9	10 10	18 4	23 48	2♈ 3	8♉59	17 4
	17	19 53	27 55	3♓41	11 54	18 49	26 54
	25	29 39	7♒46	13 33	21 45	28 39	6♋43
♂	1	24♎56	10♏28	22♏ 2	28♏15	24♏11	13♏58
	13	1♏13	15 43	25 25	27R57	20R 4	11R58
	25	7 10	20 20	27 38	25 51	15 55	11D55
♃	1	26♐ 2	2♑41	7♑55	11♑44	12♑57	11♑21
	13	28 40	5 0	9 40	12 33	12R40	10R 5
	25	1♑15	7 7	11 5	12 56	11 57	8 36
♄	1	13♏59	15♏56	16♏21	15♏17	13♏13	11♏ 2
	13	14 54	16 17	16R 6	14R32	12R19	10R24
	25	15 37	16R23	15 38	13 40	11 28	9 57
♅	1	11♐10	12♐38	13♐26	13♐28	12♐46	11♐35
	13	11 49	13 4	13 33	13R16	12R20	11R 5
	25	12 22	13 21	13R32	12 57	11 52	10 37
♆	1	29♐22	0♑26	1♑ 9	1♑26	1♑12	0♑34
	13	29 48	0 48	1 19	1R23	1R 0	0R15
	25	0♑13	1 3	1 25	1 17	0 44	29 56
Pl.	1	1♏48	2♏ 8	1♏56	1♏16	0♏26	29♎42
☊	1	14♊30	12♊52	11♊19	9♊41	8♊ 6	6♊27
		SUN	WED	THURS	SUN	TUES	FRI

Noon		JUL	AUG	SEP	OCT	NOV	DEC
☉	1	9♋49	9♌24	9♍13	8♎29	9♏15	9♐29
	9	17 27	17 4	16 59	16 22	17 16	17 37
	17	25 4	24 45	24 46	24 18	25 19	25 44
	25	2♌43	2♍27	2♎35	2♏15	3♐25	3♑54
☿	1	19♋42	6♍37	2♍12	1♎14	22♏33	29♐54
	7	1♌19	11 10	0R 3	11 58	1♐28	0R11
	13	11 46	13 18	3D 0	22 19	10 2	24♐18
	19	21 2	12R21	10 26	2♏15	18 5	16 51
	25	29 3	8 16	20 26	11 48	25 6	14D35
	31	5♍40	2 57	• • •	21 3	• • •	17 34
♀	1	14♋ 6	22♌14	0♎22	7♏ 9	14♐54	20♑51
	9	23 56	2♍ 5	10 11	16 45	24 35	0♒25
	17	3♌47	11 55	20 0	26 40	4♑13	9 47
	25	13 37	21 45	29 48	6♐24	13 49	19 0
♂	1	12♏36	22♏ 6	8♐14	27♐26	19♑26	11♒53
	13	15 13	27 46	15 36	5♑45	28 19	21 1
	25	19 14	4♐11	23 23	14 20	7♒20	0♓11
♃	1	7♑50	4♑22	3♑ 8	4♑45	8♑55	14♑39
	13	6R20	3R33	3D28	6 6	11 3	17 15
	25	5 0	3 9	4 13	7 48	13 25	19 58
♄	1	9♏49	10♏ 0	11♏40	14♏24	17♏54	21♏28
	13	9R42	10 29	12 39	15 42	19 20	22 50
	25	9D49	11 11	13 47	17 5	20 46	24 5
♅	1	10♐25	9♐39	9♐37	10♐21	11♐47	13♐32
	13	10R 2	9R32	9 50	10 51	12 28	14 16
	25	9 46	9D33	10 9	11 25	13 10	15 0
♆	1	29♐46	29♐ 3	28♐41	28♐47	29♐24	0♑21
	13	29R28	28R51	28D39	28 58	29 45	0 47
	25	29 11	28 43	28 43	29 13	0♑ 9	1 15
Pl.	1	29♎20	29♎28	0♏ 7	1♏ 8	2♏22	3♏30
☊	1	4♊52	3♊13	1♊35	29♉59	28♉21	26♉46
		SUN	WED	SAT	MON	THURS	SAT

	d.	JAN	FEB	MAR	APR
☽	1	20♐28	6♒25	27♒17	11♈53
	3	15♑27	0♓18	21♓ 1	6♉10
	5	9♒47	24 2	14♈52	1♊ 2
	7	3♓40	17♈53	9♉ 4	26 45
	9	27 24	12♉17	4♊ 0	23♋40
	11	21♈30	7♊50	0♋10	22♌ 0
	13	16♉35	5♋ 7	28 32	21♍34
	15	13♊12	4♌18	27♌38	21♎31
	17	11♋37	4♍46	28♍ 9	20♏42
	19	11♌24	5♎10	28♎13	18♐19
	21	11♍28	4♏12	26♏41	14♑14
	23	10♎41	1♐23	23♐15	8♒51
	25	8♏24	26 57	15♑17	2♓44
	27	4♐41	21♑26	12♒22	26 30
	29	29 52	15♒23	6♓ 6	20♈35
	31	24♑21	• • •	29 53	• • •

	d.	MAY	JUN	JUL	AUG
☽	1	15♉16	3♋28	11♌34	4♎49
	3	10♊42	0♌59	9♍57	3♏25
	5	7♋ 0	29 59	8♎37	0♐48
	7	5♌21	27♍25	6♏38	27 4
	9	2♍23	25♎59	3♐52	22♑28
	11	1♎16	23♏58	0♑18	17♒13
	13	0♏21	21♐12	25 56	11♓24
	15	28 53	17♑26	20♒43	5♈11
	17	26♐14	12♒34	14♓54	28 54
	19	22♑10	6♓50	8♈41	23♉ 4
	21	16♒52	0♈39	2♉36	18♊18
	23	10♓50	24 38	27 18	15♋15
	25	4♈39	19♉21	23♊24	14♌ 5
	27	28 53	15♊18	21♋13	14♍12
	29	23♉56	12♋38	20♌25	14♎23
	31	20♊ 2	• • •	20♍ 7	13♏27

	d.	SEP	OCT	NOV	DEC
☽	1	27♏25	3♑30	19♒56	22♓13
	3	24♐ 5	28 54	14♓ 0	15♈56
	5	19♑32	23♒19	7♈43	9♉52
	7	14♒10	17♓13	1♉34	4♊30
	9	8♓16	10♈56	25 49	0♋ 3
	11	2♈ 4	4♉45	20♊44	26 34
	13	25 46	28 43	16♋28	23♌53
	15	19♉40	23♊41	13♌ 4	21♍51
	17	14♊16	19♋34	11♍ 8	20♎13
	19	10♋10	16♌58	10♎ 4	18♏45
	21	7♌51	15♍58	9♏30	17♐ 2
	23	7♍21	16♎ 3	8♐38	14♑33
	25	7♎50	16♏ 5	6♑39	10♒53
	27	7♏57	14♐57	3♒ 7	5♓58
	29	6♐37	12♑ 7	28 9	0♈ 4
	31	• • •	7♒40	• • •	23 46

STATIONS	☿	♀	♂	♃
	11JAN	NONE	6 APR	1 MAY
	0♑23		28♏21	12♑58
	12APR		20JUN	30AUG
	6♉42		11♏42	3♑ 8
	6 MAY	♄	♅	♆
	26♈19	25FEB	19MAR	4 APR
	15AUG	16♏23	13♐34	1♑26
	13♍23	14JUL	18AUG	12SEPT
	7SEPT	9♏42	9♐32	28♐39
	0♍ 2	SIDER Pl. TIME		1 JAN
	5 DEC	6 HRS 39M 22S MIDN		
	0♑49	18 HRS 41M 20S NOON		
	25DEC	LEAP YEAR		1984
	14♐31			

Noon		JAN	FEB	MAR	APR	MAY	JUN
☉	1	11♑ 2	12♒35	10♓51	11♈43	11♉ 4	10♊56
	9	19 10	20 42	18 52	19 35	18 48	18 35
	17	27 19	28 47	26 51	27 25	26 31	26 14
	25	4♒28	6♓50	4♈47	5♉14	4♊13	3♋52
☿	1	18♐25	0♒18	19♓45	15♈23	14♈19	3♊32
	7	24 42	10 2	0♈53	10R39	20 59	16 35
	13	2♑18	20 14	10 29	7 20	29 8	29 38
	19	10 38	0♓57	16 48	6D57	8♉38	11♋53
	25	19 28	12 9	18R36	9 28	19 25	22 55
	31	28 42	. . .	16 6	. . .	1♊26	. . .
♀	1	26♒55	29♓13	19♈30	15♈36	6♈48	25♈42
	9	5♓45	6♈18	21 56	10R41	9 41	2♉53
	17	14 18	12 31	22R 0	7 8	14 14	10 34
	25	22 28	17 33	19 30	6D 0	19 58	18 37
♂	1	5♓32	29♓ 5	19♈58	12♉28	3♊33	24♊42
	13	14 41	8♈ 6	28 46	20 59	11 49	2♋43
	25	23 48	17 1	7♉27	29 24	19 58	10 39
♃	1	21♑35	28♑49	5♒ 4	11♒ 2	15♒ 9	16♒57
	13	24 23	1♒34	7 32	12 55	16 11	16R51
	25	27 12	4 13	9 49	14 29	16 48	16 18
♄	1	24♏47	27♏ 9	28♏ 6	27♏36	25♏53	23♏36
	13	25 51	27 43	28R 6	27R 2	25R 0	22R49
	25	26 44	28 2	27 51	26 17	24 6	22 11
♅	1	15♐24	16♐56	17♐47	17♐56	17♐21	16♐12
	13	16 3	17 22	17 57	17R47	16R57	15R45
	25	16 38	17 42	17R59	17 31	16 29	15 14
♆	1	1♑30	2♑35	3♑17	3♑37	3♑26	2♑49
	13	1 57	2 56	3 29	3R36	3R14	2R31
	25	2 22	3 13	3 35	3 30	2 59	2 11
Pl.	1	4♏22	4♏45	4♏35	3♏57	3♏ 8	2♏21
☊	1	25♉ 7	23♉29	22♉ 0	20♉21	18♉46	17♉ 7
		TUES	FRI	FRI	MON	WED	SAT

Noon		JUL	AUG	SEP	OCT	NOV	DEC
☉	1	9♋35	9♌11	8♍59	8♎15	9♏ 1	9♐15
	9	17 13	16 50	16 45	16 8	17 2	17 22
	17	24 51	24 31	24 32	24 4	25 5	25 30
	25	2♌29	2♍14	2♎22	2♏ 1	3♐10	3♑39
☿	1	2♌35	24♌27	21♌36	14♎57	1♐ 1	3♐13
	7	10 50	20R54	1♍13	24 48	7 59	28♏52
	13	17 34	16 13	12 19	4♏13	13 11	0♐41
	19	22 27	13 21	23 38	12 41	14R56	6D21
	25	25 2	14D34	4♎33	21 44	11 2	13 50
	31	24R47	20♌16	. . .	29 45		22 10
♀	1	24♉52	29♊ 0	5♌10	11♍28	19♎51	27♏27
	9	3♊25	8♋11	14 45	21 18	29 51	7♐30
	17	12 10	17 28	24 24	1♎12	9♏52	17 34
	25	21 5	26 52	4♍ 8	11 8	19 54	27 38
♂	1	14♋36	4♌44	24♌34	13♍34	3♎ 3	21♎46
	13	22 26	12 27	2♍11	21 8	10 34	29 13
	25	0♌13	20 7	9 47	28 40	18 3	6♏36
♃	1	15♒52	12♒25	8♒43	7♒ 8	8♒30	12♒25
	13	14R43	10R52	7R45	7D17	9 48	14 32
	25	13 19	9 26	7 13	7 55	11 28	16 54
♄	1	21♏56	21♏30	22♏36	24♏54	28♏11	1♐43
	13	21R35	21D45	23 23	26 6	29 35	3 7
	25	21 28	22 13	24 22	27 23	1♐ 0	4 28
♅	1	15♐ 1	14♐ 9	14♐ 0	14♐37	15♐57	17♐40
	13	14R37	14R 0	14D10	15 4	16 36	18 24
	25	14 17	13D58	14 26	15 36	17 18	19 7
♆	1	2♑ 2	1♑17	0♑53	0♑57	1♑31	2♑28
	13	1R43	1R 5	0R51	1D 7	1 52	2 54
	25	1 26	0 56	0D54	1 21	2 15	3 21
Pl.	1	1♏57	2♏ 2	2♏39	3♏38	4♏52	6♏ 1
☊	1	15♉32	13♉54	12♉15	10♉40	9♉ 1	7♉26
		MON	THURS	SUN	TUES	FRI	SUN

d.		JAN	FEB	MAR	APR
☽	1	5♉41	20♊21	28♊14	16♌44
	3	0♊ 2	16♋46	24♋37	15♍42
	5	25 30	14♌49	22♌53	15♎55
	7	22♋17	13♍58	22♏36	16♏12
	9	20♌10	13♎15	22♎40	15♐24
	11	18♍35	11♏54	21♏57	12♑58
	13	16♎59	9♐34	19♐53	8♒58
	15	15♏ 4	6♑20	16♑28	3♓47
	17	12♐42	2♒19	11♒58	27 51
	19	9♑47	27 34	6♓41	21♈32
	21	6♒ 7	22♓ 6	0♈48	15♉ 9
	23	1♓30	16♈ 0	24 32	8♊59
	25	25 56	9♉36	18♉ 7	3♋25
	27	19♈43	3♊27	12♊ 0	28 51
	29	13♉25	. . .	6♋44	25♌45
	31	7♊44	. . .	2♌57	. . .

d.		MAY	JUN	JUL	AUG
☽	1	24♍17	17♏52	26♐10	16♒32
	3	24♎ 8	17♐29	24♑26	12♓28
	5	24♏23	16♑13	21♒27	7♈ 8
	7	23♐52	13♒44	17♓ 0	1♉ 7
	9	21♑47	8♓57	11♈20	24 47
	11	17♒58	3♈16	5♉ 3	18♊55
	13	12♓46	26 57	28 49	14♋ 8
	15	6♈41	20♉39	23♊17	10♌47
	17	0♉18	14♊50	18♋49	8♍43
	19	24 1	9♋50	15♌29	7♎21
	21	18♊10	5♌45	13♍ 0	6♏ 1
	23	13♋ 1	2♍32	11♎ 2	4♐18
	25	8♌47	0♎ 8	9♏15	2♑ 2
	27	5♍40	28 27	7♐31	29 7
	29	3♎48	27♏16	5♑36	25♒26
	31	3♏ 1	. . .	3♒ 7	20♓50

d.		SEP	OCT	NOV	DEC
☽	1	3♈11	5♉37	19♊46	23♋17
	3	27 17	29 12	13♋56	18♌32
	5	20♉55	22♊59	9♌ 1	14♍53
	7	14♊42	17♋31	5♍32	12♎37
	9	9♋19	13♌27	3♎45	11♏45
	11	5♌21	11♍ 8	3♏28	11♐48
	13	3♍ 4	10♎26	3♐51	11♑42
	15	2♎ 7	10♏33	3♑ 0	10♒19
	17	1♏39	10♐22	1♒59	7♓ 6
	19	0♐45	8♑58	28 30	2♈12
	21	28 55	6♒ 5	23♓31	26 12
	23	26♑ 0	1♓49	17♈36	19♉47
	25	22♒ 5	26 32	11♉14	13♊32
	27	17♓18	20♈35	4♊52	7♋48
	29	11♈45	14♉16	28 48	2♌47
	31	. . .	7♊53	. . .	28 32

STATIONS	☿	♀	♂	♃
	25MAR	14MAR	NONE	5JUN
	18♈39	11♈10		16♒58
	17APR	25APR		3OCT
	6♈44	6♈ 0		7♒ 7
	28JUL	♄	♅	♆
	25♌19	8MAR	24MAR	6APR
	21AUG	28♏ 8	17♐59	3♑37
	13♌13	26JUL	24AUG	14SEPT
	19NOV		13♐58	0♑51
	15♐ 0	SIDER. TIME		1JAN
	8DEC	6HRS 42M 21S		MIDN
	28♏47	18HRS 44M 19S		NOON
		COMMON YEAR		1985

Noon		JAN	FEB	MAR	APR	MAY	JUN
☉	1	10♑46	12♒20	10♓36	11♈28	10♉49	10♊42
	9	18 56	20 27	18 37	19 21	18 34	18 22
	17	27 5	28 32	26 36	27 11	26 18	26 0
	25	5♒14	6♓35	4♈33	4♉59	3♊59	3♋38
☿	1	23♐37	12♒40	28♓37	18♓ 9	19♈38	21♊57
	7	2♑27	23 16	1♈18	20 45	29 58	3♋33
	13	11 36	4♓ 9	28♓47	25 42	11♉26	13 40
	19	21 2	14 51	23R25	2♈23	23 55	22 11
	25	0♒48	24 9	19 5	10 25	7♊ 1	28 58
	31	10 56	• • •	18D 0	• • •	19 53	• • •
♀	1	6♑27	15♒25	20♓29	28♈58	5♊44	13♋ 5
	9	16 31	25 27	0♈27	8♉49	15 27	22 35
	17	26 35	5♓29	10 24	18 39	25 6	2♌ 1
	25	6♒38	15 29	20 19	28 25	4♋43	11 23
♂	1	10♏53	29♏33	15♐43	2♑10	15♑16	22♑46
	13	18 11	6♐35	22 19	7 52	19 9	22R59
	25	25 23	13 38	28 39	12 59	21 51	21 26
♃	1	18♒22	25♒25	2♓ 7	9♓19	15♓27	20♓14
	13	21 0	28 17	4 58	11 54	17 32	21 30
	25	23 46	1♓10	7 45	14 20	19 28	22 23
♄	1	5♐13	7♐59	9♐26	9♐33	8♐16	6♐ 4
	13	6 24	8 45	9 40	9R11	7R28	5R13
	25	7 27	9 18	9R40	8 37	6 36	4 26
♅	1	19♐32	21♐ 8	22♐ 4	22♐22	21♐52	20♐47
	13	20 12	21 37	22 17	22R15	21R30	20R18
	25	20 49	21 59	22 22	22 1	21 4	19 49
♆	1	3♑37	4♑42	5♑26	5♑48	5♑39	5♑ 4
	13	4 3	5 4	5 38	5R48	5R28	4R46
	25	4 31	5 21	5 46	5 43	5 14	4 27
Pl.	1	6♏55	7♏21	7♏14	6♏39	5♏49	5♏ 2
☊	1	5♉48	4♉ 9	2♉40	1♉ 2	29♈26	27♈48
		WED	SAT	SAT	TUES	THURS	SUN

Noon		JUL	AUG	SEP	OCT	NOV	DEC
☉	1	9♋22	8♌57	8♍45	8♎ 1	8♏46	9♐ 0
	9	16 58	16 37	16 31	15 54	16 47	17 7
	17	24 37	24 17	24 18	23 49	24 50	25 15
	25	2♌15	2♍ 0	2♎ 7	1♏47	2♐55	3♑24
☿	1	3♌46	25♋52	4♍39	26♎20	29♏ 6	19♏ 0
	7	6 12	26D49	16 13	4♏56	27R 3	26 30
	13	5R53	1♌43	27 11	12 53	20 3	5♐ 1
	19	3 1	10 7	7♎30	20 0	13 54	13 57
	25	28♋56	20 56	17 12	25 43	13D56	23 6
	31	26 4	2♍41	• • •	28 56	• • •	2♑25
♀	1	18♌20	23♍10	24♎41	16♏50	15♏ 2	5♏28
	9	27 31	1♎44	1♏47	19 40	10R16	8D12
	17	6♍35	10 3	8 10	20R19	6 48	12 44
	25	15 30	18 2	13 36	18 28	4 54	18 36
♂	1	20♑ 5	12♑14	14♑ 8	26♑ 2	13♒53	3♓39
	13	16R43	11D25	17 59	2♒29	21 36	11 54
	25	13 32	12 36	23 6	9 33	29 35	20 13
♃	1	22♓39	22♓13	19♓ 5	15♓16	13♓ 3	13♓52
	13	22R51	21R16	17R31	14R 5	13D 1	15 0
	25	22 35	19 58	15 58	13 18	13 28	16 32
♄	1	4♐ 5	3♐ 5	3♐35	5♐25	8♐24	11♐50
	13	3R32	3D 6	4 10	6 28	9 44	13 15
	25	3 11	3 20	4 57	7 39	11 8	14 39
♅	1	19♐35	18♐38	18♐22	18♐52	20♐ 6	21♐46
	13	19R 9	18R26	18D29	19 16	20 44	22 29
	25	18 48	18 22	18 42	19 46	21 24	23 13
♆	1	4♑17	3♑32	3♑ 5	3♑ 7	3♑39	4♑34
	13	3R58	3R18	3R 2	3 16	3 59	5 0
	25	3 41	3 9	3D 4	3 29	4 22	5 27
Pl.	1	4♏35	4♏37	5♏11	6♏ 8	7♏21	8♏32
☊	1	26♈13	24♈34	22♈56	21♈20	19♈42	18♈ 6
		TUES	FRI	MON	WED	SAT	MON

d.		JAN	FEB	MAR	APR
☽	1	11♍42	3♏19	14♏ 7	7♑21
	3	8♎42	1♐28	12♐26	4♒57
	5	6♏41	29 59	10♑30	1♓34
	7	5♐38	28♑27	8♒ 8	27 14
	9	5♑ 5	26♒15	5♓ 3	22♈ 4
	11	4♒ 6	22♓49	0♈59	16♉12
	13	1♓49	18♈ 0	25 43	9♊55
	15	27 49	12♉ 6	19♉55	3♋38
	17	22♈23	5♊46	13♊36	27 53
	19	16♉ 8	29 42	7♋31	23♌15
	21	9♊47	24♋30	2♌20	20♍11
	23	3♋59	20♌32	28 32	18♎47
	25	29 4	17♍45	26♍15	18♏33
	27	25♌ 7	15♎46	25♎ 5	18♐29
	29	21♍58	• • •	24♏18	17♑35
	31	19♎24	• • •	23♐12	• • •

d.		MAY	JUN	JUL	AUG
☽	1	15♒17	3♈44	7♉ 1	21♊ 3
	3	11♓33	28 6	0♊43	15♋ 1
	5	6♈40	21♉54	24 23	9♌37
	7	0♉59	15♊32	18♋22	4♍58
	9	24 50	9♋19	12♌53	0♎ 5
	11	18♊30	3♌28	8♍ 3	27 58
	13	12♋16	28 17	4♎ 4	25♏44
	15	6♌32	24♍ 8	1♏13	24♐20
	17	1♍47	21♎25	29 41	23♑28
	19	28 30	20♏19	29♐17	22♒21
	21	26♎57	20♐28	29♑10	20♓11
	23	26♏52	20♑46	28♒11	16♈31
	25	27♐17	19♒55	25♓32	11♉26
	27	26♑56	17♓13	21♈ 8	5♊26
	29	24♒56	12♈44	15♉28	29 11
	31	21♓10	• • •	9♊12	23♋18

d.		SEP	OCT	NOV	DEC
☽	1	5♌38	9♍18	28♎38	6♐14
	3	0♍ 3	6♎18	27♏57	6♑38
	5	27 28	4♏24	27♐38	6♒25
	7	24♎43	3♐ 7	26♑42	4♓37
	9	22♏34	1♑50	24♒35	1♈ 7
	11	20♐50	0♒ 7	21♓13	26 17
	13	19♑16	27 40	16♈46	20♉38
	15	17♒31	24♓24	11♉33	14♊34
	17	15♓ 7	20♈13	5♊46	8♋19
	19	11♈40	15♉ 9	29 37	2♌ 7
	21	7♉ 1	9♊21	23♋20	26 12
	23	1♊22	3♋ 9	17♌21	20♍58
	25	25 11	26 59	12♍11	16♎57
	27	19♋ 4	21♌27	8♎27	14♏40
	29	13♌37	17♍ 8	6♏31	14♐11
	31	• • •	14♎25	• • •	14♑46

STATIONS	☿	♀	♂	♃
	8 MAR	17OCT	10JUN	14JUL
	1♈18	20♏24	23♑ 7	22♓51
	31MAR	27NOV	13AUG	10NOV
	17♓56	4♏54	11♑25	13♓58
	11JUL	♄	♅	♆
	6♌25	21MAR	30MAR	9 APR
	4 AUG	9♐42	22♐22	5♑49
	25♋24	9 AUG	29AUG	16SEP
	3 NOV	3♐ 4	18♐21	3♑ 2
	29♏ 9	SIDER	Pl. TIME	1 JAN
	23NOV	6H 41M	24S	MIDN
	13♏ 6	18H 43M	22S	NOON
		COMMON	YEAR	1986

Noon		JAN	FEB	MAR	APR	MAY	JUN
☉	1	10♑31	12♒ 5	10♓22	11♈13	10♉35	10♊28
	9	18 41	20 11	18 23	19 6	18 20	18 8
	17	26 50	28 17	26 21	26 56	26 3	25 46
	25	4♒58	6♓20	4♈18	4♉45	3♊45	3♋24
☿	1	3♑58	25♒41	6♓42	14♓10	3♉46	3♋10
	7	13 30	5♓13	1R32	22 14	16 30	9 59
	13	23 15	12 15	14♒58	1♈ 3	14 29	14 35
	19	3♒18	14 24	1D58	10 58	11♊49	16 41
	25	13 37	10R51	6 34	21 53	22 43	16R 6
	31	23 59	• • •	12 57	• • •	1♋50	• • •
♀	1	24♏31	25♐59	27♑52	4♓34	10♈39	18♉14
	9	1♐59	4♑53	7♒14	14 9	20 19	27 54
	17	9 59	13 58	16 53	23 46	15 0	7♊38
	25	18 23	23 12	26 12	3♈24	9♉42	17 23
♂	1	25♓ 6	16♈15	6♉ 7	27♉11	17♊ 9	7♋23
	13	3♈29	25 5	14 19	5♊11	25 1	15 7
	25	11 52	3♉22	22 28	13 11	2♋50	22 50
♃	1	17♓35	23♓23	29♓42	7♈ 9	14♈15	20♈53
	13	19 38	26 0	2♈33	10 2	16 56	23 7
	25	21 57	28 46	5 27	12 52	19 29	25 6
♄	1	15♐26	18♐31	20♐25	21♐ 9	20♐22	18♐25
	13	16 43	19 28	20 54	21R 0	19R43	17R32
	25	17 54	20 13	21 7	20 38	18 56	16 41
♅	1	23♐37	25♐17	26♐19	26♐43	26♐21	25♐19
	13	24 18	25 47	26 34	26R39	26R 0	24R50
	25	24 56	26 12	26 42	26 28	25 35	24 21
♆	1	5♑42	6♑49	7♑34	7♑58	7♑53	7♑19
	13	6 9	7 10	7 47	8R 0	7R43	7R 2
	25	6 35	7 29	7 56	7 56	7 29	6 42
Pl.	1	9♏28	9♏56	9♏53	9♏19	8♏31	7♏42
☊	1	16♈27	14♈49	13♈20	11♈41	10♈ 6	8♈27
		THUR	SUN	SUN	WED	FRI	MON

Noon		JUL	AUG	SEP	OCT	NOV	DEC
☉	1	9♋ 8	8♌43	8♍31	7♎46	8♏31	8♐45
	9	16 45	16 22	16 16	15 39	16 32	16 51
	17	24 23	24 3	24 3	23 34	24 35	25 0
	25	2♌ 1	1♍45	2♎ 3	1♏32	2♐40	3♑ 8
☿	1	13♋17	20♋51	19♍44	3♏ 9	14♏37	27♏ 7
	7	9R44	1♌ 9	14 52	8 56	27D32	6♐ 7
	13	7 33	13 1	9♎17	12 35	1♏30	15 29
	19	8D11	25 13	18 2	12R39	8 51	24 53
	25	12 10	6♍57	26 3	7 51	17 36	4♑24
	31	19 22	18 0	• • •	0 35	• • •	14 2
♀	1	24♊43	2♌44	11♍ 3	18♎20	26♏56	4♑15
	9	4♋29	12 36	20 59	28 18	6♐53	14 11
	17	14 17	22 28	0♎55	8♏15	16 51	24 6
	25	24 17	2♍22	10 52	18 13	26 48	4♒ 0
♂	1	26♋40	16♌26	6♍ 9	25♍19	15♎16	4♏49
	13	4♌20	24 4	13 48	3♎ 1	23 3	12 42
	25	11 59	1♍42	21 28	10 45	0♏53	20 37
♃	1	26♈ 0	29♈10	29♈27	26♈53	22♈50	20♈ 5
	13	27 31	29 39	28R43	25R21	21R28	19R46
	25	28 41	29R40	27 35	23 44	20 26	19D56
♄	1	16♐17	14♐47	14♐40	16♐ 0	18♐36	21♐52
	13	15R33	14R33	15 2	16 52	19 51	23 17
	25	15 0	14D34	15 37	17 55	21 11	24 37
♅	1	24♐ 7	23♐ 6	22♐43	23♐ 5	24♐13	25♐49
	13	23R40	22R51	22D46	23 27	24 49	26 32
	25	23 17	22 44	22 57	23 54	25 29	27 16
♆	1	6♑33	5♑46	5♑18	5♑17	5♑46	6♑40
	13	6R13	5R32	5R14	5 24	6 5	7 5
	25	5 55	5 22	5D14	5 37	6 28	7 32
Pl.	1	7♏13	7♏12	7♏42	8♏38	9♏51	11♏ 2
☊	1	6♈52	5♈14	3♈35	2♈ 0	0♈21	28♓46
		WED	SAT	TUE	THU	SUN	TUE

d.		JAN	FEB	MAR	APR
☽	1	0♒ 1	21♓46	29♓35	17♉15
	3	29 34	18♈45	26♈34	12♊ 6
	5	27♓14	14♉ 3	22♉ 2	6♋ 9
	7	23♈ 5	8♊15	16♊22	29 58
	9	17♉39	2♋ 0	10♋10	24♌ 8
	11	11♊33	25 49	4♌ 3	19♍11
	13	5♋16	20♌ 2	28 30	16♎ 0
	15	29 7	14♍50	23♍47	12♏56
	17	23♌16	10♎19	19♎59	11♐16
	19	17♍53	6♏39	16♏62	9♑55
	21	13♎17	3♐59	14♐49	8♒22
	23	9♏54	2♐27	13♑ 8	6♓17
	25	8♐ 4	1♒44	11♒43	3♈30
	27	7♑43	1♓ 6	10♓ 7	29 54
	29	7♒58	• • •	7♈49	25♉25
	31	7♓34	• • •	4♉25	• • •

d.		MAY	JUN	JUL	AUG
☽	1	20♊ 5	4♌13	6♍42	22♎58
	3	14♋ 5	28 2	1♎ 6	19♏17
	5	7♌52	22♍28	26 42	17♐19
	7	1♍59	18♎11	24♏ 3	16♑57
	9	27 5	15♏40	23♐16	17♒21
	11	23♎37	14♐54	23♑42	17♓37
	13	21♏45	15♑ 4	24♒ 0	15♈33
	15	21♐ 0	14♒55	22♓58	12♉ 5
	17	20♑26	13♓28	20♈ 8	7♊ 9
	19	19♒12	10♈29	15♉46	1♋18
	21	16♓52	6♉12	10♊20	25 3
	23	13♈27	1♊ 2	4♋20	18♌50
	25	9♉ 9	25 17	28 5	12♍53
	27	4♊ 7	19♋10	21♌50	7♎27
	29	28 28	12♌52	15♍48	2♏47
	31	22♋22	• • •	10♎20	29 14

d.		SEP	OCT	NOV	DEC
☽	1	12♐57	21♑44	15♓ 1	22♈42
	3	11♑24	20♒32	12♈51	19♉ 4
	5	10♒56	19♓28	10♉ 2	14♊41
	7	10♓43	17♈52	6♊15	9♋31
	9	9♈44	15♉ 9	1♋24	3♌37
	11	7♉15	11♊ 5	25 38	27 17
	13	3♊ 8	5♋46	19♌22	21♍ 5
	15	27 46	29 42	13♍15	15♎43
	17	21♋40	23♌28	7♎59	11♏51
	19	15♌24	17♍41	4♏ 3	9♐49
	21	9♍29	12♎48	1♐37	9♑13
	23	4♎12	9♏ 4	0♑16	9♒ 4
	25	29 44	6♐22	29 14	8♓14
	27	26♏11	4♑22	27♒48	6♈11
	29	23♐32	2♒40	25♓37	2♉54
	31	• • •	0♓58	• • •	28 44

STATIONS	☿	♀	♂	♃
	20FEB 14♓29	NONE	NONE	21AUG 29♈48
	15MAR 0♓ 1			17DEC 19♈46
	22JUN 16♋49	♄	♅	♆
	16JUL 7♋24	1 APR 21♐10	3APR 26♐44	11APR 8♑ 0
	18OCT 13♏12	21AUG 14♐32	3 SEP 22♐43	20SEP 5♑14
	7 NOV 27♎25	SIDER Pl. TIME		1 JAN
		6H 40M 27S		MIDN
		18H 42M 25S		NOON
		COMMON YEAR		1987

Noon		JAN	FEB	MAR	APR	MAY	JUN
☉	1	10♑16	11♒50	11♓ 7	11♈58	11♉19	11♊12
	9	18 26	19 56	19 8	19 50	19 4	18 51
	17	26 35	28 2	27 7	27 41	26 47	26 30
	25	4♒43	6♓ 6	5♈ 3	5♉29	4♊29	4♋ 8
☿	1	15♑10	27♒59	14♒56	24♓ 5	23♉36	26♊45
	7	25 29	25R34	19 47	4♈ 9	4♊46	25R16
	13	5♒23	18 56	25 51	16 5	13 56	22 8
	19	14 52	13 45	4♓ 7	28 22	20♊48	19 13
	25	23 8	12D51	12 50	11♉ 8	25 9	18D10
	31	27 45	• • •	22 25	• • •	27 0	• • •
♀	1	12♒37	20♓24	24♈25	27♉48	23♊ 7	28♊27
	9	21 57	14♈56	3♉25	5♊31	27 24	24R21
	17	2♓14	9 23	12 11	12 39	14 57	19 26
	25	11 57	18 41	20 41	19 1	0R22	15 33
♂	1	25♏15	15♐56	5♑26	26♑21	16♒25	6♓25
	13	3♐14	24 59	13 32	4♒26	23 18	13 43
	25	11 15	2♑ 4	21 38	12 27	2♓ 1	20 36
♃	1	20♈15	23♈29	28♈32	5♉15	12♉20	19♉38
	13	21 11	25 23	0♉46	8 3	15 11	22 20
	25	22 31	27 34	3 39	10 54	18 1	24 55
♄	1	25♐31	28♐52	1♑13	2♑28	2♑12	0♑36
	13	26 53	14 57	1 52	2R32	1R43	29♐45
	25	28 10	0♑53	2 19	2 22	1 3	28 52
♅	1	27♐41	29♐23	0♑32	1♐ 2	0♑44	29♐47
	13	28 23	29 56	0 49	1R 0	0R26	29R19
	25	29 2	0♑23	0 59	0 51	0 3	28 29
♆	1	7♑33	8♑56	9♑44	10♑10	10♑ 4	9♑32
	13	8 15	9 18	9 57	10 11	9R55	9R15
	25	8 41	9 37	10 6	10R 8	9 41	8 56
Pl.	1	12♏ 0	12♏31	12♏30	11♏58	11♏10	10♏21
☊	1	28♓ 8	25♓29	23♓57	22♓18	20♓43	19♓ 5
		FRI	MON	TUE	FRI	SUN	WED

Noon		JUL	AUG	SEP	OCT	NOV	DEC
☉	1	9♋51	9♌26	9♍15	8♎31	9♏17	9♐31
	9	17 28	17 6	17 1	16 24	17 18	17 38
	17	25 6	24 47	24 48	24 20	25 21	25 46
	25	2♌45	2♍29	2♎37	2♏17	3 26	3♑55
☿	1	19♊52	7♌35	2♎21	26♎37	22♎17	9♐35
	7	24 26	19 53	10 21	22R28	1♏23	19 0
	13	1♋41	1♍26	17 20	15 37	10 58	28 26
	19	11 23	12 6	22 56	11 43	20 36	7♑54
	25	22 59	21 56	26 25	14D 2	15 7	17 22
	31	5♌30	0♎56	• • •	20 54	• • •	26 36
♀	1	14♊ 6	25♊46	23♋46	26♌29	2♎58	9♏48
	9	14D22	2♋ 5	2♌ 8	5♍44	12 45	19 44
	17	16 51	9 8	10 47	15 7	22 32	14♐53
	25	21 2	16 44	19 41	24 38	2 23	9 40
♂	1	23♓54	7♈18	11♈12	4♈14	0♈ 1	6♈40
	13	14 50	10 16	9R15	1R17	1D33	11 26
	25	4♈53	11 26	6 0	29♓55	4 38	16 52
♃	1	26♉ 9	1♊41	5♊15	6♊ 2	3♊49	29♉54
	13	28 28	3 21	5 55	5R31	2R20	28R24
	25	0♊35	4 40	6 7	4 33	0 43	27 12
♄	1	28♐26	26♐34	25♐55	26♐45	28♐44	2♑ 2
	13	27R37	26R 9	25D 5	27 28	0♑ 7	3 24
	25	26 54	25 56	26 28	28 21	1 22	4 49
♅	1	28♐35	27♐31	27♐ 2	27♐19	28♐22	29♐56
	13	28R 7	27R15	27D 4	27 39	28 57	0♑38
	25	27 43	27 5	27 12	28 5	29 35	1 21
♆	1	8♑46	7♑59	7♑29	7♑27	7♑56	8♑48
	13	8R27	7R45	7R25	7 35	8 14	0 38
	25	8 9	7 34	7 25	7 47	8 36	9 40
Pl.	1	9♏50	9♏47	10♏17	11♏11	12♏22	13♏34
☊	1	17♓29	15♓51	14♓12	12♓37	10♓59	9♓23
		FRI	MON	THU	SAT	TUE	THU

d.		JAN	FEB	MAR	APR
☽	1	11♊15	26♋57	17♌37	1♎59
	3	5♋57	20♌41	11♍18	26 39
	5	0♌ 4	14♍20	5♎16	22♏ 9
	7	23 48	8♎13	29 46	18♐33
	9	17♍26	2♏47	24♏ 9	15♑53
	11	11♎29	28 36	21♐43	14♒ 8
	13	6♏39	26♐ 6	19♑42	13♓ 5
	15	3♐32	25♑22	18♒58	12♈14
	17	2♑20	25♒42	18♓55	10♉51
	19	2♒30	25♓52	18♈30	8♊14
	21	2♓47	24♈47	16♉47	4♋ 7
	23	2♈ 0	21 57	13♊22	28 40
	25	29 36	17♊31	8♋26	22♌28
	27	25♉42	11♋58	2♌30	16♍10
	29	20♊19	5♌48	26 8	10♎23
	31	14♋59	• • •	19♍55	• • •

d.		MAY	JUN	JUL	AUG
☽	1	5♏32	24♐45	2♒45	26♓22
	3	1♐45	23♑ 6	2♓ 3	25♈ 3
	5	28 55	6♒40	0♈46	22♉23
	7	26♑42	20♓ 0	28 33	18♊26
	9	24♒53	17♈54	25♉25	13♋28
	11	23♓15	15♉16	21♊24	7♌47
	13	21♈33	11♊57	16♋34	1♍34
	15	19♉25	7♋44	10♌57	25 8
	17	16♊21	2♌31	4♍45	18♎52
	19	12♋ 3	27 29	28 20	13♏13
	21	6♌34	21♍ 8	22♎15	8♐45
	23	0♍22	14♎ 5	17♏11	5♑57
	25	24 5	9♏ 2	13♐41	4♒54
	27	18♎26	5♐32	11♑57	5♓ 2
	29	13♏58	3♑36	11♒35	12♈44
	31	10♐51	• • •	11♓34	4♉28

d.		SEP	OCT	NOV	DEC
☽	1	18♉29	0♋43	10♌ 4	11♍50
	3	15♊14	19 31	3♍54	5♎28
	5	10♋32	11♌42	27 29	29 35
	7	4♌51	7♍20	21♎28	24♏41
	9	28 36	0♎57	16♏11	20♐57
	11	22♍11	24 57	11♐48	18♑12
	13	15♎54	19♏33	8♑14	16♒ 2
	15	10♏36	14♐56	5♒22	14♓ 7
	17	5♐ 5	11♑14	3♓11	12♈16
	19	1♑17	8♒40	1♈40	10♉23
	21	29 1	7♓17	0♉34	8♊10
	23	28♒19	6♈49	29 15	5♋10
	25	28♓24	6♉29	26♊57	1♌ 1
	27	28♈25	5♊15	23♋10	25 42
	29	27♉11	2♋25	17♌58	19♍34
	31	• • •	27 54	• • •	13♎13

STATIONS	☿	♀	♂	♃
	3 FEB	24MAY	28AUG	26SEPT
	28♒ 9	0♋24	11♈27	6♊ 8
	25FEB	6 JUL	29OCT	
	12♒46	13♊56	29♓53	
	1 JUN	♄	♅	♆
	26♊47	12APR	7 APR	14APR
	26JUN	2♑33	1♑ 3	10♑12
	18♊11	2SEPT	7SEPT	21SEPT
	30SEP	25♐56	27♐ 3	7♑25
	27♎ 3	SIDER Pl. TIME		1 JAN
	21OCT	6HRS	39M 30S	MIDN
	11♎39	18HRS	41M 28S	NOON
		LEAP YEAR		1988

1989

	Noon	JAN	FEB	MAR	APR	MAY	JUN
☉	1	11♑ 3	12♒36	10♓53	11♈44	11♉ 5	10♊58
	9	18 12	20 43	18 54	19 36	18 50	18 37
	17	27 21	28 48	26 52	27 27	26 33	26 16
	25	5♒30	6♓52	4♈48	5♉15	4♊15	3♋53
☿	1	28♑ 5	27♑15	16♒32	8♈33	1♊38	28♉41
	7	6♒ 8	26D 9	25 4	20 50	5 47	28D20
	13	11 16	29 2	4♓20	3♉17	6 47	0♊38
	19	10R42	4♒25	14 19	14 55	5R 3	5 28
	25	4 22	11 20	25 2	24 36	1 47	12 34
	31	27♑55	• • •	6♈33	• • •	28♈55	• • •
♀	1	18♐25	27♑13	2♓14	10♈51	17♉58	26♊ 3
	9	28 26	7♒14	12 13	20 46	27 49	5♋51
	17	8♑26	17 14	22 12	0♉41	7♊40	15 37
	25	18 27	27 14	2♈ 9	10 34	17 29	25 22
♂	1	20♈27	7♉27	24♉ 1	12♊55	1♋25	16♋37
	13	26 47	14 28	0♊41	20 18	8 51	28 4
	25	3♉27	21 37	8 37	27 43	16 17	5♌33
♃	1	26♉41	26♉20	28♉42	3♊33	9♊39	16♊41
	13	26R10	27 4	0♊ 6	5 52	12 20	19 28
	25	26D 7	28 13	2 7	8 21	15 4	22 14
♄	1	5♑39	9♑ 9	11♑25	13♑33	13♑51	12♑43
	13	7 3	10 22	12 37	13 51	13R35	11R58
	25	8 24	11 26	13 13	13R55	13 5	11 8
♅	1	1♑47	3♑31	4♑41	5♑18	5♑ 7	4♑15
	13	2 29	4 4	5 1	5R19	4R51	3R47
	25	3 9	4 33	5 14	5 12	4 29	3 18
♆	1	9♑56	11♑ 4	11♑52	12♑20	12♑18	11♑47
	13	10 24	11 27	12 6	12 23	12R 9	11R30
	25	10 50	11 46	12 16	12R21	11 56	11 12
Pl.	1	14♏34	15♏ 7	15♏ 7	14♏39	13♏52	13♏ 2
☊	1	7♓45	6♓ 7	4♓37	2♓59	1♓24	29♒45
		SUN	WED	WED	SAT	MON	THU

	Noon	JUL	AUG	SEP	OCT	NOV	DEC
☉	1	9♋37	9♌12	9♍ 1	8♎17	9♏ 3	9♐16
	9	17 15	16 52	16 47	15 10	17 4	17 23
	17	24 54	24 33	24 34	24 5	25 7	25 31
	25	2♌31	1♍46	2♎23	2♏ 3	3♐11	3♑40
☿	1	21♊47	23♌48	5♎56	26♍17	3♏12	20♐43
	7	2♋52	4♍ 7	9 38	26D48	13 3	14 50
	13	15 18	13 29	10R24	2♎42	22 41	8♑58
	19	28 9	21 51	7 19	11 34	2♐ 9	16 58
	25	10♌31	29 9	1 12	21 28	11 28	23 55
	31	21 59	5♎ 6	• • •	1♏35	• • •	25♒50
♀	1	2♌40	10♍10	17♎ 5	21♏53	25♐56	23♑56
	9	12 23	19 45	26 29	1♐22	4♑17	29 33
	17	22 4	29 18	5♏48	9 49	11 52	3♒46
	25	1♍44	8♎18	15 2	18 31	19 2	6 6
♂	1	9♌17	28♌42	18♍22	7♎43	28♎11	18♏28
	13	16 47	5♍47	26 4	15 35	6♏14	26 44
	25	24 18	13 54	3♎49	23 31	14 22	5♐ 5
♃	1	23♊36	0♋18	5♋57	9♋39	10♋51	9♋ 3
	13	26 17	2 39	7 41	10 28	10R28	7R40
	25	28 52	4 48	9 5	10 51	9 37	6 5
♄	1	10♑41	8♑33	7♑22	7♑38	9♑21	12♑ 8
	13	9R48	7R57	7D18	8 8	10 22	13 27
	25	8 59	7 31	7 28	8 51	11 31	14 48
♅	1	3♑ 4	1♑57	1♑22	1♑31	2♑28	3♑57
	13	2R36	1R33	1R20	1 48	3 0	4 39
	25	2 10	1 26	1D26	2 12	3 38	5 22
♆	1	11♑ 2	10♑14	9♑42	9♑38	10♑ 4	10♑55
	13	10R42	9R59	9R37	9 44	10 22	11 20
	25	10 24	9 47	9D36	9 55	10 43	11 46
Pl.	1	12♏29	12♏23	12♏49	13♏41	14♏52	16♏ 3
☊	1	28♒10	26♒32	24♒53	23♒17	21♒39	20♒ 4
		SAT	TUE	FRI	SUN	WED	FRI

	d.	JAN	FEB	MAR	APR
☽	1	25♎11	10♐25	18♐39	7♒40
	3	19♏49	7♑10	15♑10	6♓22
	5	15♐47	5♒32	13♒21	6♈26
	7	13♑11	5♓ 1	13♓10	6♉48
	9	11♒39	4♈42	13♈28	6♊13
	11	10♓29	3♉39	12♉57	3♋51
	13	9♈ 5	31♊26	11♊18	29 40
	15	7♉ 9	27 58	7♋48	24♌ 9
	17	4♊30	23♋27	2♌55	17♍56
	19	1♋ 4	18♌ 5	27 9	11♎33
	21	26 47	12♍ 9	20♍55	5♏23
	23	21♌36	5♎51	14♎34	29 40
	25	15♍39	29 31	7♏78	24♐35
	27	9♎19	23♏37	2♐32	20♑20
	29	3♏ 6	• • •	27 39	17♒13
	31	27 40	• • •	23♑56	• • •

	d.	MAY	JUN	JUL	AUG
☽	1	15♓28	9♉11	17♊34	7♌ 8
	3	15♈ 0	8♊25	15♋ 9	2♍22
	5	15♉ 3	6♋43	11♌31	26 44
	7	14♊27	3♌28	6♍35	20♎33
	9	12♋14	28 41	0♎43	14♏21
	11	8♌11	22♍48	24 27	8♐43
	13	2♍43	16♎30	18♏29	4♑14
	15	26 29	10♏27	13♐21	1♒11
	17	20♎ 9	5♐ 7	9♑22	29 33
	19	14♏12	0♑43	6♒34	28♓46
	21	8♐55	27 13	4♓39	28♈ 2
	23	4♑21	24♒28	3♈ 9	26♉39
	25	0♒33	22♓18	1♉39	24♊13
	27	27 35	20♈37	29 49	20♋42
	29	25♓36	19♉11	27♊24	16♌14
	31	24♈30	• • •	24♋ 8	10♍57

	d.	SEP	OCT	NOV	DEC
☽	1	23♍ 4	25♎36	10♐20	14♑19
	3	16♎57	19♏19	4♑45	9♒50
	5	10♏40	13♐17	29 56	6♓18
	7	4♐37	7♑57	26♒23	4♈ 2
	9	29 23	3♒51	24♓29	3♉ 6
	11	25♑ 0	1♓27	24♈12	2♊56
	13	23♒20	0♈50	24♉42	2♋28
	15	22♓43	1♉20	24♊34	0♌40
	17	22♈51	1♊ 5	22♋46	27 6
	19	22♉32	0♋25	18♌61	22♍ 1
	21	20♊55	27 20	13♍46	16♎ 0
	23	17♋44	22♌40	7♎41	9♏43
	25	13♌13	16♍57	1♏22	3♐44
	27	7♍48	10♎45	25 14	28 21
	29	1♎50	4♏28	19♐30	23♑44
	31	• • •	28 18	• • •	19♒54

STATIONS	☿	♀	♂	♃
	17 JAN	30DEC	NONE	21JAN
	11♒54	6♒25		26♉ 5
	7FEB			30OCT
	26♑ 4			10♋53
	14MAY	♄	♅	♆
	6♊51	25APR	11APR	16APR
	6 JUN	13♑56	5♑20	12♑23
	28♉10	13SEP	11SEP	23SEP
	13SEP	7♑18	1♑10	9♑37
	10♎34	SIDER Pl. TIME		1 JAN
	5 OCT	6H 42M 30S		MIDN
	25♍44	18H 44M 28S		NOON
		COMMON YEAR		1989

Noon	JAN	FEB	MAR	APR	MAY	JUN
☉ 1	10♑49	12♒22	10♓38	11♈30	10♉51	10♊45
9	18 59	20 29	18 39	19 22	18 36	18 23
17	27 7	28 34	26 38	27 13	26 18	26 2
25	5♒15	6♓37	4♈35	5♉ 1	3♊ 1	3♋41
☿ 1	25♑38	17♑15	26♒18	24♈54	14♉47	16♉21
7	20R36	24 6	6♓32	5♉10	11R 5	23 23
13	13 6	1♒58	17 27	12 43	8 24	2♊17
19	9 45	10 36	29 2	16 48	8D 9	12 55
25	11D24	19 49	11 4	17R17	10 34	24 58
31	16 15	• • •	22 0	• • •	15 21	• • •
♀ 1	6♒13	21♑53	28♑31	25♒ 3	27♓ 2	2♉25
9	3R52	20D57	4♒13	3♓13	6♈ 0	11 44
17	29♑28	22 30	10 52	11 41	15 6	21 8
25	24 45	26 7	18 13	20 23	24 18	0♊35
♂ 1	10♐ 0	2♑ 6	22♑30	15♒29	7♓54	0♈53
13	18 30	10 48	0 81	24 26	16 51	9 36
25	27 4	19 34	9♒76	3♓25	25 44	18 10
♃ 1	5♋ 8	1♋41	0♋50	2♋48	7♋ 1	12♋55
13	3R35	1R 1	1 15	4 16	9 10	15 27
25	2 17	0 48	2 7	6 2	11 30	18 5
♄ 1	15♑39	19♑16	22♑ 9	24♑25	25♑19	24♑44
13	17 4	20 35	23 10	24 58	25R16	24R 8
25	18 28	21 47	24 2	25 15	24 30	23 24
♅ 1	5♑47	7♑33	8♑48	9♑31	9♑27	8♑40
13	6 30	8 8	9 10	9 35	9R14	8R14
25	7 10	8 39	9 25	9R31	8 54	7 45
♆ 1	12♑ 2	13♑11	14♑ 0	14♑31	14♑31	14♑ 2
13	12 30	13 34	14 15	14 34	14R23	13R46
25	12 54	13 54	14 26	14R33	14 11	13 27
Pl. 1	17♏ 5	17♏41	17♏45	17♏18	16♏33	15♏43
☊ 1	18♒25	16♒47	15♒18	13♒39	12♒ 4	10♒25
	MON	THU	THU	SUN	TUE	FRI

Noon	JUL	AUG	SEP	OCT	NOV	DEC
☉ 1	9♋23	8♌59	8♍48	8♎ 3	8♏48	9♐ 0
9	17 20	16 38	16 33	15 56	16 49	17 8
17	24 39	24 39	24 0	23 51	24 52	25 16
25	2♌17	2♍20	2♎ 9	1♏49	2♐57	3♑25
☿ 1	7♋54	4♍14	21♍10	22♍54	15♏16	29♐21
7	20 19	11 43	15R54	3♎ 4	24 38	6♑ 5
13	2♌27	17 46	10 49	13 37	3♐47	9 49
19	14 2	21 56	9D55	24 0	12 42	7R58
25	24 0	23 33	14 27	4♏ 1	21 19	15 36
31	2♍52	21R49	• • •	13 41	• • •	24♐34
♀ 1	7♊42	14♋54	22♌47	15♍ 4	8♏46	16♐26
9	16 2	23 24	2♍40	9♎58	18 48	26 29
17	26 49	4♌22	12 34	19 58	28 51	8♑31
25	6♋26	14 11	22 31	15 0	8♐54	16 34
♂ 1	22♈22	12♉57	0♊30	12♊ 1	13♊33	3♊59
13	0♉36	20 13	5 57	14 10	10R32	0R12
25	8 31	26 55	10 20	14R23	6 13	28♉ 5
♃ 1	19♋25	26♋20	2♌56	8♌23	12♌17	13♌35
13	22 6	28 58	5 15	10 9	13 8	13R18
25	24 34	1♌30	7 24	11 36	13 33	12 33
♄ 1	22♑59	20♑44	19♑ 5	18♑45	19♑57	22♑22
13	22R 6	19R58	18R47	19 2	20 47	23 35
25	21 13	19 21	18D42	19 33	21 48	24 55
♅ 1	7♑31	6♑21	5♑20	5♑43	6♑33	7♑57
13	7R 2	6R 1	5R36	5 29	7 3	8 38
25	6 35	5 45	5D39	6 18	7 38	9 20
♆ 1	13♑17	12♑29	11♑56	11♑49	12♑12	13♑ 1
13	12R58	12R13	11R49	11 54	12 29	13 26
25	12 39	12 0	11D48	12 4	12 50	13 52
Pl. 1	15♏ 7	14♏58	15♏21	16♏11	17♏21	18♏33
☊ 1	8♒50	7♒12	5♒33	3♒58	2♒19	0♒44
	SUN	WED	SAT	MON	THU	SAT

d.	JAN	FEB	MAR	APR
☽ 1	3♓16	25♈34	6♉12	29♊27
3	0♈37	23♉57	4♊55	26♋43
5	28 47	22♊ 9	2♋47	22♌43
7	27♉28	19♋53	29 44	17♍48
9	26♊27	16♌45	25♌48	12♎16
11	24♋45	12♍44	21♍ 6	6♏18
13	21♌48	7♎33	15♎42	0♐ 5
15	17♍27	1♏43	9♏43	23 53
17	11♎56	25 28	3♐29	18♑ 8
19	5♏47	19♐31	27 28	13♒25
21	29 38	14♑25	22♑16	10♓24
23	24♐ 5	10♒10	18♒30	9♈16
25	19♑27	8♓20	16♓30	9♉30
27	15♒55	7♈ 5	15♈57	9♊53
29	13♓21	• • •	15♉56	9♋ 5
31	11♈20	• • •	15♊16	

d.	MAY	JUN	JUL	AUG
☽ 1	6♌33	24♍ 4	26♎58	10♐54
3	2♍25	18♎21	20♏47	5♑ 0
5	27 11	12♏11	14♐36	29 51
7	21♎20	5♐56	8♑48	25♒40
9	15♏10	29 59	3♒36	22♓28
11	8♐56	24♑ 3	29 12	20♈ 6
13	2♑49	19♒18	25♓43	18♉19
15	27 10	15♓23	23♈16	16♊48
17	22♒28	12♈52	21♉48	15♋13
19	19♓14	11♉49	20♊59	13♌14
21	17♈48	11♊44	20♋ 6	10♍14
23	17♉53	11♋35	18♌23	6♎10
25	18♊21	10♌15	15♍17	1♏ 0
27	17♋51	7♍14	10♎46	25 3
29	15♌36	2♎38	5♏ 9	18♐49
31	11♍35	• • •	29 0	12♑59

d.	SEP	OCT	NOV	DEC
☽ 1	25♑23	29♒ 5	19♈10	27♉13
3	21♒ 6	26♓39	19♉10	27♊46
5	18♓ 9	25♈38	19♊22	27♋31
7	16♈19	25♉11	18♋34	25♌37
9	15♉ 0	24♊18	16♌13	22♍ 0
11	13♊34	22♋23	12♍28	17♎ 3
13	11♋40	19♌22	7♎40	11♏16
15	9♌ 6	15♍25	2♏10	5♐ 3
17	5♍51	10♎43	26 10	28 43
19	1♎46	5♏21	19♐53	22♑30
21	26 50	29 24	13♑32	16♒42
23	21♏ 6	23♐ 5	7♒30	11♓43
25	14♐52	16♑48	2♓24	7♈59
27	8♑40	11♒12	28 50	5 54
29	3♒12	7♓ 0	27♈12	5♊22
31	• • •	4♈38	• • •	5♋38

STATIONS

☿	♀	♂	♃
1 JAN	9 FEB	22OCT	26FEB
25♑48	20♑55	14♊34	0♋48
21JAN			1 DEC
9♑42			13♌36
24APR	♄	♅	♆
17♉30	6 MAY	15APR	18APR
18MAY	25♑20	9♑35	14♑35
7♉55	25SEP	17SEP	17SEP
27AUG	18♑42	5♑36	5♑36
23♍28	SIDER. TIME		1 JAN
19SEP	6H 41M 33S		MIDN
9♍37	18H 43M 31S		NOON
16DEC	COMMON YEAR		1990
10♑ 0			

THE STELLAR ZODIAC

The "tropical" or "moving" or "equinox" zodiac is the one that now, as for centuries past, is almost unanimously used for astrology, except in India. It begins at the vernal equinox, so that positions given in an ephemeris or table of houses (which use the tropical zodiac) correspond exactly to geocentric celestial longitude as understood by astronomers.

But the vernal equinox moves round a circle among the "fixed" or remote, stars in about 26,000 years, in reverse direction of the signs. Thus, after a sufficient length of time, a different sign of this zodiac will cover any given group of stars.

A very few leading European astrologers in modern times prefer to use the stellar, or fixed, or sidereal, zodiac, the traditional zodiac in Hindu astrology. This begins at a particular point among the fixed stars, so that each sign of this stellar zodiac will always cover the same part of the "remote star-pattern". The two zodiacs, of course, coincided at some past date. Exactly when, is much disputed. The difference between the two zodiacs increases at the rate of (roughly) a degree every 72 years. The rate, that is the "precession of the equinoxes", is not in dispute. But the distance from (for example) 0° of Aries in the tropical zodiac to 0° of Aries in the stellar zodiac, at a given date, depends on an extremely controversial estimate of the date when both zodiacs in reality were the same. The difference between them at any given date is called the "ayanamsa" for that date. Various authorities differ by some four or five degrees on the amount of this ayanamsa. About the greatest value assigned to it is that which is the result of considering the star Spica Virginis as 0~0. This is the majority view among Hindu authorities. Dr. V. B. Raman, the Hindu writer of the present day best known to English readers, adopts an "average" ayanamsa of about 3° less. Mr. Cyril Fagan, leading European authority on the subject, as a result of much scholarly, and original, research in astronomical archaeology, now regards as corresponding to 29~0 the same star, Spica Virginis.

The ayanamsa for each year from 1870 to 1960, inclusive, given in the table below, is based on Mr Fagan's reckoning. It ignores the small amount of precession during a single year, but, for any reader wishing to experiment with the stellar zodiac, will give a result as close as consistent with the use of condensed ephemeris and tables of houses. After casting the horoscope, simply deduct the ayanamsa from every zodiacal longitude; cusps of houses, and positions of planets etc., alike. For Dr. Raman's ayanamsa, take 2°28' from the ayanamsa given in the table below, for any date.

TABLE OF AYANAMSA

year	°	'	year	°	'	year	°	'	year	°	'	year	°	'	year	°	'	year	°	'
1885	23	14	1900	23	27	1915	23	39	1930	23	52	1945	24	4	1960	24	17	1975	24	29
1886	23	15	1901	23	28	1916	23	40	1931	23	53	1946	24	5	1961	24	18	1976	24	30
1887	23	16	1902	23	29	1917	23	41	1932	23	54	1947	24	6	1962	24	18	1977	24	31
1888	23	17	1903	23	29	1918	23	42	1933	23	54	1948	24	7	1963	24	19	1978	24	32
1889	23	18	1904	23	30	1919	23	43	1934	23	55	1949	24	8	1964	24	20	1979	24	32
1890	23	18	1905	23	31	1920	23	44	1935	23	56	1950	24	9	1965	24	21	1980	24	33
1891	23	19	1906	23	32	1921	23	44	1936	23	57	1951	24	9	1966	24	22	1981	24	34
1892	23	20	1907	23	33	1922	23	45	1937	23	58	1952	24	10	1967	24	23	1982	24	35
1893	23	21	1908	23	33	1923	23	46	1938	23	59	1953	24	11	1968	24	23	1983	24	36
1894	23	22	1909	23	34	1924	23	47	1939	23	59	1954	24	12	1969	24	24	1984	24	37
1895	23	23	1910	23	35	1925	23	48	1940	24	0	1955	24	13	1970	24	25	1985	24	37
1896	23	23	1911	23	36	1926	23	49	1941	24	1	1956	24	14	1971	24	26	1986	24	38
1897	23	24	1912	23	37	1927	23	49	1942	24	2	1957	24	14	1972	24	27	1987	24	39
1898	23	25	1913	23	38	1928	23	50	1943	24	3	1958	24	15	1973	24	27	1988	24	40
1899	23	26	1914	23	38	1929	23	51	1944	24	4	1959	24	16	1974	24	28	1989	24	41
1900	23	27	1915	23	39	1930	23	52	1945	24	4	1960	24	17	1975	24	29	1990	24	41

according to all current systems of house—division
for all geographical latitudes from 0° to 60° north

Ascendant and M.C. in degrees and minutes, for all systems; intermediate cusps for the Regiomontanus and Campanus and Placidus systems and for Natural Graduation, in whole degrees (not needed for using the Porphyry and Equal House Systems).

NOTE

When the sign changes in a column, the new sign is given, for Asc. or M.C., between the degrees and the minutes, as: 4♌23— but in the case of an intermediate cusp (11, 12, 2, or 3) the new sign is given before the degrees, as: ♌4 (the same as 4♌0) which may not so readily catch the eye. Therefore great care must be taken always to cast the eye up the column to be sure where the sign last changed before the entry wanted.

ZERO LATITUDE

THE M.C.: this, being the same at all latitudes, may be taken from a table for any other latitude.

THE ASCENDANT: at latitude 0° this is always the same as the M.C. at sidereal time 6h. later (or 18h. earlier).

INTERMEDIATE CUSPS (11, 12, 2, 3): in the systems of Regiomontanus, Campanus, and Placidus, which are all alike at lat. 0°, cusps 11, 12, 2, and 3, respectively, are the same as the M.C. at sidereal times later by 2h., 4h., 8h., 10h., respectively, or earlier by 22h., 20h., 16h., 14h., respectively. In the Natural Graduation system they are as shown below.

0° Lat.   Natural Graduation Intermediate Cusps

Sid. Time h m	11 ♉	12 Ⅱ	2 ♌	3 ♍	Sid. Time h m	11 ♍	12 ♎	2 ♐	3 ♐	Sid. Time h m	11 ♈	12 ♈	2 ♓	3 ♉
0 0	0	0	0	0	8 0	29	1	1	29	16 0	1	29	29	1
0 24	6	6	6	6	8 24	♎5	7	7	♑5	16 24	7	♒5	♈5	7
0 48	13	12	12	13	8 48	11	13	13	11	16 48	13	11	11	13
1 12	19	17	17	19	9 12	17	19	19	17	17 12	19	17	17	19
1 36	25	23	23	25	9 36	23	25	25	23	17 36	24	24	24	24
2 0	♉1	29	29	♎1	10 0	29	♏1	♑1	29	18 0	♒0	♈0	♉0	Ⅱ0
2 24	7	♍5	♍5	7	10 24	♏5	7	7	♑5	18 24	6	6	6	6
2 48	13	11	11	13	10 48	11	13	13	11	18 48	12	13	13	12
3 12	19	17	17	19	11 12	17	19	19	17	19 12	17	19	19	17
3 36	24	24	24	24	11 36	24	23	23	25	19 36	23	25	25	23
4 0	♊1	29	29	♏1	12 0	♏0	♐0	♑0	♑0	20 0	29	♈1	Ⅱ1	29
4 24	7	♌5	♎5	7	12 24	6	6	6	6	20 24	♓5	7	7	♋5
4 48	13	11	11	13	12 48	12	13	13	12	20 48	11	13	13	11
5 12	19	17	17	19	13 12	19	17	17	19	21 12	17	19	19	17
5 36	24	24	24	24	13 36	25	23	23	25	21 36	23	25	25	23
6 0	♌0	♍0	♍0	♐0	14 0	♐1	29	29	♓1	22 0	29	♉1	♋1	29
6 24	6	6	6	6	14 24	7	♑5	♓5	7	22 24	♈5	7	7	♌5
6 48	12	13	13	12	14 48	13	11	11	13	22 48	11	13	13	11
7 12	17	19	19	17	15 12	19	17	17	19	23 12	17	19	19	17
7 36	23	25	25	23	15 36	25	23	23	25	23 36	24	24	24	24
8 0	29	♎1	♐1	29	16 0	♑1	29	29	♉1	24 0	♉0	Ⅱ0	♌0	♍0

10° N. Lat. — Cusps of Houses — 0h. – 12h.

Sid. Time h. m.	M.C. long. ♈	Asc. 1 ♊	REG. 11 ♉	12 Ⅱ	2 ♌	3 ♍	CAMP. 11 ♉	12 Ⅱ	2 ♌	3 ♍	PLAC. 11 ♉	12 Ⅱ	2 ♌	3 ♍	NAT.GR. 11 ♉	12 Ⅱ	2 ♌	3 ♍
0 0	0 0	4 1	3	5	0	29	3	5	1	29	3	5	0	29	1	3	3	1
0 12	3 16	6 45	7	8	4	♍2	6	8	4	♍2	6	7	3	♍2	4	6	6	4
0 24	6 32	9 29	10	11	7	5	9	10	7	5	9	10	6	5	7	9	9	7
0 36	9 48	12 12	13	14	10	8	12	13	10	9	12	13	9	8	10	12	12	10
0 48	13 3	14 56	16	17	12	11	15	16	12	12	15	16	12	11	13	15	15	13
1 0	16 17	17 40	19	20	15	14	19	19	15	15	19	19	15	14	17	17	17	17
1 12	19 30	20 24	22	23	18	17	22	22	18	18	22	22	17	17	20	20	20	20
1 24	22 42	23 8	25	25	21	21	25	25	21	21	25	24	20	20	23	23	23	23
1 36	25 53	25 53	28	28	24	24	28	28	24	24	27	27	23	24	26	26	26	26
1 48	29 3	28 39	Ⅱ1	♋1	27	27	Ⅱ1	♋1	27	27	Ⅱ0	♋0	27	27	29	29	29	29
2 0	2♉11	1♋25	4	4	♍0	♎0	4	3	♍0	♎0	3	3	29	♎0	Ⅱ2	♋2	♍2	♎2
2 12	5 18	4 12	7	7	3	3	6	6	3	3	6	5	♍2	3	5	4	4	5
2 24	8 23	6 59	10	9	6	6	9	8	6	7	9	8	5	6	8	7	7	8
2 36	11 26	9 48	13	12	9	9	12	11	9	10	12	11	8	10	11	10	10	11
2 48	14 28	12 38	15	14	12	11	15	14	12	13	15	14	11	13	14	13	13	14
3 0	17 29	15 28	18	17	15	16	18	17	15	16	18	16	14	16	17	16	16	17
3 12	20 26	18 20	21	20	18	19	21	19	18	19	20	19	18	19	20	19	19	20
3 24	23 23	21 13	24	23	21	22	23	22	21	22	23	22	21	22	23	22	22	23
3 36	26 19	24 7	26	26	24	25	26	25	24	25	26	25	24	25	26	25	25	26
3 48	29 13	27 2	29	28	27	28	29	28	27	29	29	28	27	28	29	28	28	29
4 0	2Ⅱ5	29 58	♋2	♌0	♎0	♏1	♋2	♌1	♎0	♏1	♋1	♌0	♎0	♏1	♋2	♌0	♎0	♏2
4 12	4 57	2♌55	5	3	3	4	4	3	4	4	4	3	4	3	5	3	3	5
4 24	7 47	5 33	8	6	6	6	7	6	7	7	7	6	6	8	7	6	6	7
4 36	10 36	8 52	10	9	9	9	10	9	10	10	10	9	9	11	10	9	9	10
4 48	13 24	11 51	13	12	12	13	13	12	13	13	12	12	12	13	13	12	12	13
5 0	16 11	14 51	16	15	15	16	15	15	16	16	15	15	16	16	16	15	15	16
5 12	18 58	17 56	19	18	18	19	18	17	19	19	18	17	19	19	19	18	18	19
5 24	21 44	20 54	21	21	21	22	21	20	22	22	21	20	22	22	22	21	21	22
5 36	24 30	23 56	24	24	24	25	24	23	25	25	23	23	25	25	24	24	24	24
5 48	27 15	26 56	27	27	27	28	27	26	28	28	26	26	28	28	27	27	27	27
6 0	0♋0	0♎0	♌1	♍0	♏0	♐0	29	29	♏1	♐1	29	29	♏1	♐1	♌0	♍0	♏0	♐0
6 12	2 45	3 2	4	3	3	3	♌2	♍2	4	3	♌2	♍2	4	4	3	3	3	3
6 24	5 30	6 4	6	6	6	6	5	5	6	5	5	5	6	7	6	6	6	5
6 36	8 16	9 1	9	9	9	8	8	9	9	9	8	8	10	9	8	9	9	8
6 48	11 2	12 8	12	12	12	11	11	11	12	12	11	11	13	12	11	12	12	11
7 0	13 49	15 9	14	15	15	14	14	14	15	15	14	14	15	15	14	15	15	14
7 12	16 36	18 9	17	18	18	17	17	17	18	17	17	18	18	18	17	18	18	16
7 24	19 24	21 8	20	21	21	20	20	20	21	20	19	21	21	20	20	21	22	19
7 36	22 13	24 7	23	24	23	22	23	23	24	23	22	24	24	23	23	24	25	22
7 48	25 3	27 5	26	27	26	25	26	27	27	26	26	27	27	26	25	27	28	25
8 0	27 55	0♏2	29	♎0	29	28	29	♎0	♐0	29	28	♎0	♐0	29	28	♎0	♐0	27
8 12	0♌47	2 58	♏2	3	♐2	♑1	♏2	3	2	♑1	♏2	3	3	♑1	♏1	2	3	♑0
8 24	3 41	5 53	5	6	5	3	5	6	5	4	5	6	5	4	4	5	5	3
8 36	6 37	8 47	8	9	7	6	8	9	7	6	8	9	8	7	7	8	8	6
8 48	9 34	11 40	11	12	10	8	11	12	11	9	11	12	11	10	10	11	11	9
9 0	12 31	14 32	14	15	13	12	14	15	13	12	13	14	13	12	13	14	14	12
9 12	15 32	17 22	17	18	16	15	17	18	16	15	17	19	16	15	16	17	17	15
9 24	18 34	20 12	21	21	18	18	20	21	19	18	20	22	19	18	19	20	20	18
9 36	21 37	23 1	24	24	21	20	23	24	21	20	24	25	22	21	22	23	23	21
9 48	24 42	25 48	27	27	24	23	26	27	24	23	27	28	25	24	25	25	26	25
10 0	27 49	28 35	♎0	♏0	27	26	♎0	♏0	27	26	♎0	♏1	27	27	28	28	28	28
10 12	0♍57	1♏21	3	3	29	29	3	3	♑0	29	3	4	♑0	♐0	♎1	♏1	♑1	♐1
10 24	4 7	4 7	6	6	♑2	♐2	6	6	3	♐2	6	7	3	3	4	4	4	4
10 36	7 18	6 52	9	9	5	5	9	8	6	5	10	9	5	5	7	7	7	7
10 48	10 30	9 36	11	12	8	8	12	11	8	8	13	13	8	8	10	10	10	10
11 0	13 43	12 20	16	15	10	11	15	15	11	11	16	16	11	11	13	13	12	13
11 12	16 57	15 4	19	18	13	14	18	17	14	14	19	18	14	15	17	15	15	17
11 24	20 12	17 48	22	21	16	17	21	20	16	18	22	21	17	18	20	18	18	20
11 36	23 28	20 31	25	23	19	20	25	23	19	21	25	24	20	21	23	21	21	23
11 48	26 44	23 15	28	26	22	23	28	25	22	24	28	27	23	24	26	24	24	26
12 0	0♎0	25 59	♏1	29	25	27	♏1	28	25	27	♏2	♐0	25	27	29	27	27	29

206

10° N. Lat. Cusps of Houses 12h. – 24h.

Sid. Time	M.C. long.	Asc. 1	REGIOMONTA. 11	12	2	3	CAMPANUS 11	12	2	3	PLACIDUS 11	12	2	3	NAT. GRAD. 11	12	2	3
h m	≏	♐	♏	♐	♑	≈	♏	♐	♑	≈	♏	♐	♑	≈	≏	♏	♐	≈
12 0	0 0	25 59	1 29 25 27				1 28 25 27				2 0 25 26				29 27 27 29			
12 12	3 16	28 44	3 ♐2 28 ⋊0				4 ♐1 28 ⋊0				4 3 28 ⋊0				♏3 ♐0 ≈0 ⋊2			
12 24	6 32	1♍29	6 5 ≈1 3				7 4 ≈1 4				8 5 ≈1 3				5 3 3 5			
12 36	9 48	4 15	9 7 4 6				10 7 5 7				11 8 4 7				9 5 5 9			
12 48	13 3	7 2	13 10 7 10				13 10 8 10				13 11 7 10				12 8 8 12			
13 0	16 17	9 50	16 13 10 13				16 13 11 14				16 14 10 13				15 11 11 15			
13 12	19 30	12 29	19 16 13 16				19 15 14 17				19 16 14 17				18 14 14 18			
13 24	22 42	15 29	22 18 16 20				21 18 17 20				22 19 17 20				21 17 17 21			
13 36	25 53	18 21	25 21 19 23				24 21 20 24				25 22 20 23				28 20 20 24			
13 48	29 3	21 15	28 24 23 27				27 23 23 27				28 25 23 27				27 23 23 27			
14 00	2♏11	24 10	♏0 27 26 ♈0				♏0 26 26 ♈0				♏1 27 26 ♈0				♏0 26 26 ♈0			
14 12	5 18	27 7	3 29 29 3				3 29 29 4				4 ♐0 29 3				3 29 29 4			
14 24	8 23	0≈6	6 ♑2 ⋊2 7				6 ♑2 ⋊3 7				7 3 ⋊3 7				6 ♑2 ⋊2 7			
14 36	11 26	3 8	9 5 6 10				8 5 6 11				9 6 6 10				10 5 5 10			
14 48	14 28	6 12	11 8 9 14				11 8 10 14				12 8 9 13				13 8 8 13			
15 0	17 28	9 18	14 10 13 17				14 11 13 17				15 11 13 17				16 11 11 16			
15 12	20 26	12 26	17 13 16 20				17 14 17 21				18 14 16 20				19 14 14 19			
15 24	23 23	15 37	20 16 20 24				19 16 20 24				20 17 20 23				22 17 17 22			
15 36	26 19	18 50	22 19 23 27				22 19 24 27				23 20 23 27				25 21 20 25			
15 48	29 13	22 5	25 22 26 ♋0				25 22 27 ♋0				26 23 27 ♋0				28 24 24 28			
16 0	2♐5	25 23	28 25 ♈0 3				28 24 ♈0 4				29 25 ♈0 3				♏1 27 27 ♏1			
16 12	4 57	28 43	♐1 28 4 7				♑0 27 4 7				♑2 28 3 6				3 ♈0 ♈0 3			
16 24	7 47	2⋊6	3 ≈1 7 10				3 ≈1 7 10				4 ≈1 7 9				6 3 4 7			
16 36	10 37	5 30	6 4 10 13				6 4 11 13				7 4 10 12				9 7 7 10			
16 48	13 24	8 56	8 7 14 16				9 7 14 16				10 7 14 15				12 10 10 12			
17 0	16 11	12 24	12 10 17 19				12 10 18 19				12 10 17 19				15 13 13 15			
17 12	18 58	15 54	15 13 21 22				14 13 21 22				15 14 21 22				18 15 17 18			
17 24	21 44	19 24	18 16 24 25				17 16 25 25				18 17 24 25				21 20 20 21			
17 36	24 30	22 56	20 19 28 28				20 19 28 28				21 20 27 27				24 23 24 24			
17 48	27 15	26 28	23 23 ♋1 ♍1				23 22 ♋1 ♍0				24 23 ♋1 ♍0				27 27 27 27			
18 0	0♑0	0♈0	26 26 4 4				26 25 5 4				27 26 4 3				♍0 ♈0 ♋0 ♍0			
18 12	2 45	3 32	29 29 7 7				29 29 8 7				≈0 29 7 6				3 3 3 3			
18 24	5 30	7 4	≈2 ⋊2 11 10				≈2 ⋊2 11 10				3 ⋊3 10 9				6 6 7 6			
18 36	8 16	10 36	5 6 14 13				5 6 14 13				5 6 13 12				9 9 10 9			
18 48	11 2	14 7	8 9 17 15				8 9 17 16				8 9 16 15				12 13 13 12			
19 0	13 45	17 36	11 13 20 18				11 13 21 19				11 13 20 18				15 16 17 15			
19 12	16 36	21 4	14 16 23 21				14 16 24 21				15 16 23 20				18 20 20 18			
19 24	19 23	24 30	17 20 26 24				17 19 27 24				18 20 26 23				21 23 23 21			
19 36	22 13	27 54	20 23 29 26				20 23 ♍0 26				21 23 29 26				23 27 27 24			
19 48	25 3	1♍17	23 26 ♍2 29				23 26 3 29				24 27 ♍2 29				27 ♈0 ♍0 27			
20 0	27 55	4 37	27 ♈0 5 ♌2				26 ♈0 6 ♌2				27 ♈0 5 ♋1				29 3 3 29			
20 12	0≈47	7 55	⋊0 4 8 5				⋊0 3 9 5				⋊0 3 7 4				⋊2 6 6 ♌2			
20 24	3 41	11 10	3 7 11 8				3 7 12 8				3 7 10 7				5 10 9 5			
20 36	6 37	14 23	6 10 14 10				7 10 14 10				7 10 13 10				8 13 13 8			
20 48	9 34	17 34	10 14 17 13				10 14 17 13				10 14 16 12				11 16 16 11			
21 0	12 32	20 43	13 17 20 16				13 17 20 16				13 17 19 15				14 19 19 14			
21 12	15 32	23 49	16 21 23 19				16 20 23 19				17 21 22 18				17 22 22 17			
21 24	18 34	26 52	20 24 25 21				19 24 26 22				20 24 24 21				20 25 25 21			
21 36	21 37	29 54	23 28 28 24				23 27 28 24				23 27 27 23				23 28 28 24			
21 48	24 42	2♍3	27 ♐1 ♌1 27				26 ♐0 ♌1 27				27 ♐1 ♌0 26				26 ♐1 ♌1 27			
22 0	27 49	5 51	♈0 4 4 ♍1				♈0 4 4 ♍0				♈0 4 3 29				29 4 4 ♍0			
22 12	0⋊57	8 46	3 7 7 4				3 7 7 3				3 7 5 ♌2				♈2 7 7 3			
22 24	4 7	11 39	7 11 9 6				6 10 9 6				7 10 8 5				6 10 10 6			
22 36	7 18	14 31	10 14 12 9				10 13 12 8				10 13 11 8				9 13 13 9			
22 48	10 30	17 21	14 17 14 12				13 16 15 11				13 16 14 11				12 16 16 12			
23 0	13 43	20 10	17 20 17 14				16 20 17 14				17 20 16 14				15 19 19 15			
23 12	16 57	22 58	20 23 20 17				20 23 20 17				20 23 19 17				18 22 22 18			
23 24	20 12	25 45	24 26 23 20				23 26 23 20				23 26 22 19				21 24 24 22			
23 36	23 28	28 31	27 29 26 23				26 29 25 23				27 29 25 22				25 27 27 25			
23 48	26 44	1≈16	♉0 ♊2 28 26				28 ♊2 28 26				♉0 ♊2 27 26				28 ♊0 ♌0 28			
24 0	0♈0	4 1	3 5 ♌0 29				♉3 5 ♌1 29				3 5 ♌0 29				♉1 3 3 ♊1			

Sid. Time h m	M.C. long.	Asc. 1	REGIOMONTA. 11	12	2	3	CAMPANUS 11	12	2	3	PLACIDUS 11	12	2	3	NAT. GRAD. 11	12	2	3
0 0	0 0	8 14	5	9	4	0	3	7	5	2	4	7	3	29	2	6	6	2
0 12	3 16	10 56	8	12	7	3	6	10	8	5	7	10	5	♏2	5	9	9	5
0 24	6 32	13 36	11	15	9	6	9	13	11	8	10	13	8	5	8	12	12	8
0 36	9 48	16 16	15	18	12	9	13	16	13	10	13	16	11	8	11	15	15	8
0 48	13 3	18 56	18	21	15	12	16	19	16	13	17	19	14	11	14	18	18	14
1 0	16 17	21 36	21	23	18	15	19	22	19	16	20	22	17	15	17	20	20	17
1 12	19 30	24 15	24	26	20	18	22	25	22	19	23	25	19	18	21	23	23	21
1 24	22 42	26 54	27	29	23	21	25	27	24	22	26	27	22	21	24	26	26	24
1 36	25 53	29 13	♊0	♋2	26	24	28	♋0	27	25	29	♋0	25	24	27	28	28	27
1 48	29 3	2♋12	3	4	29	27	♊1	3	♍0	28	♊2	3	28	27	♊0	♋1	♋1	♍0
2 0	2♊11	4 52	6	7	♍1	♎0	4	6	3	♎2	5	6	♏1	♎0	3	4	4	3
2 12	5 18	7 32	9	10	4	3	7	8	6	5	8	8	4	3	6	7	7	6
2 24	8 23	10 13	12	13	7	6	10	11	8	8	10	11	6	6	9	10	10	9
2 36	11 26	12 54	15	15	10	9	13	14	11	11	13	14	9	9	12	13	13	12
2 48	14 28	15 36	18	18	13	12	16	16	14	14	16	16	12	12	15	15	15	15
3 0	17 29	18 18	20	20	16	15	19	19	17	17	19	19	15	15	18	18	18	18
3 12	20 26	21 1	23	23	19	18	22	22	20	20	22	22	18	19	20	21	21	20
3 24	23 23	23 44	26	26	21	21	24	24	23	23	25	25	21	22	23	24	24	23
3 36	26 19	26 28	29	29	24	24	27	27	26	26	27	27	24	25	26	26	26	26
3 48	29 13	29 13	♍1	♍1	27	27	♌0	♍0	29	29	♌1	♍0	27	28	29	29	29	29
4 0	2♌5	1♍58	4	4	♎0	♏0	3	3	♎2	♏2	3	3	♎0	♏1	♌2	♍2	♎2	♏2
4 12	4 57	4 44	7	7	3	3	5	5	4	4	6	5	3	4	5	5	5	5
4 24	7 47	7 31	10	9	6	6	8	8	7	7	8	8	6	7	8	8	8	8
4 36	10 36	10 18	13	12	9	9	11	11	10	10	11	11	9	10	11	10	10	11
4 48	13 24	13 6	16	15	11	12	14	13	13	13	14	14	12	13	13	13	13	13
5 0	16 11	15 54	18	18	14	14	16	16	16	16	16	17	15	15	16	16	16	16
5 12	18 58	18 43	21	20	17	17	19	19	19	19	19	19	18	18	19	19	19	19
5 24	21 44	21 32	23	23	20	20	22	22	22	22	22	22	21	21	22	22	22	22
5 36	24 30	24 21	26	26	23	23	24	24	24	24	25	25	24	24	24	24	24	24
5 48	27 15	27 11	29	29	26	26	27	27	27	27	28	28	26	27	27	27	27	27
6 0	0♎0	0♎0	♎2	♏1	29	28	♎0	♏0	♏0	♐0	♎0	♏1	29	♐0	♎0	♏0	♏0	♐0
6 12	2 45	2 49	4	4	♏1	♐1	3	3	3	3	3	4	2	3	3	3	3	3
6 24	5 30	5 39	7	7	4	4	6	6	5	5	6	6	5	5	6	6	6	6
6 36	8 16	8 28	10	10	7	7	8	8	8	8	9	9	8	8	8	8	8	8
6 48	11 2	11 17	13	13	10	9	11	11	11	11	12	12	11	11	11	11	11	11
7 0	13 49	14 6	16	16	12	12	14	14	14	14	15	15	13	14	14	14	14	14
7 12	16 36	16 54	18	19	15	15	17	17	17	16	17	18	16	16	17	17	17	17
7 24	19 24	19 42	21	21	18	17	20	20	19	19	20	20	19	19	19	20	20	19
7 36	22 13	22 29	24	24	21	20	23	23	22	22	23	24	22	22	22	22	22	22
7 48	26 3	26 16	27	27	23	23	26	26	25	25	26	27	25	24	25	25	25	25
8 0	27 55	28 2	♏0	♎0	26	26	28	29	28	27	29	♏0	27	27	28	28	28	28
8 12	0♏47	0♏47	3	3	29	29	♏1	♎1	♐1	♑0	♏2	3	♐0	♑0	♏1	♎1	♐1	♑1
8 24	3 41	3 32	6	6	♐1	♑1	4	4	4	3	5	6	3	3	4	4	4	4
8 36	6 37	6 16	9	9	4	4	7	7	6	6	8	9	5	6	6	6	6	6
8 48	9 34	8 59	12	11	7	7	10	10	9	8	11	12	8	8	9	9	9	9
9 0	12 31	11 42	15	14	10	10	13	13	12	11	15	15	11	11	12	12	12	12
9 12	15 32	14 24	18	17	12	12	16	16	14	14	18	18	14	14	15	15	15	15
9 24	18 34	17 6	21	20	15	15	19	19	17	17	21	21	16	17	18	17	17	18
9 36	21 37	19 47	24	23	17	18	22	22	20	20	24	24	19	20	21	20	20	21
9 48	24 42	22 28	27	26	20	21	26	24	23	23	27	26	22	22	24	23	23	24
10 0	27 49	25 8	♐0	29	23	24	28	27	25	26	♐0	29	24	25	27	26	26	27
10 12	0♐57	27 48	3	♏1	26	27	♐2	♏0	28	27	3	♏2	27	28	♐0	29	28	♑0
10 24	4 7	0♐27	6	4	28	♑0	5	3	♑1	♒2	6	5	♑0	♒1	3	♏1	♑1	3
10 36	7 18	3 6	9	7	♑1	3	8	6	3	5	9	8	3	4	6	4	4	6
10 48	10 30	5 45	12	10	4	6	11	8	5	8	12	11	5	7	9	7	7	9
11 0	13 43	8 24	15	12	7	9	14	11	8	11	15	13	8	10	12	10	10	12
11 12	16 57	11 4	18	15	9	12	17	14	11	14	19	16	11	13	16	12	12	16
11 24	20 12	13 44	21	18	12	15	20	17	14	17	22	19	14	17	19	15	15	19
11 36	23 28	16 24	24	21	15	19	23	19	17	20	25	22	17	20	22	18	18	22
11 48	26 44	19 3	27	23	18	22	24	22	20	24	28	25	20	23	25	21	21	25
12 0	0♑0	21 46	♑0	26	21	25	29	25	23	27	♑1	27	23	26	28	24	24	28

SID. TIME	M.C. long.	Asc.	REGIOMONTA. 11	12	2	3	CAMPANUS 11	12	2	3	PLACIDUS 11	12	2	3	NAT. GRAD. 11	12	2	3
h m	♎	♐	♏	♏	♑	♒	♎	♏	♑	♒	♏	♏	♑	♒	♎	♏	♑	♒
12 0	0 0	21 46	0 26	21	25		29 25	23	27		1 27	23	26		28 23	23	28	
12 12	3 16	24 28	3 29	24	29		2 27	26	0		4 0	26	29		1 26	26	1	
12 24	6 32	27 11	6 1	27	2		4 0	29	4		7 3	29	3		4 29	29	4	
12 36	9 48	29 56	9 4	0	5		7 3	2	7		10 5	2	6		8 2	2	8	
12 48	13 3	2♏41	12 7	3	9		10 5	5	11		13 8	5	9		11 5	5	11	
13 0	16 17	5 29	14 10	7	12		13 8	8	14		15 11	8	13		14 8	8	14	
13 12	19 30	8 18	17 12	10	16		16 11	12	18		18 14	11	16		17 11	11	17	
13 24	22 42	11 9	20 15	13	19		19 14	15	21		21 16	14	20		20 14	14	20	
13 36	25 53	14 2	23 17	16	23		22 16	18	25		24 19	18	23		23 17	17	23	
13 48	29 3	16 58	26 20	20	27		24 19	22	28		27 22	21	27		26 20	20	26	
14 0	2♏11	19 55	28 23	23	0		27 22	25	2		29 24	23	0		29 23	23	29	
14 12	5 18	22 56	1 26	27	4		0 24	29	5		2 28	27	3		2 26	26	2	
14 24	8 23	26 0	4 28	0	7		3 27	2	9		5 0	1	7		5 29	29	5	
14 36	11 26	29 6	7 1	4	11		5 0	6	12		8 3	5	10		9 2	2	9	
14 48	14 28	2♐16	9 4	8	14		8 3	9	15		11 5	8	14		12 5	5	12	
15 0	17 29	5 29	12 7	11	18		11 5	13	18		14 8	12	17		15 8	8	15	
15 12	20 26	8 45	15 9	15	21		14 8	17	22		16 11	15	21		18 11	11	18	
15 24	23 23	12 5	17 12	19	25		16 11	21	25		19 14	19	24		21 15	15	21	
15 36	26 19	15 28	20 15	22	28		19 14	24	29		22 17	23	27		24 18	18	24	
15 48	29 13	18 55	23 18	26	1		22 17	28	3		24 20	26	1		27 21	21	27	
16 0	2♐5	22 25	26 21	0	4		25 20	2	7		27 23	0	4		0 25	24	0	
16 12	4 57	25 59	29 24	4	8		27 23	6	10		0 26	4	7		3 28	28	4	
16 24	7 47	29 36	1 27	8	11		0 26	10	13		3 29	7	10		6 1	1	6	
16 36	10 36	3♑16	4 0	11	15		3 29	13	16		5 2	11	13		9 5	5	9	
16 48	13 24	7 0	7 3	15	18		6 2	17	20		8 5	15	17		12 8	8	12	
17 0	16 11	10 45	10 7	19	21		9 5	20	23		11 8	18	20		15 12	12	15	
17 12	18 58	14 33	12 10	22	24		11 8	24	26		14 11	22	23		18 15	15	18	
17 24	21 44	18 23	15 13	26	27		14 11	27	28		17 14	25	26		21 19	19	21	
17 36	24 30	22 15	18 16	0	0		17 14	1	2		20 18	29	29		24 23	23	24	
17 48	27 15	26 7	21 20	3	3		20 18	5	5		22 21	3	2		27 26	26	27	
18 0	0♑0	0♑0	24 23	7	6		23 22	8	8		25 23	6	5		0 0	0	0	
18 12	2 45	3 53	27 27	10	9		26 25	12	11		28 27	9	8		3 4	4	3	
18 24	5 30	7 45	0 0	14	12		29 29	15	14		1 1	12	10		6 7	7	6	
18 36	8 16	11 37	3 4	17	15		2 3	19	16		4 5	16	13		9 11	11	9	
18 48	11 2	15 27	6 8	20	18		5 6	22	19		7 8	19	16		12 15	15	12	
19 0	13 49	19 15	9 11	23	20		8 9	25	22		10 12	22	19		15 18	18	15	
19 12	16 36	23 0	12 15	27	23		11 13	28	25		13 15	25	22		18 22	22	18	
19 24	19 20	26 44	15 19	0	26		14 17	1	0		17 19	28	25		21 25	25	21	
19 36	22 13	0♒24	19 22	3	29		17 21	4	0		20 23	1	27		24 29	29	24	
19 48	25 3	4 1	22 26	6	1		20 25	7	3		23 26	4	0		27 2	2	27	
20 0	27 55	7 35	26 0	9	4		24 29	10	6		28 0	7	1		0 6	6	0	
20 12	0♒47	11 5	29 4	12	7		27 2	13	9		29 4	10	6		3 9	9	3	
20 24	3 41	14 42	2 8	15	10		0 6	16	11		3 7	3	8		6 12	12	6	
20 36	6 37	17 55	5 11	18	13		4 9	19	14		9 13	8	11		9 16	16	9	
20 48	9 34	21 15	9 15	21	15		8 13	22	17		9 15	8	14		12 19	19	12	
21 0	12 31	24 31	12 19	23	18		11 17	25	19		13 18	11	16		15 22	22	15	
21 12	15 32	27 44	16 22	26	21		14 21	27	22		16 22	14	20		18 25	25	18	
21 24	18 34	0♓54	19 26	29	23		18 25	0	25		20 25	16	22		21 29	29	21	
21 36	21 37	4 0	23 0	2	26		21 28	3	28		23 29	19	25		24 1	1	24	
21 48	24 42	7 4	26 3	4	29		25 1	6	0		27 3	22	28		27 4	4	27	
22 0	27 49	10 5	0 7	7	2		28 5	8	3		0 6	24	0		0 7	7	0	
22 12	0♓57	13 2	4 10	10	4		2 8	11	6		3 9	28	3		3 11	11	3	
22 24	4 7	15 58	7 14	13	7		5 12	14	9		7 12	0	6		7 14	14	7	
22 36	7 18	18 51	11 17	15	10		9 15	16	12		10 16	3	9		10 17	17	10	
22 48	10 30	21 42	14 20	18	13		12 18	19	14		14 19	5	12		13 19	19	13	
23 0	13 43	24 31	18 23	20	16		16 22	21	17		17 22	8	15		16 22	22	16	
23 12	16 57	27 19	21 27	23	18		19 25	24	20		21 25	24	20		21 25	11	17	
23 24	20 12	0♈4	25 0	26	21		23 28	27	23		24 28	14	20		22 28	28	22	
23 36	23 28	2 49	28 3	29	24		26 1	0	26		27 1	17	23		25 1	1	25	
23 48	26 44	5 32	1 6	1	27		0 3	3	29		1 4	20	26		29 4	4	29	
24 0	0♈0	8 14	5 9	4	0		3 7	5	2		4 7	23	29		2 7	7	2	

Sid. Time	M. C. long.	Asc. 1	REGIOMONTA. 11	12	2	3	CAMPANUS 11	12	2	3	PLACIDUS 11	12	2	3	NAT. GRAD. 11	12	2	3
h m	° '	♉	♊	♊	♌	♍	♉	♊	♌	♍	♉	♊	♌	♍	♉	♊	♌	♍
0 0	0 0	10♉31	5	11	6	1	3	8	8	3	4	9	4	1	3	8	8	3
0 12	3 16	13 10	9	14	8	3	6	11	10	6	8	12	7	3	6	11	11	6
0 24	6 32	15 48	12	17	11	6	9	14	13	9	11	15	9	6	8	14	14	9
0 36	9 48	18 26	15	20	14	9	13	17	15	11	14	18	12	9	12	16	16	12
0 48	23 23	21 2	19	23	16	12	16	20	18	14	17	20	15	12	15	19	19	15
1 0	16 17	23 39	22	25	19	15	19	23	21	17	20	23	18	15	18	22	22	18
1 12	19 30	26 15	25	28	22	18	22	26	24	20	23	26	20	18	21	25	25	21
1 24	22 42	28 51	28	♋1	25	21	25	28	26	23	26	29	23	21	24	27	27	24
1 36	25 53	1♋27	♋1	4	27	24	28	♋1	29	26	29	♋2	26	24	27	♋0	♍0	27
1 48	29 3	4 3	4	6	♍0	27	♋1	4	♍2	29	♋2	4	29	27	♋0	3	3	♎0
2 0	2♊11	6 39	7	9	2	♎0	4	7	5	♎2	5	7	♍1	♎0	3	5	5	3
2 12	5 18	9 15	10	12	5	3	7	9	7	5	8	10	4	3	6	8	8	6
2 24	8 23	11 54	13	14	8	6	10	12	10	8	11	12	7	6	9	11	11	9
2 36	11 26	14 28	16	17	11	9	13	15	13	11	14	15	10	9	12	14	14	12
2 48	14 28	17 5	19	20	13	12	16	17	16	14	17	18	13	12	15	17	17	15
3 0	17 29	19 43	22	22	16	15	19	20	18	17	20	21	16	15	18	19	19	18
3 12	20 26	22 21	24	25	19	18	22	23	21	20	23	23	18	18	21	22	22	21
3 24	23 23	25 0	27	28	22	21	24	25	24	23	25	26	21	21	24	25	25	24
3 36	26 19	27 39	♌0	♌0	24	24	27	28	27	26	28	29	24	24	25	27	27	25
3 48	29 13	0♍18	3	3	27	27	♌0	♌1	♎0	29	♌1	♌1	27	27	29	♌0	♎0	29
4 0	2♋5	2 58	5	6	♎0	29	3	3	3	♋2	4	4	♎0	♍0	♋2	3	3	♋2
4 12	4 57	5 39	8	8	3	♍2	5	6	5	5	6	7	3	3	5	5	5	5
4 24	7 47	8 20	11	11	6	5	8	9	8	8	9	9	6	6	8	8	8	8
4 36	10 36	11 1	13	14	8	8	11	11	11	11	12	12	9	9	11	11	11	11
4 48	13 24	13 43	16	16	11	11	14	14	13	13	14	15	12	12	13	13	13	13
5 0	16 11	16 25	19	19	14	14	16	16	16	16	17	18	14	15	16	16	16	16
5 12	18 58	19 8	22	22	17	17	19	19	19	19	20	20	17	18	19	19	19	19
5 24	21 44	21 51	24	24	19	19	22	22	22	22	23	23	20	21	22	22	22	22
5 36	24 30	24 34	27	26	22	22	25	25	24	25	25	26	23	24	25	25	25	25
5 48	27 15	27 17	♍0	♍0	25	25	28	27	27	27	28	29	26	26	27	27	27	27
6 0	0♌0	0♎0	2	2	28	28	♎0	♍0	♎0	♏0	♍1	♍1	29	29	♍0	♍0	♎0	♏0
6 12	2 45	2 43	5	5	♏0	♏0	3	3	3	3	4	4	♏1	♏2	3	3	3	3
6 24	5 30	5 26	8	8	4	3	6	5	5	6	7	7	4	5	5	5	5	5
6 36	8 16	8 9	11	11	6	6	9	8	8	9	10	7	7	8	8	8	8	8
6 48	11 2	10 52	13	13	8	8	11	11	10	11	12	13	10	10	11	11	11	11
7 0	13 49	13 35	16	16	11	11	14	14	13	14	15	16	12	13	14	14	14	14
7 12	16 36	16 17	19	19	14	14	17	17	16	18	18	18	15	16	17	17	17	17
7 24	19 24	18 59	22	22	16	17	20	19	18	19	21	21	18	18	19	19	19	19
7 36	22 13	21 40	25	24	19	19	23	22	21	22	24	24	21	21	22	22	22	22
7 48	25 3	24 21	28	27	22	22	25	25	24	25	27	27	23	24	25	24	24	25
8 0	27 55	27 2	♏1	♎0	24	25	28	28	27	27	♏0	♎0	26	26	28	27	27	28
8 12	0♍47	29 42	2	3	♏0	27	♏1	♎0	29	♐0	3	3	29	29	♏1	♎0	♏0	♏1
8 24	3 39	2♏41	6	6	4♐0	♐0	4	3	♐2	3	6	6	♐1	♐2	3	2	2	3
8 36	6 37	5 0	7	8	3	7	6	5	6	9	9	4	5	6	5	5	6	
8 48	9 34	7 39	12	11	8	6	10	9	7	8	12	12	7	7	9	8	8	9
9 0	12 31	10 17	15	14	11	8	13	12	10	11	15	14	9	10	12	11	11	12
9 12	15 22	12 55	18	17	14	11	16	14	12	14	18	17	12	13	15	14	14	15
9 24	18 34	15 32	21	19	16	14	19	17	15	17	21	20	15	16	18	16	16	18
9 36	21 37	18 6	24	22	19	17	22	20	18	20	24	23	18	19	21	19	19	21
9 48	24 42	20 45	27	25	22	20	25	23	20	23	27	26	20	22	24	21	21	24
10 0	27 49	23 21	♐0	28	24	23	28	25	23	26	♎0	29	23	25	27	24	24	27
10 12	0♎57	25 57	3	♐0	27	26	♎1	28	25	29	3♐1	26	28	♎0	27	27	♏0	
10 24	4 7	28 33	6	4	♐0	29	4♏	1	29	♐2	6	4	28	♏1	3♐0	♐0	3	
10 36	7 18	1♐9	9	6	2	♐2	7	3	♐0	5	9	7	♐1	4	6	3	3	6
10 48	10 30	3 45	12	8	5	5	10	6	2	8	12	10	4	7	9	5	5	9
11 0	13 43	6 21	15	11	8	8	13	9	5	11	15	12	17	10	12	8	8	12
11 12	16 57	8 58	18	14	10	11	15	11	8	14	18	15	10	13	15	11	11	15
11 24	20 12	11 34	21	16	13	15	19	14	11	18	21	18	12	16	18	14	14	18
11 36	23 28	14 12	24	19	16	18	21	17	15	21	24	21	15	19	21	16	16	21
11 48	26 44	16 50	27	22	18	21	24	19	18	24	27	23	18	22	24	19	19	24
12 0	0♏0	19 29	♐0	24	21	25	27	22	21	28	♏0	26	21	26	28	22	22	28

Sid. Time	M.C.	Asc.	REGIOMONTA.				CAMPANUS				PLACIDUS				NAT. GRAD.			
h m	long. ♎	1 ♐	11	12	2	3	11	12	2	3	11	12	2	3	11	12	2	3
12 0	0 0	19 29	29	24	26	25	27	22	21	28	0	26	21	26	28	22	22	28
12 12	3 16	22 10	♏2	27	22	28	♏0	25	24	♓1	3	29	24	29	♏1	25	24	♓1
12 24	6 32	24 51	5	♐0	25	♓1	3	27	27	4	6	♐1	27	♓2	4	28	27	4
12 36	9 48	27 34	8	2	28	5	6	♐0	=1	8	9	4	=0	6	7	♐0	=0	7
12 48	13 3	0♏18	11	5	=1	8	9	3	4	11	12	7	3	9	10	3	3	11
13 0	16 17	3 5	14	8	5	12	12	5	7	15	15	9	7	13	13	6	6	14
13 12	19 30	5 53	17	10	8	15	14	8	10	18	18	12	10	16	16	9	9	17
13 24	22 42	8 43	19	13	11	19	17	10	14	22	21	15	13	20	19	12	12	20
13 36	25 53	11 36	22	16	15	23	22	13	17	26	23	18	16	23	22	15	15	23
13 48	29 3	14 32	25	18	18	26	23	16	21	29	26	20	20	26	26	18	17	26
14 0	2♏11	17 31	28	21	22	♈0	26	18	25	♈3	29	23	23	♈0	29	21	20	29
14 12	5 18	20 32	♈0	24	25	4	29	21	28	6	♈2	26	27	4	♐2	24	24	♈2
14 24	8 23	23 37	3	26	29	7	♐1	24	♓2	10	5	28	♈0	7	5	27	27	5
14 36	11 26	26 46	6	29	♓3	11	4	26	6	14	7	♏1	4	10	8	♈0	♈0	6
14 48	14 28	29 58	8	=2	7	15	7	29	10	17	10	4	8	14	11	3	3	12
15 0	17 29	3=14	11	5	10	18	9	♓3	13	21	13	7	11	17	14	7	6	14
15 12	20 26	6 34	14	7	14	22	12	5	17	24	16	10	15	21	17	10	9	18
15 24	23 23	9 58	17	10	18	25	15	8	21	28	18	12	19	24	20	13	13	21
15 36	26 19	13 17	19	13	22	29	18	10	25	♉1	21	15	22	28	23	17	16	23
15 48	29 13	17 0	22	16	26	♉2	20	13	29	4	24	18	26	♉1	26	20	20	27
16 0	2♐5	20 37	25	19	♈0	5	23	16	♈3	8	26	21	♈0	4	29	24	23	♉0
16 12	4 57	24 18	27	22	4	9	26	19	7	11	29	24	4	8	♉2	27	26	3
16 24	7 47	28 4	♈0	25	8	12	28	22	11	14	♉2	27	8	11	6	=0	♈0	6
16 36	10 36	1♈54	2	28	12	15	♈1	25	15	18	5	=0	11	14	9	4	4	9
16 48	13 24	5 47	6	=1	16	19	4	28	19	21	7	3	15	17	12	7	7	12
17 0	16 11	9 44	8	5	20	22	7	=2	23	24	10	7	19	20	15	11	11	15
17 12	18 58	13 43	11	8	23	25	10	5	26	27	13	10	22	23	18	15	15	18
17 24	21 44	17 25	14	11	27	28	12	8	♉0	♊0	16	13	26	26	21	18	18	21
17 36	24 30	21 49	17	15	♉1	♊1	15	12	4	3	19	16	♉0	29	24	22	23	24
17 48	27 15	25 54	20	18	5	4	18	15	8	6	22	20	3	♊2	27	26	27	27
18 0	0♑0	0♈0	23	22	8	7	21	19	11	9	25	23	6	9	=0	♈0	♉0	♊0
18 12	2 45	4 6	26	25	12	10	24	22	14	12	28	27	10	8	3	4	4	3
18 24	5 30	8 11	29	29	15	13	27	26	18	15	=1	♈0	14	11	6	8	8	6
18 36	8 16	12 35	=2	♈3	19	16	=0	29	21	18	4	4	17	14	9	12	12	9
18 48	11 2	16 17	5	7	22	19	3	♈3	24	20	7	8	20	18	12	15	15	12
19 0	13 49	20 16	8	10	25	22	6	7	28	23	10	11	23	20	15	19	19	15
19 12	16 36	24 13	11	14	29	24	9	11	♊1	26	13	15	27	23	18	23	22	18
19 24	19 24	28 ·6	15	18	♊2	27	13	15	4	29	16	19	♊0	25	21	26	26	21
19 36	22 13	1♉56	18	22	5	♋0	16	19	7	♋2	19	22	3	28	24	♈0	♊0	24
19 48	25 3	5 42	21	26	8	3	19	23	10	4	22	26	6	♋1	27	4	3	28
20 0	27 55	9 23	25	♈0	11	5	23	27	13	7	26	♈0	9	4	♈0	7	7	♋1
20 12	0=47	13 0	28	4	14	8	26	♈1	16	10	29	4	12	6	3	10	10	4
20 24	3 41	16 43	♈1	8	12	11	29	5	19	12	♈2	8	15	9	6	14	13	7
20 36	6 37	20 2	5	12	20	13	♈2	9	22	15	6	11	18	12	9	17	17	10
20 48	9 34	23 26	8	16	23	16	6	12	25	18	9	15	20	14	12	21	20	13
21 0	12 31	26 46	12	20	25	19	9	16	28	21	13	19	23	17	15	24	23	16
21 12	15 32	0♊1	15	23	28	22	13	20	♋0	23	16	22	26	20	18	27	27	19
21 24	18 34	3 14	19	27	♋1	24	17	24	3	26	20	26	29	23	22	♉0	♋0	22
21 36	21 37	6 23	23	♉1	4	27	20	28	6	29	23	♉0	♋2	25	25	3	3	25
21 48	24 42	9 28	26	5	6	♋0	23	♉1	8	♋2	26	5	4	28	28	7	6	28
22 0	27 49	12 29	♈0	8	9	2	27	5	11	4	♈0	8	7	♋1	♈1	10	9	♋1
22 12	0 57	15 28	4	12	12	5	♈1	8	14	7	4	12	10	4	4	13	12	4
22 24	4 7	18 24	7	15	14	8	4	12	16	10	7	15	12	7	7	16	15	8
22 36	7 18	21 17	11	19	17	11	8	16	19	13	11	19	15	9	10	18	18	11
22 48	10 30	24 7	15	22	20	13	11	19	22	15	15	22	18	12	13	21	21	14
23 0	13 43	26 55	18	25	22	16	15	23	24	18	18	25	21	15	16	24	24	16
23 12	16 57	29 42	22	29	25	19	19	26	27	21	22	29	23	18	20	27	27	20
23 24	20 12	2♋26	25	♊2	28	22	22	29	♋0	24	25	♊2	26	21	23	♊0	♋0	23
23 36	23 28	5 9	29	5	♋0	25	26	♊2	2	27	29	5	29	24	26	3	3	26
23 48	26 44	7 50	♉2	8	3	28	♉0	5	5	♋0	♉2	8	♋1	27	29	6	5	29
24 0	0♈0	10 31	5	11	6	♍1	2	8	8	3	5	11	4	♍0	♊2	8	8	♍2

Sid. Time h m	M.C. long ♈	Asc. ♉	REGIOMONTA. 11 ♉	12 Ⅱ	2 ♌	3 ♍	CAMPANUS 11 ♉	12 Ⅱ	2 ♌	3 ♍	PLACIDUS 11 ♉	12 Ⅱ	2 ♌	3 ♍	NAT.GRAD. 11 ♉	12 Ⅱ	2 ♌	3 ♍
0 0	0 0	12 56	6 13	7	1		2	9	10	4	5	11	5	0	3	10	10	3
0 12	3 16	15 32	10 16	9	4		5	12	13	7	8	14	8	3	6	13	13	6
0 24	6 32	18 8	13 19	12	7		9	15	15	10	11	17	11	6	9	16	16	9
0 36	9 48	20 42	16 22	15	10		12	18	18	13	15	19	13	9	12	18	18	12
0 48	13 3	23 16	20 25	18	13		15	21	20	16	18	22	16	12	15	21	21	15
1 0	16 17	25 49	23 28	20	16		19	24	23	19	21	25	19	15	18	24	24	18
1 12	19 30	28 21	26 ♊0	23	18		22	27	26	22	24	28	21	18	21	26	26	21
1 24	22 42	0♌53	29 3	25	21		25	29	28	24	27	♌1	24	21	24	29	29	25
1 36	25 53	3 25	Ⅱ2 6	28	24		28	♌2	♍1	27	Ⅱ0	3	27	24	27	♌2	♍2	28
1 48	29 3	5 57	5 9	♍1	27		Ⅱ1	5	4	♌0	3	6	29	27	Ⅲ1	4	4	♎1
2 0	2♉11	8 29	8 11	3	♎0		4	8	6	3	6	9	♍2	♎0	4	7	7	4
2 12	5 18	11 1	11 14	6	3		7	10	9	6	9	11	5	3	7	10	10	7
2 24	8 23	13 33	14 17	9	6		10	13	12	9	12	14	7	6	10	12	12	10
2 36	11 26	16 5	17 19	11	9		13	16	14	12	15	17	10	9	12	15	15	12
2 48	14 28	18 37	20 22	14	12		16	18	17	15	18	19	13	12	15	17	17	15
3 0	17 29	21 10	23 24	17	14		19	21	20	18	21	22	16	15	18	20	20	18
3 12	20 26	23 43	26 27	19	17		22	23	23	21	23	25	19	18	21	23	23	21
3 24	23 23	26 16	28 29	22	20		24	26	25	24	26	27	22	21	24	26	26	24
3 36	26 19	28 50	♌1 ♌2	25	23		27	29	28	27	29	♌0	24	24	27	28	28	27
3 48	29 13	1♍24	4 5	27	26		♌0	♌1	♎1	♍0	♌2	3	27	27	♌0	♌1	♎1	♍0
4 0	2Ⅱ5	3 59	7 7	♎0	29		3	4	4	2	4	5	♎0	♍0	2	4	4	2
4 12	4 57	6 34	9 10	3	♍2		5	6	7	5	7	8	3	3	5	6	6	5
4 24	7 47	9 9	12 12	5	4		8	9	10	8	10	11	6	6	8	9	9	8
4 36	10 36	11 44	15 15	8	7		11	11	12	11	13	13	8	9	11	11	11	11
4 48	13 24	14 20	17 18	11	10		14	14	14	14	15	16	11	11	14	14	14	14
5 0	16 11	16 56	20 20	13	13		16	16	17	16	18	19	14	14	16	17	17	16
5 12	18 58	19 33	23 23	16	16		19	19	19	19	21	21	17	17	19	19	19	19
5 24	21 44	22 10	25 25	19	18		22	22	22	22	24	24	20	20	22	22	22	22
5 36	24 30	24 48	28 28	21	21		24	25	25	25	26	27	22	23	25	25	25	25
5 48	27 15	27 23	♌1 ♍1	24	24		27	27	27	27	29	29	25	25	27	27	27	27
6 0	0♋0	0♎0	4 3	27	26		♌0	♍0	♍0	♋0	♍2	♍2	28	28	♌0	♍0	♍0	♋0
6 12	2 45	2 37	6 6	29	29		3	3	3	3	5	♎1	♍1	♎1	3	3	3	3
6 24	5 30	5 12	9 9	♍2	♍2		5	5	5	6	7	8	3	4	5	5	5	5
6 36	8 16	7 50	12 11	5	5		8	8	8	10	10	10	6	6	8	8	8	8
6 48	11 2	10 27	14 14	7	7		11	11	10	11	13	13	9	9	12	11	11	12
7 0	13 49	13 4	17 17	10	10		14	13	13	14	16	16	11	12	14	13	13	14
7 12	16 36	15 40	20 19	12	13		16	16	16	16	19	19	14	15	16	16	16	16
7 24	19 24	18 16	23 22	15	15		19	19	19	19	22	22	17	17	19	19	19	19
7 36	22 13	20 51	26 25	18	18		22	21	21	22	24	24	19	20	22	21	21	22
7 48	25 3	23 26	28 27	20	21		25	24	24	25	27	27	22	23	25	24	24	25
8 0	27 55	26 1	♍1 ♎0	23	23		28	27	27	27	♍0	♎0	25	26	27	26	26	27
8 12	0♌47	28 36	4 3	25	26		♍0	29	29	♑0	3	3	27	28	♍0	29	29	♑0
8 24	3 41	1♍10	7 5	28	29		3	♎2	♑2	3	6	6	♑0	♑1	3	2	2	3
8 36	6 37	3 44	10 8	♎1	♑2		5	5	5	6	9	8	3	4	6	4	4	6
8 48	9 34	6 17	13 11	3	4		9	8	7	8	12	11	5	7	9	7	7	9
9 0	12 31	8 50	16 13	6	7		12	10	10	11	15	14	8	9	12	10	10	12
9 12	15 32	11 23	18 16	8	10		15	13	12	14	18	17	11	12	15	12	12	15
9 24	18 34	13 55	21 19	11	13		18	16	15	17	21	20	13	15	18	15	15	18
9 36	21 37	16 27	24 21	13	16		21	18	18	20	24	22	16	18	20	18	18	20
9 48	24 42	18 59	27 24	16	19		24	21	20	23	27	25	19	21	23	20	20	23
10 0	27 49	21 31	♎0 27	19	21		27	24	23	26	♎0	28	29	24	26	23	23	26
10 12	0♍57	24 3	3 29	21	25		♎0	26	26	29	3	♎1	24	27	29	26	26	29
10 24	4 7	26 35	6 ♍2	24	28		3	29	28	♍2	6	3	♎0	♑2	♎2	28	28	♍3
10 36	7 18	29 7	9 5	27	♑1		5	♎2	♑0	5	9	6	29	3	5	♎1	♑1	6
10 48	10 30	1♑39	12 7	♑0	4		8	4	2	8	12	9	♑2	6	8	4	4	9
11 0	13 43	4 11	14 10	2	7		11	7	5	11	15	11	5	9	11	7	6	12
11 12	16 57	6 44	17 12	5	10		14	9	8	15	18	14	8	12	15	9	9	15
11 24	20 12	9 18	20 15	8	14		17	12	11	18	21	17	11	15	18	12	12	18
11 36	23 28	11 52	23 18	11	17		20	15	15	21	24	19	13	19	21	15	14	21
11 48	26 44	14 28	26 20	14	20		23	17	18	24	27	22	17	22	24	17	17	24
12 0	0♎0	17 4	29 23	17	24		26	20	21	28	♍0	25	19	25	27	20	20	27

212

Sid. Time h m	M.C. long ♎	Asc. 1 ♎	REGIOMONTA. 11 ♏	12 ♐	2 ♒	3 ♎	CAMPANUS 11 ♏	12 ♐	2 ♒	3 ♎	PLACIDUS 11 ♎	12 ♏	2 ♒	3 ♎	NAT. GRAD. 11 ♏	12 ♐	2 ♒	3 ♎
12 0	0 0	17 4	29	23	17	24	26	20	21	28	0	25	19	25	27	20	20	27
12 12	3 16	19 41	♏2	5	20	27	29	22	24	♓2	3	27	22	23	♏0	23	23	♓1
12 24	6 32	22 20	4	28	23	♓1	♏2	25	27	5	6	♑0	25	♓2	3	26	25	4
12 36	9 48	25 1	7	♐1	26	4	5	27	≈0	9	9	3	29	5	6	28	28	7
12 48	13 3	27 43	10	3	29	8	7	♑0	3	12	11	5	≈2	9	9	♐1	≈1	10
13 0	16 17	0♑28	13	6	≈2	11	10	3	7	16	14	8	5	12	12	4	4	13
13 12	19 30	3 14	16	18	10	15	13	5	10	20	17	11	8	16	16	7	6	16
13 24	22 42	6 4	18	11	9	19	16	8	13	23	20	13	12	19	19	10	9	19
13 36	25 53	8 55	21	13	13	23	19	10	17	27	23	16	15	23	22	13	12	23
13 48	29 3	11 50	24	16	16	26	22	13	21	♈1	25	19	19	26	25	16	15	26
14 0	2♏11	14 49	26	19	20	♈0	25	16	24	4	28	21	22	♈0	28	19	18	29
14 12	5 18	17 51	29	21	24	4	28	18	28	8	♐1	24	26	4	♐1	22	21	♈2
14 24	8 23	20 56	♐2	24	28	7	♑0	21	♓2	12	4	27	29	7	4	25	24	5
14 36	11 26	24 6	5	27	♓1	11	3	24	6	15	6	29	♓3	11	7	28	28	8
14 48	14 28	27 20	7	♑0	5	15	6	26	10	19	9	♏2	7	14	10	♏2	♈1	11
15 0	17 29	0≈39	10	2	9	19	9	29	14	22	12	5	11	18	13	5	4	14
15 12	20 26	4 3	13	5	12	21	11	♒2	18	26	15	8	14	41	16	8	7	17
15 24	23 23	7 31	15	8	18	26	14	5	23	29	17	11	18	25	20	11	11	20
15 36	26 19	11 5	18	11	22	29	17	7	27	♉3	20	13	12	28	23	15	14	23
15 48	29 13	14 44	21	14	24	♉3	19	10	♈1	6	23	17	26	♉2	26	18	18	26
16 0	2♐5	18 29	23	17	♈0	6	22	13	5	10	26	19	♈0	5	29	22	21	29
16 12	4 57	22 19	26	20	4	10	25	16	9	13	28	22	4	8	♒2	25	25	♉2
16 24	7 47	26 14	29	23	8	13	28	19	13	16	♒1	25	8	11	5	29	29	5
16 36	10 36	0♓14	♒2	26	12	16	♑0	22	17	19	4	29	12	15	8	≈3	♈2	8
16 48	13 24	4 20	4	29	17	20	3	25	21	23	7	≈2	16	18	11	6	6	12
17 0	16 11	8 29	7	≈2	21	23	6	29	25	26	9	5	19	21	14	10	10	15
17 12	18 58	12 42	10	6	25	26	9	≈2	29	29	12	8	23	24	18	14	14	18
17 24	21 44	15 33	13	9	29	29	11	5	♉3	♊2	15	12	27	27	20	17	17	20
17 36	24 30	21 18	16	13	♉2	♊2	14	9	7	5	18	15	♉1	♊0	23	22	22	24
17 48	27 15	25 38	19	16	6	5	17	12	11	8	21	19	4	3	27	26	26	27
18 0	0♑0	0♈0	21	20	10	8	20	16	4	11	24	22	8	6	≈0	♈0	♈0	♊0
18 12	2 45	4 22	25	24	14	11	23	19	18	14	27	26	11	9	3	4	4	3
18 24	5 30	8 42	28	28	17	14	28	23	21	17	≈0	29	15	12	6	8	8	6
18 36	8 16	14 27	≈1	♈1	21	17	29	27	25	20	3	♈3	18	15	10	13	13	10
18 48	11 2	17 18	4	5	24	20	≈2	♈1	28	22	6	7	22	18	12	16	16	12
19 0	13 49	21 31	7	9	28	29	5	5	♊1	25	9	11	25	21	15	20	20	16
19 12	16 36	25 40	10	13	♊1	26	8	9	4	28	12	14	28	23	18	24	24	19
19 24	19 24	29 46	14	18	4	28	12	13	7	♋1	15	18	♊1	26	22	28	27	22
19 36	22 13	3♉46	17	22	7	♋1	15	17	11	3	19	22	5	29	25	♈1	♊1	25
19 48	25 3	7 41	20	24	10	4	18	21	14	6	22	26	8	♋2	28	5	5	28
20 0	27 55	11 31	24	♈0	13	7	22	25	17	9	25	♈0	11	4	♓1	9	8	♋1
20 12	0≈47	15 16	27	6	16	9	25	29	19	12	28	4	14	7	4	12	12	4
20 24	3 41	18 55	♓1	8	19	12	28	♈3	22	14	♓2	8	17	10	7	16	15	7
20 36	6 37	22 29	9	12	22	15	♓2	7	25	17	5	12	19	12	10	19	19	10
20 48	9 34	25 27	8	17	25	17	5	11	28	20	9	16	22	15	13	23	22	14
21 0	12 31	29 21	11	21	29	20	9	16	♋1	22	12	19	25	18	16	26	26	16
21 12	15 32	2♊40	15	25	♋0	23	12	20	4	25	16	23	28	21	19	29	29	20
21 24	18 34	5 54	19	29	3	25	16	23	6	28	19	27	♋1	24	22	♉3	♋2	23
21 36	21 37	9 4	23	♉2	6	28	20	27	9	♌0	23	♉1	3	26	25	6	5	26
21 48	24 42	12 9	26	6	9	♋1	23	♉1	12	3	26	4	6	29	28	9	8	29
22 0	27 49	15 11	♈0	10	11	4	27	5	14	6	♈0	8	9	♌2	♈1	12	12	♌2
22 12	0♓57	18 10	4	14	14	6	♈1	9	17	9	4	11	11	5	4	15	14	5
22 24	4 7	21 7	7	17	17	9	4	13	19	11	7	15	14	7	7	18	17	8
22 36	7 18	23 56	11	21	19	12	8	16	22	14	11	18	17	10	11	21	20	11
22 48	10 30	26 46	15	24	22	14	12	20	25	11	14	22	17	13	14	24	23	14
23 0	13 43	29 24	19	28	24	17	15	23	27	20	18	25	22	16	17	26	26	18
23 12	16 57	2♊17	22	♊1	27	20	19	26	♌0	23	21	28	25	19	20	29	29	21
23 24	20 12	4 59	26	4	29	23	22	♊0	2	26	25	♊1	27	22	23	♊2	♌2	23
23 36	23 28	7 42	29	7	♌2	26	26	3	5	28	28	4	♌0	24	26	5	4	27
23 48	26 44	10 19	♉3	10	5	28	29	6	8	♍1	♉2	8	3	27	29	8	7	♍0
24 0	0♈0	12 56	6	13	7	♍1	♉2	9	10	4	5	11	5	≈0	♉3	10	10	♏3

Sid. Time h m	M.C. long. ♈	Asc. 1 ♉	REGIOMONTA. 11 ♉	12 Ⅱ	2 ♌	3 ♍	CAMPANUS 11 ♉	12 Ⅱ	2 ♌	3 ♍	PLACIDUS 11 ♉	12 Ⅱ	2 ♌	3 ♍	NAT. GRAD. 11 ♉	12 Ⅱ	2 ♌	3 ♍
0 0	0 0	15 1	7	16	9	2	1	10	12	5	5	12	6	1	3	12	11	4
0 12	3 16	17 35	11	19	11	4	5	13	15	8	9	15	9	3	6	15	14	7
0 24	6 32	20 7	14	21	14	7	8	16	17	11	12	18	12	6	9	17	17	10
0 36	9 48	22 38	17	24	16	10	12	19	20	14	15	21	14	9	12	20	20	13
0 48	13 3	25 9	21	27	19	13	15	22	22	17	19	24	17	12	16	23	23	16
1 0	16 17	27 38	24	29	21	16	18	25	25	20	22	27	20	15	19	25	25	19
1 12	19 30	♊ 8	27	♋2	24	19	21	27	28	23	25	29	22	18	22	28	28	22
1 24	22 42	2 36	♊0	5	26	21	25	♋0	♍0	26	28	♋2	25	21	25	♋1	♍0	25
1 36	25 53	5 5	3	8	29	24	28	3	3	29	♊1	5	27	24	28	3	3	28
1 48	29 3	7 33	6	♋0	♍1	27	♊1	6	5	♎1	4	8	♍0	27	♊1	6	6	♎1
2 0	2♊11	♋0 1	9	13	4	♎0	4	8	8	4	7	10	3	♎0	4	9	8	4
2 12	5 18	12 29	12	16	7	3	7	11	11	7	10	13	6	3	7	11	11	7
2 24	8 23	14 57	15	18	9	6	10	13	13	10	13	16	8	6	10	14	13	10
2 36	11 26	17 25	18	21	12	9	13	16	16	13	16	18	11	9	13	16	16	13
2 48	14 28	19 54	21	23	14	11	16	19	18	15	19	21	14	12	16	19	18	16
3 0	17 29	22 22	24	26	17	14	18	21	21	19	21	23	16	15	19	21	21	19
3 12	20 26	24 51	26	28	20	17	22	24	24	22	24	26	19	18	21	24	24	21
3 24	23 23	27 20	29	♋1	22	20	24	26	26	24	27	29	22	21	24	26	26	24
3 36	26 19	29 49	♋2	4	25	23	27	29	29	27	♋0	♋1	25	24	27	29	29	27
3 48	29 13	♍2 19	5	6	27	26	♋0	♋1	♎2	♏2	2	4	28	27	♋0	♋1	♎1	♏0
4 0	2♉5	4 48	8	9	♎0	28	3	4	4	3	5	6	♎0	29	3	4	4	3
4 12	4 57	7 19	10	11	3	♏1	5	7	7	6	8	9	2	♏2	5	7	7	5
4 24	7 47	9 49	13	14	5	4	8	9	10	9	11	12	5	5	8	9	9	8
4 36	10 36	12 20	16	16	8	7	11	12	12	11	13	14	8	8	11	12	12	11
4 48	13 24	14 51	18	19	10	9	13	14	15	14	16	17	11	11	14	15	15	14
5 0	16 11	17 22	21	21	13	12	16	17	17	17	19	20	14	14	16	17	17	16
5 12	18 58	19 53	24	24	16	15	19	19	20	20	22	22	16	17	19	20	20	19
5 24	21 44	22 25	26	26	18	18	22	22	23	22	24	25	19	19	22	22	22	22
5 36	24 30	24 56	2	29	21	20	24	24	25	25	27	27	22	22	25	25	25	25
5 48	27 15	27 28	♌1	♍1	23	23	27	27	28	28	♌0	♍0	24	25	27	27	27	27
6 0	0♋0	♋0 0	4	4	26	26	29	♍0	♏0	♐0	2	3	27	28	♌0	♍0	♏0	♐0
6 12	2 45	2 32	7	7	29	28	♌2	2	3	2	5	6	♏0	♐0	3	3	3	3
6 24	5 30	5 4	10	9	♏1	♐1	5	5	6	5	8	8	3	3	5	5	5	5
6 36	8 16	7 35	12	12	4	4	7	7	8	8	11	11	5	6	8	8	8	8
6 48	11 2	10 7	15	14	6	6	10	10	11	11	13	14	8	8	11	10	10	11
7 0	13 49	12 38	18	17	9	9	13	13	13	14	16	16	10	11	14	13	13	14
7 12	16 36	15 9	21	20	11	12	15	15	16	17	19	19	13	14	16	15	15	16
7 24	19 24	17 40	23	22	14	14	18	18	18	19	22	22	16	17	19	18	18	19
7 36	22 13	20 11	26	25	16	17	21	20	20	22	25	25	18	19	22	21	21	22
7 48	25 3	22 41	29	27	19	20	24	23	23	25	28	28	21	22	25	23	23	25
8 0	27 52	25 12	♍2	♎0	♏2	22	26	26	26	27	♍1	♎0	24	25	27	26	26	27
8 12	0♌47	27 41	4	3	24	25	♍0	28	29	♑0	3	2	26	28	♍0	28	28	♑0
8 24	3 41	0♌11	7	5	26	28	3	♎1	♐1	3	6	5	29	♑0	3	♎1	♐1	3
8 36	6 37	2 40	10	8	29	♑1	5	4	4	6	9	8	♐1	3	6	4	4	6
8 48	9 34	5 9	13	10	♐2	4	8	6	6	9	12	11	4	6	9	6	6	9
9 0	12 31	7 38	16	13	4	6	11	9	9	11	15	14	7	9	11	9	9	11
9 12	15 32	10 6	19	16	7	9	14	12	11	14	18	16	9	11	14	12	11	14
9 24	18 34	12 35	21	18	9	12	17	14	14	17	21	19	12	14	17	14	14	17
9 36	21 37	15 3	24	21	12	15	20	17	16	20	24	22	14	17	20	17	17	20
9 48	24 42	17 31	27	23	14	18	23	19	19	23	27	24	17	20	23	19	19	23
10 0	27 49	19 59	♎0	26	17	21	26	22	22	26	♎0	27	20	23	26	21	22	26
10 12	0♍57	22 57	3	29	20	24	29	25	24	29	3	♐0	22	26	29	24	25	29
10 24	4 7	24 55	6	♏1	22	27	♎2	27	27	♒2	6	3	25	29	♎2	27	27	♒2
10 36	7 18	27 24	9	4	25	♒0	4	♐0	♑0	5	9	5	28	♒2	5	♐0	♑0	5
10 48	10 30	29 52	11	6	28	4	7	2	2	8	12	8	♒1	5	8	2	2	8
11 0	13 43	2♎22	14	9	♑1	6	10	5	5	12	15	10	3	5	11	5	5	11
11 12	16 57	4 51	17	11	3	9	13	8	8	15	18	13	6	11	14	7	7	14
11 24	20 12	7 22	20	14	6	12	16	10	11	18	21	16	9	15	17	10	10	18
11 36	23 28	9 53	23	16	9	16	19	13	15	22	24	18	12	18	20	13	13	21
11 48	26 44	12 25	26	19	11	19	22	15	18	25	21	21	15	21	23	16	15	24
12 0	0♎0	14 59	28	21	14	23	25	18	21	29	24	24	18	25	26	19	18	27

Sid. Time	M.C. long.	Asc. 1	REGIOMONTA. 11	12	2	3	CAMPANUS 11	12	2	3	PLACIDUS 11	12	2	3	NAT. GRAD. 11	12	2	3
h m	♎	♐	♎	♏	♑	♒	♎	♏	♑	♒	♎	♏	♑	♒	♎	♏	♑	♒
12 0	0 0	14 59	28	21	15	23	25	18	20	29	29	24	18	25	26	19	18	27
12 12	3 16	17 33	♏1	24	18	26	27	20	24	♓2	♏2	27	21	28	29	21	21	♓0
12 24	6 32	20 10	4	26	21	♓0	♏0	23	27	6	5	29	24	♓1	♏3	24	23	3
12 36	9 48	22 48	7	29	24	4	3	25	♒0	9	8	♐1	27	5	6	27	26	6
12 48	13 3	25 28	9	♐1	27	7	6	28	3	13	11	4	♒0	8	9	♐0	29	9
13 0	16 17	28 10	12	4	♒0	11	9	♐1	7	17	14	7	4	12	12	3	♒2	13
13 12	19 30	0♑55	15	7	4	15	10	3	10	21	17	9	7	16	15	5	5	16
13 24	22 42	3 42	17	9	7	19	13	6	4	25	19	12	10	19	18	8	8	19
13 36	25 53	6 33	20	12	11	22	16	8	18	28	22	14	14	23	21	11	10	22
13 48	29 3	9 26	23	14	15	26	18	11	22	♈2	25	17	17	26	24	14	13	25
14 0	2♏11	12 24	26	17	18	♈0	21	13	26	6	28	20	21	♈0	27	17	16	28
14 12	5 18	15 25	28	20	22	4	24	16	♓0	9	♐0	22	25	4	♐0	20	20	♈1
14 24	8 23	18 31	♐1	22	26	8	27	19	4	13	3	25	28	7	3	24	23	4
14 36	11 26	21 41	4	25	♓0	11	♐0	21	8	17	6	28	♓2	11	7	27	26	8
14 48	14 28	24 56	6	28	4	15	3	24	12	20	9	♒1	6	14	10	♒0	29	11
15 0	17 29	28 17	9	♑0	8	19	6	27	16	24	11	3	10	18	13	3	♓2	14
15 12	20 26	1♒43	12	3	13	23	9	29	20	27	14	6	14	22	16	6	6	17
15 24	23 23	5 15	14	6	17	26	11	♏2	24	♏1	17	9	18	25	19	10	9	20
15 36	26 19	8 53	17	9	21	♉0	14	5	28	4	19	11	22	29	22	13	13	23
15 48	29 13	12 37	20	12	26	4	16	8	♈3	8	22	15	26	♉2	25	17	16	26
16 0	2♐5	16 28	22	15	♈0	7	19	11	7	11	25	18	♈0	5	28	20	20	29
16 12	4 57	20 25	25	18	4	11	22	14	11	15	28	21	4	9	♒2	24	23	♉0
16 24	7 47	24 29	28	21	9	14	25	17	15	18	♑0	24	8	12	5	28	27	5
16 36	10 36	28 39	♑1	24	13	17	28	20	20	21	3	27	12	15	8	♒2	♈1	8
16 48	13 24	2♓55	3	27	17	21	♏1	23	24	24	6	♒0	16	19	11	6	5	11
17 0	16 11	7 16	6	♒0	22	24	3	26	28	28	9	4	20	22	14	9	9	14
17 12	18 58	11 43	9	4	26	27	6	29	♉2	♊1	11	7	24	25	17	14	13	17
17 24	21 44	16 13	12	7	♉0	♊0	9	♈2	6	4	14	10	28	28	20	18	17	21
17 36	24 30	20 47	15	11	4	3	12	6	9	7	17	14	♉2	♊1	24	22	22	24
17 48	27 15	25 23	18	15	8	6	14	9	13	10	20	17	5	4	27	26	26	27
18 0	0♑0	0♈0	21	18	12	9	17	13	17	13	23	21	9	7	♒0	♈0	♈0	♊0
18 12	2 45	4 37	24	22	15	12	20	16	20	16	26	25	13	10	3	4	4	3
18 24	5 30	9 13	27	26	19	15	23	20	24	28	29	28	16	13	6	8	8	6
18 36	8 16	13 47	♑0	♓0	23	18	26	24	27	21	♓2	♓2	20	16	9	13	12	10
18 48	11 2	18 17	3	4	26	21	29	28	♊1	24	5	6	23	19	13	17	17	13
19 0	13 49	22 44	6	8	♊0	24	♒2	♓2	24	27	8	10	26	21	16	21	21	16
19 12	16 36	27 5	9	13	3	27	6	6	7	♋0	11	14	♊0	24	19	25	25	19
19 24	19 24	1♉21	13	17	6	29	9	10	10	2	15	18	3	27	22	29	28	22
19 36	22 13	5 31	16	21	9	♋2	12	14	13	5	18	22	6	♋0	25	♈3	♊2	25
19 48	25 3	9 35	19	26	12	5	15	18	16	8	21	26	9	2	28	7	6	28
20 0	27 55	13 32	23	♈0	15	8	19	23	19	11	25	♈0	12	5	♓1	11	10	♋2
20 12	0♒47	17 23	26	4	18	10	22	27	22	13	28	4	15	8	3	14	13	5
20 24	3 41	21 7	♓0	9	21	13	26	♈1	25	16	♓1	8	19	11	7	18	17	8
20 36	6 37	24 45	4	13	24	16	29	5	28	19	5	12	21	13	10	21	20	11
20 48	9 34	28 17	7	17	27	18	♓3	10	♋1	21	8	16	24	16	13	25	24	14
21 0	12 31	1♊43	11	22	♋0	21	6	14	3	24	22	20	27	19	16	28	27	17
21 12	15 33	5 4	15	26	2	24	10	18	6	27	16	24	29	21	19	♉1	♋0	20
21 24	18 34	8 19	19	♉0	5	26	13	22	9	29	19	28	♋2	24	22	4	3	23
21 36	21 37	11 29	22	4	8	29	17	26	11	♌2	23	♉2	5	27	25	7	6	26
21 48	24 42	14 35	26	8	10	♌2	21	♈0	14	4	26	5	8	♌0	29	11	10	♋0
22 0	27 49	17 36	♈0	12	13	4	25	4	17	8	♈0	9	10	2	♈2	14	13	3
22 12	0♓57	20 36	4	15	16	7	28	8	19	10	4	13	13	5	5	17	16	6
22 24	4 7	23 27	8	19	18	10	♈2	12	23	13	7	16	16	8	8	20	19	9
22 36	7 18	26 18	11	23	21	13	6	16	24	16	11	20	18	11	11	23	22	12
22 48	10 30	29 5	15	26	23	15	9	20	29	19	14	23	21	14	14	25	25	15
23 0	13 43	1♋50	19	♊2	26	18	13	23	29	21	18	26	23	17	17	28	28	18
23 12	16 57	4 32	23	3	29	21	17	27	♌2	24	22	♊0	26	19	20	♊1	♌0	21
23 24	20 12	7 12	26	6	♌1	23	20	♉0	9	27	25	3	29	22	24	4	3	24
23 36	23 18	9 50	♉0	9	4	26	24	3	7	♍0	29	6	♌1	25	27	6	6	27
23 48	26 44	12 37	4	12	6	29	28	6	10	3	♉2	9	3	28	♋0	9	9	♍1
24 0	0♈0	15 1	7	15	9	♍2	♉1	9	12	6	5	12	6	♍1	3	12	11	4

Sid. Time h	m	M.C. long. ♈	Asc. 1 ♉	REGIOMONTA. 11 ♉	12 ♊	2 ♌	3 ♍	CAMPANUS 11 ♉	12 ♊	2 ♌	3 ♍	PLACIDUS 11 ♉	12 ♊	2 ♌	3 ♍	NAT. GRAD. 11 ♉	12 ♊	2 ♌	3 ♍
0	0	0 0	17 16	8	18	10	2	0	10	15	17	6	14	8	1	3	14	13	4
0	12	3 16	19 46	12	21	13	5	4	13	17	10	9	17	10	4	7	16	16	7
0	24	6 32	22 15	15	23	15	8	7	16	20	12	13	20	13	7	9	19	18	10
0	36	9 48	24 42	18	26	17	10	11	19	22	15	16	23	15	10	12	21	21	13
0	48	13 3	27 9	22	29	20	13	14	22	25	18	19	26	18	12	16	24	24	16
1	0	16 17	29 35	25	♋2	22	16	18	25	27	21	22	28	20	15	19	27	26	19
1	12	19 30	2♌ 1	28	5	25	19	21	28	♏0	24	26	♎1	23	18	22	29	29	22
1	24	22 42	4 25	♍1	7	27	22	24	♍1	2	27	29	4	26	21	25	♋2	♍2	25
1	36	25 53	6 49	5	10	♍0	24	27	3	5	♎0	2	7	28	24	28	5	4	28
1	48	29 3	9 14	8	12	2	27	♍1	6	7	2	5	9	♏1	27	♍1	7	7	♎1
2	0	2♉11	11 38	11	15	5	♎0	4	9	10	5	8	12	3	♎0	4	10	9	4
2	12	5 18	14 1	14	18	7	3	7	11	12	8	11	14	6	3	7	12	12	7
2	24	8 23	16 25	17	20	10	6	10	14	15	11	14	17	9	6	10	15	15	10
2	36	11 26	18 49	19	23	12	8	13	17	17	14	17	20	11	9	13	17	17	13
2	48	14 28	21 13	22	25	15	11	16	19	20	17	19	22	14	12	16	20	20	16
3	0	17 29	23 37	25	28	17	14	18	21	22	20	22	25	17	15	19	23	22	19
3	12	20 26	26 1	28	♌0	20	17	21	24	25	22	25	27	19	18	22	25	25	22
3	24	23 23	28 25	♋1	3	22	20	24	27	28	25	28	♏0	22	20	24	27	27	25
3	36	26 19	0♍50	3	5	25	22	27	29	♎0	28	♎1	2	25	23	27	♌0	♎0	27
3	48	29 13	3 15	6	8	27	25	♎0	♌2	3	♏1	3	5	27	26	♎0	2	2	♏0
4	0	2♊ 5	5 40	9	10	♎0	23	2	4	5	4	6	8	♎0	29	3	5	5	3
4	12	4 57	8 5	12	13	3	♏0	5	7	8	6	9	10	3	♏2	6	7	7	6
4	24	7 47	10 30	14	15	5	3	8	9	11	9	11	13	5	5	8	10	10	8
4	36	10 36	12 56	17	17	8	6	10	12	13	12	14	15	8	8	11	12	12	11
4	48	13 24	15 22	19	20	10	9	13	14	16	15	17	18	11	10	14	15	15	14
5	0	16 11	17 48	22	22	13	11	16	17	18	17	20	20	13	13	17	17	17	17
5	12	18 58	20 14	25	25	15	14	19	19	21	20	22	23	16	16	19	20	20	19
5	24	21 44	22 41	27	27	18	17	22	22	23	23	25	26	19	19	22	22	22	22
5	36	24 30	25 7	♌0	♍0	20	19	24	24	26	25	28	28	21	21	25	25	25	25
5	48	27 15	27 34	3	2	23	22	27	27	28	28	♎0	♏1	24	24	27	27	27	27
6	0	0♋ 0	0♍ 0	5	5	25	25	29	29	♏1	♐1	3	3	27	27	♏0	♎0	♏0	♎0
6	12	2 45	2 26	8	7	28	27	♏2	♍2	3	4	6	6	29	♎0	3	3	3	3
6	24	5 30	4 53	11	10	♏0	♐0	5	4	6	6	9	9	2	2	5	5	5	5
6	36	8 16	7 19	13	12	3	3	7	7	9	9	11	11	4	5	8	8	8	8
6	48	11 2	9 46	16	15	5	5	10	9	11	11	14	14	7	8	11	10	10	11
7	0	13 49	12 12	19	17	8	8	13	12	14	14	17	17	10	10	13	13	13	13
7	12	16 36	14 38	21	20	10	11	15	14	16	17	20	19	12	13	16	15	15	16
7	24	19 24	17 4	24	22	13	13	18	17	19	19	22	22	15	16	19	18	18	19
7	36	22 13	19 30	27	25	15	16	21	20	21	22	25	25	17	19	22	20	20	22
7	48	25 3	21 55	♍0	27	17	18	24	22	24	25	28	27	♎0	21	24	23	23	24
8	0	27 55	24 20	2	♎0	20	21	26	25	26	28	♐1	♎0	22	24	27	25	23	27
8	12	0♌47	26 45	5	3	22	24	29	27	29	♐0	4	3	29	27	♏0	28	28	♐0
8	24	3 41	29 10	8	5	25	27	♐2	♎0	♐1	3	7	5	28	29	3	♍0	♏0	3
8	36	6 37	1♎35	10	8	27	29	5	2	4	6	10	8	♐0	♏2	5	3	3	6
8	48	9 34	3 59	13	10	♐0	♏2	8	5	6	9	12	11	3	5	8	5	5	8
9	0	12 31	6 23	16	13	2	5	11	8	9	12	15	13	5	8	11	8	8	11
9	12	15 32	8 47	19	15	5	8	14	10	11	14	18	16	8	11	14	10	10	14
9	24	18 34	11 11	22	18	7	11	17	13	14	17	21	19	10	13	17	13	13	17
9	36	21 37	13 35	24	20	10	13	20	15	16	20	24	21	13	16	20	15	15	20
9	48	24 42	15 59	27	23	12	16	23	18	19	23	27	24	16	18	23	18	18	23
10	0	27 49	18 22	♎0	25	15	19	26	20	21	26	♎0	27	18	22	26	21	20	26
10	12	0♍57	20 46	3	28	18	22	29	23	24	29	3	29	21	25	29	23	23	29
10	24	4 7	23 11	6	♏0	20	25	♏2	25	27	♐3	6	2	23	28	♎2	25	25	♐2
10	36	7 18	25 35	8	3	23	29	4	28	♐0	6	9	4	26	♏1	5	29	28	5
10	48	10 30	27 59	11	5	25	♐2	7	♏1	2	9	12	7	29	4	8	♏1	♐1	8
11	0	13 43	0♏25	14	8	28	5	10	3	5	12	15	10	♐2	8	11	4	3	11
11	12	16 57	2 51	17	10	♐1	8	12	6	8	16	18	12	4	11	14	6	6	14
11	24	20 12	5 18	20	13	4	12	15	8	11	19	20	15	7	14	17	9	8	17
11	36	23 28	7 45	22	15	7	15	18	11	14	23	23	17	10	17	20	12	11	20
11	48	26 44	10 14	25	17	9	18	20	13	17	26	26	20	13	21	23	14	14	23
12	0	0♎ 0	12 44	28	20	12	22	23	16	20	♐0	29	22	16	24	26	17	16	27

Sid. Time h m	M.C. long. ≙	Asc. ♐	REGIOMONTA. 11	12	2	3	CAMPANUS 11	12	2	3	PLACIDUS 11	12	2	3	NAT. GRAD. 11	12	2	3
12 0	0 0	12 44	28	20	12	22	23	15	20	29	29	22	16	24	26	17	16	27
12 12	3 16	15 15	♍0	22	15	26	26	18	23	♈3	♏2	25	19	28	29	20	19	♈0
12 24	6 32	17 43	3	25	18	29	29	21	27	7	5	23	22	♓1	♏2	22	22	3
12 36	9 48	20 23	6	27	22	♓4	♏1	23	≙0	11	8	♑0	25	5	5	25	24	6
12 48	13 3	23 0	9	♑0	25	7	4	26	4	14	10	3	29	8	8	27	26	9
13 0	16 17	26 57	11	2	28	10	7	28	7	18	13	5	≙2	12	11	♑0	29	12
13 12	19 30	29 40	14	5	≙2	14	10	♑1	11	22	16	8	5	15	14	3	≙2	15
13 24	22 42	1♑6	17	7	5	18	12	3	15	26	19	10	9	19	17	6	5	19
13 36	25 53	3 54	19	10	9	22	15	6	18	♈0	21	13	12	23	20	9	8	22
13 48	29 3	6 46	22	12	13	26	18	8	22	3	24	15	16	26	23	12	11	25
14 0	2♏11	9 41	25	15	16	♈0	21	11	26	7	27	18	20	♈0	27	15	14	28
14 12	5 18	12 41	27	18	20	4	23	14	♈0	11	♈0	21	23	4	♈0	18	17	♈1
14 24	8 23	15 46	♑0	20	24	8	26	16	4	14	2	23	27	7	3	22	21	4
14 36	11 26	18 56	3	23	29	12	28	19	8	18	5	26	♓1	11	6	25	24	7
14 48	14 28	22 11	2	25	♓3	16	♏1	21	13	22	8	29	5	15	9	28	27	10
15 0	17 28	25 33	8	28	7	20	4	24	17	26	10	♑2	9	18	12	♈1	♓0	13
15 12	20 26	29 0	11	♑1	12	23	6	26	21	29	13	4	13	22	15	5	3	17
15 24	23 23	2≙35	13	4	16	27	9	29	26	♉3	16	7	17	25	18	8	7	20
15 36	26 19	6 17	16	7	21	♉1	12	♑2	♈0	6	19	10	22	29	21	12	10	23
15 48	29 13	10 6	18	7	25	4	15	5	5	10	21	13	26	♉2	25	15	14	26
16 0	2♐5	14 3	21	12	♈0	8	18	9	13	♑0	24	16	♈0	6	28	18	18	♉0
16 12	4 57	18 8	24	15	5	12	20	10	14	17	27	19	4	9	♉1	23	22	3
16 24	7 47	22 41	27	18	9	15	23	14	18	20	29	22	8	13	5	27	26	6
16 36	10 36	26 42	29	22	14	18	25	17	22	23	♉2	25	13	16	8	≙1	♈0	9
16 48	13 24	1♏11	♈2	25	18	22	28	20	26	26	5	59	17	19	12	5	4	13
17 0	16 11	5 47	5	28	23	25	♑1	23	♉1	♈0	8	≙2	21	22	15	9	8	16
17 12	18 58	10 29	8	≙2	27	28	4	26	5	3	11	5	25	26	18	13	12	19
17 24	21 44	15 17	11	5	♉1	♈1	6	29	9	6	13	9	29	29	21	18	17	22
17 36	24 30	20 9	1	8	6	5	9	≙3	12	9	16	12	♉3	♈2	24	22	21	25
17 48	27 15	25 4	16	13	10	8	12	6	16	12	19	16	7	5	27	26	26	27
18 0	0♑0	0♈0	19	16	14	11	15	10	20	15	22	20	10	8	♈0	♈0	♈0	♈0
18 12	2 45	4 56	22	20	17	14	18	14	24	18	25	23	14	11	3	4	4	3
18 24	5 30	9 51	25	24	21	17	21	17	27	20	28	27	18	14	6	9	9	6
18 36	8 16	14 43	29	29	25	19	24	21	♉1	23	≙1	♈1	21	17	9	13	13	9
18 48	11 2	19 31	≙2	♈3	28	22	27	25	4	26	4	5	25	19	12	17	17	12
19 0	13 49	24 13	5	7	♉2	25	≙0	29	8	29	8	9	28	22	15	22	21	15
19 12	16 36	28 49	8	12	5	28	3	♈3	11	♉2	11	13	♉1	25	18	26	25	18
19 24	19 24	3♉18	12	16	8	♉1	7	8	14	4	14	17	5	28	21	♈0	29	22
19 36	22 13	7 19	15	21	12	3	10	12	17	7	17	22	8	♉1	25	4	♉3	25
19 48	25 3	11 52	18	25	15	6	13	16	≙0	10	21	26	11	3	28	8	7	29
20 0	27 55	15 57	22	♈0	18	9	16	21	23	12	24	♈0	14	6	♉1	12	12	♉3
20 12	0≙47	19 54	26	5	21	12	20	25	25	15	28	4	17	9	4	16	15	6
20 24	3 41	23 43	29	9	23	14	23	29	28	18	♉1	8	20	11	8	20	19	9
20 36	6 37	27 25	♉4	14	26	17	27	♈4	♉0	20	5	13	23	14	11	23	22	18
20 48	9 34	1♐0	7	18	29	19	♈0	8	3	23	8	17	26	17	14	26	26	15
21 0	12 32	4 27	10	23	♉2	22	4	13	6	26	12	21	28	20	17	♉0	29	18
21 12	15 32	7 49	14	27	5	25	8	17	9	29	15	25	♉1	22	20	4	♉2	21
21 24	18 34	11 4	18	♉1	7	27	11	22	12	♊1	19	29	4	25	23	7	5	24
21 36	21 37	14 14	22	6	10	♊0	15	26	14	4	23	♉3	7	28	26	10	8	27
21 48	24 42	17 19	26	10	12	3	19	♈0	17	7	26	7	9	♊0	29	13	11	♊0
22 0	27 49	20 19	♈0	14	15	5	23	4	19	9	♈0	10	12	3	♊2	16	15	3
22 12	0♏57	23 14	4	17	18	8	26	8	22	12	4	14	14	6	5	19	18	7
22 24	4 7	26 6	8	21	20	11	♈1	12	24	15	7	18	17	9	8	22	21	10
22 36	7 18	28 54	12	25	23	13	4	16	27	17	11	21	20	11	12	25	24	13
22 48	10 30	0≙20	16	28	25	16	8	20	29	20	15	25	22	14	15	28	27	16
23 0	13 43	3 20	♊2	23	♊2	23	18	23	♊2	23	18	28	25	17	18	♊1	♊0	19
23 12	16 57	7 0	23	5	♊0	21	15	27	5	26	22	♊1	28	20	21	4	3	22
23 24	20 12	9 37	27	8	3	24	19	♊0	7	29	25	5	♊0	22	24	6	5	25
23 36	23 28	12 12	♊1	12	5	27	23	3	12	♋1	29	8	2	25	27	9	8	28
23 48	26 44	14 45	15	8	♍0		26	7	12	4	♊2	11	5	28	♊0	11	10	♏1
24 0	0♐0	17 16	8	18	10	2	♊0	10	15	7	6	14	8	♋1	3	14	13	4

217

42° N. Lat.   Cusps of Houses   0h. – 12h.

Sid. Time	M.C. long.	Asc. 1	REGIOMONTA. 11	12	2	3	CAMPANUS 11	12	2	3	PLACIDUS 11	12	2	3	NAT. GRAD. 11	12	2	3
h m			♉	♊	♌	♍	♈	♊	♌	♍	♉	♊	♌	♍	♉	♊	♌	♍
0 0	0 0	19 43	9	20	12	3	29	11	17	8	7	16	9	1	4	16	15	5
0 12	3 16	22 8	13	23	14	6	♉3	14	19	11	10	19	11	4	7	18	17	8
0 24	6 32	24 33	16	26	16	8	7	17	22	13	13	22	14	7	10	21	20	11
0 36	9 48	26 56	20	29	19	11	10	20	24	17	17	25	16	10	13	24	23	14
0 48	13 3	29 18	23	♊2	21	14	13	23	27	19	20	28	19	13	16	26	25	17
1 0	16 17	♊40	26	4	24	16	17	25	29	22	23	♋0	21	16	19	28	27	20
1 12	19 30	4 0	♋0	7	26	19	20	28	♍2	25	27	3	24	18	22	♋1	♍2	22
1 24	22 42	6 21	3	10	28	22	24	♍1	4	28	♍0	6	27	21	25	4	4	25
1 36	25 53	8 51	6	12	♍1	25	27	4	7	♎1	3	8	29	24	29	6	6	29
1 48	29 3	11 0	9	16	3	27	♍0	6	9	4	6	11	♍2	27	♍2	9	8	♎2
2 0	2♋11	13 20	12	17	6	♎0	3	9	12	6	9	14	4	♎0	5	11	10	5
2 12	5 18	15 39	15	20	8	3	6	12	14	9	12	16	7	3	7	14	13	8
2 24	8 23	17 58	18	22	11	5	9	14	17	12	15	19	9	6	10	16	16	11
2 36	11 26	20 17	21	25	13	8	12	17	19	15	18	21	12	9	13	18	18	14
2 48	14 28	22 36	24	26	15	11	15	19	22	18	20	24	14	12	16	21	21	16
3 0	17 28	24 55	27	29	18	14	18	22	24	21	23	26	17	14	19	23	23	19
3 12	20 26	27 15	29	♌2	20	16	21	24	27	23	26	29	20	17	22	26	25	22
3 24	23 23	29 34	♌2	4	23	18	24	27	29	26	29	♌1	22	20	25	28	28	25
3 36	26 19	1♍54	5	7	25	22	27	29	♎2	29	♌1	4	25	23	28	♌1	♎1	28
3 48	29 13	4 13	7	9	28	24	29	♌2	4	♏2	4	6	27	26	♌0	3	3	♏0
4 0	2♊5	6 33	10	12	♎0	29	♌2	4	7	4	7	9	♎0	29	3	6	6	3
4 12	4 57	8 53	13	14	2	♏0	5	7	9	7	10	11	3	♏1	6	8	8	6
4 24	7 47	11 13	15	16	5	3	8	9	12	10	12	14	5	4	9	10	10	9
4 36	10 35	13 39	18	19	7	5	10	12	14	13	15	16	8	7	12	13	13	11
4 48	13 24	15 54	21	21	10	8	13	14	17	16	18	19	10	10	14	15	15	14
5 0	16 12	18 15	23	24	12	10	16	17	19	18	20	21	13	13	17	18	18	16
5 12	18 58	20 36	26	26	15	13	19	19	22	21	23	24	16	15	19	20	20	19
5 24	21 44	22 57	29	28	17	16	22	21	24	23	26	27	18	18	22	23	23	21
5 36	24 30	25 18	♏1	♏1	19	18	24	24	27	26	28	29	21	21	25	25	24	24
5 48	27 15	27 39	4	3	22	21	27	26	29	29	♏1	♏2	23	23	27	28	28	27
6 0	♋0 0	♏0 0	6	6	24	24	29	29	♏2	♐1	4	4	26	26	♏0	♏0	♏0	♏0
6 12	2 45	2 21	9	8	27	26	♏2	♏1	4	4	7	7	28	29	3	2	2	3
6 24	5 30	4 42	12	11	29	29	5	4	7	7	9	9	♏1	♐2	6	5	5	6
6 36	8 16	7 3	14	13	♏2	♐1	7	6	9	12	12	12	3	4	8	7	7	8
6 48	11 2	9 24	7	15	4	4	10	8	11	12	15	14	5	7	11	10	10	11
7 0	13 48	11 45	20	18	6	7	12	11	14	15	17	17	8	9	13	12	12	13
7 12	16 36	14 6	22	20	9	9	15	13	16	17	20	20	11	12	16	15	15	16
7 24	19 25	16 21	25	23	11	12	18	16	19	20	23	22	14	15	19	17	17	19
7 36	22 13	18 47	27	25	14	15	21	18	21	23	26	25	16	18	22	19	19	22
7 48	25 3	21 7	♐0	28	16	17	23	21	24	25	29	27	19	20	24	22	23	24
8 0	27 55	23 27	3	♎0	18	20	26	23	26	28	♐1	♎0	21	23	27	24	24	27
8 12	0♌47	25 47	6	2	21	23	29	26	29	♐1	4	3	24	26	♐0	27	27	♐0
8 24	3 41	28 6	8	5	23	25	♐1	28	♐1	4	7	5	26	28	2	29	29	2
8 36	6 37	0♏26	11	7	26	28	4	♎1	4	7	10	8	29	♐1	5	♎2	♐2	5
8 48	9 34	2 45	14	10	28	♐1	7	3	6	19	13	10	♐1	4	8	4	4	8
9 0	12 32	5 5	16	12	♐0	3	10	6	9	12	16	13	4	7	11	7	7	11
9 12	15 32	7 24	19	15	3	6	12	8	11	15	18	16	6	10	14	9	9	14
9 24	18 34	9 43	22	17	5	9	15	11	14	18	21	16	9	12	16	12	12	17
9 36	21 37	16 2	25	19	8	12	18	13	16	21	24	18	11	15	20	14	15	19
9 48	24 42	14 21	27	22	10	15	21	16	19	24	27	21	13	18	22	17	16	13
10 0	27 49	16 40	♎0	24	13	18	24	18	21	27	♎0	23	17	21	25	19	19	25
10 12	0♏57	19 0	3	27	15	21	26	21	24	♑0	3	26	19	24	28	22	21	28
10 24	4 7	21 9	5	29	18	24	29	23	27	3	6	28	22	27	♎1	24	24	♏1
10 36	7 18	23 39	8	♏2	20	27	♑2	26	29	6	9	♏1	24	♑0	5	26	26	5
10 48	10 30	26 0	11	4	23	♑0	5	28	♑2	10	12	3	27	4	8	28	29	8
11 0	13 43	28 20	14	6	26	4	8	♏1	5	13	14	6	♑0	7	10	♏2	♑1	11
11 12	16 57	0♐42	16	9	28	7	11	3	8	16	17	9	2	10	13	5	4	14
11 24	20 12	3 4	19	11	♑1	10	14	6	11	20	20	11	5	13	16	8	7	16
11 36	23 28	5 27	22	14	4	14	17	8	14	23	23	13	8	17	19	10	9	20
11 48	26 44	7 52	24	16	7	17	20	11	17	27	26	16	11	20	22	13	12	23
12 0	0♎0	10 17	27	18	10	21	23	13	20	♓1	29	19	14	23	25	15	14	26

Sid. Time	M. C. long.	Asc.	REGIOMONTA.				CAMPANUS				PLACIDUS				NAT. GRAD.			
h m	♎	♐	11 ♎	12 ♏	2 ♑	3 ♒	11 ♎	12 ♏	2 ♑	3 ♓	11 ♎	12 ♏	2 ♑	3 ♒	11 ♎	12 ♏	2 ♑	3 ♒
12 0	0 0	10 18	27	18	10	21	22	13	20	1	29	21	14	23	25	15	14	26
12 12	3 16	12 45	♏0	21	13	25	25	16	23	4	♏1	24	17	27	28	18	17	29
12 24	6 32	15 13	3	23	16	28	27	18	27	8	4	26	20	♓0	♏1	21	19	♓2
12 36	9 48	17 44	5	26	19	♓2	♏0	21	♒0	12	7	29	23	4	4	24	22	6
12 48	13 3	20 17	8	28	22	6	3	22	3	16	10	♏1	27	8	7	26	25	9
13 0	16 17	22 52	10	♏0	26	10	6	26	7	19	13	4	♒0	11	10	29	27	12
13 12	19 30	25 31	13	3	29	14	8	28	11	23	15	6	3	15	13	♐2	♒0	15
13 24	22 42	28 12	16	5	3	18	11	♐1	15	27	18	9	7	19	16	4	3	18
13 36	25 53	0♑56	18	8	6	22	14	3	19	♈1	21	11	10	22	♒0	7	6	21
13 48	29 3	3 45	21	10	10	26	16	5	23	5	23	14	14	26	23	10	9	24
14 0	2♏11	6 37	24	13	14	♈0	19	8	27	9	26	16	18	♈0	26	13	11	27
14 12	5 18	9 34	26	15	18	4	22	11	♓1	13	29	19	22	4	29	16	14	♈2
14 24	8 23	12 37	29	18	22	8	25	13	5	16	♈2	22	26	8	♓2	19	17	4
14 36	11 26	15 45	♐1	20	27	12	27	16	10	20	4	24	♓0	11	5	22	20	7
14 48	14 28	18 57	4	23	♓1	16	♈0	18	14	24	7	27	4	15	8	25	24	10
15 0	17 28	22 20	7	26	6	20	2	21	19	28	9	29	8	19	11	29	27	13
15 12	20 26	25 45	9	28	10	24	5	23	23	♉1	12	♑2	12	22	14	♑2	♓0	16
15 24	23 23	29 26	12	♑1	15	28	8	26	28	5	15	5	17	26	17	5	4	19
15 36	26 19	3♒9	15	4	20	♉2	10	29	♈3	8	18	8	21	♉0	20	9	7	22
15 48	29 13	7 3	17	7	25	4	13	♑2	8	11	20	11	26	3	24	13	11	25
16 0	2♐5	11 7	20	10	♈0	9	16	4	12	15	23	14	♈0	7	27	16	15	28
16 12	4 57	15 20	23	13	5	13	18	7	17	19	26	17	4	10	♑0	20	19	♉1
16 24	7 47	19 43	25	16	10	16	21	10	22	22	28	20	9	13	4	24	23	4
16 36	10 35	24 17	28	19	15	20	24	13	26	25	♑1	23	13	17	7	28	28	7
16 48	13 24	29 0	♑1	22	20	23	27	16	♉0	28	4	27	18	20	11	=1	♈2	11
17 0	16 12	3♓53	3	26	24	26	29	19	5	♊2	7	♒0	22	23	14	6	6	14
17 12	18 58	8 55	6	29	29	♊0	♑2	22	9	5	10	3	26	27	17	11	11	17
17 24	21 44	14 4	9	=3	♉3	3	5	26	13	8	12	7	♉0	♊0	20	16	16	20
17 36	24 30	19 19	12	6	8	6	8	29	17	11	15	10	4	3	23	21	20	23
17 48	27 15	24 39	15	10	12	9	10	=3	21	14	18	14	8	6	27	25	25	27
18 0	0♑0	0♈0	18	14	16	12	13	7	24	17	21	18	12	9	=0	♈0	♉0	♊0
18 12	2 45	5 21	21	18	20	15	16	10	26	12	24	22	16	12	3	5	3	3
18 24	5 30	10 41	24	22	24	18	19	14	♊1	22	27	26	19	15	7	10	9	7
18 36	8 16	15 56	27	27	27	21	22	18	5	25	=0	♈0	23	18	10	14	14	10
18 48	11 2	21 5	=0	♈1	♊1	24	25	22	9	28	4	4	27	20	13	19	19	13
19 0	13 48	26 7	4	6	4	27	28	26	12	♋1	7	8	♊0	23	16	24	24	16
19 12	16 36	1♉0	7	10	8	29	=1	♈0	15	3	10	12	3	26	19	28	29	19
19 24	19 25	5 43	10	15	11	♋2	5	4	18	6	13	17	7	29	23	♈2	♊2	23
19 36	22 13	10 17	14	20	14	5	8	9	21	9	17	21	9	♋1	26	7	6	27
19 48	25 3	14 40	17	25	17	7	11	13	23	11	20	26	13	4	29	11	10	♋0
20 0	27 55	18 53	21	♈0	20	10	15	18	26	14	23	♈0	16	7	♈2	15	14	3
20 12	0=47	22 57	25	5	23	13	18	23	27	17	27	4	19	10	5	17	17	7
20 24	3 41	26 51	28	10	26	15	22	27	♋2	19	♈0	9	22	12	8	23	21	10
20 36	6 37	0♊35	♈2	15	29	18	25	♈2	4	22	4	13	25	15	11	26	25	12
20 48	9 34	4 15	6	20	♋2	21	29	6	7	25	8	18	28	18	14	29	28	16
21 0	12 32	7 40	10	24	4	23	♈2	11	10	27	11	22	♋0	20	17	♉3	♋1	19
21 12	15 32	11 3	14	29	7	26	6	16	12	♌0	15	26	3	23	20	6	5	22
21 24	18 34	14 15	18	♉3	10	29	10	20	15	3	19	♉0	6	26	23	10	8	25
21 36	21 37	17 23	22	8	12	♌1	14	25	17	5	22	4	8	28	26	13	11	28
21 48	24 42	20 26	26	12	15	4	17	29	20	8	26	8	11	♌1	♈0	16	14	♌1
22 0	27 49	23 23	♈0	16	17	6	21	♉4	22	11	♈0	12	14	4	3	19	17	4
22 12	0♓57	26 15	4	20	20	9	25	8	25	13	4	16	16	7	6	22	20	7
22 24	4 7	29 4	8	24	23	12	29	12	27	16	8	20	19	9	9	24	23	10
22 36	7 18	1♋48	♈3	28	26	14	♈3	16	♌0	19	11	23	21	12	12	27	26	14
22 48	10 30	4 29	16	♊1	28	17	7	20	2	22	15	27	24	15	15	♊0	28	17
23 0	13 43	7 8	20	4	29	20	11	23	5	24	19	♊0	26	17	18	3	♌1	20
23 12	16 57	9 43	24	8	♌2	22	15	27	7	27	22	3	29	20	21	5	4	23
23 24	20 12	12 16	28	11	4	25	18	♋0	10	♍0	26	7	♌1	23	24	8	7	26
23 36	23 28	14 47	♊2	14	7	27	22	4	12	3	♊0	10	4	26	28	11	9	29
23 48	26 44	17 15	5	17	9	♍0	26	7	15	5	3	13	6	29	♊1	13	12	♍2
24 0	0♈0	19 42	9	20	12	3	♍0	10	17	8	7	16	9	♍1	4	16	15	5

Sid. Time		M.C. long.	Asc. 1	REGIOMONTA.				CAMPANUS				PLACIDUS				NAT. GRAD.			
				11	12	2	3	11	12	2	3	11	12	2	3	11	12	2	3
h	m	♈	♉	♉	♊	♌	♍	♈	♊	♌	♍	♉	♊	♌	♍	♉	♊	♌	♍
0	0	0 0	21 42	10 23	13	3	29	11	19	9	7	18	10	2	4	18	16	5
0	12	3 16	24 4	14 25	15	6	♉2	14	21	12	11	21	12	4	7	20	19	8
0	24	6 32	26 24	17 28	18	9	6	17	24	15	14	24	15	7	10	23	21	11
0	36	9 48	28 44	21 ♋1	20	11	9	20	6	18	17	26	17	10	13	25	24	14
0	48	13 3	1♊ 2	24 4	22	14	13	23	29	20	21	29	20	13	17	28	27	17
1	0	16 17	3 20	28 6	25	17	16	26	♍1	23	24	♋2	22	16	20	♋0	29	20
1	12	19 30	5 37	♊1 9	27	19	20	29	3	26	27	5	25	19	23	2	♍2	23
1	24	22 42	7 54	4 12	29	22	23	♋1	5	29	♊0	7	27	21	26	5	4	26
1	36	25 53	10 10	7 14	♍2	25	26	4	8	♍2	3	10	♍0	24	29	7	7	29
1	48	29 3	12 26	10 17	4	27	29	7	11	5	7	13	2	27	♊2	10	9	♍2
2	0	2♉11	14 4	13 19	6	♎0	♊3	9	13	7	10	15	5	♎0	5	13	12	5
2	12	5 18	16 57	15 22	9	3	6	12	16	10	13	18	7	3	8	15	14	8
2	24	8 23	19 12	18 24	11	5	9	14	18	13	15	20	10	6	11	17	17	11
2	36	11 26	21 27	21 26	13	8	12	17	20	16	18	23	12	9	14	19	19	14
2	48	14 28	23 42	24 29	16	11	15	19	23	18	21	25	15	11	16	22	22	17
3	0	17 28	25 57	27 ♌1	18	13	18	22	25	21	24	28	17	14	19	24	24	19
3	12	20 26	28 13	♊0 3	20	16	20	24	28	24	27	♌0	20	17	22	27	26	22
3	24	23 23	0♋28	3 6	23	19	23	27	♎0	27	♌0	3	22	16	25	29	29	25
3	36	26 19	2 44	6 8	25	21	25	29	3	♍0	3	5	25	23	28	♌1	♎1	28
3	48	29 13	4 59	9 11	28	24	28	♌2	5	2	6	8	27	26	♋0	4	4	♍1
4	0	2♊ 5	7 15	11 13	♎0	27	♋1	4	8	5	8	10	♎0	28	3	6	6	3
4	12	4 57	9 31	14 15	2	29	4	7	10	8	10	12	3	♍1	6	9	8	6
4	24	7 47	11 47	17 18	5	2	7	9	12	10	13	15	5	4	9	11	11	9
4	36	10 35	14 3	19 20	7	5	9	11	15	13	16	17	8	7	11	13	13	11
4	48	13 24	16 20	22 22	10	7	12	14	17	16	18	20	10	9	14	16	16	14
5	0	16 12	18 36	24 25	12	10	15	16	20	18	21	22	13	12	17	18	18	17
5	12	18 58	20 53	27 27	14	12	18	19	22	21	24	25	15	15	19	20	20	19
5	24	21 44	23 10	29 29	17	15	20	21	24	24	27	27	18	18	22	23	23	22
5	36	24 30	25 26	♌2 ♍2	19	18	23	23	27	27	29	♍0	20	20	25	25	25	25
5	48	27 15	27 43	5 9	21	20	26	25	29	♍0	♌2	2	23	23	27	28	28	27
6	0	0♋ 0	0♌ 0	7 6	24	23	28	28	♍2	2	4	5	28	26	♌0	♍0	♍0	♎0
6	12	2 45	2 17	10 9	26	25	♌1	♍1	4	5	7	7	28	28	3	2	3	3
6	24	5 30	4 34	12 11	28	28	4	3	6	8	10	10	♍0	♎1	5	5	5	5
6	36	8 16	6 50	15 13	♍1	♍1	6	5	9	10	12	12	3	3	8	7	7	7
6	48	11 2	9 7	18 16	3	3	8	8	11	13	15	15	5	6	11	10	10	11
7	0	13 48	11 24	20 18	5	6	12	10	14	16	18	17	8	9	13	12	12	13
7	12	16 36	13 40	23 20	8	8	14	13	16	18	21	20	10	12	16	14	14	16
7	24	20 26	15 47	25 23	10	11	17	15	19	21	23	22	13	14	19	17	17	19
7	36	22 13	18 13	28 25	12	13	20	18	21	24	26	25	15	17	21	19	19	21
7	48	25 3	20 29	♍1 28	15	16	22	20	23	26	29	27	18	20	24	22	21	24
8	0	27 55	22 45	3 ♎0	17	19	25	22	26	29	♍2	♎0	20	22	27	24	24	27
8	12	0♋57	25 1	6 2	19	21	28	25	28	♏2	4	3	22	24	29	26	26	♏0
8	24	3 41	27 16	9 5	22	24	♍0	27	♏0	4	7	5	25	27	♍2	29	29	2
8	36	6 37	29 32	11 7	24	27	3	♎0	3	7	10	8	27	♏0	5	♎1	♏1	5
8	48	9 34	1♍47	14 10	27	♎0	6	2	5	10	13	10	♏0	3	8	4	3	8
9	0	12 32	4 3	17 12	29	3	9	5	8	13	16	13	2	6	11	6	6	11
9	12	15 32	6 18	19 14	♎1	6	12	7	10	15	19	15	5	9	14	8	8	13
9	24	18 24	8 33	22 17	4	9	14	10	13	18	21	18	7	12	16	11	10	16
9	36	21 37	10 48	25 19	6	12	17	12	15	21	24	20	10	15	19	13	13	19
9	48	24 42	13 3	27 21	8	15	20	14	18	24	27	23	12	17	22	16	15	22
10	0	27 49	15 56	♎0 24	11	17	23	17	20	27	♎0	25	15	20	25	18	18	25
10	12	0♏57	17 34	3 26	13	20	26	19	23	♏1	3	28	17	23	27	21	20	28
10	24	4 7	19 50	5 28	16	23	28	21	26	4	6	♏0	20	26	♎1	24	23	♏1
10	36	7 18	22 6	8 ♏1	18	26	♎1	24	28	7	9	3	23	♏0	4	26	25	4
10	48	10 30	24 23	11 3	21	29	4	26	♏1	10	11	5	25	3	7	28	28	7
11	0	13 43	26 40	13 5	24	♏2	7	29	4	14	14	8	28	6	10	♏1	♏0	10
11	12	16 57	28 58	16 8	26	6	10	♏1	7	17	17	10	♏1	9	13	3	3	13
11	24	20 12	1♏15	19 10	29	9	12	4	10	21	20	13	4	13	16	6	5	17
11	36	23 28	3 36	21 12	♏2	13	15	6	13	24	23	15	6	16	19	9	7	20
11	48	26 44	5 56	24 15	5	16	18	8	16	28	26	18	9	19	22	11	10	23
12	0	0♏ 0	8 18	27 17	7	20	21	11	19	♐1	28	20	12	23	26	14	12	26

220

Sid. Time	M.C. long.	Asc. 1	REGIOMONTA. 11	12	2	3	CAMPANUS 11	12	2	3	PLACIDUS 11	12	2	3	NAT. GRAD. 11	12	2	3
h m	♎	♏	♎	♏	♑	♒	♎	♏	♑	♒	♎	♏	♑	♒	♎	♏	♑	♒
12 0	0 0	8 18	27	17	7♐	20	21	11	19	1	28	20	12	23	25	14	12	26
12 12	3 16	10 42	29	19	10	24	23	13	22	5	♏1	22	15	26	28	17	15	29
12 24	6 32	13 7	♏2	22	12	28	26	16	26	9	4	25	18	♓0	♐1	19	17	♓2
12 36	9 48	15 34	5	24	17	♓1	29	18	29	12	7	27	22	4	3	22	20	5
12 48	13 3	18 3	7	27	20	5	♏2	20	≈3	17	9	♐0	25	7	7	24	23	8
13 0	16 17	20 34	10	29	23	9	4	23	6	20	12	2	28	11	10	27	25	12
13 12	19 30	23 9	12	♐1	27	13	7	25	10	24	15	5	≈2	15	13	♐0	28	14
13 24	22 42	25 46	15	4	≈0	17	10	28	14	28	18	7	5	19	16	3	≈1	18
13 36	25 53	28 27	18	6	4	22	12	♐0	18	♓2	20	10	9	22	19	5	3	21
13 48	29 3	1♏12	20	8	8	26	15	3	23	6	23	12	13	26	22	8	6	24
14 0	2♏11	4 1	23	11	12	♈0	18	5	27	10	26	15	17	♈0	25	11	9	27
14 12	5 18	6 55	25	13	16	4	21	8	♓1	14	28	17	20	4	28	14	12	♈0
14 24	8 23	9 55	28	16	20	8	23	10	6	18	♐1	20	25	8	♐1	17	15	3
14 36	11 26	13 0	♐1	18	25	13	26	13	11	22	4	23	29	11	4	20	18	6
14 48	14 28	16 13	3	21	♓0	17	28	15	16	25	6	25	♓3	15	7	23	21	10
15 0	17 28	19 32	6	24	4	21	♐1	18	20	29	9	28	7	19	10	27	25	13
15 12	20 26	23 0	8	26	9	25	4	20	25	♓3	12	♏1	12	23	13	♐0	28	16
15 24	23 23	26 36	11	29	14	29	6	23	♈0	6	14	4	16	26	17	3	♓1	19
15 36	26 19	0≈22	13	♒2	20	♓2	9	25	5	10	17	6	21	♓0	20	7	5	22
15 48	29 13	4 18	16	5	25	6	12	28	10	13	20	9	25	4	23	11	9	25
16 0	2♐5	8 26	19	7	♈0	10	14	♏1	15	17	22	12	♈0	7	26	14	13	28
16 12	4 57	12 45	21	10	5	14	17	4	20	20	24	15	5	11	29	18	17	♈1
16 24	7 47	17 16	24	13	10	17	20	6	25	23	27	18	9	14	♒2	22	21	4
16 36	10 35	22 0	27	17	16	21	22	9	29	27	♒0	22	14	17	6	27	26	7
16 48	13 24	26 56	♒0	20	21	24	24	12	♉4	♊0	3	25	18	21	9	♒1	♈0	10
17 0	16 12	2♓4	3	23	26	28	28	15	8	3	6	28	23	24	13	5	5	13
17 12	18 58	7 24	6	27	♉0	♊1	♏1	19	12	6	9	≈2	27	27	16	10	10	17
17 24	21 44	12 54	9	♒0	5	4	3	22	16	9	12	5	♉1	♊0	20	15	15	20
17 36	24 30	18 31	12	4	10	7	6	25	20	12	15	9	5	3	23	20	20	23
17 48	27 15	24 14	15	8	14	10	9	29	24	15	17	13	10	7	27	25	25	27
18 0	0♑0	0♈0	17	12	18	13	12	≈2	28	18	20	17	13	10	≈0	♈0	♉0	♊0
18 12	2 45	5 44	20	16	22	15	15	♊1	♊1	21	23	20	17	13	3	5	5	4
18 24	5 30	11 29	23	20	26	18	18	10	5	24	26	25	21	15	7	10	10	7
18 36	8 16	17 6	26	25	♊0	21	21	14	8	27	≈0	29	25	18	10	15	15	10
18 48	11 2	22 36	29	♈0	3	24	24	18	11	♊0	3	♓3	28	21	13	20	20	14
19 0	13 48	27 55	≈2	4	6	27	27	22	14	3	6	7	♊2	24	17	25	25	17
19 12	16 36	3♉4	6	9	10	♋0	≈0	26	17	6	9	12	5	27	20	♈0	29	21
19 24	19 25	8 0	9	14	13	3	3	♈1	20	8	13	16	8	♋0	23	4	♊3	24
19 36	22 13	12 44	13	20	17	6	6	5	23	11	16	21	12	3	26	9	7	28
19 48	25 3	17 15	16	25	20	9	10	10	26	14	19	25	15	6	29	13	11	♋1
20 0	27 55	21 34	20	♈0	23	11	13	15	29	16	23	♈0	18	8	♈3	17	15	4
20 12	0♑47	25 42	24	5	25	14	17	20	♋2	19	26	5	21	10	6	21	19	7
20 24	3 41	29 38	28	10	28	17	20	25	4	22	♈0	9	24	13	9	25	23	11
20 36	6 37	3♊24	♈1	16	♋1	19	24	♈0	7	24	4	14	26	16	12	28	26	14
20 48	9 34	7 0	5	21	4	22	27	4	10	27	7	18	29	18	15	♉2	♋0	17
21 0	12 32	10 28	9	26	6	24	♈1	9	12	♌0	11	23	♋2	21	17	5	3	20
21 12	15 32	13 47	13	♉0	9	27	5	14	15	2	15	27	5	24	20	9	6	23
21 24	18 34	17 0	17	5	12	29	8	19	17	5	19	♉1	7	27	23	12	10	26
21 36	21 37	20 5	22	10	14	♌2	12	24	20	8	22	5	10	29	27	15	13	29
21 48	24 42	23 5	26	14	17	5	16	28	22	10	26	10	13	♌2	♈0	18	16	♌2
22 0	27 49	25 59	♉0	18	19	7	20	♋3	25	12	♉0	13	15	4	3	21	19	5
22 12	0♒57	28 48	4	22	22	10	24	7	27	15	5	17	18	7	6	24	22	8
22 24	4 7	1♌33	8	26	24	12	28	12	♌0	17	8	21	20	10	9	27	25	11
22 36	7 18	4 14	13	♋0	26	15	♈2	16	2	20	11	25	23	12	12	29	27	14
22 48	10 30	6 51	17	3	29	18	6	20	5	22	15	28	25	15	15	♊2	♌0	17
23 0	13 43	9 26	21	6	♌1	20	10	23	7	26	19	♊2	28	18	18	5	3	20
23 12	16 57	11 57	25	10	3	23	13	27	9	28	23	5	♌0	21	22	7	6	23
23 24	20 12	14 26	29	13	6	25	17	♋0	12	♍1	26	8	3	23	25	10	9	27
23 36	23 38	16 43	♉2	17	8	28	21	4	14	4	♋0	12	5	26	28	12	11	29
23 48	26 44	19 18	6	20	11	♍1	25	7	17	7	4	15	8	29	♋1	15	14	♍2
24 0	0♈0	21 42	10	23	13	3	29	11	19	9	7	18	10	♍2	4	18	16	5

Sid. Time	M.C. long.	Asc. 1	REGIOMONTA. 11	12	2	3	CAMPANUS 11	12	2	3	PLACIDUS 11	12	2	3	NAT. GRAD. 11	12	2	3
h m	♈	♉	♉	♊	♌	♍	♉	♊	♌	♍	♉	♊	♌	♍	♉	♊	♌	♍
0 0	0 0	23 50	12	25	14	4	27	11	21	10	8	20	11	2	4	19	18	6
0 12	3 16	26 8	15	28	16	6	♉1	14	23	13	11	23	14	5	8	22	20	9
0 24	6 32	28 24	18	♋1	19	9	5	17	26	16	15	26	16	8	11	24	23	12
0 36	9 48	0♋39	22	3	21	12	8	20	28	19	18	28	18	10	14	27	25	15
0 48	13 3	2 54	25	6	23	14	12	23	♍0	22	22	♋1	21	13	17	29	28	18
1 0	16 17	5 7	29	9	26	17	15	26	3	24	25	4	23	16	20	♋1	♍1	21
1 12	19 30	7 20	♊2	11	28	19	19	29	5	27	28	6	26	19	23	4	3	24
1 24	22 42	9 32	5	14	♍0	22	22	♋1	8	29	♊1	9	28	22	26	6	5	27
1 36	25 53	11 44	8	16	2	25	26	4	10	♎3	4	12	♍0	24	29	9	8	♎0
1 48	29 3	13 56	12	19	5	27	29	7	13	6	7	14	3	27	♊2	11	10	3
2 0	2♉11	16 7	15	21	7	♎0	♊2	9	15	8	11	17	5	♎0	5	13	13	6
2 12	5 18	18 18	18	23	9	3	5	12	17	11	13	19	8	3	8	16	15	8
2 24	8 23	20 30	21	26	12	5	8	15	19	14	17	22	10	6	11	18	18	11
2 36	11 26	22 41	23	28	14	8	11	17	22	16	19	24	13	8	14	20	20	14
2 48	14 28	24 52	26	♌0	16	11	14	19	24	19	22	27	15	11	17	23	22	17
3 0	17 29	27 3	29	3	18	13	17	22	27	22	25	29	18	14	19	25	25	20
3 12	20 26	29 14	♋2	5	21	16	20	24	29	25	28	♌2	20	17	22	27	27	23
3 24	23 23	1♋45	4	7	23	18	23	27	♎1	28	♌1	4	23	20	25	♌0	♎0	26
3 36	26 19	3 36	7	10	25	21	26	29	4	♍0	3	6	25	22	28	2	2	28
3 48	29 13	5 47	10	12	28	24	28	♌2	6	3	6	9	28	25	♋1	4	4	♍1
4 0	2♊5	7 59	12	14	♎0	26	♋1	4	9	6	9	11	♎0	28	3	7	7	3
4 12	4 57	10 11	15	16	2	29	4	6	11	8	11	14	2	♍1	6	9	9	6
4 24	7 47	12 23	18	19	5	♍1	7	9	13	11	14	16	5	3	9	11	11	9
4 36	10 36	14 34	20	21	7	4	9	11	16	14	17	18	7	6	11	14	14	12
4 48	13 24	16 46	23	23	9	7	12	13	18	16	19	21	10	9	14	16	16	14
5 0	16 11	18 58	25	26	12	9	15	16	21	19	22	23	12	12	17	18	18	17
5 12	18 58	21 5	28	28	14	12	17	18	23	22	25	26	15	14	19	21	21	19
5 24	21 44	23 23	♌0	♍0	16	14	20	21	25	24	27	28	17	17	22	23	23	22
5 36	24 30	25 35	3	2	18	17	23	22	28	27	♌0	♍0	20	20	25	25	25	25
5 48	27 15	27 48	6	5	21	19	25	25	♎0	♎0	2	3	22	22	27	28	28	27
6 0	0♋0	0♍0	8	7	23	22	28	28	2	2	5	5	25	25	♍0	♍0	♍0	♍0
6 12	2 45	2 12	11	9	25	24	♌0	♍0	5	5	8	8	27	28	3	2	2	2
6 24	5 30	4 25	13	12	28	27	3	2	8	8	10	10	♍0	♎0	5	5	5	5
6 36	8 16	6 37	16	14♍0	♎0	6	5	10	10	13	13	2	3	8	7	7	8
6 48	11 2	8 55	18	16	2	2	8	7	12	13	16	15	4	5	11	9	9	11
7 0	13 49	11 2	21	18	4	5	11	9	14	15	18	18	7	8	13	12	12	13
7 12	16 36	13 14	23	21	7	7	14	11	17	18	21	20	9	11	16	14	14	16
7 24	19 24	15 26	26	23	9	10	16	14	19	21	24	23	12	13	18	16	16	18
7 36	22 13	17 37	29	25	11	12	19	16	21	23	27	25	14	16	21	19	19	21
7 48	25 3	19 49	♍1	28	14	15	22	18	24	26	29	28	16	19	24	21	21	24
8 0	27 55	22 1	4	♎0	16	18	24	21	26	29	♍2	♎0	19	21	27	24	23	27
8 12	0♋47	24 13	6	2	18	20	27	24	29	♏1	5	2	21	24	29	26	26	29
8 24	3 41	26 24	9	5	20	23	♍0	26	♏1	4	8	5	24	27	♍2	28	28	♏2
8 36	6 37	28 35	12	7	23	26	2	29	3	7	10	7	26	29	5	♎0	♏0	5
8 48	9 34	1♏46	14	9	25	28	5	♎1	6	10	13	10	29	♏2	7	4	4	6
9 0	12 13	2 57	17	12	27	♏1	8	3	8	13	16	12	♏1	5	10	5	5	10
9 12	15 32	5 8	19	14	♏0	4	11	6	11	16	19	15	3	8	13	8	7	13
9 24	18 34	7 19	22	16	2	7	13	8	13	19	22	17	6	11	16	10	10	16
9 36	21 37	9 30	25	18	4	9	16	11	15	22	24	20	8	14	19	12	12	19
9 48	24 42	11 42	27	21	7	12	19	13	18	25	27	22	11	17	22	15	14	22
10 0	27 49	13 43	♎0	23	9	15	22	15	21	28	♎0	25	13	19	24	17	17	25
10 12	0♌57	16 4	3	25	11	18	25	18	23	♏1	3	27	16	23	27	20	19	28
10 24	4 7	18 16	5	28	14	21	27	20	26	4	6	♏0	18	26	♎0	22	21	♏1
10 36	7 18	20 28	8	♏0	16	25	♎0	22	28	8	8	2	21	29	3	25	24	4
10 48	10 30	22 40	11	2	19	28	3	25	♏1	11	11	4	24	♏2	6	27	26	7
11 0	13 43	24 53	13	44	21	♏1	6	27	4	15	14	7	26	5	9	29	28	10
11 12	16 57	27 6	16	7	24	5	8	♏0	6	18	17	9	29	8	12	♏2	♏1	13
11 24	20 12	29 21	18	9	27	8	11	2	10	21	20	12	♐2	12	15	5	3	16
11 36	23 28	1♐36	21	11	29	11	14	4	13	25	22	14	4	15	18	7	6	19
11 48	26 44	3 52	24	14	♐2	15	17	7	16	29	25	16	7	19	21	10	8	22
12 0	0♎0	6 10	26	16	5	19	20	9	19	♐3	28	19	10	22	24	12	11	26

222

Sid. Time h m	M.C. long.	Asc. 1	REG. 11	12	2	3	CAMP. 11	12	2	3	PLAC. 11	12	2	3	NAT. 11	12	2	3
12 0	0 ♎ 0	6 10	26	16	5	18	20	9	19	3	28	19	10	22	24	12	11	27
12 12	3 16	8 29	29	18	8	23	22	11	23	6	♏1	21	13	26	27	15	13	✕0
12 24	6 32	10 49	♏1	20	11	27	25	13	26	10	3	24	16	29	♏0	17	16	2
12 36	9 48	13 11	4	23	14	✕1	28	16	=0	14	6	26	20	✕3	3	2♉	18	5
12 48	13 3	15 56	7	25	17	5	♏1	18	3	18	9	28	23	7	6	23	21	8
13 0	16 17	18 3	9	27	21	9	4	21	7	22	12	♏1	26	11	9	25	23	♊1
13 12	19 30	20 33	12	♑0	24	13	7	23	11	26	14	3	=0	15	12	28	26	14
13 24	22 42	23 6	14	2	28	17	9	25	15	♈0	17	6	3	18	15	♏1	28	17
13 36	25 53	25 42	17	4	=1	21	11	28	19	4	20	8	7	22	18	4	=1	19
13 48	29 3	28 22	19	7	5	26	14	♑0	24	8	22	11	11	26	21	7	4	22
14 0	2♏11	1♈ 7	22	9	9	=0	17	2	28	12	25	13	14	♈0	24	9	7	25
14 12	5 18	3 57	24	11	14	4	19	5	✕3	16	28	16	19	4	27	12	10	27
14 24	8 23	6 52	27	14	19	9	22	7	8	20	♑0	18	23	8	♑0	15	13	♈1
14 36	11 26	9 53	♑0	16	23	13	25	10	13	24	3	21	27	12	3	18	16	4
14 48	14 28	13 2	2	19	28	17	27	12	18	27	5	24	✕2	15	6	21	19	8
15 0	17 29	16 18	5	21	✕3	21	♑0	15	23	♉1	8	26	6	19	10	24	22	12
15 12	20 26	19 44	7	24	8	25	3	17	28	5	11	29	11	23	13	28	25	15
15 24	23 23	23 19	10	27	13	29	5	20	♈3	9	14	♑2	16	27	16	♏1	29	18
15 36	26 19	27 4	12	29	19	♉3	8	22	9	12	16	4	21	♉1	19	4	✕3	21
15 48	29 13	1= 1	15	♑2	24	7	10	25	14	15	19	7	25	4	22	8	6	24
16 0	2♐ 5	5 12	18	5	♈0	12	13	28	19	19	21	10	♈0	8	25	12	10	27
16 12	4 57	9 36	20	8	6	15	16	·♈0	24	22	24	13	5	11	29	16	15	♉0
16 24	7 47	14 15	23	11	11	19	18	3	28	25	27	16	9	15	♑2	21	19	4
16 36	10 36	19 10	26	14	17	22	21	6	♉3	28	29	20	14	18	5	25	24	7
16 48	13 24	24 20	28	17	22	25	24	9	8	♉2	♏2	23	19	22	9	=0	28	10
17 0	16 11	29 47	♑1	21	27	29	26	12	12	5	5	26	24	25	12	4	♈3	13
17 12	18 58	5✕28	4	24	♉2	♊2	29	15	16	8	8	=0	28	28	16	9	8	16
17 24	21 44	11 23	7	28	7	5	♏2	18	20	11	11	3	♉3	♊1	19	14	14	20
17 36	24 30	17 29	9	=1	11	8	5	21	24	14	14	7	4	4	23	20	19	23
17 48	27 15	24 52	12	5	16	11	8	25	28	17	17	11	11	7	26	25	25	27
18 0	0♑ 0	0♈ 0	15	9	21	14	10	28	♊1	20	19	14	16	11	0 ✕0	♉0	♊0	
18 12	2 45	5 8	18	14	25	17	13	=2	5	23	23	19	19	13	3	5	5	4
18 24	5 30	12 31	22	19	29	20	16	6	8	25	26	23	23	17	7	11	10	7
18 36	8 16	18 37	25	23	♉2	23	19	10	12	28	29	27	27	19	11	16	16	11
18 48	11 2	24 32	28	28	6	26	22	14	15	♋1	=2	✕2	♊0	22	14	22	21	14
19 0	13 49	0♉13	=1	✕2	9	29	25	18	18	4	5	6	4	25	17	27	26	18
19 12	16 36	5 40	5	8	13	♋1	28	22	22	6	8	11	7	28	20	♈2	♊1	21
19 24	19 24	10 50	8	13	16	4	=2	27	24	9	12	16	10	♋1	23	7	5	25
19 36	22 13	15 45	12	19	19	7	5	✕2	27	12	14	21	14	3	27	11	9	28
19 48	25 3	20 24	15	24	22	9	8	6	♋0	14	19	25	17	6	✕0	15	14	♋1
20 0	27 55	24 48	18	♈0	25	12	11	2	17	22	22	♈0	20	9	3	20	18	5
20 12	0=55	28 59	23	6	28	15	15	16	5	20	26	5	23	11	6	24	21	8
20 24	3 41	2♊56	27	11	♋1	17	19	21	8	22	29	9	26	13	9	27	25	11
20 36	6 37	6 16	✕1	17	3	20	22	27	10	25	✕3	14	28	17	13	♉1	29	14
20 48	9 34	10 16	5	22	6	23	26	♈2	13	28	7	19	♋1	20	16	5	♋2	17
21 0	12 31	13 42	9	27	9	25	29	7	15	♋0	11	24	4	22	19	8	6	21
21 12	15 32	16 58	13	♉2	11	28	✕3	12	18	3	15	28	6	25	22	11	9	24
21 24	18 34	20 7	17	7	14	♌0	7	17	20	5	18	♉3	9	27	25	14	12	27
21 36	21 37	23 8	21	11	16	3	11	22	23	8	22	7	12	♌0	28	17	15	♌0
21 48	24 42	26 3	26	16	19	6	15	27	25	11	26	11	14	2	♈1	20	18	3
22 0	27 49	28 53	♈0	21	21	8	19	♉1	28	13	♈0	16	17	5	3	24	21	6
22 12	0✕57	1♊38	4	25	23	11	23	6	♌0	16	4	19	19	8	6	26	24	9
22 24	4 7	4 18	9	29	26	13	26	11	2	19	8	23	22	10	9	29	26	12
22 36	7 18	6 54	13	♊2	28	16	♈0	15	4	21	12	♊2	24	13	13	♊2	29	15
22 48	10 30	9 27	17	6	♌0	18	4	19	6	24	15	♊0	27	16	16	4	♌2	18
23 0	13 43	11 57	21	9	3	21	8	23	9	27	19	4	29	18	19	7	5	21
23 12	16 57	14 24	25	13	5	23	12	27	11	♍0	23	7	♌2	21	22	11	7	24
23 24	20 12	16 49	29	16	7	26	16	♊0	13	2	27	10	4	24	25	14	10	27
23 36	23 28	19 11	♉3	19	10	29	20	4	16	5	♉1	14	6	27	28	18	12	♍0
23 48	26 44	21 31	7	22	12	♍1	24	8	18	8	4	17	9	29	♉1	22	15	3
24 0	0♈ 0	23 50	12	25	14	4	27	11	20	10	8	20	11	♍2	4	26	18	6

Sid. Time	M. C. long.	Asc.	REGIOMONTA.				CAMPANUS				PLACIDUS				NAT. GRAD.			
h m	♈	♊	11 ♉	12 Ⅱ	2 ♌	3 ♏	11 ♈	12 Ⅱ	2 ♌	3 ♏	11 ♉	12 Ⅱ	2 ♌	3 ♏	11 ♉	12 Ⅱ	2 ♌	3 ♏
0 0	0 0	25 22	12	27	15	4	27	11	22	11	8	21	12	2	5	21	19	6
0 12	3 16	27 36	16	♑0 17		7	♌0 14		25	14	12	24	14	5	8	23	21	9
0 24	6 32	29 49	19	2	19	9	4	17	27	17	15	27	17	8	11	26	24	12
0 36	9 48	2♏1	23	5	22	12	8	21	♏0	20	19	♌0	19	11	14	28	26	15
0 48	13 2	4 12	26	7	24	14	11	24	2	22	22	2	21	13	17	♋1	29	18
1 0	16 17	6 23	Ⅱ0	10	26	17	15	28	4	25	25	5	24	16	20	3	♏1	21
1 12	19 30	8 33	3	13	28	20	18	♌0	7	28	29	8	26	19	23	5	4	24
1 24	22 42	10 42	6	15	♏1	22	21	2	9	♎1	Ⅱ2	10	29	22	26	7	6	27
1 36	25 53	12 51	9	17	3	25	24	5	11	3	5	13	♏1	24	29	10	9	♎0
1 48	29 3	14 59	13	20	5	27	27	8	14	6	8	15	3	27	Ⅱ2	12	11	3
2 0	2♉11	17 8	16	22	7	♎0	Ⅱ1	11	16	9	11	18	6	♎0	5	14	14	6
2 12	5 18	19 16	19	25	10	3	5	13	18	12	14	20	8	3	8	16	16	9
2 24	8 23	21 24	21	27	12	5	8	16	21	14	17	23	11	6	11	19	18	13
2 36	11 26	23 32	24	29	14	8	11	18	23	17	20	25	13	8	14	21	19	16
2 48	14 28	25 40	27	♏1	16	10	14	21	25	20	23	28	15	11	17	24	21	19
3 0	17 28	27 48	♌0	4	19	13	18	23	28	23	26	♏0	18	14	20	26	22	23
3 12	20 26	29 56	3	6	21	16	20	26	♎0	25	29	2	20	17	22	28	24	26
3 24	23 23	2♎4	5	8	23	18	23	28	2	28	♎1	5	23	19	25	♏0	27	29
3 36	26 19	4 13	8	11	25	21	27	♎1	4	♏1	4	7	25	22	28	2	29	♏1
3 48	29 13	6 21	11	13	28	23	♌0	3	7	4	7	10	28	25	♎1	5	♏2	3
4 0	2Ⅱ5	8 29	13	15	♎0	26	2	5	10	7	9	12	♎0	28	3	7	5	6
4 12	4 57	10 38	16	17	2	29	4	7	12	9	12	14	2	♏0	6	10	7	8
4 24	7 47	12 47	18	19	5	♏1	7	10	14	12	15	17	5	3	9	12	10	11
4 36	10 36	14 56	21	22	7	4	10	12	16	14	17	19	7	6	11	15	13	13
4 48	13 24	17 5	24	24	9	6	12	14	18	17	20	21	10	8	14	17	16	15
5 0	16 11	19 14	26	26	11	9	15	17	21	19	23	24	12	11	17	19	19	17
5 12	18 58	21 23	28	28	14	11	18	19	24	22	26	26	15	14	19	21	21	19
5 24	21 44	23 32	♎1	♏1	16	14	20	21	26	25	28	29	17	16	22	23	23	22
5 36	24 30	25 41	4	3	18	16	23	23	28	27	♎0	♏1	19	19	25	25	25	25
5 48	27 15	27 51	6	5	20	19	26	25	♏1	♐0	3	3	22	22	27	28	28	28
6 0	0♋0	0♎0	9	7	23	21	28	28	3	3	6	6	24	24	♏0	♎0	♏0	♐0
6 12	2 45	2 9	11	10	25	24	♎1	♏1	5	5	8	8	27	27	3	2	2	3
6 24	5 30	4 19	14	12	27	26	3	3	8	8	11	11	29	♐0	5	5	5	5
6 36	8 16	6 28	16	14	29	29	6	5	10	10	14	13	♏1	2	8	7	7	8
6 48	11 2	8 37	19	16	♏2	♐2	9	8	12	13	16	15	4	5	10	9	9	10
7 0	13 49	10 46	21	19	4	4	11	10	15	16	19	18	6	7	13	11	11	13
7 12	16 36	12 55	24	21	6	6	14	12	17	18	22	20	9	10	15	14	14	15
7 24	19 24	15 4	26	23	8	9	17	15	19	21	24	23	11	13	18	16	16	18
7 36	22 13	17 13	29	25	11	12	20	17	22	24	27	25	13	15	20	19	18	21
7 48	25 3	19 22	♏1	28	13	14	23	20	24	27	♏0	28	16	18	22	22	21	24
8 0	27 55	21 31	4	♎0	15	17	25	22	26	29	2	♎0	18	21	24	25	23	27
8 12	0♌47	23 39	7	2	17	19	28	24	29	♑2	5	2	20	23	27	27	25	♑0
8 24	3 41	25 47	9	5	19	22	♏0	26	♐1	5	♏0	4	23	26	♏0	29	28	2
8 36	6 37	27 56	12	7	22	25	3	28	3	8	11	7	25	29	3	♎1	♐0	5
8 48	9 34	0♏4	14	9	24	27	6	♎1	5	11	13	10	28	♑1	6	4	2	7
9 0	12 32	2 12	17	11	26	♑0	8	4	8	13	16	12	♐0	4	9	6	4	10
9 12	15 32	4 20	20	14	29	3	11	6	11	16	19	15	2	7	12	8	7	13
9 24	18 34	6 28	22	16	♐1	6	14	8	13	19	22	17	5	10	15	10	9	16
9 36	21 37	8 36	25	18	3	9	17	11	16	22	24	19	7	13	18	12	11	19
9 48	24 42	10 44	27	20	5	11	19	13	18	25	27	22	10	16	21	14	14	22
10 0	27 49	12 52	♐0	23	8	14	22	15	21	29	♐0	24	12	19	24	16	16	25
10 12	0♏57	15 1	3	25	10	17	25	18	23	♒2	3	27	15	22	27	19	19	28
10 24	4 7	17 9	5	27	13	21	28	20	26	5	6	29	17	25	♐0	21	21	♒1
10 36	7 18	19 18	8	29	15	24	♐0	22	28	8	8	♐1	20	28	3	23	23	4
10 48	10 30	21 27	10	♏2	17	27	3	25	♑1	11	11	4	22	♒1	6	26	25	7
11 0	13 43	23 37	13	4	20	♒0	6	27	4	15	14	6	25	5	9	29	27	10
11 12	16 58	25 48	16	6	23	4	9	29	7	19	17	9	28	8	12	♏1	♒0	13
11 24	20 12	27 59	18	8	25	7	11	♏2	10	23	19	11	♑0	11	15	3	3	16
11 36	23 28	0♐11	21	11	28	11	14	4	13	26	22	13	3	15	18	6	5	19
11 48	26 44	2 24	23	13	♑0	14	17	6	16	♒0	25	16	6	18	21	9	7	22
12 0	0♎0	4 38	26	15	3	18	19	8	19	3	28	18	9	22	24	11	9	25

Sid. Time	M. C. long.	Asc. 1	REGIOMONTA. 11	12	2	3	CAMPANUS 11	12	2	3	PLACIDUS 11	12	2	3	NAT. GRAD. 11	12	2	3
h m	♎	♐	♎	♏	♑	♒	♎	♏	♑	♓	♎	♏	♑	♒	♎	♏	♑	♒
12 0	0 0	4 38	26 15	3	18		19 8	19	3		28 18	9	22		24 11	9	25	
12 12	3 16	6 54	28 17	6	22		22 10	23	7		♏0 20	12	24		27 14	12	28	
12 24	6 32	9 11	♏1 18	9	26		25 12	26	11		3 23	15	29		♏0 16	14	♓2	
12 36	9 48	11 30	4 22	12	♓0		28 15	♎0	15		6 25	18	♓3		3 19	17	5	
12 48	13 3	13 51	6 24	15	6		♏0 18	3	19		8 21	21	7		5 21	19	8	
13 0	16 17	16 14	9 26	19	8		2 20	7	23		11 ♏0	25	10		8 24	22	11	
13 12	19 30	18 40	11 28	22	13		5 22	11	27		14 2	28	14		11 27	24	14	
13 24	22 42	21 9	14 ♐1	26	17		7 25	16	♈1		16 4	♋1	18		14 29	26	17	
13 36	25 53	23 42	16 3	29	21		10 27	20	5		19 7	6	22		17 ♐2	29	21	
13 48	29 3	26 18	19 5	♒3	26		13 29	24	9		22 10	9	26		20 5	♒2	24	
14 0	2♏11	28 59	21 8	7	♈0		16 ♐1	29	13		24 12	13	♈0		23 8	5	27	
14 12	5 18	1♑55	24 10	12	4		10 3	♓4	17		27 14	18	4		26 11	8	♈0	
14 24	8 23	4 36	26 12	16	9		21 6	9	22		♈0 17	22	8		29 14	10	3	
14 36	11 26	7 34	29 15	21	13		24 8	14	25		2 20	26	12		♓2 17	13	6	
14 48	14 48	10 39	♐1 17	26	17		26 11	19	28		5 22	♓1	16		6 20	16	9	
15 0	17 29	13 52	4 20	♓1	22		29 13	25	♉2		7 25	6	20		9 23	20	12	
15 12	20 26	17 14	7 22	7	26		♓2 16	♈0	6		10 28	10	23		12 26	23	15	
15 24	23 23	20 47	9 25	12	♉0		4 18	6	10		13 ♑0	15	27		16 29	26	18	
15 36	26 19	24 31	12 27	18	4		7 21	11	13		15 3	20	♉1		18 ♒3	♓0	21	
15 48	29 13	28 28	14 ♒1	24	8		9 23	16	17		18 6	25	5		21 7	4	24	
16 0	2♐5	2♒9	17 3	♈0	12		12 26	21	20		21 9	♈0	8		24 10	7	27	
16 12	4 57	7 6	19 6	6	16		15 28	26	23		23 12	5	12		28 14	12	♉0	
16 24	7 47	11 50	22 9	12	19		17 ♒1	♉1	27		26 15	10	15		♒1 18	17	3	
16 36	10 36	16 51	25 12	18	23		20 4	6	♉0		29 18	15	19		5 23	21	6	
16 48	13 24	22 12	27 15	23	26		23 7	10	3		♒1 21	20	22		8 25	26	9	
17 0	16 11	27 52	♑0 19	29	♐0		25 10	15	6		4 25	24	25		12 ♒3	♈1	13	
17 12	18 58	3♓50	3 22	♉4	3		28 13	19	9		7 28	29	29		16 7	7	16	
17 24	21 44	10 6	6 26	9	6		♒2 16	23	12		10 ♎2	♉4	♊2		19 13	12	19	
17 36	24 30	16 35	9 29	14	10		4 19	27	15		13 6	8	5		23 18	18	23	
17 48	27 15	23 15	11 ♒3	18	13		6 23	♐0	18		16 9	12	8		27 24	24	27	
18 0	0♐0	0♈0	15 7	23	15		9 27	4	21		19 13	17	11		♎0 ♈0	♉0	♊0	
18 12	2 45	6 45	17 12	27	19		12 ♊0	7	24		22 18	21	14		3 6	5	3	
18 24	5 30	13 25	20 16	♊1	21		15 4	11	27		25 22	24	17		7 13	12	7	
18 36	8 16	19 54	24 21	4	24		18 7	14	♋0		28 26	28	20		11 18	17	11	
18 48	11 2	26 10	27 26	8	27		21 12	17	2		♎1 ♈1	♊1	23		14 23	23	14	
19 0	13 49	2♉8	♎0 ♈1	11	♋0		24 16	20	5		5 6	5	26		18 29	28	19	
19 12	16 36	7 48	2 7	15	3		27 20	23	8		8 10	9	29		22 ♈4	♊3	24	
19 24	19 24	13 9	7 12	17	5		♎0 25	26	10		11 15	12	♋1		25 9	7	27	
19 36	22 13	18 10	11 18	21	8		4 29	29	13		15 20	15	4		27 13	12	♋0	
19 48	25 3	22 54	14 24	24	11		7 ♈4	♋2	16		18 25	18	7		♈1 18	16	4	
20 0	27 55	27 51	18 0	27	13		10 9	4	18		22 ♈0	21	9		4 23	20	7	
20 12	0♎47	1♊32	22 6	♋0	16		14 14	7	21		25 5	24	12		6 26	24	9	
20 24	3 41	5 29	26 12	3	18		17 19	9	23		29 10	27	15		9 ♋0	27	12	
20 36	6 37	9 13	♋0 18	5	21		21 25	12	26		♈3 15	♋0	17		12 4	♋1	15	
20 48	9 34	12 46	6 23	8	23		23 ♈0	o4	29		7 20	2	20		15 7	4	18	
21 0	12 31	16 8	8 29	10	26		28 6	17	♋1		10 24	4	23		18 10	7	21	
21 12	15 32	19 21	13 ♋4	13	29		♓2 11	19	4		14 29	8	25		21 14	10	25	
21 24	18 34	22 26	17 9	15	♌1		6 16	22	7		18 ♋4	10	28		24 17	13	28	
21 36	21 37	25 24	21 14	18	4		10 21	24	9		22 8	13	♋0		28 20	16	♌2	
21 48	24 42	28 5	26 18	20	6		13 26	27	12		26 12	15	3		♈0 23	19	4	
22 0	27 49	15 1	♈0 23	22	9		17 ♉1	29	15		♈0 17	18	6		3 25	22	6	
22 12	0♏57	3 42	4 27	25	11		21 6	♋1	17		4 21	21	8		6 28	25	9	
22 24	4 7	6 18	9 ♊1	27	14		25 11	4	20		8 24	23	11		10 ♊1	28	12	
22 36	7 18	8 51	13 4	29	16		29 15	6	22		12 28	25	14		13 3	♌1	16	
22 48	10 30	11 20	17 8	♌2	19		♈3 19	8	25		16 ♊2	28	17		16 6	3	19	
23 0	13 43	13 46	22 11	4	21		7 23	11	28		20 5	♌0	19		19 9	6	22	
23 12	16 57	16 9	26 15	6	24		11 27	13	♍0		24 9	2	22		22 11	9	25	
23 24	20 12	18 0	♊0 18	8	26		15 ♊1	15	3		27 12	5	24		25 14	11	27	
23 36	23 28	20 49	4 21	11	29		19 5	17	6		♋1 15	7	27		28 16	14	♍0	
23 48	26 44	23 6	8 24	13	♍2		23 8	19	9		5 18	10	♍0		♉2 18	16	3	
24 0	0♈0	25 22	12 27	15	4		27 11	22	11		8 21	12	2		5 21	19	6	

Sid. Time	M.C. long.	Asc. 1	REGIOMONTA. 11	12	2	3	CAMPANUS 11	12	2	3	PLACIDUS 11	12	2	3	NAT. GRAD. 11	12	2	3
h m	♈	♉	♉	♊	♌	♍	♈	♊	♌	♍	♉	♊	♌	♍	♉	♊	♌	♍
0 0	0 0	26 10	12 28	16	4		26 11	23	12		9 22	12	2		5 21	19	7	
0 12	3 16	28 22	16 ♋1	18	7		♉0 14	25	14		12 25	15	5		8 24	22	10	
0 24	6 32	0♌34	20 3	20	9		4 17	28	17		16 28	17	8		11 26	24	13	
0 36	9 48	2 44	23 6	22	12		7 20	♍0	20		19 ♋1	19	11		14 28	27	16	
0 48	13 3	4 53	27 8	24	14		10 23	3	23		22 3	22	13		17 ♋1	♍0	18	
1 0	16 17	7 2	♍0 11	27	17		14 26	5	25		26 6	24	16		20 3	2	21	
1 12	19 30	9 10	3 13	29	20		18 29	7	28		29 9	27	19		23 5	4	24	
1 24	22 42	11 18	7 16	♍1	22		21 ♋2	9	♍0		♊2 11	29	22		26 8	6	27	
1 36	25 53	13 25	10 18	3	25		24 4	12	4		5 14	♍1	24		29 10	9	♎0	
1 48	29 3	15 32	13 21	5	27		28 7	14	6		9 16	4	27		♊2 12	12	3	
2 0	2♉11	17 39	16 23	8	♎0		♊1 10	16	9		12 19	6	♎0		5 15	14	6	
2 12	5 18	19 46	19 25	10	3		4 12	19	12		15 21	8	3		8 17	16	9	
2 24	8 23	21 52	22 28	12	5		7 15	21	15		18 23	11	6		11 19	19	12	
2 36	11 26	23 59	25 ♌0	14	8		10 18	23	17		20 26	13	8		14 22	21	14	
2 48	14 28	26 5	28 2	17	10		13 20	26	20		22 28	16	11		17 24	24	17	
3 0	17 28	28 12	♋0 5	19	13		16 23	28	23		26 ♌1	18	14		20 26	26	20	
3 12	20 26	0♊18	3 7	21	16		19 25	♎0	26		29 3	20	17		22 28	28	23	
3 24	23 23	2 25	6 9	23	18		22 27	3	28		♋2 5	23	19		25 ♌1	♎1	25	
3 36	26 19	4 31	8 11	26	21		25 29	5	♍1		4 8	25	22		28 3	3	28	
3 48	29 13	6 38	11 13	28	23		28 ♎2	8	4		7 10	28	25		♌1 5	5	♍1	
4 0	2♊15	8 45	14 16	♎0	26		♌0 4	10	6		10 12	♎0	28		3 7	7	4	
4 12	4 57	10 52	16 18	2	28		3 6	12	9		12 15	2	♍0		6 10	10	6	
4 24	7 47	12 59	19 20	4	♍1		6 8	15	12		15 17	5	3		9 12	12	9	
4 36	10 37	15 7	21 22	7	3		8 11	17	14		18 19	7	6		11 14	14	11	
4 48	12 24	17 14	24 24	9	6		11 13	19	17		20 22	10	8		14 16	16	14	
5 0	16 11	19 22	26 27	11	8		14 15	22	20		23 24	12	11		17 19	19	17	
5 12	18 58	21 29	29 29	13	11		17 18	24	22		25 27	14	14		20 21	21	20	
5 24	21 44	23 37	♌1 ♍1	16	13		19 20	26	25		28 29	17	16		22 23	23	22	
5 36	24 30	25 45	4 3	18	16		22 22	28	28		♌1 ♍1	19	19		25 25	25	25	
5 48	27 15	27 52	6 5	20	19		24 25	♍0	♎0		3 4	22	21		27 28	28	27	
6 0	0♋0	0♎0	9 8	22	21		27 27	3	3		6 6	24	24		♌0 ♍0	♍0	♎0	
6 12	2 45	2 8	11 10	25	24		29 29	5	6		9 8	26	26		3 2	2	3	
6 24	5 30	4 15	14 12	27	26		♎2 ♍2	8	9		11 11	29	29		5 5	5	5	
6 36	8 16	6 23	17 14	29	29		5 4	10	11		14 13	♍1	♐2		8 7	7	8	
6 48	11 2	8 31	19 17	♍1	♐1		8 6	12	13		16 16	3	5		10 9	9	10	
7 0	13 45	10 38	22 19	3	4		10 9	15	16		19 18	6	7		13 11	11	13	
7 12	16 36	12 46	24 21	6	6		13 11	17	19		22 20	8	10		16 13	14	16	
7 24	19 23	14 53	27 23	8	9		16 13	19	22		24 23	11	12		18 16	16	19	
7 36	22 13	17 1	29 26	10	11		18 16	22	24		27 25	13	15		21 18	18	21	
7 48	25 3	19 8	♍2 28	12	14		21 18	24	27		29 28	15	18		24 20	20	24	
8 0	27 55	28 15	4 ♎0	14	16		24 20	27	♑0		♍2 ♎0	18	20		26 23	23	27	
8 12	0♌47	23 22	7 2	17	18		26 23	29	2		5 2	20	23		29 25	25	29	
8 24	3 41	25 29	9 4	19	22		29 25	♏1	5		8 5	23	25		♍2 27	27	♏2	
8 36	6 37	27 35	12 7	21	24		♏2 27	3	7		11 7	25	28		5 ♎0	29	5	
8 48	9 34	29 42	14 9	23	27		4 ♎0	6	11		13 10	27	♏1		7 2	♐2	8	
9 0	12 32	1♏48	17 11	25	♑0		7 2	8	14		16 12	29	4		10 4	3	10	
9 12	15 32	3 55	20 13	28	2		10 4	11	17		19 14	2	7		13 7	6	13	
9 24	18 34	6 1	22 16	♐0	5		13 7	13	20		22 17	4	10		16 9	9	16	
9 36	21 37	8 8	25 18	2	7		15 9	16	23		24 19	7	12		19 11	11	19	
9 48	24 42	10 14	27 20	5	11		18 11	18	26		27 22	9	15		21 14	13	22	
10 0	27 49	12 21	♏0 22	7	14		21 14	21	29		♏0 24	11	18		24 16	15	25	
10 12	0♏57	14 28	3 25	9	16		24 16	23	♒2		3 26	14	21		27 19	18	28	
10 24	4 7	16 35	5 27	12	20		26 18	26	6		6 29	16	25		♎0 21	20	♐1	
10 36	7 18	18 42	8 29	14	23		29 21	29	9		8 ♏1	19	28		3 23	22	4	
10 48	10 30	20 50	10 ♏1	17	27		♏2 23	♐1	13		11 3	21	♒1		6 26	25	7	
11 0	13 43	22 58	13 3	19	♒0		5 25	4	16		14 6	24	4		9 28	27	10	
11 12	16 57	25 7	16 6	22	3		7 28	7	19		17 8	27	8		12 ♏1	29	13	
11 24	20 12	27 16	18 8	24	6		10 ♐0	10	23		19 11	29	11		14 3	♑2	14	
11 36	23 28	29 26	21 10	27	10		13 2	13	26		21 13	♒2	14		17 5	4	19	
11 48	26 44	1♐38	23 13	29	14		16 4	16	♒0		25 15	5	18		20 8	26	22	
12 0	0♎0	3 50	26 14	♒2	18		18 7	19	4		28 18	8	21		23 11	9	25	

226

Sid. Time	M.C. long.	Asc. 1	REGIOMONTA. 11	12	2	3	CAMPANUS 11	12	2	3	PLACIDUS 11	12	2	3	NAT. GRAD. 11	12	2	3
12 0	0 0	3 50	26	14	2	18	18	7	19	4	28	18	8	21	23	11	9	25
12 12	3 16	6 4	28	17	5	22	21	9	23	7	♏0	20	11	25	26	13	12	28
12 24	6 32	8 19	♏1	19	8	26	24	11	27	11	3	22	14	29	29	15	14	♓2
12 36	9 48	10 36	3	21	11	♓0	27	14	≏0	15	6	25	17	♓3	♏2	18	16	5
12 48	13 3	12 55	6	23	14	4	29	16	4	19	8	27	21	6	5	20	18	8
13 0	16 17	15 17	8	25	17	8	♏2	18	7	23	11	29	24	10	8	23	21	11
13 12	19 30	17 40	11	28	21	13	5	21	12	27	14	♐2	27	14	11	26	23	14
13 24	22 42	20 7	13	♑0	15	17	7	23	16	♈1	16	4	≏1	18	14	29	26	17
13 36	25 53	22 38	16	2	28	21	10	25	20	5	19	7	5	22	17	♐2	28	20
13 48	29 3	25 12	19	5	≏2	26	13	28	25	9	21	9	9	26	20	4	≏1	23
14 0	2♏11	27 51	21	7	6	♈0	15	♑0	♓0	13	24	11	13	♈0	23	7	4	26
14 12	5 18	0♑34	24	9	11	4	18	3	4	17	26	14	17	4	26	10	6	♈0
14 24	8 23	3 24	26	12	15	9	20	5	9	22	29	16	21	8	29	13	9	3
14 36	11 26	6 19	29	14	20	13	23	7	15	25	♐2	19	26	12	♐2	16	12	6
14 48	14 28	9 22	♑1	17	25	17	25	9	20	29	5	21	♑0	16	5	19	15	9
15 0	17 28	12 33	4	19	♈1	22	28	12	25	♓3	7	24	5	20	8	22	18	12
15 12	20 26	15 53	6	22	6	26	♏1	15	♈0	6	10	27	10	24	11	25	22	15
15 24	23 13	19 24	9	24	12	♈0	4	17	6	10	12	29	15	27	15	29	26	18
15 36	26 19	23 7	11	27	18	4	6	20	11	13	15	♑2	20	♑1	18	♑2	29	21
15 48	29 13	27 3	14	29	24	8	9	22	16	17	18	5	25	5	21	6	♓3	24
16 0	2♐5	1≏14	16	♑2	♈0	12	12	25	22	20	20	8	♈0	9	24	9	7	27
16 12	4 57	5 41	19	5	6	16	14	27	26	24	23	11	5	12	28	14	11	♉0
16 24	7 47	10 27	22	8	12	20	17	♑0	♈1	27	25	14	10	16	♏1	18	16	3
16 36	11 36	15 32	24	11	18	24	20	3	6	♏0	28	17	15	19	4	23	21	6
16 48	13 24	20 55	27	14	24	27	23	6	♏1	3	♏1	21	20	22	8	28	26	10
17 0	16 11	26 45	♑0	17	29	♊0	25	9	16	6	4	24	25	26	11	≏2	♈0	13
17 12	18 58	2♓53	2	21	♉5	3	28	13	20	9	7	27	♉0	29	15	8	6	16
17 24	21 44	9 20	5	25	10	7	♏0	15	23	12	10	≏1	4	♊2	19	13	12	20
17 36	24 30	16 4	8	28	15	10	3	18	27	15	12	5	9	5	23	19	18	23
17 48	27 15	22 59	11	≏2	19	13	6	22	♊1	18	15	9	13	9	26	24	24	27
18 0	0♑0	0♈0	14	6	24	16	8	25	5	21	18	13	17	12	≏0	♈0	♉0	♊0
18 12	2 45	7 1	17	11	28	19	11	29	8	24	21	17	21	15	3	6	6	4
18 24	5 30	13 56	20	15	♊2	23	14	≏2	12	27	25	21	25	18	7	12	11	8
18 36	8 16	20 40	23	20	5	25	18	6	15	♋0	28	26	29	20	10	18	17	11
18 48	11 2	27 7	27	25	9	28	21	10	18	3	≏1	♓0	♊3	23	14	24	23	15
19 0	13 49	3♉15	≏0	♓1	13	♋0	24	14	21	6	4	5	6	26	17	♈0	29	19
19 12	16 36	9 2	3	6	16	3	27	18	24	8	7	10	9	29	21	4	♊3	22
19 24	19 24	14 28	6	12	19	6	≏0	23	27	11	11	15	13	♋2	24	9	7	26
19 36	22 13	19 33	10	18	22	8	3	27	♋0	13	14	20	16	4	27	14	11	29
19 48	25 3	24 19	14	24	25	11	7	♓2	2	16	18	25	19	7	♈0	19	16	♋0
20 0	27 55	28 46	18	♈0	28	14	10	6	5	8	21	♈0	22	10	3	23	20	6
20 12	0≏47	2♊57	22	6	♋1	16	13	12	8	21	25	5	25	12	6	27	24	9
20 24	3 41	6 53	26	12	3	19	17	18	10	24	29	10	28	15	9	♋1	27	12
20 36	6 37	10 36	♈0	18	6	21	20	24	13	26	♓3	15	♋1	18	12	4	♊1	16
20 48	9 34	14 7	4	24	8	24	24	29	15	29	6	20	3	20	15	8	5	19
21 0	12 32	17 27	8	29	11	26	27	♈4	18	♋2	10	25	6	23	18	12	8	22
21 12	15 32	21 38	13	♉5	13	29	♈1	9	20	4	14	♋0	9	25	21	15	11	25
21 24	18 34	23 41	17	10	16	♋1	5	14	23	7	18	4	11	28	24	18	14	28
21 36	21 37	26 36	21	15	18	4	9	20	25	10	22	9	14	♋1	27	21	17	♋1
21 48	24 42	29 26	26	19	21	6	13	25	28	13	26	13	16	3	♈0	24	20	4
22 0	27 49	2♋9	♈0	24	23	9	17	♉0	♋0	15	♈0	17	19	6	4	26	23	7
22 12	0♏57	4 48	4	28	25	11	21	5	2	17	4	21	21	9	7	29	26	10
22 24	4 7	7 22	9	♊2	27	14	25	9	5	20	8	25	23	11	10	♋2	29	13
22 36	7 18	9 53	13	5	♋0	17	29	14	7	23	12	29	26	14	13	4	♋1	16
22 48	10 30	12 20	17	9	2	19	♈3	18	9	25	16	♊3	28	16	16	7	4	19
23 0	13 43	14 43	22	13	5	22	7	22	12	28	20	6	♊1	19	19	9	7	22
23 12	16 57	17 5	26	16	7	24	11	26	14	♋1	24	9	3	22	22	12	9	25
23 24	20 12	19 24	♉0	19	9	27	14	♊0	16	4	27	13	5	24	25	14	12	28
23 36	23 28	21 41	4	22	11	29	18	4	18	6	♊1	16	8	27	28	17	14	♋1
23 48	26 44	23 56	8	25	13	♋2	22	8	21	9	5	19	10	♋0	♉2	19	17	4
24 0	0♏0	26 10	12	28	16	4	26	11	23	11	9	22	12	2	5	21	19	7

Sid. Time	M.C. long	Asc. 1	REGIOMONTA. 11	12	2	3	CAMPANUS 11	12	2	3	PLACIDUS 11	12	2	3	NAT. GRAD. 11	12	2	3
h m	♈	♊	♉	♊	♌	♍	♈	♊	♌	♍	♉	♊	♌	♍	♉	♊	♌	♍
0 0	0 0	26 35	13 28	16	4		26 11	24	12		9 22	13	3		5 22	20	7	
0 12	3 16	28 46	16 s1 18	7			♉0 14 26 15				12 25 15 5				8 24 22 10			
0 24	6 32	0♌56	20 4 20 9				3 17 28 18				16 28 17 8				11 26 24 13			
0 36	9 48	3 6	24 6 22 12				7 20 ♍0 20				19 s1 20 11				14 29 27 16			
0 48	13 3	5 14	27 9 25 15				11 23 3 23				23 4 22 13				17 s1 29 19			
1 0	16 17	7 22	♊11 11 27 17				14 26 5 26				26 6 24 16				20 3 ♍2 22			
1 12	19 30	9 29	4 14 27 20				18 29 7 28				29 9 27 19				23 6 4 25			
1 24	22 42	11 36	7 16 ♍1 22				21 s1 10 ♎1				♊3 11 29 22				26 8 7 27			
1 36	25 53	13 42	10 19 3 25				24 4 12 4				6 14 ♍1 24				29 10 9 ♎0			
1 48	29 3	16 6	13 21 6 27				28 6 14 7				9 17 4 27				♊12 13 11 3			
2 0	2♉11	17 55	16 23 8 ♎0				♉1 9 17 9				12 19 6 ♎0				5 15 14 6			
2 12	5 18	20 1	19 26 10 3				4 12 19 12				15 21 9 3				8 17 16 9			
2 24	8 23	22 6	22 28 12 5				7 14 21 15				18 24 11 6				11 19 18 11			
2 36	11 26	24 12	25 ♌0 14 8				10 17 24 18				21 26 13 8				13 21 21 14			
2 48	14 28	26 18	28 3 17 10				13 19 26 20				23 29 16 11				16 23 23 16			
3 0	17 28	27 42	s1 5 19 13				16 22 28 23				26 ♌1 18 14				19 25 25 19			
3 12	20 26	0♍29	3 7 21 15				19 24 ♎1 26				29 3 20 17				22 28 28 22			
3 24	23 23	3 5	6 9 23 18				22 27 3 28				s2 6 23 19				25 ♌0 ♎0 25			
3 36	26 19	4 41	9 12 26 21				25 29 5 ♍1				5 8 25 22				28 3 2 28			
3 48	29 13	6 47	11 14 28 23				28 ♌2 8 4				7 10 28 25				s1 5 5 ♍1			
4 0	2♊5	8 53	14 16 ♎0 26				s0 4 10 7				10 13 ♎0 27				4 7 7 4			
4 12	4 57	10 59	17 18 2 28				3 7 12 9				13 15 2 ♍0				6 10 10 6			
4 24	7 47	13 6	19 20 4 ♍1				6 9 15 12				15 17 5 3				9 12 12 9			
4 36	10 36	15 12	22 22 7 3				8 11 17 14				18 20 7 6				12 14 14 12			
4 48	13 24	17 19	24 25 9 6				♊11 13 19 17				20 22 10 8				15 16 16 14			
5 0	16 11	19 26	27 27 11 8				14 15 22 20				23 24 12 11				17 19 19 17			
5 12	18 58	21 32	29 29 13 11				16 18 24 23				26 27 14 13				20 21 21 20			
5 24	21 44	23 39	♌2 ♍1 16 13				19 20 26 25				28 29 17 16				22 23 23 22			
5 36	24 30	25 46	4 3 18 16				22 22 29 28				♌1 ♍1 19 19				25 26 26 25			
5 48	27 15	27 53	7 6 20 18				24 25 1 ♏0				3 4 22 21				27 28 28 27			
6 0	0♋0	0♎0	9 8 22 21				27 27 3 3				6 6 24 25				♌0 ♍0 ♏0 ♐0			
6 12	2 45	2 7	12 10 24 23				♌0 29 6 6				9 8 26 27				3 2 2 3			
6 24	5 30	4 14	14 12 27 26				2 ♍2 8 8				11 11 29 29				5 5 5 5			
6 36	8 16	6 21	17 14 29 28				5 4 10 11				14 13 ♏1 ♐2				8 7 7 8			
6 48	11 2	8 28	19 17 ♏1 ♐1				8 6 12 14				17 16 3 4				10 9 9 10			
7 0	13 49	10 34	22 19 3 3				10 8 15 16				19 18 6 7				13 11 11 13			
7 12	16 36	12 41	24 21 5 6				13 11 17 19				22 20 8 10				16 14 14 16			
7 24	19 24	14 48	27 23 8 8				15 13 19 22				25 23 10 12				18 16 16 18			
7 36	22 13	16 54	27 26 10 11				18 15 21 25				27 25 13 16				21 18 18 21			
7 48	25 3	19 1	♍2 28 12 18				21 18 24 28				♍0 28 15 17				24 20 20 24			
8 0	27 55	21 7	4 ♎0 14 16				23 20 26 ♐0				3 ♎0 17 20				26 23 23 26			
8 12	0♌47	23 13	7 2 16 19				26 22 29 3				5 2 20 23				29 25 25 29			
8 24	3 41	25 19	9 4 18 21				29 25 ♐1 5				8 5 22 26				♍2 28 27 ♐2			
8 36	6 37	26 55	12 7 21 24				♍2 27 4 8				11 7 24 28				5 ♎0 ♐0 5			
8 48	9 34	29 31	15 9 23 27				4 29 6 11				13 10 27 ♐1				8 2 2 8			
9 0	12 32	2♍18	17 11 25 29				7 ♎2 8 14				16 12 29 4				10 5 5 11			
9 12	15 32	3 42	20 5 27 ♐2				10 4 11 17				19 14 ♐1 6				13 7 7 14			
9 24	18 34	5 48	22 16 ♐0 5				12 6 13 20				22 17 3 9				16 10 9 17			
9 36	21 37	7 54	25 18 2 8				15 9 16 23				24 19 6 12				19 12 12 19			
9 48	24 42	9 59	27 20 4 11				18 11 18 26				27 21 8 15				21 14 13 22			
10 0	27 49	12 5	♎0 22 7 14				21 13 21 29				♎0 24 11 18				24 16 15 25			
10 12	0♍57	13 54	3 24 9 17				23 16 2 =2				3 26 14 21				27 18 18 28			
10 24	4 7	16 18	5 27 11 20				26 18 26 6				6 29 16 24				♎0 21 20 =1			
10 36	7 18	18 24	8 29 14 23				29 21 28 9				8 ♏1 19 27				3 23 22 4			
10 48	10 30	20 31	10 ♏1 16 26				♎2 23 ♐1 12				11 3 21 =1				6 26 24 7			
11 0	13 43	22 38	13 3 19 29				4 26 4 16				14 6 24 4				8 28 27 10			
11 12	16 57	24 46	15 5 21 =3				7 28 7 19				17 8 26 7				11 ♏0 29 13			
11 24	20 12	26 54	18 8 24 6				10 ♏0 10 23				19 10 29 11				14 3 ♐2 16			
11 36	23 28	29 4	21 10 26 10				13 2 13 27				22 12 ♐2 14				17 5 5 19			
11 48	26 44	1♐14	23 12 29 14				15 4 16 ♑0				25 15 5 18				20 8 7 22			
12 0	0♎0	3 25	26 14 ♑2 17				18 7 19 4				27 17 8 21				23 10 8 25			

Sid. Time	M.C. long.	Asc. 1	REGIOMONTA. 11	12	2	3	CAMPANUS 11	12	2	3	PLACIDUS 11	12	2	3	NAT. GRAD. 11	12	2	3
h m	♎	♐	♎	♏	♑	♒	♎	♏	♑	♓	♎	♏	♑	♒	♎	♏	♑	♒
12 0	0 0	3 25	26	14	2	19	18	7	19	4	27	17	8	21	23	10	8	25
12 12	3 16	5 38	28	16	5	21	21	9	23	8	♏0	20	11	25	26	13	11	28
12 24	6 32	7 53	♏1	18	8	25	24	12	27	12	3	22	14	29	29	15	13	♒1
12 36	9 48	10 9	3	21	11	29	26	14	♈1	16	5	24	17	♓2	♏2	18	15	5
12 48	13 3	12 24	6	22	14	♓4	29	16	4	20	8	27	20	6	5	20	18	8
13 0	16 17	14 47	8	25	17	8	♏2	18	7	24	11	29	23	10	8	23	20	11
13 12	19 30	17 9	11	27	21	12	4	20	12	28	13	♐1	27	14	11	26	23	14
13 24	22 42	19 36	13	♐0	24	17	17	23	16	♒2	16	3	♌1	18	14	28	25	17
13 36	25 53	22 5	16	2	28	21	10	25	21	6	19	6	4	22	17	♐1	27	20
13 48	29 3	24 38	18	4	♒2	26	12	27	25	10	21	8	8	26	20	4	♎0	23
14 0	2♏11	22 15	21	7	5	♈0	15	♈0	♈0	14	24	11	12	♈0	23	7	3	26
14 12	5 18	29 58	23	9	11	4	18	2	5	17	27	14	17	4	26	10	6	29
14 24	8 23	2♑46	26	11	15	9	20	4	10	21	29	16	21	8	29	12	9	♈2
14 36	11 26	5 40	28	14	20	13	23	7	16	25	♐2	19	25	12	♈2	15	12	5
14 48	14 28	8 42	♐1	16	25	18	26	9	21	29	4	21	♏0	16	4	18	15	8
15 0	17 28	11 57	3	19	♓0	22	28	12	26	♉3	7	24	5	20	7	21	18	11
15 12	20 26	15 11	6	21	6	26	♏1	14	♈1	6	10	26	10	24	11	25	21	14
15 24	22 23	18 35	8	24	12	♉1	3	17	7	10	12	29	15	28	14	27	25	17
15 36	26 19	22 22	11	26	18	5	6	19	12	14	15	♑2	20	♉2	17	♏1	28	20
15 48	29 13	26 18	13	29	24	9	9	22	18	17	17	5	25	5	21	5	♒1	23
16 0	2♐5	0♉28	16	♉2	♈0	13	11	24	23	21	20	3	♈0	9	24	8	3	27
16 12	4 57	4 41	19	5	6	16	24	27	28	♉4	23	11	5	12	27	12	12	♉0
16 24	7 47	9 42	21	8	12	20	17	♑0	♉2	27	25	14	10	16	♉1	17	19	3
16 36	10 36	14 49	24	11	18	24	19	3	7	♉0	28	17	15	19	5	21	25	6
16 48	13 24	20 18	27	14	24	27	22	5	12	3	♉1	20	20	23	9	25	♉2	10
17 0	16 11	26 9	29	17	♉0	♊1	25	8	16	6	4	23	25	26	12	♉0	8	13
17 12	18 58	2♈21	♉2	21	5	4	27	16	20	9	7	27	♉0	29	16	6	12	26
17 24	21 44	8 55	5	24	10	7	♏0	15	24	12	9	♒1	5	♊3	19	12	17	19
17 36	24 30	15 46	8	28	15	10	3	18	28	15	12	4	9	6	23	18	21	23
17 48	27 15	22 50	11	♒2	19	13	6	21	♉2	18	15	8	13	9	26	24	26	25
18 0	0♑0	0♈0	14	6	24	16	8	24	6	21	18	12	18	12	♎0	♈0	♉0	♊0
18 12	2 45	7 10	17	11	28	19	11	28	9	24	21	17	22	15	3	6	6	4
18 24	5 30	14 14	20	15	♊2	22	14	♈1	13	♊2	24	21	26	18	7	12	12	8
18 36	8 16	21 5	23	20	6	25	17	6	16	♋0	27	25	29	21	10	19	18	11
18 48	11 22	27 39	26	25	9	28	20	10	19	2	♒1	♈0	♊3	23	14	25	24	15
19 0	13 49	4♉51	29	♈0	13	♋1	23	14	22	5	4	5	♊1	26	19	♈1	♊0	19
19 12	16 36	10 42	♈3	6	16	3	27	18	25	8	7	10	10	29	20	6	4	22
19 24	19 24	15 11	6	12	19	6	♐0	23	27	10	11	15	13	♋2	24	11	9	26
19 36	22 13	20 18	10	18	22	9	3	28	♋0	13	13	20	16	5	27	15	13	29
19 48	25 3	25 19	14	24	25	11	6	♈2	3	16	16	25	19	7	♈0	20	17	♋3
20 0	27 25	29 32	17	♈0	28	14	9	7	6	19	21	♈0	22	10	3	25	22	6
20 12	0♒47	3♊42	21	6	♋1	17	13	12	8	21	25	5	25	13	7	28	25	10
20 24	3 41	7 38	25	12	4	19	16	18	11	24	28	10	♊2	18	10	♉2	28	13
20 36	6 37	11 25	29	18	6	22	20	23	13	27	♈2	15	♋1	18	13	5	♋2	16
20 48	9 34	14 49	♈4	24	9	24	24	28	11	29	6	20	4	20	16	9	5	19
21 0	12 32	18 9	8	♉0	11	27	27	♉4	18	♋2	10	25	6	23	19	12	9	23
21 12	15 32	21 18	12	5	14	29	♐1	9	21	4	14	♉0	9	26	22	15	12	26
21 24	18 34	24 20	17	10	16	♋2	5	14	23	7	18	5	11	28	25	18	14	29
21 36	21 37	27 14	21	15	19	4	9	19	26	10	22	9	14	♊1	28	21	17	♋1
21 48	24 42	0♊2	26	19	21	7	12	25	28	12	26	13	16	2	♈1	24	20	4
22 0	27 49	2 45	♈0	24	23	9	16	♉0	♈0	15	♈0	18	19	6	4	27	23	8
22 12	0♓57	5 22	4	28	26	12	20	5	3	18	4	22	21	9	7	29	26	11
22 24	4 7	7 55	9	♉3	28	♋2	24	9	5	20	8	26	24	11	10	♉2	29	14
22 36	7 18	10 24	13	6	♊0	17	28	14	7	23	12	29	26	14	13	5	♌1	17
22 48	10 30	12 51	18	9	3	19	♉2	18	10	25	16	♉3	29	17	16	8	4	20
23 0	13 43	15 13	22	13	5	22	6	23	12	28	20	7	♌1	19	19	10	7	23
23 12	16 57	17 36	26	16	7	24	10	26	14	♏1	24	10	3	22	22	12	10	26
23 24	20 12	19 51	♉1	19	9	27	14	♉0	17	4	28	13	6	25	25	15	12	29
23 36	23 28	22 7	5	22	12	29	18	4	19	♏1	♉2	16	8	27	29	17	15	♏1
23 48	26 44	24 22	9	25	14	♌2	22	7	22	9	5	19	10	♎0	♉2	20	17	4
24 0	0♈0	26 35	12	28	16	4	26	11	24	12	9	22	13	3	5	22	20	7

Sid. Time	M.C. long.	Asc. 1	REGIOMONTA. 11	12	2	3	CAMPANUS 11	12	2	3	PLACIDUS 11	12	2	3	NAT. GRAD. 11	12	2	3
h m	♈	♉	♉	♊	♋	♍	♈	♉	♋	♍	♈	♉	♋	♍	♉	♊	♋	♍
0 0	0 0	26 59	13	29	16	5	26	10	24	12	9	23	13	3	5	22	20	6
0 12	3 16	29 10	17	♋2	18	7	29	14	26	15	12	26	15	5	8	24	22	9
0 24	6 32	1♏19	20	4	20	10	♋3	17	28	18	16	29	18	8	11	27	25	13
0 36	9 48	3 28	24	7	23	12	7	20	♍1	20	19	♋1	20	11	14	29	28	16
0 48	13 3	5 35	27	9	25	15	10	23	3	23	23	4	22	13	17	♋1	♍0	19
1 0	16 17	7 42	21	12	27	17	14	26	5	26	26	7	24	16	20	4	3	22
1 12	19 30	9 49	4	14	29	20	17	29	8	29	29	9	27	19	23	6	5	24
1 24	22 42	11 55	7	17	♍1	22	21	♋1	10	♏1	♊3	12	29	22	26	8	7	27
1 36	25 53	14 0	11	19	4	25	24	4	12	4	6	14	♍2	24	29	11	10	29
1 48	29 3	16 6	14	22	6	27	27	7	15	7	9	17	4	27	♊2	13	13	♍2
2 0	2♊11	18 11	17	24	8	♍0	♊1	10	17	10	12	19	6	♍0	5	15	15	6
2 12	5 18	20 16	20	26	10	3	4	12	19	12	15	22	9	3	8	17	17	9
2 24	8 23	22 21	23	28	12	5	7	14	22	15	18	24	11	6	11	20	19	12
2 36	11 26	24 26	25	♌1	14	8	10	16	24	18	21	26	14	8	14	22	21	16
2 48	14 28	26 31	28	3	16	10	13	19	26	21	24	29	16	11	17	26	23	19
3 0	17 28	28 35	♋1	5	19	13	16	21	29	23	27	♌1	18	14	20	26	26	22
3 12	20 26	0♍40	4	7	21	15	19	24	♏1	26	29	4	20	17	23	29	29	24
3 24	23 23	2 45	6	10	23	18	22	26	3	29	♋2	6	23	19	25	♌1	♏1	27
3 36	26 19	4 51	9	12	26	20	24	29	6	♏1	5	8	25	22	28	3	3	29
3 48	29 13	6 56	12	14	28	23	27	♌1	8	4	8	11	28	25	♋1	5	5	♏1
4 0	2♌5	9 1	14	16	♏0	25	♌0	4	10	7	11	13	♏0	27	4	8	7	4
4 12	4 57	11 7	17	18	2	28	3	6	13	9	13	15	2	♏0	6	10	10	6
4 24	7 47	13 12	19	20	4	♏1	5	8	15	12	15	18	5	3	9	12	12	9
4 36	10 36	15 18	22	23	7	3	8	11	7	14	18	20	7	5	12	14	14	12
4 48	13 24	17 24	25	25	9	6	11	13	20	17	21	22	10	8	14	16	16	14
5 0	16 11	19 30	27	27	11	♏0	14	16	22	20	23	24	12	11	17	18	19	17
5 12	18 58	21 36	♌0	29	13	11	17	18	24	23	26	27	14	13	20	20	21	20
5 24	21 44	23 42	2	♍1	15	13	19	20	27	26	28	29	16	16	23	23	23	22
5 36	24 30	25 48	4	4	18	15	21	22	29	28	♍1	♍2	19	19	25	25	26	25
5 48	27 15	27 54	7	6	20	18	24	25	♏1	♐1	4	4	21	21	28	28	28	27
6 0	0♍0	0♎0	9	8	22	21	26	27	4	4	6	6	24	24	♍0	♍0	♍0	♐0
6 12	2 45	2 6	12	10	24	23	29	29	6	7	9	9	26	26	3	2	2	3
6 24	5 30	4 12	14	12	26	26	♍2	♍1	8	10	11	11	28	29	5	5	5	5
6 36	8 16	6 18	17	14	29	28	5	4	11	12	14	14	♏1	♐2	8	7	7	8
6 48	11 2	8 24	19	16	♏1	♐1	7	6	13	14	17	16	3	4	10	9	9	10
7 0	13 49	10 30	22	19	8	3	10	8	15	16	19	18	6	7	13	11	11	13
7 12	16 36	12 36	24	21	5	5	12	11	18	17	22	20	8	9	16	14	14	16
7 24	19 24	14 42	27	23	7	8	16	13	20	22	25	23	10	12	18	16	16	18
7 36	22 13	16 48	29	26	10	11	18	15	22	24	27	25	12	15	21	18	18	21
7 48	25 3	18 53	♏2	28	12	13	20	17	25	27	♏0	28	15	17	24	20	20	24
8 0	27 55	20 59	5	♎0	14	16	23	20	27	29	3	♎0	17	19	26	23	22	26
8 12	0♎47	23 4	7	2	16	18	26	22	29	♑2	5	2	19	22	29	25	25	29
8 24	3 41	25 9	10	5	18	21	28	24	♐2	5	8	5	22	25	♏2	27	27	♑2
8 36	6 37	27 15	12	7	20	24	♏1	27	4	8	11	8	24	28	4	29	29	5
8 48	9 34	29 20	15	9	23	26	4	29	6	11	13	10	26	♑1	7	♎2	♐1	8
9 0	12 32	1♏25	17	11	25	29	7	♎1	9	14	16	12	29	3	10	4	4	10
9 12	15 32	3 29	20	13	27	♑2	9	4	11	17	19	14	♑1	6	13	6	6	13
9 24	18 34	5 34	22	15	29	5	12	6	14	20	22	16	4	9	16	9	8	16
9 36	21 37	7 39	25	18	♑2	8	15	8	16	23	24	19	6	12	18	11	11	19
9 48	24 42	9 44	27	20	4	10	17	11	18	26	27	21	8	15	21	13	13	22
10 0	27 49	11 49	♎0	22	6	13	20	13	21	29	♎0	24	11	18	24	16	15	25
10 12	0♏57	13 54	3	24	8	16	23	15	23	♒2	3	26	13	21	27	18	17	28
10 24	4 7	16 0	5	26	11	19	26	18	26	6	6	28	16	24	♎0	21	19	♒1
10 36	7 18	18 5	8	29	13	23	29	20	29	9	8	♑1	18	27	3	23	22	4
10 48	10 30	20 11	10	♐1	16	26	♎1	22	♒1	12	11	3	21	♒1	5	25	24	7
11 0	13 42	22 18	13	3	18	♒0	4	25	4	16	14	6	23	4	8	28	26	11
11 12	16 57	24 45	15	5	21	3	7	27	7	20	17	8	26	7	11	♏0	29	14
11 24	20 12	26 32	18	7	23	6	10	29	10	23	19	10	29	11	14	3	♐1	17
11 36	23 28	28 41	20	10	26	10	13	♏2	13	27	22	12	♒1	14	17	5	3	20
11 48	26 44	0♐50	23	12	28	13	15	4	16	♒1	25	15	4	18	20	7	6	23
12 0	0♏20	3 1	25	14	♒1	17	18	6	19	4	27	17	7	21	23	10	8	25

230

Sid. Time h m	M.C. long	Asc. 1	REGIOMONTA. 11	12	2	3	CAMPANUS 11	12	2	3	PLACIDUS 11	12	2	3	NAT. GRAD. 11	12	2	3
12 0	0 0	3 1	25	14	1	17	18	6	19	4	27	17	7	21	23	10	8	25
12 12	3 16	5 13	28	16	4	21	21	8	23	8	♍0	19	10	25	26	12	10	28
12 24	6 32	7 26	♍1	18	7	25	24	11	27	12	3	22	13	29	29	15	13	♈1
12 36	9 48	9 41	3	20	10	29	26	13	≈0	16	5	24	16	♓2	♍2	18	15	4
12 48	13 3	11 58	6	23	13	♓4	29	15	4	20	8	26	20	6	5	20	17	7
13 0	16 17	14 17	8	25	16	8	♍2	18	8	24	11	29	23	10	8	23	20	11
13 12	19 30	16 39	11	27	19	12	4	20	13	28	13	♏1	27	14	11	25	22	14
13 24	22 42	19 4	13	29	22	17	7	22	17	♈2	16	4	≈0	18	14	28	25	17
13 36	25 53	21 32	15	♓2	27	21	10	25	22	6	19	6	4	22	14	♏1	27	20
13 48	29 3	24 4	18	4	≈1	25	12	27	26	10	21	8	8	26	20	3	≈0	23
14 0	2 11	26 40	21	6	5	♈0	15	29	♓1	14	24	11	12♈	0	23	6	3	26
14 12	5 18	29 21	23	8	9	5	18	♓2	6	18	26	13	16	4	26	9	5	29
14 24	8 23	2♍ 8	26	11	14	9	20	4	11	22	29	16	21	8	29	12	8	♈2
14 36	11 26	5 1	28	13	19	13	23	6	16	23	♓2	18	25	12	♓2	15	11	5
14 48	14 28	8 1	♏1	16	24	18	26	9	22	29	4	21	♈0	16	5	18	14	8
15 0	17 28	11 10	3	18	♈0	22	28	11	27	♉3	7	23	5	20	8	21	17	11
15 12	20 26	14 28	6	21	6	26	♏1	13	♈2	7	9	26	10	24	11	24	21	14
15 24	23 23	17 56	8	23	11	♉1	4	16	7	10	12	29	15	28	14	28	24	17
15 36	26 19	21 37	11	26	17	5	6	18	13	14	14	♍0	20	♉1	17	♍1	28	20
15 48	29 13	25 32	13	28	24	9	9	21	18	17	17	4	25	5	21	5	♓2	23
16 0	2♍ 5	29 43	16	♍1	♈0	13	12	24	23	21	19	7	♈0	9	24	8	5	26
16 12	4 57	4♍10	18	4	6	17	14	27	28	24	22	10	5	12	27	13	10	♉0
16 24	7 47	8 58	21	7	13	20	17	♍0	♉3	28	25	13	10	16	♍1	17	15	3
16 36	10 36	14 6	24	10	19	24	20	3	8	♊1	28	16	15	19	4	22	20	6
16 48	13 24	19 37	26	13	25	27	22	5	12	4	♍1	20	20	23	7	26	25	9
17 0	16 11	25 32	29	16	♉0	♊0	25	8	17	7	3	23	25	26	11	≈1	♈0	12
17 12	18 58	1♍50	♍2	19	6	4	28	11	21	10	6	27	♉0	29	15	7	6	16
17 24	21 44	8 29	5	22	11	7	♍0	14	25	13	9	≈0	5	♊3	19	12	12	19
17 36	24 30	15 28	8	27	16	11	3	17	29	16	12	4	9	6	22	18	18	23
17 48	27 15	22 40	10	≈1	21	14	5	20	♍3	19	15	8	14	7	26	24	24	26
18 0	0♍ 0	0♈ 0	13	5	25	17	8	24	7	22	18	12	18	12	≈0	♈0	♍0	♊0
18 12	2 45	7 20	16	9	29	20	11	27	10	25	21	16	22	15	4	6	6	4
18 24	5 30	14 32	19	14	♊3	22	14	≈1	13	27	24	21	20	18	7	12	12	8
18 36	8 16	21 31	23	19	8	25	17	5	16	♋0	27	25	♍0	21	11	18	17	11
18 48	11 2	28 10	26	24	11	28	20	9	19	3	≈1	♈0	3	24	14	24	23	15
19 0	13 49	4♍28	≈0	♈0	14	♋1	23	13	22	6	4	5	7	27	18	♈0	29	19
19 12	16 36	10 23	3	5	17	4	26	17	25	8	7	10	10	29	21	5	♊4	23
19 24	19 24	15 54	6	11	20	6	29	21	28	11	11	15	14	♋2	24	10	9	28
19 36	22 13	21 2	10	17	23	9	≈2	25	♋1	14	14	20	17	5	27	15	13	♋0
19 48	25 3	25 50	13	24	26	12	6	♈1	3	16	18	25	20	8	♈1	20	17	3
20 0	27 55	0♍17	17	♈0	29	14	9	6	6	19	21	♍0	23	11	4	24	22	6
20 12	0≈47	4 28	21	6	♋2	17	13	12	9	22	25	5	26	13	7	28	25	10
20 24	3 41	8 23	25	13	4	19	16	17	11	24	29	10	29	15	10	♉2	29	13
20 36	6 37	12 4	29	19	7	22	20	23	14	27	♍2	15	♍1	18	13	6	♋3	16
20 48	9 34	15 32	♓4	25	9	24	23	28	16	29	6	20	4	21	16	9	6	19
21 0	12 32	18 50	8	♉0	12	27	27	♈3	19	♌2	10	25	7	23	19	13	9	22
21 12	15 32	21 59	12	6	14	29	♈1	9	21	5	14	♍0	9	26	22	16	12	25
21 24	18 34	24 59	17	11	17	♌2	5	14	23	7	18	5	12	28	25	19	15	28
21 36	21 37	27 52	21	16	19	4	9	19	26	10	22	9	14	♍1	28	22	18	♍1
21 48	24 42	0♍39	25	21	22	7	12	24	28	13	26	14	17	4	♈1	25	21	4
22 0	27 49	3 20	♈0	25	24	9	16	♉0	♍1	15	♈0	18	19	6	4	27	24	7
22 12	0♓57	5 56	5	29	26	12	20	4	3	18	4	22	22	9	7	♊0	27	10
22 24	4 7	8 28	9	♊3	28	15	23	9	5	21	8	26	24	11	10	3	29	13
22 36	7 18	10 56	13	8	♌1	17	27	13	8	23	12	♍0	26	14	13	5	♍2	16
22 48	10 30	13 21	18	11	3	19	♈1	18	10	26	16	3	29	17	16	8	5	19
23 0	13 43	15 43	22	14	5	22	5	22	12	29	20	7	♍1	19	19	10	7	22
23 12	16 57	18 2	26	17	7	25	9	26	15	♍1	24	10	4	22	22	13	10	25
23 24	20 12	20 19	♉1	20	10	27	13	29	17	4	28	14	6	28	25	15	12	28
23 36	23 28	22 24	5	23	12	♍0	17	♊3	19	6	♉1	17	8	27	29	17	14	♍1
23 48	26 44	24 47	9	26	14	3	21	7	22	9	5	20	11	♍0	♉2	20	17	4
24 0	0♍ 0	26 59	13	29	16	5	25	10	24	12	9	23	13	3	5	22	20	6

53° N. Lat.   Cusps of Houses   0h. – 12h.

Sid. Time	M.C. long.	Asc.	REGIOMONTA.				CAMPANUS				PLACIDUS				NAT. GRAD.			
h m	♈	1 ♉	11 ♉	12 ♊	2 ♌	3 ♍	11 ♈	12 ♊	2 ♌	3 ♍	11 ♉	12 ♊	2 ♌	3 ♍	11 ♉	12 ♊	2 ♌	3 ♍
0 0	0 0	27 50	13	0	17	5	25	11	24	12	9	24	13	3	5	23	21	7
0 12	3 16	29 59	17	3	19	7	29	14	27	15	13	27	16	5	8	25	23	9
0 24	6 32	2♉ 6	21	5	21	10	♉3	17	29	18	16	29	18	8	11	27	25	12
0 36	9 48	4 13	24	8	23	12	6	20	♊1	21	20	♋2	20	11	14	♋0	28	14
0 48	13 3	6 19	28	10	25	15	10	23	4	25	23	5	23	14	17	2	♌0	19
1 0	16 17	8 24	♊1	13	27	17	14	26	6	26	27	7	25	16	20	4	3	20
1 12	19 30	10 28	5	15	♏0	20	17	29	8	29	♊0	10	27	19	23	6	5	23
1 24	22 42	12 33	8	18	2	22	21	♋1	11	♎2	3	13	29	22	26	9	8	27
1 36	25 53	14 37	11	20	4	25	24	4	13	4	6	15	♍2	25	29	11	10	♍0
1 48	29 3	16 40	14	22	6	27	27	7	15	7	9	18	4	27	♊2	13	12	3
2 0	2♉11	18 44	17	25	8	♌0	♊1	9	18	10	12	20	6	♍0	5	15	15	6
2 12	5 18	20 47	20	27	10	3	4	12	20	13	15	22	9	3	8	18	17	9
2 24	8 23	22 50	23	29	13	5	7	14	22	15	18	25	11	5	11	20	19	12
2 36	11 26	24 53	26	♌1	15	8	10	17	24	18	21	27	13	8	14	22	22	14
2 48	14 28	26 57	29	4	17	10	13	19	27	21	24	29	16	11	17	24	24	17
3 0	17 28	29 0	♋2	6	19	13	16	22	29	24	27	♍2	18	14	20	27	26	20
3 12	20 26	1♍ 3	4	8	21	15	19	24	♎1	26	♋0	4	21	16	22	29	29	3
3 24	23 23	3 7	7	10	23	18	21	26	4	29	2	6	23	19	24	♌1	♎1	26
3 36	26 19	5 10	10	12	26	20	24	29	6	♍2	5	9	25	22	27	4	3	28
3 48	29 13	7 14	12	14	28	23	27	♌1	8	4	8	11	28	25	♋0	6	5	♏1
4 0	2♊ 5	9 17	15	17	♎0	25	♌0	3	11	7	11	13	♎0	27	3	8	8	4
4 12	4 57	11 21	17	19	2	28	3	5	13	10	13	16	2	♍0	6	10	10	6
4 24	7 47	13 25	20	21	4	♍0	5	8	15	13	16	18	5	3	9	12	12	9
4 36	10 36	15 29	22	23	7	3	8	11	18	15	18	20	7	5	12	14	14	12
4 48	13 24	27 33	25	25	9	5	10	13	20	18	21	23	9	8	14	17	17	14
5 0	16 11	19 38	27	27	11	8	13	15	22	20	24	25	12	10	17	19	19	17
5 12	18 58	21 42	♌0	♎0	13	10	16	17	24	23	26	27	14	13	20	21	21	20
5 24	21 44	23 47	2	2	15	13	19	20	27	25	29	♍0	16	15	23	23	23	22
5 36	14 30	25 51	5	4	17	15	21	22	29	28	♌1	♍2	19	18	24	26	26	25
5 48	27 15	27 56	7	6	20	18	24	24	♏1	♐1	4	4	21	21	27	28	28	27
6 0	0♋0	0♎0	10	8	22	20	27	26	4	3	66	6	24	24	♌0	♍0	♏0	♐0
6 12	2 45	2 4	12	10	24	23	29	29	6	6	9	9	26	26	3	2	2	3
6 24	5 30	4 9	15	13	26	25	♌2	♍1	8	8	12	11	28	29	5	4	4	5
6 36	8 16	6 13	17	15	28	28	4	3	11	11	14	13	♏1	♐1	8	7	7	8
6 48	11 2	8 18	20	17	♏0	♐0	7	6	13	14	17	16	3	4	9	10	9	10
7 0	13 49	10 22	22	19	3	3	10	8	15	16	20	18	5	6	13	11	11	13
7 12	16 36	12 27	25	21	5	5	12	9	17	19	22	21	7	9	16	13	13	16
7 24	19 24	15 31	27	23	7	8	15	11	20	21	25	23	10	12	18	16	16	18
7 36	22 13	16 35	♍0	26	9	10	17	14	22	23	27	25	12	14	21	18	18	21
7 48	25 3	18 39	2	28	11	13	20	17	24	26	♍0	28	14	17	23	20	20	23
8 0	27 55	20 43	5	♏0	13	15	23	19	26	28	3	♎0	17	19	26	22	22	26
8 12	0♌47	22 46	7	2	16	18	26	22	29	♑1	5	2	19	22	29	25	24	29
8 24	3 41	24 50	10	4	18	20	28	24	♐1	4	8	5	21	25	♏3	27	27	♑2
8 36	6 37	26 53	12	7	20	23	♏1	26	4	8	11	7	24	28	5	29	29	5
8 48	9 34	28 57	15	9	22	26	4	28	6	11	14	9	26	♑0	8	♎1	♐1	7
9 0	12 32	1♏0	17	11	24	28	6	♎1	8	14	16	12	28	3	10	4	3	10
9 12	15 32	3 3	20	13	26	♑1	9	3	11	17	19	14	♐1	6	13	6	6	13
9 24	18 34	5 7	22	15	29	4	12	5	13	20	22	17	3	9	15	8	8	16
9 36	21 37	7 10	25	17	♐1	7	15	8	16	23	25	19	5	12	18	11	10	19
9 48	24 42	9 13	27	20	3	10	18	10	18	26	27	21	8	15	21	13	12	22
10 0	27 49	11 16	♏0	22	5	13	20	12	21	29	♏0	24	10	18	24	15	15	25
10 12	0♍57	13 20	3	24	8	16	23	15	23	♒3	3	26	12	21	27	17	17	28
10 24	4 7	15 23	5	26	10	19	26	17	26	6	5	28	15	24	♏0	19	19	♒1
10 36	7 18	17 27	8	28	12	22	28	19	28	9	8	♏1	17	27	2	21	21	4
10 48	10 30	19 32	10	♏0	15	25	♎1	22	♑1	13	11	3	20	♒0	5	23	24	7
11 0	13 43	21 36	13	3	17	29	4	24	4	16	14	5	23	3	8	27	26	10
11 12	16 57	23 41	15	5	20	♒2	6	26	7	20	17	8	25	♑1	11	♏0	28	13
11 24	20 12	25 47	18	7	22	6	9	29	10	24	19	10	28	10	14	2	♑1	16
11 36	23 28	27 54	20	9	25	9	12	♏1	13	27	22	12	♑1	14	17	14	3	19
11 48	26 44	0♐1	23	11	27	13	15	3	16	♒1	25	14	3	17	20	7	5	22
12 0	0♎0	2 10	25	13	♑0	17	18	5	19	5	27	17	6	21	23	9	7	25

Sid. Time	M.C. long.	Asc. 1	REGIOMONTA. 11	12	2	3	CAMPANUS 11	12	2	3	PLACIDUS 11	12	2	3	NAT. GRAD. 11	12	2	3
h m	♎	♐	♎	♏	♑	♒	♎	♏	♑	♓	♎	♏	♑	♒	♎	♏	♑	♒
12 0	0 0	2 10	25	13	0	17	18	5	19	5	27	17	6	21	23	9	7	25
12 12	3 16	4 20	28	16	3	21	20	8	23	9	♏0	19	9	25	26	12	10	29
12 24	6 32	6 31	♏0	18	6	25	23	10	27	13	3	21	12	28	29	14	12	♓2
12 36	9 8	8 44	3	20	9	29	26	12	♒1	17	5	24	15	♓2	♏2	17	14	6
12 48	13 3	10 59	5	22	12	♓3	28	15	4	20	8	26	19	6	5	19	17	10
13 0	16 17	13 16	8	24	15	8	♏1	17	8	24	11	29	23	10	8	22	19	13
13 12	19 30	15 35	10	26	19	12	4	19	13	28	13	♌1	26	14	11	25	21	16
13 24	22 42	17 57	13	29	22	16	6	21	17	♈3	16	3	29	18	13	27	24	19
13 36	25 53	20 23	15	♌1	26	21	9	24	22	7	18	5	♒3	22	16	♑0	26	21
13 48	29 3	22 52	18	3	♒0	25	11	26	26	11	21	8	7	26	19	3	29	24
14 0	♐11	25 26	20	5	4	♈0	14	28	♈1	14	24	10	11	♈0	22	5	♒1	27
14 12	5 18	28 4	23	8	8	5	17	♈1	6	18	26	12	15	4	25	8	4	29
14 24	8 23	0♑48	25	10	13	9	20	3	12	22	29	15	20	8	28	11	7	♈2
14 36	11 26	3 38	28	12	18	14	22	5	17	26	♌1	17	24	12	♌1	14	10	5
14 48	14 28	6 36	♑0	15	23	18	26	8	22	♉0	4	20	29	16	4	17	13	8
15 0	17 28	9 42	3	17	29	22	28	10	28	4	6	23	♓4	20	7	20	16	11
15 12	20 26	12 57	5	20	♓4	27	♑0	13	♈3	9	9	25	9	24	10	23	19	14
15 24	23 23	16 23	8	22	11	♉1	3	15	9	11	11	27	14	28	13	27	23	17
15 36	26 19	20 2	10	25	17	5	5	18	14	13	13	♑1	19	♉2	17	♑0	26	20
15 48	29 19	23 55	13	27	23	9	8	20	20	17	17	3	25	5	20	3	♓0	23
16 0	2♐5	28 4	15	♑0	♈0	13	11	23	25	21	19	6	♈0	9	23	7	4	26
16 12	4 57	2♒31	18	3	7	17	13	25	♉0	25	22	9	5	13	27	12	9	29
16 24	7 47	7 20	20	6	13	21	16	28	4	28	25	12	11	16	♒0	16	14	♉3
16 36	10 36	12 31	23	9	19	24	18	♑1	9	♉1	28	15	16	20	4	20	19	6
16 48	13 24	18 7	26	12	24	28	21	4	14	4	♒0	19	21	23	7	25	24	9
17 0	16 11	24 9	28	15	♉1	♊1	24	6	19	8	3	22	26	27	11	♒0	29	12
17 12	18 58	0♓38	♒1	19	7	5	27	9	22	11	6	26	♉1	♊0	15	6	♈5	16
17 24	21 44	7 32	4	22	12	8	29	13	26	13	9	29	6	3	18	12	11	19
17 36	24 30	14 47	7	26	17	11	♒2	16	♊0	16	12	♒3	10	6	22	18	17	22
17 48	27 15	22 19	10	♒0	22	14	5	19	4	19	15	8	15	9	26	24	23	26
18 0	0♑0	0♈0	13	4	26	17	8	22	8	22	18	11	19	12	♒0	♉0	♉0	♊0
18 12	2 45	7 41	6	8	♊0	20	11	26	11	25	21	15	23	15	4	6	6	4
18 24	5 30	15 13	19	13	4	23	14	♒0	14	28	24	20	27	18	7	13	12	8
18 36	8 16	22 28	22	18	8	26	17	4	17	♉1	27	24	♊1	21	11	19	18	12
18 48	11 2	29 22	25	23	11	29	20	7	21	3	♒0	29	4	24	15	25	24	15
19 0	13 49	5♉51	29	29	15	♋2	22	11	24	6	3	♓4	8	27	18	♈2	♊0	19
19 12	16 36	11 53	♒2	♉5	18	4	26	16	26	9	7	9	11	♋0	21	7	5	23
19 24	19 24	17 29	6	11	21	7	29	21	29	11	10	14	15	2	24	12	9	26
19 36	22 13	22 40	9	17	24	10	♒2	26	♋2	14	14	19	18	5	27	16	14	♋0
19 48	24 58	27 29	13	22	27	12	5	♉0	5	17	17	25	21	8	♈1	21	19	3
20 0	27 55	1♊56	17	♈0	♋0	15	9	5	8	19	21	♈0	24	11	4	26	23	7
20 12	0♒41	6 5	21	7	3	17	12	11	10	22	25	5	27	13	7	♉0	26	10
20 24	3 41	9 58	25	13	5	20	16	16	13	25	28	11	29	16	9	3	♋0	14
20 36	6 37	13 37	29	19	8	22	19	21	15	27	♓2	16	♋3	19	12	7	3	17
20 48	9 34	17 3	♓3	24	10	25	23	27	18	♋0	6	21	5	21	15	11	7	20
21 0	12 32	20 18	8	♉1	13	27	26	♈2	21	2	10	26	7	24	18	14	10	23
21 12	15 32	23 24	12	7	15	♋0	♈0	8	23	5	14	♉1	10	26	21	17	13	26
21 24	18 34	26 22	16	12	18	2	4	14	25	8	18	6	13	29	24	20	16	29
21 36	21 37	29 12	21	17	20	5	8	19	27	10	22	10	15	♋1	27	23	19	♋2
21 48	24 42	1♋56	25	22	22	7	12	24	♋0	13	26	15	18	4	♈0	26	22	5
22 0	27 49	4 34	♈0	26	25	10	15	29	2	16	♈0	19	20	6	4	29	25	8
22 12	0♓57	7 8	5	♊0	27	12	20	♈4	4	18	4	23	22	9	7	♊2	27	11
22 24	4 7	9 37	9	4	29	15	24	8	6	21	8	27	25	12	10	4	♋0	14
22 36	7 18	12 3	14	8	♋1	17	28	13	9	24	12	♏1	27	14	13	6	3	17
22 48	10 30	14 25	18	11	4	20	♈2	17	11	26	16	4	29	17	16	9	5	19
23 0	13 43	16 44	22	15	6	22	6	22	13	29	20	8	♋1	20	19	11	8	22
23 12	16 57	19 1	27	18	8	25	10	26	16	♍2	24	11	4	22	22	13	11	24
23 24	20 12	21 16	♉1	21	10	27	14	29	18	4	28	15	6	25	25	16	13	27
23 36	23 28	23 29	5	24	12	♍0	18	♊2	20	7	♉2	18	9	27	29	18	16	♍0
23 48	26 44	25 40	9	27	14	2	22	7	22	10	5	21	11	♍0	♊2	21	18	3
24 0	0♈0	27 50	13	♋0	17	5	25	11	25	12	9	24	13	3	5	23	21	7

Sid. Time h m	M.C. long.	Asc. 1	REGIOMONTA. 11	12	2	3	CAMPANUS 11	12	2	3	PLACIDUS 11	12	2	3	NAT. GRAD 11	12	2	3
0 0	0 0	28 42	14	1	17	5	25	11	25	13	9	25	14	3	5	24	22	7
0 12	3 16	0♌48	18	4	19	7	29	14	28	15	13	28	16	6	8	26	24	10
0 24	6 32	2 54	21	6	21	10	♉2	17	♍0	18	17	♋0	18	8	11	29	26	13
0 36	9 48	4 59	25	9	24	12	6	20	2	21	20	3	21	11	14	♋1	29	16
0 48	13 3	7 3	29	11	26	15	10	23	5	24	24	6	23	14	17	3	♍1	19
1 0	16 17	9 6	♉2	14	28	17	13	26	7	27	27	8	25	16	20	5	3	22
1 12	19 30	11 9	5	16	♍0	20	17	29	9	29	♋0	11	27	19	23	7	6	25
1 24	22 42	13 11	9	19	2	22	20	♋1	11	♎2	4	13	♍0	22	26	9	8	28
1 36	25 23	15 14	12	21	4	25	23	4	14	5	7	16	2	25	♋0	12	10	♎1
1 48	29 3	17 15	15	23	6	27	27	7	16	8	10	18	4	27	3	14	13	3
2 0	2♉1	19 17	18	25	8	♎0	♍0	8	18	10	13	21	7	♎0	6	16	15	6
2 12	5 18	21 19	21	28	11	3	3	12	20	13	16	23	9	3	8	18	17	9
2 24	8 23	23 20	24	♌0	13	5	6	14	23	16	19	25	11	5	11	20	20	12
2 36	11 26	25 22	27	2	15	8	9	17	25	18	22	28	14	8	14	23	22	15
2 48	14 28	27 23	29	4	17	10	12	19	27	21	25	♌0	16	11	17	25	24	17
3 0	17 28	29 25	♌2	6	19	13	16	22	♎0	24	27	2	18	14	20	27	27	20
3 12	20 26	1♍27	5	9	21	15	18	24	3	27	♌0	5	21	16	23	29	29	23
3 24	23 23	3 28	7	11	24	18	21	26	5	29	3	7	23	19	26	♍1	♎1	26
3 36	26 19	5 30	10	13	26	20	24	28	7	♏2	6	9	25	22	28	3	3	28
3 48	29 19	7 32	13	15	28	23	27	♍1	9	5	8	12	28	24	♍1	5	6	♏1
4 0	2♍5	9 34	15	17	♎0	25	♍0	3	11	7	11	14	♎0	27	4	8	8	4
4 12	4 57	11 36	17	19	2	28	3	6	13	10	14	16	2	♏0	7	10	10	7
4 24	7 47	13 39	20	21	4	♍0	5	8	16	12	16	18	5	2	9	12	12	9
4 36	10 36	15 41	23	24	6	3	8	10	18	15	19	21	7	5	12	15	14	12
4 48	13 24	17 43	25	26	9	5	10	12	20	18	21	23	9	8	14	17	17	15
5 0	16 11	19 46	28	28	11	7	13	14	22	20	24	25	12	10	17	19	19	17
5 12	18 58	21 49	♌0	♍0	13	10	15	17	25	23	27	27	14	13	20	21	21	20
5 24	21 44	23 52	3	2	15	12	18	19	27	25	29	♍0	16	15	22	23	23	22
5 36	24 30	25 54	5	4	17	15	21	21	29	28	♎2	2	19	18	25	26	26	25
5 48	27 15	27 57	8	6	19	17	24	24	♏1	♐1	4	4	21	21	28	28	28	27
6 0	0♎0	0♎0	10	8	22	20	26	26	4	3	7	7	23	23	♌0	♍0	♎0	♏0
6 12	2 45	2 3	13	11	24	22	29	28	6	6	9	9	26	26	3	2	2	3
6 24	5 30	4 6	15	13	26	25	♎2	♏1	8	9	12	11	28	28	5	4	4	5
6 36	8 16	6 8	18	15	28	27	4	3	11	12	15	14	♏1	♐1	8	7	7	8
6 48	11 2	8 11	20	17	♏0	♐0	7	5	13	14	17	16	3	3	10	9	9	10
7 0	13 49	10 14	23	19	2	2	10	8	15	17	20	18	5	6	13	11	11	13
7 12	16 36	12 17	25	21	4	5	12	10	18	20	22	21	7	9	16	13	13	16
7 24	19 24	14 19	27	24	6	·7	15	12	20	22	25	23	9	11	18	16	16	18
7 36	22 13	16 21	♍0	26	9	10	17	15	23	25	28	25	12	14	21	18	18	21
7 48	25 3	18 24	2	28	11	13	20	17	25	28	♍0	28	14	16	24	20	20	23
8 0	27 55	20 26	5	♎0	13	15	23	19	27	♐0	3	♎0	16	19	26	22	23	26
8 12	0♏51	22 28	7	2	15	17	26	21	29	3	6	2	18	22	29	25	25	29
8 24	3 41	24 30	10	4	17	20	29	24	♐1	6	8	5	21	24	♍1	27	27	♐2
8 36	5 37	26 32	12	6	19	23	♏2	26	4	9	11	7	23	27	4	29	29	4
8 48	9 34	28 33	15	9	21	25	4	28	6	12	14	9	25	♐0	7	♎3	♐1	7
9 0	12 32	0♏35	17	11	24	28	6	♎0	8	15	16	12	28	3	10	5	3	10
9 12	15 32	2 37	20	13	26	♐1	9	3	11	18	19	14	♐0	5	12	7	5	13
9 24	16 34	4 38	22	15	28	3	11	5	13	21	22	16	2	8	15	9	7	16
9 36	19 37	6 40	25	17	40	6	14	7	16	23	25	19	5	11	18	11	10	19
9 48	24 42	8 41	27	19	2	9	17	9	18	26	27	21	7	14	21	13	12	22
10 0	27 49	10 43	♎0	22	5	12	20	12	21	29	♎0	23	9	17	24	15	14	24
10 12	0♐57	12 45	3	24	7	15	22	14	23	≈3	3	26	12	20	26	18	16	27
10 24	4 7	13 46	5	26	9	18	25	17	26	6	6	28	14	23	29	20	18	≈0
10 36	7 18	16 49	8	28	11	21	28	19	29	10	8	♏0	17	26	♎2	23	21	4
10 48	10 30	18 51	10	♍0	14	24	≈1	29	♐1	13	11	3	19	≈0	5	25	23	7
11 0	13 43	20 54	13	2	16	28	3	23	4	16	14	5	22	3	8	28	25	10
11 12	16 57	22 57	15	4	19	≈1	6	26	7	20	16	7	24	6	11	♏0	27	13
11 24	20 12	25 1	18	6	21	5	9	28	10	24	19	9	27	10	14	3	♐1	16
11 36	23 28	27 6	20	9	24	9	12	♏0	13	28	22	12	♐0	13	17	5	2	19
11 48	26 44	29 11	23	11	26	12	14	2	16	×1	24	14	2	17	20	7	4	22
12 0	0≈0	1♐18	25	13	29	16	17	5	19	5	27	16	5	21	23	9	6	25

Sid. Time	M.C. long.	Asc. 1	REGIOMONTA. 11	12	2	3	CAMPANUS 11	12	2	3	PLACIDUS 11	12	2	3	NAT. GRAD. 11	12	2	3
h m	♎	♏	♎	♏	♐	♐	♎	♏	♐	♑	♎	♏	♑	♎	♎	♏	♐	♎
12 0	0♎0	1♏17	25	13	29	16	17	5	19	4	27	16	5	21	23	19	6	25
12 12	3 16	3 25	28	15	♒2	20	20	7	23	8	♏0	18	8	24	26	11	9	28
12 24	6 32	5 34	♏0	17	5	24	23	9	27	12	2	21	11	28	29	14	11	♓1
12 36	9 48	7 45	3	19	8	28	25	12	♒0	17	5	23	14	♓2	♏2	16	13	4
12 48	13 3	9 57	5	21	11	♓3	28	14	4	21	8	25	18	6	5	19	15	8
13 0	16 17	12 12	7	24	14	7	♏1	16	8	25	10	28	21	10	7	21	18	11
13 12	19 30	14 29	10	26	17	12	3	18	13	29	13	♏0	25	14	10	24	20	14
13 24	22 42	16 49	12	28	21	16	6	20	17	♈3	15	2	28	18	13	27	23	17
13 36	25 53	19 11	15	♏0	25	21	8	22	22	7	18	5	♒2	22	16	29	25	17
13 48	29 2	21 48	17	2	28	25	11	25	27	11	21	7	6	26	19	♉2	27	23
14 0	2♏11	24 8	20	5	3	♈0	14	27	♒2	15	23	9	10	♈0	22	4	♒0	26
14 12	5 18	26 44	22	7	♈7	5	16	♏0	7	19	26	12	15	4	25	7	3	29
14 24	8 23	29 25	25	9	12	9	19	2	13	23	28	14	19	8	28	10	6	♈2
14 36	11 26	2♏12	27	11	17	14	22	4	18	27	♈1	17	24	12	♏1	13	9	5
14 48	14 28	5 6	♈0	14	22	18	24	7	24	♉1	3	19	29	16	4	16	12	8
15 0	17 28	8 8	2	16	28	23	27	9	29	4	6	22	♓3	20	7	19	14	11
15 12	20 26	11 20	5	19	♓4	27	♏0	11	♈4	8	9	24	8	24	10	22	17	14
15 24	23 23	14 43	7	21	10	♉2	2	14	10	11	11	27	14	28	13	26	20	17
15 36	26 19	18 19	10	24	17	6	5	16	15	15	14	♏0	19	♉2	16	29	24	20
15 48	29 19	22 10	13	26	23	10	8	19	20	18	16	2	25	6	19	♒2	27	22
16 0	2♐5	26 17	15	29	♈0	14	10	21	26	22	19	5	♈0	9	22	6	♉0	25
16 12	4 57	0♏44	17	♒2	7	18	13	24	♈1	25	22	8	5	13	26	10	6	29
16 24	7 47	5 32	20	5	13	21	16	27	6	28	24	11	11	17	♏0	15	11	♉2
16 36	10 36	10 46	23	8	20	25	18	29	11	♊2	27	14	16	20	3	19	16	5
16 48	13 24	16 26	25	11	26	29	21	♒2	16	5	♏0	18	22	24	6	24	22	9
17 0	16 11	22 36	28	14	♉2	♊2	23	5	20	8	3	21	27	27	10	29	27	12
17 12	18 58	♏1 0	♒1	17	7	5	26	8	24	11	5	♐1	♊0	♊0	14	♋5	♈4	16
17 24	21 44	6♓26	3	21	13	9	29	11	28	14	8	28	6	4	18	11	11	19
17 36	24 30	14 1	6	25	18	12	♒2	15	♉2	17	11	♒2	11	7	22	17	17	23
17 48	27 15	21 55	9	28	23	15	4	18	6	20	14	6	15	10	26	24	24	26
18 0	0♑0	0♈0	12	♈3	27	18	7	21	9	23	17	10	20	13	♎0	♈0	♉0	♊0
18 12	2 45	8 5	15	7	♊2	21	10	25	12	26	20	15	24	16	4	7	6	4
18 24	5 30	15 49	18	12	5	24	13	28	15	28	23	19	28	19	7	13	13	8
18 36	8 16	23 34	21	17	9	27	16	♒2	18	♋1	26	24	♊2	21	11	20	19	12
18 48	11 2	0♉44	24	22	13	29	19	6	11	3	♎0	29	5	25	15	26	25	16
19 0	13 49	7 24	28	28	16	♋2	22	10	25	♋0	3	♈3	9	♋0	18	♈3	♊1	20
19 12	16 36	13 34	♒1	♈4	19	5	25	15	27	9	6	8	12	♋0	21	8	6	23
19 24	19 24	19 14	5	10	22	7	♒1	19	♋0	12	10	14	16	3	24	13	11	27
19 36	22 13	24 28	9	17	25	10	5	24	3	15	17	19	19	6	28	18	15	♋0
19 48	25 3	29 16	12	23	28	13	9	29	6	17	19	25	22	8	♓1	23	20	4
20 0	27 55	4♉43	16	♈0	♋1	15	8	♈3	8	20	21	♈0	25	11	4	28	24	7
20 12	0♑41	7 50	20	7	4	17	11	9	11	23	24	5	28	14	6	♉1	28	11
20 24	3 41	11 41	24	13	6	20	15	14	13	25	28	11	♋0	16	9	5	♊1	14
20 36	6 37	15 17	28	20	9	23	18	20	16	28	♓2	16	3	19	12	8	4	17
20 48	9 34	18 40	♓3	26	11	25	22	25	18	♌0	6	22	6	21	15	12	8	20
21 0	12 32	21 52	7	♉2	14	28	26	♈1	21	3	10	27	8	23	19	16	11	23
21 12	15 32	24 54	12	8	16	♌0	29	6	23	6	14	♉1	11	26	22	18	14	26
21 24	18 34	27 48	16	13	19	3	♓3	12	26	8	18	6	13	28	25	21	17	29
21 36	21 37	0♊35	21	18	21	5	7	17	28	11	22	11	16	♌2	28	24	20	♌2
21 48	24 42	3 16	25	23	23	8	11	23	♌0	13	26	15	18	3	♈1	26	23	5
22 0	27 49	5 52	♈0	27	25	10	15	28	3	16	♈0	20	21	6	24	28	26	8
22 12	0♒58	8 12	5	♊2	28	13	19	♉3	5	19	4	24	23	9	27	♊1	29	10
22 24	4 7	10 41	9	5	♌0	15	23	7	7	21	8	28	25	11	10	4	♋3	12
22 36	7 18	13 11	14	9	2	18	27	12	9	24	12	♊2	28	14	13	7	6	14
22 48	10 30	15 31	18	13	4	20	♈1	17	11	27	16	5	♌0	16	16	10	10	16
23 0	13 43	17 48	23	16	6	23	5	21	14	29	20	9	2	19	19	12	14	18
23 12	16 57	20 3	27	19	9	25	9	25	16	♏2	24	12	5	22	22	15	15	21
23 24	20 12	22 15	♉2	22	11	27	13	29	19	5	28	16	7	24	25	17	17	25
23 36	23 28	24 26	6	25	13	♍0	17	♊3	21	♌0	♉2	19	9	27	29	19	18	29
23 48	26 44	27 35	10	28	15	2	20	7	23	10	6	22	12	♍0	♉2	21	20	♍3
24 0	0♈0	28 43	14	♋1	17	5	25	11	25	13	9	25	14	3	5	24	22	7

Sid. Time	M. C. long.	Asc. 1	REGIOMONTANA. 11	12	2	3	CAMPANUS 11	12	2	3	PLACIDUS 11	12	2	3	NAT. GRAD. 11	12	2	3
h m	♈	♋	♉	♋	♌	♍	♈	♊	♌	♋	♈	♊	♌	♍	♉	♊	♋	♍
0 0	0 0	29 36	14	2	18	5	24	10	26	13	10	26	14	3	5	24	22	8
0 12	3 16	1♌41	18	5	20	8	28	13	28	16	13	29	17	6	8	27	24	11
0 24	6 32	3 44	22	7	22	10	♂2	16	♍1	19	17	♋1	19	8	11	29	27	14
0 36	9 48	5 47	26	10	24	13	6	19	3	22	21	4	21	11	15	♋2	29	17
0 48	13 3	7 49	29	12	26	15	9	22	5	24	24	7	23	14	18	4	♍2	20
1 0	16 17	9 50	♊2	15	28	18	13	25	7	27	27	9	26	16	21	6	4	22
1 12	19 30	11 51	6	17	♍0	20	16	28	10	♠0	♋1	12	28	19	24	8	6	25
1 24	22 42	13 51	9	19	2	23	20	♋1	12	2	4	14	♍0	22	27	10	9	28
1 36	25 53	15 52	13	22	5	25	23	4	14	8	7	17	2	25	♍0	12	11	♎1
1 48	29 3	17 52	16	24	7	28	27	7	16	8	10	19	5	27	3	14	14	4
2 0	2♉11	19 52	19	26	9	♎0	♍0	10	19	11	13	21	7	♎0	6	16	16	6
2 12	5 18	21 51	22	28	11	2	3	12	21	13	16	24	9	3	9	19	18	9
2 24	8 23	23 51	25	♍1	13	5	6	14	23	16	19	26	12	5	11	21	20	12
2 36	11 26	25 51	27	3	15	7	9	17	26	19	22	28	14	8	14	23	22	15
2 48	14 28	27 51	♋0	5	17	10	12	19	28	21	25	♍1	16	11	17	25	25	18
3 0	17 28	29 51	3	7	19	12	15	22	♎0	24	28	3	18	14	20	27	27	20
3 12	20 26	1♌50	5	9	22	15	18	24	3	27	♋1	5	21	16	3	♌0	29	23
3 24	23 23	3 50	8	11	24	17	21	26	5	29	3	8	23	19	26	2	♎1	26
3 36	26 19	5 51	11	13	26	20	24	29	7	♍2	6	10	25	22	28	4	4	29
3 48	29 19	7 51	13	16	28	22	27	♍1	10	5	9	12	28	24	♋1	6	6	♍1
4 0	2♊ 5	9 51	16	18	♎0	25	♋0	3	12	8	11	14	♎0	27	4	8	8	4
4 12	4 57	11 52	18	20	2	27	2	6	14	10	14	17	2	♍0	6	10	10	7
4 24	7 47	13 52	21	22	4	♍0	5	8	16	13	17	19	5	2	9	13	12	9
4 36	10 36	15 53	23	24	6	2	7	11	18	15	19	21	7	5	11	15	15	12
4 48	13 24	17 54	26	26	8	5	10	13	21	18	22	23	9	7	14	17	17	15
5 0	16 11	19 55	28	28	11	7	13	15	23	21	24	26	12	10	17	19	19	17
5 12	18 58	21 56	♌0	♍2	13	10	15	18	25	23	26	28	14	13	20	21	21	20
5 24	21 44	23 57	3	2	15	12	18	20	27	26	29	♎0	16	15	22	23	23	22
5 36	24 30	25 58	6	5	17	14	21	22	♍0	29	♍2	2	18	18	25	26	26	25
5 48	27 15	28 0	8	7	19	17	23	24	2	♍1	5	5	21	20	27	28	28	27
6 0	0♋ 0	0♎ 0	11	9	21	19	26	26	4	4	7	7	23	23	♌0	♍0	♍0	♎0
6 12	2 45	2 0	13	11	23	22	29	28	6	6	10	9	25	25	3	2	2	3
6 24	5 30	4 2	16	13	25	24	♍1	♍1	9	9	12	12	28	28	5	4	4	5
6 36	8 16	6 3	18	15	28	27	4	3	11	12	15	14	♍0	♎1	8	7	7	8
6 48	11 2	8 4	20	17	♍0	29	7	5	13	14	17	16	2	4	10	9	9	10
7 0	13 49	10 5	23	19	2	♎2	9	7	15	17	20	18	4	6	13	11	11	13
7 12	16 36	12 6	25	22	4	4	12	9	18	20	23	21	7	8	16	13	13	16
7 24	19 24	14 7	28	24	6	7	15	12	20	22	25	23	9	11	18	15	15	18
7 36	22 13	16 8	♍0	26	8	9	17	14	22	25	28	25	11	13	21	18	17	21
7 48	25 3	18 8	3	28	10	12	20	16	24	28	♍0	28	13	16	24	20	19	24
8 0	27 55	20 9	5	♎0	12	14	22	19	27	♍0	3	♎0	16	19	26	22	22	26
8 12	0♌41	22 9	8	2	14	17	25	♋1	29	3	6	2	18	21	29	24	24	29
8 24	3 41	24 9	10	4	17	19	28	23	♍2	6	8	5	20	24	♍2	26	26	♑2
8 36	6 37	26 10	13	6	19	22	♍0	25	4	9	11	7	22	27	4	29	28	5
8 48	9 34	29 10	15	8	21	25	3	28	7	12	14	9	25	29	7	♎1	♎1	7
9 0	12 32	0♏ 9	18	11	23	27	6	♎0	9	15	16	12	27	♑2	10	3	3	10
9 12	15 32	2 9	20	13	25	♏0	9	2	12	18	19	14	29	5	12	5	5	13
9 24	18 34	4 9	23	15	27	3	11	5	14	21	22	16	♑2	8	15	8	7	16
9 36	21 37	6 9	25	17	29	5	14	7	16	24	25	18	4	11	18	10	9	19
9 48	24 42	8 9	28	19	♎2	8	17	9	19	27	27	21	6	14	21	12	11	21
10 0	27 49	10 9	♎0	21	4	11	19	11	21	♎0	♎0	23	9	17	24	14	14	24
10 12	0♏57	12 8	2	23	6	14	22	14	24	4	3	25	11	20	26	17	16	28
10 24	4 7	14 8	5	25	8	17	25	16	27	7	5	28	13	23	29	19	18	♒1
10 36	7 18	16 9	7	28	10	21	28	18	♏0	11	8	♏0	16	26	♎2	21	20	5
10 48	10 30	18 9	10	♏0	13	24	♎0	20	3	14	11	2	18	29	5	24	22	8
11 0	13 43	20 10	12	2	15	28	3	23	6	18	14	4	21	♒3	8	26	25	11
11 12	16 57	22 11	15	4	18	♏1	6	25	9	21	16	7	23	6	11	28	27	14
11 24	20 12	24 13	17	6	20	4	11	♏0	14	28	19	9	26	9	16	3	♑1	19
11 36	23 28	26 16	20	8	23	8	11	♏0	14	28	22	11	29	13	16	3	♑1	19
11 48	26 44	28 19	22	10	25	12	14	2	17	♒2	24	13	♑1	17	19	6	3	22
12 0	0 0	0♏24	25	12	28	16	17	4	20	6	27	16	4	20	22	8	6	25

Sid. Time	M.C. long.	Asc.	REGIOMONTA.				CAMPANUS				PLACIDUS				NAT. GRAD.			
h m	♎	1 ♐	11 ♎	12 ♏	2 ♑	3 ♒	11 ♎	12 ♏	2 ♑	3 ♒	11 ♎	12 ♏	2 ♑	3 ♒	11 ♎	12 ♏	2 ♑	3 ♒
12 0	0 0	0 24	25	12	28	16	17	4	20	6	27	16	4	20	22	8	6	25
12 12	3 16	2 29	27	14	♍1	20	19	7	25	10	♍0	18	7	24	25	11	8	28
12 24	6 32	4 36	♍0	17	3	24	22	9	29	14	2	20	10	28	28	13	10	♓1
12 36	9 48	6 44	2	19	6	28	25	11	♒3	18	5	22	13	♓2	♍1	15	12	4
12 48	13 3	8 54	5	21	9	♓2	27	13	7	22	7	25	17	6	4	17	15	7
13 0	16 17	11 6	7	23	12	7	♍0	15	11	26	10	27	20	10	7	20	17	10
13 12	19 30	13 20	10	25	16	11	3	18	16	♓0	13	29	23	14	10	23	19	14
13 24	22 42	15 37	12	27	19	16	6	20	20	4	15	♑2	27	18	13	26	22	17
13 36	25 53	17 57	14	29	23	21	8	22	24	8	18	4	♒1	22	16	28	24	20
13 48	29 3	20 20	17	♑2	27	25	11	24	28	12	20	6	5	26	19	♑1	27	23
14 0	2♏11	22 48	19	4	♒1	♈0	13	26	♓2	16	23	9	9	♈0	22	3	29	26
14 12	5 18	25 20	22	6	6	5	16	29	8	20	25	12	14	4	25	6	♒2	29
14 24	8 23	27 57	24	8	10	9	19	♈1	13	23	28	14	18	8	27	9	4	♈2
14 36	11 26	0♍41	27	10	15	14	21	4	19	27	♈1	16	23	12	♑0	12	7	5
14 48	14 28	3 31	29	13	21	19	24	6	25	♉0	4	18	28	16	3	15	10	8
15 0	17 28	6 30	♑2	15	27	23	27	8	♈0	4	6	21	♓3	20	6	18	13	11
15 12	20 26	9 38	4	18	♓3	28	29	11	6	8	8	23	8	24	9	21	16	14
15 24	23 23	12 57	7	20	9	♉2	♈2	13	11	11	11	26	13	28	13	24	20	17
15 36	26 19	16 30	9	23	16	6	4	16	17	15	13	29	19	♉2	16	28	23	20
15 48	29 19	20 17	12	25	23	10	7	18	23	19	16	♏1	24	6	19	♏1	27	23
16 0	2♐5	24 21	14	28	0♈	14	10	20	28	23	19	4	♈0	10	22	5	♈0	♑0
16 12	4 57	28 46	17	♏1	7	18	12	23	♉2	26	21	7	6	13	25	9	5	29
16 24	7 47	3♏34	19	3	14	22	15	26	7	29	24	10	11	17	29	14	10	♉2
16 36	10 36	8 49	22	6	21	26	18	29	11	♉2	27	13	17	21	♉2	18	15	5
16 48	13 24	14 34	25	9	27	29	20	♉2	15	5	29	17	22	24	6	23	21	8
17 0	16 11	20 51	27	12	♉3	♊2	23	5	20	8	♉2	20	27	27	10	27	26	12
17 12	18 58	27 43	♑0	16	9	6	26	8	24	11	5	23	♉2	♊1	14	=4	♈2	15
17 24	21 44	5♍10	3	19	15	9	29	10	28	14	8	27	7	4	18	10	9	19
17 36	24 20	13 7	5	23	20	13	♏1	13	♊3	17	11	=1	12	7	22	17	16	22
17 48	27 15	21 27	8	27	24	16	4	16	7	20	14	5	16	10	26	23	23	26
18 0	0♑0	0♈0	11	=1	29	19	7	19	11	23	17	9	21	13	=0	♈0	♈0	♊0
18 12	2 45	8 33	14	16	♊3	22	10	23	14	26	20	14	25	16	4	7	7	4
18 24	5 30	16 53	17	10	7	25	13	28	17	29	23	18	29	19	7	14	14	8
18 36	8 16	24 50	21	15	11	27	16	=2	20	♋1	26	23	♊3	22	11	21	20	12
18 48	11 2	2♉17	24	21	14	♋0	19	6	23	4	29	28	7	25	15	28	26	16
19 0	13 49	9 9	28	27	18	3	22	10	25	7	=3	♈3	10	28	18	♈5	♊3	20
19 12	16 36	15 26	=1	♈3	21	5	25	15	28	10	6	8	13	♋1	22	10	7	24
19 24	19 24	21 11	4	9	24	8	28	19	♋1	12	9	13	16	3	25	15	12	27
19 36	22 13	26 26	8	16	27	11	=1	23	4	15	13	19	20	6	28	20	16	♋1
19 48	25 3	1♊14	12	23	29	13	4	27	7	18	17	24	23	9	♈1	25	21	5
20 0	27 55	5 39	16	♈0	♋2	16	7	♓2	10	20	20	♈0	26	11	4	♉0	25	8
20 12	0=41	9 43	20	7	5	18	11	7	12	23	24	6	29	14	7	4	29	11
20 24	4 41	13 30	24	14	7	21	15	13	14	26	28	11	♋1	17	10	8	♉2	14
20 36	6 37	17 3	28	21	10	23	19	19	17	28	♓2	17	4	19	13	11	6	17
20 48	9 34	20 22	♓2	27	12	26	22	24	19	♌1	6	22	7	22	16	14	9	20
21 0	12 32	23 30	7	♈3	15	28	26	♈0	22	3	10	27	9	24	19	17	12	23
21 12	15 32	26 34	11	9	17	♌1	♈0	5	24	6	14	♉2	12	26	22	20	15	26
21 24	18 34	29 19	16	15	20	3	3	11	26	9	18	7	14	29	25	23	18	29
21 36	21 37	2♊3	21	20	22	6	7	16	29	11	22	12	17	♌2	28	26	21	♌2
21 48	24 42	4 40	25	24	24	8	11	22	♌1	14	26	16	19	5	♈1	28	24	5
22 0	27 49	7 12	♈0	29	26	11	14	27	4	16	♈0	21	21	7	4	♈1	27	8
22 12	0♓57	9 40	5	♊3	28	13	18	♉2	6	19	4	25	24	10	7	3	29	11
22 24	4 7	12 3	9	7	♌1	16	22	6	8	22	8	29	26	12	10	6	♉2	14
22 36	7 18	14 23	14	11	3	18	26	10	10	25	12	♊3	28	15	13	8	4	17
22 48	10 30	16 40	19	14	5	20	♈0	15	13	27	16	7	♌1	17	16	11	7	20
23 0	13 43	18 54	23	18	7	23	24	19	15♍	0	20	10	3	20	20	13	10	23
23 12	16 57	21 3	8	21	9	25	8	23	17	3	24	13	5	22	23	15	12	26
23 24	20 12	23 16	♉2	24	11	28	12	27	19	5	28	16	8	25	26	18	14	29
23 36	23 28	25 24	6	27	13♍	0	16	♊2	22	8	♉2	20	10	28	29	20	17	♍2
23 48	26 44	27 51	10	29	16.	3	20	6	24	11	6	23	12	♍0	♉2	22	19	5
24 0	0♈0	29 36	14	♋2	18	5	24	10	26	13	10	26	14	3	5	24	22	8

237

Sid. Time		M.C. long.	Asc. 1	REGIOMONTA.				CAMPANUS				PLACIDUS				NAT. GRAD.			
h	m	♈	♌	11 ♉	12 ♊	2 ♌	3 ♍	11 ♈	12 ♊	2 ♌	3 ♍	11 ♉	12 ♊	2 ♌	3 ♍	11 ♉	12 ♊	2 ♌	3 ♍
0	0	0 0	0 32	15	3	18	5	24	10	27	14	10	27	15	3	5	25	23	8
0	12	3 16	2 34	19	6	20	8	28	13	29	17	14 ♋0	17	6		8	27	25	10
0	24	6 32	4 35	23	9	22	10	♉2	16	♏1	20	17	2	19	9	12	29	27	13
0	36	9 48	6 36	26	11	24	13	5	19	4	22	21	5	21	11	15 ♋2	♍0		16
0	48	13 3	8 36	29	13	27	15	9	22	6	25	25	8	24	14	18	4	2	19
1	0	16 17	10 35	♊3	16	29	18	13	25	8	28	28	10	26	17	21	6	4	22
1	12	19 30	12 34	7	18	♏1	20	16	28	10	♎0	♊1	13	28	19	24	8	7	25
1	24	22 42	14 32	10	20	3	23	19	♋1	13	3	5	15	♏0	22	27	10	9	28
1	36	25 53	16 31	13	23	5	25	23	4	15	6	8	17	3	25	♊0	13	11	♎1
1	48	29 3	18 29	16	25	7	28	26	7	17	9	11	20	5	27	3	15	14	4
2	0	2♉11	20 27	19	27	9	♎0	♊0	9	19	11	14	22	7	♎0	6	17	16	7
2	12	5 18	22 25	22	29	11	2	3	12	22	14	27	25	9	3	9	19	19	9
2	24	8 23	24 23	25	♌1	13	5	6	14	24	17	20	27	12	5	11	21	21	12
2	36	11 26	26 21	28	4	15	7	9	17	26	20	23	29	14	8	14	23	23	15
2	48	14 28	28 19	♋1	6	17	10	12	19	28	22	26	♌1	16	11	17	25	26	18
3	0	17 28	0♍17	3	8	20	12	15	21	♎1	25	28	4	19	13	20	28	28	21
3	12	20 26	2 15	6	10	22	15	18	24	3	28	♌1	6	21	16	23	♌0	♎0	23
3	24	23 23	4 13	9	12	24	17	21	26	5	♏0	4	8	23	19	26	2	2	26
3	36	26 19	6 12	12	14	26	20	24	29	7	3	7	10	25	21	28	4	4	29
3	48	29 19	8 10	14	16	28	22	27	♌1	10	6	9	13	28	24	♌1	6	6	♏1
4	0	2♊5	10 9	16	18	♎0	25	29	3	12	8	12	15	♎0	27	4	8	8	4
4	12	4 57	12 8	19	20	2	27	♉2	5	14	11	15	17	2	29	6	11	11	7
4	24	7 47	14 6	21	22	4	♏0	5	8	17	14	17	19	5	♏2	9	13	13	9
4	36	10 36	16 5	24	24	6	2	7	10	19	16	20	21	7	5	11	15	15	12
4	48	13 24	18 4	26	27	8	4	10	12	21	19	22	24	9	7	14	17	17	14
5	0	16 11	20 3	29	29	10	7	13	14	23	22	25	26	11	10	17	19	19	17
5	12	18 58	22 3	♌1	♏1	13	9	15	17	26	25	27	28	14	12	20	21	21	20
5	24	21 44	24 2	4	3	15	12	18	19	28	27	♌0	♋0	16	15	23	24	24	22
5	36	24 30	26 1	6	5	17	14	21	21	♏0	29	2	3	18	17	26	26	26	25
5	48	27 15	28 1	9	7	19	17	23	23	2	♐2	5	5	21	20	28	28	28	27
6	0	0♋5	0♎0	11	9	21	19	26	26	4	4	7	7	23	23	♌0	♍0	♏0	♐0
6	12	2 45	1 59	13	11	23	21	29	28	7	7	10	9	25	25	3	2	2	3
6	24	5 30	3 59	16	13	25	24	♌1	♍0	9	10	13	12	27	28	5	4	4	5
6	36	8 16	5 58	18	15	27	26	4	2	11	12	15	14	♏0	♐0	8	7	6	8
6	48	11 2	7 57	21	17	29	29	6	5	14	15	18	16	2	3	10	9	9	10
7	0	13 49	9 57	23	20	♏1	♐1	9	7	16	18	20	19	4	5	13	11	11	13
7	12	16 36	11 56	26	22	3	4	12	9	18	20	23	21	6	8	16	13	13	16
7	24	19 24	13 55	28	24	6	6	14	11	21	23	25	23	9	10	18	15	15	18
7	36	22 13	15 54	♍0	26	8	9	17	14	23	26	28	25	11	13	21	17	17	21
7	48	25 3	17 52	3	28	10	11	20	16	25	28	♍1	28	13	15	23	20	19	24
8	0	27 55	19 51	5	♎0	12	14	23	18	27	♑1	♍3	♎0	15	18	26	22	22	26
8	12	0♌41	21 50	8	2	14	16	25	20	29	4	6	2	17	21	29	24	24	29
8	24	3 41	23 48	10	4	16	18	28	23	♐2	7	9	5	20	23	♏1	26	26	♑2
8	36	6 37	25 47	13	6	18	21	♍0	25	4	10	11	7	22	26	4	28	28	5
8	48	9 34	27 45	15	8	20	24	3	27	6	13	14	9	24	29	7	♎1	♐0	7
9	0	12 32	29 43	18	10	22	27	5	29	9	16	17	11	26	♑2	9	3	2	10
9	12	15 32	1♍41	20	13	24	29	8♎	2	11	18	19	14	29	4	12	5	4	13
9	24	18 34	3 39	23	15	26	♑2	11	4	13	22	22	16	♐1	7	15	7	6	16
9	36	21 37	5 37	25	17	29	5	13	6	16	25	25	18	3	10	18	9	8	19
9	48	24 42	7 35	28	19	♐1	8	16	8	18	28	27	21	5	13	21	12	11	21
10	0	27 49	9 33	♎0	21	3	11	19	11	20	♒1	♎0	23	8	16	23	14	13	24
10	12	0♍57	11 31	2	23	5	14	22	13	22	4	3	25	10	19	26	16	15	28
10	24	4 7	13 29	5	25	7	17	24	15	25	8	5	27	13	22	29	19	17	♒1
10	36	7 18	15 28	7	27	9	20	27	17	28	11	8	♏0	15	25	♎2	21	19	5
10	48	10 30	17 26	10	29	12	23	♎0	20	♑1	14	11	2	17	29	5	23	21	8
11	0	13 43	19 25	12	♏1	14	27	3	22	4	18	13	4	19	♒2	8	26	23	11
11	12	16 57	21 24	15	3	17	♒1	5	24	7	21	16	6	22	5	10	28	25	14
11	24	20 12	23 24	17	6	19	4	7	26	10	25	19	9	25	9	13	♏0	28	17
11	36	23 28	25 25	20	8	21	7	10	29	13	28	21	11	28	13	16	2	♑0	19
11	48	26 44	27 26	22	10	24	11	13	♏1	16	♓1	24	13	♑0	16	19	5	2	22
12	0	0♎0	29 28	25	12	27	15	16	3	20	5	27	15	3	20	22	7	5	25

Sid. Time	M.C.	Asc.	REGIOMONTA.				CAMPANUS				PLACIDUS				NAT. GRAD.			
h m	long.	1	11	12	2	3	11	12	2	3	11	12	2	3	11	12	2	3
	♎	♏	♎	♏	♐	≈	♎	♏	♑	♓	♎	♏	♑	♓	♎	♏	♑	≈
12 0	0 0	29 28	25 12	27 15			16 3	19 6			25 15	3 20			22 7	5 25		
12 12	3 16	1♏31	27 14	29 19			19 5	24 10			29 17	6 24			22 10	7 28		
12 24	6 32	3 35	♏0 16	♑2 23			22 8	28 14			♏2 20	9 27			28 12	9 ♓1		
12 36	9 48	5 41	2 18	5 27			24 10	≈2 18			5 22	12 ♓1			♏1 15	11 4		
12 48	13 3	7 48	4 20	8 ♓2			27 12	7 22			7 24	15 5			4 17	14 7		
13 0	16 17	9 57	7 22	11 6			♏0 14	11 26			10 26	19 9			7 20	16 10		
13 12	19 30	12 9	9 24	14 11			2 16	16 ♈0			12 29	22 13			9 22	18 14		
13 24	22 42	14 23	12 26	18 16			5 19	20 4			15 ♏1	26 18			12 25	21 17		
13 36	25 53	16 29	14 28	22 20			8 21	24 8			17 3	≈0 22			15 27	23 20		
13 48	29 3	19 0	17 ♏1	25 25			10 23	29 12			20 5	4 26			18 ♏0	25 23		
14 0	2♏11	21 23	19 3	≈0 ♈0			13 25	♓3 16			23 8	8 ♈0			21 3	28 26		
14 12	5 18	23 52	21 5	4 5			16 28	9 20			25 10	12 4			24 5	≈0 29		
14 24	8 23	26 25	24 7	9 10			18 ♏0	14 24			28 13	17 8			27 8	3 ♈2		
14 36	11 26	29 5	26 9	14 14			21 3	20 28			♏0 15	22 12			♏0 11	6 5		
14 48	14 28	1♐51	29 12	19 19			23 5	26 ♉2			3 17	27 17			3 14	9 8		
15 0	17 28	4 46	♏1 14	26 24			26 7	♈2 6			5 19	♓2 21			6 16	11 11		
15 12	20 26	9 38	4 17	♓2 28			29 9	7 9			8 22	8 25			9 19	15 14		
15 24	23 23	11 4	6 19	8 ♉3			♏1 11	13 12			10 25	14 29			12 23	18 17		
15 36	26 19	16 30	9 21	15 7			4 14	19 16			13 28	20 ♉3			15 26	22 20		
15 48	29 19	18 15	11 24	23 11			6 16	24 20			15 ♑0	24 6			18 ♏0	25 23		
16 0	2♐5	22 16	14 27	♈0 15			9 19	♉0 23			18 3	♈0 10			21 3	28 26		
16 12	4 57	26 38	16 29	7 19			12 22	4 26			21 6	6 14			25 7	♓3 29		
16 24	7 47	1≈24	18 ♑2	15 23			14 25	9 29			23 9	10 17			28 12	8 ♉2		
16 36	10 36	6 39	21 5	22 26			17 28	13 ♊3			26 12	16 21			♑2 17	13 5		
16 48	13 24	12 27	24 8	28 29			19 ♑0	17 6			29 15	22 25			6 21	19 8		
17 0	16 11	18 52	27 11	♉4 ♊3			22 3	21 9			♑2 19	28 28			9 26	24 11		
17 12	18 58	25 56	29 14	11 7			25 6	25 12			4 22	♉3 ♊1			13 ≈3	♈1 15		
17 24	21 44	3♓41	♑2 18	16 10			28 9	♊0 15			7 26	8 5			18 10	8 19		
17 36	24 30	12 3	5 22	21 13			♑0 12	4 18			10 ≈0	13 8			22 16	15 23		
17 48	27 15	20 53	8 25	26 16			3 15	8 21			13 4	18 11			26 23	23 26		
18 0	0♑0	0♈0	11 ♑0	♊0 19			6 18	12 24			16 8	22 14			♑0 ♓0	♉0 ♊0		
18 12	2 45	9 7	14 4	5 22			9 22	15 27			19 12	26 17			4 7	7 4		
18 24	5 30	17 57	17 9	8 25			12 26	18 29			22 17	♊0 20			8 14	14 8		
18 36	8 16	26 19	20 14	12 28			15 ≈0	21 ♋2			25 22	4 23			11 22	20 12		
18 48	11 2	4♉4	23 19	16 ♋1			18 4	24 5			29 27	8 26			15 29	27 17		
19 0	13 49	11 8	27 26	19 3			21 9	27 8			≈2 ♓2	11 28			19 ♈6	♊4 21		
19 12	16 36	17 33	≈1 ♓2	22 6			24 13	29 10			5 8	15 ♋1			22 11	9 24		
19 24	19 24	23 21	4 8	25 9			27 17	♋2 13			9 13	18 4			25 16	13 28		
19 36	22 13	28 36	7 15	28 12			≈1 21	5 16			13 19	21 7			28 21	18 ♋2		
19 48	25 3	3♊32	11 23	♋1 14			4 26	8 18			16 24	24 9			♓1 26	22 5		
20 0	27 55	7 44	15 ♈0	3 16			7 ♓0	11 21			20 ♈0	27 12			4 ♉2	27 9		
20 12	0≈41	11 45	19 7	6 19			10 5	13 23			24 6	♋0 15			7 5	♋0 12		
20 24	3 41	13 30	23 15	9 21			14 10	16 26			27 11	2 17			10 8	3 15		
20 36	6 37	18 56	27 22	11 24			18 16	18 29			1 17	5 20			13 11	7 18		
20 48	9 34	20 22	♓2 28	13 26			21 21	20 ♍1			5 22	8 22			16 15	10 21		
21 0	12 32	25 14	5 ♉4	16 29			25 26	23 4			9 28	10 25			19 19	14 24		
21 12	15 32	28 9	11 10	18 ♌1			29 ♈2	25 6			13 ♉3	13 27			22 22	16 27		
21 24	18 34	0♋55	16 16	20 4			♓3 ♈7	♋0 11			18 8	15 ♍0			25 24	19 ♌0		
21 36	21 37	3 35	20 21	23 6			6 15	♌0 11			22 13	17 2			28 27	22 3		
21 48	24 42	6 8	25 26	25 9			10 21	2 14			6 18	20 5			♈1 29	25 6		
22 0	27 49	8 37	♈0 ♊0	27 11			14 27	5 17			♈0 22	22 7			4 ♊2	28 9		
22 12	0♓57	11 0	5 5	29 13			18 ♉1	7 20			4 26	25 10			7 5	♌0 12		
22 24	4 7	13 21	10 8	♌1 16			22 6	9 22			8 ♊0	27 13			10 7	3 15		
22 36	7 18	15 18	14 18	4 18			26 10	11 25			12 4	29 16			13 10	5 18		
22 48	10 30	17 51	19 16	6 21			♈0 14	13 28			17 8	♌1 18			17 13	8 21		
23 0	13 43	20 3	24 19	8 23			4 19	15 ♏1			21 11	4 20			20 15	10 23		
23 12	16 57	22 12	28 22	10 26			8 23	17 3			25 15	6 23			23 17	13 26		
23 24	20 12	24 19	2 25	12 28			12 27	20 6			29 18	8 25			26 19	15 29		
23 36	23 28	26 25	7 28	14 ♏0			16 ♊2	22 9			♉3 21	10 28			29 21	18 ♏2		
23 48	26 44	29 29	11 ♋1	16 3			20 6	25 11			6 24	13 ♏1			♉2 23	20 5		
24 0	0♈0	0♌32	15 3	18 5			24 10	27 14			10 27	15 3			5 25	23 8		

Sid. Time	M. C. long.	Asc. 1	REGIOMONTA. 11	12	2	3	CAMPANUS 11	12	2	3	PLACIDUS 11	12	2	3	NAT. GRAD. 11	12	2	3
h. m	♈	♌	♉	♋	♌	♍	♈	♊	♌	♍	♉	♊	♌	♍	♉	♊	♌	♍
0 0	0 0	1 30	16	5	19	6	23	10	28	14	11	28	15	3	5	26	23	8
0 12	3 16	3 29	27	21	8	27	13	♍0	17		14	♋1	18	6	9	28	26	11
0 24	6 32	5 28	23	10	23	10	♉0	16	2	20	18	4	20	9	12	♋0	28	14
0 36	9 48	7 26	27	12	25	13	3	19	4	22	22	6	22	11	15	2	♍0	17
0 48	13 3	9 24	♍0	15	27	15	7	22	7	25	25	9	24	14	18	5	3	20
1 0	16 17	11 21	3	17	29	18	10	25	9	28	28	11	26	17	21	7	5	23
1 12	19 30	13 18	7	19	♏1	20	14	28	11	♎1	♊2	14	29	19	24	9	7	26
1 24	22 42	15 14	11	21	3	23	18	♋1	13	3	5	16	♏1	22	27	11	10	29
1 36	25 53	17 11	14	24	5	25	21	4	16	6	8	18	3	25	♍0	13	12	♎2
1 48	29 3	19 7	17	26	7	28	25	6	18	9	11	21	5	27	3	15	14	4
2 0	2♉11	21 3	20	28	9	♎0	29	9	20	11	15	23	7	♎0	6	17	16	7
2 12	5 18	22 59	23	♐0	11	2	♊2	12	22	14	14	25	10	3	9	19	19	10
2 24	8 23	24 25	26	2	14	5	5	14	25	17	21	28	12	5	12	21	21	12
2 36	11 26	26 51	29	4	16	7	8	17	27	19	23	♐0	14	8	14	23	23	15
2 48	14 28	28 47	♋1	6	18	10	11	19	29	22	26	2	16	11	17	25	25	18
3 0	17 28	0♍44	4	8	20	12	14	21	♏1	25	29	4	19	13	20	27	28	20
3 12	20 26	2 40	7	11	22	15	17	24	4	27	♋2	6	21	16	23	♍0	♎0	23
3 24	23 23	4 36	9	13	24	17	20	26	2	♏0	5	9	23	19	26	2	2	26
3 36	26 19	6 33	12	15	26	20	23	28	6	3	7	11	25	21	29	4	4	29
3 48	29 19	8 30	15	17	28	22	26	♎1	8	6	10	13	28	24	♋2	6	6	♏1
4 0	2♊5	10 26	17	19	♎0	24	29	3	12	8	12	15	♎0	27	4	9	8	4
4 12	4 57	12 23	19	21	2	27	♋2	5	15	11	15	18	2	29	6	11	11	7
4 24	7 47	14 20	22	23	4	29	4	7	17	13	18	20	5	♏2	9	13	13	9
4 36	10 36	16 18	25	25	6	2	7	10	20	16	20	22	7	4	12	15	15	12
4 48	13 24	18 15	27	27	8	4	9	12	22	19	23	24	9	7	14	17	17	14
5 0	16 11	20 12	29	29	10	7	12	14	24	21	25	26	11	9	17	19	19	17
5 12	18 58	22 10	♎2	♏1	12	9	14	16	26	24	28	29	14	12	20	21	21	20
5 24	21 44	24 7	4	3	14	12	17	19	28	26	♎0	♏1	16	15	22	23	24	22
5 36	24 30	26 5	7	5	16	14	19	21	♏1	29	3	3	18	17	25	25	26	25
5 48	27 15	28 2	9	7	19	17	22	23	3	♐2	5	5	20	20	27	27	28	27
6 0	0♋0	0♎0	12	9	21	19	25	25	5	4	8	7	23	22	♏0	♍0	♏0	♐0
6 12	2 45	1 58	14	11	23	21	28	28	7	7	10	10	25	25	3	2	2	3
6 24	5 30	3 55	16	14	25	23	21	♍0	9	10	13	12	27	27	5	4	4	5
6 36	8 16	5 53	19	16	27	26	3	2	11	12	15	14	29	♐0	6	6	6	8
6 48	11 2	7 50	21	18	29	28	6	4	14	15	18	16	♏1	2	10	9	9	10
7 0	13 49	9 48	23	20	♏1	♐1	9	6	16	18	21	19	4	5	13	11	11	13
7 12	16 36	11 45	26	22	3	3	11	9	18	20	23	21	6	7	16	13	13	16
7 24	19 24	13 42	28	24	5	5	14	11	20	23	26	23	8	10	18	15	15	18
7 36	22 13	15 40	♏1	26	7	8	17	13	23	25	28	25	10	12	21	17	17	21
7 48	25 3	17 37	3	28	9	11	20	15	25	28	♏1	28	12	15	24	19	19	23
8 0	27 55	19 54	5	♎0	11	13	22	18	27	♏1	3	♎0	15	18	26	22	21	26
8 12	0♌41	21 30	8	2	13	16	24	20	29	3	6	2	17	20	29	24	23	29
8 24	3 41	23 27	10	4	15	18	27	22	♏2	7	9	5	19	23	♏1	26	26	♑2
8 36	6 37	25 24	13	6	17	21	29	24	4	10	11	7	21	25	4	28	28	4
8 48	9 34	27 20	15	8	19	23	♏2	27	6	13	14	9	24	28	7	♎0	♑0	7
9 0	12 32	29 16	18	10	21	26	5	29	9	16	17	11	26	♏1	9	2	2	10
9 12	15 32	1♏13	20	12	24	28	8	♎1	11	19	19	14	28	4	12	5	4	13
9 24	18 34	3 9	23	14	26	♏1	10	3	14	22	22	16	♑0	7	15	7	6	16
9 36	21 37	5 5	25	16	28	4	13	6	16	25	25	18	2	9	18	9	8	18
9 48	24 42	7 1	28	19	♑0	7	16	8	18	28	27	20	5	12	20	11	11	21
10 0	27 49	8 57	♎0	21	2	10	18	10	21	♑1	♎0	23	7	15	23	14	13	24
10 12	0♍57	10 53	2	23	4	13	21	12	24	4	3	25	9	19	26	16	15	27
10 24	4 7	12 49	5	25	6	16	24	14	26	7	5	27	12	22	29	18	17	♑0
10 36	7 18	14 46	7	27	9	19	27	17	29	11	8	29	14	25	♎2	21	19	3
10 48	10 30	16 42	10	29	11	23	29	19	♑2	15	11	♏1	16	28	4	23	21	7
11 0	13 43	18 39	12	♏1	13	27	♎2	21	5	18	13	4	19	♑2	7	25	23	11
11 12	16 57	20 36	15	3	15	♒0	5	23	8	22	16	6	21	5	10	27	25	14
11 24	20 12	22 34	17	5	18	3	7	25	11	26	19	8	24	8	13	♏0	28	17
11 36	23 28	24 32	20	7	20	7	10	28	14	♒0	21	10	26	12	16	2	♑0	19
11 48	26 44	26 31	22	9	23	10	13	♏0	17	3	24	12	28	16	19	4	2	22
12 0	0≏0	28 30	24	11	25	14	16	2	20	7	27	15	♒2	19	22	7	4	25

Sid. Time	M.C. long.	Asc. 1	REGIOMONTA. 11	12	2	3	CAMPANUS 11	12	2	3	PLACIDUS 11	12	2	3	NAT. GRAD. 11	12	2	3
h m	♋	♎	♏	♐	♒	♓	♎	♏	♐	♒	♎	♏	♐	♒	♎	♏	♒	♓
12 0	0 0	28 30	24 11	25	14	16	2 20	7	27	15	2 19	22	7	4 25
12 12	3 16	0 ♏31	27 13	28 19	18	4 24	11	29 17	5 23	25	9	7 28
12 24	6 32	2 33	29 15	♑1 23	21	7 29 15	♏2 19	8 27	28 12	9 ♓1
12 36	9 48	4 36	♏2 17	3 27	24	9 ≈3 19	4 21	11 ♓1	♏0 14	11	4
12 48	13 3	6 40	4 19	6 ♓1	26 11	7 23	7 24	14	5	3 16	12	7
13 0	16 17	8 46	7 21	9 6	29 13 12	27	9 26 17	9	6 19 15 10
13 12	19 30	10 55	9 24	13 11	♏2 16	16 ♈1	12 28 21	13	9 22 17 13
13 24	22 42	13 5	12 26 16 16	4 18 21	5	14 ♑0 25 17	12 24 19 16
13 36	25 53	15 19	14 28 20 20	7 20 25	9	17 2 29 22	14 27 22 19
13 48	29 3	17 35	17 ♑0 24 25	10 22 ♐0 13	20 5 ≈3 26	17 ♑0 24 22
14 0	2 ♏11	19 55	19 2 28 ♈0	12 24 4 17	22 7 7 ♈0	20 2 26 26
14 12	5 18	22 20	21 4 ≈2 5	15 27 10 21	25 9 11 4	23 5 29 29
14 24	8 23	24 49	23 6 7 10	18 29 16 24	27 12 16 8	26 7 ≈2 ♈2
14 36	11 26	27 24	26 9 12 14	20 ♐1 22 28	♑0 14 21 13	29 10 4 5
14 48	14 28	0 ♈6	28 11 18 19	23 4 27 ♑2	2 16 26 17	♐2 13 6 8
15 0	17 28	2 55	♑1 13 24 24	25 6 ♈3 6	5 19 ♓1 21	5 15 9 11
15 12	20 26	7 49	3 15 ♓1 29	28 8 9 9	7 21 7 25	8 18 13 14
15 24	23 23	9 4	5 18 7♉ 3	♑1 11 15 13	10 24 13 29	11 22 16 18
15 36	26 19	14 32	8 20 15 7	3 13 21 17	12 26 18 ♉3	14 25 20 21
15 48	29 19	16 4	11 23 22 11	6 15 27 20	15 28 24 7	17 28 23 24
16 0	2 ♐5	19 59	13 25 ♈0 16	9 18 ♉2 24	18 ♒2 ♑0 11	21 ♒2 26 28
16 12	4 57	24 17	16 28 8 20	11 21 7 27	20 5 6 14	24 6 ♓1 ♉0
16 24	7 47	29 0	18 ♒1 15 23	14 23 11 ♈0	23 8 12 18	28 11 7 3
16 36	10 36	4 ≈14	21 3 23 27	17 26 15 3	25 11 17 22	♒1 15 12 6
16 48	13 24	10 4	23 6 29 ♈0	19 29 19 6	28 14 23 25	5 20 17 8
17 0	16 11	16 35	26 9 ♉6 3	22 ≈2 23 9	♒1 17 29 28	9 24 22 11
17 12	18 58	23 52	28 13 12 7	25 5 27 12	4 21 ♉4 ♈2	13 ≈1 29 15
17 24	21 44	1 ♓57	♒1 16 18 11	27 7 ♈2 15	7 25 9 5	17 9 ♈7 19
17 36	24 30	10 47	4 20 23 14	♈0 10 6 18	9 29 14 8	21 16 15 22
17 48	27 15	20 13	7 24 28 17	3 13 10 21	12 ≈3 19 11	26 23 22 26
18 0	0 ♑0	0 ♈0	0 ♈0 10 28 ♈2 20	5 16 14 25	15 7 23 15	≈0 ♈0 29 ♈0
18 12	2 45	9 47	13 ≈2 6 23	8 20 17 27	19 11 27 18	4 8 7 4
18 24	5 30	19 13	16 7 10 26	11 24 20 ♋0	22 16 ♈1 21	8 15 14 9
18 36	8 16	28 3	19 12 14 29	14 29 23 3	25 21 5 23	11 23 21 13
18 48	11 2	6 ♉8	13 18 17 ♉1	17 ≈3 25 5	28 26 9 26	15 ♈0 29 17
19 0	13 49	13 25	27 24 21 4	20 7 28 8	≈2 ♈1 13 29	19 8 ♈6 22
19 12	16 36	19 56	≈0 ♈1 24 7	23 11 ♋1 11	5 7 16 ♋2	22 12 10 25
19 24	19 24	25 46	3 5 27 9	26 16 ·3 13	8 13 19 4	25 16 14 29
19 36	22 13	1 ♊0	7 15 29 12	≈0 20 6 16	12 18 22 7	28 19 19 ♋2
19 48	25 3	5 43	10 22 ♋2 15	3 24 9 19	16 24 25 10	♈1 23 24 6
20 0	27 55	10 1	14 ♈0 5 17	6 28 12 21	19 ♈0 28 12	4 27 28 9
20 12	0 ≈41	13 56	19 8 7 19	10 ≈4 15 24	23 6 ♋1 15	7 ♉2 ♋2 12
20 24	3 41	15 28	23 15 10 22	13 10 17 27	27 12 4 18	10 6 5 15
20 36	6 37	20 56	27 23 12 25	17 15 19 29	♈1 17 6 20	13 11 8 18
20 48	9 34	22 11	♈1 29 15 27	21 21 22 ♋2	5 23 9 23	16 16 11 21
21 0	12 32	27 5	6♉ 6 17 29	24 27 24 4	9 29 11 25	19 21 15 25
21 12	15 23	29 54	11 12 19 ♋2	28 ♉3 26 7	13 ♉4 14 28	22 23 17 28
21 24	18 34	2 ♋36	16 18 21 4	♈1 9 29 10	17 9 16 ♋0	25 26 20 ♋1
21 36	21 37	5 11	20 23 24 7	5 15 ♋1 12	22 14 18 3	28 28 23 4
21 48	24 42	7 40	25 28 26 9	9 21 3 15	26 19 21 5	♈1 ♋1 26 7
22 0	27 49	10 5	♉0 ♋2 28 12	13 26 6 18	♉0 23 23 8	4 4 28 10
22 12	0 ♓57	12 25	5 6 ♋0 14	17 ♋1 8 20	4 27 25 10	7 6 ♋1 13
22 24	4 7	14 11	10 10 3 16	21 5 10 23	8 ♊1 28 13	11 8 3 15
22 36	7 18	16 55	14 14 4 19	25 10 12 26	13 5 ♋0 15	14 10 6 18
22 48	10 30	19 5	19 17 6 21	29 14 14 28	17 9 2 18	17 12 9 21
23 0	13 43	21 14	24 21 8 23	♈3 19 17 ♊1	13 4 21 21	20 15 11 24
23 12	16 57	24 30	29 24 11 26	7 23 19 4	16 6 23 24	23 17 13 27
23 24	20 12	27 32	♉3 27 13 28	11 27 21 7	19 9 26 29	26 20 16 ♍0
23 36	23 28	29 32	7 29 15 ♍1	15 ♉2 23 10	22 11 28 ♉3	29 22 18 2
23 48	26 44	0 ♍29	11 ♋2 17 3	19 6 25 12	25 13 ♍1 8	♉2 24 21 5
24 0	0 ♈0	♊ 30	16 5 19 6	23 10 28 14	28 15 3 12	5 26 23 8

Sid. Time h m	M.C. long.	Asc. 1	REGIOMONTA. 11	12	2	3	CAMPANUS 11	12	2	3	PLACIDUS 11	12	2	3	NAT. GRAD. 11	12	2	3
0 0	0 0	2 29	16	6	19	6	23	10	29	15	11	28	16	4	6	27	24	8
0 12	3 16	4 26	20	9	22	8	27	13	♏1	18	14	♋3	18	7	9	29	6	11
0 24	6 32	6 23	24	11	23	11	♉0	16	3	21	18	5	20	9	12	♋1	29	14
0 36	9 48	8 18	28	13	25	13	4	19	5	23	22	7	22	11	15	3	♏1	17
0 48	13 3	10 14	♉1	16	27	15	7	22	8	26	26	10	25	14	18	5	3	20
1 0	16 17	12 0	4	18	29	18	11	25	10	29	29	12	27	17	21	7	5	23
1 12	19 30	14 3	8	20	♏1	20	15	28	12	≏2	♍2	15	29	19	24	10	8	26
1 24	22 42	15 58	12	22	4	23	18	♋1	14	4	6	17	♏1	22	27	12	10	29
1 36	25 53	17 52	15	25	6	25	22	3	16	7	9	19	3	25	♍0	14	12	≏1
1 48	29 3	19 46	18	27	8	28	25	6	19	10	12	22	6	27	3	16	15	4
2 0	2♉11	21 40	21	29	10	≏0	29	9	21	12	15	24	8	≏0	6	18	17	7
2 12	5 18	23 34	24	♈1	12	2	♍2	12	23	15	18	26	10	3	9	20	19	10
2 24	8 23	25 28	27	3	14	5	5	14	25	17	21	28	12	5	12	22	21	12
2 36	11 36	27 23	29	5	16	7	8	16	27	20	24	♈1	14	8	14	24	24	15
2 48	14 28	29 17	♉2	7	18	10	11	19	≏0	23	27	3	17	11	17	26	26	18
3 0	17 28	1♈11	5	9	20	12	14	21	2	26	♍0	5	19	13	20	28	28	21
3 12	20 26	4 6	8	11	22	15	17	23	4	28	2	7	21	16	23	♋1	≏0	23
3 24	23 23	5 0	10	13	24	17	20	26	6	♏1	5	9	23	19	26	3	2	26
3 36	26 19	6 55	13	15	26	19	23	28	9	4	8	12	26	21	28	5	5	29
3 48	29 19	8 50	15	17	28	22	26	♏1	11	6	10	14	28	23	♋1	7	7	♏1
4 0	2♉5	10 45	18	19	≏0	24	29	3	13	9	13	16	≏0	26	4	9	9	4
4 12	4 57	12 40	20	22	2	27	♍2	5	16	12	16	18	2	29	7	11	11	7
4 24	7 47	14 35	23	23	4	29	4	7	17	14	18	20	4	♏1	9	13	13	10
4 36	10 36	16 30	25	25	6	♏1	7	10	19	17	21	22	7	4	12	15	15	12
4 48	13 24	18 25	27	27	8	4	10	12	22	20	23	25	9	6	14	17	17	14
5 0	16 11	20 21	♍0	29	10	6	12	14	24	22	26	27	11	9	17	19	19	17
5 12	18 58	22 17	2	♏1	12	9	14	16	26	25	28	29	13	12	20	22	22	20
5 24	21 44	24 13	5	4	14	11	17	18	28	28	♏1	♍1	16	14	22	24	24	22
5 36	24 30	26 8	7	6	16	13	20	21	♏0	♎0	3	3	18	17	25	26	26	25
5 48	27 15	28 4	10	8	18	16	22	23	3	3	6	6	20	19	27	28	28	27
6 0	0♋0	0≏0	12	10	20	18	25	25	5	5	8	8	22	22	♍0	♍0	♍0	♍0
6 12	2 45	1 56	14	12	22	20	28	27	7	7	11	10	24	24	2	2	2	3
6 24	5 30	3 52	17	14	24	23	♋1	29	9	9	13	12	27	27	5	4	4	5
6 36	8 16	5 47	19	16	26	25	3	♍2	12	12	16	14	29	29	8	6	6	8
6 48	11 2	7 43	21	18	29	28	6	4	14	14	18	17	♏1	♎2	10	8	12	10
7 0	13 49	9 39	24	20	♏1	♏0	9	6	16	17	21	19	3	4	13	11	11	13
7 12	16 36	11 35	26	22	3	3	11	8	18	20	24	21	5	7	15	13	13	16
7 24	19 24	13 30	29	24	5	5	14	11	21	23	26	23	8	9	18	15	15	18
7 36	22 13	15 25	♏1	26	7	7	16	13	23	25	29	26	10	12	21	17	17	21
7 48	25 3	17 20	3	28	8	10	19	15	25	28	♏1	28	12	14	24	19	19	24
8 0	27 55	19 15	6	≏0	11	12	22	17	27	♍1	4	≏0	14	17	26	21	21	26
8 12	0♌41	21 10	8	2	13	15	24	20	29	3	5	2	16	19	29	23	23	29
8 24	3 41	23 5	11	4	15	17	27	22	♍2	8	9	4	18	22	♍1	26	25	♑2
8 36	6 37	25 0	13	6	17	20	29	24	4	11	11	7	21	25	4	28	27	4
8 48	9 34	25 54	15	8	19	22	♍2	26	6	14	14	9	23	28	7	≏0	♑0	7
9 0	12 32	28 49	18	10	21	25	5	29	8	17	17	11	25	♑0	9	2	2	10
9 12	15 32	0♍43	20	12	23	28	8	≏1	10	20	19	13	27	3	12	4	4	13
9 24	18 34	2 37	23	14	25	♍1	10	3	13	23	22	16	29	6	15	7	6	15
9 36	21 37	4 32	25	16	27	3	13	5	15	26	25	18	♑2	9	18	9	8	18
9 48	24 42	6 26	28	18	29	6	16	7	17	29	27	20	4	12	20	11	10	21
10 0	27 49	8 20	≏0	19	♍1	9	18	9	20	♎1	≏0	22	6	15	23	13	12	24
10 12	0♍57	10 14	2	22	3	12	21	11	23	5	3	24	8	18	26	15	14	28
10 24	4 7	12 8	5	24	5	15	24	14	26	8	5	27	11	21	29	18	16	≏1
10 36	7 18	14 2	7	26	7	18	26	16	29	12	8	29	13	24	≏1	20	18	4
10 48	10 30	15 57	10	29	10	22	29	18	♑2	16	11	♏1	15	28	4	22	20	7
11 0	13 43	17 51	12	♏1	12	26	≏2	20	5	19	13	3	18	≏1	7	25	22	11
11 12	16 57	19 46	15	3	14	29	5	23	8	23	16	5	20	4	10	27	25	14
11 24	20 12	21 42	17	5	17	≏2	8	25	11	27	19	8	23	8	13	29	27	16
11 36	23 28	23 37	19	7	19	6	10	27	14	♎0	21	10	25	12	16	♏2	29	19
11 48	26 44	25 34	22	8	21	10	12	29	17	3	23	12	27	16	19	4	♑1	22
12 0	0≏0	27 31	24	11	24	14	15	♏1	20	7	26	14	♑2	19	22	6	3	25

Sid. Time	M. C. long.	Asc. 1	REGIOMONTA. 11	12	2	3	CAMPANUS 11	12	2	3	PLACIDUS 11	12	2	3	NAT. GRAD. 11	12	2	3
h m	♎	♏	♏	♎	♏	♐	♎	♎	♏	♍	♏	♎	♏	♌	♏	♏	♏	♐
12 0	0 0	27 31	24 11	24 14	15 1	20 7	26 14	1 19	21 6	3 24
12 12	3 16	29 29	27 13	26 18	18 4	24 11	29 16	3 23	24 8	6 28
12 24	6 32	1 ♐28	29 15	29 22	21 6	29 15	♏2 18	6 27	27 11	7 ♈1
12 36	9 48	3 28	♏1 17	♍2 26	23 8	♌3 19	4 21	9 ♈1	♏0 13	9 4
12 48	13 3	5 30	3 19	5 ♈1	26 11	8 24	7 23	13 5	3 16	12 7
13 0	16 17	7 33	6 21	7 6	29 14	12 28	9 25	16 9	6 18	14 10
13 12	19 30	9 38	9 23	11 11	♏1 16	17 ♈2	12 27	19 13	9 21	16 13
13 24	22 42	11 45	11 25	14 15	4 18	21 6	14 29	23 17	11 23	18 17
13 36	25 53	13 55	13 27	18 20	6 20	26 10	17 ♐2	27 22	14 26	20 20
13 48	29 3	16 7	16 29	23 25	9 22	♏0 14	19 4	♍1 26	17 28	23 23
14 0	2♏11	18 23	18 ♈1	26 ♈0	12 24	5 18	22 6	5 ♈0	20 ♏0	25 26
14 12	5 18	20 43	20 3	♎0 5	15 26	11 22	24 8	10 4	23 3	27 29
14 24	8 23	23 8	23 5	5 10	17 28	17 26	27 11	15 8	26 6	♎0 ♈2
14 36	11 26	25 38	25 7	10 14	20 ♐1	23 29	29 13	20 13	29 9	2 5
14 48	14 28	28 15	28 10	16 19	22 3	29 ♐3	♐2 15	25 17	♐2 11	5 8
15 0	17 28	0 ♍58	♈0 12	22 24	25 5	♏6 6	4 18	♍1 21	5 14	7 11
15 12	20 26	3 51	3 14	29 29	28 7	11 10	7 20	6 25	8 17	10 14
15 24	23 23	6 55	5 17	♈6 ♐4	♐0 10	17 14	9 23	12 29	11 19	14 17
15 36	26 19	10 11	7 19	14 8	3 12	23 17	12 25	18 ♐3	14 22	17 20
15 48	29 19	13 42	10 21	22 12	5 14	29 21	14 28	24 7	17 25	21 23
16 0	2♐5	17 31	12 24	♈0 16	8 17	♈4 25	17 ♏1	♐0 11	20 28	24 26
16 12	4 57	21 43	15 26	8 20	11 19	9 29	19 3	6 14	23 ♏1	29 29
16 24	7 47	26 21	17 29	16 24	14 22	13 ♏1	22 6	12 18	27 3	♈4 ♏2
16 36	10 36	1 ♎31	20 ♍2	24 28	16 25	18 4	25 9	18 22	♏1 6	9 5
16 48	13 47	7 21	22 5	♐1 ♏1	19 28	22 7	28 13	24 26	4 9	14 18
17 0	16 11	13 57	25 7	8 4	22 ♏1	27 10	♐0 16	29 29	8 12	19 11
17 12	18 58	21 26	28 11	14 8	25 3	♏1 13	9 19	♍5 ♏2	12 16	28 14
17 24	21 44	29 52	♍1 14	20 12	27 6	5 16	6 23	10 6	17 19	♈6 18
17 36	24 30	9 ♈14	3 18	25 15	♏0 9	8 19	9 27	15 9	21 23	14 22
17 48	27 15	19 24	6 22	♍0 18	3 12	12 22	12 ♎1	20 12	25 26	22 26
18 0	0♍0	0♈0	9 26	4 21	5 19	15 25	15 5	25 15	♎0 ♏0	♍0 ♏0
18 12	2 45	10 36	12 ♍0	8 24	8 19	18 28	18 10	29 18	4 8	8 4
18 24	5 30	20 46	15 5	12 27	11 23	21 ♏1	21 15	♏3 21	8 16	15 9
18 36	8 16	0♍8	18 10	16 29	14 27	24 3	24 20	7 24	12 24	23 13
18 48	11 2	8 34	22 16	19 ♍2	17 ♎1	27 6	28 25	11 27	15 ♈2	♍0 18
19 0	13 49	16 3	26 22	23 5	20 5	29 9	♏1 ♈1	14 ♍0	19 11	9 22
19 12	16 36	22 39	29 29	25 8	23 9	♍2 11	9 6	17 2	22 16	12 26
19 24	24 23	28 29	♍2 ♈6	28 10	26 14	5 14	8 12	21 5	25 21	17 ♈1
19 36	22 13	3 ♉39	6 14	♎1 13	29 18	8 17	12 18	24 8	28 26	19 ♏3
19 48	25 3	8 17	10 22	4 15	♎2 22	11 19	16 24	27 10	♈1 ♉1	25 7
20 0	27 55	12 29	14 ♈0	6 18	5 26	13 22	19 ♏0	28 13	4 5	♍0 10
20 12	0♎41	16 18	18 4	8 20	9 ♈2	16 25	23 6	♎3 16	7 10	3 13
20 24	3 41	19 49	22 16	11 23	13 8	18 27	27 12	5 18	10 13	7 16
20 36	6 37	26 7	26 24	13 25	17 14	20 ♍0	♍1 18	7 21	13 16	10 19
20 48	9 34	24 6	♈1 ♉0	16 27	20 19	23 2	5 24	10 23	16 19	13 22
21 0	12 32	29 2	6 8	18 ♍0	24 25	25 5	9 29	12 26	19 23	16 26
21 12	15 32	1♉45	11 14	20 2	28 ♈1	27 8	13 ♈5	15 28	22 26	19 29
21 24	18 34	4 22	15 20	22 5	♈1 7	♏0 10	17 10	17 ♍1	25 28	21 ♍2
21 36	21 37	6 52	20 25	25 7	5 13	2 13	22 15	19 3	28 ♏1	24 5
21 48	24 42	9 17	25 ♍0	27 10	9 19	4 16	26 20	22 6	♈1 3	27 7
22 0	27 49	11 37	♏0 ♈4	29 12	12 25	7 18	♏0 25	24 8	4 5	♍0 10
22 12	0♍57	13 53	5 8	♍1 14	16 ♉0	9 21	4 29	26 11	7 7	2 13
22 24	4 7	16 5	10 12	3 17	21 4	11 23	8 ♍3	28 13	10 10	5 16
22 36	7 18	18 15	15 16	5 19	25 9	13 26	13 7	♎1 16	14 12	7 19
22 48	10 30	20 22	19 19	7 21	29 13	15 29	17 11	3 18	17 14	10 21
23 0	18 43	22 27	24 23	9 24	♈3 18	18 ♏1	21 14	5 21	20 16	12 24
23 12	16 57	24 30	29 25	11 26	7 22	20 4	25 17	7 24	23 18	14 27
23 24	20 12	26 32	♉4 28	13 29	11 27	22 7	29 21	9 26	26 21	17 ♍0
23 36	23 28	28 32	8 ♎1	15 ♍1	15 ♍1	24 9	♉3 24	12 29	29 23	19 3
23 48	26 44	0♎31	12 4	17 3	19 6	26 13	7 27	14 ♍1	♉2 25	22 6
24 0	0♈0	2 29	16 6	19 6	23 10	29 15	11 28	16 4	6 27	24 8

60° N. Lat.   Cusps of Houses   0h. − 12h.

Sid. Time h m	M.C. long. ♈	Asc. 1 ♌	REGIOMONTA. 11 ♉	12 ♊	2 ♌	3 ♍	CAMPANUS 11 ♈	12 ♊	2 ♍	3 ♍	PLACIDUS 11 ♉	12 ♊	2 ♌	3 ♍	NAT. GRAD. 11 ♉	12 ♊	2 ♌	3 ♍
0 0	0 0	4 34	18	9	21	6	22	9	1	15	12	2	17	4	6	29	25	9
0 12	3 16	6 26	22	11	23	9	26	12	3	18	16	6	19	7	9	♋1	27	12
0 24	6 32	8 17	26	14	25	11	29	15	5	21	20	8	21	9	12	3	29	15
0 36	9 48	10 8	♍0	16	27	13	♉3	17	7	23	23	10	23	12	15	5	♍1	18
0 48	13 3	11 58	3	18	28	16	6	20	10	26	27	12	25	14	18	7	3	21
1 0	16 17	13 49	7	20	♍0	18	10	23	12	29	♍0	15	28	17	21	9	5	23
1 12	19 30	15 39	10	22	2	20	14	26	14	♎2	4	17	♍0	20	24	11	7	26
1 24	22 42	17 28	13	25	4	23	17	29	16	5	7	19	2	22	27	13	10	29
1 36	25 53	19 18	16	27	6	25	21	♋2	18	7	10	21	4	25	♍0	15	13	♎2
1 48	29 3	21 8	19	29	8	28	25	5	20	10	15	24	6	28	3	17	15	5
2 0	2♉11	22 58	22	♋1	10	♎0	28	8	23	12	17	26	8	♎0	6	19	18	7
2 12	5 18	24 48	25	3	12	2	♋11	11	25	15	20	28	10	2	9	21	20	10
2 24	8 23	26 38	28	5	14	5	4	13	27	18	23	♌0	13	5	12	23	22	13
2 36	11 26	28 28	♋1	7	16	7	7	15	29	20	26	2	15	8	15	25	24	15
2 48	14 28	0♍18	4	9	18	10	10	18	♎1	23	28	4	17	10	18	27	26	18
3 0	17 28	2 8	6	11	20	12	13	20	3	26	♌1	6	19	13	20	29	29	21
3 12	20 26	3 59	9	13	22	14	16	23	5	28	4	9	21	16	23	♍1	♎1	24
3 24	23 23	5 50	11	15	24	17	19	25	7	♍1	6	11	23	18	26	3	3	26
3 36	26 19	7 41	14	17	26	19	22	28	9	4	9	13	26	21	28	5	5	29
3 48	29 19	9 31	17	19	28	21	25	♌0	11	6	12	15	28	23	♌1	7	7	♍2
4 0	2♊5	11 23	19	21	♎0	24	28	2	14	9	14	17	♎0	26	4	9	9	4
4 12	4 57	13 14	21	23	2	26	♋1	4	16	12	17	20	2	28	7	11	11	7
4 24	7 47	15 5	24	25	4	28	4	7	19	15	19	21	4	♍1	9	14	13	10
4 36	10 36	16 57	26	27	6	♍1	6	9	21	17	22	23	7	4	12	16	15	12
4 48	13 24	18 48	29	28	8	3	9	11	23	20	24	25	9	6	14	18	18	15
5 0	16 11	20 40	♌1	♍0	10	5	11	13	25	23	27	28	11	9	17	20	20	17
5 12	18 58	22 32	3	2	12	8	14	15	28	26	29	♍0	13	11	20	22	22	20
5 24	21 44	24 24	6	4	14	10	17	17	♍0	28	♍2	2	15	14	22	24	24	22
5 36	24 30	26 16	8	6	16	12	19	19	2	♍1	4	4	17	16	25	26	26	25
5 48	27 15	28 8	11	8	18	15	22	21	4	3	7	6	19	19	27	28	28	27
6 0	0♋0	0♎0	13	10	20	17	25	24	6	5	9	8	22	21	♌0	♍0	♍0	♍0
6 12	2 45	1 52	15	12	22	19	27	26	8	7	11	10	24	23	3	2	2	3
6 24	5 30	3 44	18	14	24	22	♌0	28	11	10	14	13	26	26	5	4	4	5
6 36	8 16	5 36	20	16	26	24	3	♍0	13	13	16	15	28	28	8	6	6	8
6 48	11 2	7 28	22	18	28	27	5	3	15	15	19	17	♍0	♍1	10	8	8	10
7 0	13 49	9 20	25	20	♍0	29	8	5	17	18	21	19	2	3	13	10	10	13
7 12	16 36	11 12	27	22	2	♍1	11	7	19	21	24	21	5	6	15	12	12	16
7 24	19 22	13 3	29	24	3	4	13	9	22	23	26	23	7	8	18	15	14	18
7 36	22 13	14 55	♍2	26	5	6	16	11	24	26	29	26	9	11	21	17	16	21
7 48	25 3	16 46	4	28	7	9	18	13	26	29	♍2	28	11	13	23	19	18	24
8 0	27 55	18 37	6	♎0	9	11	21	15	28	♍1	4	♎0	13	16	26	21	21	27
8 12	0♌41	20 29	9	2	11	13	24	18	♍0	4	7	2	15	18	28	23	23	29
8 24	3 41	22 19	11	4	13	16	26	20	3	7	9	4	17	21	♍1	25	25	♏2
8 36	6 37	24 10	13	6	15	19	29	22	5	11	12	7	19	24	3	27	27	4
8 48	9 34	26 1	16	8	17	21	♍2	24	8	14	14	9	21	26	6	29	29	7
9 0	12 32	27 52	18	10	19	24	4	26	10	17	17	11	24	29	9	♎1	♏1	10
9 12	15 32	29 42	20	12	21	26	7	28	12	20	20	13	26	♏2	12	4	3	12
9 24	18 34	1♏32	23	14	23	29	9	♎0	15	23	22	15	28	4	14	6	5	15
9 36	21 37	3 22	25	16	25	♏2	12	2	17	26	25	17	♏0	7	17	8	7	18
9 48	24 42	5 12	28	18	27	5	15	5	19	29	28	19	2	10	20	10	9	21
10 0	27 49	7 2	♎0	17	29	8	17	7	22	♏2	♎0	21	4	13	23	12	11	24
10 12	0♍57	8 52	2	22	♏1	11	20	9	25	6	2	24	6	15	25	14	13	27
10 24	4 7	10 42	5	24	3	14	23	12	28	9	5	26	9	20	28	17	14	♏0
10 36	7 18	12 32	7	26	5	17	26	14	♏1	12	8	28	11	23	♎1	19	17	4
10 48	10 30	14 21	10	28	7	20	28	16	4	16	10	♍0	13	26	4	21	19	7
11 0	13 43	16 11	12	♍0	10	23	♎1	18	7	19	13	2	15	♏0	7	23	21	11
11 12	16 57	18 2	14	2	12	27	4	20	10	23	17	5	18	3	9	26	23	13
11 24	20 12	19 52	17	3	14	♏0	6	23	13	27	18	7	20	6	12	28	25	16
11 36	23 28	21 43	19	5	16	4	9	25	16	♏0	21	9	22	10	15	♏0	27	19
11 48	26 44	23 34	21	7	18	8	12	27	19	4	23	11	24	14	18	2	29	22
12 0	0♎0	25 26	24	9	21	12	15	29	21	♏8	26	13	28	18	21	5	♏1	24

244

Sid. Time	M.C. long.	Asc. 1	REGIOMONTA. 11	12	2	3	CAMPANUS 11	12	2	3	PLACIDUS 11	12	2	3	NAT. GRAD. 11	12	2	3
h m ≏	♏	≏	♏	♐	♒	♓	≏	≏	♑	♓	≏	♏	♐	♒	≏	♏	♑	♓
12 0	0 0	25 26	24	9	21	12	15	29	21	8	26	13	28	18	21	5	1	24
12 12	3 16	27 18	26	11	23	16	17	♏2	24	12	29	15	♍0	22	24	7	3	27
12 24	6 32	29 11	29	13	26	21	20	4	28	16	♏1	17	3	26	26	9	5	✗1
12 36	9 48	1♐5	♏1	15	29	25	22	7	=2	20	4	19	6	♍0	29	12	7	4
12 48	13 3	3 0	3	17	♍1	✗0	25	9	6	25	6	21	9	4	♏2	14	9	7
13 0	16 17	4 56	5	19	4	4	28	11	10	29	9	24	13	8	5	16	11	10
13 12	19 30	6 54	8	21	7	9	♏0	13	15	♈3	11	26	16	13	88	19	13	13
13 24	22 42	8 54	10	23	10	14	3	15	20	7	14	28	20	17	10	21	15	16
13 36	25 53	10 55	12	25	14	20	6	17	26	11	16	♐0	24	21	13	23	17	19
13 48	29 3	12 59	15	27	18	25	8	19	✗1	15	19	2	28	26	16	26	20	23
14 0	2♏11	15 6	17	29	22	♈0	11	22	7	19	21	4	=2	♈0	19	28	22	26
14 12	5 18	17 16	19	♐1	26	5	14	24	13	23	23	6	7	4	22	♐1	24	29
14 24	8 23	19 30	22	3	=1	10	16	26	19	27	26	9	12	9	25	4	26	42
14 36	11 26	21 49	24	5	6	16	19	28	26	♉0	28	11	17	13	27	6	29	5
14 48	14 28	24 13	27	7	12	21	21	♐0	♈2	4	♐1	13	23	17	♐0	9	=1	8
15 0	17 28	26 44	29	10	18	26	24	3	9	7	3	15	28	22	3	11	3	11
15 12	20 26	29 22	♐1	12	25	♉0	27	5	15	11	6	18	4	26	6	13	6	14
15 24	23 23	2♍10	4	14	✗3	5	29	7	21	15	8	20	11	♉0	9	17	9	17
15 36	26 19	5 10	6	16	11	9	♐2	9	27	19	11	23	17	4	12	20	12	20
15 48	29 19	8 23	9	18	20	14	4	12	♉3	22	13	25	23	8	15	23	15	23
16 0	2♐5	11 54	11	21	♈0	18	7	14	8	26	16	28	♈0	18	18	26	18	26
16 12	4 57	15 47	13	23	10	22	10	17	14	29	18	♍0	7	16	21	♍0	22	28
16 24	7 47	20 7	16	26	19	26	12	19	18	♊2	21	3	13	20	25	4	26	♉1
16 36	10 36	25 2	19	29	27	♊0	15	22	22	5	24	6	19	23	29	9	✗1	4
16 48	13 24	0=42	21	♍1	♉5	3	18	24	27	8	26	9	26	27	♍2	13	7	7
17 0	16 11	7 17	24	4	12	7	20	27	♊1	11	29	13	♉2	♍0	6	18	13	10
17 12	18 58	15 13	26	7	18	10	23	29	5	14	♍2	16	7	4	10	24	21	14
17 24	21 44	24 13	29	10	24	13	26	♍2	9	17	4	20	13	7	15	=1	29	18
17 36	24 30	4✗55	♍2	14	29	16	28	5	12	20	7	24	18	10	20	10	♈9	22
17 48	27 15	17 1	5	18	♊4	19	♍1	8	15	23	10	28	23	14	25	19	19	26
18 0	0♍0	0♈0	8	22	8	22	4	11	19	26	13	=2	28	17	=0	♉0	♉0	♍0
18 12	2 45	12 59	11	26	12	25	7	14	22	29	16	7	♊2	20	4	11	11	4
18 24	5 30	25 5	14	=1	16	28	10	18	25	♉2	20	12	6	23	8	21	20	9
18 36	8 16	5♉47	17	6	20	♋1	13	21	28	4	23	17	10	26	12	♈1	29	14
18 48	11 2	14 47	20	12	23	4	16	25	♊0	7	26	23	14	28	16	9	♊6	19
19 0	13 49	22 43	23	18	26	6	19	29	3	10	=0	28	17	♊1	♉0	17	12	24
19 12	16 36	29 18	27	25	29	9	22	=3	6	12	3	✗4	21	4	23	22	17	28
19 24	24 23	4♉58	♉0	♋3	♋1	11	25	7	8	15	7	10	24	6	26	27	21	♊1
19 36	22 13	9 53	4	11	4	14	28	12	11	18	10	17	27	9	29	♉2	26	5
19 48	25 3	14 13	8	20	7	17	=1	17	13	20	14	23	♉0	12	✗2	7	♊0	8
20 0	27 55	18 6	12	9	9	19	4	22	16	23	18	♊0	2	14	5	12	4	12
20 12	0=41	21 37	16	10	11	21	8	27	18	26	22	7	5	17	8	15	7	15
20 24	3 41	24 50	21	19	14	24	12	✗3	20	28	26	13	7	19	11	18	10	18
20 36	6 37	27 50	25	27	16	26	15	9	23	♉1	✗0	19	10	22	13	21	13	21
20 48	9 34	0♋38	✗0	♉5	18	29	19	15	25	4	4	26	12	24	16	24	16	24
21 0	12 32	3 16	4	12	20	♉1	23	22	27	6	8	♉2	15	27	19	27	19	27
21 12	15 32	5 47	9	18	22	3	26	28	29	9	13	7	18	♉0	22	29	21	♉0
21 24	18 34	8 11	14	24	25	6	✗0	♈4	♉2	11	17	13	19	♉2	25	♉1	24	3
21 36	21 37	10 30	20	29	27	8	4	11	4	14	21	18	21	4	28	4	26	5
21 48	24 42	12 44	25	♉4	29	11	7	17	6	16	24	23	24	7	♈1	6	29	8
22 0	27 49	14 54	♈0	8	♉1	13	11	23	8	19	♈0	28	26	9	4	8	♉2	11
22 12	0✗57	17 1	5	12	3	15	15	29	10	22	4	♈2	28	11	7	10	4	14
22 24	4 7	19 5	10	16	5	18	19	♈4	13	24	9	6	♉0	14	11	13	6	17
22 36	7 18	21 6	16	20	7	20	23	10	15	27	13	10	2	16	14	15	8	19
22 48	10 30	23 6	21	23	9	22	27	15	17	♍0	17	14	4	19	17	17	10	22
23 0	13 43	25 4	26	26	11	25	♈1	20	19	2	22	17	6	21	20	19	12	25
23 12	16 57	27 0	♉0	29	13	27	5	24	21	5	26	21	9	24	23	21	15	28
23 24	20 12	28 55	5	♉1	15	29	9	28	23	8	♉0	24	11	26	26	23	17	♍1
23 36	23 28	0♍49	9	4	17	♍2	13	♉2	25	10	4	27	13	29	29	25	20	4
23 48	26 44	2 42	14	7	19	4	17	6	28	13	8	♋0	15	♍2	♉2	27	22	6
24 0	0♍0	4 34	18	9	21	6	22	9	12	15	12	2	17	4	6	29	25	9

C L O S E R P R E C I S I O N
TABLES FOR FINDING APPROXIMATE MINUTES ON MINOR CUSPS
AND FOR FINDING CAMPANUS AND NATURAL GRADUATION MIDCUSPS.

Regiomontanus, Campanus, Placidus, cusps 11, 12, 2,3,and Campanus midcusps, same as Ascendants at fictitious latitudes and at time (sidereal) diminished (for cusps etc. between 10 and 1), or (below Asc.) increased, by time differences. Tables below give fictitious lats. and (for Campanus) time differences. For Regiomontanus and Placidus, time diffs. are, 4h. for cusps 11 and 3, 2h. for 12 and 2.

Midcusps denoted thus: 10/11 = midcusp between cusps 10 and 11.

Natural Graduation, Q is degrees of zodiac from M.C. to Asc. Table below gives values of A,B,a,b, for different values of Q. When Q exceeds 90° take columns as named at FOOT; otherwise, as named at TOP. Then M.C.+A = cusp 11; Asc.− A = 12; Asc.+B = 2; cusp 4−B = 3. Midcusps 11/12 and 2/3: halve degrees between cusps.
M.C.+a = midcusp 10/11; Asc.−a = 12/1; Asc.+b = 1/2; cusp 4−b = 3/4.

FICTITIOUS LATITUDES FOR REGIOMONTANUS AND PLACIDUS

real lat.	REGIOMONTANUS 11and3	12and2	PLACIDUS 11and3	12and2	real lat.	REGIOMONTANUS 11and3	12and2	PLACIDUS 11and3	12and2
10°	5° 2'	8°41'	3°23'	6°43'	50°	30°47'	45°54'	22°31'	39°12'
20	10 19	17 30	6 57	13 41	52	32 37	47 56	24 10	41 22
30	16 6	26 34	10 59	21 9	54	34 31	50 0	26 0	43 37
35	19 18	31 14	13 17	25 10	56	36 33	52 5	27 59	45 58
40	22 40	36 0	15 56	29 32	58	38 40	58 11	30 14	48 26
45	26 34	40 54	18 57	34 10	60	40 54	56 18	32 47	51 3

FICT. LATS. (° ') and TIME DIFFS. (h m s). CAMPANUS

real lat.	10/11and3/4 °	h m s	11 and 3 °	h m s	11/12and2/3 °	h m s	12 and 2 °	h m s	12/1 and1/2 °	h m s
10°	2 35	5 0 52	4 59	4 1 31	7 3	3 1 45	8 39	2 1 32	9 39	1 0 53
20	5 5	5 1 40	9 51	4 6 4	14 0	3 7 7	17 14	2 6 16	19 26	1 0 56
30	7 27	5 7 45	14 29	4 13 44	20 42	3 12 26	25 40	2 14 45	28 53	1 8 42
35	8 32	5 10 29	16 40	4 18 45	23 56	3 18 43	29 47	2 20 87	33 39	1 12 27
40	9 27	5 13 36	18 45	4 24 34	27 2	3 30 11	33 59	2 28 2	38 4	1 17 7
45	10 33	5 17 5	20 42	4 31 9	30 0	3 38 56	37 46	2 39 0	43 5	1 23 22
50	11 26	5 20 56	22 31	4 38 34	32 33	3 48 4	41 34	2 47 39	47 44	1 30 31
52	11 46	5 22 32	23 13	4 41 44	33 52	3 53 31	43 3	2 52 39	49 34	1 33 5
54	12 51	5 24 12	23 52	4 45 1	34 54	3 58 9	44 29	2 57 59	51 24	1 38 1
56	12 23	5 27 38	24 56	4 48 26	35 53	4 3 13	45 54	3 3 40	53 13	1 42 25
58	12 41	5 29 29	25 7	4 5 57	36 51	4 8 31	47 17	3 9 49	55 0	1 47 12
60	12 57	5 29 29	25 40	4 55 35	37 46	4 13 51	48 35	3 17 44	56 47	1 52 45

NATURAL GRADUATION

Q	A	B	a	b	...	Q	A	B	a	b	...
°	° '	° '	° '	° '	°	°	° '	° '	° '	° '	°
38	15 10	36 22	9 13	14 19	142	64	23 22	34 44	12 50	15 39	116
40	15 51	36 33	9 33	14 31	140	66	23 56	34 27	13 3	15 40	114
42	16 12	36 33	9 53	14 42	138	68	24 30	34 9	13 16	15 40	112
44	17 12	36 29	10 12	14 51	136	70	25 3	33 51	13 28	15 39	110
46	17 51	36 25	10 30	15 0	134	72	25 35	33 31	13 39	15 38	108
48	18 30	36 19	10 48	15 7	132	74	26 7	33 11	13 50	15 36	106
50	19 8	36 11	11 5	15 14	130	76	26 38	32 50	14 1	15 33	104
52	19 46	36 2	11 21	15 20	128	78	27 9	32 28	14 11	15 30	102
54	20 24	35 52	11 38	15 25	126	80	27 39	32 5	14 20	15 27	100
56	21 0	35 41	11 53	15 30	124	82	28 8	31 41	14 29	15 22	98
58	21 36	35 28	12 8	15 33	122	84	28 37	31 17	14 38	15 18	96
60	22 12	35 15	12 23	15 36	120	86	29 5	30 52	14 45	15 12	94
62	22 48	35 0	12 37	15 38	118	88	29 33	30 26	14 55	15 6	92
64	23 22	34 44	12 50	15 39	116	90	30 0	30 0	15 0	15 0	90
..	B	A	b	a	Q	..	B	A	b	a	Q

Adapted from the much fuller table privately published by author

LATITUDES AND LONGITUDE-EQUIVALENTS FOR NEARLY A THOUSAND PLACES
and simple table to estimate lat. and long.-equiv. of places omitted
ZONE AND STANDARD TIMES OF MOST COUNTRIES AND STATES
and dates of many changes in these between 1870 and 1952
DATES OF CALENDAR-CHANGE IN COUNTRIES USING OLD-STYLE AFTER 1870
AND FOREIGN SUMMER-TIME OR DAYLIGHT-SAVING DETAILS FROM 1916 TO 1951

EXPLANATIONS:

PLACES LISTED. British Isles: towns of over 30,000 pop.(Eng.and Ws.)
or 20,000 (Scotl.and Irel.) when today's younger adults born; County
Towns, and main towns of the chief small islands, even if pop. much
less.
    Europe, British Commonwealth, and U.S.A.: over 100,000 pop.; nat-
ional Capitals (and some capitals of provinces, states etc.) even if
pop. much smaller.
    Rest of the world: cities over 500,000 pop., most capitals, some
islands or their chief towns.
    All subject to discretionary (and possibly inadvertent)exceptions
— especially where majority of pop.not literate in a Europ.language.

LAT, thus: 5ln30 = 51°30′ north; 5ls30 = 51°30′ south.

LONG.-EQUIV.:Geog.longitude expressed as time (+1 h. = 15°east; -1 h.
  = 15°west); amount by which local differs from Greenwich mean or
sidereal time.

ZONE TIMES (whole or half-hours only) given in column headed 'h';
  date of adoption (where known) in col. headed 'from';
  but other STANDARD TIMES (involving minutes and / or seconds)thus:
1h23m35s, or (to nearest minute) 1h35m — farther to the left, with
no attention to width of column.
    PRESENT STANDARD TIME (early 1952) given first; standard times for
past years, if different and known, given after, in BACKWARD order of
date of adoption or use.
    PLUS (+) means fast on Greenwich; subtract,to get Greenwich time.
    MINUS (-) means slow on Greenwich; add,to get Greenwich time.
  ʃ means 'except for some part(s) of this'(country etc.).
  NAME underlined means 'has used some variation, summer-time or the
like, in certain years of 1916-1951'.

SUMMER OR DAYLIGHT-SAVING TIME. Began on date given before the / or
// or ⚹ or ⚹ or ⚹, and ended on date following that sign;
  the sign / means single summer time (1 h. advance);
  the sign ⚹ means only a half-hour advance;
  the sign // means double summer time - total advance of 2 h.;
  the sign ⚹ means semi-double — total advance of 1½ hours;
  the sign ⚹ means twenty minutes advance only.
THE TIME WHEN CLOCKS CHANGED (by law),if known,shown thus :
  a = 1 a.m.; b = 2 a.m.; c = 3 a.m.;
  x = 10 p.m.; y = 11 p.m.; z = 12 p.m. (not 0 a.m.); so that
  y24Ap/a23Se would mean: 1 h.summer time from 11 p.m. on the
24th of April till 1 a.m. on the 23rd of September. Times thus
shown are intended as expressed in STANDARD time,but sometimes are
doubtful, especially for the ending of summer time etc.

DATES ABREVIATED FOR WIDTH OF COL, thus:12Ja32 = 12 January 1932;
  but 12Ja92 = 12 January 1892(all years between 1870 and 1952).
Months: first two letters, but note: Ja, Je, JL (not Jl) are used
for January, June, July; Mh, My for March, May; oc (not Oc) used
for October (small L or capital O confusable with one and zero).

IN SOUTH LATITUDES 'summer' is from a late month one civil year to
an early month the next year; so,under 1920, oc/Mh means 'to Mh1921'.
CONT.(instead of a date)=continuous from preceding, or into following, year.

PLACE	LAT.	m	s	PLACE	LAT.	m	s	PLACE	LAT.	m	s
Aberdare	51n32	-13	40	Chester	53n12	-11	36	Greenock	55n57	-19	0
Aberdeen	57n 9	- 8	24	Chesterfld	53n14	- 5	40	Grimsby	53n34	- 0	16
Abertil-				Chorley	53n39	- 9	32	Guildford	51n14	- 2	16
lery	51n45	-12	40	Clackman'n	56n 6	14	56	Haddington	55n57	-11	8
Aberyst-				Clonmel	52n21	-30	52	Halesowen	52n27	- 8	12
wyth	52n25	-20	20	Clydebank	55n55	-17	36	Halifax	53n42	- 7	28
Accringtn	53n45	- 9	28	Coatbridge	55n52	-16	4	Hamilton	55n47	-16	8
Acton, Mx	51n31	- 1	4	Colchester	51n53	+ 3	32	Hanley	53n 2	- 8	44
Airdrie	55n52	-15	48	Cork	52n54	-33	52	Harrogate	53n59	- 6	12
Aldershot	51n15	- 3	8	Coulsdon	51n19	- 0	28	Hartlepool	54n42	- 4	40
Appleby	54n35	-10	0	Coventry	52n25	- 6	0	Hastings	50n51	+ 2	16
Arbroath	56n34	-10	20	Cowes, IOW	50n45	- 5	12	HaverfordW	51n47	-17	52
Armagh	54n21	-26	20	Crewe	53n 5	- 9	52	Hendon	51n36	- 0	52
Ashton	53n30	- 8	28	Crosby, Gt	53n28	-12	8	Hereford	52n10	-11	0
Aylesbury	51n49	- 3	16	Croydon	51n22	- 0	24	Heston	51n29	- 0	23
Ayr	55n26	-18	28	Cupar	56n19	-12	0	Hornsey	51n37	- 0	28
Ballymena	54n52	-25	4	Dagenham	51n33	+ 0	40	Hove	50n50	- 0	48
Banff	51n40	-10	8	Darlington	54n32	- 6	8	Huddersfld	53n39	- 7	8
Bangor	53n14	-16	28	Darwen	53n45	- 5	52	Hull	53n45	- 1	20
Barking	51n33	+ 0	20	Derby	52n56	- 5	52	Huntingdon	52n21	- 0	44
Barnes	51n28	- 0	56	Dewsbury	53n42	- 6	28	Hyde	53n27	- 8	20
Barnsley	53n33	- 5	56	Dolgelly	52n45	-15	32	Ilford	51n34	+ 0	20
Barrow h F	54n 7	-12	52	Doncaster	53n31	- 4	32	Ilkeston	52n59	- 5	16
Barry, Glam	56n30	-11	4	Dorchester	50n43	- 9	40	Inverary	56n14	-20	20
Bath	51n21	- 9	20	Douglas	54n 9	-17	56	Inverness	57n29	-16	52
Batley	53n43	- 6	32	Dover	51n 7	+ 5	16	Ipswich	52n 4	+ 4	40
Beckenham	51n24	- 0	8	Downpatrick	54n20	-22	56	Jarrow	54n58	- 6	0
Bedford	52n 9	- 0	56	Drogheda	53n45	-25	8	Jedburgh	55n29	-10	16
Belfast	54n27	-23	40	Dublin	53n24	-25	0	Keighley	53n52	- 7	36
Bexley	51n26	+ 0	36	Dudley	52n31	- 8	20	Kiddermin-			
Bilston	52n33	- 8	12	Dumbarton	56n 5	-18	40	ster	52n24	- 8	52
Birkenh'd	53n23	-12	8	Dumfries	55n 4	-14	32	Kidare	53n10	-27	40
Birm'gham	52n29	- 7	28	Dundalk	54n 0	-25	24	Kilkenny	52n35	-29	0
Blackburn	53n45	- 8	56	Dundee	56n28	-11	52	Kingston	51n25	- 1	12
Blackpool	53n49	-12	12	Dunfermline	56n 6	-13	48	Kingstown	53n17	-24	36
Blaydon	54n58	- 7	48	Duns	55n47	- 9	24	Kinross	56n12	-13	40
Blyth	55n 8	- 6	0	Durham	54n47	- 6	16	Kirkcaldy	57n 7	-12	36
Bodmin	50n29	-18	52	Ealing	51n33	- 0	32	Kirkcudb't	54n50	-12	12
Bolton	53n36	- 9	56	Eastbourne	50n46	+ 5	8	Kirkwall	58n59	-11	48
Bootle	53n27	-11	56	East Ham	51n32	+ 0	12	Lanark	55n44	-15	8
Bournem'th	50n44	- 7	28	Ebbw Vale	51n47	-12	40	Lancaster	54n 3	-11	12
Bradford	53n48	- 7	0	Eccles	53n28	- 9	24	Leeds	53n48	- 6	12
Brecon	51n57	-13	32	Edinburgh	55n57	-12	48	Leicester	52n39	- 4	32
Brentford	51n29	- 1	16	Edmonton	51n37	- 0	12	Leigh Lancs	53n29	- 6	8
Brighton	50n49	- 0	36	Elgin	57n39	-13	12	Lerwick	60n10	- 4	40
Bristol	51n27	-10	12	Enfield	51n40	- 0	20	Lewes	50n52	+ 0	4
Bromley, Kt	51n25	+ 0	4	Ennis	52n51	-35	56	Leyton	51n34	- 0	4
Burnley	53n47	- 9	0	Enniskillen	54n20	-30	36	Lifford	54n50	-30	40
Burton o T	52n48	- 6	42	Epsom	51n20	- 1	8	Limerick	52n30	-35	0
Bury	53n27	- 0	28	Erith	51n28	+ 0	48	Lincoln	53n15	- 2	8
Caerphilly	51n35	-12	0	Eston	54n34	- 4	28	Linlithgow	55n58	-14	28
Cambridge	52n13	+ 0	28	Exeter	50n44	-14	8	Lisburn	54n31	-24	12
Cannock	52n43	- 8	4	Falkirk	56n 0	-15	8	Liverpool	53n24	-11	56
Canterbury	51n17	+ 4	20	Falmouth	50n10	-20	20	Llandudno	53n20	-15	40
Cardiff	51n28	-13	4	Finchley	51n36	- 0	40	Llanelly	51n41	-16	36
Carlisle	54n54	-11	40	Folkestone	51n 5	+ 4	44	Llangefni	53n16	-17	6
Carlow	52n50	-27	40	Forfar	56n39	-11	32	LONDON:City	51n31	- 0	24
Carmarthen	51n55	-17	12	Galway	53n17	-36	16	Battersea	51n28	- 0	40
Carnarvon	53n 8	-17	0	Gellygaer	51n41	-13	4	Bermonds.	51n30	- 0	16
Carrick/Sh	53n57	-32	20	Gateshead	54n58	- 6	24	Bethnal Gn	51n31	- 0	12
Castlebar	53n52	-37	12	Gillingham	51n24	+ 2	12	Camberwel	51n28	- 0	16
Cavan	53n29	-23	28	Glasgow	55n52	-17	0	Chelsea	51n29	- 0	44
Chatham	51n23	+ 2	8	Gloucester	51n52	- 8	56	Deptford	51n29	- 0	8
Chelmsford	51n42	+ 1	52	Gosport	50n48	- 8	32	Finsbury	51n34	- 0	24
Cheltenham	51n53	+ 8	20	Gravesend	51n27	+ 1	28	Fulham	51n28	- 0	52

PLACE	LAT.	m	s	PLACE	LAT.	m	s	PLACE	LAT.	m	s
LONDON (contin.)				Oakham	52n41	– 2	56	Stafford	52n43	– 8	24
Greenw'ch	51n31	0	0	Oldbury	52n59	– 8	0	Stirling	56n 7	–15	44
Hackney	51n33	– 0	12	Oldham	53n33	– 8	32	Stockton-			
Hammersm.	51n30	– 0	56	Omagh	54n36	–29	16	on-Tees	54n34	– 5	20
Holborn	51n31	– 0	28	Orpington	51n23	– 0	24	Stoke-on-T	53n 1	– 8	44
Islington	51n32	– 0	24	Oxford	51n45	– 5	4	Stonehaven	56n58	– 8	52
Kensingtn	51n30	– 0	38	Paisley	55n51	–17	44	Stornoway	58n13	–25	28
Lambeth	51n30	– 0	28	Peebles	55n39	–12	44	Streatham	51n26	– 0	32
Lewisham	51n28	– 0	4	Pembroke	51n40	–17	36	Sunderland	54n55	– 5	28
Maryleb.	51n31	– 0	40	Perth	56n23	–13	44	Sutton Sur.	51n22	– 0	48
Paddingtn	51n31	– 0	40	Peterboro'	52n36	– 0	56	Swansea	51n37	–15	40
Poplar	51n31	– 0	4	Plymouth	50n23	–16	32	Swindon	51n33	– 7	0
StPancras	51n32	– 0	28	Pontypool	51n42	–12	8	Swinton	53n29	– 5	20
Shoreditch	51n32	– 0	20	Pontypridd	51n35	–13	16	Taunton	51n 1	–12	24
Southwark	51n31	– 0	16	Poole	50n43	– 7	56	Tralee	53n16	–38	48
Stepney	51n31	– 0	8	Portadown	54n25	–25	48	Trim	53n34	–27	8
Stoke N'n	51n34	– 0	16	Portsmouth	50n48	– 4	24	Tullamore	53n16	–30	0
Wandsworth	51n27	– 0	48	Port Talbot	51n35	–15	4	Tunbr.Ws.	51n 8	+ 1	4
Westminst.	51n31	– 0	28	Presteign	52n17	–12	0	Twickenham	51n27	– 1	20
Woolwich	51n29	+ 0	16	Preston	52n44	– 9	52	Tynemouth	55n 1	– 5	40
Londonderry	55n0	–29	24	Ramsgate	51n20	+ 5	40	Uxbridge	51n33	– 1	56
Longford	53n44	–31	12	Reading	51n27	– 3	52	Wakefield	53n41	– 6	0
Lowestoft	52n29	+ 7	0	Reigate	51n14	– 0	52	Wallasey	53n25	–12	20
Lurgan	55n48	–25	20	Renfrew	55n23	–17	40	Wallsend	54n59	– 6	8
Macclesfld	53n16	– 8	32	Rhondda	51n39	–13	56	Walsall	52n34	– 7	52
Maidstone	51n17	– 2	4	Richmond	51n27	– 1	12	Waltham-			
Manchester	53n29	– 9	4	Rochdale	53n37	– 8	44	stow	51n38	– 0	16
Mansfield	53n 8	– 4	48	Rochester	51n24	+ 2	4	Warrington	53n25	–10	32
Margate	51n23	– 5	32	Romford	51n35	+ 0	40	Warwick	52n17	– 6	20
Maryboro'	53n 2	–29	16	Roscommon	53n39	–32	48	Wednesbury	52n33	– 8	0
Middlesbo.	54n35	– 4	56	Rutherglen	55n49	–16	48	Welshpool	52n40	–12	36
Mitcham	51n24	– 0	40	Ryde IOW	50n44	– 4	44	Wembley	51n33	– 1	16
Mold	53n10	–12	36	St Helens	53n21	–11	0	W,Bromwich	52n31	– 8	0
Monaghan	54n10	–28	0	St Helier	49n11	–33	36	West Ham	51n33	+ 0	8
Monmouth	51n44	–12	0	Salford	53n30	– 9	8	Wexford	52n20	–25	52
Motherwell	55n47	–15	56	Salisbury	51n 4	– 7	12	Wicklow	52n58	–24	12
Mullingar	53n32	–29	24	Scarboro'	54n17	– 1	40	Widnes	53n22	–11	0
Nairn	57n30	–15	20	Scunthorpe	53n36	– 2	20	Wigan	53n33	–10	32
Neath	51n32	–15	12	Selkirk	53n32	–11	24	Wigtown	54n45	–17	0
Nelson	53n52	– 8	56	Shepley	53n36	– 6	48	Willesden	51n32	– 0	56
N'castle/T	54n59	– 6	24	Shrewsbury	52n43	–11	0	Wimbledon	51n26	– 0	52
" " under L.	53n 1	– 8	56	Skye	57n20	–25	20	Winchester	51n 4	– 5	12
Newmarket	52n15	+ 1	40	Sligo	54n17	–34	20	Windsor	51n29	– 2	28
Newport IOW	50n43	– 5	12	Slough	51n30	– 2	20	Wolver-			
" " " Mon.	51n35	–12	0	Southall	51n31	– 1	32	hampton	52n35	– 8	24
Newry	54n11	–25	40	Southamptn	50n55	– 5	36	Wolverton	52n 5	– 3	12
Newtown				Southend/S	51n33	+ 2	48	Wood Grn.	51n36	– 0	28
ards	54n36	–22	44	Southgate	51n38	– 0	28	Worcester	52n11	– 8	52
Northamptn	52n15	– 3	46	Southport	53n39	–11	56	Worthing	50n49	– 1	32
Nottingham	52n57	– 4	32	Southsea	50n47	– 4	16	Yarmouth	50n43	+ 5	52
Norwich	52n38	+ 5	12	S.Shields	55n 0	– 5	40	Yeovil	50n57	–10	28
Nuneaton	52n32	– 5	52	Spenboro'	53n44	– 6	44	York	53n58	– 4	16

Longitude-equivalents above are given to the nearest four sec.

NOTE – HOROSCOPES FOR THOSE BORN IN LONDON

Greater-London births are about a quarter of those in all England. So improving their accuracy goes a long way to improving English astrology. For whole-degree approximate charts, 51°30′N., 0° long., is perhaps near enough for them all. Using this, as (alas) too often is done, when Ascendant is professedly correct to nearest minute, is an utter absurdity, however, for the whole of Greater London's 700 or so square miles! So, above, London suburban towns are treated as any of the other towns of Britain, and Boroughs are given under LONDON.

This is believed to be the first time any astrological work of reference has given data for any part of London but one.

PLACE	Country	LAT.	h	m	s
AARAU	Switz	47n23	+ 0	32	12
ABERCORN	N.Rho	8s47	+ 2	5	20
ACCRA	Gd Ct	5n38	- 0	0	48
ADDIS ABABA	Abyss	9n 2	+ 2	34	52
ADELAIDE	S.Aus	34s54	+ 9	14	24
ADEN	Arab.	12n58	+ 3	4	0
AGRA	India	27n 7	+ 5	12	20
AHMADABAD	India	23n 3	+ 4	50	32
AIX LA CH.	Rhinel	50n46	+ 0	24	28
AJACCIO	Cors.	41n55	+ 0	34	48
AJMER	India	26n22	+ 4	58	40
AKRON,Ohio	USA	41n 8	- 5	26	0
ALBANY, NY	USA	42n38	- 4	56	0
ALEPPO	Syria	36n14	+ 2	29	4
ALESSANDRIA	Italy	44n55	+ 0	34	28
ALEXANDRIA	Egypt	31n 9	+ 1	59	32
ALGIERS	Alger	36n50	+ 0	11	40
ALICE SPRINGS	Aus	23s36	+ 8	55	32
ALLAHABAD	India	25n22	+ 5	43	28
ALMA ATA	USSR	43n28	+ 5	7	52
ALTDORF	Switz	46n53	+ 0	34	32
ALTONA	Germ.	53n33	+ 0	39	48
AMIENS	Fr'ce	49n53	+ 0	9	12
AMOY	China	24n30	+ 7	52	40
AMRITSAR	India	31n47	+ 4	59	12
AMSTERDAM	Neth.	52n2	+ 0	19	40
ANDORRA	Andor	42n30	+ 0	5	56
ANGERS	Fr'ce	47n29	- 0	2	20
ANGRA DE H.	Azor.	38n40	- 1	48	20
ANKARA	Turk.	39n52	+ 2	11	56
ANTANANARIV.	Madag	19s 0	+ 3	9	20
ANTIOCH	Syria	36n 4	+ 2	24	40
ANTOFAGASTA	Chile	23s30	- 4	41	40
ANTWERP	Belg.	51n14	+ 0	17	32
ARNHEM	Neth.	51n58	+ 0	23	36
ASTRAKHAN	USSR	46n13	+ 3	12	0
ASUNCION	Parag	25s15	- 3	50	20
ATHENS	Gr'ce	37n59	+ 1	35	8
ATLANTA,Geo	USA	33n45	- 5	37	20
ATLANTIC C,NJ	USA	39n26	- 4	58	0
AUCKLAND	N.Z.	36s54	+11	47	4
AUGSBURG	Germ.	48n23	+ 0	43	40
BAGDAD	Iraq	33n18	+ 2	58	0
BAHIA	Braz.	10s40	- 2	25	48
BAHIA BLANCA	Arg.	38s30	- 4	9	20
BAKU	USSR	40n22	+ 3	19	4
BALTA	USSR	47n59	+ 1	58	0
BALTIMORE Md	USA	39n23	- 5	6	20
BANGALORE	India	12n59	+ 5	10	32
BANGKOK	Siam	13n45	+ 6	42	20
BARCELONA	Spain	41n22	+ 0	8	40
BARELI	India	28n20	+ 5	18	0
BARI	Italy	41n 8	+ 1	7	28
BARMEN	Germ.	51n17	+ 0	28	52
BASLE	Switz	47n33	+ 0	30	16
BASRA	Iraq	30n34	+ 3	11	20
BATAVIA	Java	6s10	+ 7	7	20
BATHURST,NSW	Aus	13n23	+ 1	6	32
BATHURST	Gamb.	33s33	+ 1	47	20
BEIRUT	Leb.	33n54	+ 2	22	8
BELGRADE	Yugos	44n50	+ 1	22	4
BELIZE	Br.Ho	17n30	- 5	52	8
BELLINZONA	Switz	46n12	+ 0	36	8
BELLO HORIZ.	Braz.	19s50	- 2	57	40
BERGEN	Norw.	60n2	+ 0	21	20
BERLIN	Germ.	52n34	+ 0	53	
BERNE	Switz	46n58	+ 0	29	52
BIELITZ	Pol.	49n50	+ 1	16	4
BLOEMFCNTN	S.Afr	29s 9	+ 1	44	52
BOCHUM	Germ.	51n28	+ 0	29	8
BOGOTA	Colmb	4n30	- 4	58	0
BOLOGNA	Italy	44n29	+ 0	45	24
BOMBAY	India	19n 0	+ 4	51	40
BONN	Germ.	50n43	+ 0	28	16
BORDEAUX	Fr'ce	44n50	- 0	2	4
BOSTON,Mass	USA	42n25	- 4	44	20
BOULOGNEsurM	Fr'ce	50n43	+ 0	6	32
BOURGES	Fr'ce	47n 5	+ 0	9	24
BRATISLAVA	Czech	48n10	+ 1	8	24
BREMEN	Germ.	53n 6	+ 0	35	4
BRESCIA	Italy	45n36	+ 0	40	48
BRESLAU	Germ.	51n 8	+ 1	8	0
BREST	Fr'ce	48n26	- 0	18	0
BRIDGEPORTCon	USA	41n14	- 4	53	20
BRIDGE TOWN	Barb.	13n 0	- 4	0	0
BRISBANE Qns	Aus	27s30	+10	12	0
BRNO(Brünn)	Czech	49n11	+ 1	6	32
BRUGES	Bel.	51n13	+ 0	12	48
BRUNSWICK	Germ.	52n15	+ 0	42	0
BRUSSELS	Bel.	50n51	+ 0	17	24
BUCHAREST	Rum.	44n25	+ 1	44	20
BÜCKEBURG	Germ.	52n17	+ 0	36	8
BUDAPEST	Hung.	47n29	+ 1	16	20
BUEN.AYRES	Arg.	34s40	- 3	54	0
BUFFALO NY	USA	42n55	- 5	15	52
BYDGOSZCZ	Pol.	53n 8	+ 1	12	0
CAGLIARI	Italy	39n15	+ 0	36	32
CAIRO	Egypt	30n 1	+ 2	4	52
CALCUTTA	India	22n32	+ 5	56	0
CAMAGUEY	Cuba	21n22	- 5	11	56
CAMDEN,NJ	USA	40n 0	- 5	0	0
CANBERRA	Aust.	35s15	+ 9	56	40
CANDIA	Crete	35n15	+ 1	40	0
CANEA	Crete	35n32	+ 1	36	4
CANTON	China	23n15	+ 7	33	20
CANTON,Ohio	USA	40n53	- 5	25	20
CAPE TOWN	S.Afr	33s58	+ 1	13	44
CARACAS	Venez	10n31	- 4	27	56
CARTAGENA	Spain	37n37	- 0	3	48
CASABLANCA	Moroc	33n30	- 0	32	0
CASSEL	Germ.	51n18	+ 0	37	40
CATANIA	Sic.	37n29	+ 1	0	24
CAWNPORE	India	26n24	+ 5	21	36
CERNAUTI	Rum.	48n18	+ 1	43	44
CETINJE	Yugos	42n35	+ 1	15	52
CHATTANOOGA	Tenn USA	35n 3	- 5	40	28
CHICAGO, Ill	USA	41n50	- 5	51	0
CHISINAU	Rum.	47n 4	+ 1	54	44
CHRISTCHURCH	NZ	43s31	+11	30	28
CHUNGKING	China	29n35	+ 7	6	32
CINCINNATI,Oh.	USA	39n 3	- 5	38	0
CIUDAD BOL.	Venez	8n 7	- 4	15	28
CLEVELAND,Oh.	USA	41n30	- 5	26	0
COLOGNE	Germ.	50n56	+ 0	28	0
COLOMBO	Cey.	6n58	+ 5	19	52
COLUMBUS,Oh.	USA	39n57	- 5	32	0
CONSTANTA	Rum.	44n12	+ 1	54	44
CONSTANTINE	Alger	36n30	+ 0	26	0
COPENHAGEN	Danm	55n43	+ 0	50	32
CORDOBA	Arg.	31s10	- 4	17	40

PLACE	Country	LAT.	h	m	s	PLACE	Country	LAT.	h	m	s
CORDOVA	Spain	37n52	− 0	19	12	HANGCHOW	China	30n10	+ 8	0	20
CRACOW	Pol.	50n 5	+ 1	19	56	HANKOW	China	30n50	+ 7	37	0
DACCA	Pak.	23n46	+ 6	2	0	HANOI	China	21n 0	+ 7	3	0
DAIREN	Manch	39n 0	+ 8	6	20	HANOVER	Germ.	52n23	+ 0	39	32
DAKAR	Seneg	14n40	− 1	9	52	HARTFORD,Conn	USA	41n15	− 4	51	8
DALLAS,Tex	USA	32n50	− 6	27	20	HAVANA	Cuba	23n 0	− 5	30	0
DAMASCUS	Syria	33n30	+ 2	25	20	HAVRE, LE	Fr'ce	49n30	+ 0	0	28
DANZIG	Danz.	54n20	+ 1	14	40	HELSINKI	Finn.	60n13	+ 1	39	52
DARMSTADT	Germ.	49n54	+ 0	34	32	HONGKONG	China	22n20	+ 7	35	40
DAYTON,Ohio	USA	39n42	− 5	56	48	HONOLULU	Hawai	21n25	−10	31	40
DELHI	India	28n35	+ 5	9	12	HOUSTON,Tex	USA	29n49	− 6	21	20
DENVER,Col	USA	39n43	− 6	59	56	HOWRAH	India	22n37	+ 5	53	8
DES MOINES,Io	USA	41n33	− 6	14	20	HSINKING	Manch	44n 0	+ 8	20	0
DESSAU	Germ.	51n50	+ 0	49	4	HYDERABAD	India	17n16	+ 5	53	52
DETMOLD	Germ.	51n56	+ 0	35	20	INDIANAPOLIS	USA	39n45	− 5	45	8
DETROIT,Mich	USA	42n20	− 5	32	20	ISTANBUL	Turk.	41n 1	+ 1	55	52
DIJON	Fr'ce	47n19	+ 0	20	16	IVANOVO VOZ.	USSR	57n 3	+ 2	43	52
DORTMUND	Germ.	51n32	+ 0	29	44	JACKSONVILLE	USA	30n20	− 5	26	40
DRESDEN	Germ.	51n 5	+ 0	54	40	JASSY	Rum.	47n15	+ 1	49	40
DUISBURG	Germ.	51n26	+ 0	27	0	JERUSALEM	Pales	31n48	+ 2	20	48
DULUTH,Minn	USA	46n47	− 6	8	40	JOHAN'BURG	S.Afr	26s15	+ 1	52	20
DURBAN	S.Afr	29s55	+ 2	4	8	JOHORE BAHRU	Joh.	1n42	+ 6	56	0
DUSSELDORF	Germ.	51n15	+ 0	27	4	JOKJAKARTA	Java	7n57	+ 7	21	20
EDMONTON,Alb	Can	53n35	− 7	33	36	KABUL	Afghan	34n33	+ 4	36	40
EL PASO,Tex	USA	31n52	− 7	5	56	KANSAS,Kan	USA	38n30	− 6	36	0
ELBERFELD	Germ.	51n15	+ 0	29	0	KANSAS,Mo.	USA	39n 0	− 6	18	0
ELIZABETH,NJ	USA	40n40	− 4	57	8	KARACHI	Pak.	24n52	+ 4	28	0
ERFURT	Germ.	51n 0	+ 0	44	0	KARLSRUHE	Germ.	49n 3	+ 0	33	20
ERIE,Pa	USA	42n 8	− 4	40	0	KATOVITZ	Pol.	50n17	+ 1	16	12
ERIVAN	Armen	40n10	+ 2	58	4	KAUNAS	USSR	54n52	+ 1	35	40
ESSEN	Germ.	51n26	+ 0	27	0	KAZAN	USSR	55n42	+ 3	16	24
EVANSVILLE,Ind	USA	37n 0	− 5	50	12	KHARKOV	USSR	49n59	+ 2	24	48
EVORA	Port.	38n34	− 0	31	40	KHARTOUM	Sudan	15n37	+ 2	10	0
FALL RIVER,Mass	USA	41n45	− 5	44	0	KIEL	Germ.	54n20	+ 0	40	40
FEZ	Moroc	44n 0	− 0	20	0	KIEV	USSR	50n26	+ 2	2	4
FLORENCE	Italy	43n46	+ 0	45	8	KINGSTON	Jam.	18n 0	− 5	7	28
FORTALEZZA	Braz.	3s50	− 2	34	40	KLAGENFURT	Austria	46n37	+ 0	57	16
Ft.DE FRANCE	Mart	14n36	− 4	4	8	KNOXVILLE	USA	35n59	− 5	36	0
Ft.WAYNE,Ind	USA	41n 0	− 5	40	8	KOBE	Japan	34n41	+ 9	0	16
Ft.WORTH,Tex	USA	32 45	− 6	29	20	KONIGSBERG	Germ.	54n42	+ 1	22	8
FRANKFURTonM	Germ	50n 7	+ 0	34	40	KORITZA	Albania	40n38	+ 1	23	12
FREETOWN	W.Afr	8n30	− 0	52	48	KREFELD	Germ.	51n20	+ 0	26	16
FUNCHAL	Madeira	32n45	− 1	8	0	KUALA LUMPUR	Malay	3n 5	+ 6	46	40
GALATI	Rum.	45n28	+ 1	52	8	KURSK	USSR	51n47	+ 2	26	12
GARY,Ind	USA	41n35	− 5	49	20	KYOTO	Japan	34n57	+ 9	3	44
GELSENKIRCHEN	Germ	51n32	+ 0	28	32	LA PAZ	Bol.	16s10	− 4	33	0
GENEVA	Switz	46n12	+ 0	24	36	LA PLATA	Arg.	34s55	− 3	52	0
GENOA	Italy	44n24	+ 0	36	0	LAGOS	Niger	6n27	+ 0	13	40
GEORGETOWN	Br.Gna	6n46	− 3	52	32	LAHORE	Pak.	31n31	+ 4	57	28
GEORGE TOWN	Pen.	0n30	+ 6	40	24	LAUSANNE	Switz	46n32	+ 0	26	28
GHENT	Belg.	51n 4	+ 0	14	52	LEGHORN	Italy	43n33	+ 0	41	20
GIBRALTAR	Gib.	36n10	− 0	21	28	LEIPZIG	Germ.	51n20	+ 0	49	20
GODTHAAB	Green.	64n15	− 3	24	40	LEMBERG	Pol.	49n50	+ 1	36	4
GOTEBORG	Swed.	57n40	+ 0	48	0	LENINGRAD	USSR	60n 0	+ 2	1	20
GRANADA	Spain	37n10	− 0	14	20	LEOPOLDVILLE	Cong	4s22	+ 1	1	20
GRAZ	Austria	47n 4	+ 1	1	44	LHASA	Tibet	29n50	+ 6	4	40
GRENADA	W.Ind	12n 5	− 4	7	0	LIEGE	Belg.	50n39	+ 0	22	16
GRONINGEN	Neth.	53n10	+ 0	26	20	LILLE	Fr'ce	50n37	+ 0	12	16
GUATEMALA	Guat.	14n41	− 6	2	20	LIMA	Peru	12s15	− 5	7	20
GUAYAQUIL	Ecua.	3s15	− 0	33	20	LINZ	Austria	48n1	+ 0	57	12
HAARLEM	Neth.	52n21	+ 0	18	36	LISBON	Port.	38n32	− 0	36	40
HALIFAX,N.S.	Can	44n38	− 4	14	12	LOANDO	Angola	8s48	+ 0	52	4
HAMBURG	Germ.	53n34	+ 0	40	8	LODZ	Pol.	51n46	+ 1	17	4
HAMILTON	Berm	32n18	− 4	18	48	LONG BEACH	Cal USA	33n45	− 7	51	20
HAMILTON,Ont.	Can.	43n16	− 5	19	36	LOS ANGELES	Cal USA	34n 1	− 7	53	20
HAMMERFEST	Norw.	70n40	+ 1	34	40	LOUISVILLE,Ky	USA	38n15	− 5	43	0

251

PLACE	Country	Lat.	h	m	s
LOUVAIN	Belg.	50n53	+ 0	18	44
LOWELL	USA	42n43	- 4	45	20
LUBECK	Germ.	53n52	+ 0	42	40
LUBLIN	Pol.	51n13	+ 1	30	16
LUCERN	Switz	47n 3	+ 0	33	4
LUCKNOW	India	26n47	+ 5	23	56
LUDWIGSHAFN	Germ.	49n30	+ 0	33	28
LUXEMBURG	Belg.	49n37	+ 0	24	28
LYNN	USA	42n30	- 0	28	0
LYONS	Fr'ce	45n44	+ 0	19	24
MACAO	Braz.	5s 0	- 3	6	0
MADRAS	India	13n 7	+ 5	21	0
MADRID	Spain	40n25	- 0	15	0
MADURA	India	9n50	+ 5	12	40
MAGDEBURG	Germ.	52n 8	+ 0	46	40
MAINZ	Germ.	50n 0	+ 0	38	8
MALACCA	St.S.	2n15	+ 6	49	0
MALMO	Swed.	55n25	+ 0	52	20
MANAGUA	Nica.	12n 7	- 5	45	0
MANDALAY	Burma	22n 3	+ 6	24	8
MANILA	Philipp.	14n10	+ 8	4	0
MANNHEIM	Germ.	49n30	+ 0	33	44
MARRAKESH	Moroc	31n38	- 0	31	56
MARSEILLES	Fr'ce	43n18	+ 0	21	40
MEDILLIN	Colum	6 25	- 5	3	20
MEERUT	India	29n 1	+ 5	11	12
MELBOURNE	Aust.	37s50	+ 9	39	52
MEMEL	Lith.	55n42	+ 1	24	40
MEMPHIS	USA	35n 9	- 6	0	0
MESSINA	Italy	38 11	+ 0	50	8
MEXICO	Mexico	19n25	- 6	37	8
MIAMI	USA	25n45	- 5	21	0
MIDDLEBURG	Neth.	51 30	+ 0	14	40
MILAN	Italy	45n28	+ 0	36	40
MILWAUKEE	USA	43n 0	- 5	52	0
MINNEAPOLIS	USA	45n 3	- 6	13	20
MINSK	USSR	53n32	+ 1	50	8
MONACO		43n43	+ 0	29	48
MONROVIA	Africa	6n20	- 0	43	20
MONS	Belg.	50n28	+ 0	15	48
MONTERREY	Mexico	25n39	- 6	41	40
MONTEVIDEO	Urug.	34s40	- 3	44	40
MONTREAL	Can.	45n32	- 6	54	24
MOSCOW	USSR	55n45	+ 2	30	24
MUKDEN	China	41n51	+ 8	13	40
MULHOUSE	Fr'ce	47n45	+ 0	28	48
MULHEIM	Germ.	47n48	+ 0	30	32
MUNICH	Germ.	48n10	+ 0	46	24
MUNSTER	Germ.	51n58	+ 0	30	24
MURCIA	Spain	38n 0	- 0	4	28
NAGASAKI	Japan	32n43	+ 8	39	48
NAIROBI	E.Afr	1s18	+ 2	27	12
NAMUR	Belg.	50n29	+ 0	19	24
NANCY	Fr'ce	48n41	+ 0	24	48
NANKING	China	32n10	+ 7	55	20
NANTES	Fr'ce	47n14	- 0	6	16
NAPLES	Italy	40n50	+ 0	55	8
NASHVILLE	USA	36n 8	- 5	47	20
NASSAU	Germ.	50n18	+ 0	31	4
NEW BEDFORD	USA	41n40	- 4	44	0
NEW HAVEN,Conn	USA	41n18	- 4	51	48
NEW ORLEANS	USA	30n 0	- 6	0	0
NEWARK,NJ	USA	40n48	- 4	57	0
NEWCASTLE	NSW Aust	32s56	+10	6	48
NIAGARA F	Ont Can	43n 7	- 5	56	32
NICE	Fr'ce	43n44	+ 0	28	56
NICOSIA	Italy	37n48	+ 0	57	28
NICTHEROY	Braz.	23s 0	- 2	52	0
NORFOLK,Va	USA	36n55	- 5	5	0
OAKLAND,Cal	USA	37n47	- 8	49	12
OBERHAUSEN	Germ.	51n28	+ 0	27	20
ODESSA	USSR	46n29	+ 2	2	24
OKLOHOMA,Ok	USA	35n28	- 6	30	0
OLDENBURG	Germ.	53n 8	+ 0	32	48
OMAHA,Neb	USA	41n15	- 6	24	0
OMSK	USSR	55n 0	+ 4	54	32
OPORTO	Port.	4ln 8	- 0	33	0
ORAN	Alger	35n40	- 0	3	10
ORENBURG	USSR	51n48	+ 3	40	40
ORLEANS	Fr'ce	47n53	+ 0	7	28
OSLO	Nor.	58n45	- 0	41	20
OSTENDE	Belg.	51n13	+ 0	12	0
OTTAWA,Ont	Can.	45n26	- 5	2	44
PANAMA	Pan.	8n59	- 5	18	8
PARA	Braz.	1s10	- 3	13	0
PARAMARIBO	D.Gna	6n10	- 3	41	40
PARIS	Fr'ce	48n52	+ 0	9	20
PATERSON,NJ	USA	41n 0	- 6	57	20
PERNAMBUCO	Braz.	8s 0	- 2	20	0
PERTH,WA	Aust.	31s52	+ 7	43	20
PERUGIA	Italy	43n 8	+ 0	49	24
PESHAWAR	Pak.	34n 8	+ 4	46	8
PHILADELPHIA	Pa USA	40n 0	- 5	1	0
PILSEN	Czech	49n45	+ 0	53	32
PITTSBURGH,Pa	USA	40n30	- 5	19	40
PNOM-PENH	Indo-Ch	11n30	+ 6	59	40
PONDICHERI	India	12n 0	+ 5	19	40
Pt.AU PRINCE	Haiti	18n40	- 6	49	20
Pt.OF SPAIN	Trin.	10n36	- 4	5	56
PORTO NOVO	W.Afr	6n30	+ 0	10	40
PORTOFERRAJO	Italy	42n50	+ 1	4	40
PORTLAND,Or	USA	45n30	- 8	10	4
POZNAN	Pol.	52n22	+ 1	8	0
PRAGUE	Czech	50n 6	+ 0	57	44
PRETORIA	S.Afr	25s45	+ 1	33	0
PROVIDENCE	USA	41n55	- 4	46	0
PUEBLO	Colom	38n17	- 6	58	36
QUEBEC	Canada	46n52	- 4	45	4
QUITO	Ecua.	0s15	- 5	15	0
RABAT	Moroc	34n 0	- 0	28	0
RANGOON	Burma	16n47	+ 6	25	0
READING,Pa	USA	40n26	- 5	3	20
REICHENBERG	Czech	50n42	+ 1	0	28
REIMS	Fr'ce	49n17	+ 0	16	8
RHODES	Rhod.	36n25	+ 1	53	8
RICHMOND,Va	USA	37n30	- 5	10	0
RIGA	Latv.	57n10	+ 1	34	0
RIO DE JAN.	Braz.	23s 0	- 2	54	0
RIYADH	Arabia	24n50	+ 3	5	12
ROSTOV on DON	USSR	47n15	+ 2	38	8
ROTTERDAM	Neth.	51n55	+ 0	17	56
ROUEN	Fr'ce	49n28	+ 0	4	16
SAARBRUCKEN	Germ.	49n17	+ 0	28	0
SAIGON	Indo-Ch	10n45	+ 7	7	0
ST.ETIENNE	Fr'ce	45n27	+ 0	17	36
ST.JOHN	Nfdld	47n20	- 3	31	20
ST.LOUIS,Mo	USA	38n39	- 6	0	52
ST.PAUL,Minn	USA	45n 0	- 6	8	12
SALEM	India	11n35	+ 5	12	48
SALONICA	Greece	40n40	+ 1	32	0
SALT LAKE C	USA	40n44	+ 1	32	0
SAMARA	USSR	53n14	+ 3	20	16

PLACE	Country	LAT.	h	m	s
SAMARKAND	USSR	39n40	+ 4	27	40
SAN ANTONIO Tex	USA	31n30	− 6	42	0
SAN DIEGO Cal	USA	32n45	− 7	8	28
SAN FR'ISCO Cal	USA	37n45	− 8	10	0
SAN JOSE	C.Rica	9n59	− 5	56	48
SAN JUAN	P.Rico	18n29	− 4	24	8
SAN MARINO	San M	45n57	+ 0	50	0
SAN SALVADOR	Salv	13n45	− 5	59	12
SANTA CRUZ	Bol.	17s25	− 4	13	0
SANTA FE	Arg.	31s30	− 4	3	56
SANTIAGO	Chile	33s25	− 4	42	0
SANTIAGO	Cuba	20n 0	− 5	3	20
SANTO DOMINGO	Dom	18n30	− 4	39	56
SANTOS	Braz.	24s 0	− 3	6	0
SAO PAOLO	Braz.	23s40	− 3	6	20
SARAGOSSA	Spain	41n40	− 0	3	24
SARATOV	USSR	51n33	+ 3	3	56
SCRANTON,Pa	USA	41n26	− 5	2	40
SCHWERIN	Germ.	53n38	+ 0	35	44
SCUTARI	Turk.	41n 0	+ 1	56	4
SEATTLE,Wash	USA	47n31	− 8	9	0
SEOUL	Korea	37n26	+ 8	27	52
SEVILLE	Spain	37n25	− 0	24	0
SHANGHAI	China	31n25	+ 8	6	0
SHOLAPUR	India	17n40	+ 5	3	44
SINGAPORE	Malay	1n20	+ 6	55	20
SION	Switz	46n13	+ 0	29	28
SMYRNA	Turk.	38n25	+ 1	48	36
SOFIA	Bulg.	42n41	+ 1	33	20
SOMERVILLE,Mass	USA	42n25	− 4	44	16
SOUTH BEND,Ind	USA	41n40	− 5	45	28
SPEZIA	Italy	44n 5	+ 0	39	16
SPOKANE,Wash	USA	47n33	− 7	49	52
SPRINGFIELD,Mass	USA	42n 6	− 4	50	20
STALINGRAD	USSR	48n40	+ 2	57	28
STETTIN	Germ.	53n26	+ 0	58	0
STOCKHOLM	Swed.	59n17	+ 1	12	12
STRASBOURG	Fr'ce	48n37	+ 0	30	48
STUTTGART	Germ.	48n50	+ 0	66	40
SVERDLOVSK	USSR	56n52	+ 4	0	48
SYDNEY,NSW	Aus.	33.55	+10	4	48
SYRACUSE,NY	USA	43n 0	− 5	4	40
SZEGED	Hung.	46n16	+ 1	4	40
TABRIZ	Pers.	37n59	+ 3	5	28
TACOMA,Wash	USA	47n14	− 8	9	52
TALCA	Chile	35s20	− 4	47	4
TALLIN	Eston	59n20	+ 1	39	20
TANGIER	Moroc	35n40	− 0	23	0
TARANTO	Italy	40n29	+ 1	9	0
TASHKENT	USSR	41n25	+ 4	37	0
TEGUICIGALPA	Hond	14n13	− 5	48	0
TEHERAN	Pers	37n40	+ 3	25	48

PLACE	Country	LAT.	h	m	s
THORSHAVN	Denm	62n 0	− 0	27	0
TIENTSIN	China	39n 5	+ 7	48	20
TIFLIS	USSR	41n45	+ 2	59	48
TIRANA	Alban	41n19	+ 1	19	12
TOKYO	Japan	35n43	+ 9	19	0
TOLEDO	Spain	39n50	− 0	16	20
TORONTO,Ont	Can	43n40	− 5	17	40
TOULON	Fr'ce	43n 7	+ 0	23	44
TOULOUSE	Fr'ce	43n36	+ 0	5	32
TOURS	Fr'ce	47n23	+ 0	26	44
TRENTON,NJ	USA	40n 6	− 5	58	40
TRICHINOPOLI	Ind	10n50	+ 5	15	0
TRIESTE	Italy	45n40	+ 0	54	48
TRIPOLI	Syria	34n52	+ 2	23	20
TROYES	Fr'ce	48n17	+ 0	16	16
TULA	USSR	54n15	+ 2	30	8
TULSA,Ok	USA	36n 6	− 6	23	52
TUNIS	Afr	36n45	+ 0	41	0
TURIN	Italy	45n 5	+ 0	30	32
TVER	USSR	56n52	+ 2	22	40
UPPSALA	Sweden	59n55	+ 1	10	0
UTICA,NY	USA	43n 0	− 5	0	48
UTRECHT	Neth.	52n 5	+ 0	20	32
VADUZ	Liech	47n10	+ 0	38	8
VALENCIA	Spain	39n28	− 0	1	24
VALETTA	Malta	35n52	+ 0	58	0
VALLADOLID	Spain	41n38	− 0	18	44
VANCOUVER,BC	Can	49n 7	− 8	11	8
VENICE	Italy	45n23	+ 0	49	20
VERONA	Italy	45n27	+ 0	44	4
VICTORIA,BC	Can	48n20	− 8	12	8
VICTORIA,	Hong-K	22n20	+ 7	45	40
VIENNA	Austria	48n12	+ 1	5	32
VILNA	Pol.	54n40	+ 1	41	20
VLADIVOSTOK	USSR	43n10	+ 8	48	0
VORONEZH	USSR	51n42	+ 2	36	40
WARSAW	Pol.	52n15	+ 1	24	4
WASHINGTON,DC	USA	39n32	− 5	8	0
WEIMAR	Germ.	51n 0	+ 0	45	20
WELLINGTON,	NZ	41s15	+11	39	4
WICHITA,Kan	USA	37n42	− 6	29	0
WIESBADEN	Germ.	56n 6	+ 0	33	0
WILMINGTON,Del	USA	39n48	− 5	2	20
WINNIPEG,Manit.	Can	49n57	− 6	29	8
WORCESTER,Mass	USA	42n35	− 4	47	20
YAROSLAVL	USSR	57n40	+ 2	39	0
YOKOHAMA	Jap.	35n30	+ 9	18	32
YONKERS,NY	USA	40n57	− 4	55	20
ZAGREB	Yugos	45n51	+ 1	4	0
ZANZIBAR	E.Afr	6s 9	+ 2	36	48
ZURICH	Switz	47n23	+ 0	34	8

LONG-EQUIV. given to nearest 4 sec

TABLE TO ESTIMATE LAT. AND LONG.—EQUIV. OF ANY PLACE BY ITS DISTANCE AND DIRECTION (ROUGHLY KNOWN) FROM A PLACE IN EITHER OF ABOVE LISTS.—e-quiv.; Miles north or south change lat.; miles east or west change long.—e-quiv.; miles north-east, north-west, south-east, south-west, change both — by the amounts shown below for number of miles and near lat.

lat. near	Miles N. or S.						Miles E. or W.						Miles N-E, N-W, S-E, or S-W												
	10		30		50		10		30		50		10				30				50				
	o	'	o	'	o	'	m	s	m	s	m	s	o	'	m	s	o	'	m	s	o	'	m	s
0	0	9	0	26	0	44	0	35	1	44	2	53	0	6	0	25	0	19	1	13	0	31	2	3
15	0	9	0	26	0	44	0	36	1	48	3	0	0	6	0	25	0	19	1	14	0	31	2	7
30	0	9	0	26	0	44	0	40	2	0	3	20	0	6	0	28	0	18	1	25	0	31	2	22
45	0	9	0	26	0	43	0	49	2	27	4	5	0	6	0	36	0	18	1	49	0	31	3	2
60	0	9	0	26	0	43	1	11	3	34	5	56	0	6	0	50	0	18	2	31	0	31	4	12

'We have great difficulty in collecting information for the lists of standard times, and often find that the legal time is not the time in general use in the country concerned.' — Remark by a spokesman of the Nautical Almanac Office of the Royal Observatory (Greenwich), at Herstmonceux Castle, Sussex, replying to telephone call from author in London regarding suspected errors in the NAUTICAL ALMANAC.

Whenever at all possible, family inquiries are advisable in every case in which the exact kind of time used in recording a birth is not unambiguously specified.

Despite every possible care, and systematic inquiries in official quarters of a large number of nationalities, and the expenditure, for these few pages, of an amount of time, relatively to the space to be filled, over 1,000 per cent more than for any other part of the book — some of the details that follow, both for standard time and about the use of summer time etc., remain subject to doubt or amendment.

Just one example from a very large number:

SIERRA LEONE. Koppenstätter's valuable book, ZONEN UND SOMMERZE-ITEN (preface dated 1937), gives standard time as 1 hour slow on G.M.T., with date of adoption unknown, and gives use of summer time as apparently confined to a single year, 1935, namely, clocks advanced, on standard time, by 40 minutes, from (an unknown day of) June to (an unknown day of) September, and then discontinued ('beendet').
Irene Hume Taylor's SUPPLEMENT (covering years from 1936 to 1942, inclusive) to the completely unobtainable, else probably equally valuable, work, Curran and Taylor's WORLD SUMMER TIME (1935), says clocks advanced 40 min. from (unknown day of) June to (unknown day of) Sept. in the years 1936-1942 inclusive.
THE NAUTICAL ALMANAC, 1951 (and some other recent years), published under the aegis of the Astronomer Royal by H.M. Stationery Office annually, gives standard time as 0h. (= G.M.T.), with an asterisk denoting a place where 'Variations of this time have been used in recent years for summer time or other purposes.'
Prolonged efforts to discover, first, at what date the standard or zone time was changed from -1h. to 0h., and, secondly, for how many years after 1942 the '40 min.' summer-time advance was used, finally resulted thus:
The British Colonial Office, responsible for Sierra Leone affairs and legislation, after looking into the matter, reported that, by a fortunate coincidence, the author's inquiry was made on the very day on which that office had received from the B.B.C. a note ('Correction of World Time, no.2') stating that the standard time was 'now' 0h. and was the only clock time all round the year, no variation for the purpose of summer time being 'now' used. Asked as from what date this applied, they did not know, but referred the author to the B.B.C., as the Colonial Office's own source of information.
The B.B.C. (Overseas Information Dept.) kindly communicated their own information — the text of a Public Relations Officer's report, in which an ordinance of 1932 was quoted, making the legal time: -1h, 1 June to 31 August each year, and -0h.40m. (a 20 minutes advance) from 1 Sep. to 31 May; with the further information that this remained in operation till 1939, when it was superseded by standard time 0h., with no summer time.
On further inquiries being pressed at the Colonial Office, their legal department eventually reported that they had found the ordinance (same as quoted by B.B.C.), but that it was republished in 1946 and was still (1952) in force, and had this year (1952) at last been 'accepted' by Greenwich, after much correspondence.

Some caution must evidently be used, and some uncertainty admitted, in following even the most authoritative works of reference, and in regard to exact house-cusps in some foreign charts.

STATE etc.	from	h
ADEN		+ 3
formerly +2h59m54s		
ALASKA	20Au00	
Central zone		-10
inc. Valdez,		
Seward,Anchorage.		
Ketchikan zone,		- 8
including S.E.		
coast ?,Cross Sd.,		
Douglas,Juneau,		
Kimsham Cove,		
Petersburg.		
S.E.coast north		
of above		- 9
West coast,Nome		
zone, and the		
Aleutians		-11
ALBANIA	1914	+ 1
ALGERIA	2Mh11	0
15Mh91 +0h5m5s		
ANGOLA	1Ja12	+ 1
ANTIGUA	1Ja11	- 4
ARGENTINE	1My20	- 4
	1No94	-4h17m
AUSTRALIA		
BrokenHill	1My09	+ 9½
	25Ja96	+ 9²
	1Fe95	+10
Capital Ter.		+10
New South Wales,		
exc.Brok.H.1945		+10
	1My95	+ 9½
	25Ja96	+ 9²
	1Fe95	+10
North.Ter.	1Fe95	+ 9½
Queensld.	1Fe95	+10²
South Aus.	1My95	+ 9½
Victoria	1Fe95	+10²
West.Aus.	1Fe95	+ 8
AUSTRIA	loc91	+ 1
AZORES	1Ja12	- 1
BAHAMAS		- 5
BARBADOES	1932	- 4
BASUTOLAND	1895	+ 2
BECHUANALAND		+ 2
BELGIAN CONGO		
Eastern	1Ja35	+ 2
inc.Lusambo,		
Stanleyville,		
Costermansville,		
Elizabethville.		
Western	1Ja12	+ 1
inc.Leopoldville,		
Coquilhatville.		
BELGIUM	3Se44	0
(Germ.)	17My40	+ 1
(Indep.)	11No18	0
(Germ.) ?	-7Au14	+ 1
(Indep.)	1My92	0
BERMUDA	1Ja30	- 4
formerly -4h19m		
BOLIVIA	21Mh32	- 4
formerly -4h32m		
BORNEO,Br.N.	1oc04	+ 8
(Borneo continued)		
(Borneo continued)		
BORNEO,Du.	194-?	+ 8
formerly		+ 7½
BRAZIL	1Ja14	
Central zone		- 4
East zone,coast		- 3
West zone		- 5
BULGARIA	30No94	+ 2
BURMA	1920	+ 6
CAMEROONS	1Ja20	+ 1
CANADA	?18No91	
Alberta	1Se06	- 7
B.Columbia		- 8
Manitoba		- 8
N.Brunswick	15Je02	- 4
	9De83	- 5
Nova Scot.	18Ja84	- 4
Ontario	1895	
E.of 90°W.		- 5
W.of 90°W.		- 6
P.Edward I.	18Je02	- 4
Quebec		
E.of 68°W.		- 5
W.of 68°W.		- 6
Saskatchewan	1920	- 7
Yukon	20Au00	- 9
CEYLON	1Ja06	+ 5½
CHILE	1Se32	- 4²
	1Ja10	- 5
CHINA		
Coast ?	1Ja03	+ 8
Canton	1904	+ 8
Interior	1928	+ 8
Shanghai	1904	+ 8
Pakhoi,Hainan,		
and from Chungking		
up river		+
to Shahsze		+ 7
COLUMBIA	23No14	- 5
CORSICA	11Mh19	0
COSTA RICA	15Ja21	- 5
CRETE		+ 2
CUBA	19JL25	- 5
formerly -5h29m		
CYPRUS		+ 2
CZECHOSLOVAK.	1Ja91	+ 1
DAHOMEY	1Ja12	0
DANZIG	1Ap93	+ 1
DENMARK	1Ap94	+ 1
DOMINICA	194-?	- 5
	1Ap33	-4h40m
ECUADOR	194-?	- 5
Formerly:		
Quito etc.		-5h14m
Guayaquil etc.		-5h19m
EGYPT	1oc00	+ 2
ERITREA		+ 3
ESTONIA	1My21	+ 2
FAROES	1No08	0
FIJI		12
FINLAND	1My21	+ 2
FLORES		+ 8
FERNANDO PO		0
FORMOSA	194-?	+ 9
	1Ja96	+ 8
FRANCE	2Mh11	0
15Mh91 +0h9m5s		
GAMBIA	194-?	0
	1918	- 1
GERMANY ?	1Ap93	+ 1
Baden	1Ap92	+ 1
15Mh91 +0h34m		
Brandenbg	1Ap92	+ 1
formerly +0h54m		
Saar(Fr.)	1945?	0
(Germ.)	1Mh35	+ 1
(Fr.)	11No18	0
(Germ.)	1Ap93	+ 1
Würtembg	1Ap92	+ 1
15Mh91 +0h37m		
GIBRALTAR		0
GILBERT IS.		+12
GOLD COAST	1918	-0h20m
Gt.BRITAIN	1oc80	0
Inc.Channel Is.;		
NOT including Ireld.		
GREECE	28JL16	+ 2
GREENLAND ?		- 3
GRENADA	1JL11	- 4
GUADELOUPE	8JL11	- 4
GUATEMALA	5oc18	- 6
GUIANA,Br.	194-?	-3h45m
	1JL11	- 4
GUIANA,Du.	194-?	- 3½
formerly -3h 41m		
GUIANA,Fr.	194-?	- 3½
	1JL11	- 4²
GUINEA,Fr.	1Ja12	- 1
GUINEA,Port.	1Ja12	- 1
GUINEA,Span.		- 5
HAITI	194-?	-10
HAWAII	formerly	-10½
HOLLAND:see Netherlds		
HONDURAS,Br.	1Ap12	- 6
HONDURAS,Rep.	1Ap12	- 6
HUNGARY	loc91	+ 1
ICELAND	1Ja08	- 1
INDIA ?	1Ja06	+ 5½
Fr.India	18JL11	+ 5½
Port Ind.	1911?	+ 5½
Calcutta	1911?	+ 5½
formerly +5h53m		
INDO-CHINA,Fr.	1My31	+7
IRAN		+ 3
IRAQ	1917	+ 3
IRELAND	loc16	0
	1880	-0h25m21s
ISRAEL:see Palestine		
ITALY	1No93	+ 1
IVORY COAST		0
JAMAICA	1Fe12	- 5
JAPAN	1Ja88	+ 9
JAVA	194-?	+ 8
	1No32	+ 7½
		+ 2²
JORDAN		+ 2
KENYA	194-?	+ 3
	JJa32	+ 2½
	1JL28	+ 3²
(Korea:next page)		

STATE etc.	from	h
KOREA	1932	+ 9
	1928	+ 8½
	1De04	+ 9²
LABRADOR		− 3½
LABUAN	1oc04	+ 8²
LATVIA	1920	+ 2
LITHUANIA	1920	+ 1
formerly		+ 2
LUXEMBURG	1De18	0
	1Ap92	+ 1
LYBIA, Cyrenaica		+ 2
Tripolitana		+ 1
MADAGASCAR	1JL11	+ 3
MADEIRA	1Ja12	− 1
MALAYAN UN.	194-?	+ 7½
	1Ja33+7h33m	
	1JL05	+ 7
		+ 1
MALTA		+ 1
MANCHURIA	194-?+	9
	1Mh32+	8
	1928+	8½
	1De04+	9²
MARIANA Is.?		+ 9
Guam		+10
MARQUESAS		−10
MARSHALL Is.		+10
MARTINIQUE	1Myll	− 4
MAURETANIA	26Fe34	− 1
MAURITIUS	1Je07	+ 4
formerly		+3h 50m
MEXICO ?	1Ap32	− 6
Lower California,		
Narayet, Sonora,and		
Sinaloa	194-?	− 7
Lower California:		
	1Ap32	− 8
	1Ja22	− 7
MONACO		0
MOROCCO		0
MOZAMBIQUE	1Mh03	+ 2
NETHERLANDS	14My40+	1
	1JL37+0h20m	
	7No08 +0h19m28s	
NEW CALED.	13Ja12	+11
NEW GUINEA,Br.		+10
NEW GUINEA,Du.		+ 9
NEW HEBRID.	13Ja12	+11
NEW ZEALAND	1945	+12
	1886	+11½
NEWFOUNDLAND		− 3½
NICARAGUA ?	23Je34-	6
formerly		−5h40m
Bluefield always		
		−5h35m
NIGERIA	1Se19	+ 1
NORTH.RHODESIA	1Mh03+	2
NORWAY	1Je95	+ 1
NOVAYA ZEMLYA	1930+	4
NYASALAND		+ 2
PAKISTAN	1Ja06	+ 5½
PALESTINE	1917	+2²
PANAMA	2Ap18	− 5
PARAGUAY	10oc31	− 4
PERU	28JL08	− 5
PHILIPPINES	2My99	+ 8
POLAND	1My16	+ 1

STATE etc.	from	h
PORTO RICO	26Mh99	− 4
PORTUGAL	1Ja12	0
RIO DE ORO		+ 1
ROMANIA	24JL31	+ 2
RUSSIA	1930	
W.of 40°E.		+ 2
40°to 52½°E.		+ 3
E.of 52½°E.		+ 4
SALVADOR		− 6
SAMOA	194-?	+11
	1911	+11½
SAO THOME		0²
SANTA CRUZ		+11
SARAWAK		+ 7½
SARDINIA	1No93	+ 1²
SENEGAL	1Ja12	− 1
SEYCHELLES	Je06	− 4
SIAM	1Ap20	+ 7
SIBERIA	1930	
W.of 67½°E.		+ 4
67½ to 82½°E.		+ 5
82½ to 97½°E.		+ 6
97½ to 112½°E.		+ 7
112½ to127½°E.		+ 8
127½ to 142½°E.		+ 9
142½ to 157½°E.		+10
157½ to 172½°E.		+11
E.of 172½°E.		+12
SICILY	1No93	+ 1
SIERRA LEONE	1939?	0?
	1Ja32	− 1
SOMALILAND	1JL11	+ 3
SOUTH AFRICA:		
Cape	1No03	+ 2
	8Fe92	+ 1½
Natal	1Se94	+ 2²
Orange F.S.	1Mh30	+ 2
	8Fe92	+ 1½
Transvaal	1Mh03	+ 2
	8Fe92	+ 1½
SOUTH RHOD.	1Mh08	+ 2²
S-W.AFRICA,Br.		+ 2
SPAIN	1Ja01	0
SUDAN		+ 2
SUMATRA	194-?	+ 7
Northern	1No32	+ 6½
Sputhern	1No32	+ 7²
SWEDEN	1Ja00	+ 1
SWITZERLAND	1Je94	+ 1
SYRIA		+ 2
TANGANYIKA		+ 3
TASMANIA	1Fe95	+10
THAILAND;see Siam.		
TOGOLAND		0
TRANSJORDANIA;see Jord		
TRINIDAD	1JL11	− 4
TUNIS	9Mh11	+ 1
	15Mh91 +0h9m5s	
TURKEY	1Ja16	+ 2
UGANDA	194-?	+ 3
	1Ja30	+ 2½
	1My28	+ 3²
formerly		+ 2½
URUGUAYA	194-?	− 3½
	1My20	− 3½
UN'ONofS.AF.see S.AFR²		

STATE etc.	from	h
U.S.A.	18No83	

NOTE: brackets() mean
that what is enclosed
within them ,(?), or
(towns,different zone)
could not be verified
for years after 1940.

Alabama		− 6
Arizona(?)		− 7
(Seligman and W.		− 8)
Arkansas		− 7
California		− 8
Colorado (?)		− 7
(Springfield		− 6)
Connecticut		− 5
Delaware		− 5
D.C.	13Mh84	− 5
Florida ?	30My89	− 5
W.of85°W.		− 6
Georgia ?		− 5
(Albany,Macon,		
Atlanta,and W.		− 6)
Idaho (?)	31Mh18	− 7
(Grangeville,Cotton-		
wood,Stites,Burke,		
and west		− 8)
Formerly,without		
the exceptions		−7
Illinois		− 6
Indiana		− 6
Iowa		− 6
Kansas ?		− 6
(Syracuse,Cinamon,		
Scott Cy.,Ellis,		
Colby		−7)
Kentucky (?)		− 6
(Covington,Newpt.		−5)
Louisiana		− 6
Maine	1887	− 5
Maryland		− 5
Massachusetts		− 5
Michigan	26Ap31	− 5
	8Se85	− 6
Minnesota		− 6
Mississippi		− 6
Missouri		− 6
Montana		− 7
Nebraska ?		− 6
(inc.N.Platte,		
Stapleton,Valentine		
−west of these−		7)
Nevada(?)		− 8
(Minto,Acoma,		
Crestlin		− 7)
New Hampshire		− 5
New Jersey		− 5
New Mexico		− 7
New York state		− 5
N.Carolina (?)		− 5
(Ashville and W.		− 6)
N.Dakota	1919	− 6
formerly,		?− 6
Portal,Flaxman,		
Minot,and W.		− 7
Ohio	4Ap27	− 5
	1Ap96	− 6

STATE etc. from	h	STATE etc. from	h	STATE etc. from	h
(U.S.A.,continued)		(U.S.A.,continued)		U.S.S.R.: see Novaya	
Oklahoma	- 6	Utah ♪	- 7	Zemlya, Russia,	
Oregon (♪)	- 8	(Salt Lake Cy.,		Siberia, and	
(Backer,Seneca	- 7)	Garfield and west-	8)	Wrangel Island	
Pennsylvania	- 5	Vermont	- 5	VENEZUELA 194-?	- 4½
Rhode Island	- 5	Virginia(♪)	- 5	WRANGEL I. 1930	+12²
S.Carolina 1Ja84	- 5	(Norton and west	- 6)	YUGOSLAVIA	+ 1
Tennessee ♪	- 6	Washington state	- 8	Bosnia 1No91	
(Bristol	- 5)	W.Virginia 1Ja87	- 5	Croatia 1No91	
Texas (♪)LJa84	- 6	Wisconsin	- 6	Serbia 1884	
(El Paso,Pecos	- 7)	Wyoming	- 7	ZANZIBAR	+ 3

'PERMANENT SUMMER TIME' OR 'NEW STANDARD TIME'?

The distinction is not always very clear. For example, France is (and apparently permanently, but it might be discontinued at any moment) now (1952) using time that is one hour ahead of Greenwich, and therefore the same as Germany (Central European Time). This, however, is simply because for a number of years France has continued to use summer time all the year round, the country's standard time being in theory the same as Greenwich. It becomes a moot point whether we are to say the standard or zone time is Oh. and summer time (1 hour fast on standard time) is used continuously, or to say that(at some date difficult to fix)the standard time of France changed from Oh. to +1h and so became the same as standard time of Germany, which is not using summer time at all. The Argentine, similarly, of which the zone time is 4h. behind Greenwich, is using continuous daylight-saving or 'permanent summer' time of 1 hour, making its clocks only 3 hours behind Greenwich. In both these cases the NAUTICAL ALMANAC will,so the author has learned privately, in future issues give the clock time — 1 hour fast on Greenwich, and 3 hours slow on Greenwich, respectively - in its list of standard times, but with a distinguishing symbol to show that these times result from the combination of permanent or continous 'summer time' with an older standard time. Up to now, however, it has given the Argentine as 3 hours behind Greenwich, while giving France as using Greenwich(standard)time, marking both with a note that variations of this standard time have been used in recent - unspecified - years for summer time or other purposes. This is a correct statement for France, incorrect for the Argentine. The same error seems to have occurred in other cases, but in some of these the author has been unable to verify the true time. One or two cases where present standard time (supposed) is marked as from '194-?' in the above list, and is in advance of that given in the next line for the same country, may be examples of 'permanent summer time'mistaken for change of standard time.

CALENDAR CHANGES IN COUNTRIES USING OLD STYLE DATES AFTER 1870

New Style (Gregorian) calendar replaced Old Style (Julian), in most countries, long before 1870, and is that in which all dates are now given. To convert O.S. dates to N.S., add 12 days to dates before the first of March (Old Style) in 1900, and to dates before 1900; add 13 days to dates since 1900 and after 29th of February in 1900,1900 was a leap year by O.S., not by N.S. Calendar changes since 1870;

Bulgaria 18 September 1920,O.S.China 30 Jan. 1912, O.S.
Greece 16 July 1916, O.S.   Japan 1872.
Romania 18 March 1920, O.S.   Russia 18 March 1918,O.S.
Yugoslavia (Serbia,Croatia, Bosnia) 17 February 1920, O.S.
But the Orthodox Greek, Rumanian, Russian, Serbian, Churches would not recognise the change till May 1923 in their countries.

INITIALS USED FOR SOME ZONE TIMES

E(astern) S(tandard) T(ime): -5h; C(entral)S.T.: - 6; M(ountain)S.T: -7; P(acific) S.T.:-8; in continental U.S.A., also A(tlantic) S.T.; -4 (American possessions and Canada). W. (War) for S. in the above means all-the-year-round daylight-saving time (1 hour advance). W(est)E(uropean)Time =Greenwich time (Oh.); C(entral)E.T.: +1; and E.E.T. (East European Time): +2. D.S.T. :Daylight Saving Time, but in ephemeris here Double Summer Time.

BRITISH ISLES including all Ireland, and Channel Is.: same as Great
Britain (see ephemeris pages) except: EIRE, no Double Summer Time.
  AZORES,MADEIRA: as Portugal. AUSTRIA, DANZIG: as Germany.
  LABRADOR:as Newfoundland.   MONACO, as France.
  SAN MARINO, SARDINIA, SICILY: as Italy. HUNGARY as Germ. to 1940.
  U.S.S.R. (including Russia, Siberia. Novaya Zemlya. Wrangel I.);
'permanent' summer time (1 hour advance) in all zones since 1930.
  U.S.A., CANADA: local rules varying from town to town yearly: so
no useful information possible in space available.
IMPORTANT:unless otherwise indicated, Double Summer Time(// or1½ hour
(½),also IMPLIES single summer time. 1h.(/),throughout that year.

Country	1916	1917	1918	1919	1920
ALASKA	none?	none?	b31Mh/b27oc	b30Mh/b26oc	none
AUSTRALIA	bloc/b25Mh(	NS;b28oc/b25Mh	b27oc/b2Mh) none	none	none
BELGIUM	z30Ap/z30Se	b16Ap/b17Se	b15Ap/b16Se	y1Mh/z4oc	y15Mh/z23oc
BR.HONDU.	none	none	z25oc/z15Fe	z24oc/z14Fe	z22oc/z21Fe
BULGARIA	none	none?	none?	date?/date?	date?/date?
CHILE	none	none	z31Au/z1JL	none	none
DENMARK	a15My/a30Se	none	none	none	none
FRANCE	y14Je/a1oc	y24Mh/a7oc	y9Mh/a6oc	y1Mh/a5oc	y15Mh/a24oc
GERMANY	z30Ap/z30Se	b16Ap/b17Se	b15Ap/b16Se	none	none
HAWAII	none?	none?	b31Mh/b27oc	b30Mh/b26oc	none
HONDURAS	Repub.none	none	1oc?/15Fe	as in 1918?	as in 1918?
ICELAND	none	20Fe/25oc	20Fe/15oc	19Fe/15oc	none
ITALY	z3Je/z30Se	z31Mh/z30Se	z9Mh/z6oc	z1Mh/z4oc	z20Mh/z1oc
LUXEMBG	y10My/z30Se	y30Ap/z30Se	b15Ap/b16Se	y1Mh/a5oc	y14Fe/a23oc
MOROCCO	Tangier zone	none till	6My/7oc	none?	none?
NETHERL.	z30Ap/z30Se	b16Ap/b17Se	b14Ap/b31oc	b7Ap/b29Se	b5Ap/b27Se
N'FOUNDL.	none	b8Ap/b17Se	b14Ap/b31oc	y5Ap/y12Au	y2Ap/y31oc
NORWAY	y21My/y21oc	none	none	none	none
POLAND	z30Ap/z30Se	c16Ap/c17Se	c15Ap/c16Se	none	none
PORTUGAL	y17Je/z31oc	y28Fe/z14oc	y1Mh/z14oc	y28Fe/z14oc	y29Fe/z14oc
RUSSIA (N.S.)	none	y13My/z13Se	z29Je/z31Au	none?	none
SPAIN	none	y7Ap/z6cc	y6Ap/z5oc	y5Ap/z4oc	none
TURKEY	none?	none?	none?	none?	b28Mh/b25oc

1921-1930; PLACES OMITTED, if named above —(believed)none.1921-30					
Country	1921	1922	1923	1924	1925
BELGIUM	y14Mh/z25oc	y25Mh/z7oc	y31Mh/z6oc	y29Mh/z4oc	y4Ap/z3oc
BR.HONDU.	z1oc/z11Fe	z7oc/z10Fe	z6oc/z9Fe	z4oc/z14Fe	z3oc/z13Fe
FRANCE	y14Mh/z25oc	y25Mh/z7oc	y31Mh/z6oc	y29Mh/z4oc	y4Ap/z3oc
HOND.Rep.	(Koppenstätter says;1oc/Fe every year; not verified.)				
ICELAND	19Mh/22Je	none	none	none	none
LUXEMBG	y14Mh/z25oc	y25Mh"z7oc	y31Mh/z6oc	y29Mh"z4oc	y4Ap/z3oc
MOROCCO	Span. and Tang.zones,none till?....			y16Ap/y4oc	none?
NETHERL.	b4Ap/b28Se	b26Mh/b8oc	b1Je/b7oc	b30Mh/b5oc	b5Ap/c4oc
N'FOUNDL.	y1My/y30oc	y7My/y29oc	y6My/y28oc	y4My/y26oc	y3My/y25oc
PORTUGAL	y28Fe/z14oc	none	none	y16Ap/z14oc	none
SPAIN	y28Fe/z14oc	none	none	y16Ap/z14oc	none
TURKEY	b3Ap/b3oc	b26Mh/b8oc	b28Ap/b16Se	none?	none?
URUGUAY	(Montevideo only)none till		z1oc/z31Mh	z1oc/z31Mh	z1oc/z31Mh

Country	1926	1927	1928	1929	1930
ARGENTINE	? none till........				z30No/z31Mh
BR.HONDU.	z2oc/z12Fe	z1oc/z11Fe	z6oc/z9Fe	z5oc/z8Fe	z4oc/z14Fe
CHILE	none	z31Au/z31Mh	z31Au/z31Mh	z31Au/z31Mh	z31Au/z31Mh
CUBA	? none till		z9Je/z9oc	none?	none?
FRANCE	y17Ap/z2oc	y9Ap/z1oc	y14Ap/z6oc	y20Ap/z5oc	y12Ap/z4oc
HOND.Rep.	(see 1920-1925; same source, unchecked, same for 1926-30)				
MEXICO	? none till........				date?/z14No
MOR.Span.Tan.	y17Ap/y2oc	y9Ap/y1oc	y14Ap/y6oc	none	none
NETHERL.	b15Ap/b3oc	b15Ap/b2oc	b15Ap/b7oc	b15Ap/b6oc	b15Ap/b5oc
N.ZEALAND	none	z6No/z4Mh {	z4No/z31De) z31De/z3Mh)	z13oc/z16Mh	z12oc/z15Mh
N'FOUNDL.	y2My/y31oc	y1My/y30oc	y6My/y28oc	y5My/y27oc	y4My/y26oc
PORTUGAL	y17Ap/z2oc	y9Ap/z1oc	y14Ap/z6oc	y20Ap/z5oc	none
SPAIN	y17Ap/z2oc	y9Ap/z1oc	y14Ap/z6oc	none	none

258

Country	1931	1932	1933	1934	1935
ARGENTIN	z31Se/z31Mh	z31oc/z28Fe	z31oc/z28Fe	z31oc/z28Fe	z31oc/z29Fe
BELGIUM	y18Ap/z3oc	y2Ap/zloc	y25Mh/z7oc	y7Ap/z6oc	y30Mh/z5oc
BRAZIL	y3oc/z31Mh	(z2oc/z31Mh	exc.Maranh.)	none.Apl933-1948 inclus.	
BR.HONDU	z2oc✗z13Fe	z7oc✗z11Fe	z6oc✗z10Fe	z5oc✗z9Fe	z4oc✗z8Fe
CHILE	z31Au/z31Mh	none till 1942, but new Zone Time 1932.			
FRANCE	y18Ap/z3oc	y2Ap/zloc	y25Mh/z7oc	y7Ap/z6oc	y30Mh/z5oc
GOLD CST	z31Au✳z31De	z31Au✳z31De	z31Au✳z31De	z31Au✳z31De	z31Au✳z31De
GREECE	none?	z5J1/blNo	none?	none?	none?
HONDURAS	Republic; as before,ending 31De32?			?	?
LUXEMBRG	apparently the same as Belgium each year				
MEXICO	z30Ap/z29Se	z31Mh/z30Se	z31Mh/z30Se	z31Mh/z30Se	z31Mh/z30Se
NETHERL.	b15My/b4oc	b22My/b2oc	b15My/b8oc	b15My/b7oc	b15My/b6oc
N.ZEAL'D	z11oc✗z20Mh	z9oc✗b19Mh	b8oc✗b29Ap	b30Se✗b28Ap	b29Se✗b26Ap
N'FOUNDL	y3Ap/y20oc	y1Ap/y30oc	y7Ap/y29oc	y6Ap/y28oc	y5Ap/y27oc
PORTUGAL	y18Ap/z8oc	y2Ap/zloc	none	y7Ap/z5oc	y30Mh/z5oc
ROMANIA	none?	none?	z21My/a2oc	z1Ap/aloc	z6Ap/a6oc
SARAWAK	none until?........				z13Se✳z13De
SIER.LEO	z31Mh✳z31Au	z31Mh✳z31Au	z31Mh✳z31Au	z31Mh✳z31Au	z31Mh✳z31Au
URUGUAY	none?	none?	z28oc✗z31Mh	z27oc✗z30Mh	z26oc✗z28Mh

Country	1936	1937	1938	1939	1940
ARGENTIN	z31oc/z28Fe	z31oc/z28Fe	z31oc/z28Fe	z31oc/z29Fe	z30Se/CONT.
BELGIUM	y18Ap/z3oc	y3Ap/z2oc	y26Mh/zloc	y15Ap/z19No	b26Fe/c20My
	using German zone and summer time from 20My 1940.				
BR.HONDU	z3oc✗z13Fe	z2oc✗z12Fe	zloc✗z11Fe	z7oc✗z10Fe	z5oc✗z9Fe
CUBA	none until ?........				z1Je/z31Au
DENMARK	none until ...1940b30Ap,then as Germany,includ.				b30Ap/CONT.
FALKL.Is	z27Se/z27Mh	z26Se/z19Mh	z24Se/z18Mh	z30Se/z23Mh	z27Se/z22Mh
FRANCE	y18Ap/z3oc	y3Ap/z2oc	y26Mh/zloc	y15Ap/z19No	y24Fe/CONT.
	and in occupied areas (including Paris)				y15Je/date?
GERMANY	none until..........				c1Ap/CONT.
GOLD CST	z31Au✳z31De	z31Au✳z31De	z31Au✳z31De	z31Au✳z31De	z31Au✳z31De
HONDURAS	Rep. apparently every year(?), –?oc✗about middle of Fe.				
ITALY	none until........				15Je/CONT.
LUXEMBRG	same as Belgium,unless for few days diff.1940,beg.Germ.t				
MEXICO	z31Mh/z30Se	z31Mh/z30Se	z31Mh/z30Se	z31Mh/z30Se	z31Mh/CONT.
NETHERL.	b15My/b4oc	b22My/b3oc	b15My/b2oc	b15Ap/bloc	b19Ap/CONT.
	but note that from 26My1940,new zone time must be taken.				
N.ZEAL'D	b27Se/b25Ap	b25Se✗b24Ap	b25Se✗b30Ap	b24Se✗b29Ap	b29Se✗b27Ap
N'FOUNDL	z10My/z4oc	z9My/z3oc	z8My/z2oc	z14My/zloc	z12My/z6oc
NORWAY	none until..........				bllAu/CONT.
PALESTINE	none till TWO periods in 1940; 30My/30Se AND 17No/CONT.				
PERU	?	23Se?/31Mh	24Se/25Mh	23Se/24Mh	26Se/29Mh
POLAND	none until..........				23Je/CONT.
PORTUGAL	y18Ap/z3oc	y2Ap/z2oc	y26Mh/zloc	y15Ap/z7oc	y24Fe/z5oc
SARAWAK	z13Se✳z13De	z13Se✳z13De	z13Se✳z13De	z13Se✳z13De	z13Se✳z13De
SIER.LEO	z31Mh✳z31Au	z31Mh✳z31Au	z31Mh✳z31Au	z31Mh✳z31Au	z31Mh✳z31Au
SPAIN	none	y16Je/z2oc	y16Ap/zloc	y15Ap/z7oc	y13Ap/CONT.
SWITZERL	none until..........				2No/date?
TURKEY	none until TWO periods in 1940; z30Je/z5oc AND z30No/CONT.				
URUGUAY	z31oc✗z26Mh	z3oc✗z25Mh	z28oc✗z24Mh	z28oc✗z29Mh	z26oc✗z28Mh

Country	1941	1942	1943	1944	1945
ARGENTIN	CONT./CONT.	CONT./z31Je43	z15oc/CONT.	CONT./CONT.	to 23Mh46
AUSTRALI	1942;blJa/b29Mh42 AND b27Se/b28Mh43;1943 exc.W.A.b3oc/b26Mh				
BELGIUM	German zone and summer time until..			b3Ap/c16Se	b2Ap/c16Se
BR.HONDU	z4oc✗z8Fe	z3oc✗z14Fe	z2oc✗z13Fe	zloc✗z11Fe	z7oc✗z10Fe
BULGARIA	no summer time;temporary new zone (+1h only)4Ap43/3Ap44.				
CZECHOSL	none	none	b29Mh/b4oc	b3Ap/b2oc	b2Ap/bloc
DENMARK	As Germany except..........				b2Ap/b15Au
FALKL.Is	z27Se/z20Mh?	apparently none after 1941..........			
FRANCE	b25Fe/✗5oc	y8Mh/✗a2No	a29Mh/b4oc	a3Ap/✗y7oc	
GERMANY	b25Fe?/b5oc?	CONT./a2No?	b29Mh/b4oc	a3Ap/y7oc	
GOLD CST	z31Au✳z31De	z31Au✳z31De	z31Au✳z31De	z31Au✳z31De	z31Au✳z31De
GREECE	25Ap/date?(zone+1h only;2Fe42-29Mh43 4oc43-3Ap44,2oc-31oc44)				
HONDURAS	Rep. apparently, every year(?) –?oc✗about middle of Fe.				
HUNGARY	7Ap/2No	29Mh/4oc	3Ap/4oc	3Ap/2No	y1My/y1No
ICELAND	2Fe/24oc?	8Mh/25oc	7Mh/23oc	5Mh/22oc	4Mh/22oc

259

	1941	1942	1943	1944	1945
ITALY {	CONT./CONT.	CONT./b2No	z29Mh/b4oc	z1Ap/z16Se	z31Mh/z15Se
	(but in 1943, Brit. and allied-occupied areas				z29Mh/z26Se)
NETHERL.	CONT./CONT.	CONT./b2No	b29Mh/b7oc	b3Ap/b4oc	b3Ap/c16Se
N.ZEALAND	b28Se/b26Ap	b27Se/b25Ap	b26Se/b30Ap	b24Se/b29Ap	(new Zone T)
N'FOUNDL.	z11My/z1No	z1Mh/CONT.	z30My/z25Se	z10JL/z28Se	CONT./z7oc
NORWAY	CONT./CONT.	CONT./x1No	b29Mh/b4oc	b3Ap/b2oc	z1Ap/cloc
PALESTINE	CONT./date!	date!/date!	date!/date!	date!/date!	date!/date!
POLAND	CONT./CONT.	CONT./b2No	b29Mh/b4oc	b3Ap/z31No	z28Ap/z31oc
PORTUGAL	y6Ap/z5oc	y11Mh/z25oc	y13Mh/z31oc	y11Mh/z29oc	y10Mh/z28oc
SIER.LEO.	z31Mh×z31De	z31Mh×z31De	z31Mh×z31De	z31Mh×z31De	z31Mh×z31De
SPAIN	CONT./CONT.	y25My/zkSe	y17Ap/aloc	y15Ap/aloc	y14Ap/a30Se
SWITZERL.	z4My/z5oc	z3My/z4oc	none	none	none
TURKEY	CONT./z2oSe	z31Mh/CONT.	CONT./date!	date!/date!	date!/date!
URUGUAY	24oc/27Mh	14De/13Ap43	13Ap/CONT.	CONT./CONT.	CONT./15Mh46

Country	1946	1947	1948	1949	1950
ARGENTIN.	z30Se/CONT.	CONT./CONT.	CONT./CONT.	CONT./CONT.	CONT./CONT.
BELGIUM	b19My//c7oc	CONT./CONT.	CONT./CONT.	CONT./CONT.	CONT./CONT.
BRAZIL	none	none	none	z30No/z30Ap	z30No/z31Mh
BR.HOUNDU.	z6oc/z9Fe	z5oc/z8Fe	z3oc/z14Fe	z2oc/z12Fe	z1oc/z11Fe
CHILE	y25Se/y21My	(none after	21My47) none	none	none
CZECHOSL.	(z6My/(8oc!)	z19Ap/z4oc	z17Ap/z2oc	z9Ap/z1oc	none
	(Note: 1946. clocks 1 hour SLOW on standard time				1De-26Fe
DENMARK	z30Ap/z31Au	z3Ap/z9Au	z7My/z7Au	z9Ap/z1oc	none
FRANCE	CONT./CONT.	CONT./CONT.	CONT./CONT.	CONT./CONT.	CONT./CONT.
GERMANY {	b14Ap/b7oc	b6Ap/b5oc	b18Ap/b31oc	b10Ap/b1oc	none
	and, in 1947, b11My/b29Je				
GOLD COST	z31Au×z31De	z31Au×z31De	z31Au×z31De	z31Au×z31De	z31Au×z31De
HONDURAS	REPUBLIC every year (!)		-oc/ about middle of Fe.		
HUNGARY	z31Mh/z6oc	25Ap/z4oc	23Ap/3oc	29Ap/2oc	none
ICELAND	z3Mh/z27oc	z5Ap/z26oc	z3Ap/z23oc	z2Ap/z30oc	z1Ap/z22oc
ISRAEL	(Palestine 1946-1947 (?)		none	27Ap/31oc	15Au/14Se
MEXICO	(Mexico City only) none till 1950:				14Mh/-!Mh51
N'FOUNDL.	z5My/z10oc	z4My/z5oc	z9My/z3oc	z1My/z2oc	z30Ap/z24Se
POLAND	z13Ap/z5oc	z3My/z4oc	z17Ap/z2oc	z9Ap/z1oc	none
PORTUGAL	y6Ap/z5oc	y5Ap/z4oc	b4lp/c3oc	b3Ap/c2oc	none
SIER.LEO	z31Mh×z31Au	z31Mh×z31Au	z31Mh×z31Au	z31Mh×z31Au	z31Mh×z31Au
SPAIN	y13Ap/a29Se	CONT./CONT.	CONT./CONT.	y23Ap/aloc	CONT./CONT.
TURKEY	z1Je/z30Se	z19Ap/z4oc	z17Ap/z2oc	z9Ap/z1oc	z21Ap/z7oc
URUGUAY	CONT./CONT.	CONT./CONT.	CONT./CONT.	CONT./CONT.	CONT./CONT.

Country	1951	1952	1953	1954	1955
ARGENTIN.	CONT./CONT.	CONT./CONT.	CONT./CONT.	CONT./CONT.	CONT./CONT.
BELGIUM	CONT./CONT.	CONT./CONT.	CONT./CONT.	CONT./CONT.	CONT./CONT.
BRAZIL	z30No/z3Mh	z1De/z1Mh	none	none	none
BR.HONDU.	z7oc/z10Fe	z5oc/z15Fe	z4oc/z14Fe	z3oc/12Fe	z5oc/z11Fe
FRANCE	CONT./CONT.	CONT./CONT.	CONT./CONT.	CONT./CONT.	CONT./CONT.
GOLD COST	z31Au/z31De	z1Se/1Ja	z1Se/1Ja	z1Se/1Ja	z1Se/1Ja
GREECE	none	1JL/31oc	none	none	none
ICELAND	1Ap/28oc	6Ap/26oc	5Ap/25oc	4Ap/24oc	3Ap/23oc
ISRAEL	31Mh/10No	19Ap/18oc	12Ap/12Se	12Je/12Se	11Je/10Se
N'FOUNDL.	z30Ap/z24Se	z27Ap/z28Se	z26Ap/z27Se	z25Ap/z26Se	z24Ap/z25Se
PORTUGAL	61Ap/c7oc	6Ap/5oc	rAp/4oc	4Ap/3oc	3Ap/2oc
SIER.LEO	z31Mh×z31De	none	none	none	none
SPAIN	CONT./CONT.	CONT./CONT.	CONT./CONT.	CONT./CONT.	CONT./CONT.
TURKEY	z21Ap/z60c	none	none	none	none
URUGUAY	CONT./CONT.	CONT./CONT.	CONT./CONT.	CONT./CONT.	CONT./CONT.

Country	1956	1957	1958	1959	1960
ARGENTIN	Cont./Cont.	Cont./Cont.	Cont./Cont.	Cont./Cont.	Cont./Cont.
BR. HONDU.	60c/9Fe	50c/8Fe	40c/14Fe	30c/13Fe	20c/11Fe
EGYPT	none·	30Ap/10c	30Ap/30Se	30Ap/30Se	30Ap/10c
ICELAND	1Ap/280c	7Ap/10c	30Ap/260c	5Ap/250c	3Ap/230c
ISRAEL	2Je/29Se	27Ap/21Se	none	none	none
N'FOUNDL.	29Ap/30Se	29Ap/29Se	28Ap/28Se	26Ap/27Se	24Ap/300c
PORTUGAL	1Ap/70c	7Ap/10c	6Ap/50c	5Ap/50c	3Ap/20c
URUGUAY	none	none	none	24My/14No	16Ja/5Mh

Country	1961	1962	1963	1964	1965
ARGENTIN	Cont./Cont.	Cont./Cont.	Cont./10c	15De63/1Mh	150c64/1Mh
BRAZIL	none	none	230c63/1Mh	none	31Ja/31Mh
BR. HONDU.	70c61/10Fe	60c62/9Fe	50c63/8Fe	30c64/13Fe	30c65/12Fe·
CANADA } N'FOUNDL. } NEW YORK }	30Ap/290c	29Ap/280c	28Ap/270c	26Ap/250c	25Ap/310c
CUBA	none	none	1Je/10c	31My/10c	23My/30c
EGYPT	30Ap/30Se	30Ap/30Se	30Ap/30Se	30Ap/30Se	30Ap/10c
ICELAND	2Ap/220c	1Ap/280c	7Ap/270c	5Ap/250c	4Ap/240c
PORTUGAL	2Ap/10c	1Ap/70c	7Ap/60c	5Ap/40c	4Ap/30c
TURKEY	none	15J1/Cont.	Cont./290c	15My/10c	none
URUGUAY	none	none	none	none	3Ap/25Se

Country	1966	1967	1968	1969	1970
ARGENTIN	150c65/1Mh	0c66/Mh67	Se67/Ap68	0c68/Ap69	Oct69/Indef
BRAZIL	1De65/Fe67	No67/Mh68	none	none	none
BR. HONDU.	10c66/11Fe	0c67/Fe68	0c68/Fe69	0c69/Fe70	0c70/Fe71
CUBA	7My/10c	Ap/0c	Ap68/----	----/Se70	none
EGYPT	1My/10c	My/0c	My/0c	My/0c	My/0c
ITALY	21My/25Se	My/Se	My/Se	June/Se	June/Se
BELGIUM	none	none	none	none	none
CANADA	Ap/0c	Ap/0c	Ap/0c	Ap/0c	Ap/0c
N'FOUNDL.	Ap/0c	Ap/0c	Ap/0c	Ap/0c	Ap/0c
U.S.A.	Each Year	Last Sunday In April/Last Sunday in Oct. (1 Hour)			
ICELAND	Ap/0c	Ap/0c	Ap/? Standard Time changed to G.M.T.		
PORTUGAL	Ap/ Permanent Summer Time throughout Year 1 Hour				
URUGUAY	none	none	?/De	?/?	Ap 1 ?

ADDITIONAL STANDARD—TIME AND SUMMER—TIME DATA: FILL IN BELOW
Paste in additional leaves when this and next page are filled.

NOTES

NOTES

NOTES

NOTES

NOTES

NOTES

NOTES

NOTES

NOTES

NOTES

NOTES

NOTES